Paradox

Programming

UNLEASHED

Mike Prestwood

PUBLISHING

201 West 103rd Street
Indianapolis, IN 46290

To my wife Lisa, our daughter Felicia, and our new baby boy; the three most important people in my life.

Copyright © 1996 by Sams Publishing

FIRST EDITION

International Standard Book Number: 0-672-30895-9

Library of Congress Catalog Card Number: 95-72328

99 98 97 96   4 3 2 1

Interpretation of the printing code: the rightmost double-digit number is the year of the book's printing; the rightmost single digit, the number of the book's printing. For example, a printing code of 96-1 shows that the first printing of the book occurred in 1996.

Composed in AGaramond and MCPdigital by Macmillan Computer Publishing

Printed in the United States of America

Publisher	*Richard K. Swadley*
Acquisitions Manager	*Greg Wiegand*
Development Manager	*Dean Miller*
Managing Editor	*Cindy Morrow*
Marketing Manager	*Gregg Bushyeager*

Acquisitions Editor
Brad Jones

Development Editor
Michael Watson

Software Development Specialist
Cari Skaggs

Production Editor
Jill D. Bond

Copy Editors
Chuck Hutchinson
Susan Christophersen

Technical Reviewers
Chris Levesque
Randy Spitz

Editorial Coordinator
Bill Whitmer

Technical Edit Coordinator
Lynette Quinn

Formatter
Frank Sinclair

Editorial Assistants
Sharon Cox
Andi Richter
Rhonda Tinch-Mize

Cover Designer
Tim Amhrein

Book Designer
Gary Adair

Production Team Supervisor
Brad Chinn

Production
Steve Adams, Carol Bowers, Georgiana Briggs, Mona Brown, Jason Hand, Sonja Hart, Mike Henry, Ayanna Lacey, Clint Lahnen, Kevin Laseau, Steph Mineart, Cheryl Moore, Nancy Price, Bobbi Satterfield, SA Springer, Josette Starks, Andrew Stone, Susan Van Ness, Todd Wente, Colleen Williams

Overview

Contents

Part II ObjectPAL Basics

Part III   The Display Managers and More

Part IV   Exploring ObjectPAL

Part V   Special Topics

Acknowledgments

A book of this nature demands input from as many different people as possible. I'm lucky enough to have worked with many talented engineers over the years. Their contributions and their openness to my inquiries are greatly appreciated.

The following software engineers deserve mention for either giving me ideas on style and content, contributing clip-objects, or just giving me support: James Arias-LaRheir, Tarik Ghbeish, Keith Bigelow, David Orriss, Jr., Dave Jemmott, Bryan Valencia, Fernando Chilvarguer, and Carlos Yoshimoto.

Thanks goes to Cari Skaggs for helping me put the CD-ROM together. Thank you to Chuck Hutchinson for editing chapters 30 through 36 and Susan Christophersen for editing the appendixes that are on the CD-ROM. I probably could go on for another page or two, but let me finish with a big thank you to Sams Publishing for giving me this opportunity and guidance. In particular, thanks goes to Brad Jones, Michael Watson, and Jill Bond for their support and guidance.

About the Author

Mike Prestwood, Author

Mike Prestwood is currently the Product Manager of the mortgage division of The Money Store. He leads three teams of developers developing client/server applications in ObjectPAL, Delphi, and C++ to Interbase 4 and Informix 8.

In the past, Mike Prestwood has worked for Borland International, Inc. Mike reached the highest technical position possible in Technical Support: Consulting Engineer. His duties at Borland included serving as Advanced Training Coordinator, member of the SQL team, and a SysOp on CompuServe.

As the Advanced Training Coordinator for the Paradox team, Mike was responsible for putting together training courses for SQL, advanced ObjectPAL, and more. Mike taught a 40-hour, week-long ObjectPAL course, and helped put together 21 advanced ObjectPAL training courses for Paradox technical support (more than 100 engineers).

Mike supported Paradox 1.0 for Windows since before it shipped. He answered questions on the Paradox Help desk and SQL lines, and he reviewed technical bulletins about Paradox. Mike has also answered questions from Borland's international subsidiaries through Borland's international BBS. Before joining the Paradox technical support team, Mike was part of the ObjectVision technical support team for one and one-half years.

Mike is also the author of the Sams books, *What Every Paradox for Windows Programmer Should Know* and *What Every Paradox 5 for Windows Programmer Should Know*, the predecessors to this book. Mike also contributed to the Sams book, *Paradox 5 for Windows Developer's Guide*, Second Edition, by James Arias-LaRheir.

You can send e-mail to Mike on CompuServe at 73704,2233. On the Internet, send e-mail to mprestwood@impex.com. In addition, you can visit the World Wide Web site of Prestwood Enterprises and download the latest files and updates for this book (http:\\www.impex.com/prestwood).

Introduction

This book is for anyone who wants to learn or get better at ObjectPAL and is ready to tackle ObjectPAL with a hands-on approach. This includes beginner, intermediate, and advanced ObjectPAL programmers, and everyone who wants to write a database application with Paradox. Through instruction and example, you will learn the intricacies of ObjectPAL and how to write a complete database application.

If you already know the basics of ObjectPAL, this book is a good source for ideas, tricks, tips, short code routines, undocumented features, and advanced concepts. This book doesn't document every feature of Paradox—that's the job of the manuals—nor does it show you how to use interactive features, except for occasional interactive solutions to programming problems. That is the job of beginner-level Paradox books.

The goal of this book is to add to the manuals with as little duplication as possible to present a complete study of ObjectPAL. It teaches you how to use ObjectPAL and how to bring all the elements of Paradox together to develop a complete application. This book concentrates on ideas, solutions, and learning ObjectPAL. If you own several ObjectPAL books, I'm confident you will find this book to be most useful with many more advanced examples and discussions presented in clear English.

What You Should Know Before Reading This Book

This book assumes that you understand interactive Paradox. If you can create a table, form, report, and query, you fall into this category. Although you don't need to know how to use every interactive feature of Paradox, you must be familiar with the majority of its interactive— non-ObjectPAL—features. Be sure to check out the important appendixes that are on the book's CD-ROM.

Part I: Design Fundamentals

Part I addresses some of the elements of interactive Paradox and the part of the software development life cycle that comes before you start coding. It presents many concepts the ObjectPAL programmer needs to keep in mind when developing an application including the Paradox environment, designing tables, and form design. This part of the book is intended to help developers get ready to code in ObjectPAL.

Part II: ObjectPAL Basics

Part II is a formal study of the concepts and ideas behind ObjectPAL. It introduces you to ObjectPAL, the ObjectPAL Editor, and presents all the concepts and ideas used in ObjectPAL in a logical, step-by-step approach.

This part of the book is intended to help bring the beginning ObjectPAL programmer to an intermediate level. The beginning ObjectPAL programmer should consider rereading Part II, perhaps after reading the entire book. Intermediate and advanced users will enjoy a concise review of the ObjectPAL basics, perhaps filling in some holes in their knowledge.

Part III: The Display Managers and More

Part III continues your quest into ObjectPAL by giving you control of the various categories of ObjectPAL: application, forms, reports, TableViews, queries, and reports.

Part IV: Exploring ObjectPAL

Part IV is the "meat and potatoes" of this book. This part explores almost every area of developing in ObjectPAL.

This part of the book is for every level of ObjectPAL programmer. To work towards becoming an advanced ObjectPAL programmer, beginning and intermediate ObjectPAL programmers should go straight through Part III, whereas advanced ObjectPAL programmers may want to use this part for reference.

Part V: Special Topics

Part V concludes the discussion of ObjectPAL by exploring advanced topics. In addition to revisiting the event model, it covers topics such as debugging, networking, SQL, and delivering your application. All ObjectPAL programmers should read Part V.

Conventions Used in This Book

Whenever code elements are referred to in text, the element is in monospace. This includes methods, events, procedures, keywords, and Object variables. In addition, if the command is a method or procedure, it is followed with ( ). You can easily tell the difference between an event, such as open and the ObjectPAL runtime library method with the same name—open(). For example, "You can use the open() method in the open event to open another form.

The New 7 Feature icon highlights new features to version 7.

The New Term icon indicates new terms that are defined in the surrounding text. The term being defined is *italicized.*

The Disc icon box indicates forms and directories that are on the CD-ROM that accompanies this book.

TIP

Tips are just fun facts to know and tell or hints that can help you do things smarter and faster.

NOTE

Notes contain important information that pertains to the surrounding text.

On the book's CD-ROM, you will find the following important appendixes: A, "Specifications of Paradox for Windows"; B, "Database Quick Reference"; C, "Prestwood's Coding Convention"; and D, "Converting an Existing Paradox 5 Application."

PART

IN THIS PART

Design Fundamentals

The Paradox Development Environment

1

The definition of the word *paradox* seems to fit the software rendition well. A paradox is something that appears to contradict itself or be contrary to common sense but might be true. The name applies well to the Paradox database development environment because it is very powerful, yet easy to learn and use. With Paradox 7, you can quickly prototype an application for a client and then turn the prototype into the full application—this is known as *Rapid Application Development* (RAD). Paradox 7 brings RAD development to a new height of simplicity and power.

ObjectPAL stands for *Object Paradox Application Language*. The acronym portion of the name PAL comes from the DOS version of Paradox. Borland decided to add the term object to the name because ObjectPAL is an object-based, event-driven programming environment that is much more advanced than its PAL predecessor.

Before jumping into ObjectPAL, you need to review a few concepts. The first few chapters deal with issues such as planning, table design, and interactive form design. These chapters also discuss interactive issues that an ObjectPAL programmer needs to keep in mind. The rest of this chapter gives you an overview of the design process and gives you ideas about how a database application should look.

The goal of this chapter is to talk about Paradox from an overall development perspective. It begins with a discussion of why you should use Paradox. Then, it moves into a discussion of types of applications and which types of applications Paradox is suitable for. This chapter then follows up with this idea, introducing the CD and the types of applications on it.

Why Should You Use Paradox?

A *database* is an organized collection of information. For Paradox users, this meaning is stretched to mean a set of related tables (usually in the same directory). Paradox is much more than a simple database program. Every version of Paradox has made complex databases accessible to the average user. In my opinion, Paradox has three levels of usability: easy database access, complex database access, and database application development. A database application is a cohesive set of files. Your database, with all its tables, forms, queries, reports, and anything else that you include within the scope of the files, including utilities and accessories, makes up your database application.

Easy database access enables you to create simple database tables and to enter and browse through data quickly with the traditional table window or a more flexible form. In addition, you can print in table and form view by selecting File | Print. Or, you can create more complex printing with a report.

Complex database access enables you to ask complex questions about your data. In Paradox, you can set a filter in a form or ask a question of your data with a query. After you find the answer, you can use crosstabs, graphs, and advanced reports to communicate the answer to your users.

Database application development includes bringing all the elements that display data—table views, forms, and reports—into a cohesive presentation. The application development side of Paradox brings a friendly user interface to the end user and a powerful language called ObjectPAL to the programmer. Both of these elements together enable you to better control the application environment. Developing an application in Paradox is a process of taking small steps.

As a DBMS, Paradox is capable of using either local tables (Paradox or dBASE) and remote tables (such as Oracle and Sybase). This means that, as a Paradox or dBASE developer, you can read and write Paradox and dBASE tables and indexes without importing them. This is important. Some developers get confused about this issue and ask how to convert a dBASE table to a Paradox table or vice versa. The answer is, you don't. If you need to copy the data from dBASE to Paradox format, or vice versa, then simply copy it.

In addition to local table structures such as Paradox and dBASE, you can use any of the SQL servers supported by the *Borland Database Engine* (*BDE*). As of this writing, this includes Borland's Interbase, Oracle, Sybase, Microsoft SQL, DB/2, and Informix. Also, the BDE engine is ODBC compliant. This means that you can use almost any ODBC driver to connect to almost anything, including text files, BTrieve, and Excel spreadsheets.

What Type of Development Tool Is Paradox for Windows?

Now that Borland has moved both dBASE and Paradox to the Windows environment and released the development tool Delphi, which should you use? All three support dBASE and Paradox table formats and act as a front-end to SQL servers. (This is accomplished by the BDE engine, which all three use.) Which table structure is better is still a factor, but is no longer the deciding issue. The decision now centers around which development environment you prefer.

Tables, dBASE, and Paradox

Paradox handles Paradox tables best and dBASE handles dBASE tables best. For example, with dBASE for Windows, you can store a graphic in a binary field, and dBASE for Windows knows that it's a graphic and displays it. Paradox for Windows does not. It simply displays <BLOB Binary>. Another example is that the Paradox table supports an OLE field type. Because Paradox supports OLE 2 and dBASE does not, Paradox handles this Paradox table field better. Each DBMS—Paradox and dBASE—handles its own native table structures best. Because the Paradox table structure is superior to the dBASE table structure, and because Paradox handles Paradox tables best, my choice of development environment is Paradox for Windows. For more on dBASE and Paradox table structures, see the section, "dBASE Tables versus Paradox Tables" in Chapter 2.

Design Methodology

It's important to understand the elements of ObjectPAL. If you don't keep the big picture in mind, however, the end product suffers. With this book, you will learn the skills to develop in ObjectPAL and a short introduction to the complete software development life cycle.

The Software Development Life Cycle

The software development cycle is introduced and discussed in Chapter 36. For the sake of this discussion, I define the software development life cycle as follows:

1. Gather Requirements
2. Design Database
3. Design Software
4. Code Software
5. Debug Software
6. Test Software
7. User Accepts Product
8. Deploy Application

This book is primarily concerned with the coding and debugging phases of the software development cycle. Occasionally, I digress into another area when the subject is something that a programmer needs to know to be more productive, or is something that helps you understand how Paradox and ObjectPAL fit into the software development life cycle.

More on design methodology and the software development life cycle later, in Chapter 36.

Forms Are Your Application

In Paradox for DOS, the script is the center of your application design, and the form is used to present data. In C programs, your code is the center of your application design, and windows are created to display data. A form in Paradox for Windows is used to present data, but it also doubles as the center of your application. A form has many objects that you can use to develop an application. It's important that you have a good grasp of what these objects can do. A table frame is an object used to display multiple records on a form. A field is a multipurpose object that enables you to display a single value from a table. It also enables you to show users extra bits of information, calculated values, and other values not stored directly in the table. An object such as a button, field, or box is an item that the user interacts with to create events. The more you know about Paradox's objects, the better your application will be. Chapter 3 shows you a good technique for developing forms.

A form stores the code for an application. For large applications, it is a good idea to break it into multiple forms or use libraries to store extra code. (Storing and centralizing code is discussed later in Chapter 23.) When you deliver your form, Paradox compiles it into what is actually a Windows DLL with a .FDL extension.

Screen Resolution

The main window in Paradox is the desktop. The desktop is the highest level of interaction with all Paradox objects. The desktop varies its size depending on your screen resolution. The desktop is also known as your application workspace. In ObjectPAL, there is an application variable type for manipulating Paradox's application workspace. The application variable is discussed in Chapter 13.

Forms designed for one screen resolution don't necessarily look good under a different resolution. If you will be porting applications from one machine to another, you should use the same resolution on both systems. (Also, be sure to use the same fonts on both systems.) If it's impossible to use the same resolution, develop the form for the lowest common resolution—for example, VGA (640 by 480) rather than SVGA (800 by 600). Later, in Part III, you will revisit this topic and see several ObjectPAL solutions.

Forms Versus Pages

A form can consist of multiple pages, and an application can consist of multiple forms. It's often difficult to decide when to add a page or start a new form. In general, think about adding a new page to the existing form first. If a new page won't work, add a new form. Because every page of a form must be the same size, usually size dictates whether to use a new page or form.

When all the forms and pages are the same size, then I let the data model dictate whether to add a new page or a new form. The general rule is one data model per form. When the data model gets in the way, then start a new form. For example, in a typical invoicing system, you might link Orders to Customers. You could use one form with this data model and simply add pages until another data model is indicated. For example, suppose that you need to have a page or form for the user to browse through the Customer table. The preceding data model does not work because the Customer table is the second table in a one-to-one relationship; it is restricted by the Orders table. Common sense tells you to create a new form with a new data model; that is, a data model with just the Customer table in it. (Table relationships are discussed more in the next chapter.)

The Main Form

A typical application consists of tables, indexes, forms, reports, queries, and possibly scripts or libraries. This presents a problem to the user: how to start up the application. The common practice for developers is to give the main form the same name as the directory that contains it; for example, C:\SECRETS3\SECRETS3.FDL. If you stick with this practice, the users of your Paradox applications will soon learn how to start them up. For more coding conventions such as this, refer to Appendix C on the disc.

Types of Applications

This section discusses types, or categories, of applications, introduces the files on the disc, and discusses how those files fall into these categories. It's just as important to study the files on the disc as it is to study the code, techniques, and concepts presented in this book. In fact, the programs on the disc provide you with a wealth of code.

What's on the CD-ROM

Before jumping into the formal discussion, you should see what Paradox is capable of. Sometimes it's nice to see what a product can do. As they say, "Seeing is believing." Knowing what a product can do is half the battle. This section demonstrates the capabilities of Paradox by showing you what comes on the CD-ROM that accompanies this book. If you haven't done so yet, take a few minutes now to install it.

> **NOTE**
>
> Whenever I refer to a directory in this book that is part of the disc, I refer to the subdirectory under the SECRETS3 directory. For example, when you see \APPS\INVOICE\INVOICE.FSL, the actual path is C:\SECRETS3\APPS\INVOICE\INVOICE.FSL. (This example assumes that you installed the SECRETS3 directory at the root level of C:\).

The disc that comes with this book includes several types of files: support files for the examples, answers to the examples, clip-objects, utilities, and sample applications. You can access all the support files through one main form, SECRETS3.FSL, which loads MAINMENU.FSL (see Figure 1.1). All the forms are nondelivered (.FSL) forms (except for the Paradox Desktop demo). All the code in the sample applications is commented and uses a consistent naming convention for naming objects and variables.

FIGURE 1.1.

MAINMENU.FSL is your gateway to the book's support files.

While on the Main menu, click the Configuration button to move to the configuration screen. While on the Configuration screen, you can install some of the more useful utilities to your Tools menu, or click on the SECRETS3.TXT button to view the text file for the latest information (see Figure 1.2). Also, press F1 while on the Main menu to view the SECRETS3.HLP Windows help file.

FIGURE 1.2.

SECRETS3.TXT: Late-breaking information on the book.

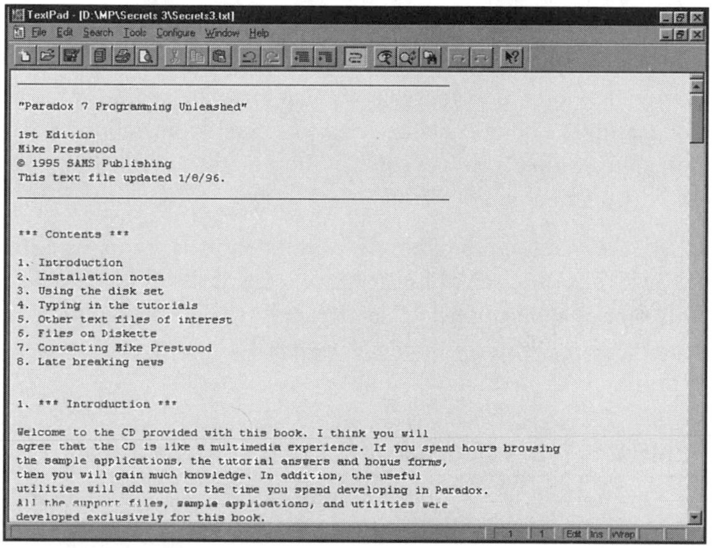

The example support files arc in the TUTORIAL directory. Before going through any example, set your working directory to the TUTORIAL directory. The answers to all examples are in the ANSWERS directory. If you have any problems with an example, run the answer from the ANSWERS directory. In addition, the ANSWERS directory is a fun directory to browse. Use the form \ANSWERS\ANSWERS.FSL to browse the files (see Figure 1.3).

FIGURE 1.3.

\ANSWERS\ANSWERS.FSL enables you to easily browse the example files for this book.

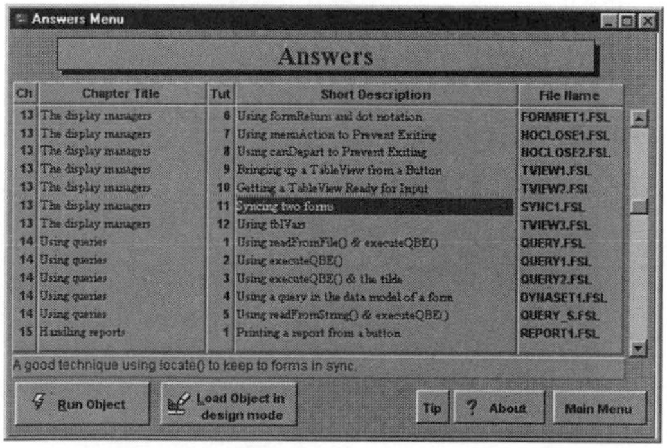

The clip-objects are in the DEV-SRC directory (which is short for *development source*). Use the form \APPS\APPS.FSL to browse the files. Each of the sample applications is in a subdirectory below the \APP directory. Use the form \APPS\APPS.FSL to browse the files.

Also on the disc are Appendixes A, B, C, and D.

Suitable Applications for Paradox

Studying the different types of applications could be a whole book by itself. In fact, discussing how to develop the various parts of just one type of application could take up a whole book. For example, a book could be devoted to developing all the nuances of an invoicing application. This section addresses some of the issues involved in developing the types of applications for which Paradox is best suited.

There are many types of applications. Because Paradox is a database management system (DBMS), it's best suited for developing databases. This doesn't mean that databases are the only type of application you can develop. In fact, you can develop many types of applications with Paradox. Table 1.1 discusses how well suited Paradox is for developing each type of application.

Table 1.1. Types of applications and Paradox.

Category	Suitability	Comments
Manager system	Sometimes yes	Suitable when one of the applications is written in Paradox
Database	Yes	Paradox's strong point
Informational	Yes	Paradox's strong point
Kiosk	Yes	Paradox's strong point
Educational	Usually yes	Educational software often uses tables
Desk accessory	Sometimes yes	Suitable only when a Paradox application is used
Games	No	A few interesting games can be created, however
Prototype	Yes	Prototyping applications in Paradox is very fast

Usually, choosing a tool is easy. When you are asked to do a certain project or when you get an inspiration to develop an application, usually you know what tool you should use. Clearly, Paradox isn't the best tool for every category of software. For example, you probably would not wish to write a file utility with it. If a project involves extensive amounts of data, Paradox will likely be well suited for the job. ObjectPAL is the powerful backbone of Paradox and, therefore, can be the backbone of a large DBMS. Paradox also is useful for prototyping an application that you plan to write in C or Pascal. Prototyping is the process of application development, in which small parts or the general structure of an application are designed and tested. These models are used as the basis for building the finished system. If you are going to develop applications, it is important to know what tool—or developing environment—to use.

Manager Systems

A *manager system* is an application that manages other applications. For example, the MAINMENU.FSL form in the main \SECRETS3 directory manages all the sample applications and forms that come with this book (refer to Figure 1.1). The MAINMENU.FSL form is your gateway to all of the files and subdirectories in the \SECRETS3 directory. MAINMENU.FSL uses a splash screen (SECRETS3.FSL), a main menu, and a help screen. These three elements give this manager system a professional touch. The code in the splash screen—SECRETS3.FSL—contains timers that offer interesting effects.

In general, Paradox isn't the best tool for developing a manager system. When one or more of the managed applications is written in Paradox, however, you might consider using it.

> **NOTE**
>
> Take the time now to open and browse through each application on the disc. Perhaps spend at least five minutes per application. It is important to become familiar with what Paradox can do. Don't worry about the code at this point—just learn what is on the disc. More specifically, learn what features are demonstrated in each application.

Database Applications

A database is any clearly identified collection of data. One example is a telephone book. In Paradox terms, a database is a set of related tables. It is a cohesive set of files—specifically, all the tables, forms, queries, reports, and anything else that you include within the scope of the files. This includes utilities, accessories, and so on.

A superset of a database application is a Database Manager System (DBMS). Typically, a DBMS differs from a database application only in its completeness. A DBMS is a collection of hardware and software that organizes and provides access to a database. Paradox is a perfect tool for both a database application and a DBMS. Several of the applications on the disc demonstrate this category of an application. These applications are as follows:

> **Mail Merge**
> **Version:** 2.0
> **Working directory:** \APPS\DDE-WORD
> **File to open:** DDE-WORD.FSL

The Mail Merge demonstrates an interesting technique for doing mail merge. It uses a DDE link to Word for Windows (see Figure 1.4).

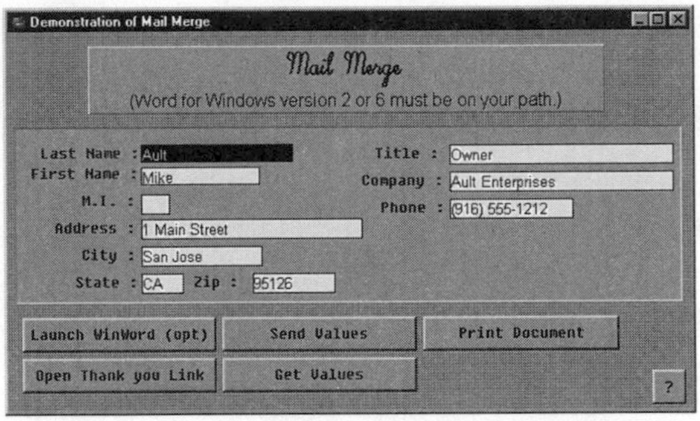

FIGURE 1.4.

DDE-WORD.FSL demonstrates using DDE to Word for Windows.

The People Keeper
Version: 1.0
Working directory: \APPS\PEOPLE
File to open: PEOPLE.FSL

The People Keeper tracks various information on people (see Figure 1.5). This application has an interesting data model that demonstrates linking several types of table relationships (these relationships are discussed in Chapter 2).

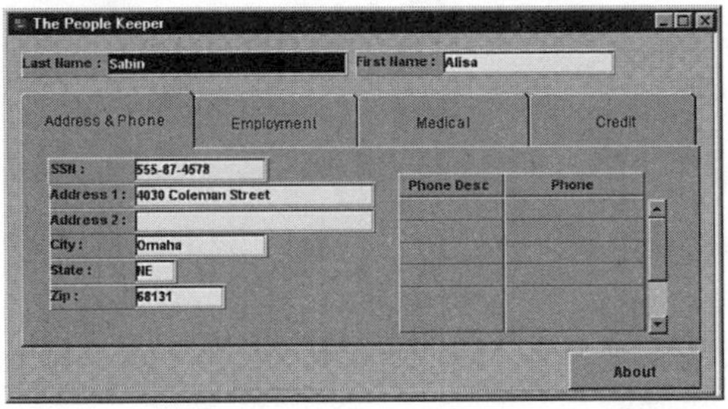

FIGURE 1.5.

PEOPLE.FSL demonstrates a medium-sized data model.

The Invoice System
Version: 2.0
Working directory: \APPS\INVOICE
File to open: INVOICE.FSL

The Invoice System is a multiform application that resides in the APPS\INVOICE directory. It contains a simple invoicing application that gets you started (see Figure 1.6). The Invoice System is not intended to be a complete invoicing application. You can use the Invoice System application as a template for your own invoicing system. I recommend that you use it for at least one hour. Study its code thoroughly before you alter it to your liking.

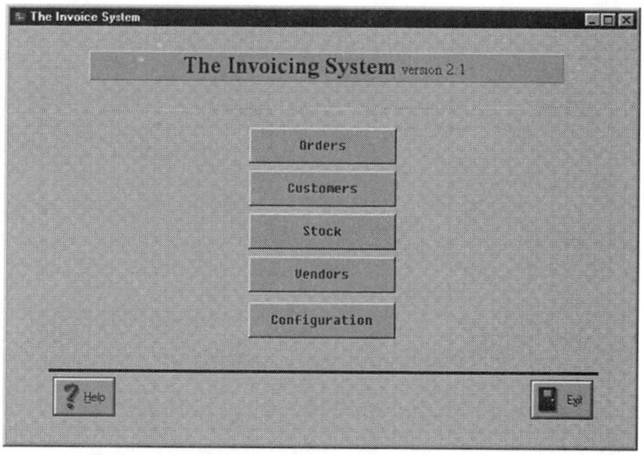

FIGURE 1.6.

*The main menu form of the
Invoice System application.*

Kiosk Applications

You've probably seen *kiosk applications* in airports, malls, and museums. They are stands with a monitor and some type of keyboard. You might use them to find your way, locate a store, or learn about a particular dinosaur. Generally, kiosk applications are user-friendly. They're similar to informational applications. A kiosk application is geared toward people who aren't computer users, however. It has a simple user interface, and the user can't exit the application.

Graphics and Multimedia

Paradox is suitable for some types of databases that traditional database managers don't handle well. You can use the Formatted Memo, Graphic, and OLE field types to store formatted text, bitmaps, sound, and movies. For example, you can use the Graphic field type to store graphics in your application easily. The MMEDIA.FSL sample application demonstrates this.

> **Multimedia Demo**
> **Version:** 1.0
> **Working directory:** \APPS\MMEDIA
> **File to open:** MMEDIA.FSL
>
> You can use this multimedia application as a template for your own multimedia application. Simply collect text, pictures, animations, and sounds on a particular subject and paste them into the appropriate fields (see Figure 1.7).

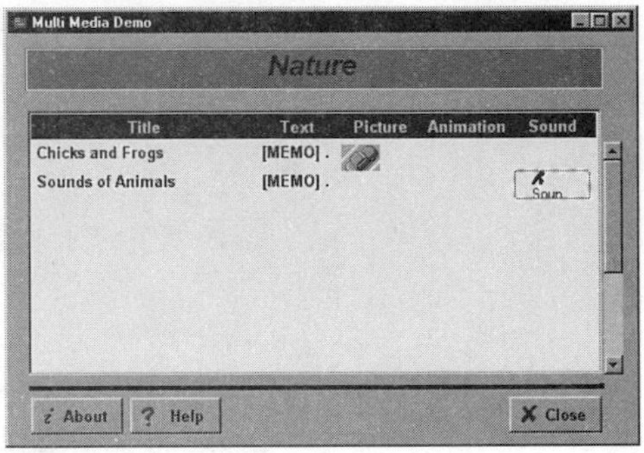

FIGURE 1.7.
MMEDIA.FSL is a simple
multimedia application.

Informational Applications

Database applications display, alter, and add data. Informational applications are a subcategory of database applications. They provide information, but they don't enable the user to alter the data presented to them.

> **Paradox 7 Reference Material**
> **Version:** 1.1
> **Working directory:** \APPS\REF
> **File to open:** REF.FSL

The APPS\REF directory contains reference material generated by ObjectPAL methods and procedures. You use the REF.FSL form to access various reference tables in the same directory. You can use these tables to look up various commands, properties, error messages, and more. Figure 1.8 shows REF.FSL, and Figure 1.9 shows one of the reports included with Paradox 7 Reference Material.

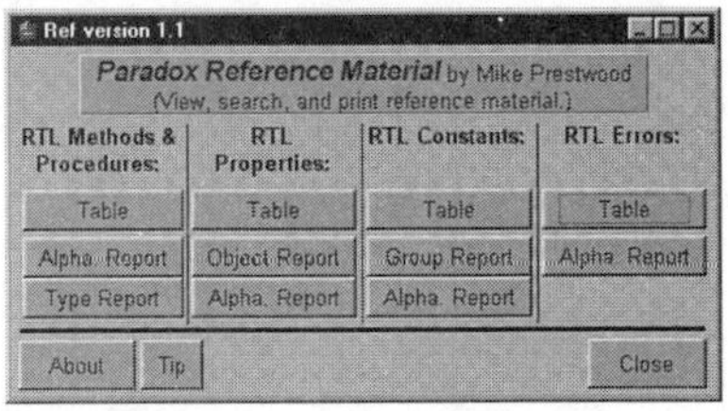

FIGURE 1.8.
REF.FSL provides easy
access to Paradox reference
material.

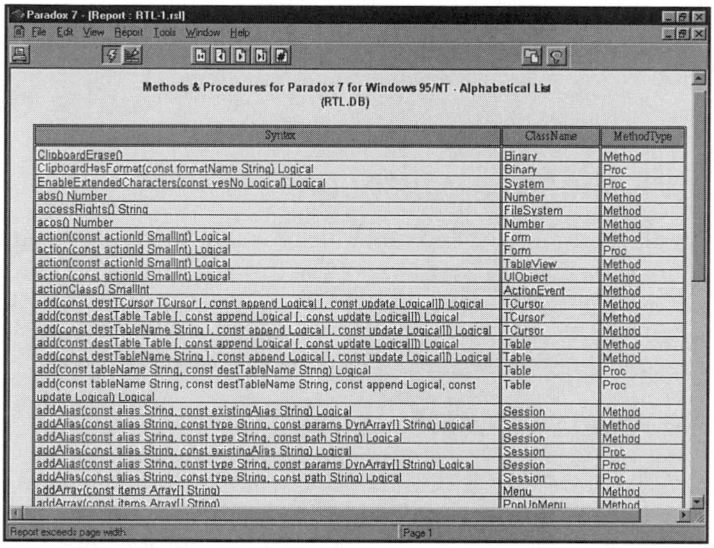

Methods & Procedures for Paradox 7 for Windows 95/NT - Alphabetical List
(RTL.DB)

Syntax	ClassName	MethodType
ClipboardErase()	Binary	Method
ClipboardHasFormat(const formatName String) Logical	Binary	Proc
EnableExtendedCharacters(const yesNo Logical) Logical	System	Proc
abs() Number	Number	Method
accessRights() String	FileSystem	Method
acos() Number	Number	Method
action(const actionId SmallInt) Logical	Form	Method
action(const actionId SmallInt) Logical	Form	Proc
action(const actionId SmallInt) Logical	TableView	Method
action(const actionId SmallInt) Logical	UIObject	Method
actionClass() SmallInt	ActionEvent	Method
add(const destTCursor TCursor [, const append Logical [, const update Logical]]) Logical	TCursor	Method
add(const destTable Table [, const append Logical [, const update Logical]]) Logical	TCursor	Method
add(const destTableName String [, const append Logical [, const update Logical]]) Logical	TCursor	Method
add(const destTable Table [, const append Logical [, const update Logical]]) Logical	Table	Method
add(const destTableName String [, const append Logical [, const update Logical]]) Logical	Table	Method
add(const tableName String, const destTableName String) Logical	Table	Proc
add(const tableName String, const destTableName String, const append Logical, const update Logical) Logical	Table	Proc
addAlias(const alias String, const existingAlias String) Logical	Session	Method
addAlias(const alias String, const type String, const params DynArray[] String) Logical	Session	Method
addAlias(const alias String, const type String, const path String) Logical	Session	Method
addAlias(const alias String, const existingAlias String) Logical	Session	Proc
addAlias(const alias String, const type String, const params DynArray[] String) Logical	Session	Proc
addAlias(const alias String, const type String, const path String) Logical	Session	Proc
addArray(const items Array[] String)	Menu	Method
addArray(const items Array[] String)	PopUpMenu	Method

FIGURE 1.9.
REF.FSL Report, Methods sorted alphabetically.

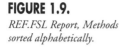

Utility Applications

Another category of applications that Paradox is well equipped to handle is utilities. A *utility* is an application that helps the developer run, create, or analyze other applications. For a small utility, the best tools to use are C or Pascal because a utility written in C or Pascal compiles into a single executable—that is, .EXE—file. You can develop two types of utilities with ObjectPAL. One type is a utility that helps developers create, modify, or analyze an application; the other type is a utility that helps end users run or use applications.

Because of the vast array of database commands and support for local tables (Paradox and dBASE) and remote tables (SQL), Paradox is a great candidate for database utilities.

Paradox Desktop
Version: 3.0 Demo
Working directory: `\APPS\DESKTOP`
File to open: DESKTOP.FDL

Paradox Desktop version 3.0 is an add-on utility for Paradox 7 for Windows 95/NT. This utility helps the Paradox 7 for Windows 95/NT developer and includes dozens of features, such as The Launcher, Paradox Task List, The Inspector, and The Status Pad. The Launcher enables you to launch a new instance of Paradox for Windows with a new private directory and working directory. Paradox Task List enables you to easily switch between instances of Paradox and to switch to forms or reports in the current instance of Paradox. This is particularly handy when you accidentally hide a form or report. The Inspector enables you to inspect forms, libraries, scripts, and tables for source code, link information, object names, object properties, and table structures. The Status Pad displays information about the currently active form, the currently selected object(s), Paradox 7, and Windows 95/NT (see Figure 1.10).

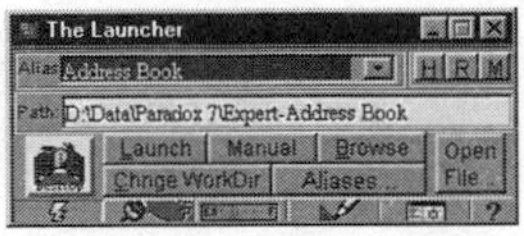

FIGURE 1.10.
*Paradox Desktop version
3.0 demo.*

Educational Applications

Another category of software for which Paradox is perfectly suited is *educational software*. Most educational software uses some type of database to store the information. Paradox, of course, has the database power. With its capability to manipulate objects during runtime, Paradox is perfect for developing educational software.

Desk Accessories

A term originally used in the Macintosh world, *desk accessory* refers to a small application that adds functionality to an application. Adding this type of application to your Paradox application is a good idea. It's not a good idea, however, to develop a desk accessory in Paradox for use outside of Paradox, because Paradox takes such a long time to load—usually 17 to 25 seconds. A programming language that creates executables would be good for non-Paradox-based applications because they can load much faster than Paradox. Sometimes it's a matter of using the right tool for the job.

Games

Paradox isn't suited for all games. You wouldn't develop a "shoot 'em up" game in Paradox because the game would run too slowly. Paradox is a suitable tool for educational games or games with a lot of data, however. The disc that comes with this book contains another game, Felicia, that demonstrates an appropriate match of tool and game.

> **Felicia**
> **Version:** 2.0
> **Working directory:** \APPS\FELICIA
> **File to open:** FELICIA.FSL
>
> The FELICIA.FSL form, shown in Figure 1.11, is a child's keyboard game. All the keys are disabled except for the letters and the numbers. When the user presses a letter key, a random sound is generated and both the uppercase and lowercase forms of that letter are displayed. If a number key is pressed, the number is displayed and a random three-note melody is played. To keep the youngster's attention, a picture of a horse scrolls across the top.

FIGURE 1.11.

The Felicia game for children.

Summary

In this chapter, you learned that Paradox is a database development tool with an event-driven, object-based programming language called ObjectPAL. In addition, you learned that Paradox is just a part of the complete software development life cycle. Although Paradox is best suited for database applications, there are many other types of applications that you can build. Paradox is also suitable for informational, kiosk, and educational applications. Also, certain other types of applications such as desk accessories and games can sometimes be built with Paradox.

The next two chapters deal with the development theory behind tables and forms. For example, they do not show you how to set up a one-to-many table relationship, but do tell you why. You will learn what a many-to-many table relationship is, when to use cascade delete, the six steps to developing a great form, and more.

Tables and Developing

2

The *table* is a tool that you, the developer, use to store data. In your continuing quest to study the fundamentals of design, this chapter discusses constructing a database; that is, creating tables with relationships in mind. It discusses all three types of database relationships and their variations—the one-to-one (1:1) relationship, the one-to-many (1:M) relationship, and the many-to-many (M:M) relationship. This chapter also helps you decide which table structure to use, namely, Paradox or dBASE. Finally, this chapter covers a few of the interesting characteristics of both dBASE and Paradox tables. First, however, consider the importance of aliases to the developer.

Aliases

NEW
Term

In the past, when you developed an application and moved the data, you had to redefine all your links (a link establishes a relationship between tables by connecting corresponding fields). If you moved one of the tables to another directory path, you created a big problem. The usual solution was to break and then create the link again. An *alias* is the name you assign to a directory path and implement to solve this big problem. Paradox uses aliases to refer to a location of files, such as a directory or SQL server.

In Paradox terms, the location that is pointed to by the alias often is called a *database*. Although aliases might be new to you, they are a great time saver. They make using hundreds of tables, queries, and forms in many different directories and on different servers manageable. There's tremendous value in having the capability to select File | Open | Table and browse through the aliases that you set up. In addition, you can use aliases in your code to refer to files. If you move the files, you just need to define the new path in the alias.

When Paradox first starts up, a dialog box that enables you to easily add or create an alias to a set of files or tables appears.

Using an alias offers the following benefits:

- Long path names are shortened to a single user-defined word.
- Your applications are instantly relocatable. ObjectPAL code can refer to objects by means of an alias. For example, when the path of your tables changes, redefine the alias to point to the new path.
- You can use multiple sets of data with the same application. After an application is set up with an alias, you can redefine your alias to point to a different path; instantly, you are working with a different set of data. This makes it possible to develop an application on your local drive and then switch the tables it uses to network tables and even to an SQL server with little modification.

You can set up aliases on a system by selecting Tools | Alias Manager. An even easier way is to use the *BDE Configuration Utility.* You can use the Aliases tab to easily browse through existing aliases and set the paths of existing aliases or add a new alias. I find it easier to use the BDE Configuration Utility to add and alter aliases (see Figure 2.1).

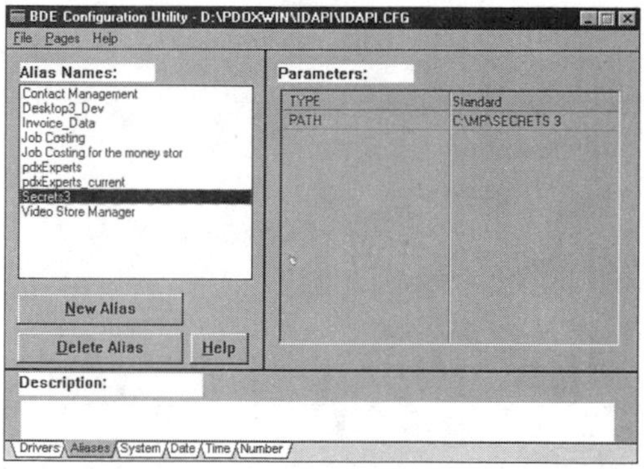

FIGURE 2.1.

The Aliases tab from the BDE Configuration Utility.

When you're ready to start structuring your tables, you need to decide where you want to place them. You have two choices: the current working directory or another directory. If you're developing a single-user application, it makes sense to put all the files in the same directory if you will never need to move the tables to a network directory. If you are developing what might become a multi-user application, consider separating the tables from the rest of the application and using an alias to refer to the tables. Using an alias makes your application more relocatable. Because Paradox doesn't search for a table, you must develop your application with tables in the current working directory or use an alias. Hard-coding table paths usually is a mistake because it then becomes more difficult to move the tables.

TIP

Put your tables in a directory different from the one that contains the forms, reports, and libraries. Use an alias to refer to the tables. This makes your application instantly a network-compatible application by making the tables relocatable. When you install the application onsite, you simply have to ask where to put the data and where to put the application. The application can be local or on the network. Place the data files where they need to be, and change the alias path. If you eventually want to move your data onto a SQL server, then you will have less code to rewrite.

TIP

If you are developing an application using local tables and you know you are eventually going to move the data onto a SQL server, then do yourself a favor and spend a few hours studying the field and table naming rules of your target SQL server before you create your first table. While creating your local tables, use a naming convention that uses common rules. If you use the naming rules in common between the two database types, then you will save yourself time when you move your data to the SQL server because SQL servers often have different naming rules than Paradox.

The *Invoicing System* uses the aforementioned technique of using aliases. The forms are in the \APPS\INVOICE directory and the data is in the \ANSWERS directory. It uses two aliases to manage the files: the Invoice alias points to the forms and reports, and the Invoice_Data alias points to the data files. See Appendix C for more suggestions on developing software with Paradox.

Public and Project Aliases

You can create either a *public* or *project* alias. Project aliases are stored in PDOXWORK.CFG file, which is loaded whenever you change working directories. You can think of project aliases as aliases that belong to a certain project stored in a specific working directory.

Paradox and dBASE Field Types

Why talk about Paradox and dBASE field types in a book on ObjectPAL? Partially because ObjectPAL is the backbone language to the Paradox DBMS, and understanding the field types into which you can store data is important. The main reason to discuss these field types, however, is so that you can become familiar with which types of data can go into which type of field. Later in this chapter, table field types and ObjectPAL data types will be discussed. For now, browse and study the following field types. Pay attention to the field types that are new to you. In particular, study what data can go in what field, and study each field type's maximum and minimum value limits. Understanding the type of data that can go into fields will help you better understand the ObjectPAL data types.

Alpha (A)—A general-purpose field type that can contain up to 255 letters, numbers, special characters, and other printable ASCII characters. The Paradox 3.5, 4, 5, and 7 table structures can use this field type. It is similar to the Character field type in dBASE.

Autoincrement (+)—This is a special field type that contains unique non-editable numbers. Paradox begins with the number 1 and adds one number for each record in the table. You can specify the starting number by specifying the minimum value during the creation of a table. Deleting a record does not change the field values of other records. This field type can be very useful when designing tables, and especially is useful for adding an artificial unique primary key to a table. (See "Primary Keys," later in this chapter.) This field type is valid for Paradox 5 and 7 tables only.

BCD (#)—First consider what a BCD field is supposed to do. Paradox BCD fields contain numeric data in a BCD (Binary Coded Decimal) format. Use BCD fields when you want to perform calculations with a higher level of precision than that available with the use of other numeric fields (up to 32 digits after the decimal point).

Calculations on BCD fields are not performed as quickly as those on other numeric fields. In Paradox, the BCD field type is provided only for compatibility with other applications that use BCD data. Paradox correctly interprets BCD data from other applications that use the BCD type. When Paradox performs calculations on BCD data, however, it converts the data to the numeric float type, and then converts the result back to BCD. This field type is valid with Paradox 5 and 7 tables only.

Binary (B)—This is a field used by programmers to store custom data that Paradox cannot interpret. For example, a binary field can be used for sound and animation. You can store any type of binary data in a binary field type; however, Paradox does not know what to do with data in a binary field. You have to add routines to your program to use the binary data. You can specify the amount of the binary data stored in the table (0–240 characters). This field type is valid with Paradox 1, 5, and 7 tables and dBASE 5 tables.

Bytes (Y)—Only advanced users who need to work with data that Paradox cannot interpret should use the Bytes field type because Paradox does not know how to interpret bytes fields. You can read and write the data in Bytes fields with ObjectPAL; for example, to store bar codes or magnetic strips. However, you will have to rely on other routines to manipulate the data (for example, functions in DLLs). Unlike binary fields, bytes fields are stored in the Paradox table (rather than in the separate .MB file), allowing for faster access. You can specify from 1–255 bytes. This field type is valid for Paradox 5 and 7 tables.

Character (C)—A dBASE character field can contain up to 254 characters (including blank spaces). This field is valid for dBASE III+, IV, and V. This field is similar to the Paradox Alpha field type.

Date (D)—Paradox 7 Date fields can contain any valid date from January 1, 9999 BC, to December 31, 9999 AD. This field type is valid for dBASE III+, IV, V, and Paradox 3.5, 4, 5, and 7.

Float (F)—dBASE provides two ways to store numeric data. The float number type contains numeric data in a binary floating-point format. Use the float number type on fields that will not require precise calculations to be performed on them; some degree of precision is lost during calculation. Float number fields are best used to contain whole numbers, or numbers of up to two decimal places. The size of a dBASE float number field can be from 1 to 20. This field type is valid for dBASE IV and V.

Formatted Memo (F)—Paradox-formatted memo fields are like memo fields, except that you can format the text. You can alter and store the text attributes typeface, style, color, and size. You can specify the amount of data stored in the table (0–240 characters). This field type is valid for Paradox 4, 5, and 7 Tables.

Graphic (G)—Paradox graphic fields contain pictures in .BMP, .PCX, .TIF, .GIF, and .EPS file formats. Not all graphic variations are available. Currently, for example, you cannot store a 24-bit .TIF graphic. When you paste a graphic into a graphic field,

Paradox converts the graphic into the .BMP format. You can specify how much of the data is stored in the table (0–240 characters). This field type is valid for Paradox for Windows 1, 5, and 7 tables.

Logical (L)—Paradox logical fields contain values representing True or False (yes or no). By default, valid entries include T and F (case is not important). This field type is valid for Paradox 5 and 7, and dBASE III+, IV, V.

Long Integer (I)—Paradox long integer fields are 32-bit signed integers that contain whole numbers in the range 2,147,483,647 to –2,147,483,647. Long integer fields require more space to store than Short fields. This field type is valid for Paradox 5 and 7.

Memo (M)—This is a special type of BLOB field used for storing text. *BLOB* is an acronym for *binary large object*. A BLOB is not a field type, but rather a data type. Field types that can contain BLOBs include binary, memo (both Paradox and dBASE), formatted memo, graphic, and OLE. You can specify how much of the binary data is stored in the table (1–240 characters). This data type is valid for Paradox 4, 5, and 7, and dBASE III+, IV, and V.

Money ($)—Paradox money fields, like number fields, can contain only numbers. They can hold positive or negative values. By default, however, money fields are formatted to display decimal places and a money symbol. Regardless of the number of decimal places displayed, Paradox recognizes up to six decimal places when performing internal calculations on money fields. Valid for Paradox 3.5, 4, 5, and 7, this field type was called Currency in versions of Paradox before verion 5.

Number (N)—This is a field that can contain only numbers from –10307 to +10308, with 15 significant digits. A number field can contain some valid nonnumerical characters, such as a decimal point or a minus sign. This field type is available in Paradox 3.5, 4, 5, and 7, and dBASE III+, IV, and V table structures.

dBASE number fields contain numeric data in a Binary Coded Decimal (BCD) format. Use number fields when you need to perform precise calculations on the field data. Calculations on number fields are performed more slowly but with greater precision than are calculations on float number fields. The size of a dBASE number field can be from 1 to 20. Remember, however, that BCD is in Paradox for Windows only for compatibility and is mapped directly to the Number field type.

OLE (O)—Use the OLE field to store data generated by an OLE server, such as images, sound, documents, and so on. The OLE field provides you with a way to view and manipulate this data without leaving Paradox. Paradox 5 now supports OLE 1 and OLE 2. You can specify how much of the binary data is stored in the table (0–240 characters). This field is valid for Paradox for Windows 1, 5, and 7, and dBASE 5.

Short (S)—This is a Paradox field type that can contain integers from –32,767 through 32,767. A short number field type uses less disk space than does the number field type. It's perfect for storing ages, years of employment, invoice numbers, item numbers, and so on. It is valid for Paradox 3.5, 4, 5, and 7.

Time (T)—Paradox time fields contain times of day, stored in milliseconds since midnight and limited to 24 hours. This field type is valid for Paradox 5 and 7.

TimeStamp (@)—Paradox time stamp fields contain a value comprised of both date and time values. Rules for this field type are the same as those for date fields and time fields. This field type is valid for Paradox 5 and 7.

TIP

To enter today's date, current time, or both into a Date, Time, or Datetime fields, press the spacebar repeatedly until Paradox enters the data.

NOTE

The BLOB types are binary, memo, formatted memo, graphic, and OLE. The value you specify in the Create Table dialog box refers to the amount of the BLOB data Paradox stores in the table. The entire BLOB is stored outside the table in a file with the same name as the table but with a .MB file extension. For example, the BLOB data for My Table.db is stored in My Table.mb.

Primary Keys

Paradox enables you to manage many types of data in its fields. A *field* in Paradox terms is a single value in a record—for example, City. The entire City column of a table is considered the City field. In addition to standard types of data, such as text, number, date, and currency, you can store a variety of data, such as graphic, OLE, and binary. With Paradox table structures, Borland gives you a variety of data types including Time, TimeStamp, BCD, and Autoincrement.

The *structure* of a table is the arrangement of fields in a table: their data types, indexes, validity checks, and so on. Now, more than ever, deciding on table structure and relationships is a crucial element of developing an application. Develop tables in two steps: decide on data components and then decide on the table relationships. The first step in deciding table relationships is to decide which fields need to be a part of the primary key.

A *record* is the horizontal row in a Paradox table that represents a set of data for that item, such as a person's address information. A primary key sorts your table and makes each record unique. A primary key isn't required but it is highly recommended. In fact, I suggest that every table you create should contain a primary key. A key on a Paradox table orders records and ensures unique records and allows *referential integrity*, which is a way of ensuring that the ties between similar data in separate tables can't be broken. Referential integrity is defined at the table level in Paradox. Establishing a key has several effects. It prevents duplicate records, sorts records, enables use of the table in a detail link, and speeds general access to the table.

A Paradox primary key can consist of more than one field. These fields are treated as one—a composite. A *composite key* or *index* is a key or index composed of two or more fields of a table. A composite primary key must be made up of the first fields of the table. Use composite key fields when a table contains no single field in which every value is unique. Together, the combination of the fields in the key sorts the table. Define the primary key from the first field through however many fields will make each record unique.

When a table has a composite key field, duplicate values are permitted in an individual key field as long as the values are not duplicated across all the key fields. In other words, the key fields, taken as a group, must uniquely identify a record. To sort tables that have composite key fields, Paradox starts with the first field and then sorts the following fields. Paradox's primary key also promotes normalized table structures (more on this later in this chapter).

Should you go crazy and key most or all the fields in a table? No. Your goal is always to find the least number of fields that will make each record unique.

Primary Keys and Secondary Indexes

An *index* is a file that determines the order in which a table displays records. It also enables objects such as UIObjects, TCursors, and Table variables to point to any record. A *secondary index* is an extra index primarily used for linking, querying, and sorting tables. Paradox tables can have a primary key and as many secondary indexes as you want, whereas a dBASE table can have only indexes—that is, files with .MDX or .NDX extensions. In general, you can refer to any file that sorts a table as an index.

> **TIP**
>
> Tables need indexes to speed them up. In Paradox, get used to the idea of creating maintained and case-sensitive secondary indexes. Accepting and doing this simple step will greatly improve the overall speed of your application—especially queries. When you move up to writing applications that access SQL servers, remember that creating indexes also speeds them up.

What are the differences between version 5 tables and version 7 Paradox tables? In version 7, secondary indexes are now more flexible. The new sort index options under Secondary Index are Unique and Descending. To convert a Paradox 4 or Paradox 5 table to a Paradox 7 table structure, you must use one of the new Paradox 7 table features, either when you create the table or restructure it.

Using a Primary Key

To demonstrate the proper use of primary keys and secondary indexes, develop a typical address table. In the following development cycle, you will see how a table may change over time as you realize what truly makes each record unique. This is a natural process. You can learn from this example that you do not have to finalize your table structures too early in the development cycle.

In a typical table consisting of addresses, you might index on the combination of first and last name. This combination of first name and last name makes every record in the table unique. The following is a typical address table with * representing the composite primary key:

```
1:  First Name*
2:  Last Name*
3:  Address
4:  City
5:  State
6:  Zip
7:  Phone
```

This table, however, first sorts by first name and then by last name. Abe Smith will come before Bobby Brown. For a more standard sort, you might sort by last name and then first name. If you need to search by first name, create a secondary index that consists of first names so that you can search and sort by a person's last name, first name, or last and first names. The following is a typical address table with a more standard sort order. It has a secondary index represented by **.

```
1:  Last Name*
2:  First Name*      **
3:  Address
4:  City
5:  State
6:  Zip
7:  Phone
```

After entering records for a few days, you may discover that you have two identical names, such as John Smith. Because the combination of last name and then first name no longer makes each record unique, you come to the conclusion that it is a good idea to include the person's middle initial. With large amounts of data, you might even include the street address. This takes into account people who have the same name, but who live at separate addresses. It also enables you to keep track of people's home and work addresses. Following is an example of a fully unique address table with a secondary index on First Name:

```
1:  Last Name*
2:  First Name*         **
3:  Middle Initial*
4:  Address*
5:  City
6:  State
7:  Zip
8:  Phone
```

In most cases, keying from the first field through however many fields needed to make each record unique works. This technique is awkward at times, however. Consider the previous case in which you have included one's address to force each record to be unique. The unique primary key now contains two types of data (a person's name and address). The key now consists of four fields and therefore takes up more disk space than a key with fewer fields. A different approach, perhaps slightly more elegant, involves using a single, unique field entry, such as a Social Security number field to make each record unique and using secondary indexes for alternate sorting and searching. Following is an example of a fully unique address table with two composite secondary indexes:

```
1:   SSN*
2:   Last Name          1 **       2 ***
3:   First Name         2 **       1 ***
4:   Middle Initial     3 **
5:   Address
6:   City
7:   State
8:   Zip
9:   Phone
```

If this table is developed for the government, then you might discover that the government actually reuses Social Security numbers. Therefore, if you need to keep a history, you may need to find another unique identifier, such as Birth Date:

```
1:   Social Security Number*
2:   Birth Date*
3:   Last Name          1 **       2 ***
4:   First Name         2 **       1 ***
5:   Middle Initial     3 **
6:   Address
7:   City
8:   State
9:   Zip
10:  Phone
```

If, for example, it is illegal to ask for a customer's Social Security number in your state, then the preceding table structure will not work. Because of a business rule, you might have to find another keying solution. The following presents a final solution, an autoincrementing key or artificial key:

```
1:   ID*
2:   Last Name          1 **       2 ***
3:   First Name         2 **       1 ***
4:   Middle Initial     3 **
5:   Address
6:   City
7:   State
8:   Zip
9:   Phone
10:  Social Security Number
11:  Birth Date
```

In this final solution, a random unique identifier is used to make each record unique. The Autoincrement field is perfect for this situation. The new Autoincrement field type is a special field type that contains unique non-editable numbers. Paradox begins with the number 1 and adds one number for each record in the table. This field type can be very useful when designing tables. In particular, it is useful for adding an artificial, unique, primary key to a table.

In general, try to avoid this final solution and use it only as a last resort. Using an artificial, unique, primary key generally is considered a bad idea. Have you ever gone into a store and been asked whether you know your customer number? Sometimes it's your phone number or your Social Security number, but sometimes it's a random number that you were expected to remember (and you probably didn't). If you use this last solution, make sure that you build an easy-to-use, effective way to quickly look up a customer's ID number.

As you can see, deciding which fields to include in a table is only half the battle. The other half of the battle is deciding what makes each record unique.

Printing a Table's Structure

Now that you have created your table structure, suppose that you want to print the structure of it to study and to keep in a safe place. Paradox doesn't have a direct command for printing the structure of a table. In versions 1.0 and 4.5 of Paradox for Windows, whenever you restructured a table or viewed its structure with the Info Structure option, a table named STRUCT.DB was created in your private directory. Many users grew accustomed to printing that table to print a table's structure. In versions 5 and 7, no :PRIV:STRUCT.DB table is created. The following is a brief tutorial on how to print the structure of a table in Paradox.

Step By Step

1. Select Tools | Utilities | Info Structure.
2. Select a table. The Structure Information dialog box appears.
3. Choose the Save As button.
4. Name the table (perhaps use :PRIV:STRUCT.DB). This creates a table with the name you entered.
5. Select File | Open | Table, and open the table you created in steps 3 and 4.
6. Select File | Print. To format the data, you could select Quick Report instead.

Follow the preceding instructions. Then design a few reports based on :PRIV:STRUCT.DB and add your own style to your structure printouts. Perhaps save your favorite report as STRUCT.RSL. If you stick with saving structures as :PRIV:STRUCT.DB, then you can simply open your favorite STRUCT.RSL report to view the table's structure; otherwise, you have to use the Change Table option of the Open Document dialog box.

> Paradox Desktop 3.0 enables you to easily print a table's structure or all the tables in a directory. A working demo version of Paradox Desktop is included on the disc that accompanies this book.

Relating Tables

The following material reviews the concepts and theories behind setting up table relationships. If you need help linking tables with the data model, refer to the *Paradox User's Guide.* Advanced database developers will appreciate this review of table relationships.

When you hear developers talk about table relationships, you hear things such as "the two tables are linked in a one-to-many." What they really are describing is the theoretical number of records possible in each table. The term *one-to-many* translates into the following: For every unique record in the first table, the second table can have many records. Examine a few cases to clearly understand relating tables, the terminology, and the theory behind relating tables.

The One-to-One Relationship (1:1)

Suppose that you're working with two tables that are both keyed on the Social Security number (the field name is SSN). One table contains personal information; the other contains medical information. You want to pull data from both of them and display that information as though it came from one database. You need to relate the two tables based on a common field or common fields—in this case, SSN.

After you relate these two tables in a 1:1 relationship, the medical database will display the correct record whenever you display a record from the personal database. Whenever you want to relate two tables, they must have one or more fields in common.

Now for the theory. Although you may not see a good reason that you can't dump all the information from both tables into a single table, there is one. In general database theory, it's a good idea to group data into smaller tables based on logical splits of the data such as address, employee, and medical information.

If you dump all the data into one huge table, managing the data can get out of control and the tables can grow unnecessarily. Imagine a table with address, employee, and medical information in it. It is a single table with perhaps 50 fields in it. Every time you create a new entry and store just address information or work information, the database reserves room on your hard drive for all 50 fields, even though the majority of the fields are empty!

Now, imagine that this table is broken into three tables: ADDRESS.DB, EMPLYEE.DB, and MEDICAL.DB. If you enter a record into the Address table, no room is necessarily reserved in the Employee and Medical tables. Breaking large tables into several tables can save disk space and makes working with your data faster and easier to analyze.

An Example of a 1:1 Relationship

A 1:1 relationship is really just a large table split into multiple tables and linked on a common field or fields. In the following table relationship, for every record in Customer, there can be only one record in Custnote. The form \ANSWERS\DM_1-1.FSL and data model file \ANSWERS\DM_1-1.DM demonstrate this table relationship (see Figure 2.2).

```
Customer.db                    Custnote.db
1:   Customer No* ===>          Customer No*
2:   Name                       Notes
3:   Street                     Picture
4:   City
5:   State
6:   Zip
7:   Country
8:   Phone
```

FIGURE 2.2.

This form DM_1-1.FSL demonstrates a 1:1 relationship.

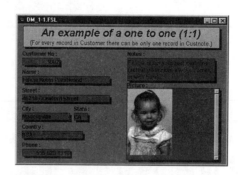

The One-to-Many Relationship (1:M)

A *master table* in a multitable relationship is the primary table of your data model. If there is only one table in your data model, it is the master table.

A *detail table* in a multitable relationship is the table whose records are subordinate to those of the master table. A detail table is also called a *slave* table, a *child* table, or a *many* table. A clearer way to state this is as follows: for every record in the master table, there can be many records in the detail table.

An Example of a 1:M Relationship

When you look at an invoice from a store, you typically are seeing a master table and its detail records; the end product of tables set up in a series of 1:1 and 1:M relationships. This next example shows two tables from a typical invoicing system. For every order in the Orders table, there can be many line items in the Lineitem table. Note that the two tables are linked on Order No and that the Lineitem table uses a composite primary key. The form \ANSWERS\DM_1-M.FSL and data model file \ANSWERS\DM_1-M.DM demonstrate this table relationship (see Figure 2.3).

```
Orders.db                    Lineitem.db
1:  Order No* ------------>>  Order No*
2:  Customer No              Stock No*
3:  Sale Date                Selling Price
4:  Ship Date                Qty
5:  Total Invoice
6:  Amount Paid
7:  Balance Due
8:  Payment Method
```

FIGURE 2.3.

This form DM_1-M.FSL demonstrates a 1:M relationship.

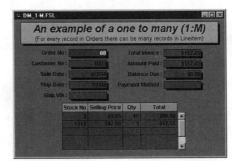

The Many-to-One Relationship (M:1)

Usually, when discussing table relationships, you're talking about the primary key. More specifically, however, you should be talking about the fields on which the tables are linked. The next example does not use an index on the first table; it demonstrates a M:1 relationship. At first glance, this may seem like a 1:1 relationship, but on closer inspection, it actually is a M:1. You can have many records in Orders with the same Customer No for any one Customer No in the Customer table. The Customer No field in the Orders table in this case is called a *foreign key.* The form \ANSWERS\DM_M-1.FSL and data model file \ANSWERS\DM_M-1.DM demonstrate this table relationship (see Figure 2.4).

```
Orders.db                    Customer.db
1:  Order No*
2:  Customer No <<--------   Customer No*
3:  Sale Date                Name
4:  Ship Date                Street
5:  Total Invoice            City
6:  Amount Paid              State
7:  Balance Due              Zip
8:  Payment Method           Country
9:                           Phone
```

FIGURE 2.4.

This form DM_M-1.FSL demonstrates a M:1 relationship.

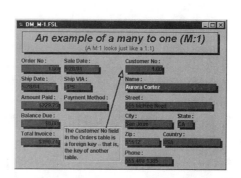

The Many-to-Many Relationship (M:M)

A many-to-many (M:M) relationship is when two tables share a common field or fields. Both can have multiple values based on the field(s) in common. Following is an example of a M:M relationship; Figure 2.5 shows the form equivalent.

```
Phone.db          Credit.db
1:  SSN* <<---->>  SSN*
2:  Phone Desc*    Credit Card*
3:  Phone          Number
4:                 Expiration
5:                 Credit Limit
```

The form \ANSWERS\DM_M-M.FSL and data model file \ANSWERS\DM_M-M.DM demonstrate this table relationship (see Figure 2.5).

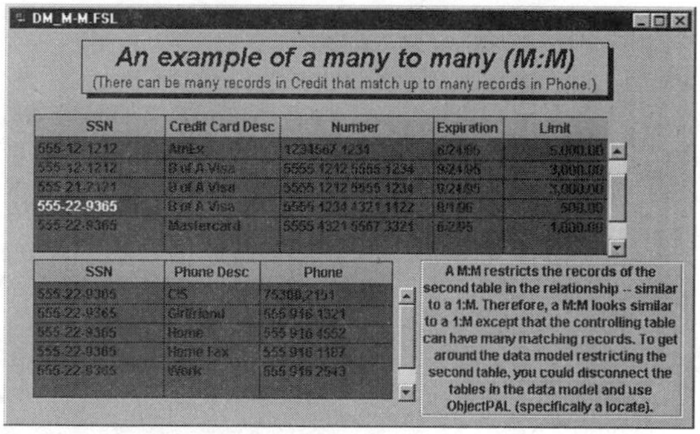

FIGURE 2.5.

The form DM_M-M.FSL is an example of a many-to-many relationship.

The preceding M:M relationship becomes clearer when you add an intermediate table and make the relationship a M:1:M (see the "An Example of a M:1:M Relationship" section, later in this chapter).

Relating Three Tables

Now that you understand the basic three table relationships, let's add a third table to the scenario and study some case examples.

An Example of a 1:1:1 Relationship

Earlier in this chapter, I mentioned breaking a large table full of address, employee, and medical information into three tables: ADDRESS.DB, EMPLOYEE.DB, and MEDICAL.DB. The following is that table relationship. The form \ANSWERS\DM_1-1-1.FSL and data model file \ANSWERS\DM_1-1-1.DM demonstrate this table relationship (see Figure 2.6).

```
1:  Address.db          Employee.db           Medical.db
2:  SSN* ---------->    SSN* -------------->   SSN*
3:  Last Name           Department            Male or Female
4:  First Name          Desk Phone            Color of Hair
5:  Address 1           Manager SSN           Color of Eyes
6:  Address 2           Start Date            Weight (lbs)
7:  City                Salary (per year)     Height
8:  State               Shift Start Time      Blood type
9:  Zip                 Shift End Time
```

NOTE

The tables in the preceding 1:1:1 example actually have more fields in the table than listed. The fields in the preceding list reflect the fields displayed on the DM_1-1-1.FSL form.

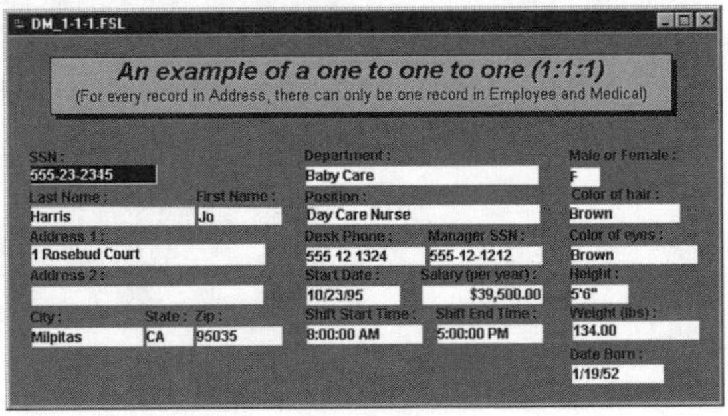

FIGURE 2.6.

This form DM_1-1-1.FSL demonstrates a 1:1:1 relationship.

An Example of a M:1:M Relationship

The next example is a followup to the M:M relationship presented earlier. This three-way table relationship is really just two 1:M relationships. For every record in the Address table, there can be many records in the Phone table and in the Credit table.

The form \ANSWERS\DM_M-1-M.FSL and data model file \ANSWERS\DM_M-1-M.DM demonstrate this table relationship (see Figure 2.7).

```
Phone.db              Address              Credit.db
1:  SSN* <<----       SSN*        ---->>   SSN*
2:  Phone Desc*       Last Name             Credit Card*
3:  Phone             First Name            Number
4:                    Address 1            Expiration
5:                    Address 2            Credit Limit
6:                    City
7:                    State
8:                    Zip
```

FIGURE 2.7.

*This form DM_M-1-
M.FSL demonstrates a
M:1:M relationship.*

A Deceiving Example of a M:1:M Relationship

As stated earlier, a typical invoicing system is simply a series of 1:1 and 1:M table relationships. The next example is of a M:1:M relationship. More precisely, it is a M:1 between Orders and Customer and a 1:M between Orders and Lineitem. There can be many records in the Orders table for every one record in the Customer table. For every record in the Orders table, there can be many records in the Lineitem table. The Customer No field in the Orders table is a *foreign key,* that is, the key of another table. The form \ANSWERS\DM_M-1-M2.FSL and data model file \ANSWERS\DM_M-1-M2.DM demonstrate this table relationship.

**New
Term**

```
1:   Orders.db              Customer.db        Lineitem.db
2:   Order No* -------------------->>          Order No*
3:   Customer No <<--------  Customer No*       Stock No*
4:   Sale Date              Name               Selling Price
5:   Ship Date              Street             Qty
6:   Total Invoice          City
7:   Amount Paid            State
8:   Balance Due            Zip
9:   Payment Method         Country
10:                         Phone
```

An Example of a 1:M:M Relationship

The next example is a 1:M:M (or more precisely, a 1:M with a 1:M). This example uses the same tables as the preceding example, but it views the data differently. A secondary index is used on the Orders table. The form \ANSWERS\DM_1-M-M.FSL and data model file \ANSWERS\DM_1-M-M.DM demonstrate this table relationship (see Figure 2.8).

```
 1:  Customer.db         Orders.db                  Lineitems.db
 2:                      Order No*       ------>> Order No*
 3:  Customer No* -->>   Customer No**              Stock No*
 4:  Name                Sale  Date                 Selling Price
 5:  Street              Ship Date                  Qty
 6:  City                Ship Via                   Total
 7:  State               Total Invoice
 8:  Zip                 Amount Paid
 9:  Country             Balance Due
10:  Phone               Payment Method
```

A good technique to use when you present this much data is to show the user only one or two identifying fields from each table and to use another page or form to show the details.

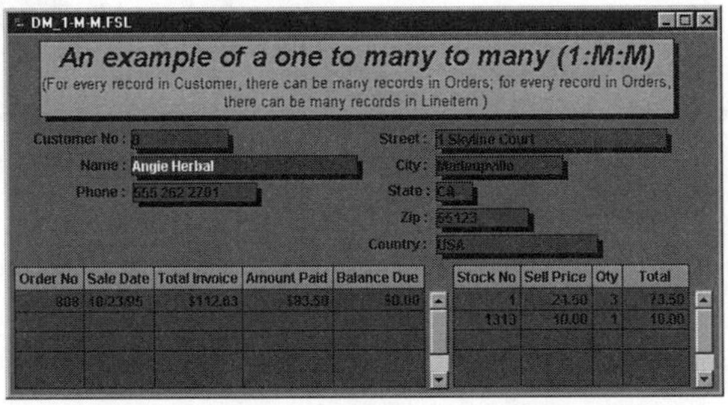

FIGURE 2.8.

This form DM_1-M-M.FSL demonstrates a 1:M:M relationship.

An Example of a 1:M:1 Relationship

Take a look at a table relationship that often throws developers off. In this scenario, you are developing the table structure for a clothing manufacturer. You have two tables: types of material and outfit patterns (MATERIAL.DB and PATTERNS.DB). You need to connect any one record in the Material table to any one record in the Patterns table. Initially, this sounds like a M:M, but it is not. After you start developing this table relationship, you will discover that you need a third intermediate table, as in the following:

```
1:  Material.db        Outfits.db              Patterns.db
2:  Cloth ID*  -->>    Cloth ID*
3:  Cloth Desc         Pattern ID* <<----      Pattern ID*
4:  Cost               Total cost              Pattern Desc
5:                                             Cost
```

This three-table relationship is a 1:M:1. For every record in the Material table, you can have many records in the Outfits table; and for every record in the Patterns table, you can have many records in the Outfits table. The file ANSWERS\DM_1-M-1.FSL demonstrates this table relationship.

The Recursive Relationship

NEW
Term

The last table relationship to be demonstrated is a *recursive relationship*. A recursive relationship is when a single table is used as though it were two tables. In certain table structures, a single table contains all the fields needed to link to itself in a 1:M relationship. For example, take a look at the following table:

```
Employee.db
1:   SSN*
2:   Department
3:   Desk Phone
4:   Manager SSN     **
5:   Start Date
6:   Salary (per year)
7:   Shift Start Time
8:   Shift End Time
```

Any one Manager SSN field can link to many records defined by the SSN field. To do this relationship, you need a primary key and a secondary index. Putting a table multiple times in a data model enables you to do a recursive relationship. To aid in visualizing this relationship, use a *table alias* in the data model.

In a data model, a table alias is an alternate name for a table. A table alias enables you to rename a table in a data model. This enables you to refer to the table in the data model by the table alias rather than the table name. This is important in ObjectPAL when you need to refer to a table in a data model. Rather than referring to the table name, you can refer to the table alias. This way, if you change the underlying table, you do not have to change your code if it refers to a table alias.

Table aliases also help when using a recursive relationship in a data model. You can give the same table that appears multiple times in your data model different table aliases. This doesn't have any real advantages except to help clarify your data model. The form \ANSWERS\DM_EMP1.FSL and data model file \ANSWERS\DM_EMP1.DM demonstrate this table relationship (see Figure 2.9).

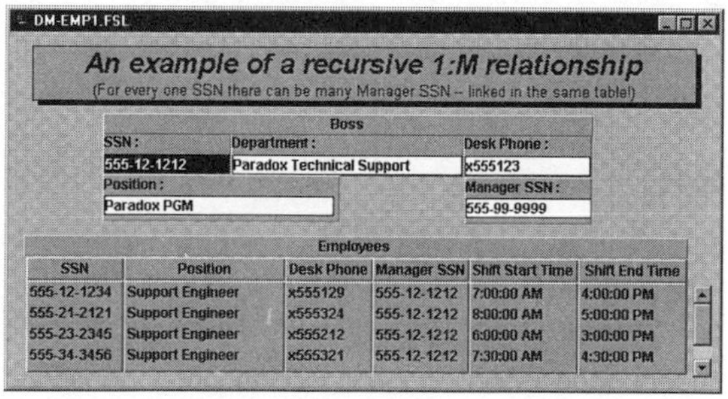

FIGURE 2.9.

The form DM_EMP1.FSL demonstrates a recursive one-to-many relationship.

The recursive relationship is easier to understand if you look at a variation of it, as follows:

```
Emp2.db
1:  Manager SSN*
2:  Employee SSN*              **
3:  Department
4:  Desk Phone
5:  Start Date
6:  Salary (per year)
7:  Shift Start Time
8:  Shift End Time
```

Now you can easily see that the combination of Manager SSN and Employee SSN makes each record unique. In addition, there is a secondary index on Employee SSN, so you can still use the table in the same manner as the previous example. The form \ANSWERS\DM_EMP2.FSL and data model file \ANSWERS\DM_EMP2.DM demonstrate this table relationship.

> **NOTE**
>
> Another technique for doing a recursive relationship in Paradox is to use a live query in the data model and link from the query to the table. For more information about live queries, refer to the *Paradox User's Guide*.

Normalizing a Data Structure

Now that you have laid down a foundation for creating and relating tables, this section discusses normalizing data. A *normalized data structure* arranges data to minimize data redundancy. This, in turn, usually leads to a database that uses less disk space, is easier to extract data, and sometimes is faster. When you normalize data, you decompose one big flat file table into multiple relational tables. Each record includes the smallest number of fields necessary to establish a category. Rather than dumping all possible fields into a large table, normalized tables distribute information over many tables. This saves disk space each time a user doesn't need to use a particular table. In addition, normalized tables provide more flexibility in terms of analysis. Normalized data should be your goal at all times. It enables you to optimize disk space, analyze data better, and make data easier to manipulate.

In this method of organizing information, you group fields into categories in which each record contains the least number of fields necessary to establish a unique group. A normalized data model is not required in Paradox, but it is highly recommended. The normalization process discussed next is broken into three steps: remove identical records, remove repeating groups, and move fields that do not relate to the key to another table. These three steps are commonly known as the first three normal forms. Although several other rules for normalizing data are common, it generally is agreed that the first three normal forms are sufficient for most database applications.

First Normal Form: Remove Identical Records

To put a table in first normal form, you remove all identical records. When you key a table in Paradox, you remove all duplicate records. (See the section, "Using a Primary Key," earlier in this chapter for a complete discussion.)

Second Normal Form: Remove Repeating Groups

To put a table in second normal form, you remove repeating groups—a process that is more difficult to explain. An example is used to help explain this step. In a traditional name and address table, you store a person's telephone number as part of the main table. In today's fast-paced, high-technology world, someone can have many telephone, fax, and communication numbers. A person can have several home and work numbers, as well as fax and modem numbers—perhaps even MCI and CompuServe account numbers. You could guess the maximum number of potential fields and put them in the table. (Typically, developers will put Home, Work, and Fax fields in their tables.) Some users might have no numbers, however, and some might have all three. Because when a new record is created, database products allocate disk space for all fields defined—this can be a waste of disk space.

In addition, this scheme does not work when you need to have four or more numbers. Data with the potential for so many telephone numbers should be normalized. Again, the second rule to normalizing your data is to remove repeating groups. A traditional table with a Home field, a Work field, and a Fax field repeat a single field Phone Number three times. A good solution to this problem is to break apart the two bodies of information and link them in a 1:M relationship with a data model. In other words, for every one record in the parent table, there can be many records in the child table. Following is an example of using a second table for telephone numbers:

```
Rolodex.db                  Rolodx-p.db
1:  Last Name*    ---->>   Last Name*
2:  First Name*   ---->>   First Name*
3:  Middle Name*  ---->>   Middle Name*
4:  Address 1              Phone # Name*
5:  Address 2              Phone Number
6:  City                   Phone Ext
7:  State
8:  Zip
9:  Zip Ext
10: Notes
```

Third Normal Form: Move Nonrelating Fields

The third and final normal form outlined in this chapter involves tables that have a composite primary key. If a nonkey field relies on only part of the total key, the nonkey field should be moved to a separate table. This means that every field in the table must be directly related to all the key fields—not just some of them. For example, in a typical invoicing system, the child or detail table consists of at least the following:

```
Lineitem.db
1:  Order No*
2:  Stock No*
3:  Description
4:  Selling Price
5:  Qty
```

Note that Description is related only to the Stock No field of the two-field composite index. Because Description does not directly pertain to Order No, it should be moved to another table and the two tables linked by the common field Stock No. The following structure accomplishes this:

```
Lineitem.db          Stock.db
1:  Order No*
2:  Stock No* -->    Stock No*
3:  Selling Price    Vendor No
4:  Qty              Description
5:                   Qty on Hand
6:                   Cost Price
7:                   Selling Price
```

> INVOICE.FSL uses the preceding table structures as part of its data model. It demonstrates how to use a separate table for the item description.

If you study and learn the preceding three rules of normalizing data, you will be able to create larger databases that are optimized for disk space. In addition, the data will be better organized and, therefore, easier to analyze. I suggest that you reread this section—or this entire chapter—in a month or two in order to drive the point home. In addition, consider purchasing a book on normalizing databases.

dBASE Tables Versus Paradox Tables

After you decide to use Paradox as your DBMS, you still need to decide whether to use a local table structure, such as dBASE and Paradox, or move to a DBMS server and the client server model. In general, use local tables when a smaller amount of data is being collected and use a DBMS server when either a very large amount of data is being collected, a large number of concurrent users will be accessing the data, or when a DBMS has features, such as automatic backup and recovery, that Paradox and dBASE do not offer. For a complete discussion of the client server model, see Chapter 35.

After you decide on a local table structure, you still need to decide between Paradox or dBASE table structures. You can store both Paradox and dBASE tables on either your hard drive or a networked drive. Both have their advantages and disadvantages. Although single-user applications can store the data on either your local hard drive or the network, multi-user applications usually store the data on the network. What follows is intended to help you decide, but I must tell you up front that my strong preference is the Paradox table structure.

The primary key in Paradox promotes normalized table structures. On the other hand, dBASE allows for the flexibility of non-normalized tables because it does not use the concept of a primary key. Both dBASE 5 and Paradox 7 offer flexible table structures. (Paradox 7 has many more field types, however.) In addition, the Paradox table structure enables you to use spaces, lowercase characters, and special characters in the field's name. This feature alone decided the issue for me. The Paradox table structure enables you to humanize field names.

The Paradox table structure supports so many advanced features that the choice seems clear. For example, the Paradox 7 table structure has referential integrity and supports advanced field types, such as Formatted Memo, Graphic, Time, and Autoincrement. In addition, Paradox 7 allows for unique and descending secondary indexes. dBASE, however, has the benefit of being supported on almost every platform, including DOS, Windows, OS/2, Macintosh, Amiga, and UNIX. Many products support the dBASE standard on many platforms. dBASE index expressions also permit tremendous flexibility. Refer to the "Using dBASE Expressions" section, later in this chapter.

Whether you use dBASE or Paradox tables is up to you. Each one has its advantages and disadvantages. dBASE gives you more flexible indexes and allows for compatibility across platforms. Paradox is faster, promotes normalized data structures, has referential integrity, and has more flexible field types. If, after reading this short section, you still are not sure which table structure to use, I suggest you read the rest of this chapter carefully and experiment with both structures until you decide.

Notes on the dBASE Table Structure

The following section contains notes on various important features of the dBASE table structure. The intent is to let you know about some of the key differences between the Paradox and dBASE table structures and to highlight features of each.

dBASE Tables Mark Records for Deletion

In dBASE, records are marked for deletion by the active index. They are deleted only after you pack the table. If you never pack the table, it will continue to grow. This is an advantage; it also is, however, a disadvantage that is easily overcome. You can put routines in your application to retrieve and purge deleted records. Just remember that dBASE tables must be purged of deleted records or they will continue to grow.

dBASE Allows Duplicates in the Main Index

Another difference is that with dBASE, you have the option of having duplicate key values in all the indexes except unique indexes. Even with a unique index, however, duplicate values are allowed in the table; duplicate values are prevented only in the index. After a Paradox table is keyed, it will not allow duplicates.

dBASE Record Numbers Are Not Dynamic

When you delete a record in dBASE, the record still exists in the table until you pack the table from the Restructure Table dialog box. The record number sticks with the record until the deleted records are purged. To purge deleted records from a dBASE table, restructure the table and select the Pack Table radio button.

NEW
Term

In Paradox, the record numbers are put on a heap stack, and therefore, are dynamic; in dBASE, they are not. With Paradox tables, the record numbers reorder whenever you delete a record. To accomplish this, Paradox uses the concept of a *heap stack*. A heap stack is a technique used to order a set of items in ascending order. In Paradox, the record number is a unique number that identifies each record and always starts with 1.

When you select Table | Filter for a Paradox table, the record numbers are reordered according to the new heap stack. When you do this same operation on a dBASE table, the record numbers for each record remain the same as before (compare Figures 2.10 and 2.11).

There are other less substantial differences between Paradox and dBASE tables. For example, the status bar and scroll bar behave differently, depending on which type of table you are displaying. For dBASE tables, the status bar shows you only the record number you are on, not what record number of how many, as in Paradox tables (see Figure 2.10). Finally, the scroll bar behaves oddly when you use it with dBASE tables. The scroll box appears to stick to the center of the scroll bar. You can attribute this final oddity to the fact that dBASE tables do not use a stack heap and it is difficult for Paradox to estimate where the record pointer is in relationship to the whole table.

FIGURE 2.10.

Customer table sorted by Customer.

FIGURE 2.11.

Customer table sorted by Name.

CUSTOMER	CUSTOMER	NAME	STREET	CITY	STATE	ZIP	COUN
27	1,513.00	Bernice Prestwood	Z32 999 #12A-77 A.A.	Marcoville	CA		Columbia
29	1,560.00	Bernie & Debbia Roach	15243 Underwater Fwy.	Marathon	FL	35003	U.S.A.
4	4.00	Beth Fenster	12 Lacey Drive	Milpitas	CA	95035	
22	1,354.00	Bob Holzbauer	PO Box 541	Milpitas	Gr	95035	British Wes
15	1,008.00	Brian Zunita	84 Main Street	Amyville	IL	55561	
70	6,582.00	Brigitte Parot	PO Box 6834	Marcoville	CA	PSBZ	Bermuda
5	5.00	Cassandra Leon	1 Leonkim Street	Manassas	VA	55321	
46	3,051.00	Charles Winship	1701-D N Broadway	Marcoville	CA	95443	U.S.A.
7	9.00	Chris & Mark Skinner	1 Raiders Street	Marcoville	CA	95035	USA
23	1,356.00	Daphne Homan	632-1 Third Frydenhoj	Christiansted	St	00820	US Virgin Is
1	1.00	Darcy Dunn	765 Mattos Ct.	Allentown	IL	55512	USA
44	3,041.00	David Clodges	634 Complex Ave	Pelham	AL	32145	U.S.A.
32	1,645.00	Dick & Cleo Unsicker	PO Box 5451-F	Sarasota	FL	32274	U.S.A.
62	5,165.00	E.J. Johns	3562 NW Bruce Street	Milwaukie	OR	96277	U.S.A.
18	1,221.00	Ed Wong	4-976 Sugarloaf Hwy	Kapaa Kauai	HI	94766	U.S.A.
9	23.00	Eddy Gorgen		Marcoville	CA	95035	
13	1,002.00	Felicia Robin Prestwood	46710 Crawford Street	Marcoville	CA	95035	USA
34	1,680.00	Forrest & Diane Sass	6133 1/3 Stone Avenue	St Simons Isl	GA	32521	U.S.A.
6	7.00	Glenn & Glenda Bryan	1 Skyline Court	Marcoville	CA	55123	
14	1,003.00	Henry Getz	1 Ruth Avenue	Marcoville	CA	55511	USA
19	1,222.00	Herbert & Alice Unsicker	1 Main Street	Marcoville	CA	95555	
52	3,168.00	James A. LaRheir	Blue Spar Box #3	Marcoville	CA	00820	US Virgin Is
21	1,351.00	Joe Santoro	1 Neptune Lane	Marcoville	CA	95035	Cyprus
42	2,975.00	Keith Kintamont	#73 King Salmon Way	Christiansted	St	02860	US Virgin Is

Using dBASE Expressions

One advantage that dBASE tables have over Paradox tables is that dBASE indexes are very flexible. You can write elaborate expressions using dBASE keywords in the Define Index dialog box (see Figure 2.12). The dBASE expression engine enables you to code expressions that give you a unique view to a table. Paradox tables do not use expressions as part of their indexes; Paradox indexes enable you to specify the order of fields and only have four options: Unique, Maintained, Case Sensitive, and Descending. The following are all the dBASE functions supported by the expression engine:

ABS	DTOR	LOG10	SIGN
ACOS	DTOS	LOWER	SIN
ASC	DTOS	LTRIM	SPACE
ASIN	EXP	MAX	SQRT
AT	FIXED	MIN	STR
ATAN	FLOAT	MOD	STUFF
ATN2	FLOOR	MONTH	SUBSTR
CEILING	FV	PAYMENT	TAN
CHR	IIF	PI	TRANSFORM
COS	INT	PV	TRIM
CTOD	ISALPHA	RAND	UPPER
DAY	ISLOWER	REPLICATE	VAL
DIFFERENCE	ISUPPER	RIGHT	YEAR
DIV	LEFT	ROUND	
DOW	LEN	RTOD	
DTOC	LOG	RTRIM	

Following are some examples of index expressions:

> DEPT+UPPER(LNAME) lists records by DEPT and LNAME fields. In this case, the index ignores case in the LNAME field.

> UPPER(Field1)+UPPER(Field2)+UPPER(Field3) lists records by the Field1, Field2, and Field3 fields. In the following index, case is ignored completely.

```
SUBSTR(DEPT,1,3)+SUBSTR(UPPER(LNAME),1,3)
DEPT+DTOS(DATE_HIRED)
DEPT+STR(DATE()-DATE_HIRED,4,0)
DEPT + STR(YEAR(DATE_HIRED),4,0) + STR(MONTH(DATE_HIRED),2,0) +
➥STR(DAY(DATE_HIRED),2,0)
IIF(DEPT="SALES",SUBSTR(LNAME,1,3),SUBSTR(CITY,1,3))
IIF(STATE="AZ".OR.STATE="CA",STATE+"A",STATE)
DEPT+STR(YEAR(DATE_HIRED),4,0)+STR(SALARY,7,0)
DEPT+STR(MONTH(DATE_HIRED),2,0)+STATE
DEPT+STATE+STR(100000-SALARY,8,0)
```

FIGURE 2.12.

*Entering dBASE
expressions.*

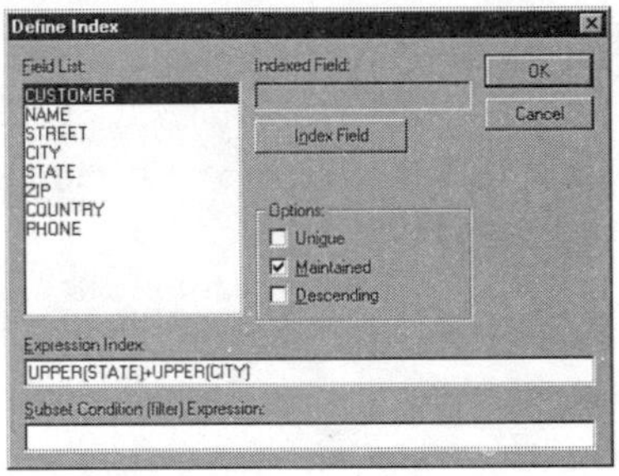

The preceding examples of index expressions show you how flexible dBASE indexes are. You are limited to expressions that have a length of no more than 220 characters and result in no more than 100 characters. The CUSTOMER.DBF in the ANSWERS directory has a few indexes defined.

WARNING

Not all dBASE structures are the same! Slight variations with the .DBF table structure, as well as drastic variations in the index, exist between different implementations. In general, all .DBF database files are similar enough in structure not to cause any problems. Indexes, however, are another story. Paradox is compatible with only .NDX and .MDX indexes. For example, you can't use Clipper .NTX indexes or FoxPRO's proprietary (.COX) indexes.

Notes on the Paradox Table Structure

As an ObjectPAL programmer, you must keep in mind the things that are better accomplished in interactive Paradox—for example, at the table level. This section talks about the various Paradox table properties. It concentrates on using pictures to aid data development and to control data. This section also discusses how various concepts of referential integrity apply to Paradox tables.

Paradox Table Properties

The Paradox table properties are important. They enable you to restrict data input, use lookup tables, add secondary indexes to sort and view your data differently, add referential integrity to ensure the data in two tables stay linked, add password security, change the table's table language, and view the dependent tables associated with a table.

Following is a quick review of table property options:

Validity Checks—These options control and guide the values a user can enter in a field. They enable you to set up default values, data input checks, required values, and more.

Table Lookup—This is a data entry tool that ensures that data from one table is entered correctly in another table.

Secondary Indexes—As discussed previously, secondary indexes are very useful in interactive mode and in ObjectPAL. Secondary indexes are useful for speeding up operations and viewing data in different ways.

New to Paradox 7, secondary indexes are Unique and Descending. These new options enable you to show your data in the following two new views.

7 NEW Feature

Referential Integrity—This enables you to ensure data across two tables. With referential integrity, you can make sure that ties between data will not be broken. For example, one option enables you to prohibit the deletion of a master table record if the child table has corresponding records.

Password Security—Full-password encryption at the table and field levels guarantees the security of your data.

Table Language—The language driver for a table determines the table's sort order and the available character sets. The default table language is set by the BDE Configuration Utility. When you create or restructure a table, you can override the default table language with the Table Language option in the Table Properties panel in the Restructure dialog box. Paradox 7 offers many language drivers, including several ANSI language drivers, that enable you to store Windows ANSI high characters.

Dependent Tables—This table property shows all the tables that are recognized as children in a referential integrity link.

Picture Strings

A *picture string* is a pattern of characters that defines what a user can type into a field during editing or data entry of a table or form. A picture string aids data entry and promotes—but does not ensure—consistent data. Picture strings are an input aid and a means of validating data.

Although picture strings can be implemented on a field at the table or form level, they are best implemented at the table level. When you add a picture to a table, any forms you create using that table will inherit the picture string. Every ObjectPAL programmer needs to keep this in mind. If you must limit what someone can enter into a field, implement the limiting factor at the table level with a validity check, if possible. You should use ObjectPAL on a form only when you determine that a picture won't work. Remember, ObjectPAL is on the form only. Unless you password-protect your table, nothing can prevent the user from selecting File | Open | Table and entering data directly into the table; in other words, bypassing your ObjectPAL code. This concept applies to all database backends, including SQL servers. One of the basic tenets of developing a good client server application is to put as much processing on the database server as possible.

Use the Picture Assistance dialog box to enter new pictures (see Figure 2.13). To get to the Picture Assistance dialog box, select the Assist button on the restructure table dialog box.

FIGURE 2.13.

The Picture Assistance dialog box.

Table 2.1 lists the picture string characters you can use to validate data.

Table 2.1. Picture string characters.

Character	Description
#	A numeric digit
?	Any letter (uppercase or lowercase)
&	Any letter (converts to uppercase)
@	Any character

Character	Description
!	Any character (converts to uppercase)
;	Interprets the next character as a literal character, not as a special picture string character
*	The character that follows can be repeated any number of times
[xyz]	The characters between square brackets are optional
{x,y,z}	Optional characters separated by commas
{}	Grouping operator
,	Alternative choices of values

Any other characters you use in a picture string are treated as a constant. Paradox automatically types the constant when the user comes to a point in the picture string in which that constant is specified. The exception is the first character, which figures since in life there are almost always exceptions. The user must tell Paradox that he or she wants to enter data by entering the first character or by pressing the spacebar for autofill.

TIP

Remember, autofill is a great feature that you should promote to your users. To automatically fill in a date field with today's date, for example, just press the spacebar a couple of times. Make sure you add this type of help to any manuals or help files you develop for your application. Autofill works with Date, Time, Timestamp, and Logical fields and does not require a picture statement.

The PICTURES.TXT file is on the disc that comes with this book in the \DEV-SRC directory. You can use the Notepad to open it and paste the settings into the Picture Assistance dialog box.

Useful pictures include the following:

```
Phone with auto fill = ###-####
Phone with auto fill (area opt) = [(###)]###-####
Phone w/1-800 optional = [{1-800-,(###)}]###-####
Flexible Phone Number = [1 (*3{#}) ]*3{#}-*4#
US 5 or 9 Zip Code = #####[-####]
US 5, US 9, or Canada zip code = *5{#}[*4#],@#@ #@#
SSN with auto fill = ###-##-####
SSN no auto fill = ###{-}##{-}####
Letters only (no spaces) = *?
Letters only (capitalize first) = &*?
```

```
Capital Letters = *&
Capital First letter = !*@
Capitalize every word 1 = *[![*?][* ]]
Capitalize every word 2 = !*[ * !,@]
Capitalize every word 3 = *{ ,.}!*{{ ,.}^{ ,.}!,@}
Capitalize every word 4 = *[[*#[ ]]![*?][@][ ]]
Capital After = !*[{ ,.,(,;,}*{ ,.,(,;,}!,@]
Time (HH:MM:SS:) = {0#,1#,2{0,1,2,3}}:{0,1,2,3,4,5}#:{0,1,2,3,4,5}#
Time with SS optional = {0#,1#,2{0,1,2,3}}:{0,1,2,3,4,5}#[:
{0,1,2,3,4,5}#]
Time (HH:MM AM) or (HH:MM PM) = {1{:,{0,1,2}:},{2,3,4,5,6,7,8,9}:}  {0,1,2,3,4,5}#
➥{AM,PM}
Date with auto fill = {##/##/##,#/##/##}
Date 2 = {##/01/##,#/01/##}
Allow Miss, Ms., Mr., or Mrs. = M{iss,s.,r{.,s.}}
Allow Dr., Doctor, Father, Miss, Mrs., Mr., Mr. & Mrs., Ms., Msgr.,    Pastor, and
➥Reverend: =
{D{r.,octor},Father,M{iss,r{s.,.[ ;& Mrs.]}, s{.,gr.}},Pastor,Reverend}
```

Using Table Lookup Effectively

When the user presses Ctrl+spacebar to display a lookup table, the Lookup Help dialog box respects the table properties set for the table. You can use this feature to jazz up the way the table lookup dialog box looks. For example, you can change the colors of a table in a table window and the changes will carry over to the table lookup dialog box. The table properties you alter are stored in the tableview file with the same name as the table and a .TV extension. When you use that table in the lookup, it will appear with the new property values.

TIP

When users press Ctrl+spacebar to display a lookup table, remember to let them know that they can use Ctrl+Z (zoom) to locate a value. This is an interactive feature that can greatly enhance the user's perception of your application.

Table Lookup Does Not Use Aliases

When you use the Table Lookup feature, use lookup tables in the same directory or subdirectory of the master table. If you do, then you can freely move the master table and lookup table to another directory without losing the lookup table. If you use a lookup table outside the master table directory, Paradox hard codes the path to the table. This creates a problem when you move data.

The reason Paradox for Windows 1.0 table structures do not support aliases when setting up lookup tables is for compatibility with Paradox for DOS 4.5. The concept of aliases does not exist in Paradox for DOS. If Paradox for Windows allowed the use of aliases in lookup tables, then Paradox for DOS would not know how to interpret the alias. Therefore, even if you specify an alias, the path (not the alias name) is stored along with the table name.

What about Paradox for Windows 5 and 7 tables? Paradox for Windows 5 and 7 tables behave the same as Paradox for Windows 1 tables do, with respect to lookup tables and aliases. Because Paradox for DOS cannot open a Paradox for Windows 5 or 7 table, I do not know why this occurs. Perhaps Borland is planning a Paradox for DOS version 5 or 7 that still will not support aliases.

Table Language and Sorting

How do you get support for special character sets in Paradox? For languages whose characters are written with an alphabet—not languages such as Chinese and Japanese—a language driver that supports the character set needs to exist, or Borland must create and release one.

In addition, the sort order of a table depends on the *language driver*. The three main language drivers with which we are concerned here in the United States are Paradox *ascii*, Paradox *intl*, and Paradox *ANSI INTL*. The Paradox intl (international) and Paradox ANSI INTL drivers sort alphabetically, mixing uppercase and lowercase; for example, aAbBBccC. The Paradox ascii (ASCII) driver sorts by the ASCII table, putting all the lowercase characters first; for example, aabbbcdAAABCCCD. It is important to know that the way in which Paradox sorts a table depends on the language driver.

NEW
Term

Secondary Indexes

Earlier in this chapter, the importance of primary keys was addressed. A secondary index is used to sort a table by any of the fields in the table (not just by the primary key). A *secondary index* is a field or group of fields that you define as an alternate sort order for a table. You can use secondary indexes to view a table in a separate sort order, link a table on a field other than the primary key, and to speed up search and locate operations. A table can have more than one secondary index and each secondary index can be a composite of fields. When you use a secondary index, you change only the view order of the records. The physical location of the records in the table does not change. Secondary indexes are flexible and include the following options: Composite, Unique, Case-sensitive, Maintained, and Ascending/Descending.

NEW
Term

> **NOTE**
>
> You cannot create a secondary index on a memo, formatted memo, binary, OLE, graphic, logical, or bytes field.

Before Paradox 4.0, most users didn't even know what a secondary index was. With Paradox 4.0 for DOS, secondary indexes became one of the options on the Main pull-down menu. In Paradox for Windows, secondary indexes are an integral part of the table structure. If you need help with secondary indexes, refer to this chapter for theory, and the *Paradox User's Guide* for interactive instructions.

Referential Integrity

Referential integrity (RI) is extremely important. Point-and-click referential integrity enables you to set up relationships between tables so that your data is always valid. *Data integrity* is a guarantee that the values in a table are valid. You can use various features of Paradox tables to protect data from misuse, including the required field option, the minimum and maximum options, and picture statements. Data integrity for autoincrementing, for example, might mean that no two records have the same key values. For referential integrity, data integrity might mean that the records in one table will always match the records in another table.

There are various types of referential integrity. Paradox supports Prohibit, Cascade, and Strict Update rules. Figure 2.14 shows a referential integrity link being set up between LINEITEM.DB and STOCK.DB. To display this dialog box, restructure the child table of a one to many, select Referential Integrity from the Table Properties drop-down edit box, and select either Define or Modify. Note the two options selected in the Update Rule panel.

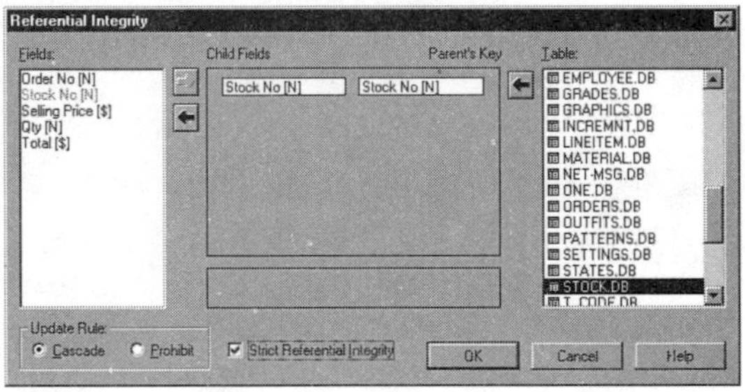

FIGURE 2.14.

The Referential Integrity dialog box, which shows a link between LINEITEM.DB and STOCK.DB.

Setting up Referential Integrity

You must be in the child table to create a referential integrity link. In addition, you must make sure that the child table contains all key fields of the parent. Besides controlling data entry, the referential integrity link provides an update feature: either Cascade or Prohibit.

Cascade enables you to update child tables when a value changes in the parent table. With Cascade referential integrity, any changes that are made to the parent table's primary key are automatically made to the child table. Therefore, if you make a change to the parent table's primary key, the child table's foreign key also is updated. Referential integrity links don't need to be made on key fields in the child table. Whenever a change is made to the parent key, the change is cascaded to all the child records that match that key. If you change the spelling of a customer's name from Smith to Smythe, for example, the data in the reference field of all the child table records that consist of this key also will change.

> **WARNING**
>
> If you delete a record in the parent table, the related records in the child tables are not deleted. Although Paradox supports cascade updates with a convenient table level feature, it does not support cascade deletes with a table level feature. See "Implementing Cascade Delete Using ObjectPAL" in Chapter 16.

Prohibit referential integrity prevents a change in the parent's key if any records match the value in the child table. You can use Prohibit in an invoicing system to prevent the invoice numbers in existing line-item entries from being changed or deleted.

New Term

Strict Referential Integrity Checkbox

Strict Referential Integrity should have been called "Prohibit Paradox 4.0" because it prevents Paradox 4.0 and its earlier versions from writing to the table because they don't support referential integrity. When the Strict Referential Integrity option in the Update Rule panel is checked, Paradox 4.0 for DOS can't alter data (refer to Figure 2.14). This feature is designed entirely for interoperatability with Paradox for DOS.

When strict integrity is selected, Paradox 4.0 and 4.5 see the table as being write-protected. Therefore, the data can be viewed in Paradox for DOS, but can't be changed. If you are going to use referential integrity, and data security is important, then you should also turn on Strict Referential Integrity.

The Parent Must Use a Primary Key

One of the requirements to use referential integrity is that the parent table has a primary key. The child table must use all the fields of the parent table's primary key.

A parent table holds the master values for the link. It has the power to change these values, delete them, and add new values. A child table depends on the values in the parent table for its matching fields. Only the ones that exist in the parent table are available to a user to alter or view in a form.

Automatic Secondary Index

A referential integrity link can be defined between the primary key in a parent table and any index in a child table. The fields must match in number, type, and size. In other words, a parent table with two fields in its primary key must link to an index—primary or secondary—with two fields of the same type in the child table. You can use composite secondary indexes on the child table in a referential integrity link.

If Paradox needs to, it will automatically create any secondary indexes needed to establish a referential link. If Paradox needs a single field secondary index, it creates Case Sensitive and Maintained and names it the same name as the field. If more than one field is needed, it names it the same name as the name you gave the referential integrity link.

Blank Field Caution

In referential integrity, blank fields are permitted to exist in the child, even when no matching blank field exists in the parent. Blank fields are considered to be outside the referential integrity link. This feature comes in handy when you want to enter a child record without matching it immediately to a parent record; you can add the link value later.

NEW
Term

You should not blank out a primary key value in the parent table, however. If you do, the corresponding fields in the child records are made blank as the change cascades from the parent. When you change the blank primary key to a nonblank value, the child records that were linked to it will remain blank. This is known as *orphaning records*. Remember, blanks in the master are considered to be outside the link.

To prevent orphaning of child records, restructure the table and use the Required Field validity check for all the key fields. In fact, it generally is considered good database design to make all the fields in a Paradox primary key Required Fields.

NOTE

Referential integrity and other settings stored in .VAL files sometimes interfere with the development of a project. This particularly is a problem when you are restructuring a child table in a referential integrity link. If this happens to you and you don't mind losing the validity checks for a table or for a set of tables, go ahead and delete or, better yet, rename them.

Be careful, however. All the validity checks will be deleted. For example, the ORDERS.DB, CUSTOMER.DB, LINEITEM.DB, STOCK.DB, and VENDORS.DB tables in the SAMPLE directory that comes with Paradox are a wonderful starting point for an invoicing system. The .VAL files—or more precisely, the table validity checks and referential integrity—might interfere, however, with you using the tables.

Summary

No matter which table structure you choose, use aliases and make sure that your data model is correct. Aliases are your ticket to portability. No matter what type of relationship you set up, your data model is simply a series of 1:1, 1:M, M:1, and M:M relationships. When you study a complex data model, examine the relationship between any two tables.

The form is a wonderful tool, but it isn't the place where data is stored: the table is. Therefore, the table is a much better place to implement data integrity. Set up data validity checks at the table level if possible. You can use pictures, table lookups, and referential integrity to implement data integrity. Only after you determine that a data restriction can't be implemented at the table level should you move to the form level and use ObjectPAL to manipulate a user's input.

Forms and Developing

3

IN THIS CHAPTER

With Paradox, you can create forms and reports visually. You can create dazzling single or multiple forms for viewing, editing, and adding data. This chapter shows you how to begin integrating design elements into a complete application. It deals with issues, problems, and solutions with design documents from a developing point of view. A *design document* is a form or a report that a developer uses to display data. This chapter also dives into special, summary, and calculated fields.

Study Applications for a Better User Interface

The user interface is the first element of your application that a user sees. Because first impressions are important, the user interface carries more weight than any other part of your application. It deserves much planning and effort. While developing Windows 95, Microsoft spent much money and time planning and testing the user interface. The efforts of Microsoft are apparent in the user-oriented design of the new operating system. If you are a Windows 3.1 developer and you are developing your first Windows 95 application, then you owe it to your users to study and learn the look and feel of Windows 95. When you deliver an application that has the look and feel of the operating system, the user is instantly familiar with your application and its user interface. Rather than trying to learn a new user interface, the user focuses on learning how to perform the task for which your application is intended.

Often when you start a new form, you already have an idea of what you want it to look like. When you're inspired, go with it and harvest your inspiration. However, even when you are inspired, plan your user interface carefully, down to the most seemingly insignificant details. With large applications, document your look and feel in an application style guide.

When you're struggling to find the right look and feel for a form or application, however, why reinvent the wheel? Software companies spend millions of dollars studying the look and feel of software. You can benefit from all this effort by looking through the software right on your machine. Take some time—perhaps now—to open up and browse through your favorite Windows 95 software applications. In general, what does the application look like? Look for consistent features. Are all the buttons the same size? If the application deals with large amounts of data, how is that data handled? Does the application use any Windows 95 style gadgets? What color scheme did they develop? What things do you like, and what do you dislike? What would you change? Be really choosey. Closely examine the details of these professionally developed applications.

Your applications should look as professional as commercial applications. The closer you get, however, the more your users will enjoy your application. You should at least choose a design concept and stick to it. Select your colors, form size, button size and location, frame style, and fonts. Don't stray from the standard that you set for a particular project. If you don't know what the look and feel should be, design with a simple version of the Windows 95-style look and feel.

Do yourself a favor and purchase a good book on user interface design and concept. To really master the Windows 95 and Windows NT look and feel, consider a user interface book specific to Windows 95 and Windows NT.

Study Objects Before You Start Designing

Paradox comes with a plethora of objects and options, including new Windows 95-specific objects. Browse through them and look at their many characteristics. Many people get caught up in a particular project and never explore the many visual features of Paradox. Spend some time studying the visual properties of objects. The objects from the Toolbar tools that you can place in forms and reports are *design objects*. The better you know the design objects of Paradox, the better your applications will look. Make sure that you know what the properties do. For example, a field has several Run Time properties. What are the differences among Read Only, Tab Stop, and No Echo? Know the properties of design objects before you start programming in ObjectPAL.

Getting the Most Out of Style Sheets

The prototyping of objects is a feature of Paradox that enables you to create great-looking and consistent forms and reports. This option enables you to save default settings, such as color, font information, ObjectPAL code, and so on. Use this feature to expedite the creation of consistent objects, complete with all the properties and ObjectPAL code. The following section discusses style sheets in general. If you need help changing the contents of the style sheet, consult the *Paradox User's Guide*.

Style sheets are a powerful tool for design development. You can maintain several different looks and switch among them before you create a design document (either a form or a report). You can set up several screen and report style sheet files (with different fonts, colors, frame styles, and so on) and save them to your working directory.

You can even use custom color schemes, which are saved as part of the Style Sheet file. You also can create your own color schemes that are independent of the Windows color palette. The possibilities are limitless.

Keep in mind, however, that many users are still bound to only 16 colors. If you have a better video card, remember that the custom colors you define probably will be dithered on lesser video cards. Therefore, it is recommended that you test your work on a standard 16-color VGA card. It's also a good idea to test your application with at least three different Windows color schemes. To check out possible color schemes, open the Display applet in the Control Panel and select the Appearance tab.

TIP

Design user interfaces using the default Windows color scheme. If you develop your applications using the default Windows color scheme, then your applications will look good with more of the predesigned Windows color schemes.

If you get into the habit of choosing a style sheet before you create the first form for a project, you guarantee a consistent look and feel for your entire application—with little or no effort.

On the disc are the following several .FT files to get you started:

FANCY.FT: A fancier custom look

CLOWN.FT: A simple colorful look

SECRETS1.FT: My preferred style sheet (no ObjectPAL code)

SECRETS2.FT: My preferred style sheet (with lots of ObjectPAL code)

SECRETS2.FP: My preferred printer style sheet

Also on the disc are two scripts for creating your own style sheets based on an existing form or report.

The Six Steps to Create a Form

Everyone has his or her own technique for developing a form. This section explores one technique. Study this technique and use it to improve your own technique for developing forms. Following are the six steps of developing a form that I use:

1. **Create the data model.** This includes gathering data components and business rules, and planning and creating the tables. See Chapter 2 for an in-depth discussion of tables and Chapter 35 for an overview of SQL.

2. **Prototype several forms.** Design several versions of one or two of the main forms of the application with the data models you created and the business rules you gathered in step 1. Let someone else decide which prototype form has the best look and feel. Create the rest of the forms.

3. **Test the built-in behavior.** Run the form and see whether the basic data model and fields are what you need. Make sure that you use the application the way that the user will. For example, search for values, insert a new record, change, and delete records.

4. **Add objects and design elements.** After you decide on the prototyped forms and test the built-in behavior, the next step is to add text objects, graphics, buttons, and so on, to get the overall visual effect you want.

5. **Add ObjectPAL.** Decide what more you want an object to do and add the appropriate code (more on this, starting with Chapter 3).

6. **Test.** Large companies thoroughly test their software, and so should you. There are many types of tests you can run, including unit testing, integration testing, and regression testing. See Chapter 36 for more on testing your application.

Step 1: Create the Data Model

You can use what Borland calls the *Data Model Designer* to create relational table links visually. You can even save and load data model files (.DM files). Whether you're working on forms, reports, or queries, all you do is draw lines between tables. The linking expert automatically does all the relational work for you by showing you how the tables can be linked. No matter how complex the relationship is, Paradox graphically displays the linked tables.

The first step in creating a form is to decide on a data model. The better you understand how the data model works and the theory behind relating tables, the easier it is for you to create forms and applications. See Chapter 2 for more information on the theory behind linking tables.

Step 2: Prototype Several Forms

Creating forms in Paradox is easy. Within a couple of hours, you could create nearly a dozen variations of a form. Design several versions of the main forms for your application and let someone else, such as the client, decide which prototype form he or she likes the look and feel of best.

When you prototype a form, set the form's properties, decide on a Style Sheet, create the form using either the data model or an Expert, decide whether you want the form to be a window or a dialog box, set the title of the form, and so on.

Set the form's properties (see Figure 3.1). Get into the habit of setting the properties of a form whenever you create one. Give it a name, take the scroll bars off, and so on. Now is a good time to choose a look and feel for your application. (Refer to the section titled "Getting the Most Out of Style Sheets" earlier in this chapter.) Figure 3.1 shows the Form Window Properties that I prefer.

FIGURE 3.1.

The Form Window Properties dialog box.

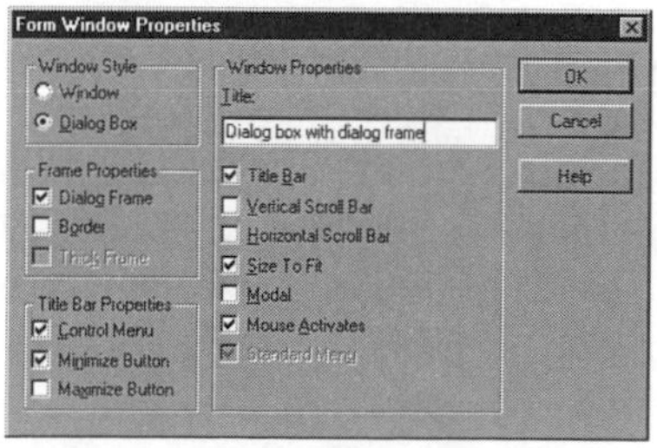

Step 3: Test the Built-In Behavior

Because Paradox has a tremendous amount of built-in functionality, exploring the built-in behavior of the form is important. Users often waste time because they don't know the built-in behavior. Sometimes, the built-in behavior is different from what they assume it is. After programming for many hours, they finally give up and either call Borland or post a message on CompuServe, only to be told that the default behavior already does what they were trying to do. In other words, if you don't know the default behavior, you might waste time duplicating it. Even worse, your added code may cause problems, prompting you to write more code to fix. This is a programming loop you must try to avoid.

Testing your form before you begin to add to it also gives you an overall sense of what you're trying to accomplish. Developers often get caught up in one detail of an application and lose sight of the big picture. Use your forms the way your users will. Your applications will have a much better look and feel.

The next step is to add objects—calculated fields, lines, graphics, boxes used to contain fields (a wonderful way to set the tab order for a group of objects), and so on. You add more objects only after you thoroughly test the built-in behavior of your newly created form.

Step 4: Add Objects and Design Elements

When first developing a form, consider using the snap to grid options to help you quickly place many objects on a form in orderly positions. The *grid* consists of horizontal and vertical lines that help you place objects. You can show or hide the grid; you also can resize it. Use Snap To Grid when you first design a form. Doing so cuts down the time needed to design the form.

Step 5: Add ObjectPAL

If you have a detailed design specification, then the next step is to alter the default behavior of the objects to behave as specified. Before adding any code to alter or add to the built-in behavior, thoroughly test how your objects and design elements operate with the built-in behavior of Paradox. The next step is to decide what more you want the form to do. Do you want the form to automatically put values in fields? Do you want it to open another form? Do you want to add pull-down menus and a custom toolbar?

Whatever ObjectPAL you decide to add, develop in small steps and test as you go. If you add code and the code doesn't work, take it out! I can't tell you how many times I have talked to programmers who swear that the problem they have is a bug in Paradox and it turns out to be their overcoding. Often, when faced with a task, you will experiment with code to see what happens. If you just keep adding code to your form in hopes of solving the problem, you will end up with a mess. Remember to remove code experiments. Also, remember to step back and remind yourself what you are trying to do, and try to think of different ways of accomplishing the same task.

> **NOTE**
>
> If you are already familiar with ObjectPAL, here is a tip. If, in experimentation, you use `sleep()`, `doDefault`, or `DisableDefault` to overcome some odd or misunderstood behavior, do not leave the commands in your code. If using the command didn't seem to make a difference, then take it out. Use commands only when they are called for.
>
> One great way to really learn the event model and the power of these—and other— commands is to experiment with adding them. Remember to take them out, however, if they did not do what you wanted.

If you really think you have found a bug in Paradox, then don't waste any time on your complicated form. Instead, try to duplicate the problem on a brand new form with no extra code on it. Only after you have duplicated the problem on a new form should you notify Borland. I believe that you will find, more times than not, that the problem is not a bug in Paradox, however.

Step 6: Test

The final step in developing a form is to test your form as a whole. You'll see whether you are done or need to go back to steps 4 and 5. You should test your ObjectPAL code as you go. In this step, you test the whole application, not its individual elements. Does the form behave the way you thought it would? Does it behave the way your users will expect it to? Does it integrate with the rest of the application? Chapter 36 discusses techniques you can use to test your own custom written software.

Notes on Creating Forms

Now that creating forms has been discussed in general abstract terms, the following section discusses specific design issues of creating forms.

Child Windows Versus Dialog Boxes

Put some thought into whether you want a form to be a child window or a dialog box. Forms that are child windows obey Microsoft's Multiple Document Interface (MDI). The MDI, for example, dictates that when you maximize one child window, all child windows are maximized.

A temporary window that requests or provides information is a *dialog box*. Many dialog boxes present options from which you must choose before you can perform an action. Other dialog boxes display warnings or error messages. Some are even utilities, such as the Paradox Desktop that comes on the disc that comes with this book.

NEW
Term

A *model dialog box* is a dialog box that the user can't leave until he or she responds to it. In general, model dialog boxes are frustrating to the user and should be avoided. Reserve the use of model dialog boxes to situations when additional information is required to complete a command or when it is important to prevent any further interaction until satisfying a condition. Use the form ANSWERS\F_SHOW.FSL to experiment with the various form types (see Figure 3.2). Each form type has different characteristics. Open F_SHOW.FSL and experiment with the various types of dialog boxes. Figures 3.3 through 3.5 show several of the various types of dialog boxes that you can design.

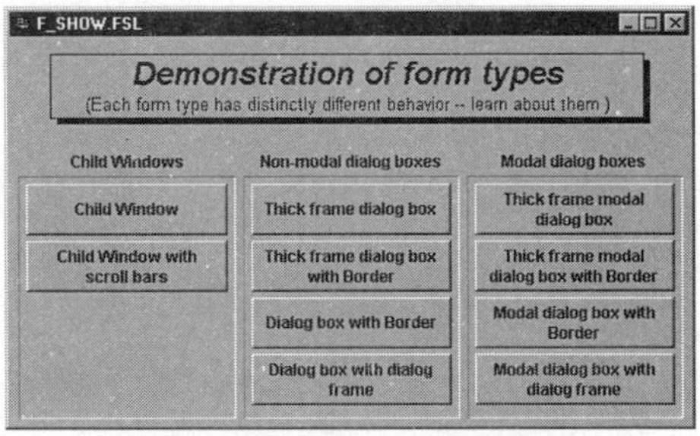

FIGURE 3.2.

ANSWERS\F_SHOW.FSL demonstrates the various form types.

FIGURE 3.3.

ANSWERS\F_DIA2.FSL demonstrates a nonmodal thick frame dialog box.

FIGURE 3.4.

ANSWERS\F_DIA4.FSL demonstrates a nonmodal dialog frame dialog box.

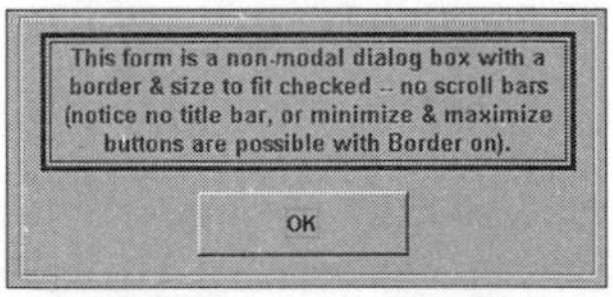

FIGURE 3.5.

ANSWERS\F_MOD3.FSL demonstrates a modal dialog box with a border.

NOTE

If you leave the form as a child window to Paradox and hide the Paradox desktop, the child window hides with it. If you want to hide the Paradox desktop so that the form is the only visual object onscreen, you must define the form as a dialog box. Remember that a form is a dialog box only when it is opened in View Data mode. If you're in Design mode, running the form isn't the same as reopening it. You must reopen it. Using forms as dialog boxes is discussed more in Chapter 13.

Spicing Up Your Forms

Windows is a wonderful color graphics environment. With the early versions of Windows, most applications had white backgrounds with black letters. Microsoft added three-dimensional buttons to version 3.1 to improve the look. Now with Windows 95, applications have come to life visually with stunning three-dimensional schemes. Keep this in mind, because your users will demand a high degree of visual appeal from your database applications. Just remember not to overdo it; keep your applications looking professional.

TIP

If you add many images to your application, make sure the images use a 16- or 256-color palette. If you use images with a 24-bit palette, then the images will slow down your application. The slowness is very apparent on lower-quality video cards and slower CPUs.

Spicing Up Your Applications

UIObjects are objects, such as circles, lines, fields, and buttons, that you can draw by using the Toolbar. You can add pictures to spice up UIObjects. Use bitmaps whenever possible. Although small bitmaps are not part of the Windows 95 look and feel, many users consider them particularly attractive; they give your application a professional look. The form ANSWERS\F_BUTTON.FSL demonstrates adding graphics to buttons (see Figure 3.6).

NEW *Term*

FIGURE 3.6.

To spice up an application, add pictures to buttons.

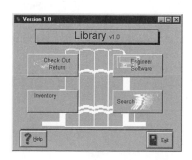

SHRINK IMAGES BEFORE YOU PASTE THEM INTO A FORM

I once added five little bitmaps to five buttons on a form. Each bitmap was about 1/2 inch by 1/2 inch. When I saved and reloaded the form, it ran incredibly slowly. I studied the situation and discovered that my form took up 960K of space. I had accidentally used five full-screen bitmaps and had Paradox shrink the graphics by selecting Magnification | Best Fit. I opened the bitmaps in Photo Styler, changed them to their actual sizes (about 1/2 inch by 1/2 inch). The size of the form shrank from 960K to 48K, and the form ran as it should.

NEW
Term

A *crosstab* is an object you place on a form or report, which enables you to summarize data in one field by expressing it in terms of two other fields. These spreadsheet-like structures are easy for the user to understand. Unfortunately, crosstabs aren't used enough by developers. There-fore, keep in mind that another way to improve the look and feel of an application is to use crosstabs to show summaries of information. In today's technological world, people are bom-barded with information. Users expect to be presented with neat little packages of informa-tion. Crosstabs are your gateway to creative summaries and graphs.

Graphs add visual excitement and flair to your forms and reports. Using a graph to represent data visually is appealing to the eye and brain. You can use many types of graphs, including line, bar, and three-dimensional pie. You can even combine line and marker graphs. Graphs change as data is changed. They are a wonderful visual aid. Most database users agree that graphs are not used enough, especially for analyzing data.

Do Not Crowd a Form

Many users use Paradox to duplicate printed forms: applications, records, and so on. Your natural inclination might be to put all the fields on a single 8.5- by-11-inch-page—just like the real form. Try to resist this temptation, because it causes problems with the user interface.

Typically, a form that mimics a form is larger than the screen, and the user must scroll around it to fill in all the data. A better user interface approach is to break the fields into categories on forms, a multipage form, or a form with the new tabbed notebook object (see Figure 3.7). When you are ready to print, use a report or a large form. Although this means some duplication of effort, your users will appreciate your extra effort with the user interface (see Figure 3.8).

FIGURE 3.7.

\APPS\PEOPLE\PEOPLE.FSL demonstrates using the tabbed notebook.

FIGURE 3.8

F_FLDS.FSL demonstrates a scrolling fields form trick.

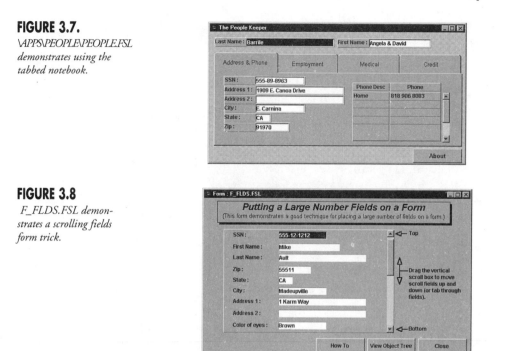

Consistency is the Key to Creating Good-Looking Forms

Choose consistent colors when you create and place objects. If you choose a white background for your forms, stick to it. If you choose another color or a special color scheme, such as a Windows 95 look, stick to it. When you design forms, a good approach is to set your colors to the Windows default by using the Control Panel.

To achieve a good user interface, you need to be consistent. Make similar objects the same size. Buttons are especially noticeable; try to use only one or two sizes for them and locate them on the right or bottom side of the form. Use a consistent line width and frame style.

At the same time, limit the number of visual elements in your application. A good-looking application doesn't have an abundance of colors or objects. Instead, good-looking applications use subtle design elements. Use patterns sparingly—only one or two styles for each application. When you select colors, feel free to choose as many as you need for the foreground, background, text, title, and user input—just be consistent. Realize, however, that just because your users have at least 16 colors, you don't have to use every color on a single form or in a single application.

Just as Microsoft has found a look and feel it likes (the Windows 95 look), you should strive to find your own style. You can create several looks and switch among them with each project, or you can develop a single look; your users may soon recognize your applications. Keep in mind, however, that the data is more important than the flashy objects around it.

> **INCREASE PRODUCTIVITY**
>
> A benefit of running multiple instances of Paradox is that you can easily copy and paste objects from one form to another. For example, I frequently develop with another instance of Paradox running with its working directory set to DEV-SRC (the developer source directory with clip objects in it that ships with the disc from this book).
>
> You can use the Paradox Desktop utility in APPS\DESKTOP\DESKTYOP.FDL or set up icons in your Paradox group to run more than one copy of Paradox. First, create more private directories in your Paradox directory. Call them PRIV2, PRIV3, and PRIV4. Next, set up three more icons with the following command lines:
>
> ```
> PDOXWIN -e -pC:\PDOXWIN\PRIV2
> PDOXWIN -e -pC:\PDOXWIN\PRIV3
> PDOXWIN -e -pC:\PDOXWIN\PRIV4
> ```
>
> In the preceding code, -p is used to specify the private directory, and -e is used to prevent writing environment changes.

Data Model and Table Lookup Notes

This section does not tell you how to use the data model; data model theory is discussed in Chapter 2 and it is assumed that you already know the basics of linking tables with the data model. Instead, this section points out some common pitfalls of the data model and table lookups with respect to forms.

Link the Correct Way

When using referential integrity, make sure that you link from the master to the detail. If you accidentally link from the detail to the master, the data model will attempt to update the child table before updating the master table; this causes the error message Master Record missing.

If you want to test this, create two tables with a single field primary key. Save the first table as REF1.DB and the second as REF2.DB. Restructure REF2.DB (the child table) and set up a Cascade Delete referential integrity link to REF1.DB (the parent table). Next, create a form and link the tables in a one-to-one relationship. The goal in this case was to update the REF2.DB child table whenever a new record is inserted or updated in REF1.DB. But because you linked the wrong way—from the child to the parent—the data model first tries to update REF2.DB, then REF1.DB. The message on the status bar is Master Record missing. To fix the form, go into design mode, open the data model, unlink the two tables, and relink them; this time link from REF1.DB (the parent table) to REF2.DB (the child table).

Do Not Hard Code Table Lookups

When you hard code a table lookup, you specify the drive, path, and table filename. As discussed in Chapter 2, aliases are not allowed on table lookups. This, unfortunately, limits the usefulness of table lookups. If your data needs to be portable, then put the table lookups in the same directory as the main data or a subdirectory below it. This second technique is called *relative directory addressing* (RDA). This enables you to move your entire data directory (along with its subdirectories) to a different location.

The Second Table in a 1-1 Relationship Is Read-Only

When you link two tables in the data model of a form, the second table is set to read-only by default. If you do this and attempt to modify the second table, you will get the error message, `Cannot modify this table`.

To change this setting, view the forms data model and right-click the detail table. The pop-up menu will show Read-Only with a checkmark next to it. Select the Read-Only property to remove the checkmark. You now will be able to edit the detail table.

Special, Summary, and Calculated Fields

Many users have trouble understanding calculated fields. For this reason, and so that you don't try to duplicate this functionality by using ObjectPAL, this next section explores how to use special, summary, and calculated fields.

Using Special or Calculated Fields

To use a special or calculated field, select the field into which you want the value to go, inspect its properties, and choose Define Field. You can use the tools in the Define Field Object dialog box to set up a special or calculated field.

When you *define* a field object, you attach it to data from a table. For example, you define a field object in a form as a field in a table. You cannot define calculated fields to a field in a table. Do not confuse defining with binding. You *bind* or *associate* an object such as a table frame or multirecord object (MRO) with a table, whereas you *define* a field.

Special Fields and Summary Fields

A *special field* is a field, placed in a design document, that contains information about a table or design. These fields are predefined by Paradox, such as Now and Table Name. Table 3.1 describes special fields, Table 3.2 describes special table fields, and Table 3.3 describes the summary fields.

Table 3.1. Special fields.

Field	Description
Now	Displays the current running time in the field. This is an excellent and easy way to add a clock to your application. Because you can't define a field to a table and also use it as a special Now field, use the `time()` method via ObjectPAL to time-stamp a record or use the new TimeStamp field type.
Today	Displays the current date in the field.
TimeStamp	Displays the current time and date in the field.
Page Number	Displays the current page number of the form.
Number of Pages	Displays the total number of pages in the current form.

Table 3.2. Special table fields.

Field	Description
Table Name	Displays the name of the table in the field. Table Name is particularly useful in reports.
Record Number	Displays the current record number in the field. Using a table's record number is particularly useful for auto-numbering records in forms and reports when you don't need to store the number with the table. Record Number obeys restricted views. That is, if the number of records is restricted by the data model, Record Number reflects this and starts numbering at 1. This makes it useful for auto-numbering items in a typical invoicing system.
Number of Records	Displays the total number of restricted records.
Number of Fields	Displays the number of fields in the table.

Table 3.3. Summary fields.

Field	Description
Sum	Adds all the values.
Count	Displays a count of all the records.
Min	Displays the smallest value for this field in the table.
Max	Displays the largest value for this field in the table.
Avg	Displays the average value for this field in the table.

Field	Description
Std	Displays the standard deviation of the values in the set.
Var	Displays the statistical variance of the values in the set.

Tutorial Auto-Incrementing a Restricted View

Suppose that you want to number the detail records in a typical invoicing system. To do this, you do not need ObjectPAL. The special table field Record Number can handle the task.

Step By Step

1. Launch Paradox, and make the TUTORIAL directory your working directory.
2. Select File | New | Form and use the Data Model/Design Layout option to link ORDERS.DB to LINEITEM.DB in a 1:M relationship. Select OK.
3. At the Design Layout screen, select By Rows in the Object Layout: panel, and select OK.
4. Add a column to the detail table frame. Your form should now look similar to Figure 3.9.

FIGURE 3.9.

Adding a column to a table frame.

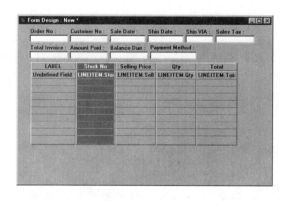

5. To display the Define Field Object dialog box for the newly added column, select the undefined field of the column you added in step 4. Right-click (or press F6) to inspect the field. Select Define Field.
6. Select the drop-down arrow of the LINEITEM.DB table and then select the Record Number special table field. Select OK.
7. Label the column Item Number if you want, and run the form. It should look similar to Figure 3.10.
8. Save the form as REC-NO.FSL.

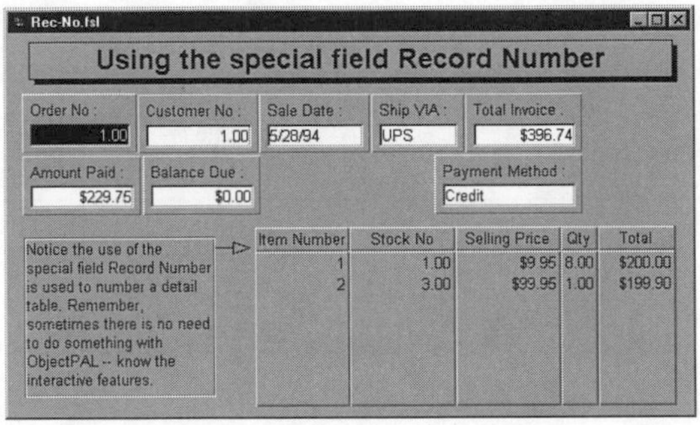

FIGURE 3.10.

The completed form from REC-NO.FSL showing the use of a table field for the line item in the first column.

Rec-No.fsl

Using the special field Record Number

Order No :	Customer No :	Sale Date :	Ship VIA :	Total Invoice :
1.00	1.00	6/28/94	UPS	$396.74

Amount Paid :	Balance Due :		Payment Method :
$229.75	$0.00		Credit

Notice the use of the special field Record Number is used to number a detail table. Remember, sometimes there is no need to do something with ObjectPAL -- know the interactive features.

Item Number	Stock No	Selling Price	Qty	Total
1	1.00	$9.95	8.00	$200.00
2	3.00	$99.95	1.00	$199.90

NOTE

If you had any problems with this tutorial (or any tutorial in this book), open up the completed form in the \SECRETS3\ANSWERS directory.

Analysis

The first column is numbered 1 through however many records there are in the restricted view. The restricted view is determined by the table relationships set up in the data model. This operation is built into Paradox. You could do this same operation in ObjectPAL, but with difficulty.

TIP

Before you code in ObjectPAL, ask yourself two questions. Does Paradox already do this? Is there a better and easier way? Remember, simple solutions for simple problems.

You also can use the Record Number table field with reports; for example, when you want the records of a report to be numbered. Special and summary fields have many uses, so make sure that you know what all these field types do. The Now special field is particularly useful. To put a clock on a form, simply place an undefined field on the form and define it as the Now special field type. Voilà! In an instant, you have created a running clock on your form.

Using Calculated Fields

NEW
Term

Calculated fields use the Calculated panel of the Define Field Object dialog box to set up a user-defined formula or to display concatenated strings. When you combine two or more alphanumeric values, you *concatenate* them. An *operator* is a symbol that represents an operation to be performed on a value or values. For example, the + operator represents addition, and the

* operator represents multiplication. The *arithmetic operators* in ObjectPAL are +, -, *, /, and ( ). Use these operators to construct mathematical expressions in queries and calculated fields. To concatenate two or more alphanumeric values in a calculated field (or ObjectPAL), for example, use the + operator. For example, the following formula

```
1:   City.value + ", " + State.value
```

concatenates three strings to form a value, such as

```
1:   Milpitas, CA
```

In addition to arithmetic operators, you can use any expression that returns a single value in a calculated field. This includes any ObjectPAL statement that returns a single value. Although you have not formally started your study of ObjectPAL, here are some fairly self-explanatory, single-command expressions you can use in a calculated field:

```
startUpDir()
privDir()
workingDir()
windowsDir()
windowsSystemDir()
isToolBarShowing()
getMouseScreenPosition()
version()
isDir("C:\\DOS")
fieldName1.value + fieldName2.value
```

Following are some combination-method expressions you can use in a calculated field:

```
size(startUpDir())
isLeapYear(today())
number(fieldName1.value) + number(fieldName2.value)

dow(today())
doy(today())
```

F_CALC.FSL demonstrates calculated and special fields (see Figure 3.11).

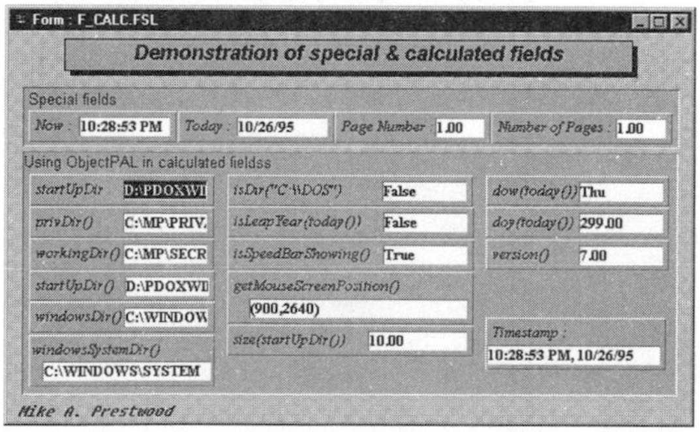

FIGURE 3.11.

*The form
ANSWERS\F_CALC.FSL.*

Using *iif()*

You can use the iif (immediate if) statement in both calculated fields and ObjectPAL to make decisions. With an iif statement, you can in essence say, "If the following expression is true, this field's value is A. Otherwise, this field's value is B."

Syntax

```
iif(Condition, ValueIfTrue, ValueIfFalse)
```

Examples

```
iif(field1.value = blank(), today, field1.value)
iif(taxable.value = "Yes", ([LINEITEM.Selling Price] * [LINEITEM.Qty]) * .06,
➡blank())
```

> **TIP**
>
> If you ever have a calculated field on a form not update when it should, then you can use the ObjectPAL method forceRefresh() to make the calculated field display the correct values. This can occur, for example, when you update a field involved with a calculated field using a TCursor. You can find more information about forceRefresh() in Chapter 18.

Special fields, special table fields, summary fields, and calculated fields are important to the ObjectPAL programmer. Many times, tasks are easier to accomplish with these fields than through ObjectPAL.

Summary

In addition to designing and creating tables, designing good forms makes your application more professional. Forms are the backbone of your application. In fact, in Paradox, forms are your application. The better you are at designing forms, the better your applications turn out.

PART

ObjectPAL Basics

An ObjectPAL
Overview

4

**NEW
*Term***

Although interactive Paradox is powerful, it still can't do some things interactively. You have to accomplish some tasks using its programming language. The Object Paradox Application Language is *ObjectPAL*. Why would you need to use ObjectPAL? You use ObjectPAL to automate or customize objects on a form. An example of a task that requires ObjectPAL is creating a custom menu system for a form. If you plan to develop a complete custom Paradox application, you probably will need to use ObjectPAL.

> **NOTE**
>
> This chapter, exclusively about ObjectPAL, is geared toward the beginning ObjectPAL programmer. If you have never programmed in ObjectPAL before, then this chapter is for you. If you have programmed in ObjectPAL a little—or a lot—then I recommend that you read it as review material. Especially important are the sections on the event model and types of commands.

ObjectPAL is for both programmers and nonprogrammers. If you have experience with another language, especially an object-oriented programming language such as C++, Pascal with objects, or Delphi, you will find ObjectPAL especially interesting. If you have never programmed, ObjectPAL is a good language to learn first because it enables you to paint objects with built-in behavior onto a form and then attach bits of code to events on the object.

You use the user interface to design forms with objects on them, such as fields, tables, and buttons. When you're happy with the way the form works interactively, you attach ObjectPAL code to the objects that require it. This system of programming falls into the category of an event-driven language. The fact that you draw objects on a form and attach code to the objects allows even the nonprogrammer to create applications easily.

Features of ObjectPAL

ObjectPAL's features include an event handler, data types, strong program control, the runtime library, user-defined commands, support for dynamic link libraries, and delivery time binding.

The event handler built into ObjectPAL cuts down the amount of time you spend programming. It also makes the language accessible to nonprogrammers. ObjectPAL has many data types, including `String`, `Number`, `SmallInt`, `Date`, `Time`, `Array`, and `DynArray`. The language supports programming control-branching, such as `if`, `for`, `while`, and `scan`. ObjectPAL also has a long list of commands called *methods* and *procedures* that a programmer can use. Methods and procedures either stand alone or work on an object, and they include commands such as `open()`, `attach()`, `moveTo()`, `setTitle()`, `getPosition()`, `setPosition()`, and `searchRegistry()`. ObjectPAL also enables you to read or set all the properties with which you are already familiar such as Color, Tab Stop, and Next Tab Stop.

As with C and Pascal, you can create your own commands with ObjectPAL. These user-created commands are called *custom methods* and *custom procedures*. Custom methods and procedures consist of methods and procedures from the runtime library and other user-defined routines. You also can make calls to dynamic link libraries (DLLs). DLLs contain functions and procedures that usually are written in C, C++, or Pascal. After you register the user-created function in ObjectPAL, you can use it as though Borland included it. This offers you almost unlimited expandability.

A Powerful High-Level Programming Language

ObjectPAL is a complete programming language. Like Basic, Pascal, and C, ObjectPAL supports variables, control structures, loops, and more. The power of ObjectPAL pleases traditional programmers. You will appreciate ObjectPAL's power to manipulate databases. The ObjectPAL language contains a rich array of functionality for managing data. You can find and manipulate values in a table. You can add records from one table to another. You can even scan a table, find every field that has a certain word, and change that word. No language can do it all, but ObjectPAL certainly comes close.

Sometimes, you might spend a few minutes in ObjectPAL, adding a few lines of code to an object on a form, and then you are done. Other times, you might spend hours coding many different objects that interact with one other. If you program in small steps and test as you go, programming in ObjectPAL can be fun and easy.

Do I Have to Learn a Programming Language?

Most of the time, ObjectPAL is easy to program; however, sometimes it can be difficult. Every programming language can be tough. At the same time, every programming language is easy if you take it in small increments. It is just a matter of how much you want to learn in a given period of time. If you want to learn all about ObjectPAL by next week, ObjectPAL is as hard as hard can get. If you're willing to spend a little time, however, it's one of the easiest languages with which to start. The goal of this chapter is for you to learn how to add small bits of ObjectPAL code to objects to accomplish specific tasks.

What Do I Need to Know to Use ObjectPAL?

An ObjectPAL master programmer must be multitalented. To become an ObjectPAL master, you must have a firm grasp of database technology and know Windows, DOS, and object-oriented programming (OOP). You must know how to use DDE, OLE, and DLLs effectively. You must be a graphic artist and a program designer. You also need to be a mind reader so that you can know what your client actually wants. In short, an ObjectPAL master must know everything there is to know about Windows programming.

But what is a mere mortal to do? In one way or another, you can incorporate almost all you've learned about computers into your application. If your strength is in application design, concentrate on that. If your strength is in graphics, concentrate on that. If you don't have a strength, do what Borland originally intended for you to do: concentrate on developing good database applications. Later, you can go back and explore all the fun, nondatabase features. The point is that whatever your previous experience is with databases, Paradox for DOS PAL programming, other programming languages, or graphics, all you know about computers will come in handy with Paradox.

What Is Elegant Programming?

Before you continue your journey into ObjectPAL, this section diverges a little and discusses the ambiguous part of every programming language. Some programmers believe that what they write often approaches art because of its sheer elegance. Elegant programming is the best way to accomplish a particular task. It can mean many things, but most often, elegant programming means a routine that takes the least amount of code to complete a task. Try to resist overcoding a task. Recall from the last chapter: if you add some code that doesn't work, take it out!

The term *elegant code* has many meanings. Fast code, for example, is elegant. Code that uses a TCursor (a pointer to a table) can, in some situations, be more elegant than code that uses a UIObject (a user interface object). A TCursor is faster because it doesn't have the overhead of screen refreshes. (In many cases, however, you can accomplish the same objective by using a UIObject—especially if it's already there.)

Code that is free of bugs and takes into account all possibilities is elegant. The least amount of code is not always the most elegant. If code does not take care of all possibilities, then it is not adequate. This is the reason you need to let some of the users of your software test the software for functionality. This type of test is usually referrred to as beta testing your software. For example, test the effect of putting blanks into date fields. Try putting negative numbers where you normally expect a positive number. If users can do it, they will!

Portable code is elegant. The capability to copy an object with code from one form to another with little modification is elegant. ObjectPAL is an Object-Based Programming (OBP) language that enables you to create objects you can copy from one form to another. In most cases, this is not automatic, but with a little creative programming, you can create objects that you can paste into other forms.

Even where you put code determines how elegant it is. The places—events—to which you attach ObjectPAL code is part of the event handler. The event handler handles all the events coming from Windows, such as key presses, mouse movements, and mouse button clicks. The event model that the event handler uses determines when your code will trigger. In ObjectPAL, *where* you code is as important as *what* you code. This book devotes Chapters 7, 8, and 30 to this subject.

Although no book can claim to have the correct answer for everything, this book does attempt to demonstrate elegant programming. This book won't always have the perfect solution for every problem; indeed, no book can make that claim. After typing in a routine, you might think of a more elegant way to code it. This is good: the challenging and fun part of programming is coming up with a better solution. The most elegant way isn't always obvious. As a programmer with limited time, you must balance your time between elegant and adequate programming.

As you will see in later chapters, a problem often has several solutions that range from simple to complicated and sometimes elegant. You learn the most by studying simple solutions first, and then more complicated solutions (rather than the other way around). You see the quickest and best way to complete a task. By seeing various levels of solutions to a problem, you learn more about elegant programming.

For example, although the Paradox table structure offers an Autoincrement field type, Chapter 16 shows you several techniques for autoincrementing a field with ObjectPAL. First, you add a record to a form. Second, you set up a simple autoincrement field. Third, you autoincrement a nonkey field. Fourth, you autoincrement the master table on a form with a one-to-many table relationship. For the most elegant solution, you add locking to the routine.

By studying simple and elegant solutions, you learn how to implement different routines under different situations. This gives you the capability to balance your time between elegant and adequate programming.

One form of elegant programming is structured programming. Refer to Appendix C for more information on structured programming and how it applies to ObjectPAL.

Setting Your ObjectPAL Level

In this section, you are going to jump right in and write some ObjectPAL. First, make sure that your ObjectPAL level is set to Beginner. To do this, start Paradox. Select Edit | Developer Preferences to display the Developer Preferences dialog box (see Figure 4.1). This is where you set the developer preferences. From the ObjectPAL Level panel of the General tab, select Beginner. Later, in the next chapter, you will switch to the Advanced level.

> **NOTE**
>
> Whether your ObjectPAL level is set to Beginner or Advanced, you can use all the ObjectPAL methods, procedures, properties, constants, keywords, and so on. The Level panel is a help filter used just for learning purposes.

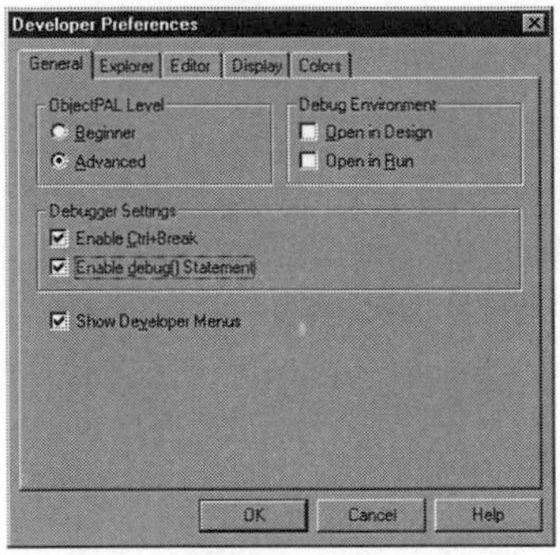

FIGURE 4.1.

*The Developer Preferences
dialog box.*

Starting ObjectPAL

NEW
Term

A *method* is the location in a form, script, or library in which you place ObjectPAL code. This code is attached to the object and defines the object's response to that event. An *event* is an action sent by the event handler that triggers an ObjectPAL *event*. For example, pushing (clicking) a button triggers pushButton, clicking on a box triggers mouseDown, and opening a form triggers init. For the sake of explanation, you can think of methods and events as being synonymous.

Code in ObjectPAL is attached to objects in these methods and events. When you right-click on an object, the Object Inspector displays options you can select. Select Object Explorer from the Object Inspector to gain access to the Object Explorer (see Figures 4.2 and 4.3). Use the Object Explorer to gain access to the ObjectPAL Editor. You type code into the ObjectPAL Editor. The Editor is closely tied to the compiler; you type commands—that is, text—into the editor that the compiler uses to compile code.

FIGURE 4.2.

*You get to the Object
Explorer by right-clicking
an object.*

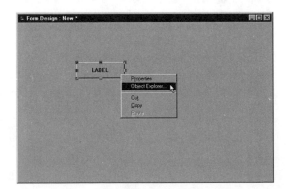

After you've opened the Object Explorer, you can edit any of the methods or events. For example, you can add code to the pushButton event of a button. The pushButton method is an event that is triggered when the user left-mouse clicks a button object. These built-in events are the events that trigger your code. Figure 4.3 shows the Object Explorer.

FIGURE 4.3.
The Object Explorer.

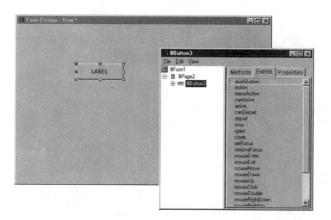

The ObjectPAL editor for version 7 is much enhanced over previous versions. In the ObjectPAL Editor, you enter code much as you would in other Windows editors, such as Notepad. The Editor has the normal features of any Windows editor: cut, copy, paste, and so on. In addition, the editor has many features specific to ObjectPAL that check your syntax, help you build a line of code, color code your syntax, and debug your code (see Figure 4.4).

NEW Feature

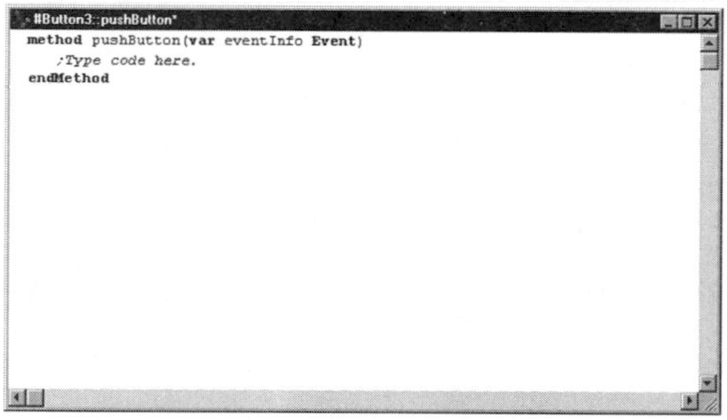

FIGURE 4.4.
The ObjectPAL Editor.

Programming a Button to Send a Message to the Status Bar

A wonderful way to jump into ObjectPAL is to see what it can do. One type of command in ObjectPAL is called a *procedure*. Procedures generally are the easiest ObjectPAL commands to use because they usually are straightforward. For example, to send a message to the status line, you use the message() procedure. Following is the syntax for message().

NEW Term

```
message ( const message String [, const message String]* )
```

To use this procedure, you type in the keyword **message** followed by an open parenthesis, and then type the string you want to show up on the status line followed by a close parenthesis, as in the following example:

```
1:   message("type string here")
```

> **NOTE**
>
> In general, do not type the code that appears as part of the body of text. It is included to illustrate what the text is talking about. Generally, every discussion is followed by a tutorial, which is where you can get your feet wet. Any exceptions to this are noted.

You also can send a message composed of many different strings. Although the online help says this is limited to 6 strings, I tested a message composed of 30 strings. Although the string concatenation symbol for ObjectPAL is the +, you can use a comma with the message() procedure. For example, the following lines of code display the same message on the status line:

```
1:   message("Hello World")         ;Displays "Hello World".
2:   message("Hello ", "World")     ;Displays "Hello World".
3:   message("Hello " + "World")    ;Displays "Hello World".
4:   message("H", "e", "l", "l", "o", " ", "W", "o", "r", "l", "d")
```

The first following few tutorials in ObjectPAL lead you step-by-step through the exercise. In most of the later tutorials, you are given only a setup description, the code for all the objects, and minimul instructions. It's important in these first few tutorials to understand how to get to the ObjectPAL Editor, and how to enter code into methods and events.

Tutorial Sending a Message to the Status Line

Suppose that you want to send a message to the status bar when a user clicks a button. This tutorial acquaints you with the pushButton event of a button and the message() procedure. When you click on the button, a message is displayed on the status bar.

> You can find the MESSAGE.FSL form on the disc in the \ANSWERS directory.

Step By Step

1. Change your working directory to the TUTORIAL directory and create a new form by selecting File | New | Form.
2. Place a button on the form with the Toolbar button. Change the label of the button to Display Message. Your form should now look like that shown Figure 4.5.
3. Right-click the button to display the Object Inspector and select Object Explorer (see Figure 4.6).

FIGURE 4.5.

Change label to Display
Message.

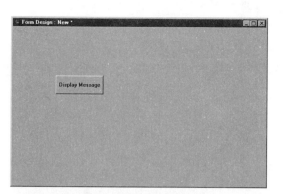

FIGURE 4.6.

*Select the Object
Explorer option.*

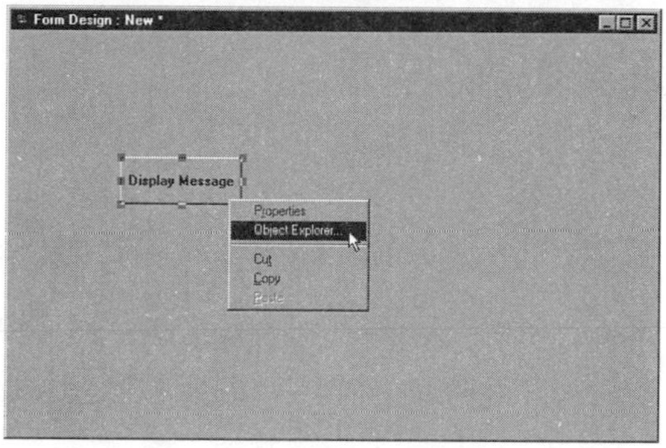

4. Select the pushButton event from the Events tab of the Method Inspector and press
   the Enter key (see Figure 4.7). Between method and endMethod, there is a blank line
   with a blinking cursor ready for you to type code.

FIGURE 4.7.

The Method Inspector.

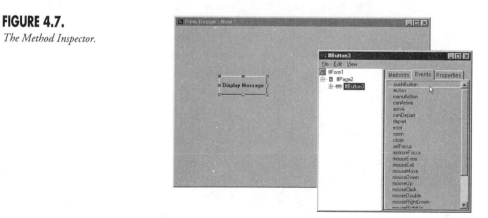

5. In the `pushButton` method, type line 3 that follows:

```
1:    ;MESSAGE :: btnMessage :: pushButton
2:    method pushButton(var eventInfo Event)
3:        message("We put some words on the status bar.")
4:    endmethod
```

6. Check your syntax by selecting Program | Check Syntax. If you have any syntax errors, correct them. (Watch out for opening and closing parentheses and quotation marks.)

7. Close the ObjectPAL Editor window.

8. Then save the form by selecting File | Save As. Save the form as MESSAGE.FSL.

9. Run the form by selecting Form | View Data.

10. Click the Display Message button. The message appears in the status bar. Figure 4.8 shows MESSAGE.FSL. Your completed form should look similar.

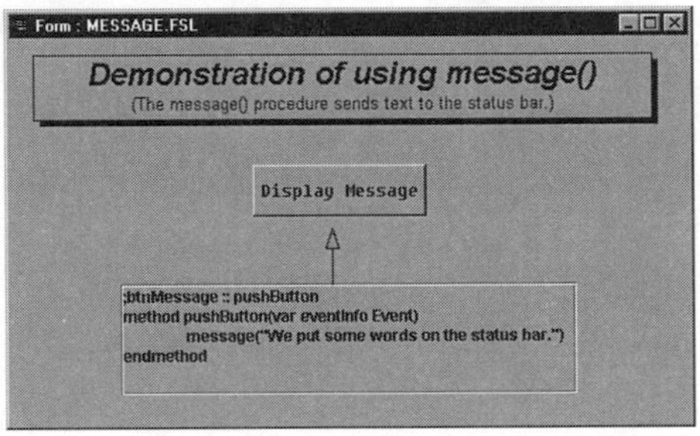

FIGURE 4.8.

MESSAGE.FSL.

Analysis

Paradox enters two of the three lines required to display a message in the status line. In step 5, line 1 identifies what form, object, and method the following code applies to. You can tell it is a remark because it starts with a ;. You never need to type this remark; it is in this book to help guide you through the tutorials. Lines 2 and 4 signify the beginning and the end of the event. Line 3 does the actual work you want it to do. It uses the `message()` procedure to display a message in the status line.

All modifiable events and custom methods start with `method` and end with `endMethod`. Take a closer look at line 2. After `method` in line 2 is its name, `pushButton`. This identifies the event to which you are attaching code; in this case, `pushButton`. Following `pushButton` is the parameter that `pushButton` takes, `var eventInfo Event`. `var` signifies that the event expects a variable. `eventInfo Event` signifies that the `eventInfo` variable is of type `Event`. For now, realize that ObjectPAL is an event-driven type of language that sends events from object to object and line 2 identifies the type of event the event handler is sending.

The Elements of ObjectPAL

Now that you have gotten your feet wet, take a closer look at ObjectPAL. ObjectPAL consists of many different elements. When you study a broad subject such as a programming language, it often is helpful to categorize what you are about to learn. The following paragraphs describe the elements of ObjectPAL.

An *event handler* is a type of programming language that has preset triggers to which the programmer can attach code. The idea of attaching code to triggers on objects puts Paradox in this category. Do not confuse the category of event handler with the term event model. An event model is the map that an event handler uses to process events. The *events* are the triggers that start your code, such as pushButton, open, and changeValue. Events are part of the event handler.

The actual words or building blocks of ObjectPAL are called *keywords*, such as doDefault, DisableDefault, method, endMethod, var, endVar, if, endIf, switch, and endSwitch. For example, an if statement is comprised of the following keywords: if, then, the optional else, and endIf. The ObjectPAL editor displays all keywords in bold. Consider keywords to be the skeleton of your code.

The *methods*—commands—act on objects, such as open(), setPosition(), and moveTo(). Examples of methods include formVariable.open("form"), theBox.setPosition(100,100), and fieldName.moveTo(). Methods differ from *procedures*, which are commands that don't have a specified object on which they work, such as close(), setTitle(), and setAliasPath(). Examples of procedures include close(), setTitle("My Application"), and setAliasPath("MyAlias", "C:\\WORK\\DATA").

In ObjectPAL, you can manipulate the *properties*—the characteristics—of objects, such as value, color, and tabStop. Examples of properties include fieldName.value = "Angie Herbal", theBox.frame.color = Blue, and buttonName.tabStop = True. Most of the properties that you set interactively by typing in values or inspecting an object can be set using ObjectPAL.

Object variables are built into the language, such as self, container, and active. Examples of using Object variables include self.color = Red, container.color = Blue, and message(active.Name).

A *constant* is a word that represents an unchanging value you can use in ObjectPAL. ObjectPaL has both predefined constants and user defined constants. Red, DataInsertRecord, and True are all constants that ObjectPAL already understands. With constants, the number the constant represents does not matter (and can change in a future version). This humanizes ObjectPAL; that is, it makes it easier to relate to. You use a meaningful word rather than a number in your code. Examples of using constants include box1.color = Red, action(DataInsertRecord), and fld3.tabStop = True. You also can use user-created constants; (more on constants later in the section entitled "Basic Language Elements and ObjectPAL").

Introducing the Event Handler

In the first example earlier in this chapter, you used the pushButton event of a button, but how do you know which event to add code to? One thing that makes ObjectPAL easy to learn is that it is an event-driven language. You can refer to the event-driven part of ObjectPAL as the event handler. In a traditional procedural language, you have to write everything, including the interface—one of the least favorite tasks for a developer.

In Paradox, you design the interface interactively with little trouble. In fact, it's fun to design forms with Paradox. With the interface out of the way, you simply attach code to enhance or restrict the interface and its built-in behavior. In most cases, you want to put the code on the object on which you want it to act. If you want a button to do something, put code on the pushButton event of the button. If you want to prevent a user from leaving a field, put code on the canDepart event of that field. Whenever you search for a place to put code, ask yourself, "What object am I working with or on?" Think of programming in ObjectPAL as attaching small bits of code to events or triggers.

Table 4.1 lists some common events to place code. This table can be valuable for beginning ObjectPAL programmers.

Table 4.1. Common places to put code.

Object	Location	Use
Form	init	Initializes variables and sets up tables.
Form	arrive	Maximizes a form and sets values in the form.
Form	menuAction	Processes menu events.
Form	action	Traps for key violations on a single table form.
Form	mouseExit	Clears the status bar if you use mouseEnter.
Page	arrive	Sets up a custom pull-down menu.
Button	pushButton	Executes code when the user selects a button.
Button	mouseEnter	Adds help by sending a message to the status bar.
Field	changeValue	Checks a new value against an old value in a table.

Every object has a default behavior that you can modify with built-in events. Most objects share the same built-in events: action, menuAction, arrive, canDepart, mouseClick, and error. Some objects have unique built-in events, such as pushButton for a button.

The Six Beginner-Level Event Methods

Whenever you're looking for a place to put code, consider ObjectPAL's six beginner-level events first. These core events are the events that Borland believes new users to ObjectPAL will use most. Table 4.2 provides a short description of each.

Table 4.2. The six beginner-level event methods.

Method	Description
action	Used when a user calls, or triggers, an event. Typically, action is used for trapping events and processing them. For example, action is useful for trapping database actions such as inserting a record, and moving in and out of edit mode.
menuAction	Called whenever a user selects a menu option. Put code in the menuAction method if you want to trap when the user selects an option from the menu, toolbar, or form control box.
arrive	arrive occurs whenever focus moves to a field. At first, arrive seems identical to setFocus, which occurs whenever focus moves to an object (and with fields this appearance is somewhat accurate). With some objects, however, it is not. Look at opening a form, for example. First, the init event is called, followed by open and arrive, and finally setFocus. arrive occurs only after open, whereas setFocus occurs whenever the form becomes active; for example, with a multiple form application. You can use arrive to instruct the user what to enter. By the way, arrive only occurs after canArrive.
canDepart	Think of canDepart as the opposite of arrive. Typically, canDepart is used for data integrity. For example, if the value is less than 100, canDepart can prevent the user from leaving the field until the correct value is entered.
mouseClick	This is triggered whenever the logical left mouse button is pressed and released when the mouse is on an object.
error	This event is triggered whenever an error occurs. The error event method is used to add to the event method action (response).

Types of Commands

ObjectPAL has several types of commands you can use in an event. This section addresses procedures, methods, keywords, and properties, which are some of the commands you can use in an event.

Identifying Procedures

You already have used a procedure in your first tutorial. A procedure is a powerful type of command; it can stand alone. In other words, a procedure would be complete on a line by itself. For example, each of the following is a procedure.

```
1:    message("Press OK to continue")

2:    msgInfo("Warning", "You are about to delete a record")

3:    isFile("C:\\DOS\\COMMAND.COM")
```

Identifying Methods

A method is a weaker type of command. It requires an object to hold it up, as in the following example:

```
1:    TaxableField.isBlank()    ;Returns True if the field is blank.
2:    f.open("FORM1")           ;Opens a form named "FORM1".
```

Another way to look at methods versus procedures is to say that a procedure always knows the object it works on or with, but a method does not. To further confuse the issue, some commands can serve as both procedures and methods, as in the following example:

```
1:    close()      ;Procedure that closes the current form.
2:    f.close()    ;A method that closes the form associated
3:                 ;with f (f is a form variable).
```

Line 1 uses the `close()` command as a procedure—it knows to close the current form. If, however, you use `close()` as a method, you need to specify an object. In line 2, `f` is a form variable you have opened previously.

NOTE

Do not confuse a command that can be both a method and procedure with the alternate syntax. Whenever you code `object.method()`, the alternate syntax enables you to code `method(object)`, as in the following example:

```
f.close()    ;Regular syntax.
close(f)     ;Alternate syntax.
```

When a single command supports the alternate syntax, which syntax should you use? Although it doesn't really matter, the regular syntax `object.doIt()`, as seen in the preceding first line, is preferred. It's more consistent with the rest of the language. Don't worry too much about these variations in syntax at this point. Syntax is revisited in Chapter 9 and you can read more about coding conventions in Appendix C.

Identifying Keywords

Keywords are words reserved for use with certain commands in ObjectPAL. They are special language construct commands that are neither procedures nor methods. Keywords include Proc, endProc, method, endMethod, doDefault, iif, and Database. A complete list of keywords appears in Chapter 9. At this point, just be aware that you shouldn't use keywords in ObjectPAL for the names of objects or variables.

Following is an example of keywords that are used properly:

```
1:    ;Button :: pushButton
2:    method pushButton(var eventInfo Event)   ;method is a keyword.
3:       if taxable.value = "Yes" then         ;if & then are keywords.
4:          tax.value = subtotal * .06
5:       else                                  ;else is a keyword.
6:          tax.value = 0
7:       endIf                                 ;endIf is a keyword.
8:    endmethod                                ;endMethod is a keyword.
```

method, if, then, else, endIf, and endMethod are all keywords. You can't give objects or variables names that are the same as these keywords. In fact, it's a good idea not to give an object or a variable the same name as any element of the ObjectPAL language. This optional rule is a good idea. It makes your code more readable and avoids possible problems. Appendix C presents many more coding conventions.

Altering Properties and Dot Notation

Objects that you place on a form have properties. You have already set many of the properties of objects; for example, when you change the color of a box on a form to blue. With ObjectPAL, you can alter an object's property with dot notation. Dot notation is the basic syntax structure used in ObjectPAL. It uses dots to separate elements in a complex statement. Following is the basic syntax structure:

```
ObjectName.property = Constant
```

The capability to alter properties while the form is running is powerful and sets Paradox above many other DBMS systems. Following are some examples of altering the properties of objects:

```
1:    box1.color = Blue            ;Change box1 to blue.
2:    box1.visible = False         ;Make box1 disappear.
3:    Last_Name.color = Yellow     ;Change field color.
4:    City.tabStop = False         ;Do not allow focus to City.
```

Dot notation also can represent a complete path to an object. The following examples set the properties of objects in other objects.

```
1:    pge3.box1.Last_Name.color = DarkGray        ;Change field color to dark
                                                   gray.
2:    f.pge3.visible = False                      ;Make a page disapear.
3:    box1.Last_Name.Frame.Style = Windows3DGroup ;Change the style of a field.
```

The example in line 3 of the preceding code represents a compound property. The path of the object is `box1.Last_Name`. The compound property is `Frame.Style`. This is confusing, especially when learning ObjectPAL. For now, understand that both the object path and the property can be composed of multiple values. The following are three instances for which dot notation is used in ObjectPAL:

- To separate an object and property, as in the following:

  `Last_Name.value = "Santwier"`

- To separate or indicate an object's path, as in the following:

  `pge2.boxSection3.Last_Name.value = "Santwier"`

- To separate an object and a method, as in the following:

  `Last_Name.moveTo()`

> **NOTE**
>
> For now, think of the containership path of an object as analogous to a directory path. When you open a file, you specify its path; for example, `C:\PDOXWIN\DATA\MYFORM.FSL`. When referring to objects, you need to specify the path of the object with dots rather than a slash, as in the following example:
>
> `pge2.boxSection3.Last_Name.`

Properties are another type of code you can use in ObjectPAL to get or alter the property of an object. Think of objects as having a set of data attached to them. Some of the properties of a field object are `value`, `color`, `font.color`, `TabStop`, `Name`, `FieldName`, `TableName`, and `Enabled`. The next example demonstrates that you can alter the properties of objects with ObjectPAL.

Changing the Color of a Box

Suppose that you want to change the color of a box when the user clicks the box. This tutorial uses the `mouseClick` method of a box to alter the property `color`. The object variable `self` is used to refer to the object to which the code is attached. This tutorial also demonstrates using dot notation.

 You can find the COLOR.FSL form on the disc in the `\ANSWERS` directory.

Step By Step

1. Change your working directory to the TUTORIAL directory, and create a new form and add a box to the form (see Figure 4.9).

FIGURE 4.9.

Setup form for tutorial.

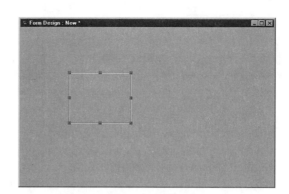

2. Right-click the box to display its Object Inspector.

3. Select Methods.

4. Open the built-in mouseClick method.

5. In the mouseClick method, enter lines 3 and 4:

```
1:      ;COLOR :: theBox :: mouseClick
2:      method mouseClick(var eventInfo MouseEvent)
3:          ;The following changes the color of self.
4:          self.color = Red
5:      endmethod
```

6. Check your syntax and save the form as COLOR.FSL.

7. Close the Edit box by clicking the close icon—that is, the arrow icon.

8. Go into View Data mode—that is, run the form—by clicking on the Toolbar lightning bolt icon. Click the box and watch the color change. Figure 4.10 shows COLOR.FSL. Your completed form should look similar (minus the button).

FIGURE 4.10.

The completed COLOR.FSL form.

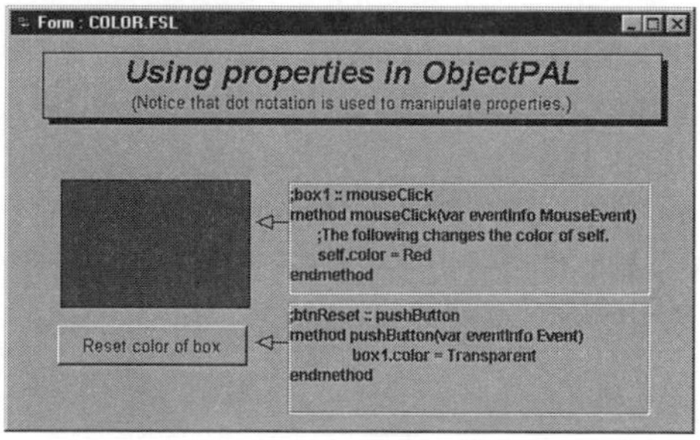

Analysis

In step 5, lines 2 and 5 begin and end the method. These lines of code are always provided for you by ObjectPAL. In line 2, note that the eventInfo variable type is MouseEvent. This is important to note and is discussed in more detail later in Chapter 7. For now, understand that

ObjectPAL is an event-driven language and, in this case, an event of type `MouseEvent` was sent to `mouseClick`. Line 3, in step 5, starts with a semicolon, followed by a comment. Lines that start with a semicolon are stripped out when the form is compiled or run. Do yourself a favor and comment all your code heavily. You'll appreciate your efforts when you go back to the code a month later. The semicolon also is a good way to disable a line of code; it's useful when you debug code. For the tutorials in this book, you do not need to type the comments.

Look at line 4, which uses a special built-in object variable, `self`, to refer to the object to which the code is attached. If you named the box `box1`, you could have used `box1.color = Red` rather than `self.color = Red`. `color` is a property of the object type `Box`. The rest of the line sets that property to a certain value or constant. A constant is a specific, unchanging value; in this case, the color `Red`. Contrast this with a variable, which is a place in memory used to store data temporarily.

One type of code that you write in ObjectPAL gets or alters the property of an object. Think of objects as having a set of data attached to them. Some of the properties of a field object are `value`, `color`, `font.color`, `tabStop`, `name`, `fieldName`, and `tableName`. As demonstrated in the previous tutorial, you can alter the properties of objects with ObjectPAL.

ObjectPAL Is Descriptive

In addition to altering an application's look by manipulating properties, there are many ObjectPAL commands that can have an effect on an application. For example, you can change the look of the desktop with the procedures `hideToolbar()` and `showToolbar()`. They hide and show the Toolbar. For example:

```
1:    hideToolbar()   ;Hide Toolbar.
2:    sleep(1000)     ;Wait for 1 second.
3:    showToolbar()   ;Show toolbar.
```

Notice how descriptive ObjectPAL is. It uses real words that describe what you're doing. Sounds easy so far, right? Well, that's because it is easy. The reason ObjectPAL has such a steep learning curve is that it's so rich in commands. Every procedure and method is as easy to understand as the previous examples, however. Because there are so many procedures, methods, and properties, it takes a while just to get a handle on ObjectPAL.

Basic Language Elements and ObjectPAL

Now that you have looked at ObjectPAL from the big picture, this next section introduces basic programming elements common to most programming languages and relates these common elements to ObjectPAL. If you have programmed in another language before, then you will particularly like this section.

NOTE

If you want to type and run the examples in this section, then use the pushButton method of a button and type the code, run the form, and select the button. (There is no need to type the comments.)

A *variable* is a place in memory used to store data temporarily. You first declare a variable and then you use it. For example, a *string* is an alphanumeric value or an expression consisting of alphanumeric characters. You can convert a number to a string with string(x) or you can declare a string variable and use it as the following code demonstrates. For example, line 2 that follows declares s as a string:

```
1:   var                        ;Begin variable block.
2:      s    String             ;Declare s as a string.
3:   endVar                     ;End variable block.
4:
5:   s = "Press OK to continue."  ;Set s to string value.
6:   message(s)                 ;Display value stored in s.
```

An *operator* is a symbol that represents an operation to be performed on a value or values. For example, the + operator represents addition, and the * operator represents multiplication. Line 8 in the code that follows multiplies x and y and then displays the result on the status line.

```
1:   var                ;Start variable block.
2:      x    Number     ;Declare x as a number.
3:      y    Number     ;Declare y as a number.
4:   endVar             ;End variable block.
5:
6:   x = 10             ;Set x to 10.
7:   y = 5              ;Set y to 5.
8:   message(x * y)     ;Displays 50 on the status line.
```

When you *concatenate* two values, you combine two or more alphanumeric values with the + operator. For example, line 9 that follows concatenates two strings and then assigns the value to s2.

```
1:   var                ;Begin variable block.
2:      s1   String     ;Declare s1 as a string.
3:      s2   String     ;Declare s2 as a string.
4:   endVar             ;End variable block.
5:
6:   s1 = "Enter name here"           ;Set s1 to string.
7:   s1.view("What is your name?")    ;View s1 in a view box.
8:
9:   s2 = "Hello " + s1               ;Set s2 to string plus s1.
10:  message(s2)                      ;Display s2 on status line.
```

Comparison operators are symbols used to compare two values in a query, in a calculated field, or in an ObjectPAL expression. The comparison operators are <, >, <=, >=, and =. For example, lines 11–13 compare x and y. Depending on which value is greater, a different message is displayed.

```
 1:    var                                      ;Begin variable block.
 2:       x      Number                         ;Declare x as a number.
 3:       y      Number                         ;Declare y as a number.
 4:    endVar                                    ;End variable block.
 5:    x = 0                                     ;Set x to 0.
 6:    x.view("Enter value for x")               ;View x in a view box.
 7:    y = 0                                     ;Set y to 0.
 8:    y.view("Enter value for y")               ;View y in a view box.
 9:
10:    switch                                    ;Begin switch block.
11:       case x > y : message("x is bigger")    ;Is x > y?
12:       case y > x : message("y is bigger")    ;Is y > x?
13:       case x = y : message("They are equal") ;Is x = Y?
14:    endSwitch                                 ;End switch block.
```

A *constant* is a specific, unchanging value. ObjectPAL uses two types of constants; those used in calculations and defined in the Const window of an object and constants predefined by ObjectPAL. For example, line 2 that follows uses a user set constant that sets the value of pi to 8 decimal points.

```
 1:    const                   ;Begin constant block.
 2:       pi = 3.14159265      ;Set the permanent value of pi.
 3:    endConst                ;End constant block.
 4:
 5:    ;Display the square root of pi.
 6:    message("The square root of pi is ", sqrt(pi))
```

You already have used predefined constants; all property values are actually predefined constants. For example, in the previous tutorial, you used self.color = Red. Red is a constant that represents a number ObjectPAL associates with the color red. You use constants with methods and procedures, such as DataNextRecord, DarkBlue, and FieldForward. Examples of constants include fieldName.action(DataNextRecord), fieldName.font.color = DarkBlue, and active.action(FieldForward).

The following line of code shows the numeric equivalent to the constant Red.

```
message("The numeric value of Red is ", SmallInt(Red))
```

Although it is academically interesting to understand the numbers behind the built-in ObjectPAL constants, always use the constants in your own coding. Never use the numbers because Borland could renumber all the constants in a future version.

A *branch* transfers program control to an instruction other than the next sequential instruction. When you used the switch block in the example for comparison operators, you branched to one line of code or another depending on a comparison. Normally, a programming language executes line after line in sequential order. This is true whether the language is a line-oriented language, such as BASIC, or a statement-oriented language, such as ObjectPAL, Pascal, or C.

In programming languages, a *control structure* is a set of keywords used to branch or loop. With control structures, you can alter the sequence of execution and add logic to your code. A *loop* is a set of instructions that is repeated a predetermined number of times or until a specified condition is met. For example, lines 6 and 7 in the code that follows are repeated 10 times as indicated in line 5.

```
1:    var                 ;Begin variable block.
2:        x      Number    ;Declare x as a number.
3:    endVar              ;End variable block.
4:
5:    for x from 1 to 10  ;Begin loop.
6:        message(x)       ;Display x.
7:        sleep(500)       ;Wait 1/2 second.
8:    endFor              ;End Loop.
```

A *logical value* is a True or False value that is assigned to an expression when it is evaluated. *Logical operators* are operators used in queries, in calculated fields, and in ObjectPAL methods. The three logical operators are and, or, and not. For example, line 2 in the code that follows declares l as a logical variable, and line 6 uses the not logical operator to display the opposite of l in a view box.

NEW
Term

```
1:    var                 ;Begin variable block.
2:        l      Logical   ;Declare l as a logical.
3:    endVar              ;End variable block.
4:
5:    l = True            ;Set l to True.
6:    view(not l)         ;Display False in view box.
```

A *subroutine* is a sequence of instructions that performs a specific task, usually more than once in a program. The sequence may be invoked many times by the current program or by multiple applications. Although ObjectPAL doesn't have actual subroutines, you can think of custom methods and custom procedures as subroutines. You can find more on this subject in Chapter 23.

NEW
Term

Hiding the Desktop

At one point or another, most users want to create a form that hides the Paradox desktop. To do this, define an Application variable and use that variable with the hide() and show() methods, as in the following example:

```
1:    var
2:        app  Application   ;App is now an application variable.
3:    endVar
```

Then use the hide() method to hide it. Unless you have defined your form as a dialog box and have reopened it, your form will disappear with the desktop. At first, hide the desktop only for a period of time; for example, three seconds:

```
1:    app.hide()
2:    sleep(3000)
3:    app.show()
```

After a variable is defined as an application, you can use any of the application-type methods on it. In addition to hide() and show(), you can use and manipulate an application variable with the following methods: bringToTop(), getPosition(), getTitle(), isMaximized(), `isMinimized()`, `isVisible()`, `maximize()`, `minimize()`, `setPosition()`, `setTitle()`, `windowClienthandle()`, and `windowHandle()`. Don't bother experimenting with these at this early stage. Just realize that you can set the title of an application, check whether it's maximized, maximize it, and get and set its position. The next example shows you how to put the `hide()` and `show()` methods to work on an Application variable.

How to Hide the Desktop

Suppose that you want to hide the desktop for five seconds using the `pushButton` method of a button. This tutorial uses the following methods and procedures: `hide()`, `show()` and `sleep()`. In addition, it acquaints you with how to declare and use a variable in ObjectPAL. Finally, it demonstrates that a form is a child window of the desktop that hides when the desktop is hidden.

You can find the APP.FSL form on the disc in the \ANSWERS directory.

Step By Step

1. Change your working directory to the TUTORIAL directory and create a new form. Add a button to the form and change its label to Hide Desktop (see Figure 4.11).

FIGURE 4.11.
*Your form should
look like this.*

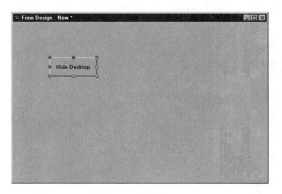

2. Open the `pushButton` event by selecting the button and pressing Ctrl+spacebar. Open the ObjectPAL Editor for the `pushButton` method.

3. Add lines 3–8 to the `pushButton` method. There is no need to type the comments after the semicolons.

```
1:    ;App :: btnHide :: pushButton
2:    method pushButton(var eventInfo Event)
3:       var
4:          app  Application      ;App is a application variable.
5:       endVar
```

```
6:      app.hide()          ;Hide the desktop.
7:      sleep(5000)         ;Wait 5 seconds.
8:      app.show()          ;Show the desktop.
9:   endmethod
```

4. While you're still in the ObjectPAL Editor, right-click to display the Editor's Object Inspector. Select Check Syntax to check your syntax.

5. Save the form as APP.FSL, close it, and then reopen it. Click the Hide Desktop button. After five seconds, Paradox should come back.

Analysis

In step 3, lines 2 and 9 mark the beginning and the end of the method. Lines 3–5 mark the variable section. In line 4, you declare app as a variable of type Application. In lines 6 and 8, you use that variable with the hide() and show() methods. Note that even though hide() and show() don't have a parameter passed to them, you still use parentheses. Parentheses are part of the basic syntax for all methods and procedures. Contrast this with properties, which never use parentheses. In line 7, you use the sleep() procedure to sleep for 5,000 milliseconds (5 seconds). You can tell that sleep() is a procedure and not a method because it has no object on which to work. A method requires an object on which to work; a procedure does not.

Line 1 of the code in step 3 is a comment that isn't part of the ObjectPAL code. (The semicolon signifies that this is a remark.) All code in the tutorials will have this remark line above it for reference. The first word of this special identifying remark is either the name of the object or the type of the object. Following the name or type is the window in which you will place the code. This window can be any of the events; for example, Var for variable window, Const for the constants window, the name of a custom method, and so on. This technique of referring to objects comes straight from the Editor window. This naming convention is consistent with what the ObjectPAL Editor displays on the title bar, which indicates where you are that follows (see Figure 4.12).

FIGURE 4.12.

The title bar of the ObjectPAL editor indicates where you are.

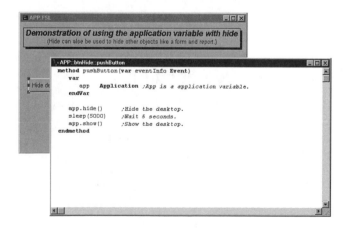

First Database Routines

All this programming theory and manipulating properties and the desktop is necessary and useful, but it probably isn't the reason you purchased Paradox. This section discusses some of the basic commands used to edit data. Old time ObjectVision users will appreciate this section because it simulates some of the most important database functions from ObjectVision.

Using *home()*, *end()*, *priorRecord()*, and *nextRecord()*

In ObjectPAL, you often have several ways to do something. For example, to go to the beginning of a table, you could use either a method or an action constant. The following two lines of code are equivalent:

```
1:    nextRecord()
2:    action(DataNextRecord)
```

These two methods represent two techniques for maneuvering through a table. Both of these methods move the pointer from the current record to the next record. The first line requires less typing and is my preferred usage. The second line represents more clearly what ObjectPAL is doing, however. The `action()` method sends a constant to the event `action`. When the constant `DataNextRecord` reaches the `action` method, `action` knows to insert a record. In addition to `nextRecord()`, there is a whole set of table-related methods, including `home()`, `end()`, and `priorRecord()`.

In addition to using the object variable `self`, which refers to the object the code is attached to, you can use `active`, which represents the object with focus. You can combine these with the two distinctly different techniques for positioning the pointer, as in the following example:

```
1:    self.nextRecord()              ;Move to the next record.
2:    active.nextRecord()            ;Move to the next record.
3:    self.action(DataNextRecord)    ;Move to the next record.
4:    active.action(DataNextRecord)  ;Move to the next record.
```

These two groups of code use two built-in object variables: `self` and `active`. `self` refers to the object that executes the code and `active` refers to the object that has focus.

Using *edit()* and *endEdit()*

When you go into edit mode (with a command such as `edit()`), it is important to note that you put the whole form into edit mode. In other words, you can go to any field of any table on any page and enter or edit values. When you issue an `endEdit()` command, the whole form is taken out of Edit mode. The `edit()` method is intelligent enough to act on the table that is connected to `self`. `active` refers to the object that currently has the focus. In a multitable form, you could use `active` to move the record pointer to the table that is attached to the selected object.

Basic Database Buttons

Suppose that you want to put eight buttons on a form that simulate the ObjectVision menu actions: Top, Bottom, Previous, Next, Edit, Store, New, and Delete (see Figure 4.13). This tutorial introduces you to the following ObjectPAL methods: `home()`, `end()`, `priorRecord()`, `nextRecord()`, `edit()`, `postRecord()`, `endEdit()`, `insertRecord()`, and `deleteRecord()`. It also introduces the `if` structure.

You can find the OV-LIKE.FSL form on the disc in the \ANSWERS directory.

Step By Step

1. Make your working directory the TUTORIAL directory and create a new form with the CUSTOMER.DB table in its data model.

2. Place eight buttons on the form. Change their labels to Top, Bottom, Previous, Next, Edit, Store, New, and Delete (see Figure 4.13).

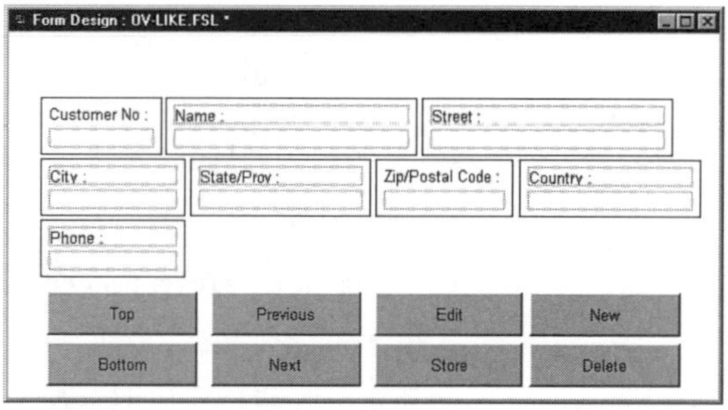

FIGURE 4.13.

The set up of the form for the tutorial Basic Database Buttons.

3. Add line 3 to the button labeled Top.

```
1:    ;OV-LIKE :: btnTop :: pushButton
2:    method pushButton(var eventInfo Event)
3:       active.home()   ;Move to the first record.
4:    endmethod
```

4. Add line 3 to the button labeled Bottom.

```
1:    ;OV-LIKE :: btnBottom :: pushButton
2:    method pushButton(var eventInfo Event)
3:       active.end()   ;Move to the last record.
4:    endmethod
```

5. Add line 3 to the button labeled Previous.

```
1:    ;OV-LIKE :: btnPrevious :: pushButton
2:    method pushButton(var eventInfo Event)
3:       active.priorRecord()    ;Move to the previous record.
4:    endmethod
```

6. Add line 3 to the button labeled Next.

```
1:    ;OV-LIKE :: btnNext :: pushButton
2:    method pushButton(var eventInfo Event)
3:        active.nextRecord()    ;Move to the next record.
4:    endmethod
```

7. Add lines 3 and 4 to the button labeled Store.

```
1:    ;OV-LIKE :: btnStore :: pushButton
2:    method pushButton(var eventInfo Event)
3:        active.postRecord()    ;Write the record to the table.
4:        endEdit()              ;End edit mode.
5:    endmethod
```

8. Add line 3 to the button labeled Edit.

```
1:    ;OV-LIKE :: btnEdit :: pushButton
2:    method pushButton(var eventInfo Event)
3:        edit()                 ;Put form into edit mode.
4:    endmethod
```

9. Add lines 3–5 to the button labeled New.

```
1:    ;OV-LIKE :: btnNew :: pushButton
2:    method pushButton(var eventInfo Event)
3:        action(MoveTopLeft)    ;Move to first field on form.
4:        edit()                 ;Put form into edit mode.
5:        active.insertRecord()  ;Insert a new blank record.
6:    endmethod
```

10. Add lines 3–7 to the button labeled Delete.

```
1:    ;OV-LIKE :: btnDelete :: pushButton
2:    method pushButton(var eventInfo Event)
3:        if deleteRecord() then
4:            message("Record deleted")
5:        else
6:            message("Could not delete record")
7:        endIf
8:    endmethod
```

11. Check the syntax, save the form as OV-LIKE.FSL, and run it. Try out all the various buttons. Your form should look similar to the \ANSWERS\OV-LIKE.FSL form (see Figure 4.14).

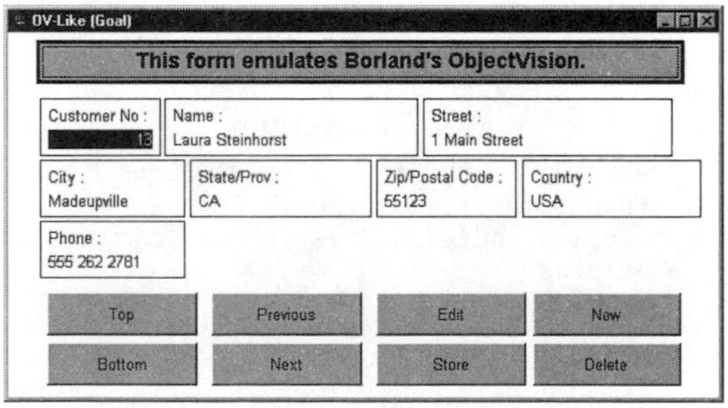

FIGURE 4.14.

The OV-LIKE.FSL form.

Analysis

In step 3, line 3 issues the home() command, which takes you to the beginning of the active table. If you have multiple tables on this form, how does home() know which table to work with? When you use a method by itself, active is implied, as in active.home().

You also could use the active variable, as in active.home(). In fact, this third variation in syntax is the clearest and the most elegant. In all these methods, the name of the object worked on is left out. This is exactly how the built-in functionality works.

In step 4, line 3 issues the end() command, which takes you to the last record in the table. In step 5, line 3 uses priorRecord() to move the pointer back one record. In step 6, line 3 uses nextRecord() to move the pointer forward one record.

In step 7, lines 3 and 4 commit the user's changes to the record and end the edit session. Both postRecord() and endEdit() were used in this example to explicitly post the change to the table and end the edit mode. Note, however, that this was done just to introduce the method postRecord(). In a real application, ending edit mode with endEdit() automatically sends DataPostRecord to the built-in action method (changes, if any, to a record are committed when you end an edit session).

In step 8, line 3 puts the form in edit mode with edit().

In step 9, with the New button, you want to get the form ready for the user edit. Move the focus to the upper-left field using the MoveTopLeft action constant with action(MoveTopLeft). Go into Edit mode and insert a record with edit() and insertRecord().

The syntax of the Delete button in step 10 deserves special attention. There are times when deleteRecord() is not a valid command. Therefore, you need to do some error checking. deleteRecord() returns a logical True or False in an if structure. If deleteRecord() is successful, the message in line 4 is sent to the status bar. deleteRecord() sometimes fails; for example, when the user isn't in Edit mode or when deleteRecord() interferes with referential integrity. Whenever deleteRecord() fails, a different message is sent to the message box in line 6.

The user can't use the pull-down menus and the toolbar whenever you use a custom menu, hide the toolbar, or use a modal dialog box. These eight buttons are very useful in such situations. Now that you have created these buttons, simply copy and paste them to other forms as needed.

Referring to Objects with *active* and by Name

The techniques shown in the previous tutorial used the object variable active and a method. They are useful for single-table forms. Most often, however, you'll create multitable forms. Therefore, you must be more precise. In the next example, you learn how to use a method on a single table in a multitable form.

Using *insertRecord()* and *deleteRecord()* with a Multi-Table Form

Until now, you've seen how to use database-type methods on a form with a single table in the data model. But what if you want to delete a record from only one table in a 1:M relationship? You can use the name of an object to refer to the underlying table, as in the following example:

```
1:    Last_Name.insertRecord() ;Insert a new blank record.
2:    LineItem.DeleteRecord()  ;Delete current record.
```

Using the name of an object enables you to specify the table with which you want to work, which is crucial when you work with multiple tables. This example puts the commands together.

Tutorial Using a UIObject Name to Refer to the Underlying Table

Suppose that you want to set up a button on a 1:M form that deletes only the currently selected detail record. This example shows you how to use dot notation in combination with a method. It also introduces the procedure msgQuestion(), which displays a message question dialog box.

You can find the DELETE.FSL form on the disc in the \ANSWERS directory.

Step By Step

1. Create a new form with a 1:M relationship between ORDERS.DB and LINEITEM.DB, and place a button on the form. Change the button's label to Delete Line Item.

2. Alter the button's pushButton method to look like the following:
   ```
   1:    ;DELETE :: btnDeleteLine :: pushButton
   2:    method pushButton(var eventInfo Event)
   3:       if msgQuestion("Warning", "Delete the current item?") = "Yes" then
   4:          edit()
   5:          Stock_No.deleteRecord()
   6:       endIf
   7:    endmethod
   ```

3. Test your syntax, correct any errors if necessary, save the form as DELETE.FSL, run the form, and click the button to delete a record in the detail table.

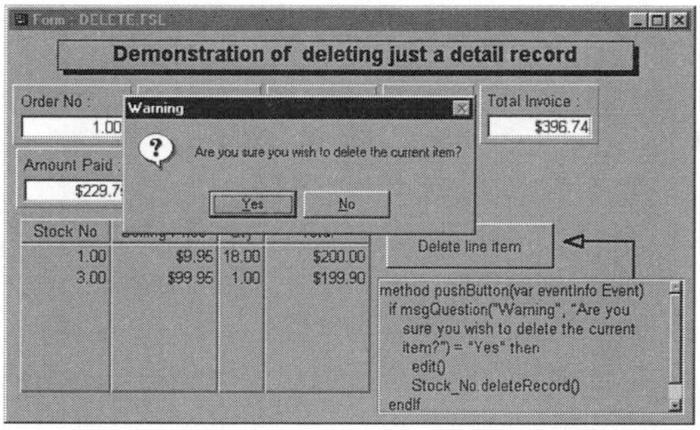

FIGURE 4.15.
DELETE.FSL. Use
msgQuestion() in an
if statement to ask the
user a question and act on
the answer.

Analysis

In step 2, line 3, the msgQuestion() procedure is used to ask the user whether he or she really wants to delete the record (see Figure 4.15). If the answer is yes, lines 4 and 5 delete the record. Otherwise, the if statement ends at line 6. To delete the record, you put the form into edit mode in line 4. In line 5, you use the name of an object to signify the table from which to delete a record. Just as easily, you could have used any other object that is connected to the table, or even the name of the table frame. Remember that when you use the name of an object with a method that uses a table, the method will use the table to which the object is connected.

Summary

This chapter introduced you to the basics of ObjectPAL. You learned a little about all the various aspects of programming in ObjectPAL. You learned that programming in an event-driven environment is about attaching code to objects. You learned the basics of ObjectPAL syntax and to refer to objects using dot notation to refer to object paths and to attach methods to objects. You also learned that methods require an object to work on while procedures know what object to work with.

If you haven't done so already, install and browse through the CD that came with this book. Now that you understand the basics of ObjectPAL, browsing existing code can be a great benefit. After you install the CD, you'll have a directory called SECRETS3. Inside the SECRETS3 directory is a main menu form called SECRETS3.FSL. Load and run this form. It's the gateway to all the secrets contained on the CD. At this stage, you'll be interested in the button called Answers to Tutorials. Take some time to browse through these sample forms. Pay special attention to the code that makes sense to you. If you come across something you don't understand, don't worry about it—just move on; the code will become clearer as you read through this book.

The ObjectPAL Editor

5

This chapter explores the ObjectPAL Editor, which is part of the Paradox integrated development environment (IDE). The IDE of Paradox consists of the ObjectPAL Editor and Debugger. This chapter is primarily concerned with the ObjectPAL Editor; the Debugger and debugging techniques are discussed in Chapter 29.

About the ObjectPAL Editor

The ObjectPAL Editor is based on Borland's award-winning C editor and has special features for use with ObjectPAL. The Editor is where you enter, edit, and check your code. Because of these features, the Editor has tremendous functionality. In fact, although you can change editors, very few people actually switch to a different editor. The better you know the Editor, the easier it will be for you to enter, edit, and debug your application.

Features of the ObjectPAL Editor include the following:

- **Writing code**: The ObjectPAL Editor is the main viewing area. This is where you write code.

- **Checking syntax**: You can easily check your syntax for typing errors and other basic mistakes before you execute your code.

- **Debugging**: With the built-in Debugger, you can inspect variables, trace execution, and step through code.

- **Reference**: When you right-click the Editor, select ObjectPAL Quick Lookup to browse the ObjectPAL language.

Entering the Editor

You move into the Editor whenever you open a script or library, or when you select a method from the Object Explorer. You get to the Object Explorer by selecting the Object Explorer option from the object's menu. (You already should be familiar with this two-step process from the last chapter.) My favorite way to get to the Editor is by selecting the object on to which I want to place code and then pressing Ctrl+spacebar. This bypasses the object's menu and takes you straight to the Object Explorer. I then press the first letter of the method I want to edit and then press Enter.

Whether you add code to a form, a library, or a script, the Editor works the same. First, you enter the Object Explorer. You then select a method to which you want to add code. The one exception to this process is a script. When you create a new script or open an existing script in Design mode, Paradox assumes that you want to edit the run method, and it automatically opens the ObjectPAL Editor for you.

The Object Explorer

To open the Object Explorer, you first need to select the object with which you want to work. Then you have the following options:

- Select an object and either click the right mouse button or press F6 to display the object's menu. Select Object Explorer.

- Select an object and press Ctrl+spacebar to go directly to the Object Explorer.

Events Tab

Every object has a set of events attached to it. Figure 5.1 shows the Events tab of the Object Explorer, which contains a list of all the available events. Select the option and press Enter, or double-click an option. You can use Ctrl+left-click and Shift+left-click to select multiple events. You can right-click an option to display a pop-up menu that contains more options (see Figure 5.1).

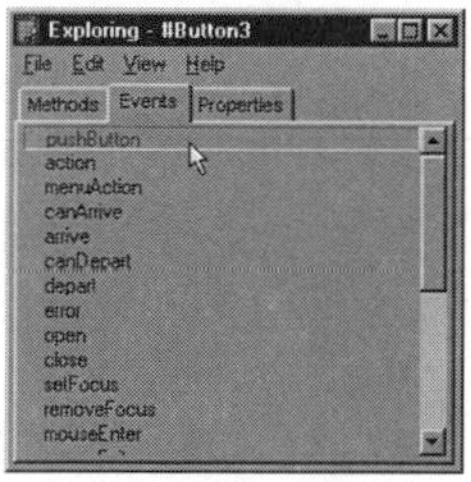

FIGURE 5.1.

The Events tab of the Object Explorer.

The list of events that the Method Inspector shows could have been called Triggers. Technically, these methods are triggers. Don't confuse the events with the methods in the runtime library. Just remember that events are triggers that dictate when—or whether—your code is executed.

> **NOTE**
>
> In this book, the term "method" can apply to either a built-in event or a command in ObjectPAL.

Methods Tab

Every object also has a set of methods attached to it. Figure 5.2 shows the Methods tab of the Object Explorer that lists the Var, Type, Const, Proc, and Uses options, which enable you to declare variables, types, constants, procedures, and external library routines to use in a method or procedure. These methods usually are referred to as Var window, Type window, and so on. The methods tab also lists an option for `<New method>` in which you can enter a new custom method.

FIGURE 5.2.

The Methods tab of the Object Explorer.

NEW Term

Custom methods are routines you create. They make a set of frequently used commands easier to use. For now, think of custom methods as being analogous to batch files in DOS. With batch files, you can use any DOS command, execute an external program, or even call another batch file. It's similar with custom methods. You can use any runtime library method or procedure, execute or call functions in DLLs, or even call other custom methods.

NEW Term

You create *custom procedures* in the Proc window. Custom procedures and custom methods are similar. They both store code you can call, and they can receive and return values. Because of the way in which they're stored, however, custom procedures are faster than custom methods. And unlike custom methods, custom procedures are private to an object. Therefore, you can't call them with dot notation from another containership hierarchy. Think of custom procedures as subroutines private to the current object and to the other objects in its containership hierarchy. Custom methods and custom procedures are discussed in greater detail in Chapter 23.

The Uses window enables you to add functionality to ObjectPAL. You can make custom methods available from libraries and functions available from DLLs. With the Uses window, ObjectPAL can be expanded virtually forever.

You use the Var window to declare a variable global to an object. You may want to do this to increase the scope of a variable. A variable declared in an object's Var window can be used by all the events, custom procedures, and so on, of that object and by all the objects that are contained by it.

You use the Const window to declare constants global to an object. A constant declared in an object's Const window can be used by all the events, custom procedures, and so on, of that object and by all the objects that are contained by it.

You define custom data types in the Type window. Just as variables and constants can be global to an object, so can custom data types. Within a custom method, you can declare the private versions of custom procedures, custom types, variables, constants, and uses. The difference between global to an object and private to a method is important. You can read more about this in Chapter 8.

Properties Tab

Finally, every object has a list of properties associated with it. Figure 5.3 shows the Properties tab of the Object Explorer, which lists the properties of a button. Notice the property names are not the same as interactive Paradox; what is listed in the Object Explorer is the ObjectPAL equivalents. Also note that any properties that are read-only are in green and have a lock icon to the left of the name.

FIGURE 5.3.

The Properties tab of the Object Explorer.

Configuring the Object Explorer

To configure the Object Explorer, select Edit | Developer Preferences from the main Paradox menu or from the Object Explorer menu. Figure 5.4 shows the Explorer tab of the Developer Preferences dialog box showing my preferred settings.

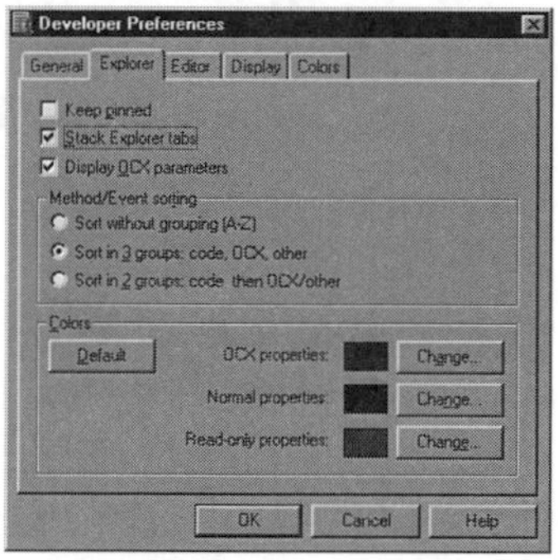

FIGURE 5.4.

The Explorer tab of the Developer Preferences dialog box.

The Object Tree Pane

The Object Explorer also enables you to display the Object Tree or Tabbed pane of a form or report. This split view enables you to view either the Object Tree, the Tabbed pane, or both. From the Object Explorer's menu, you can view the object tree by selecting View | Object Tree or both the Object Tree and the Tabbed pane by selecting View | Both (see Figures 5.5 and 5.6).

FIGURE 5.5.
The Object Tree graphically shows the object path.

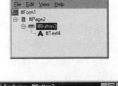

FIGURE 5.6.
The Object Explorer split view.

Key Mappings

The Editor is your tool for entering code. The better you know the Editor, the faster you can enter code. One thing you can do to expedite entering code is to memorize the keyboard short-cuts. For example, pressing Home moves you to the beginning of a line, and pressing End moves you to the end of a line.

The ObjectPAL Editor gives you three keymaps: BRIEF, Epsilon, and Paradox Default. For a complete list of shortcut keys, search Paradox help for key mappings or press Shift+F1 while on any white space in the Editor. The following section highlights some of the more interesting features of each keymap.

The Paradox Default Keymap

The Editor's default uses key bindings that match CUA mappings (with some WordStar additions). This is closest to the keystroke mappings in the Paradox 5.0 Editor. Of the three keymaps, the default is the only keymap that supports the standard menu access through hotkeys. The benefit of memorizing the keystrokes for the default map is that many of the keystrokes you memorize apply to most other Windows editors. If, however, you know the Epsilon or BRIEF keymaps, then you have a choice to make; otherwise, stick with the default keymap.

Using Bookmarks

Bookmarks are a powerful feature of any word processor. They enable you to set a marker in your code and return to it easily. The implementation in the default keymap is particularly easy to use. Set a bookmark, by pressing Ctrl+Shift+*<number>*, where *number* is a number from 0 through 9. You can move to the bookmarks you set by pressing Ctrl+*<number>*, where *number* is the number of the bookmark to which you want to move.

Moving Around

The following table lists some common keyboard shortcuts for moving around within the ObjectPAL editor. This is not a complete list, but does represent the most often used keyboard shortcuts.

Key	Action
Home	Moves cursor to start of line
End	Moves cursor to end of line
Ctrl+Left Arrow	Moves cursor left one word
Ctrl+Right Arrow	Moves cursor right one word
Ctrl+Home	Moves cursor to start of editor
Ctrl+End	Moves cursor to end of editor
F5	Goes to line
Ctrl+G	Goes to line
Ctrl+Up Arrow	Scrolls window up one line
Ctrl+Down Arrow	Scrolls window down one line
Ctrl+Page Up	Moves cursor to top of screen
Ctrl+Page Down	Moves cursor to bottom of screen
Ctrl+Backspace	Deletes the word to the left of the cursor
Ctrl+Delete	Deletes the word to the right of the cursor

Working with Code

The following table lists some common keyboard shortcuts for working with code in the ObjectPAL editor.

Key	Action
F2	Saves the source into the form; however, nothing is saved to disk
F8	Runs
F9	Checks syntax
Shift+F2	Saves the source and closes the Editor
Shift+F9	Compiles the form
Ctrl+F9	Delivers

continues

Key	Action
Insert	Toggles Insert/Overstrike mode
Ctrl+Ins	Copies to the Clipboard
Shift+Del	Cuts to the Clipboard
Shift+Ins	Pastes from the Clipboard
Ctrl+C	Copies to the Clipboard
Ctrl+X	Cuts to the Clipboard
Ctrl+V	Pastes from the Clipboard
Alt+Backspace	Undoes last action
Alt+Delete	Redoes last action
Ctrl+K+E	Toggles word under cursor to lowercase
Ctrl+K+F	Toggles word under cursor to uppercase
Ctrl+Y	Deletes current line
Ctrl+K+L	Marks current line
Ctrl+K+S	Saves form
Ctrl+K+T	Marks word under cursor

Debugger

The following table lists some common keyboard shortcuts for use within the ObjectPAL debugger. This is not a complete list, but does represent the most often used keyboard shortcuts.

Key	Action
F3	Inspects the variable at cursor (Debugger only)
F7	Steps over (Debugger only)
Shift+F3	Views callstack (toggle)
Shift+F7	Steps into (Debugger only)
Shift+F8	Runs to cursor (Debugger only)
Ctrl+F3	Toggles breakpoint
Ctrl+F5	Next warning
Ctrl+F8	Runs to `endMethod` (Debugger only)

Key	Action
Ctrl+N	Next warning
Ctrl+B	Toggles breakpoint
Ctrl+D	Delivers
Ctrl+I	Inspects the variable at cursor (Debugger only)
Ctrl+W	Adds watch of variable at cursor

Working with Blocks of Code

The following keyboard shortcuts are used with blocks of code.

Key(s)	Action
Ctrl+Shift+I	Indents block
Ctrl+Shift+U	Outdents block
Ctrl+K+B	Sets start of block (persistent blocks must be on)
Ctrl+K+C	Copies block to Clipboard
Ctrl+K+H	Hides block
Ctrl+K+I	Indents block
Ctrl+K+K	Sets end of block (persistent blocks must be on)
Ctrl+K+U	Outdents block
Ctrl+K+V	Moves block (persistent blocks must be on)
Ctrl+K+W	Writes block to file
Ctrl+K+Y	Deletes current block
Ctrl+O+C	Sets column block
Ctrl+O+G	Goes to line
Ctrl+O+I	Sets inclusive block
Ctrl+O+K	Sets non-inclusive block
Ctrl+O+L	Sets line block
Ctrl+O+O	Toggles case of block
Ctrl+K+R	Reads block from file
Ctrl+K+N	Uppercase block
Ctrl+K+O	Lowercase block

Searching

The following keyboard shortcuts are used for searching.

Key(s)	Action
Ctrl+A	Finds next
Ctrl+Z	Finds first
Ctrl+Shift+Z	Replaces first
Ctrl+S	Incremental search
Ctrl+]	Finds matching parenthesis
Ctrl+L	Replaces all
Ctrl+R	Replaces next

The Epsilon Keymap

NEW Term

A *keymap* is a description of the keyboard shortcuts. The Epsilon keymap uses key bindings that match a large part of the Epsilon editor. The following table lists the keyboard shortcuts for use with the Epsilon keymap.

> **TIP**
>
> The BRIEF and Epsilon keymaps do not allow standard menu access through hotkeys. However, you can still use F10 to access the menus. With the default keymap, you can press Alt+F+O+F for File | Open | Form. For both the Epsilon and BRIEF keymaps, you can substitute F10 for the Alt key: you can press F10+F+O+F for File | Open | Form. Another way you can gain access to the menu system is by pressing and releasing the Alt key.

Key(s)	Action
Page Up	Moves cursor up one page
Page Down	Moves cursor down one page
Backspace	Deletes character to the left of the cursor
Delete	Deletes character to the right of the cursor (On the cursor if box-shaped cursor)
Insert	Toggles Insert/Overstrike mode

Key(s)	Action
Tab	Inserts a tab, or indents to indent of previous line if Smart Tab is turned on
Ctrl+Left Arrow	Moves cursor left one word
Ctrl+Right Arrow	Moves cursor right one word
Ctrl+Home	Moves cursor to start of editor
Ctrl+End	Moves cursor to end of editor
Esc+Left Arrow	Moves cursor to start of line
Esc+Right Arrow	Moves cursor to end of line
F1	Accesses context-sensitive help
F2	Saves the source into the form; however, nothing is saved to disk
F3	Inspects the variable at cursor (Debugger only)
F5	Goes to specified line
F6	Adds watch of variable at cursor
F7	Steps over (Debugger only)
F8	Runs
F9	Undoes last action
Shift+F2	Saves the source and closes the Editor
Shift+F3	Views callstack (toggle)
Shift+F7	Steps into (Debugger only)
Shift+F8	Runs to cursor (Debugger only)
Shift+F9	Compiles the form
Ctrl+F3	Toggles breakpoint
Ctrl+F5	Displays next warning
Ctrl+F8	Runs to `endMethod` (Debugger only)
Ctrl+F9	Undoes last action
Ctrl+F10	Redoes last action
Ctrl+A	Moves cursor to start of line
Ctrl+B	Moves cursor left one column
Ctrl+D	Deletes character to the right of the cursor (Deletes character under the cursor if the cursor is box-shaped)
Ctrl+E	Moves cursor to end of line
Ctrl+F	Moves cursor right one column

continues

Key(s)	Action
Ctrl+H	Deletes character to the left of the cursor
Ctrl+K	Deletes current line and copies/appends to Clipboard
Ctrl+L	Scrolls current line to center of window
Ctrl+M	Same as Enter key
Ctrl+N	Moves cursor down one line
Ctrl+P	Moves cursor up one line
Ctrl+S	Performs incremental search
Ctrl+T	Switches the two characters on each side of the cursor
Ctrl+V	Moves cursor down one page
Ctrl+W	Deletes block and copies/appends to the Clipboard
Ctrl+Y	Pastes from Clipboard
Ctrl+Z	Scrolls up one line
Ctrl+_	Accesses context-sensitive help
Ctrl+X, (	Records key macro
Ctrl+X,)	Records key macro
Ctrl+X, E	Plays back key macro
Ctrl+X, G	Goes to specified line
Ctrl+X, I	Reads block from file
Ctrl+X, U	Undoes last action
Ctrl+X, W	Writes block to file
Ctrl+X, Tab	Indents block
Ctrl+X, Ctrl+F	Views method explorer (toggle)
Ctrl+X, Ctrl+I	Indents block
Ctrl+X, Ctrl+N	Displays next warning
Ctrl+X, Ctrl+R	Redoes last action
Ctrl+X, Ctrl+S	Saves form
Ctrl+X, Ctrl+T	Switches current and previous line
Ctrl+X, Ctrl+U	Undoes last action
Ctrl+X, Ctrl+W	Writes block to file
Ctrl+X, Ctrl+X	Exchanges cursor and block marker
Alt+B, Esc+B	Moves cursor left one column
Alt+C, Esc+C	Makes a word uppercase

Key(s)	Action
Alt+D, Esc+D	Deletes word and copies/appends to the Clipboard
Alt+F, Esc+F	Moves cursor right one word
Alt+L, Esc+L	Makes word lowercase
Alt+M, Esc+M	Moves cursor to first character on the current line
Alt+T, Esc+T	Switches the words before and after the cursor
Alt+U, Esc+U	Makes a word uppercase
Alt+V, Esc+V	Moves cursor to previous page
Alt+W, Esc+W	Copies block to Clipboard
Alt+Z, Esc+Z	Scrolls window down one line
Alt+,, Esc+,	Moves cursor to top of window
Alt+., Esc+.	Moves cursor to end of window
Alt+\, Esc+\	Deletes white space on both sides of cursor
Alt+), Esc+)	Finds the matching parenthesis
Alt+<, Esc+<	Moves cursor to start of Editor
Alt+>, Esc+>	Moves cursor to end of Editor
Alt+?, Esc+?	Accesses context-sensitive help
Alt+%, Esc+%	Replaces first occurrence
Alt+*, Esc+*	Replaces first (advanced match)
Alt+&, Esc+&	Replaces first (match string)
Alt+@, Esc+@	Sets marker to current cursor position
Alt+Backspace, Esc+Backspace	Deletes word left of cursor and copy/append to Clipboard
Alt+Tab, Esc+Tab	Indents to indent of previous line
Alt+Ctrl+B, Esc+Ctrl+B	Finds matching parenthesis
Alt+Ctrl+F, Esc+Ctrl+F	Finds matching parenthesis
Alt+Ctrl+H, Esc+Ctrl+H	Deletes the word to the left of the cursor and copies/appends to Clipboard
Alt+Ctrl+R, Esc+Ctrl+R	Searches first (backward, advanced match)
Alt+Ctrl+S, Esc+Ctrl+S	Searches first (forward, advanced match)
Alt+Ctrl+W, Esc+Ctrl+W	Appends to the keyboard (until next non-Clipboard action)
Alt+Ctrl+\, Esc+Ctrl+\	Blocks indent

The BRIEF Keymap

BRIEF was a very popular editor that many programmers are familiar with. The BRIEF keymap uses key bindings that match most of the standard BRIEF keystrokes.

Key(s)	Action
Left Arrow	Moves (or extends selection) one column left of cursor
Right Arrow	Moves (or extends selection) one column right of cursor
Up Arrow	Moves (or extends selection) one line up from cursor
Down Arrow	Moves (or extends selection) one line down from cursor
Home	Moves (or extends selection) to start on line, then start of screen, and then start of Editor
End	Moves (or extends selection) to end of line, the end of screen, and then end of Editor
Page Up	Moves (or extends selection) one page up
Page Down	Moves (or extends selection) one page down
Backspace	Deletes character to the left of the cursor
Delete	Deletes character to the right of the cursor (or under the cursor if the cursor is box-shaped)
Tab	Inserts a tab, or indents block if a block exists
Ctrl+Left Arrow	Moves (or extends selection) one word left of cursor
Ctrl+Right Arrow	Moves (or extends selection) one word right of cursor
Ctrl+Home	Moves (or extends selection) to top of screen
Ctrl+End	Moves (or extends selection) to bottom of screen
Ctrl+Page Up	Moves (or extends selection) to start of Editor
Ctrl+Page Down	Moves (or extends selection) to end of Editor
Ctrl+Backspace	Deletes the word to the left of the cursor
Alt+Backspace	Deletes the word to the right of the cursor
Shift+Home	Moves (or extends selection) to left of screen
Shift+End	Moves (or extends selection) to right of screen
Shift+Tab	Moves back to previous tab, or outdents block if a block exists
Insert	Pastes from Clipboard
Minus (Num Keypad)	Cuts block to Clipboard, cuts current line if no block is selected

Key(s)	Action
Plus (Num Keypad)	Copies block to Clipboard; copies current line if no block is selected
Star (Num keypad)	Undoes last keystrokes
F1	Not assigned, reserved for later use
F5	Finds first
F6	Replaces first
F7	Records key macro
F8	Plays back key macro
F9	Runs object
F10	Sets focus on menu
F11	Steps over (Debugger only)
F12	Steps into (Debugger only)
Alt+F2	Zooms window
Alt+F3	Inspects variable at cursor (Debugger only)
Alt+F5	Reverses search first
Alt+F6	Reverses replace first
Alt+F7	Runs to cursor (Debugger only)
Alt+F8	Runs to endMethod (Debugger only)
Alt+F10	Performs syntax check
Ctrl+F3	Views callstack
Ctrl+F4	Adds watch of variable at cursor
Ctrl+F5	Toggles case sensitive in search
Ctrl+F6	Toggles advanced match in search
Ctrl+F8	Toggles breakpoint
Ctrl+F9	Runs object
Ctrl+F10	Compiles the form
Shift+F5	Searches next
Shift+F6	Replaces next
Ctrl+B	Scrolls current line to bottom of window
Ctrl+C	Scrolls current line to center of window
Ctrl+D	Scrolls window one line down
Ctrl+E	Scrolls window one line up

continues

Key(s)	Action
Ctrl+K	Deletes to beginning of line
Ctrl+M	Same as Enter key
Ctrl+N	Displays next warning
Ctrl+S	Performs incremental search
Ctrl+T	Scrolls current line to top of window
Ctrl+U	Redoes last undo
Alt+A	Starts non-inclusive block marking
Alt+C	Starts column marking
Alt+D	Deletes line
Alt+E	Displays Object Explorer
Alt+G	Goes to line you specify
Alt+H	Displays help
Alt+I	Toggles Insert/Overwrite mode
Alt+K	Deletes to end of line
Alt+L	Starts line marking
Alt+M	Starts inclusive block marking
Alt+O	Saves form as
Alt+R	Reads block from file
Alt+S	Searches first
Alt+T	Replaces first
Alt+U	Undoes last keystrokes
Alt+W	Writes block to file, or if no block save form to disk
Alt+X	Closes Editor without saving code
Alt+ 0	Sets bookmark number 0
Alt+ 1	Sets bookmark number 1
Alt+ 2	Sets bookmark number 2
Alt+ 3	Sets bookmark number 3
Alt+ 4	Sets bookmark number 4
Alt+ 5	Sets bookmark number 5
Alt+ 6	Sets bookmark number 6
Alt+ 7	Sets bookmark number 7
Alt+ 8	Sets bookmark number 8
Alt+ 9	Sets bookmark number 9

Key(s)	Action
Alt+J+ 0	Goes to bookmark number 0
Alt+J+ 1	Goes to bookmark number 1
Alt+J+ 2	Goes to bookmark number 2
Alt+J+ 3	Goes to bookmark number 3
Alt+J+ 4	Goes to bookmark number 4
Alt+J+ 5	Goes to bookmark number 5
Alt+J+ 6	Goes to bookmark number 6
Alt+J+ 7	Goes to bookmark number 7
Alt+J+ 8	Goes to bookmark number 8
Alt+J+ 9	Goes to bookmark number 9
Ctrl+Q+[	Finds matching parenthesis
Ctrl+Q+]	Finds matching parenthesis
Ctrl+O+O	Toggles case of block

The Editor Toolbar

The Toolbar gives you quick access to many of the most-used features in the ObjectPAL Editor. Figure 5.7 shows the Editor Toolbar.

FIGURE 5.7.

The ObjectPAL Editor Toolbar.

You already are familiar with the first six and last two icons on the ObjectPAL Toolbar. The first six are the Print, Cut to Clipboard, Copy to Clipboard, Paste from Clipboard, View Data, and Design icons. The Print icon sends a copy of your code to the default printer. Use it to print copies of your code. It's equivalent to File | Print. This is a great way to archive your code—perhaps keep a binder of most frequently used code bits.

The Cut tool cuts text to the Windows Clipboard. It works like any other Windows cut tool and is equivalent to Edit | Cut. The Copy tool copies text to the Windows Clipboard. It works like any other Windows copy tool and is equivalent to Edit | Copy. The Paste tool pastes text from the Windows Clipboard. It works like any other Windows paste tool and is equivalent to Edit | Paste.

The lightning bolt is the View Data icon. This icon puts your form in View Data mode. It's equivalent to Form | View Data or F8. From the right, the two icons you are already familiar with are Experts and Project Viewer.

You use the remaining icons primarily for debugging your code. Chapter 29 discusses debugging your code. For now, the following introduces the icons.

Check Syntax - The check mark is the Check Syntax icon. Use it to check the syntax of your code. It's equivalent to Program | Check Syntax, F9, or Ctrl+Y. When you use this icon, the current editor window syntax is checked. To check all your code, use the Compile icon next to the Check Syntax icon.

NOTE

Use F9 and F8 in sequence to check your syntax and to go into Run mode quickly.

Icon	*Action*
Compile	Compiles all methods in your form, library, or script.
Go to the next Warning	If you get an error while checking your syntax, you can use the Go to the next Warning icon to see whether it is the only error.
Save source and exit the editor	The icon with an arrow is the Close icon, which saves and exits.
Add Watch	You can watch a variable by using the Watch window.
Toggle Breakpoint	A breakpoint is a place in the code where the Debugger automatically stops execution. Set a breakpoint when you debug your code. It's a good idea to set a breakpoint when you're getting an error or when part of the code doesn't seem to execute. You can place breakpoints at various spots to evaluate whether your code is executing up to that point.

The seven remaining buttons toggle various windows open and closed. Starting from the 13 button from the left, they are as follows:

- Open/Close the Object Explorer
- Open/Close the Debugger window
- Open/Close the Watches window
- Open/Close the Breakpoints window
- Open/Close the Tracer window

■ Open/Close the stack call window

■ Open/Close the ObjectPAL Quick Lookup dialog box

The Open/Close the ObjectPAL Quick Lookup (the third icon from the left) is particularly useful at this point. It toggles the ObjectPAL Quick Lookup dialog box open and closed. The ObjectPAL Quick Lookup dialog box enables you to browse all of ObjectPAL (see Figure 5.8).

FIGURE 5.8.

The ObjectPAL Quick Lookup dialog box.

The Constants tab in the ObjectPAL Quick Lookup dialog box is of particular interest. These constants are grouped by type. If you select a type of constant on the left, its available constants appear on the right.

You use these constants in many different methods. Typically, you use constants to specify colors, mouse shape, menu attributes, window styles, and printer orientation. Everything a user does interactively generates a constant.

You trap for and execute many of the constants. In particular, you can trap for any of the constants in any of the action classes in the built-in `action` method, or execute any of the action constants with the `action()` method. For example, you can trap for when the user tries to delete a record by trapping for the constant `DataDeleteRecord` in the `action` method. Also of particular mention is the `MenuCommands` class of constants; you can execute most of them with the `menuAction()` method.

> **NOTE**
>
> Rather than have to remember numbers to specify something that might change from version to version, you can use descriptive constants that Paradox evaluates for you.

The next seven icons toggle various windows open and close.

■ Object Explorer icon

■ Debugger icon

124

- Watches icon
- Breakpoints icon
- Tracer icon
- Stack windows icon
- ObjectPAL Quick Lookup icon

The Edit Menu

You use the ObjectPAL Edit menu to manipulate code. This menu contains a few more options than does the Edit menu in Design mode. Undo, Undo All Edits, and Paste From are particularly useful for manipulating code. Figure 5.9 shows the ObjectPAL Edit menu.

FIGURE 5.9.

The Edit menu from the ObjectPAL Editor.

The following list points out some of the more interesting edit options.

Option	Action
Undo	Paradox 7 now offers multiple Undo capabilities.
Undo All Edits	Restores your code to what it was before you started editing.
Delete	Deletes the code without placing it on the Windows Clipboard.
Paste From and **Copy To**	The Paste From and Copy To options are of particular interest to anyone interested in saving time. To reuse your code easily and therefore save time when you code, save code to a text file. To do this, first highlight the code, then select Edit	Copy To. The Select All option selects all the text in the current window.

> **TIP**
>
> Archive your code and save time by reusing your code! Create a directory just for pieces of code, and use Copy To and Paste From to store and retrieve code. You could even use this technique extensively and categorize code into directories.
>
> Another way to archive code is to use a dummy set of forms with the code on the appropriate object—my personal favorite.

Indent Block and **Outdent Block**	This option is particularly useful when formatting someone else's code or returning to your own code to format it. To use either of these options, select a block of text, and then select Edit	Indent Block to move the text to the right one tab or Edit	Outdent Block to move the text one tab to the left.
Block Type	This option has three sub-options: Column Block, Line Block, and Stream Block. Column Block highlights a column of text. Line Block highlights only whole lines of text (you cannot select words). Stream Block (the default) enables you to select from one character through to another character.
Record Keystrokes	Records keystrokes. Select this option again to stop recording.
Playback Keystrokes	Plays back recorded keystrokes.

The Search Menu

The Search menu enables you to search and replace code with its Find, Find Next, Replace, Replace Next, and Incremental Search options. With the possible exception of Incremental Search, these options are similar to the search-and-replace options available in word processors. The Incremental Search option enables you to search from the cursor on.

Set Bookmark and Go to Bookmark	Enables you to drop a bookmark in your code and return to it later.

TIP

You can have more than one bookmark. Through keyboard access, you can have up to 10 bookmarks and easily jump from spot to spot in your code. Set bookmarks with Control + Shift + <*number from 1 through 0*> and go to the bookmark with Control+<*number from 1 through 0*>.

Go to Line   You'll seldom use the Go to Line option. Rarely will you write code long enough to require jumping to a particular spot.

Compiling an Object

After you complete a form, script, library, or report, you can compile it with File | Deliver. This option creates another version of the file, but uses a different extension. You cannot edit this compiled version. Because of the way in which the code is stored, it's actually compiled P-Code and is faster than code that is not compiled to P-Code. Table 5.1 lists the extensions used for undelivered and delivered objects.

Table 5.1. Extensions of undelivered and delivered objects.

Type	Undelivered	Delivered
Form	FSL	FDL
Library	LSL	LDL
Script	SSL	SDL
Report	RSL	RDL

Document Source

The Document Source option from the View menu is particularly interesting. You normally edit your code in small pieces. You see only small sections of your application at a time. It sometimes is useful to view all your code at once. You can do this by selecting View | Document Source. This option creates a table called PAL$SRC.DB in your private directory, and then generates a quick report based on it. This option is particularly useful with large applications. If you create a large application, you can print all the forms, libraries, and scripts. You also can view the entire application. This also is a good way to document the application for archiving purposes.

The DEV-SRC\SOURCE.RSL report on the disc that comes with this book uses `:PRIV:PAL$SRC.DB`. You can use this report to print better looking printouts of your code.

Always Use Compiler Warnings and Compile with Debug

The Compiler Warnings option toggles the display of warning messages from the compiler. When this option is checked, messages in the status line warn you about undeclared variables and other conditions that might cause runtime errors. In addition, the Compile with Debug option allows for better error messages. You should always toggle on these two options to take advantage of extra help from the compiler.

The Help Menu

The Help menu has eight options with which you are already familiar. The Help menu is your online desk reference. You can select any menu option and press F1 for immediate information on what it does and how to use it. Context-level help at the ObjectPAL level is available. You can press F1 to get help on the closest ObjectPAL keyword.

The Editor's Pop-Up Menu

When you right-click on the Editor, the Editor's pop-up menu appears. You can check your syntax with the Check Syntax option and Compile option. After you enter your code, select Check Syntax to see whether it contains any errors.

The Object Explorer option displays the Object Explorer so that you can move quickly from one editor to another. You don't need to leave one edit window to access another.

The Keywords option helps you to piece together code. The Keywords option displays a list of some—but not all—keywords. You generally use the keywords in this list for program control. You can use this menu to insert a keyword into a method without typing the keyword.

Configuring the ObjectPAL Editor

You can configure the ObjectPAL Editor by selecting Edit | Developer Preferences (see Figure 5.10). The General, Editor, Display, and Colors tabs configure the ObjectPAL Editor. Use this dialog box to configure the ObjectPAL Editor. You have already used the Level panel to make sure your ObjectPAL level was set to Beginner. Setting it to Advanced shows the entire ObjectPAL language.

FIGURE 5.10.

The General tab from the Developer Preferences dialog box.

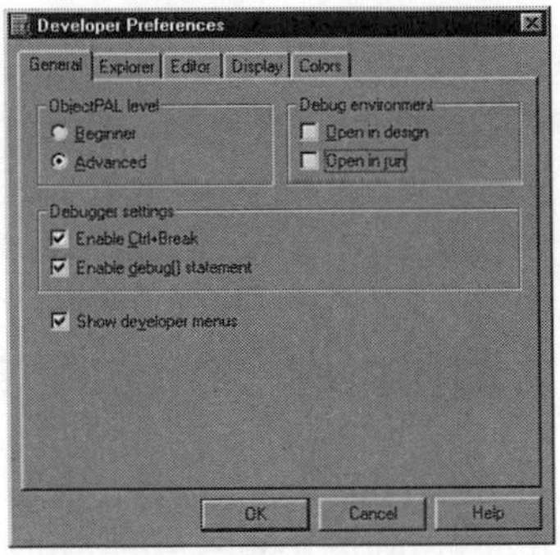

General Settings

The panels on the General tab configure various features in ObjectPAL. Refer to Figure 5.10 to see my preferred settings. The following are descriptions of the panels:

Option	Action
ObjectPAL level	Enables you to filter down the ObjectPAL Quick Lookup dialog box and Object Explorer to a subset of ObjectPAL. Even when the Beginner option is selected, you can still use all ObjectPAL commands and properties in your code.
Debug environment	Specify Open in design to open the Debugger, Watches, Breakpoints, Tracer, and Call Stack windows when you are in Design mode. Specify Open in run to open the debug environment while your application is running.
Debugger settings	Set the Enable Ctrl+Break to halt execution and go into the Debugger when you press Control+Break. When you check the Enable debug statement, you can put the debug() procedure in your code and when execution comes to it, the debugger will open as if you set a breakpoint.

> **NOTE**
>
> Check the Enable debug statement option to display more detailed error information. You can use this option even if you never use the debug() statement.

Option	Action
Show developer menus	Extends your choice of menu options in the Form Design window. This includes the Program menu and extra commands on the View and Tools menus. Otherwise, the commands will only appear in the Editor or Debugger menus.

Editor Settings

The options on the Editor tab configure behavior of the ObjectPAL and SQL editors. Figure 5.11 shows my preferred settings.

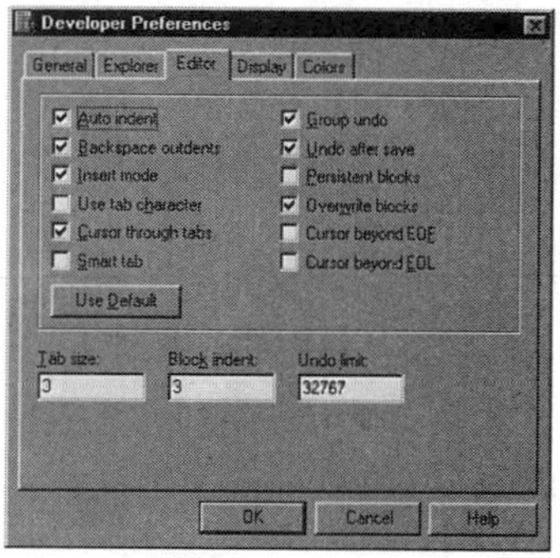

FIGURE 5.11.

The Editor tab from the Developer Preferences dialog box.

Following are descriptions of the options:

Option	Action
Auto intent	Check this option to indent the next line to the indent of the current line when you press Enter.
Backspace outdents	Aligns the insertion point to the previous indent level when you press Backspace, if the insertion point is on the first character of a line.
Insert mode	Inserts text at the insertion point without overwriting existing text. If Insert mode is not checked, text is overwritten.
Use tab character	Inserts a true ASCII 9-tab character when you indent text. If this option is not checked, Paradox inserts spaces instead. If Smart tab is enabled, this option is disabled.

continues

Option	Action
Cursor through tabs	Enables the arrow keys to move uniformly (column by column) through tabs.
Smart tab	Indents to the next character of the previous line.
Group undo	Undoes groups of your last editing commands. When this option is not checked, Paradox undoes each character you typed.
Undo after save	Enables you to perform an Edit	Undo command after a file has been saved.
Persistent Blocks	Check this option to keep marked blocks selected even when the insertion point is moved, until a new block is selected.
Overwrite blocks	Check this option to replace a marked block of text with whatever is typed next. If Persistent blocks is also checked, text you enter is added to the currently selected block.
Cursor beyond EOF	Allows the insertion point to go beyond the end-of-file character.
Cursor beyond EOL	Allows the insertion point past the last column of the line.
Use Default	Returns to the default settings of the current keymap.
Tab size	Specifies the number of columns you want between tab stops.
Block indent	Enables you to specify how many columns to indent and outdent a block.
Undo limit	Specifies the number of undo actions stored before undo information is discarded.

Display Settings

The options on the Display tab configure display preferences of the Editor. Figure 5.12 shows my preferred settings.

Following are descriptions of the options:

Keystroke mapping	Use this drop-down list to select from the three keymaps: Default, Epsilon, and BRIEF.

FIGURE 5.12.

The Display tab from the Developer Preferences dialog box.

TIP

Press Shift+F1 while in the Editor to see the keystrokes for the current keymap selected.

Prompt to save	The Editor prompts you to save changes when you close the Editor window or run a form.
BRIEF cursor shapes	Uses an underline rather than a vertical cursor in Insert mode.
Show sidebar	Shows the sidebar column to the left of your code reserved for breakpoint symbols.
Custom size	Opens the next Editor window to the size of the active Editor window (if one is open), or the size of the last Editor window open.
Hints on status bar	Shows Toolbar help messages on the status bar. When not checked, this option displays only Editor messages.
Font	Enables you to set the font and size of the Editor.

Exploring the ObjectPAL Quick Lookup Dialog Box

One of the most difficult things about ObjectPAL is getting a grasp on all it can do, especially all the thousands of combinations of types of objects, methods, method parameters, and constants. This next section is intended to ease you into ObjectPAL.

The next sections are a quick overview of the beginning-level methods, procedures, properties, and constants. Your goal is to become familiar with the beginning-level types of objects and their methods, procedures, properties, and constants.

Exploring the Tools Menu

In this section, you look at types of objects and the methods and procedures that can act on them. You'll group the 21 different beginner-level types into random pseudo-groups. For example, you'll start by lumping Date, DateTime, and Time into a category.

Part 1: The Types and Methods Tab

1. Open the ObjectPAL Editor for any object. The type of object doesn't matter. Select View | ObjectPAL Quick Lookup to display the ObjectPAL Quick Lookup dialog box.

2. From the Types and Methods tab, browse through the Date, DateTime, and Time data types by clicking them. Note the methods available for each one. Date and Time have no methods in common. DateTime, however, has methods in common with both Date and Time (see Figure 5.13).

FIGURE 5.13.

The Types and Methods tab of the ObjectPAL Quick Lookup dialog box.

Although you can't tell how all beginner-level methods and procedures act on their data types, the descriptive names for the methods give you a good idea. `daysInMonth()` returns the number of days in a month. `isLeapYear()` returns `True` if the Date or DateTime data is in a current leap year, and `False` if the data is not. `hour()` returns the hour portion of the `Time()` or `DateTime()` data format. If a method looks useful to you, select it and view its syntax.

If you need more explanation, refer to the ObjectPAL reference book or use the context-sensitive help by pressing F1.

3. Browse through `Number`, `SmallInt`, and `LongInt` methods and procedures. View their methods and procedures. Although these three data types are all types of numbers, `Number` has many more available methods and procedures. This isn't because of Beginner mode, however. When you switch to Advanced mode, the methods and procedures for `Number` are completely different from the methods and procedures for `SmallInt` and `LongInt`. If you have a variable defined as a `SmallInt` and you want to use one of the `Number` methods, you have to cast the `SmallInt` as a `Number` with either the `Number()` or `NumVal()` procedures.

4. Browse through the `AnyType`, `Logical`, and `String` types. Although `AnyType` and `Logical` have few methods and procedures, `String` has 17. (It has 35 in Advanced mode.)

5. Browse through Form and Report. These two display managers have no methods in common in Beginner mode. When you switch to Advanced mode, they have several methods and procedures in common, although they do slightly different things. Select a few of the methods and procedures whose names catch your attention, and view their syntax.

6. Browse through Table, TCursor, and UIObject. These three types have many methods in common. Their methods deal with accessing a table.

7. Browse through `ActionEvent`, `ErrorEvent`, `Event`, `MenuEvent`, `MoveEvent`, and `ValueEvent`. These types are all events, or packets of information sent from one object to another. The methods that apply to these event packets retrieve, set, or trigger them.

8. Browse through the System procedures. Select System and view the beginning-level System procedures. You'll recognize what many of these System procedures do just by looking at their names.

Part 2: The Objects and Properties Tab

Next you are going to explore the Display Objects and Properties tab (refer to Figure 5.11). In Beginner mode, the objects each have up to 36 properties, and each property has up to 17 constants. Advanced mode raises these numbers by a factor of 3 or 4. Many of these numbers are duplicates, however. For example, most objects have one or more color properties. The constants for every color property are the same 17 constants. This duplication holds true for most properties and their constants. Select Box and `frame.style` (see Figure 5.14). Note the available values that are constants.

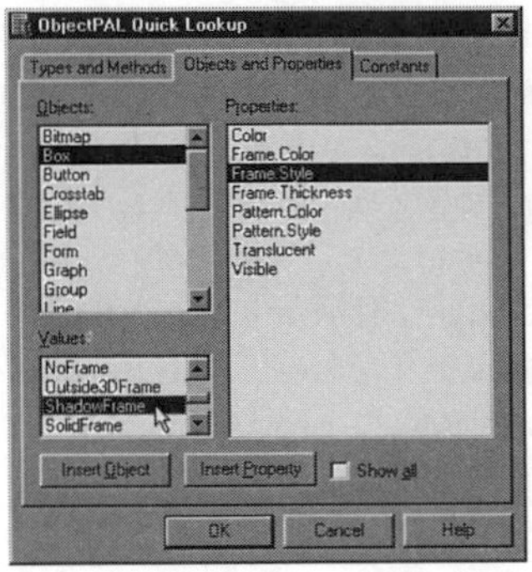

FIGURE 5.14.

The Objects and Properties tab of the ObjectPAL Quick Lookup dialog box.

Part 3: The Constants Tab

Next, you are going to explore the Constants tab.

1. In the ObjectPAL Quick Lookup dialog box, select the Constants tab.
2. Select `ActionDataCommands`. These 14 constants are the beginning-level action constants. You can use these constants with the `action` method. You will learn more about `action()` later in Chapter 24. For now, here are a few examples:

```
1:   Last_Name.action(DataLockRecord)    ;Lock a record.
2:   Last_Name.action(DataEnd)           ;Move to last record.
3:   Last_Name.action(DataBeginEdit)     ;Start edit mode.
4:   Last_Name.action(DataUnlockRecord)  ;Unlock a record.
```

3. Select `PatternStyles`. These 24 constants are the pattern styles that are available in Paradox. You can use them in ObjectPAL with dot notation to change patterns on-the-fly, as in the following example:

```
1:   theBox.Pattern.color = Yellow
2:   theBox.Pattern.Style = FuzzyStripesDownPattern
```

There are thousands of combinations of types of objects and their methods, procedures, properties, and constants. Many of them are related, however, and you can categorize them and cross-reference them mentally.

Advanced-Level ObjectPAL

Now, kick the ObjectPAL Quick Lookup into high gear and browse the rest of ObjectPAL. Select Edit | Developer Preferences and click the General tab, and toggle the ObjectPAL Level from Beginner to Advanced.

The Runtime Library in Advanced Mode

Your goal in this section is to become familiar with the advanced-level types of objects and their methods, procedures, properties, and constants.

Types of Objects

1. Display the ObjectPAL Editor from any object and select View | ObjectPAL Quick Lookup. Select Show All to list all commands. In Advanced mode, the Types section of the Types and Methods tab lists the 50-plus types of methods and procedures (see Figure 5.15).

FIGURE 5.15.

The Types and Methods tab from the ObjectPAL Quick Lookup dialog box.

2. Select the System type. The number of methods and procedures has grown from 14 in Beginner mode to more than 100 in Advanced mode. The ObjectPAL language is very robust.

3. Look at Database, FileSystem, and Session. See how they belong in a pseudo-category with System.

4. Browse through the design objects: Application, Form, Library, Query, Report, UIObject, and Script. Note the methods and procedures available to these object types.

5. Browse through the Table, TableView, TCursor, and UIObject object types. These object types are one of the reasons you bought Paradox. They are the centerpiece objects with the majority of database power. Note which object types have an `attach` method, and note their syntax. For example, UIObject has six `attach` methods, whereas TableView has none.

Summary

In this chapter, you learned about the intricacies of the ObjectPAL Editor and how it will help you develop code faster. Most of us do not want to spend hours studying the features of the Editor. Do yourself a favor and any time you have a question about a feature in the Editor, look it up in the online help. The Tools menu is of particular interest. Return to the Tools menu as often as you can while you learn ObjectPAL. After you learn the basic concepts of ObjectPAL, the Tools menu is an indispensable reference tool.

ObjectPAL Concepts

6

ObjectPAL isn't a true object-oriented programming language. It is, however, object-based programming (OBP). Take a look at objects, the three elements of Object-Oriented Programming (OOP), and see how both relate to ObjectPAL. First up is a discussion of objects.

What Are Objects?

NEW Term

Many people have trouble understanding how objects relate to programming. In normal daily existence, an object is something perceived by the senses—something material. An *object* also can be something perceived by the mind. From buttons you can place on a form to TCursors you use to get data, everything in Paradox is an object. All the elements of an ObjectPAL application are objects. Some are obvious objects, such as fields, buttons, boxes, and pages. Others are less obvious objects, such as TCursors, tables, and strings.

The biggest advantage of using object-based programming rather than procedural programming is that you can cut these independent objects from one place or container and paste them to another place or container without affecting any other objects (at least in most cases). This makes your code highly portable. For example, if you create a button that launches the Windows Calculator, you can copy it from one form to another form without affecting other objects or code. With ObjectPAL, you can reuse code more easily than you can with a procedural language such as PAL, Basic, C, or Pascal. With ObjectPAL, you can develop many self-contained routines only once.

Another advantage of object-based programming is that it is easier to maintain than a procedural programming language. Your code is contained in objects. Therefore, if something goes wrong, it generally affects only one module or part of your application. If you develop with a group of programmers, you will appreciate that each programmer's code is protected from the others' code. For example, code in one form generally will not affect code in another form.

Survey of the Six Categories of Methods and Procedures

When you study a subject as broad as the more than 1,700 ObjectPAL methods and procedures and their variations, it helps to break them into categories. The ObjectPAL methods and procedures act on objects. The objects on which the methods and procedures act fall into six categories:

- Data types
- Display managers
- Data model objects

- Design objects
- System data objects
- Event objects

Following is an overview of each of the object categories. They are discussed in detail throughout this book.

Data Types and ObjectPAL

You use data types to store data (see Table 6.1). After you store data in a particular type of variable, you can manipulate the data by using the methods associated with that type of variable. Chapter 11 discusses the data type methods and procedures in detail.

Table 6.1. Types of data.

AnyType	DynArray	OLE
Array	Graphic	Point
Binary	Logical	Record
Currency	LongInt	SmallInt
Date	Memo	String
DateTime	Number	Time

Display Managers

Display managers manage how objects are displayed. ObjectPAL has the following five display managers:

- Application
- Form
- TableView
- Report
- Script

The Application display manager is the Paradox desktop. It manages the display of the other display managers: Form, TableView, Report, and Script. A Form display manager manages all the objects that you put on it. The form is the center of every ObjectPAL application. A TableView display manager manages and displays tables. A Report display manager manages the formatted display and how table information is printed. A Script is a special display manager that has no UIObjects on it but can display information on the status bar and in message boxes. In general, you deal with display managers in ObjectPAL as a complete unit.

For example, you might maximize, minimize, or hide any of the display managers except for a Script.

Data Model Objects

You use data model objects to manipulate data in tables and databases. ObjectPAL has five types of data model objects:

- Database
- Query
- SQL
- Table
- TCursor

You use the Database methods and procedures on a database—a set of tables in a directory. For example, with Database methods and procedures, you can open a database or delete a table. You use the Query methods and procedures to execute and manipulate queries. The Table methods and procedures represent the table itself.

The Table object is distinct from a TCursor, which is a pointer to the data. It also is distinct from a table frame and a TableView, which are objects that display the data. Use the Table methods and procedures to add, copy, create, and index tables, to do column calculations, and to get information about a table's structure. Don't use Table methods to edit records, however. Use a TCursor or a table frame—a UIObject—instead.

Design Objects

Design object methods and procedures are commands used to manipulate menus, pop-up menus, and UIObjects. The three types of design objects are as follows:

- Menu
- PopUpMenu
- UIObject

You use Menu and PopUpMenu methods and procedures to build and manipulate menus. Similarly, you use UIObject—short for user interface object—methods and procedures to manipulate UIObjects. For example, when you change the color of a box to red or when you set the value of a field, you manipulate UIObject properties. UIObject methods and procedures add to this functionality. For example, they enable you to set the position of an object.

Scripts, libraries, forms, and UIObjects are the only objects that have events. The form, for example, is a display manager that behaves like a UIObject. A form has events to which you can attach code, and it responds to events. There also are methods and procedures that you can use to manipulate a form.

Many of the UIObject methods are duplicated among the TCursor methods. For example, `insertRecord()` works on both a UIObject and a TCursor. The UIObject methods that work with tables work on the underlying table by means of a visible object. Actions directed to the UIObject that affect a table are immediately visible in the object to which the table is bound.

On the other hand, TCursor methods work with a table behind the scenes as if another user were making the changes. When you work with a TCursor that affects a table to which a UIObject is bound, the result isn't visible in any UIObject until you use the `resync()` method.

System Data Objects

The types of system data objects are as follows:

- DDE
- Library
- FileSystem
- Script
- Session
- System
- TextStream

You use the DDE (dynamic data exchange) types of methods and procedures with DDE. DDE enables you to send and receive data between Windows applications (see Chapter 29 for more information on DDE). The Library methods and procedures work with libraries. A library is a place to store code (see Chapter 23 for more information on libraries). TextStream methods and procedures manipulate streams of text.

The other three categories—FileSystem, Session, and System—are used for objects outside Paradox, such as DOS-level or Windows-level procedures. FileSystem methods and procedures enable you to manipulate a FileSystem variable to provide access to and information about disk files, drives, and directories. A FileSystem variable provides a handle; that is, a variable you use in an ObjectPAL statement in order to work with a directory or a file. Session methods and procedures give you a channel to the database engine. For example, you can add and delete aliases by using Session methods. You use System procedures to display messages, find out about the user's system, get a filename with the file browser, and work with the help system.

Event Objects

Events are packets of information sent from one object to another. Events are the events in action. You use the Event methods and procedures to manipulate that packet. The following ten types of methods and procedures manipulate the various eventInfo variables:

```
Event            MouseEvent
ActionEvent      MoveEvent
```

```
ErrorEvent          StatusEvent
KeyEvent            TimerEvent
MenuEvent           ValueEvent
```

As an example, the following paragraphs discuss the `Event`, `ActionEvent`, `ErrorEvent`, and `KeyEvent` categories. The `Event` category is the base type from which the other event types are derived. Many of the methods listed in this section are used by the other event types.

You generate an `ActionEvent` primarily by editing and navigating in a table. `ActionEvent` methods and procedures enable you to get and set information in the `action` method.

An `ErrorEvent` is sent to the built-in `error` method. Use `error` to add to the built-in error behavior.

You use `KeyEvent` methods and procedures to manipulate and retrieve information about keystroke events in `keyPhysical` and `keyChar`.

`MenuEvent` methods and procedures enable you to retrieve and to set data in the `MenuEvent` event packet that is related to menu selections in the application menu bar—in other words, menu constants. For example, when the user chooses an item from the Toolbar, it triggers the `menuAction` method by sending it the appropriate menu constant. You use the methods in the `MenuEvent` class to manipulate the `MenuEvent` `eventInfo` packet.

> **NOTE**
>
> To print your own reference sheet, create and run the following one-line script:
>
> ```
> enum RTLMethods("RTL.DB")
> ```
>
> This script creates a table that lists all the runtime library methods and procedures and their variations. That's more than 1,700 commands. By using the RTL.DB, you can create and print elaborate reports and use them as reference sheets. You also can query the table to view the methods in various ways.

Is ObjectPAL OOP?

Now that you have a firm grasp of the various objects used in ObjectPAL, look at the three elements of Object Oriented Programming (OOP) and see how they relate to ObjectPAL. The three elements are encapsulation, polymorphism, and inheritance.

Encapsulation and ObjectPAL

New Term

In OOP, *encapsulation* is the bundling of methods and variables within an object so that access to the variables is permitted only through the object's own methods. ObjectPAL supports encapsulation. The code you write is stored with the object that triggers it. The code is completely independent of other objects and other code. In other words, if the object is moved inside another object or to another form, the code goes with it. This is encapsulation.

The key benefit of encapsulation is that your code is self-contained and protected from other objects. If another object needs to access variables inside your object, you can grant access through a custom method. If a group of people develop an ObjectPAL application, each programmer needs to be concerned only with his or her particular section. A section in ObjectPAL means a group of objects. If an external object needs access to something in the current object, the current object must have a method to allow it to be accessed.

For example, a team of programmers could designate one programmer to be in charge of the library for an application. (The library is where generic code is put.) When another programmer wants a routine to be included in the library, that person gives the programmer in charge of the library the specifications for the custom method; that is, what the custom method should be passed and what it should do and return. When another programmer wants to add to or alter that custom method, the programmer in charge of the library decides whether the modification is possible, given what the method already does.

Encapsulation makes it possible to bring foreign code together. With a traditional procedural language, a team of programmers must be sure not to use the same function and variable names. Because ObjectPAL supports encapsulation, you don't have to worry about the names of methods, procedures, objects, or variables. Each programmer can use his or her own variable-naming convention and not worry about the other programmers. When it comes time to bring all the sections of an application together, you simply have to worry about how the objects communicate. If you are an individual programmer, this means that you can reuse more of your code.

The capability to have duplicate names for variables and custom methods is a great relief to a programmer. For example, you can have a variable called Counter in two different places or two custom methods called cmRoutine().

Dot Notation and Encapsulation

The dot notation syntax of ObjectPAL supports encapsulation and enables you to grab values from other objects. For example, from field1 of form1, you can open form2 and grab the value in its field1 with the following code:

```
1:    var
2:       f2 Form
3:    endVar
4:
5:    f2.open("form2")
6:    field1.value = f2.field1.value
```

The rules for when you can use duplicate names and about which code can see other code refer to *scope*. (Scope is discussed in more detail later in this chapter.)

Learning Encapsulation

The goal of this tutorial is to demonstrate one element of encapsulation in ObjectPAL. Encapsulation enables you to use the same variable name in two different containers. Encapsulation is closely related to scope. In this tutorial, you refer to two variables that have the same name but are in separate containers above a button. The name of both variables is s. It is encapsulation that enables you to use duplicate named variables. This tutorial also introduces you to assigning a value to a variable and using the msgInfo() procedure.

 You can find the ENCAP.FSL form on the disc in the \ANSWERS directory.

Step By Step

1. Change your working directory to the TUTORIAL directory and create a new form with a box and a button on it.

2. Declare s as a string in the form's Var window. Do this by adding line 3 to the form's Var window.

```
1:      ;ENCAP :: Form :: Var
2:      Var
3:          s    String
4:      endVar
```

3. When the init method of the form is called, set the value of the form's version of the s variable. Do this by adding line 3 to the form's init method.

```
1:      ;ENCAP :: Form :: init
2:      method init(var eventInfo Event)
3:          s = "Text from form init"
4:      endmethod
```

4. Declare the box's version of s in the box's Var window. Do this by adding line 3 to the box's Var window.

```
1:      ;ENCAP :: Page.Box :: Var
2:      Var
3:          s    String
4:      endVar
```

5. When the open method of the box is used, set the value of the box's version of s. Do this by adding line 3 to the open method of the box.

```
1:      ;ENCAP :: Page.Box :: open
2:      method open(var eventInfo Event)
3:          s = "Text from box open event"
4:      endmethod
```

6. When the button is clicked, use the variable. Do this by adding line 3 to the pushButton method of the button.

```
1:      ;ENCAP :: Page.#Button4 :: pushButton
2:      method pushButton(var eventInfo Event)
3:          msgInfo("Value of s from button", s)
4:      endmethod
```

7. Check the syntax and save the form as ENCAP.FSL. See the "Analysis" section that follows for more instructions.

Analysis

With the button outside the box, run the form and click the button. Note that the button searches for a variable named s. The pushButton method searches for a Var block within the method block, then above the method block, then in the button's Var window, and then it searches the container's Var window, and so on. The button finally finds the variable s declared at the form level. The string variable that is declared in step 2, line 3 and set in step 3, line 3 is used by the button in step 6, line 3.

Go into Design mode, move the button inside the box, and run the form again. This time, the button uses the variable declared in the box's Var window (step 4, line 3) and set in step 5, line 3. The button now has context. The s variable's value depends on the container in which the button is contained. Containership, hierarchy, encapsulation, and scope are tightly intertwined. (Containers are discussed in more detail later in this chapter.)

Polymorphism and ObjectPAL

In OOP, the capability of the same command to be interpreted differently when used with or received by different objects is called *polymorphism*. In ObjectPAL, polymorphism is the capability of an object to act differently depending on the context in which it is being used. For example, methods require an object with which to work. Depending on the object's type, the method does different things. The following expression opens the object named Orders, depending on how varName is defined:

New Term

```
1:          varName.open("Orders")        ;varName is an object.
```

Orders can be a table, a form, a script, or many other objects. What ObjectPAL tries to open depends on what variable type you declare varName as. You can define varName to be a database, a DDE link, a form, a library, a report, a session, a TableView, a TCursor, a TextStream, or something else. As the programmer using this object-based language, you don't need to concern yourself with the details of opening these various objects. You write code that is based on this simple formula:

```
var*
    object     ObjectType         ;First declare a variable.
endVar
object.open( parameterList )   ;Then use the variable.
```

ObjectPAL takes over and handles the details. For example, to open another form, you could use the following:

```
1:    var
2:        tempVar    Form         ;tempVar is a form variable.
3:    endVar
4:
5:    tempVar.open("Orders")  ;Open form.
```

TCursors and Polymorphism

NEW
Term

A *TCursor* is a tool used to manipulate a table behind the scenes. A TCursor (table cursor) is a pointer to a record in a table. You will get a closer look at TCursors later, in Chapter 16, so this will be a brief introduction here.

If you change the variable type of `tempVar`, the same `open()` method can open something else, such as a TCursor:

```
1:   var
2:       tempVar    TCursor            ;tempVar is a TCursor.
3:   endVar
4:
5:   tempVar.open("ORDERS.DB")     ;Open a TCursor to Orders.db.
```

In the future, when Borland adds another type of object that can be opened, you won't need to learn the new syntax; you'll need to learn only the new characteristics of the object. This certainly beats learning syntax for 10 to 15 different open routines. In fact, polymorphism goes deeper than this. Throughout ObjectPAL, methods use the following syntax model:

```
object.doIt()
```

where `object` is the name of the variable or the name given to the object, and `doIt()` is what you want done. This syntax model is called *dot notation* and is highly flexible. It enables you to manipulate objects in other objects. Following are some examples of syntax that supports polymorphism:

```
1:   Container.xyz.value = 27         ;xyz can be any field.
2:   container.container.xyz.doIt()   ;doIt is a custom method.
3:   Form2Var.PageName.xyz.color = red   ;xyz can be a line or box.
```

Learning About Polymorphism

This tutorial demonstrates the existence of polymorphism in ObjectPAL. The same method, `setPosition()`, is used on the application, the page, and two UIObjects. This tutorial also introduces you to the `maximize()` method.

You can find the POLY.FSL form on the disc in the \ANSWERS directory.

Step By Step

1. Change your working directory to the TUTORIAL directory and create a new form with a box and a button on it.

2. Declare app as an application variable by adding line 3 to the form's Var window.

```
1:   ;POLY :: Form :: Var
2:   Var
3:       app    Application
4:   endVar
```

3. When the `init` event of the form is triggered, maximize and set the position of Paradox. Do this by adding lines 3 and 4 to the form's `init` event.

```
1:    ;POLY :: Form :: init
2:    method init(var eventInfo Event)
3:        app.maximize()
4:        app.setPosition(100, 100, 9000, 6000)
5:    endMethod
```

4. When the open method of the page occurs, set the page's color and position it. Do this by adding lines 3 and 4 to the open method of the page.

```
1:    ;POLY :: Page :: open
2:    method open(var eventInfo Event)
3:        self.color = Gray
4:        self.setPosition(0, 0, 7000, 3000)
5:    endmethod
```

5. When the open method of the button occurs, set its position. Do this by adding line 3 to the open method of the button.

```
1:    ;POLY :: Page.#Button4 :: open
2:    method open(var eventInfo Event)
3:        self.setPosition(2000, 1000, 2000, 1000)
4:    endmethod
```

6. When the open method of the box occurs, set its position. Do this by adding line 3 to the open method of the box.

```
1:    ;POLY :: Page.#Box3 :: open
2:    method open(var eventInfo Event)
3:        self.setPosition(100, 100, 1000, 1000)
4:    endmethod
```

7. Check the syntax, save the form as POLY.FSL, and run it. When you run this form, note the size and position of the application, the form, the page, the box, and the button change.

Analysis

In steps 3, 4, 5, and 6 the same `setPosition()` method is used. In fact, in steps 4, 5, and 6, the command is almost identical. `setPosition()` works on three different types of objects with the same command. `setPosition()`, in this sense, has context; that is, it behaves differently depending on where the code is attached.

In step 3, line 3 maximizes the application and line 4 sets its position and size. This was done to show that a maximized Paradox application doesn't have to be full screen, which is useful when you're developing for several screen resolutions. You could develop for VGA and set the position and size depending on the screen resolution.

In step 4, line 3 sets the color of the page to gray. This illustrates the difference between the page and the form. There is white space around the page. This white space is the form; the only object you can put directly on the form is a page. Every form must have at least one page, and all the objects are contained within the page.

To learn more about the commands in ObjectPAL that have polymorphism, consult the Quick Reference book. It shows clearly which commands work on more than one type of object.

Inheritance; Well, Actually, Delegation

NEW
Term

In OOP, a mechanism for automatically sharing methods and data types among objects is called *inheritance*. In ObjectPAL, an object inherits all the variables, types, and custom procedures of the objects by which it is contained.

Also, the fact that methods and procedures from one object type are derived—inherited—from other types shows the existence of inheritance in ObjectPAL. Table 6.3 depicts the online help showing the methods and procedures for the report type that are derived from the form type. The benefit of derived methods is that after you learn how to use a particular method for one type, you know how to use it on all the other objects that have inherited it.

Paradox UIObjects—objects you place on a form—don't have true inheritance. UIObjects, however, do have a form of inheritance that Borland calls delegation. You also can refer to it as *cloning*. How would UIObjects behave if they had true inheritance? Suppose that you place a button on a form, change its label, attach a method to it, and copy it. If you change the original—that is, the parent—the child also changes. This doesn't happen in Paradox. Instead, Paradox clones the original. If you change the original, nothing happens to the copy. In Paradox, the link between the parent and the child is broken after the copy is made.

Every object in Paradox supports delegation. When you copy an object, the copy is delegated the properties and methods of the parent. Be careful when you use Design | Copy To Toolbar. If the object that you copy to the Toolbar has ObjectPAL code on it, the code is copied, too.

Containers

Earlier in this chapter, a variable called container was used in a few examples. In ObjectPAL, this built-in container variable refers to the object that contains the current object. A container object completely surrounds and controls the behavior of all the objects within it. The rules of a container dictate that when you move a container, its contained objects also move. Likewise, when you delete a container, its contained objects are also deleted.

When you have objects that can contain other objects, the containership, or path, has to stop somewhere. In ObjectPAL, the form is the highest level of container. A form contains at least one page, and the page contains design objects such as fields, buttons, table frames, and bitmaps (see Figure 6.1). Note that the page contains the larger box, and that the larger box contains the circle, the smaller box, and the button. The field is contained by the small box. Remember that the form contains all these objects and that it is the highest level of container in Paradox.

FIGURE 6.1.
Containership.

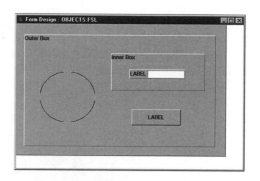

The keywords and object variables that you use with containers are as follows:

disableDefault	Stops the built-in behavior.
doDefault	Executes the built-in behavior now.
enableDefault	Allows the built-in behavior.
passEvent	Passes event up to container.
self	Refers to the object the code is on.
active	Refers to the object with focus.
container	Refers to the container.
lastMouseClicked	Last object to receive a left-mouse click.
lastMouseRightClicked	Last object to receive a right-mouse click.
subject	Refers to another object.

You can refer to a container with the container variable. For example, `message(self.container.name)` displays the name of the object that contains `self`. You can read more about the built-in object variables in Chapter 9.

Containership Hierarchy: What Contains What

Paradox employs what is called *containership*, which enables you to put a smaller object inside a larger object. You could say that the smaller object is contained by the larger object. The Object Tree visually shows you the containership hierarchy of a form. It is one of the most important tools for developing forms and writing ObjectPAL code (see Figure 6.2). The Object Tree shows you what objects contain what other objects.

NEW
Term

Use the Object Tree to rename objects quickly. Also use it to see what contains what and to see which objects have code on them. Objects that have code are underlined.

You can attach code to the objects that show up in the Object Tree. You can attach code to as many objects as you want, in any order that you want. Attaching code directly to the object with which you want to work makes ObjectPAL a great programming language to learn first.

For example, you can place a box and a circle on a form and place code in the mouseClick methods of both objects. Because the form is an event handler that follows an event model, when you run the form, Paradox takes care of trapping a mouse click when the user clicks on either the box or the circle.

FIGURE 6.2.

The Object Browser with only the Object Tree showing.

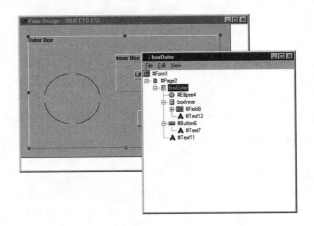

Containership Rules

The following are several rules dealing with containership:

- Deleting a container deletes all embedded objects.
- Containership determines dot notation.
- Containership enables you to have duplicate named objects in the same form.
- Noise names are not part of the containership path. A noise name is the default name Paradox gives new objects. Noise names always start with #.
- An object is embedded only if it is completely within the boundaries of the container.
- Objects inside a container can see the variables, custom methods, and custom procedures of its container.
- A container cannot see the variables, custom methods, and custom procedures of its embedded objects.

Sometimes you may want to have one object visually inside another object, but not have that object within the containership of it. Every object has a Contain Objects property which, by default, is checked. When checked, all objects within the visual boundary of the object are within the containership of the object.

Scope: What Can See What

The *scope* of an object is the range of objects that have access to it. For example, if you declare a variable in the form's Var window, that variable may be used by any object in the form, but not by objects outside the form. Scope has a definite path determined by the containership hierarchy. An object can see all the variables or constants above it and within it, but not below it. In other words, an object can't see the variables, constants, and procedures of the objects it contains. Also, an object can't see variables, constants, or procedures that are on another branch of the Object Tree. Objects that are contained can see their containers' variables, constants, and procedures. That is, they "inherit" them (and can overwrite them with their own, an OOP feature).

For example, in Figure 6.3, a box labeled Inner Box is contained by a box labeled Outer Box. Inner Box can see all its own variables and all the variables of Outer Box. Outer Box, on the other hand, can see only its own variables. It can't see the variables of Inner Box.

FIGURE 6.3.

Scope is determined by containership hierarchy.

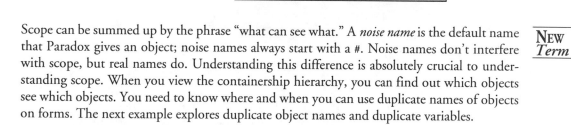

Scope can be summed up by the phrase "what can see what." A *noise name* is the default name that Paradox gives an object; noise names always start with a #. Noise names don't interfere with scope, but real names do. Understanding this difference is absolutely crucial to understanding scope. When you view the containership hierarchy, you can find out which objects see which objects. You need to know where and when you can use duplicate names of objects on forms. The next example explores duplicate object names and duplicate variables.

New
Term

Learning About Scope

The goal of this example is to demonstrate the difference between scope and containership. To do this, you will try to rename two fields the same name. You will fail at first because the scope of the objects interferes. After this fails, you will rename one of the field's containers and try again.

Step By Step

1. Change your working directory to the TUTORIAL directory and create a new form. Put two boxes on a form, then put a field in each box (see Figure 6.4).
2. Name one of the fields Field1.

FIGURE 6.4.

Set up form for tutorial.

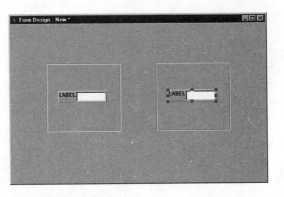

3. Try to give the other field the same name, Field1.

   You can't. Why? Aren't they in different containers? Yes and no. The two fields are in different containers, but they still can see each other because there is nothing between them except noise names. This is the difference between scope and containership. Browse the Object Tree for a visual representation of this. In Figure 6.5, note that all the names start with a pound symbol (except for the one that was renamed). This signifies that the object name is a noise name.

4. Rename either box (#Box4 in Figure 6.5) to Box2.

FIGURE 6.5.

The Object Tree inspector shows scope.

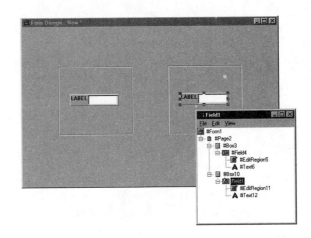

5. Rename the field inside Box2 to Field1. Now you can use a duplicate name, as Figure 6.6 shows.

FIGURE 6.6.

Now a duplicate name can be used.

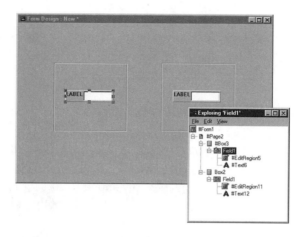

ObjectPAL Is Event Driven

How does Paradox execute all these independent routines? ObjectPAL is an event-driven language, much like ObjectVision, Visual Basic, Hypercard, and Toolbook. You paint objects onscreen and attach code directly to them. The event handler monitors what events or triggers occur, and automatically executes your code when it should, based on its event model. This mechanism of triggering events is known as an *event handler*. The plan or guideline that the event handler uses to trigger events is known as the event model.

NEW Term

To understand ObjectPAL, you first must understand the event model. Nothing else will make sense until you understand it. (Chapter 7 explores the event model in detail.) For now, keep the following points in mind:

- Every event has a target. When you click a field, it becomes the target of the event.

- Every event goes to the form first. With the form prefilter, you can intercept an event before the target gets it. If you don't place code in the form's prefilter, the event is not affected by the prefilter.

- The form sends the event to the target. The form serves as a kind of dispatcher. An event goes to the form, and then the form sends the event packet to the target object.

- Internal events stop after the target. Internal events such as open, close, and arrive go to the form and then to the target, and then they terminate.

- External events bubble. If an external event such as mouseDown, keyPhysical, and error are not trapped for at the form level or the target level—in other words, no built-in code responds to the event—the object passes the event to its container. If the container has no built-in code that traps for that external event, it is passed to its container and so on, until it reaches the form for the second time, where it stops.

■ The form can see external events twice. If an external event has no built-in code that traps for it, the form sees it twice. The prefilter equals `False` when the form is the target of the event. The prefilter also equals `False` when another object is the target of the event and the form is seeing it for the second time.

Bubbling: The Path of Events

An event has one of two definite paths: either form and then target, or form, target, and bubble back up to the form. *Bubbling* is when an event moves back up the containership path to the form. An external event such as `mouseDown` goes to the form, then to the target, and then it bubbles up the containership hierarchy until it reaches the form a second time, where it stops. The event might go through the entire path. If any of the objects in the path have built-in code that uses the event, the event might get cut short. (Your code does not stop bubbling; only built-in code does.) For example, `mouseDown` normally bubbles up to the form. If you left-click a field, however, the field knows what to do with `mouseDown` and the `mouseDown` event is not bubbled.

Most of the time, your code executes on the target. The target object executes an event such as `mouseDown`. The event goes first to the form. If the form doesn't have the appropriate code on the correct method, the event is returned to the target for execution. If the target doesn't have the appropriate code, the code is bubbled up through the containership path to the form, where it stops. The form sees the code twice—at the start and at the end—unless another object, such as the target's container, intercepts the event with built-in code, such as the preceding field example.

Now, follow what happens to a button's `pushButton` method when a user clicks it. The target object (the button) sends the `pushButton` method to the form. Because the form doesn't use a `pushButton` method, the event is returned to the target for execution. If the target (the button) doesn't have the appropriate built-in code, the event is bubbled up through the containership path to the form, where it stops. The form can see an event twice—at the start and at the end of its life cycle. You can place code anywhere on the containership path to trap for the event. In fact, you can place it several times on the path and all the code will execute.

Suppose that you want to trap for an event whenever the user arrives on a record. At the form's prefilter, you can trap for `DataArriveRecord`, as in the following:

```
 1:    method action(var eventInfo ActionEvent)
 2:       if eventInfo.isPreFilter()
 3:          then
 4:          ;This code executes for each object on the form
 5:          if eventInfo.id() = DataArriveRecord then
 6:              beep()   ;Do your stuff here
 7:          endIf
 8:       else
 9:          ;This code executes only for the form
10:       endif
11:    endmethod
```

If you are using a table frame, which has a record object, you can't move lines 5, 6, and 7 to the else part of the if structure because the record object of the table frame will use up the event and not allow it to bubble up to the else clause of the form. The action DataArriveRecord is never bubbled up to the form.

The event you're interested in applies to a table frame—one of the many other objects that are caught by the prefilter test. The comment after the then part of the if structure reads, This code executes for each object on the form. This refers to all the objects on the form except the form itself, which is tested in the else clause.

If you create a single record form—that is, a form with just fields on it—you can use the preceding else clause to trap for DataArriveRecord because it bubbles back up to the form.

Containership, Scope, and Bubbling Are Intertwined

The containership hierarchy is the branching tree represented in the Object Tree. The Object Tree enables you to see the containership hierarchy, or path, of objects. Containership hierarchy is closely related to bubbling and scope. Events go to the form and then to the target. Then, the event bubbles up the containership hierarchy. The event packet path is determined by the containership hierarchy. Scope is what can see what. Use the ObjectTree to determine the scope of objects. If an object on the containership path has been renamed, then it has defined part of the scope path. If the object has not been renamed, then it is not part of the scope path.

Summary

Whew! You have just survived, learned, and absorbed what most programmers consider the toughest aspect of ObjectPAL. This chapter covered many aspects of ObjectPAL, including objects, containers, containership hierarchy, and bubbling. The next chapter discusses the basics of the event model in detail. This chapter definitely is the toughest in this book—at least as far as concepts go. If you understood most of this chapter, great! The following are the important topics in this chapter: objects, encapsulation, polymorphism, inheritance, cloning objects, containers, containership hierarchy, and scope.

If you still don't understand a certain topic, read the section that discusses it again. Is it absolutely crucial that you understand these topics? Yes and no. Not understanding this chapter won't hold you back. However, the better you understand the concepts in this chapter, the better you will understand the big picture—and the better your applications can be.

Event Model Basics

7

IN THIS CHAPTER

Because the event model is such an important topic, it deserves two chapters. In your first look at the event model, you'll take a look at its basics. In Chapter 30, you will revisit the event model and take an in-depth view of it.

Why two chapters on the event model? Quite simply because it is the heart of Paradox. After you understand it, you will be able to program in ObjectPAL with ease.

The Event Model Makes Sense

NEW
Term

The *event model* is an important aspect of ObjectPAL. The event model is the map of when the events trigger during run mode. This section explores a simplified view of a form and the open event method. The event model is not linear, but can be used in a linear fashion. Much like a procedural language, you can attach code to the open method of the form, page, box, field, and button. The code executes in order. First the code on the form executes, then the code on the page, box, and field executes. Finally, the code on the button executes.

The goal of this next section is to show you that any single event can be linear. Specifically, it demonstrates that open occurs from the outer form object inward, object after object, in a linear fashion.

The Event Model Can Be Linear

The following section demonstrates that a single event can trigger in a linear fashion. In this tutorial, you will add a message dialog box to the open method of the form, a page, and several objects on the page.

You can find the OPEN.FSL form on the disc in the \ANSWERS directory.

Step By Step

1. Change your working directory to the TUTORIAL directory and create a new form with a box, a button, and a field on it (see Figure 7.1).

2. To display a message when the form is opened, add line 8 to the form's open method.

```
1:    ;OPEN :: Form :: open
2:    method open(var eventInfo Event)
3:       if eventInfo.isPreFilter()
4:          then
5:          ;This code executes for each object on the form
6:       else
7:          ;This code executes only for the form
8:          msgInfo("Form :: Open", "Triggered by Form ::
             Open")
9:       endif
10:   endmethod
```

3. To display a message when the page is opened, add line 3 to the page's open method.

```
1:     ;OPEN :: Page :: open
2:     method open(var eventInfo Event)
3:         msgInfo("Page :: Open", "Triggered by Page :: Open")
4:     endmethod
```

4. To display a message when the box is opened, add line 3 to the box's open method.

```
1:     ;OPEN :: Page.Box :: open
2:     method open(var eventInfo Event)
3:         msgInfo("Box :: Open", "Triggered by Box :: Open")
4:     endmethod
```

5. To display a message when the field is opened, add line 3 to the field's open method.

```
1:     ;OPEN ::Page.Box.Field :: open
2:     method open(var eventInfo Event)
3:         msgInfo("Field :: Open", "Triggered by Field :: Open")
4:     endmethod
```

6. To display a message when the button is opened, add line 3 to the button's open method.

```
1:     ;OPEN :: Page.Box.Button :: open
2:     method open(var eventInfo Event)
3:         msgInfo("Button::Open", "Triggered by Button :: Open")
4:     endmethod
```

7. Check the syntax, save the form as OPEN.FSL, and run it. Note the order of the message information boxes. Your form should look similar to \ANSWERS\OPEN.FSL (see Figure 7.2).

FIGURE 7.1.

Set up form for tutorial.

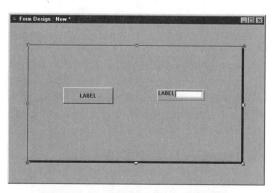

FIGURE 7.2.

\ANSWERS\OPEN.FSL shows that the event modal can be linear.

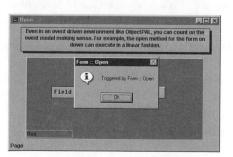

Analysis

The form is the highest container in ObjectPAL. It always contains at least one page. You place objects, such as fields, table frames, and buttons inside a page. All UIObjects, including both forms and pages, have an open event. Code in the open method is triggered whenever the object is opened. When you launch a form, first the form is opened, and then the page is opened. The code on the form's open event is triggered before the code on the page's open event. When you run this code, you'll see that msgInfo() is executed from the top container downward: the form, the page, and then UIObjects inside the page.

The five message information boxes you just saw are executed in a linear fashion. When the box and the button are on the same level, however, they both can't execute at the same time. What dictates the order of execution? The containership hierarchy determines which code is executed first. Generally, the order in which objects are placed on the page dictates which object is opened first. For an experiment, place a larger box around both of these objects and alternate moving them onto the page level. What do you expect to happen? Try it and find out.

> **NOTE**
>
> You can alter the path of objects by moving objects around in the containership hierarchy. Move objects on the same level by selecting Design | Bring to Front and Design | Send to Back.

Although ObjectPAL and Paradox can execute in a linear fashion—that is, one event executes after another—you don't program ObjectPAL in a linear fashion. When you program in Paradox, think, "What object do I want to alter?" For example, if you want to check a value in a field after the user enters it, go to that field and put code on the canDepart event method. You can use canDepart to check the field's contents before it permits the cursor to leave the field.

Default Behavior Occurs Last

The default behavior of the open event method is to open the objects within it. When exactly does an object open? All default behavior occurs just before endMethod.

Take a closer look at the events open and arrive and when the default behavior occurs. An object is always opened before it is arrived on. Therefore, code in the open method always executes before code in the arrive method. Any code that you want to execute as a form opens or before a form opens goes in the open method. Any code that you want to execute after a form opens goes in the arrive method. The arrive method is a good place for code that requires user interface objects, because UIObjects aren't opened until the end of the open method (just before endMethod).

The goal of this section is to demonstrate the differences among init, open, and arrive, and to demonstrate that the default behavior occurs just before the keyword endMethod.

You can find the LAST.FSL form on the disc in the \ANSWERS directory.

Step By Step

1. Change your working directory to the TUTORIAL directory and create a new form with a field on it. Name the field fldTest (see Figure 7.3).

2. To display a message and try to assign a value to the field fldTest when the form is opened, add lines 8 and 9 to the form's open method.

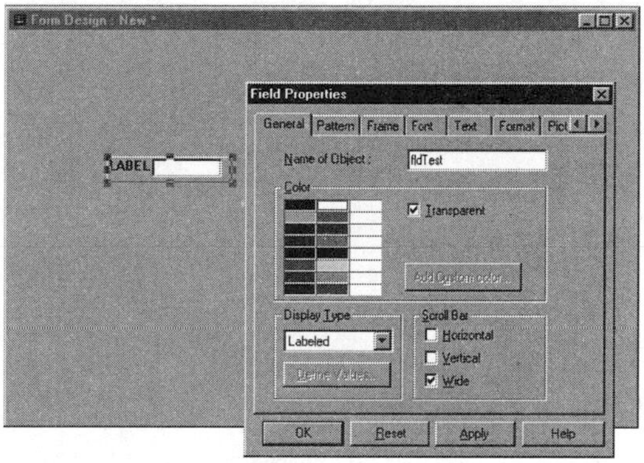

FIGURE 7.3.

Set up form for tutorial.

```
1:    ;LAST :: #Form1 :: open
2:    method init(var eventInfo Event)
3:        msgInfo("Form init method", "The form init method always occurs
➥first.")
4:    endMethod
```

3. To display a message and try to assign a value to the field fldTest when the form is opened, add lines 8 and 9 to the form's open method.

```
1:    ;LAST :: #Form1 :: open
2:    method open(var eventInfo Event)
3:        if eventInfo.isPreFilter()
4:            then
5:            ;This code executes for each object on the form
6:        else
7:            ;This code executes only for the form
8:            fldTest.value = "text from open method"
9:            msgInfo("Form", "open method")
10:       endif
11:   endmethod
```

4. To display a message when you `arrive` on the form, add line 8 to the form's `arrive` method.

```
 1:    ;LAST :: #Form1 :: arrive
 2:    method arrive(var eventInfo MoveEvent)
 3:       if eventInfo.isPreFilter()
 4:          then
 5:             ;This code executes for each object on the form
 6:          else
 7:             ;This code executes only for the form
 8:             msgInfo("Form", "arrive method")
 9:          endif
10:    endmethod
```

5. Check the syntax, save the form as LAST.FSL, and run it. Note that the message information box for the open method shows before the one for the `arrive` method. In addition, note that the value from step 2, line 8 never makes it to the field.

6. Add a `doDefault` just before the assignment in the open method (see line 8 that follows).

```
 1:    ;LAST :: #Form1 :: open
 2:    method open(var eventInfo Event)
 3:       if eventInfo.isPreFilter()
 4:          then
 5:             ;This code executes for each object on the form
 6:          else
 7:             ;This code executes only for the form
 8:             DoDefault
 9:             fldTest.value = "text from open method"
10:             msgInfo("Form", "open method")
11:          endif
12:    endmethod
```

7. Check the syntax, save the form, and run it. Note that with the `doDefault` the value does make it to the field fldTest. Your form should look similar to \ANSWERS\LAST.FSL (see Figure 7.4).

FIGURE 7.4.

\ANSWERS\LAST.FSL shows that default behavior occurs last.

Analysis

The default built-in behavior always occurs just before `endMethod`. Using keywords such as `doDefault` and `disableDefault`, you as the programmer have full control over if and when the default behavior occurs.

Event Methods Are the Event Model

Objects in ObjectPAL come with events, or triggers, for each event to which an object can respond. As stated before, the part of ObjectPAL that sets up triggers that are trapped for when the user interacts with the application is called an *event handler*.

Events specify an object's default behavior in response to a certain event. Sometimes an event is used by an object, and sometimes it's passed to another event. This using and passing of events is known as the *event model*, which is a map of the order in which events are triggered in an event handler. You cannot see this hidden code, but it is there and you can affect it, for example, with `doDefault`, `disableDefault`, and `enableDefault`.

Events can be generated by a user action, such as moving the mouse or pressing a key, or by ObjectPAL. An event generated by ObjectPAL usually is generated or called from a user's actions. So, in a sense, all events are started in one way or another by the user. Thinking of the event model in this simplified way is a good way to program. An `open` event occurs because the user chooses File | Open | Form. It's easier to think of a user opening a form, which causes the `open` method to trigger, than it is to think of the `open` event method as a method that receives an internal event generated by ObjectPAL.

Likewise, when a user clicks a button, the button's `pushButton` method is triggered, right? Wrong. `pushButton` is an internal method that is called by the external method `mouseUp` only when the cursor is inside the boundaries of the button. It's much easier, however, to think that when the user clicks a button, several events are triggered in order: `mouseDown`, `mouseUp`, `mouseClick`, and `pushButton`. There are times when it's important to understand that `mouseUp` calls `pushButton` only when the cursor is within the boundaries of the button. Even so, most of the time you can think in terms of simple user actions.

Understanding the event model is key to understanding ObjectPAL. The better you know when code executes, the better and cleaner your applications will be. Although you usually use `pushButton` when you program a button, occasionally you will want to use `mouseDown`, `mouseUp`, or `mouseClick`. Understanding what the differences are is important.

> The form \ANSWERS\BUTTON.FSL demonstrates the order of execution of a button's `mouseDown`, `mouseUp`, `mouseClick`, and `pushButton` methods. In addition, it demonstrates `mouseEnter` and `mouseExit`.

Some Event Model Rules

There are many rules that govern the event model. The following are some introductory rules to keep in mind:

- All events generate a packet of information. This event packet contains information on what generated the event, the target of the next event, and more.

Events are generated either by ObjectPAL or by a user interacting with a form. A few examples of methods for which ObjectPAL generates events are open, arrive, and depart. A few examples of methods for which a user generates events are mouseClick, keyChar, and menuAction.

■ All events go to the form first. If the target is an object other than the form, the event goes through the form's prefilter and the event is sent to the target. This is important because the prefilter of the form is a great location to code certain types of generic code.

■ Internal events are passed from the form's prefilter to the target object. Internal events, discussed in detail in the next section, are events triggered from within Paradox.

■ External events, like internal events, are passed from the form's prefilter to the target object. Unlike internal events, however, external events can bubble back up to the form.

Introducing the Form's *init* method

NEW
Feature

New to version 7 is the event method called init. The only object that supports this method is the form object itself; all other UIObjects within the form do not have this method. The chief benefit of this method, unlike all other form level methods, is that it does not have a prefilter clause. Now, you have control over what happens before the open method. In previous versions of ObjectPAL, the open method was called from a pre-wired C routine. When you access the method editor, you see the following:

```
method init (var eventInfo Event)



endMethod
```

How to use the *init* Method

The init method is called once whenever a form is opened. The default behavior of init is to call open. It is important to note that when you use disableDefault in init, the form and all the objects within the form are still opened. However, any code in the open methods of all objects does not execute. You have, in fact, disabled the code in the object's open methods. To stop a form from opening, set an error code as in the following:

```
method init(var eventInfo Event)
   if cmSomeCondition() = True then
      eventInfo.setErrorCode(CanNotArrive)    ;In place of CanNotArrive, you
                                              ;can use any non zero value.
   endIf
endMethod
```

The primary use for the init method is for initialization code. For example, if you want to set up some tables before the open method tries to open the tables, do it in init. If, after the tables are created, you want to use them in init, then call the open method with doDefault.

```
method init(var eventInfo Event)
   cmBuildTables()
   doDefault
   ;Use the tables here.
endMethod
```

Categorizing Event Methods: Internal, External, and Special

Events are triggered by internal, external, and special events. These three categories of events follow very specific rules. Table 7.1 lists the events.

Table 7.1. Event methods.

Internal	External	Special
init	mouseClick	pushButton
open	mouseDown	changeValue
close	mouseUp	newValue
canArrive	mouseDouble	
arrive	mouseRightDown	
setFocus	mouseRightUp	
canDepart	mouseRightDouble	
removeFocus	mouseMove	
depart	keyPhysical	
mouseEnter	keyChar	
mouseExit	error	
timer	status	
	action	
	menuAction	

Rules Guiding Internal Event Methods

Internal events are triggered by events generated by Paradox. A good case study example of an internal event is open. open occurs from outer container inward. The form is opened, then the page, then the objects in the page. canArrive, arrive, and setFocus also trigger from outer container in.

Their counterparts close, canDepart, and depart trigger from inner container out. To study this, suppose that you have a field inside a box on the first page of a form and you try to close the form. In what order do the various object's canDepart methods trigger? First, the canDepart for the field is triggered, or called. Then its container, the box's canDepart, is triggered, and then finally the box's container, the page canDepart, is triggered. close, canDepart, and depart are called (triggered) from inner container outward.

Like external events, internal events go first to the form and then to the target object. Unlike external and special events, internal events stop at the target. In other words, the complete path for an internal event is sent to the form and back to the object. Table 7.2 describes the internal events. The concept of bubbling back up to the form does not exist for internal events.

Table 7.2. Internal event methods.

Method	Short Description
init	Triggered once when the form is opened.
open	Triggered once for every object when the form is opened.
close	Triggered once for every object when the form is closed.
canArrive	Triggered before moving to an object.
canDepart	Triggered before moving off an object.
arrive	Triggered after moving to an object.
depart	Triggered after moving off an object.
setFocus	Occurs whenever an object gets the focus.
removeFocus	Occurs whenever an object loses the focus.
mouseEnter	Generated whenever the mouse pointer enters an object.
mouseExit	Generated whenever the mouse pointer exits an object.
timer	Triggered at a time interval specified by the programmer.

Default Behavior of Internal Events

Take a closer look at the default behavior of each internal event method. Internal event methods are always called either from other internal event methods or from an external event method. There is much built-in default behavior in Paradox. The following paragraphs describe the internal events and their default behavior.

Every object has to be opened. The open event is called only once for every object, starting with the form, then the page, then the objects contained by the page, and finally the objects contained within that container. After the first page is completely open, the process starts over with the next page in the form.

Remember that the prefilter of the form sees the open event before the target object sees it. The default code for open calls the open method for each of the objects it contains. Then, the open method for each one of those objects calls the open method for the objects it contains, and so on. The default behavior for the close method acts in the same way but in reverse. If a table is bound to the object, the object also opens the table. Any errors will abort the open process.

The OPEN2.FSL form in the \ANSWERS directory demonstrates the open method and the prefilter section of the form's open method.

The canArrive method is interesting. It occurs before movement to an object is permitted. Think of canArrive as asking permission to move to the object. Contrary to what is implied in the manuals, canArrive is not used just for restricting entrance to a field. You can use this method to execute almost any kind of code just before arriving on an object. The canArrive method blocks arrival for records beyond the end of a table—except, of course, when you are in Edit mode and the Auto-Append option is checked in the data model. Any object whose tab stop property is unchecked also is blocked.

The arrive method is executed after movement has arrived on an object. An arrive method can be called only after a canArrive method. Pages, table frames, and multirecord objects move to the first tab stop object they contain. When you arrive on a field or a record, the object is made current; if you're in Edit mode, an edit window is created for the edit region of a field. If the object is a drop-down edit list, the focus moves to the list. If the object is a radio button, the focus moves to the first button.

The setFocus method occurs every time an object gets the focus. If the object getting the focus is contained in another object, setFocus is called for each container—from the outer-most container inward. For example, if a page contains a box, which contains a field, setFocus is triggered first for the page, next for the box, and then for the field. In an edit field, the default code highlights the currently selected edit region and causes the insertion point to blink. The focus property is set to True, and the status message reports the number of the current record and the total number of records. For buttons, if the tab stop property is set, a dotted rectangle is displayed around the label.

The canDepart method is triggered before a move off an object. Field objects try to post their contents and trip changeValue. If the record is a changed record, the object tries to commit the current record. If the record is locked, the form tries to unlock it.

The removeFocus method occurs when an object loses the focus. On field objects, the flashing insertion point and highlight are removed. On a button, the dotted rectangle is removed. The object's focus property is set to False. This is called for the active object and its containers.

After canDepart and removeFocus have executed successfully, the depart method is called. Field objects close their edit windows, then repaint and clean up the screen.

The mouseEnter method is generated whenever the mouse pointer enters an object. Form, page, and button objects set the pointer to an arrow. Field objects set the pointer to an I-beam. If a button is still down, its value toggles between True and False.

The mouseExit method is generated whenever the mouse pointer exits an object. Field objects set the pointer back to the arrow.

Rules Guiding External Event Methods

External events are events generated by the user interacting with a form and by ObjectPAL. Both internal and external events go first to the form and then to the target object. External events, however, unlike internal events, bubble back up to the form. The default behavior for an external method is to pass the event to its container, which is how it bubbles up to the form. External events are generated when a user interacts with the user interface. Table 7.3 describes the external events.

Table 7.3. External event methods.

Method	Short Description
mouseMove	Occurs whenever the mouse moves.
mouseDown	Occurs when the left mouse button is pressed.
mouseUp	Occurs when the left mouse button is released.
mouseClick	Occurs when the pointer is inside an object and the left mouse button is pressed and released.
mouseDouble	Occurs when the left mouse button is double-clicked.
mouseRightDown	Occurs when the right mouse button is pressed.
mouseRightUp	Occurs when the right mouse button is released.
mouseRightDouble	Occurs when the right mouse button is double-clicked.
keyPhysical	Occurs whenever any key is pressed.
keyChar	Occurs whenever a character key is pressed.
action	Executes when a keystroke or menu option maps to an action.
menuAction	Occurs when a menu option or a toolbar icon is selected.
error	Occurs whenever an error is encountered.
status	Occurs whenever a message is displayed in the status bar.

Default Behavior of External Events

Now take a closer look at the default behavior of each external event. The following paragraphs explain the default behavior of the external events that do something in addition to bubbling their events.

The mouseDown method occurs when the left mouse button is pressed. The event packet for mouseDown contains the mouse coordinates in twips (1/1440 of an inch) relative to the last object that executed a mouseEnter method. If the object is a field that is active, the field is put into Field View. If the object is a button, its value is toggled between True and False.

The mouseRightDown method occurs when the right mouse button is pressed. It is the same as the mouseDown method, except that it uses the right mouse button instead. If the object is a formatted memo, a graphic, OLE, or an undefined field, a pop-up menu is displayed.

The mouseUp method occurs when the left mouse button is released. mouseUp is called for the last object that received a mouseDown method. Therefore, an object always sees the mouseDown and mouseUp methods in a pair. If you select text, mouseUp ends the selection. If the object is a button and the pointer is still inside the button, mouseUp calls the pushButton method. The mouseRightUp method is the same as the mouseUp method, except that it uses the right mouse button instead.

The mouseDouble method occurs when the left mouse button is double-clicked. A field object enters Field View. The mouseRightDouble method is the same as the mouseDouble method, except that it uses the right mouse button.

The movement of the mouse is tracked with the mouseMove method. Whenever the pointer is moved within an object, the mouseMove method is triggered.

The keyPhysical method occurs whenever any key is pressed and each time a key is autorepeated. keyPhysical includes all the physical keys on the keyboard, including the character keys, the function keys, and the Alt, Ctrl, and Esc keys. The keyChar method, on the other hand, triggers only when a character key is pressed. A keystroke goes first to Windows and then to Paradox, which gives it to the form's prefilter. The form sends it to the active object for processing. The object's keyPhysical determines whether the keystroke represents an action or a display character. Actions are passed to the action method, and display characters are passed to keyChar.

The keyChar method occurs whenever a character key is pressed. Actually, the keyPhysical method for the active object sends action events such as DataNextRecord to the action method, and it sends characters such as a to keyChar. If the active object is a field in Edit mode, a lock is put on the table before the first character is inserted. If the active object is a button and the character is a spacebar, the button's pushButton method is called. Remember a button can be active only if its Tab Stop option is set to True.

The `action` method is called frequently. It executes when it is sent an action keystroke from `keyPhysical`, when `menuAction` maps to a menu option, or when a method such as `DataPostRecord` calls for an action. The default behavior for `action` is extensive because all actions go through it. For example, Page Down moves to the next record, F9 toggles Edit mode, and Insert inserts a record only if the form is in Edit mode.

The `menuAction` method occurs when a menu option, a toolbar icon, or an option from the Control box is selected. The option is sent first to the form's `action` method for processing and then to the active object.

The `error` method occurs right after an error is encountered. You shouldn't test for errors with the `error` event method. Use `action` instead. An `error` is passed to its container until it gets to the form. The form might or might not display a message, depending on the severity of the error. You can trap for errors and alter the default behavior in the `action` method before the error gets to the `error` method. You can use the `error` event method to add to the built-in default error behavior.

The `status` method occurs whenever a message is displayed on the status bar. The default behavior of `status` is too extensive to be described here. In short, any time you see a message in one of the four status areas, an event has gone through the `status` event method.

The STATUS_F.FSL form in the \ANSWERS directory demonstrates filtering messages going to the status bar. It uses the `status` method to disable messages.

Introducing Special Event Methods

Special events are specific to a few objects, such as `newValue` of a field. Table 7.4 describes the special events.

Table 7.4. Special event methods.

Method	Description
`pushButton`	Occurs whenever you click a button.
`newValue`	Triggered whenever the value in a field changes.
`changeValue`	Triggered whenever the value in a table changes.

Default Behavior of the Special Event Methods

The following paragraphs explain the default behavior of the special events.

The only UIObjects that have a `pushButton` method are buttons and fields displayed as a list box. The form has a `pushButton` method because it dispatches it with its prefilter clause. `pushButton` occurs when the pointer is inside an object for both the `mouseDown` and `mouseUp` methods. In fact, `mouseUp` calls `pushButton`. Button objects visually depress and pop out. Check boxes check or uncheck. Radio buttons push in or pop out. If the `Tab Stop` property is set to `True`, the focus moves to it.

The `newValue` method is triggered after the value in a field changes. `newValue` is triggered even if the value is changed only onscreen.

The `changeValue` method on a defined field, on the other hand, is triggered by a change in a table. The `changeValue` method on an undefined field is triggered when the value in the field changes.

The `changeValue` method is triggered before a value in a table is changed. If you have code on both `changeValue` and `newValue`, the code on `changeValue` occurs first, that is, before the value changes. `newValue` is triggered after the value changes. Therefore, if you want to do validity checks on a field, `changeValue` is a good place to put them.

Learn the Event Model by Tracing It

Although the Debugger is not introduced until Chapter 29, the Tracer (one feature of the debugger) is introduced now to help demonstrate the event model.

Tracing the Event Model

In this section, you study the event action method. Your goal is to use the Tracer to demonstrate the event model and default behavior.

Step By Step

1. Create a new form by selecting File | New | Form.
2. Open the Editor window for the action method of the form.
3. Open the Tracer by selecting View | Tracer.
4. From the Tracer window, choose Properties | Built-In Events.
5. The Select Built-in Event Methods for Tracing dialog box lists all the event methods you can trace. In this dialog box, choose select All and click on OK (see Figure 7.5).
6. Make sure that Properties | Trace On is checked (see Figure 7.6).
7. Run the form (there is no need to save the form). Note how many events occur even on an empty form (see Figure 7.7).

FIGURE 7.5.

The Select Built-in Methods for Tracing dialog box.

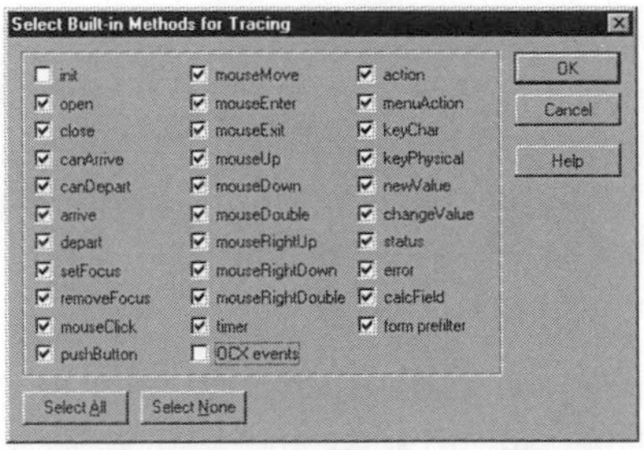

FIGURE 7.6.

The Tracer window.

FIGURE 7.7.

The Tracer tracing code.

Analysis

Tracing one or two events at a time is a great way to get acquainted with the event model. Take some time right now (about 30 minutes) to try tracing various combinations of events.

Tracing Your Own Code

This section demonstrates how to use the tracer to trace just your code. Suppose that while you are developing an application, an error occurs and you have no idea what code is causing the error.

Step By Step

1. Change your working directory to the TUTORIAL directory and open the OV-LIKE.FSL form that you created in Chapter 4. If you skipped that example (shame on you), change your working directory to the ANSWER directory and open up the OV-LIKE.FSL form (see Figure 7.8).

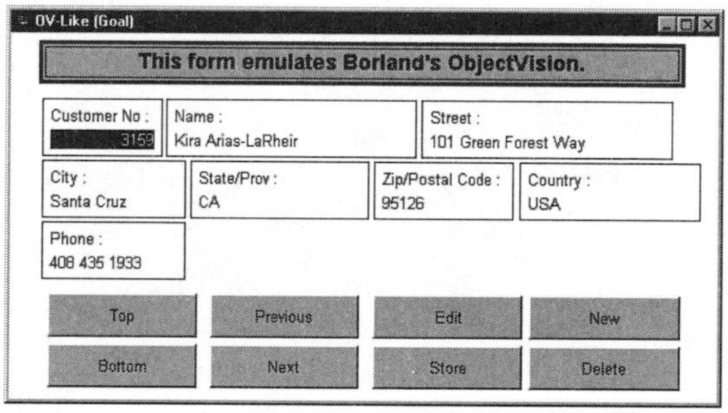

FIGURE 7.8.

Use \ANSWERS\ OV-LIKE.FSL to demonstrate tracing your code.

2. Open the Editor window for any event method.
3. Select View | Tracer to open the Tracer.
4. Select Properties | Built-In Events and make sure that no event methods are selected for tracing.
5. Make sure that Properties | Trace On and Properties | Show Code are checked.
6. Run the form, select the various buttons, and see what happens (see Figure 7.9).

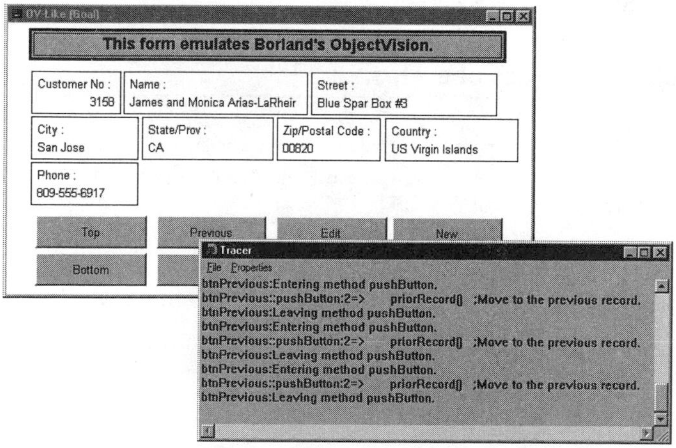

FIGURE 7.9.

Using the Tracer to trace your own code.

Analysis

You can use the Tracer for two purposes: to analyze the events and/or to analyze your code. When analyzing or debugging your code, the Tracer is great for finding the location of bugs.

Tracing execution on a large form is very time consuming. The tracer updates the screen every time it executes a line of code. As usual in a GUI, screen updates dramatically slow you down. Shrink the trace execution window as small as possible. When you want to see the trace execution, open the window. Following are the steps:

1. Run it.
2. Press Ctrl+Break.
3. Minimize it.

This solution works so well, you can now just leave the trace execution windows minimized on your screen.

Introducing the Event Packet

When you open a form interactively, many events are generated by ObjectPAL. The form opens and then the prefilter tells the page to open by sending an event to it. Understanding the sending and receiving of events is understanding the event model.

Whenever a method is called, an information packet is generated. This information packet often is passed from one method to the next. This information is called the event packet. You can read any value in the event packet with the `eventInfo` variable. Table 7.5 describes the different types of events.

Table 7.5. Types of events.

Type of event	Information about	Event methods
ActionEvent	Editing and navigating a table	action
ErrorEvent	Errors	error
Event	Base event type from which all others are derived—inherited	init,open,close, setFocus, removeFocus, newValue, and pushButton

Type of event	Information about	Event methods
KeyEvent	Keystroke events	keyChar and keyPhysical
MenuEvent	Menu selections	menuAction
MouseEvent	The mouse and pointer	mouseClick, mouseDown, mouseUp, mouseDouble, mouseRightUp, mouseRightDown, mouseRightDouble, mouseMove, mouseEnter, and mouseExit
MoveEvent	Navigating from field to field	arrive, canArrive, canDepart, and depart
StatusEvent	Messages in the status line	status
TimerEvent	Events at specified intervals	timer
ValueEvent	Changes to a field's value	changeValue

The type of eventInfo a method generates is declared in its prototype syntax. Every time you open the ObjectPAL Editor for an event, Paradox automatically prototypes the event for you: the first line of every event. For events, simply go into the method, and it will tell you on the first line the type of event the eventInfo variable is. Take a look at a button's pushButton event method:

```
1:    ;Button :: pushButton
2:    method pushButton(var eventInfo Event)
3:
4:    endmethod
```

Notice var eventInfo Event in parentheses. In this prototype, eventInfo is a variable that is declared as an Event. This is important because it tells you what types of methods can be used to extract and set information in the eventInfo variable. With pushButton, all the event methods can be used.

Next, look at the keyPhysical method of a field.

```
1:    ;Field :: keyPhysical
```

```
2:    method keyPhysical(var eventInfo KeyEvent)
3:
4:    endmethod
```

`eventInfo` is defined as a `KeyEvent`. This indicates that you can use any of the `KeyEvent` methods to extract and deal with the event information. To see a list of all the methods that work with `KeyEvent`, select View | ObjectPAL Quick Lookup to bring up the ObjectPAL Reference dialog box, and then `KeyEvent` from the Types and Methods tab (see Figure 7.10).

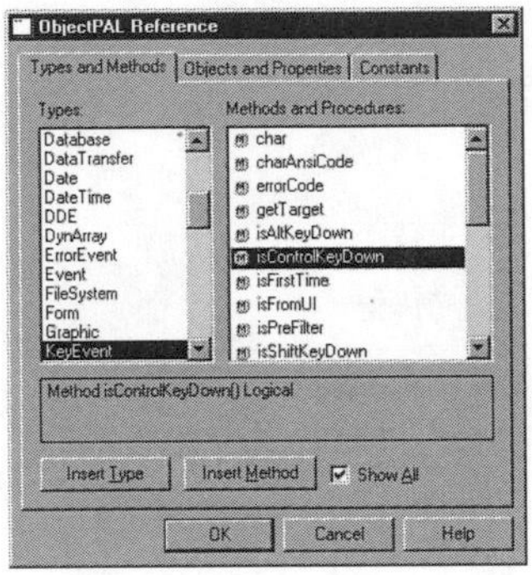

FIGURE 7.10.

*The ObjectPAL Quick
Lookup dialog box.*

You can use any of the `KeyEvent` methods in the `keyPhysical` or `keyChar` methods to deal with and alter an event created by the keyboard. For example, to prevent all Ctrl keystroke combinations on a certain field, alter the field's `keyPhysical` as follows:

```
1:    ;Field :: keyPhysical
2:    method keyPhysical(var eventInfo KeyEvent)
3:       if eventInfo.isControlKeyDown() then
4:          disableDefault
5:          msgInfo("", "Control key combinations are invalid here")
6:       endIf
7:    endmethod
```

In this routine, the Ctrl key is trapped for, and `disableDefault` prevents the default behavior.

The Path of *eventInfo* from Field to Field

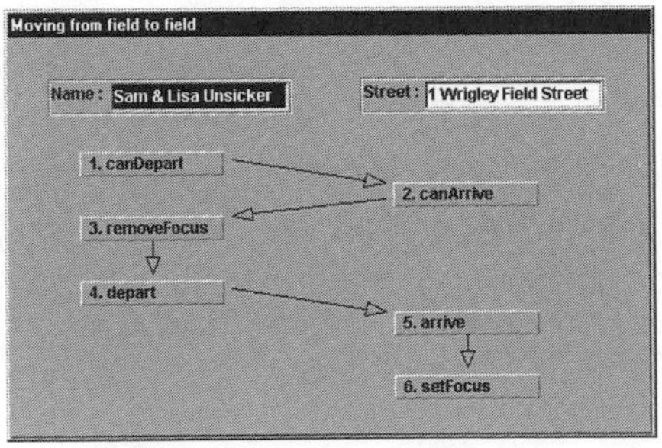

FIGURE 7.11.

*The sequence of events from
field to field.*

One important part of the event model is the sequence of execution from field to field. Figure 7.11 shows the sequence of execution of the events when moving from field to field.

Controlling Default Behavior

The default behavior for events was described earlier in this chapter. The preceding section introduced you to the eventInfo packet. To use and manipulate the default behavior, you must understand the default behavior and the eventInfo packet. You can use the following keywords and variables to control the default behavior: disableDefault, doDefault, enableDefault, and passEvent.

disableDefault prevents the built-in behavior from executing. Normally, the default behavior is executed just before endMethod. doDefault explicitly executes the default behavior ahead of time. If you have disabled the default behavior—at the beginning of the method, for example—you can re-enable it with enableDefault. passEvent passes an event to the object's container.

Summary

This chapter formally introduced you to the event model. The event model is the core piece to understanding how and where to program in ObjectPAL. Event methods are categorized in three categories: internal, external, and special. Only external event methods bubble. You also learned that you can control the default behavior with doDefault, disableDefault, enableDefault and passEvent. You will revisit the event model many times. For example, in Chapter 19 you will take a close look at the path of a key press and later, in Chapter 30, you'll revisit the event model for an advanced discussion. The next chapter discusses where you should put code.

Where to Put Code

8

One of the hardest aspects of using ObjectPAL is deciding where to place code. Novice ObjectPAL programmers tend to place code everywhere. Rather than work with the default behavior, the event model, and the data model, beginners often tend to put code in the wrong place. Later, they add more code to try to fix an inelegant approach.

Programmers who use DOS PAL and traditional procedural languages are used to writing a large amount of code. In the Windows version of Paradox, they tend to overcode to get the results they want. Understanding the system can make the difference between inelegant and elegant code.

Taking the time to understand the default behavior of objects, the event model, and the data model can save you much time. If you don't fully understand how an object works, you could end up working harder and accomplishing less. Much of this book deals with this issue. This chapter concentrates on it and offers guidelines, tips, and techniques on where and when to code.

About Coding

When new users to Paradox begin writing code in ObjectPAL, they often write tremendous amounts of code. The amount of code can become overwhelming if you don't understand the fundamentals of the product.

You usually follow certain steps whenever you develop an application. Before writing a single line of ObjectPAL code, you always should build the data model and arrange the form until it's similar to what you want. Then run the form and work with it to see what it does and doesn't do. When you find something that you want to work differently, ask yourself, "What do I want to happen?" and "When do I want it to happen?" Try to do this for only one task or object at a time. In other words, develop in small steps.

Go back and forth between Design mode and Run mode and test your work incrementally. When you're done coding and testing a single object, move to the next. By refining your application in steps, you end up with functioning code in bite-sized chunks. If you try to tackle in one step all the work that an application requires, you can easily end up frustrated, with messy code. Remember, program and test one task at a time.

Watch Out for Spaghetti Code

NEW Term

BASIC, early Pascal, and early C promoted *spaghetti code*, which is intertwined code with many repeated parts. These procedural languages required you to write line after line of code. Although modern languages don't lend themselves to spaghetti code, it's still possible to write it. During the development process, you might copy a routine from one spot to another and later find a bug in it. You would have two pieces of code to correct. This is fine if you are perfect and can remember to change both pieces of code. But this method of programming is hard on upkeep, and it makes reusing code nearly impossible. You would have to start every new project from scratch.

Use an Object-Oriented Methodology

Object-oriented programming involves compartmentalizing and reusing code. Your goal should be to avoid duplicating code by developing self-contained, reusable units. After a while, you will spend the majority of your developing time copying, pasting, and putting together previously developed units. When a bug in a certain unit turns up, you can debug that one unit, and every application from that point on that uses that unit is cleaned up or enhanced. In addition, when you enhance some code that many applications share, those applications are enhanced instantly.

Keep in mind that you can still write spaghetti code in ObjectPAL. If you duplicate parts, you inevitably introduce bugs into your application. ObjectPAL, however, promotes good programming. If you follow the rules of object-oriented methodology, develop in compartments, and avoid duplicating code, your programs will be clean.

Try to Localize Code

Because you're programming in ObjectPAL (an object-based programming language), the code should be as local to the object as possible. For example, if you're trying to decide to put code on a button or the form, then choose the button. If the situation warrants moving up to the form level, it will become obvious. There are many benefits for coding as low as possible, including the capability to copy objects with code on them from one form to another and still have it work.

> **TIP**
>
> Whenever you have a choice, try adding ObjectPAL code directly to the object to get the desired results. Do you ever want to not code locally? Yes—when you want to work with more than one of the same object. You can use a container above all the objects and put code on the object's container.

Code as Low as Possible

Put code on the lowest possible container. If you later need to use the same code elsewhere, move the code up the container path to the lowest container that both objects can see. If you follow this rule, your code will be compartmentalized and portable. By developing in compartments, you keep code segments apart. A bug introduced in one compartment is less likely to affect other parts of your application.

If you are programming a button, put all the code, including variables, on the button. This makes the button a self-contained unit that is easily copied and pasted to other forms. If you later need that same code on another button, convert it to a custom method and move it up the container path to the button's container object. A container object is an object that completely surrounds and controls the behavior of all the objects within it.

If you then decide you need to use the code with several pages within the form, then move the custom method to the form. If you need the same routine in several forms, consider putting it in a library. A library is an object that stores custom ObjectPAL code. Libraries are useful for storing and maintaining frequently used routines, and for sharing custom methods and variables among forms.

Using this general rule of coding as low to the object as possible gives you maximum access to your code and saves you time. In addition, if you later find a problem with the routine, you need to correct it in only one spot; instantly, all code that uses the routine benefits from the improvement.

Although you can write spaghetti code with an object-based language, ObjectPAL supports and promotes good object-oriented practices. By using contained objects and custom methods properly, you can keep your code clean. Develop in self-contained units whose code is protected from other objects.

When You Code, Think Levels

As I have hinted, in an ObjectPAL application, you put code on various levels. You can put code on objects, on the object's container, on the page, on the form, or even in a library. When you place code in your application, imagine that you are placing your code at various levels. The levels of coding are as follows:

- Script
- Library
- Form
- Page
- Container in a page (a box object, for example)
- Object on a page or in a container (a field object, for example)
- Elements of an object (the record object of a table frame, for example)
- The table level (picture strings and other validity checks, for example)

Script Level

A script is an object consisting of ObjectPAL code that a user can run independently of a form or that can be called from ObjectPAL. Unlike forms and reports, scripts have no objects.

Unlike libraries, scripts can be run without ObjectPAL. You will hardly ever use the script level in a project. It's useful, however, for enabling the user to execute code without opening a form. You occasionally might use the script level to start off an application—perhaps for setting up data for a form, such as adding or deleting records. Another use for scripts is to enable the user to run part of the code without launching the whole application. You will seldom use either of these techniques.

Library Level

A library is a good place to put code that you need to call from multiple forms. Many ObjectPAL programmers think of the library as a way to code above the highest container—the form. Libraries are discussed in Chapter 23. For now, just remember that a library is a place to put code that is shared among forms.

Three Form Levels

The form actually has three mental levels to place code: the init, the prefilter, and the form level. The init method occurs first and is the first place to consider placing code when you are placing code at the form level. All events go through the form's prefilter, and external events can go to the form twice. First, the event is prefiltered, and then it is sent to the target and can bubble back up to the form. If you want to intercept another object's event, use the form's prefilter. Think of the prefilter as a special level and the else part of the form's if statement as the form level. For example, if you want to do something after the form is opened, use the else portion of the form's built-in arrive method.

If you want to trap for an error so that you can do something in addition to the built-in behavior, use the form's else portion of the error method. If you want to trap for an error before it happens, then most likely the built-in action method is where you will want to code. If you want to write generic code that does something every time you arrive on any one of a set of fields, then use the prefilter of the form's arrive method.

Review of the *init, open,* and *arrive* Methods of a Form

Immediately before the open event, the init method occurs; immediately after, the arrive method occurs. The form's arrive is a good place to put code that you want executed when the form is first opened and whenever it is selected. For example, you could maximize the form and display a message upon arriving with the following code:

```
1:    ;Form :: arrive
2:    method arrive(var eventInfo MoveEvent)
3:       if eventInfo.isPreFilter()
4:          then
5:             ;This code executes for each object on the form
6:
7:       else
```

```
 8:          ;This code executes only for the form
 9:          maximize()
10:          msgInfo("Our database", "Welcome")
11:      endif
12:    endmethod
```

With this code, the form maximizes and displays the message every time the form is opened and selected. Compare the preceding routine to the following routine. They both accomplish the same thing: they maximize the application desktop and display a message when the form is opened. The following open version requires a doDefault, however:

```
 1:    ;Form :: open
 2:    method open(var eventInfo Event)
 3:       if eventInfo.isPreFilter()
 4:          then
 5:          ;This code executes for each object on the form
 6:
 7:       else
 8:          ;This code executes only for the form
 9:          maximize()
10:          doDefault
11:          msgInfo("Our database", "Welcome")
12:       endif
13:    endmethod
```

Note in line 10 that doDefault is added after the maximize line. Without the doDefault, the message would interrupt the opening of the form, and the form would look peculiar. For this reason, the arrive method is considered better because it is more elegant.

Review of the Form's Prefilter

People often have trouble using events prefiltered at the form level. If you have 50 fields on a form and want to set the colors on the arrive of each one, it doesn't make sense to add the code to every field's arrive method. Even if the code that sets colors is in a custom method, you don't need to call the custom method in each arrive. The form's prefilter enables the programmer to write code that intercepts the arrive for each object and performs the work for each object. Rather than modify 50 fields, the programmer has to deal with only one generic method at the form level. If you want to set the color of every object in the Box class when the form opens, you could do the following:

```
 1:    ;Form :: open
 2:    method open(var eventInfo Event)
 3:       var UIObj UIObject endVar
 4:       if eventInfo.isPreFilter()
 5:       then
 6:          ;This code executes for each object on the form
 7:          eventInfo.getTarget(UIObj)
 8:          if UIObj.class = "Box" then
 9:             UIObj.color = Red
10:          endIf
11:       else
```

```
12:             ;This code executes only for the form
13:
14:        endif
15:    endmethod
```

Using the form's prefilter to work on a group of objects is an important technique. With it, you can cut down on the amount of code you need to write.

\ANSWERS\GETTARG.FSL also demonstrates how to use the form's prefilter.

Using the Form's Prefilter

Suppose that you or your users are having a hard time seeing which field is currently active. One solution is to make the field highlight yellow while it is active. This section demonstrates how to alter the appearance of a field whenever it has focus using the form's prefilter.

You can find the PREFILT.FSL form on the disc in the \ANSWERS DIRECTORY.

Step By Step

1. Change your working directory to the TUTORIAL directory and create a quick form based on the CUSTOMER.DB table. Figure 8.1 shows what the quick form should look like after you create it.

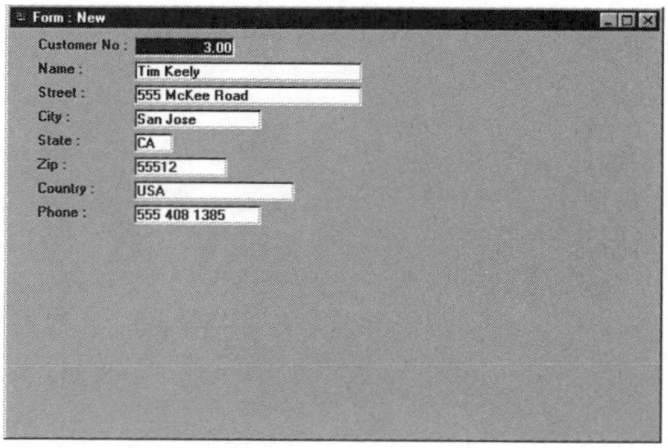

FIGURE 8.1.

The quick form should look like this after you create it.

2. Add lines 3–5 and 8–11 to the form's arrive method.

```
1:    ;PREFILT ::Form :: arrive
2:    method arrive(var eventInfo MoveEvent)
3:       var
4:       ui      UIObject              ;Declare ui as a UIObject.
5:       endVar
```

```
 6:        if eventInfo.isPreFilter() then
 7:            ;// This code executes for each object on the  form:
 8:            eventInfo.getTarget(ui)        ;Set ui to target.
 9:            if ui.class = "Field" then    ;Is ui a field, then
10:                ui.color = Yellow         ;change it to yellow.
11:            endIf
12:        else
13:            ;// This code executes only for the form:
14:
15:        endif
16:    endmethod
```

3. Add lines 3–5 and 8–11 to the form's canDepart method.

```
 1:    ;PREFILT :: Form :: canDepart
 2:    method canDepart(var eventInfo MoveEvent)
 3:        var
 4:            ui      UIObject        ;Declare ui as a UIObject.
 5:        endVar
 6:        if eventInfo.isPreFilter() then
 7:            ;// This code executes for each object on the form:
 8:            eventInfo.getTarget(ui)        ;Set ui to target.
 9:            if ui.class = "Field" then    ;Is ui a field, then
10:                ui.color = Transparent    ;make it transparent.
11:            endIf
12:        else
13:            ;// This code executes only for the form:
14:
15:        endif
16:
17:    endmethod
```

4. Check the syntax, save the form as PREFILT.FSL, and run it. Move from field to field using the Tab key or mouse and note that the active field changes color. Figure 8.2 shows what they should look like.

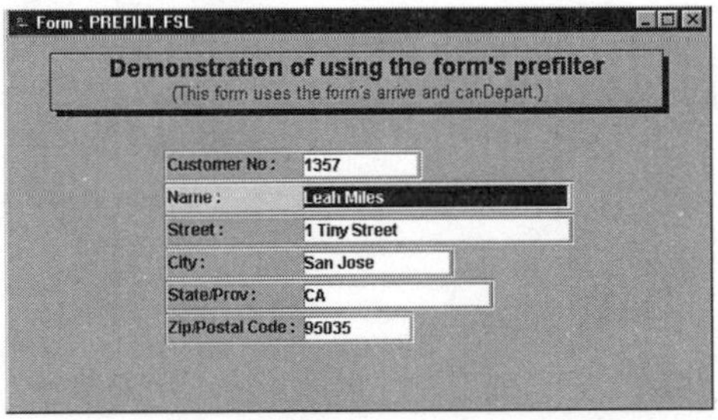

FIGURE 8.2.

The PREFILT.FSL form demonstrates using the form's prefilter.

Analysis

In step 2, line 4, a UIObject variable ui is declared. In line 8, a handle to the target object is put in the UIObject variable ui. Line 9 uses the handle to test whether it is a field by comparing the property class to the string Field. If they are the same, then a UIObject variable is used to change the field's color to yellow.

Step 4 is the same as step 3 except for location—the code is in the form's `canDepart`—and it changes the color back to transparent.

You can use the form's prefilter whenever you want to work with a group of objects. A group of objects can be categorized by class, color, font, and so on. You can check for all objects in a certain class or for objects with a certain name. You also can check for multiple criteria. For example:

```
1:    ;Form :: isPreFilter
2:    if UI.class = "Field" then
3:        if UI.name <> "Last_Name" then
4:            UI.color = Red
5:        endIf
6:    endIf
```

The prefilter of the form's `arrive` method is a good place for setting colors or other settings that need to be initialized at the beginning of a session, such as user configuration settings. You could write settings to a table or to an .INI file, read them in when the form is opened, and set all the object properties with this technique. More often, however, you will use the other events, such as `action` and `menuAction`, to manipulate a group of objects. Remember that all the form-level events have a prefilter you can use.

NOTE

Have you ever noticed that the status bar continues to display the last message even when it's no longer needed? For most applications, this is what you want. Occasionally, however, you might want a cleaner look. You can put `message("")` in the form-level `mouseExit` method to turn off messages when a user leaves an object. In addition to cleaning up the status bar whenever you leave an object, this technique enables you to put a message on the `mouseEnter` methods of objects you want to inform the user of. For example:

```
;Button :: mouseEnter
message("This button exits the application")
```

The Page Level

Normally, your first choice for high-level code should be either a library or the page level. Why not the form level? Because the form level forces the prefilter to fire for every object. In general, avoid the form level `else` portion for faster applications. When you have a multipage form and you need to distinguish between pages, use the page level. A classic example of this is when building menus. Generally, an application will need a different menu for every page. In this case, the page's `arrive` method is the perfect location to build a menu.

In addition, use the menuAction trigger of the page when you build a custom menu and need to trap for the user's selection. This enables you to have different menus for different pages of a form. If you need the same menu choices on all the pages of a form, use the form-level menuAction method. To learn more about menus, see Chapter 25.

The Container Level: Using a Container to Hold Objects

Sometimes it's advantageous to put a container, such as a box object, in a page. Put objects inside the container, and put code at the container level that deals with the objects it contains.

The Container Level: Grouping Objects to Centralize Code

In addition to putting a box around objects, you could group them. This puts an invisible box type object around the objects. If you want to test something about a group of objects, you can group them and test them with the arrive and canDepart methods, for example. In a typical 1:M invoicing system, you might want to verify that a telephone number has been entered, but only when the user attempts to leave the header information. You can group the header field objects and test the telephone field on the canDepart method of the grouped objects. For example:

```
1:    ;Group :: canDepart
2:    if Phone.isBlank() then
3:       beep()
4:       message("Enter a phone number.")
5:       eventInfo.setErrorCode(CanNotDepart)
6:    endIf
```

Grouping Objects to Centralize Code

This section demonstrates how to return the values 0 through 9, depending on which object the user clicks. This tutorial uses the technique of grouping objects to centralize code on the grouped object.

You can find the GROUP.FSL form on the disc in the \ANSWERS DIRECTORY.

Step By Step

1. Change your working directory to the TUTORIAL directory, create a new form, and place 10 text objects with the values 0 through 9. Then, group them by selecting all of them and choosing Design | Group (see Figure 8.3).

FIGURE 8.3.

GROUP.FSL demonstrates grouping objects to centralize code.

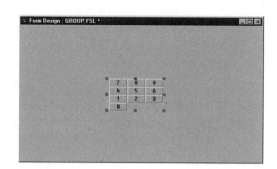

2. Add lines 3–11 to the mouseDown of the grouped object.

```
 1:    ;GROUP :: Group :: mouseDown
 2:    method mouseDown (var eventInfp MouseEvent)
 3:       var
 4:          obj  UIObject
 5:       endVar
 6:
 7:       eventInfo.getObjectHit (obj)
 8:       obj.color = Yellow
 9:       message ("You pressed the number , obj.value)
10:       sleep (100)
11:       obj.color = Gray
12:    endmethod
```

3. Check the syntax, save the form as GROUP.FSL, and run it. When you click on one of the nine text objects, it changes color and displays the correct value in the status bar.

Analysis

Line 4 declares a UIObject variable that is used in line 7 to get the intended object of a mouse action—in this case, the objects in the grouped object. Line 8 changes the object that is clicked to the color yellow, and line 9 notifies the user which object is hit (see Figure 8.4). Line 10 sleeps for one-tenth of a second so that the user can see the object highlighted. Line 11 sets the color back to gray.

Rather than use the message() procedure in line 9 to notify the user of which object was clicked, you might want to use the data for something more practical. For example, you could turn this routine into a calculator. Figure 8.5 shows how this technique is used in the Dialer application to capture the letter of the alphabet that the user types. Chapter 23 gives you more tips and techniques for writing more elegant code.

FIGURE 8.4.
*GROUP.FSL after an
object has been clicked.*

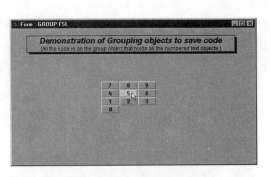

FIGURE 8.5.
*DIALER.FSL uses a group
to centralize code.*

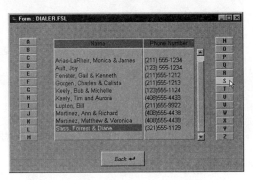

The Object Level Often Is Best

The optimal place to put code—and also the first place you should think about putting code—is directly on the object itself. Most of the time, you put objects such as fields, buttons, and table frames within a page or in a container and attach code directly to them. See the section, "Using `mouseEnter` and `mouseExit`," later in this chapter.

The Elements of Objects Also Is a Level

The lowest level for code is on the elements of an object. Many objects are actually composed of several objects. A field object is composed of a text label object and an edit region object (see Figure 8.6). When you put code on a field, you have a choice of 27 events at the field level, 10 at the edit region level, and 25 at the text label level. In the case of a field, you rarely use the edit region and text levels.

A button has two levels where you can attach code: the button object and the text object it contains. You usually use the `pushButton` event with buttons.

Figure 8.7 shows the Object Tree of a table frame. Note that a two-column table frame is composed of seven objects. Normally, you wouldn't place code on the header or on the column labels. That leaves three levels where you can place code on a table frame: the field level, the record level, and the table-frame level.

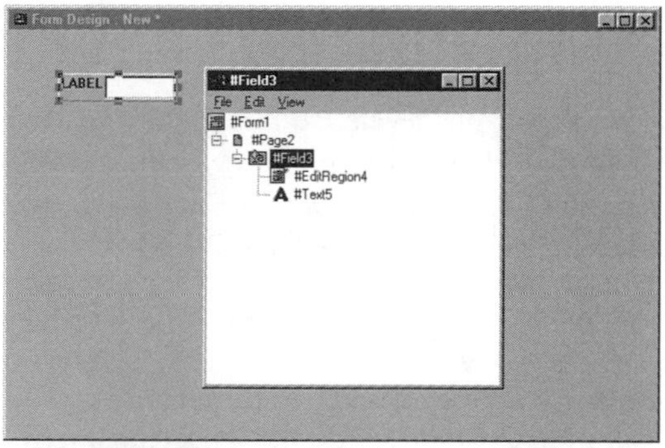

FIGURE 8.6.

The Object Tree of a field.

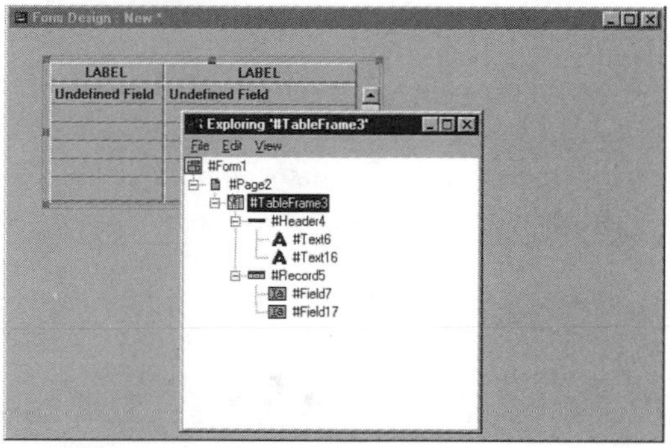

FIGURE 8.7.

The Object Tree of a table frame.

Figure 8.8 shows the Object Tree of a crosstab. A crosstab is composed of seven objects. Therefore, it has seven places where you can attach code.

Thinking of attaching code to various levels of an application or object is easier than randomly guessing where to put code. It gives you an idea of what can see what. Whenever a routine isn't behaving properly, ask yourself, "Is there a better level or location for this routine?" Sometimes, especially when you're dealing with multiple objects, the answer is yes.

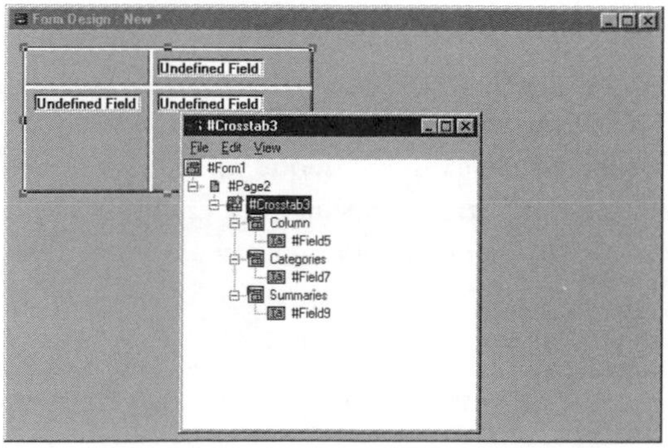

FIGURE 8.8.

The Object Tree of a crosstab.

Declaring Variables at Different Levels

The concepts of various levels, containership, and what can see what are important in ObjectPAL. One of the most important elements of ObjectPAL code placement is where to declare a variable. The discussion of scope and instance in this section also applies to the other object windows: Const, Type, Uses, and Proc.

The place where you declare a variable determines the scope and instance of a variable. The term *scope* means *accessiblity*. The scope of the variable means what other objects, if any, can see it. The scope of a variable—that is, the range of objects that have access to it—is defined by the objects in which it is declared, and by the containership hierarchy. Objects can access only their own variables and the variables defined in the objects that contain them. The scope of a variable depends on where it is declared.

The *instance* of the variable means how long the variable exists. For example, if you declare a TCursor variable within a button and you want to use the same TCursor variable in another button, you could declare the TCursor in both buttons, which is a waste of resources. Or you could move the declaration to higher ground—that is, to a place where both buttons can see and reuse one variable. In the case of two buttons on a page, the page level is a good choice. All the objects on the page, including the two buttons, have access to page-level variables.

Declare Private Variables Within a Method

After you choose which object to declare a variable on, you must decide whether you want the variable to be private to a method or global to the object. Variables declared within a method are visible only to that method and are dynamic; that is, they are accessible only while that method executes. They are initialized (reset) each time the method executes. A private variable can be seen only by the event in which it is declared. Its scope is limited. Therefore, if you want to use the variable in only a single method, use a variable that is private to the method.

If you declare a variable within a method (either within or above method...endMethod), then the variable is private to the method; that is, no other methods or objects can see or use the variable. In essence, the variable is private to the method.

Most often, the first place you choose to put a variable is inside method...endMethod. When you do this, the variable's scope is limited to the method and its existence is only for the duration of the method. Use this technique when no other objects need to use the variable and the variable can be initialized each time. For example, you can put both the variable declaration and the code in the same method window, as in the following:

```
1:    ;Btn1 :: pushButton
2:    method pushButton(var eventInfo Event)
3:       var                      ;Private variables are declared
4:          s    String           ;inside method/endMethod.
5:       endVar
6:
7:       s = "Hello World"
```

```
8:      msgInfo("", s)
9:    endMethod
```

The first technique is easier to read; all code is located in the same place. In addition, the variable is a private, or local. More specifically, the variable is local to only this method; no other events of this object or of another object can see the variable.

Declare Global Variables in the Var Window

The Var window of an object creates a variable that is global to the object. Variables declared in an object's Var window are visible to all methods attached to that object, and to any objects that object contains. A variable declared in an object's Var window is attached to the object and is static, accessible as long as the object exists.

A variable with broader scope in ObjectPAL is said to be global to the object. Any object can access it from that point down in the containership hierarchy. Do not confuse the concept of a variable being global to an object with a global variable in other languages. A variable that is global to an object in ObjectPAL is global only to that object and not to any other objects.

After you choose the object, you have three places in which you can declare a variable: in the Var window of the object, inside the method...endMethod structure of a method, or above the method...endMethod structure.

As an alternative to putting the variable declaration with the code, you can put the variable in the Var window and the code in the method, as in the following:

```
1:    ;Btn2 :: Var
2:    var              ;Global to an object variables
3:       s   String    ;are declared in the Var window
4:    endVar           ;of the object.
```

```
1:    ;Btn2 :: pushButton
2:    method pushButton(var eventInfo Event)
3:       s = "Hello World"
4:       msgInfo("", s)
5:    endMethod
```

This second technique uses a variable that is global to the object. It is more elegant if you need to use the variable elsewhere. The variable is global to the object; all the other methods of the object and of the objects it contains can see the variable. In other words, the scope you need for a particular variable is the determining factor. If no other object needs the variable, declare it privately.

Are there any exceptions to this rule? Yes. In the preceding example, either inside method...endMethod or in the Var window is equally elegant because the button's pushButton method occurs only once for each click of the button, which doesn't tax the system. In fact, you can declare a variable in any custom or event that executes once. Methods such as pushButton, open, and arrive are prime candidates for declaring variables privately inside method...endMethod.

In the case of an event such as newValue, which is triggered many times by many different events, the second technique of separating the variable in the Var window from the code in the event is more elegant. Typically, newValue is triggered so many times during a session that redeclaring a variable each time doesn't make sense. A variable could be redeclared thousands of times in a newValue method.

Var window variables are declared for the instance of the object. Therefore, they are more elegant in most cases. It's better programming practice to declare your variables only once so that the system won't be taxed. The declaring of variables in the Var window occurs only once, and it occurs even before the open method of the object. If you want to see this for yourself, put the following code on a button and run the form. The message box will display the correct variable declaration.

```
1:    ;Button :: open
2:    method open(var eventInfo Event)
3:       msgInfo("", data Type(o))
4:    endmethod
```

```
1:    ;Button :: Var
2:    var
3:        o    OLE
4:    endVar
```

When you declare variables, you usually use one of the two techniques just discussed. The scope and instance of the variable is the determining factor. In general, it's a good rule of thumb to use the Var window as your first choice. Move the declaration from the Var window (which is global to the object) to within method...endMethod (which is private to the method) only when needed. By putting variables in the Var window of an object, more events have access to it.

Declaring Variables Outside a Method

What if you want the scope of a variable to be private to a method, but have its instance be for the duration of the object? Is this possible? Yes. Variables declared before the word method in a method...endMethod block are visible only to that method and are static. This technique has the benefit of declaring the variable only once—that is, when the object is created—yet the variable remains private to the method. In addition, its existence is for the duration of the object.

```
1:    ;Button :: pushButton
2:    var
3:        O    OLE    ;Private variable declared only once.
4:
5:    endVar
6:    method pushButton(var eventInfo Event)
7:       msgInfo("", DataType(O))
8:    endmethod
```

This third technique is not used often enough. It is an elegant way to declare a variable private to a method, because the variable is declared only once. Declare permanent variables in either the Var window (scope that is global to the object with an instance of the duration of the object) or above the method...endMethod (scope that is private to the method with an instance of the duration of the object).

Variable Level Summary

After you decide that you need a variable that is global to an object—in other words, you have decided to use the Var window of an object—you must decide the level on which you want to declare the variable, such as the form, the page, the object's container, or the object. The answer depends on what you want the scope of the variable to be. In a way, it depends on how global you need the variable to be. In general, I declare the variable either at the form level or at the lowest possible container. If you declare a variable at the form level, you don't have to worry about the scope of the variable because the variable is global to the form. That is, all objects in the form can see it.

The better of these two approaches is to declare variables in the Var window of the lowest possible container. You can move them up the containership path when a broader scope is needed. For example, if you're going to use a variable on a button, declare it on the button. Declare the variable in the event itself: for example, within pushButton. If you use it in another of the button's events, for example, mouseEnter, move it to the button's Var window.

If you later need that variable for another object on that page or on another page in the form, move the variable back to the Var window of the page or form. In general, declare the variable on as low a level as possible, and use the Var window whenever you need the same variable with two different events or two different objects.

Study the Event Methods in Combination

An excellent technique for placing code on an object is to place code in "before and after" combinations. Many events have counterparts: for example, open and close, arrive and depart, canArrive and canDepart, and mouseEnter and mouseExit. If you need to code in a "before and after" maneuver, think and code in one of these method combinations. For example, occasionally you might need to create a table when a form is opened and delete it when the form is exited. The open and close combination is a good place to do this. open and canDepart might be even better, but that's up to you as the programmer.

mouseEnter and *mouseExit*

Whenever you want something to occur when the pointer is within the boundaries of an object, use the mouseEnter and mouseExit combination.

Using *mouseEnter* and *mouseExit*

Suppose that you want to display a message on the status bar whenever the mouse pointer is over a button. To do this, use the message() procedure in the mouseEnter and mouseExit event methods.

You can find the M-ENTER.FSL form on the disc in the \ANSWERS directory.

Step By Step

1. Change your working directory to the TUTORIAL directory and create a new form with a button on it. Change the label of the button to Close (see Figure 8.9).

FIGURE 8.9.

Setup form for tutorial.

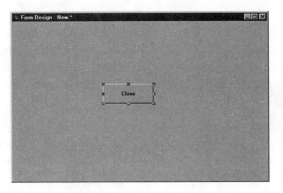

2. Add commands to the button. In this case, close the form by adding line 3 to the pushButton method.

```
1:    ;M-ENTER :: Button :: pushButton
2:    method pushButton(var eventInfo Event)
3:        close()
4:    endmethod
```

3. Place the message on the status bar by adding line 3 to the mouseEnter of the button.

```
1:    ;M-ENTER ::Button :: mouseEnter
2:    method mouseEnter(var eventInfo MouseEvent)
3:        message("This button closes the form")
4:    endmethod
```

4. Remove the message from the status bar by adding line 3 to the mouseExit of the button.

```
1:    ; M-ENTER ::Button :: mouseExit
2:    method mouseExit(var eventInfo MouseEvent)
3:        message("")
4:    endmethod
```

5. Check the syntax, save the form as M-ENTER.FSL, and run it. Move your cursor over the button and keep an eye on the status bar.

Analysis

In step 2, line 3 closes the current form. Note that close() is used as a procedure in this case—it knows what object to work with.

In step 3, line 3, the `mouseEnter` method sends a message to the status bar whenever the mouse pointer enters the boundaries of the button.

In step 4, line 3 posts a new message, the null character.

Rather than use the `mouseExit` method of every object, you can put code in the prefilter of the form's `mouseExit` method. Remember that external commands always bubble up. Therefore, putting `message("")` at the form level clears the status bar whenever the mouse leaves an object.

open Versus arrive

An object is always opened first, then `arrived` on. Therefore, `open` occurs before `arrive`. Remember that the default behavior happens last. When you `open` an object, the code on the form's built-in `open` method executes, and the form is opened. If you put code that deals with a UIObject in the `open` method, the code might not execute correctly because the objects don't exist yet. You could put `doDefault` before your code to execute the default behavior, or you could move your code to the `arrive` method.

`open` is a good place to initialize a variable, create a table, and deal with the form—for example, to maximize or resize it. `arrive` is a good place to set the properties of the objects on the form—for example, the values of the field objects.

newValue Versus changeValue

`newValue` occurs whenever the value for an edit region changes value onscreen. This occurs whether or not the field is defined. `changeValue` occurs with both defined and undefined fields but behaves quite differently for each. `changeValue` on an undefined field occurs whenever the value in it changes. With defined fields, however, it occurs only after a field is read from a table and changed by the user.

`changeValue` is a good place to do something based on a change in the table value. For example, you could perform some operation when payment type changes from cash to credit. If you want something to happen whenever a user changes a value in a field—undefined or defined—use `changeValue`.

keyChar Versus keyPhysical

The `keyChar` and `keyPhysical` events trap for the user pressing keys on the keyboard. `keyChar` traps for only the character keyboard keys; that is, the keys that print characters to the screen. `keyPhysical` traps for all the keyboard keys, both character keys and physical keys. `keyPhysical` filters the keyboard first and passes printable characters to the screen.

Use `keyChar` to trap for character keys, such as A, B, 1, 2, (, and ;. Use `keyPhysical` to trap for keys such as Esc, F1, F8, and Tab. If you need to trap for both physical and character keys in a routine, use only `keyPhysical` because it can trap for both.

action, menuAction, and error

Use action to trap for table actions, such as DataInsertRecord and DataPostRecord. Whenever a user does something related to the table, such as inserting a record, deleting a record, an action constant is sent to the action method. Use menuAction to catch user selection of menus, the Toolbar, and the control box. Whenever a user selects a menu option or clicks a button on the Toolbar, a menu constant is sent to the menuAction event of the form. You could use the error method to trap for errors, but because the built-in error method is always called after errors occur, use action instead. A good use for error is to add to the built-in error behavior; for example, to log all errors to a table.

Examples of Where to Put Code

Good examples are valuable. The following examples of where to put code might not be the most elegant, but they're good:

- **Field validation**: Validate fields at the object level with canDepart or changeValue.

- **Record validation**: Validate records at the record level with action or canDepart.

- **Initialize variables**: Initilize variables in the form's init method. In general, avoid the form's open method except for routines that deal with every object in the form.

- **Universal constants**: Declare often used constants in a library and use the extended Uses syntax. (For more information about universal constants, see Chapter 23.)

- **Universal custom types**: Define often used custom types in a library and use the extended Uses syntax. (For more information about universal custom types, see Chapter 23.)

- **Scripts**: If you have a routine that needs to be called by code and run independently by a user, then use a script. (For more information about scripts, see Chapter 23.)

TIP

Before you construct a certain behavior, be sure that the built-in behavior doesn't already do what you need with a great deal more sophistication. Knowing what Paradox does is important to the programmer. ObjectPAL is a rich and powerful language. If you duplicate functionality, you're wasting time. Always ask yourself, "What already happens in this event?"

Summary

Where code is placed in the event model is important. When coding in any event-driven environment, think levels. In ObjectPAL this extends from the library through objects on a form. Ultimately, you must find the perfect place to put your code. Only through trial and error—and some experimentation—will you learn the good and bad places to put code. The guidelines presented in this chapter will get you started.

Syntax

9

This chapter addresses syntax, the object variables, case sensitivity, and coding conventions. These topics may not seem related, but they all have to do with knowing how to type code in and making what you code readable and reuseable.

Dot Notation and *object.doIt*

The `object.doIt()` syntax style of ObjectPAL is important. The section "Object-Oriented Programming" in Chapter 6 mentioned that this style of syntax is easier to remember than a dozen different syntax variations for a single command. This next section builds on the idea that ObjectPAL is easy to remember, and compares ObjectPAL with everyday language.

In the real world, you can rudely say to people:

> Hey. Do it. Now.
> You. Do it. Pick up trash.
> Lisa. Do it. Swim.
> Glenn, Les. Go Golf.

To turn these statements into ObjectPAL code, you would write them as follows:

```
1:    var
2:        Hey, You, Lisa, Glenn    People
3:    endVar
4:
5:    Hey.doIt("Now")
6:    You.doIt("Pick up trash")
7:    Lisa.doIt("Swim")
8:    Les.doIt("Golf")
9:    Glenn.doIt("Golf")
```

In this example, in effect you program a human type or class of object. If Borland ever adds a human type or class of object to ObjectPAL, you could program a button as follows:

```
1:    method pushButton(var eventInfo Event)
2:        var
3:            p                Person
4:            pm1, pm2         PersonMovement
5:            house, store     Building
6:        endVar
7:
8:        p = "Lisa"
9:        p1 = "Swim"
10:       p2 = "Run"
11:       house.p.doIt(p1)
12:       store.p.doIt(p2)
13:   endmethod
```

With dot notation, you can tell two different people named Lisa in two different locations what to do.

Introduction to the Alternate Syntax

Because ObjectPAL's core syntax is taken directly from PAL (Paradox Application Language), Paradox for DOS programmers will be familiar with many of the commands. PAL is a procedural language; ObjectPAL is an object-based, event-driven language. Therefore, the syntax of Paradox has migrated from the DOS version to the Windows version to more closely resemble Pascal and C.

Although ObjectPAL's `object.doIt()` syntax is its syntax template, ObjectPAL does have an alternate syntax. Following is the template for the standard syntax:

`object.methodName(argument [, argument])`

Now, following is the template for the alternate syntax:

`methodName(object, argument [, argument])`

For example, the following three statements all close the current form:

```
1:     close()           ;This uses close as a procedure.
2:     self.close()      ;This is the standard syntax.
3:     close(self)       ;This is the alternate syntax.
```

Here is another example that demonstrates manipulating strings. The following two lines of code are equivalent:

```
1:     s = test.subStr(2, 3)     ;Regular syntax.
2:     s = subStr(test, 2, 3)    ;Alternate syntax.
```

If you want to try these syntax variations, put the following code on a button:

```
1:     ;Button :: pushButton
2:     method pushButton(var eventInfo Event)
3:        var
4:           s,s1,s2    String
5:        endVar
6:
7:        s = "Mike Ault"
8:        s1 = s.subStr(1,4)
9:        s2 = subStr(s,6,4)
10:       msgInfo("Syntax 1", s1)
11:       msgInfo("Syntax 2", s2)
12:    endmethod
```

The Alternate Syntax Uses Dot Notation

Just like the regular syntax, the alternate syntax can use dot notation. For example, the following two lines of code are equivalent:

```
1:     pge1.tfCustomer.Last_Name.moveTo()
2:     moveto(pge1.tfCustomer.Last_Name)
```

Although ObjectPAL gives you this freedom when you write code, be consistent. Whenever you have a choice, use the regular `object.methodName()` style of syntax. If you do this, your code will be more consistent. If your code is more consistent, it will be easier for others to read and easier for you to understand two months after you've coded it.

Using the Alternate Syntax in a Calculated Field

How do you use `round()` in a Calculated Field? Most of the Number type methods will work in a calculated field. The syntax is as follows:

methodname(*fieldname.value*)

For example, to use `round()` and `truncate()`, you need to use ObjectPAL's alternate syntax. The syntax for `round()` and `truncate()` is as follows:

truncate(*number*, *places*)   ;*Truncate the value in number.*

round(*number*, *places*)   ;*Round the value in number.*

where *places* is the number of decimal places you want to round or truncate to.

For example, if the field being rounded is `Total_Invoice`, and it needs to be rounded to two decimal places, an example of a calculated field that rounds the total is as follows:

```
1:    Round(Total_Invoice.value, 2)
```

This also can be incorporated into more complex calculated fields, as in the following:

```
1:    Round(SUM(Total_Invoice.value), 2)
```

The preceding rounds the grand total of the field `Total_Invoice`.

ObjectPAL and Case Sensitivity

When is Paradox case sensitive? Paradox is case sensitive with string comparisons and locates. For example, `Yes` is not the same as `YES` when you compare strings. When you locate a record, `Lupton` is not the same as `lupton` or `LUPTON`. Case sensitivity applies even when you check against parts of the ObjectPAL language if the part is in a string. For example, `box` isn't the same as `Box`. You can check which class an object belongs to with the following:

```
1:    var ui UIObject endVar
2:    eventInfo.getTarget(ui)
3:    if ui.class = "Box" then
4:        ;Put your code here. For example:
5:        message(ui.name)
6:    endIf
```

If you accidentally typed box or BOX, the routine would fail. Therefore, you need to watch your string comparisons. You can use ignoreCaseInStringCompares() and ignoreCaseInLocate() procedures, however, to force case insensitivity, as in the following example:

```
1:    var ui UIObject endVar
2:    eventInfo.getTarget(ui)
3:    ignoreCaseInStringCompares(Yes)
4:    if ui.class = "box" then
5:       ;Put your code here. For example:
6:       message(ui.name)
7:    endIf
```

Other than string compares and locates, ObjectPAL syntax is not case sensitive. The mixture of uppercase and lowercase characters you use when writing ObjectPAL keywords, methods, procedures, variables, and so on, is up to you. Appendix C goes into detail on this subject.

Further Details of Variables

Declaring variables already has been introduced by implication because variables have been used in many examples before now. In addition, Chapter 8 went into detail about where to declare variables. What follows in this section is a formal introduction/review of declaring variables in ObjectPAL. You declare variables in a var block, as in the following example:

```
1:    var          ;Start of variable block.
2:                 ;Declare variables here.
3:    endVar       ;End of variable block.
```

When you declare variables of the same type, you can either put them on the same line or separate lines. The choice is yours; it does not matter to the compiler. For example, the following declares four variables: two numbers and two strings.

```
1:    var
2:       s1     String    ;You can declare like variables on
3:       s2     String    ;separate lines, or
4:       n1,n2  Number    ;on the same line separated by commas.
5:    endVar
```

Following are some examples of how variables are declared:

```
1:    si    SmallInt     ;Declare si as a small integer. This
2:                       ;is useful for smaller numbers.
3:    s     String       ;Declare s as a string.
4:    f     Form         ;Declare f as form.
5:    app   Application   ;Declare an application variable
6:                       ;when you want to deal with the
7:                       ;desktop. For example,
8:                       ;to maximize or hide the
9:                       ;application.
10:   t     Time         ;Declare t as type
11:                      ;time to deal with time.
```

Following are some examples of using variables in expressions:

```
1:     x = x + 1
2:     s = "Nicole Kimberly Prestwood"
3:     s = "The new value is " + string(x)
4:     s = "The time is " + string(t)
5:     message(s)
```

Using Constants

As already stated, an ObjectPAL constant is a value that represents a number. A constant is a specific, unchanging value used in calculations and defined in a const block very similar to a variable block. Just as variables have scope and instance in ObjectPAL, so do constants. The following declares a constant with private scope; the instance of the constant is for the duration of the object.

```
1:     ;Button :: pushButton
2:     const
3:        youngest = "Veronica Renee Martinez"
4:     endConst
5:     method pushButton(var eventInfo Event)
6:        view(youngest, "New family member")
7:     endmethod
```

The value of constants, of course, doesn't change. You use these constants in ObjectPAL statements to do a variety of tasks.

> **NOTE**
>
> Two advantages of using constants is that they humanize your code and help make managing your code easier. They humanize your code by making your code easier to read. A constant named tax is easier to remember and understand than 8.125. Constants help you maintain your code by centralizing values. If the tax rate in your area changes from 8.125 to 8.5, you change the constant in one location. In the preceding example, when a new younger member of my family arrives, I just change the one constant and the change is propagated throughout. Imagine having to change it throughout your code.

Using Properties

One reason ObjectPAL is powerful is that you can change the properties of an object. You are already familiar with various properties of objects; you have set them in previous examples and in interactive Paradox. This section explores the syntax used to manipulate them in ObjectPAL. You can set most of an object's properties while the form is running—another feature that sets Paradox apart from other database systems. You can set not only the value of a field and the color of a box, but also the size and position of objects, the alignment, tab stop, and so on.

The Apostrophe and Dot Notation

There is a problem when you use properties. What if you want to change the color of a box named *color*? This is an ambiguous use of ObjectPAL. Furthermore, what if there is an object inside the box named *color*, too (see Figure 9.1). This really is an ambiguous use of ObjectPAL. The following is what ObjectPAL does with various commands when you run the form:

```
1:    color.color = Red          ;Error (invalid property).

2:    color.color.color = Red    ;Change inner box to red.
```

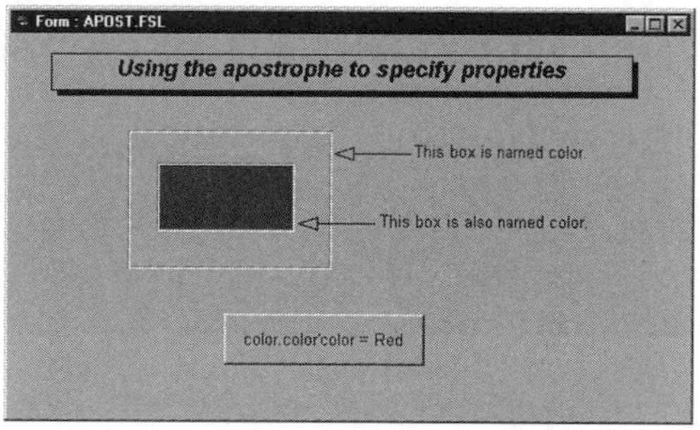

FIGURE 9.1.

Do not name an object the same name as a property.

How do you write code that changes the outer box? Do this using the apostrophe (‘), as in the following example:

```
1:    color'color = Red          ;Change outer box to red.
2:    color.color'color = Red    ;Change inner box to red.
```

Using the apostrophe makes your code incredibly easy to read. The real solution in this case, of course, is to not use any part of ObjectPAL to name objects. Should you start doing this in your code? This is completely up to you. I have not adopted using the apostrophe in my own coding convention yet because it has not been widely used or accepted by the developing community. If you name your objects carefully, then there is no need to use it. But one more time: it does make your code incredibly easy to read and I truly hope it eventually catches on, especially with the use of compound properties.

About Compound Properties

Just as there are compound objects in ObjectPAL, there are also compound properties. A *compound property* is a property that has several parts to it separated by dots. For example, Table 9.1 lists some sample compound properties.

NEW Term

Table 9.1. Sample compound properties.

Compound Property	Sample Usage
`design.SizeToFit`	`box1.design.SizeToFit = True`
`font.style`	`fld1.font.style = FontAttribBold`
`Background.Pattern.Style`	`grph1.Background.Pattern.Style = CrosshatchPattern`
`List.Value`	`fld1.lst1.list.value = "Bill Lupton"`

The Built-In Object Variables

ObjectPAL offers built-in variables in addition to its events. These variables are predefined by Paradox for you to use in your ObjectPAL routines. The built-in object variables are an integral part of ObjectPAL. Like so much of ObjectPAL, they are self-explanatory. In fact, you've already used several of them. The built-in object variables are `self`, `subject`, `container`, `active`, `lastMouseClicked`, and `lastMouseRightClicked`. Use the built-in object variables as much as possible. They make your code very readable and more portable.

Using *self*

With one exception, `self` always refers to the object to which the code is attached. The exception is when `self` is used in a library. When `self` is used in a library, it always refers to the object that calls the custom method. The technique of using `self` in a library is discussed in Chapter 23. For now, concentrate on using `self` within code on an object like a field.

Use `self` whenever possible; it makes your routines more generic. Use `self` whenever code refers to itself. If you have a choice between the following two lines of code, always choose the one that uses `self`:

```
1:    Last_Name.value = "Hoffman"
2:    self.value = "Hoffman"
```

If you later change the name of the *Last_Name* field, you don't have to change the name used in the code. In addition, if you copy or move the code to an object with a different name, it will still work. Finally, when you copy an object with code attached to it, the code is more likely to work if you use `self`.

Using *subject*

When `self` is used in a library, it refers to the calling object. Wouldn't it be nice if you could do the same with custom routines in a form? You can with `subject`. With dot notation and `subject`, you can have a routine work on another object. Custom methods and `subject` are discussed later in Chapter 23.

Using *container*

When you use container in your code, it refers to the object that contains the object to which the code is attached. If you have a small box inside a large box and you execute the following code attached to the small box, the large box turns red:

```
1:    ;SmallBox :: mouseClick
2:    container.color = red
```

Using *active*

active refers to the object that is currently active; in other words, the last object to receive a moveTo() command. Usually, it's the object that currently has the focus; that is, the object ready to be edited. In the following example, active is used to indicate the object that has the focus:

```
1:    active.nextRecord()
```

In a multitable form (a form with several tables bound to it), this line of code acts differently, depending on which object has the focus.

```
1:    lastMouseClicked and lastMouseRightClicked
```

Using *LastMouseClicked* and *LastMouseRightClicked*

LastMouseClicked refers to the last object to receive a mouseDown/mouseUp combination. A mouseDown/mouseUp combination occurs whenever the user presses the left mouse button while the pointer is over an object. This variable enables you to deal with the user's most recent mouse clicks without writing special code. lastMouseRightClicked is the same as lastMouseClicked, except that the right mouse button is pressed.

Using Object Variables

In this section, you use the object variables: self, active, lastMouseClicked, and lastMouseRightClicked. The goal is to build a somewhat crazy form that uses the ObjectPAL built-in object variables.

You can find the OPALVAR.FSL form on the disc in the \ANSWERS directory.

Step By Step

1. Change your working directory to the TUTORIAL directory and create a new form with the Customer table in the data model. Add three boxes and a button, as indicated in Figure 9.2.

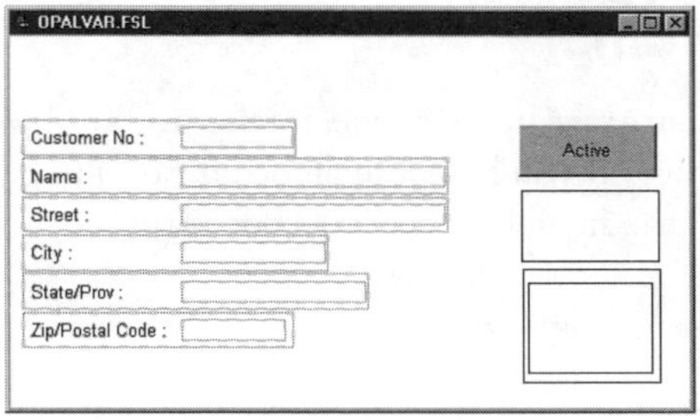

FIGURE 9.2.

After you've set up your form, it should look like this.

2. Toggle the color of self and container when the user clicks the small box. Do this by adding lines 3–9 to the mouseClick method of the small box.

```
1:    ;OPALVAR :: SmallBox :: mouseClick
2:    method mouseClick(var eventInfo MouseEvent)
3:        if self.color = Red then
4:            self.color = Green
5:            container.color = White
6:        else
7:            self.color = Red
8:            container.color = Gray
9:        endIf
10:   endmethod
```

3. To display the name of the object when the mouse is clicked, add line 3 to the page's mouseDown.

```
1:    ;OPALVAR :: Page :: mouseDown
2:    method mouseDown(var eventInfo MouseEvent)
3:        message(lastMouseClicked.name)
4:    endmethod
```

4. To display the name of the object when the mouse is right-clicked, add line 3 to the page's mouseRightDown.

```
1:    ;OPALVAR :: Page :: mouseRightDown
2:    method mouseRightDown(var eventInfo MouseEvent)
3:        message(lastMouseRightClicked.name)
4:    endmethod
```

5. To display the active field's name and value in the status bar when the user clicks a button, add line 3 to the pushButton method of the button.

```
1:    ;OPALVAR :: Button :: pushButton
2:    method pushButton(var eventInfo Event)
3:        message(active.name + ": " + active.value)
4:    endmethod
```

6. Check the syntax, save the form as OPALVAR.FSL, and then run it. Click the single box to the right (see Figure 9.3). Click the small box inside the larger box. The mouse click toggles the colors of the two boxes. If you click any of the three boxes on the right, the name of the box is displayed in the status bar. Click the button. Note the name and the value of the current object in the status bar.

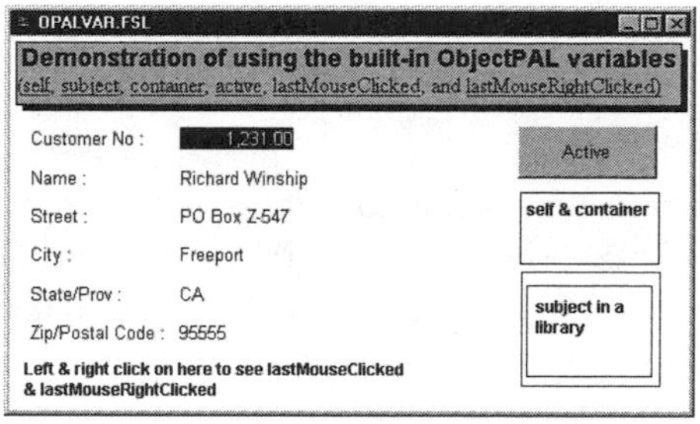

FIGURE 9.3.
*Your form should look
similar to this.*

Analysis

In step 2, lines 3–9 toggle the color of `self` (the small box) and `container` (the large box) when the small box is clicked. Line 3 checks the current color of the small box. Then, based on that current color, lines 4, 5, 7, and 8 change the colors.

Step 3, line 3 and step 4, line 3 use the fact that external methods bubble up to the form. Line 3 in step 3 displays the name of the last object that was left-clicked. Line 3 in step 4 displays the name of the last object that was right-clicked.

Step 5, line 3 uses `active` to display in the status bar the name and value of the current field whenever the user clicks the button.

TIP

The built-in object variables—`self`, `subject`, `container`, `active`, `lastMouseClicked`, and `lastMouseRightClicked`—are used in developing generic routines. Generic routines are important. The more generic routines you use, the less coding you have to do.

NOTE

You can use any property that applies to the type of object with which you are working. Properties that don't apply won't work. For example, because buttons don't have frames or color properties, `self.color = Red` doesn't work on a button.

Coding Conventions

A *coding convention* consists of the rules you use to type your code, name objects, and so on. Every programming language is flexible in how you use it. For example, the idea to use the built-in object variables `self`, `subject`, and `container` as much as possible can be part of a

NEW
Term

coding convention. How you personally use these flexible areas of the language is your own personal coding convention, such as the names you choose to name variables, UIObjects, forms, and so on.

Developing a consistent coding convention is very important. With a good, consistent coding convention, your code is much easier to read and, in the long run, saves you time. It needs to be simple and easy to remember. You might want to take some time now to read Appendix C, which is comprised of my own personal coding convention. Please feel free to use, study, and adopt it.

Summary

In this chapter, you learned that ObjectPAL is not case sensitive and flexible. For example, you learned that you can use the apostrophe to separate an object and property. The apostrophe is particularly useful when using compound properties. A programming language's syntax is something you learn as you go along. The syntax is the structure of the language. With the guidelines presented in this chapter, you now have a foundation of knowledge about ObjectPAL syntax on which to build. Whenever you type a routine, you are practicing and learning syntax.

The next chapter continues your voyage into ObjectPAL syntax. It deals with all the control structures available to the ObjectPAL programmer.

Control Structures

10

In programming languages, *control structures* are keywords used to alter the sequence of execution and add logic to your code. All programming languages contain control structures. They are a fundamental element of any programming language.

Normally, a programming language executes line after line in sequential order. This is true whether the language is a line-oriented language, such as BASIC, or a statement-oriented language, such as C. A branch transfers program control to an instruction other than the next sequential instruction.

A set of instructions that is repeated a predetermined number of times or until a specified condition is met is called a *loop*. Control structures enable you to branch and loop based on whether a certain condition is True. They also enable you to add logic to your code. The techniques you learn in this chapter will help you when you learn other programming languages. Although the syntax might vary, the control structures in ObjectPAL apply to other languages.

The Details of Branching

Branching involves testing a condition and doing something based on the result of that test. It enables you to code a Logical decision into your application. ObjectPAL has four types of branching: iif, if, switch, and try.

Using *iif*

iif() (short for *immediate if*) returns one of two values, depending on the result of a Logical expression. iif() enables you to branch within a single statement. You can use iif() wherever you use any other expression. iif() is especially useful where an if statement is illegal, such as in calculated fields and reports. The syntax for an iif() is as follows:

iif (Condition, TrueValue, FalseValue)

For example,

```
1:    ans = iif(Total > 100, Yes, No)
```

The True and False sections of iif() simply return a value. They don't execute commands.

The Details of the *if* Statement

You're familiar with the if statement because you have used it several times in the examples of this book. if executes one set of commands or another, depending on the result of a Logical expression. When ObjectPAL comes to an if statement, it evaluates whether the expression is true. If the expression is true, ObjectPAL executes the statements in the TrueStatements sequence. If the expression isn't true, ObjectPAL skips the TrueStatements sequence. Then, if the optional else keyword is present, ObjectPAL executes the FalseStatements sequence. In both cases, execution continues after the endIf keyword.

For example:

```
if Condition then        ;If condition, then
    TrueStatements       ;execute these statements.
[else                    ;Otherwise,
    FalseStatements]     ;execute these statements.
endIf
```

The following is an example of an `if` statement using the `else` clause:

```
1:    if self.value < 0 then          ;If negative, then set
2:        self.font.color = Red       ;the font color to red, &
3:        message("Value is negative") ;display a message.
4:    else
5:        self.font.color = Black     ;Otherwise, color is black
6:        message("")                 ;and clear message.
7:    endIf
```

The `if` statement is highly flexible; you can nest `if` statements. Nesting an `if` statement means that any statement in `TrueStatements` or `FalseStatements` sequences also can be an `if` statement, as in the following example:

```
if Condition1 then       ;If condition1, then
    TrueStatements1      ;execute these statements.
else                     ;Otherwise,
    if Condition2 then   ;if Condition2, then
    TrueStatements2      ;execute these statements.
    endIf                ;End inside if block.
endIf                    ;End outside if block.
```

The following is an example of a nested `if` statement:

```
1:    if skillLevel = "Beginner" then
2:        if skillBox.color = "Red" then
3:            skillBox.color = "Green"
4:        endIf
5:    endIf
```

The following two examples demonstrate how to use compound conditions with and and or:

```
if Cond1 and Cond2 then  ;If both are true, then
    TrueStatements       ;execute these statements.
else                     ;Otherwise,
    FalseStatements      ;execute these statements.
endIf                    ;End of if block.
```

For example:

```
1:    if self.value > 0 and self.value < 10 then
2:        self.font.color = Yellow
3:        message("Balance is low")
4:    endIf
```

```
if Cond1 or Cond2 then   ;If either are True, then
    TrueStatements       ;execute these statements.
else                     ;Otherwise,
    FalseStatements      ;execute these statements.
endIf                    ;End of if block.
```

For example:

```
1:    if x = 1 or x = 2 then
2:        message("True")
3:    else
4:        message("False")
5:    endIf
```

One of the examples, "Basic Database Buttons," in Chapter 4, used the following keyword sequence:

```
1:    if   deleteRecord() then
2:        message("Record deleted")
3:    else
4:        message("Could not delete record")
5:    endIf
```

Line 1 tries to delete a record. If the delete is successful, the code after the then keyword and before the else keyword is executed. If the delete fails, the code after the else keyword and before the endIf keyword is executed.

If you wanted to check the data of a field before the user leaves it, you could use an if statement in the canDepart event of the field that you want to check. Essentially, canDepart asks for permission to leave the field. In other words, the canDepart event is triggered just before the cursor leaves the field, as in the following example:

```
1:    if self.value > 100 then
2:        eventInfo.setErrorCode(canNotDepart)
3:        msgStop("!!! Warning !!!","Value too large.")
4:    endIf
```

This example has more than one line of code between the if and endIf keywords. Take a close look at line 2. eventInfo is a variable. In essence, this eventInfo variable represents a packet that ObjectPAL sends from object to object. setErrorCode() is a method that works on this packet. In this case, setErrorCode() uses the CanNotDepart error constant to set the error code in the packet to the error code CanNotDepart. You can inspect this error code with the errorCode() method. Setting the error code in the packet in this way prevents the cursor from leaving the field.

The *switch* Block

You can use nested if statements to execute one set of commands out of many sets. ObjectPAL offers a better way, however, to make compound decisions: the switch block. switch executes a set of alternative statement sequences, depending on which of several conditions is met.

switch uses the values of the condition statements in each case to determine which sequence of statements to execute. Each case works like a single if statement, and the switch structure works like multiple, compound, or nested if statements.

As soon as the first case evaluates to True, the corresponding sequence of statements is executed and the remaining cases are skipped. If no case evaluates to True and the optional otherWise clause is present, the statements in otherWise are executed. If no case evaluates to True and no otherWise clause is present, switch has no effect. Following is the syntax:

```
switch
    case Condition1   :Statements1
    [case Condition2   :Statements2] ;Repeat as needed.
    [otherWise         :Statements3]
endSwitch
```

For example:

```
1:    switch
2:        case AmountField < 0      : message("We're in the red")
3:        case AmountField < 10     : message("Balance is very low")
4:        case AmountField < 100    : message("Balance is low")
5:        case AmountField > 1000   : message("Go spend some money")
6:        otherWise                 : message("Balance is looking good")
7:    endSwitch
```

This first example is formatted well because each resulting sequence of commands was short enough to fit nicely on a single line of code, but how do you keep your code readable when you need to use multiple lines of code in the resulting sequence? This next example shows how you can use compound expressions and execute multiple statements, and still keep the code very readable.

```
1:    switch
2:        case Field1 < 0 and Field2 = True
3:            :  ans = 1
4:                message("One")
5:                Page1.moveTo()
6:        case Field1 < 0 and Field2 = False
7:            :  ans = 2
8:                message("Two")
9:                Page2.moveTo()
10:        case Field1 >= 0 and Field2 = True
11:            :  ans = 3
12:                message("Three")
13:                Page3.moveTo()
14:        case Field1 >= 0 and Field2 = False
15:            :  ans = 4
16:                message("Four")
17:                Page4.moveTo()
18:    endSwitch
```

The *try* Block

Use try as your basic ObjectPAL error recovery tool. With try, you can attempt to execute a block of code. If all the commands succeed, execution skips to just after the endTry keyword. If any one command generates a critical error, the recovery block executes starting just after the onFail keyword.

Following is the syntax:

```
try
      [Statements]        ;The transaction block.
      [fail()]            ;Optional.
onFail
      [Statements]        ;The recovery block.
      [reTry]             ;Optional.
endTry
```

You can call the keyword reTry to execute the transaction block again, as in the following example:

```
 1:     var
 2:         nCounter    Number
 3:     endVar
 4:
 5:     nCounter = 1
 6:
 7:     try
 8:         Last_Name.postRecord()
 9:     onFail
10:       sleep(250)
11:       if nCounter >= 5 then
12:           msgStop("Warning", "Could not post record")
13:       else
14:           nCounter = nCounter + 1
15:           reTry
16:       endIf
17:     endTry
```

A method or procedure that generates a warning error or returns a False does not cause the onFail block to execute. You can raise warning errors to critical errors by using errorTrapOnWarnings(), as in the following example:

```
 1:     errorTrapOnWarnings(Yes)     ;Raise warning errors to critical
 2:                                  ;so try will catch them.
```

In addition, you can use the keyword fail() to force a branch to the onFail portion. Use this technique to force a block of code to fail, such as when a method or procedure returns a False. For example, type the following line of code in the pushButton method of a button.

```
 1:     ;Button :: pushButton
 2:     method pushButton(var eventInfo Event)
 3:         try
 4:             if not isfile("C:\\NOFILE.TXT") then fail() endIf
 5:             message("File exists.")
 6:         onFail
 7:             message("File does not exist.")
 8:         endTry
 9:     endMethod
```

You can nest fail() inside several procedure calls, far from where the block begins. If you decide in a recovery block that the error code is not what you expected, or if the error code is too serious to be handled in the current onFail block, call fail() again to pass it up to the next try block's onFail clause.

If no higher-level try block exists, the whole application fails. It cancels existing actions, closes resources, and causes a critical error. This is done by the implicit try block that ObjectPAL wraps around every method (see Figure 10.1).

FIGURE 10.1.

The error message you get when you call fail() *and* fail() *has no place to fail to.*

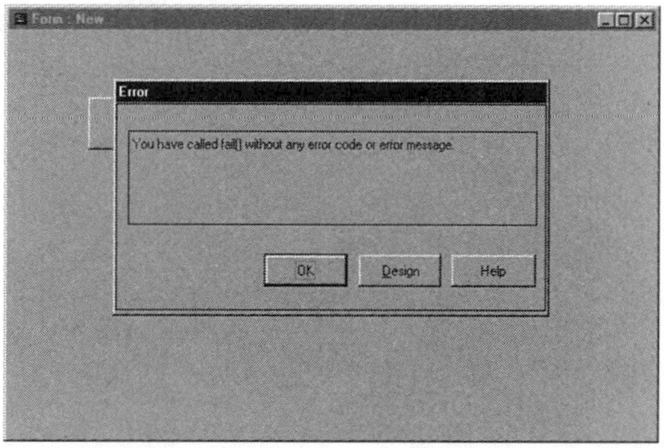

> **NOTE**
>
> ObjectPAL has two levels of errors that you need to keep in mind when using a try statement: warning and critical errors. Only critical errors generated in the try section will cause ObjectPAL to fail to the onFail section. To raise warning errors to critical errors, use errorTrapOnWarnings(Yes). The try statement and errors are discussed further in Chapter 29.

Using *try* to Test a Date in an Undefined Field

Suppose that you want to test whether the value in an undefined field is a valid date. How can you tell whether the user has typed a valid date into an undefined field? ObjectPAL doesn't have an isDate type method, so how do you test? One way to test whether the user typed in a valid date is to try to cast the value as a date. If the test fails, you know that the date isn't valid. Although blanks are normally a legal date, in this example, blanks are not allowed.

> You can find the TRY.FSL form on the disc in the \ANSWERS directory.

Step By Step

1. Change your working directory to the TUTORIAL directory and create a new form. Put an undefined field and a button on a new form. Label the button Test Date and name the field fldDate, and change its label to Enter date (see Figure 10.2).

FIGURE 10.2.

Set up form for tutorial.

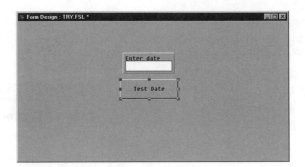

2. Add lines 3–9 to the pushButton method of the button.

```
 1:    ;TRY :: Button :: pushButton
 2:    method pushButton(var eventInfo Event)
 3:       try
 4:          if fldDate.isBlank() then fail() endIf
 5:          date(fldDate.value)
 6:          msgInfo("", "Valid date")
 7:       onFail
 8:          msgInfo("Warning", "Invalid date")
 9:       endTry
10:    endmethod
```

3. Check the syntax, save the form as TRY.FSL, and run it. Enter various dates into the field. Test each date after you've entered it by clicking on the button (see Figure 10.3). For example, try 1/8/65, 10/33/93, 001/1/1991, and a blank. This form uses isBlank() and a try structure to test whether the data typed into an undefined field is valid.

FIGURE 10.3.

ANSWERS\TRY.FSL demonstrates how to validate a date.

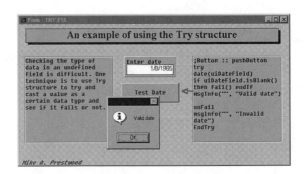

Analysis

In step 2, lines 3–9 make up the try block. Line 3 begins the structure with the keyword try. Line 4 uses an if statement along with the isBlank() method to test whether something was entered. If nothing was entered, the fail() procedure forces a fail, and the execution skips to onFail in line 7. If something was entered, the execution drops through to line 5. Line 5 attempts to cast the value in the fldDate field as a date. If the value is cast as a date, execution continues to line 6, which displays a message information box. After line 6 displays the message, the execution skips to endTry in line 9. If the casting of the fldDate field with the Date() procedure in line 5 fails, the execution skips to onFail in line 7.

Remember that, in a try structure, if any command in the try portion generates a critical error, the execution skips to onFail. If you don't care about blank entries, you can leave out the if statement, as in the following example:

```
1:    ;Button :: pushButton
2:    try                              ;Begin try block.
3:        date(fldDate.value)          ;Cast fldDate as a date.
4:        msgInfo("", "Valid date")    ;Display a message box.
5:    onFail                           ;Begin onFail block.
6:        msgInfo("", "Invalid date")  ;Display a message box.
7:    endTry                           ;End try block.
```

You can use a try block to add function to ObjectPAL. For example, this section showed you how to add an isDate() type of method. A try block is also a great way to put error checking into your application. You could surround a piece of code with a try structure and display a generic message if any command fails.

The Details of Looping

When you program, you often need to repeat a number of commands. One of the most important aspects of a programming language is its capability to loop—that is, to go through a series of commands a certain number of times. ObjectPAL has four ways to loop: scan, for, forEach, and while.

Using the *loop* and *quitLoop* Keywords

Because all four loops have two keywords in common, loop and quitLoop, this section addresses these before getting into the four loops. loop passes program control to the top of the nearest loop. When loop is executed within a for, forEach, scan, or while structure, it skips the statements between it and endFor, endForEach, endScan, or endWhile and returns to the beginning of the structure.

quitLoop exits a loop to the nearest endFor, endForEach, endScan, and so on. quitLoop immediately exits to the nearest for, forEach, endScan, or endWhile keyword. Execution continues with the statement that follows the nearest endFor, endForEach, endScan, or endWhile. quitLoop causes an error if it's executed outside a for, forEach, scan, or while structure.

The *while* Loop

A while loop enables you to execute a set of commands while a condition is true. Specifically, while repeats a sequence of statements as long as a specified condition evaluates to True. At the end of the set of commands, the condition is tested again. In a typical while loop, you must make the condition False somewhere in the set of commands.

```
while Condition       ;Test condition, if true
   [Statements]       ;execute these statements.
                      ;Don't forget to make
                      ;the condition false some place.
endWhile              ;Go back to while.
```

while starts by evaluating the Logical expression Condition. If Condition is False, the execution continues after endWhile. If Condition is True, Statements are executed. When the program comes to endWhile, it returns to the first line of the loop, which re-evaluates Condition. Statements are repeated until Condition evaluates to False.

Using a *while* Loop

This example demonstrates a simple while loop that counts to 10. It uses a counter variable to keep track of how many times to cycle through the loop.

You can find the LOOPS.FSL form on the disc in the \ANSWERS directory.

Step By Step

1. Change your working directory to the TUTORIAL directory and create a new form with a button labeled While loop.

2. Add lines 3–14 to the pushButton method of the While loop button.

   ```
   1:   ;LOOPS :: Button :: pushButton
   2:   method pushButton(var eventInfo Event)
   3:      var
   4:         Counter    SmallInt    ;Counter is a SmallInt.
   5:      endVar
   6:
   7:      Counter = 0               ;Variables must be
   8:                                ;initialized.
   9:      While Counter < 10        ;Start of while loop.
   10:        message(Counter)       ;Display Counter.
   11:        sleep(250)             ;Sleep for 1/4 second.
   12:        Counter = Counter + 1  ;Increments counter.
   13:      endWhile                 ;End of while loop.
   14:      message("Final value for Counter is " +
             StrVal(Counter))
   15:   endmethod
   ```

3. Check the syntax, save the form as LOOPS.FSL, and run the form. Click the While Loop button. Watch the status bar count from 0 to 9 in the loop and display the number 10 after the loop is finished (see Figure 10.4).

FIGURE 10.4.

Using for *and* while
loops.

Analysis

In step 3, line 4 declares Counter as a SmallInt variable. In line 7, Counter is initialized to 0. (All variables must be initialized before you use them.) Lines 9–13 form the while loop. When Counter is less than 10, lines 10–12 are executed. In line 12, the Counter variable is incremented. If you leave this line out, the counter will loop forever. (You'll have to use Ctrl+Break to exit the loop.) With while loops, you have to make the condition False at some point. This example uses a simple Counter variable that eventually makes the condition in line 9 False, which in turn ends the loop. Execution continues after endWhile.

This example uses a while loop as a counter. Normally, you would use a for loop for a loop that has a counter. while loops are useful for executing a set of commands as long as a condition is True. For example, you might execute a set of commands while the left character of a string is equal to Sm or while a box's color is red. The important thing to remember about a while loop is that it's your responsibility to make the condition False to exit the loop.

The *for* Loop

Use a for loop to execute a sequence of statements a specific number of times. You don't have to increment the counter in a for loop, as you must in a while loop.

```
for Counter [from startVal] [to endVal] [step stepVal]
    Statements
endFor
```

The three values startVal, endVal, and stepVal are values or expressions that represent the beginning, ending, and increment values. for executes a sequence of statements as many times as the counter specifies. The specific number of times is stored in Counter, and it is controlled by the optional from, to, and step keywords. You can use any combination of these keywords to specify the number of times that the statements in the loop should be executed. You don't have to declare Counter explicitly, but a for loop runs faster if you do. If you previously didn't assign a value to Counter, from creates the variable and assigns the value of startVal to it.

You can use `for` without the `from`, `to`, and `step` keywords. If `startVal` is omitted, the counter starts at the current value of `Counter`. If `endVal` is omitted, the for loop executes indefinitely—not too practical! Finally, if `stepVal` is omitted, the counter increments by 1 each time through the loop, as in the following example:

```
1:    ;Button :: pushButton
2:    for Counter from 1 to 3        ;Count from 1 to 3.
3:       Counter.view()              ;Execute these statements.
4:    endFor                         ;End for block.
```

Using the *for* Loop

This section demonstrates two `for` loops: with and without `step`. The first `for` loop counts to 5, and the second `for` loop counts to 20 by .5.

You can find the LOOPS.FSL form on the disc in the \ANSWERS directory.

Step By Step

1. Change your working directory to the TUTORIAL directory and open the LOOPS.FSL form you created in the previous example (or create it now). Place two buttons on the form and name one Simple for loop and the other For loop using step (see Figure 10.4 shown previously).

2. Add lines 3–9 to the `pushButton` method of the Simple for loop button.

```
 1:    ;LOOPS :: Button1 :: pushButton
 2:    method pushButton(var eventInfo Event)
 3:       var
 4:          Counter      SmallInt          ;Declare Counter.
 5:       endVar
 6:       for Counter from 1 to 5           ;Start of for loop.
 7:          msgInfo("Counter", Counter)  ;Commands to loop.
 8:       endFor                            ;End of for loop.
 9:       message("Note the final value for Counter is " +
              string(Counter))
10:    endmethod
```

3. Add lines 3–15 to the `pushButton` method of the For loop using step button.

```
 1:    ;LOOPS :: Button2 :: pushButton
 2:    method pushButton(var eventInfo Event)
 3:       var
 4:          Counter, CountTo    Number
 5:       endVar
 6:
 7:       CountTo = 20
 8:       CountTo.view("Enter a number")
 9:
10:       for Counter from 0 to CountTo Step .5
11:          message(Counter)
```

```
12:          sleep(250)
13:      endFor
14:
15:      message("Note the final value for Counter after loop
                 is " + string(Counter))
16:  endmethod
```

4. Check the syntax, save the form, and run it. Click the Simple for loop and For loop using step buttons. Watch the status bar as they loop.

Analysis

In step 2, line 4 declares Counter as a SmallInt variable. You also could use Number, LongInt, or AnyType. In fact, you could choose not to declare Counter at all, but that would be poor programming. Lines 6–8 make up the for loop. Line 6 sets up the Counter variable to count from 1 to 5 at the default increment step of 1.

Between for and endFor, you put all the commands that you want to loop through five times. In this case, a message information dialog box is displayed. Line 8 ends the for loop. Remember that, in a for loop, all the commands between for and endFor are executed once every time the loop is executed. Line 9 displays the final value for Counter, which is always one increment beyond the CountTo value.

In step 3, line 4 declares Counter and CountTo variables of type Number. Because of containership and encapsulation, you can use the same name (Counter) in both buttons. Line 7 initializes CountTo to 20, and line 8 displays it so that the user can either accept it or change it. Line 10 sets up the Counter variable to count from 0 to the value stored in CountTo at the increment step of .5.

Lines 10–13 make up the for loop. Line 11 displays the Counter in the status bar, and line 12 sleeps for a quarter second. Line 15 reminds you that the Counter value is always one increment beyond the value used in the last loop.

Using the *forEach* Loop

A forEach loop works similarly to a for loop. You use a forEach loop to move through the elements in a DynArray. (Chapter 11 discusses the DynArray data type and forEach loops.)

Using the *scan* Loop

You bought Paradox so that you could view, enter, and manipulate data. For the ObjectPAL programmer, the scan loop is very easy to use, and it's a powerful tool for manipulating the data in a table. In many ways, using a scan loop is similar to using a query in Interactive mode. In fact, there are occasions when using a scan loop is faster than doing a complicated query.

The scan loop is an extremely powerful tool that you can use to manipulate a whole table or, with the for keyword, a subset of a table. The scan loop scans a TCursor and executes ObjectPAL instructions. The syntax for a scan loop is as follows:

```
scan tcVar [for booleanExpression]:
    Statements
endScan
```

The colon at the end of the first line is required. It separates the first line from the following statements. scan starts with the first record in a TCursor and moves from record to record, executing Statements for every record. scan automatically moves from record to record through the table, so you don't need to call action(DataNextRecord) within your statements. When an indexed field is changed by a scan loop, the changed record moves to its sorted position in the table. Therefore, it's possible to encounter the same record more than once. As with all the loops discussed in this chapter, be sure to put statements that occur only once before the loop.

The for expression is used to filter the records. Only the records that match the expression are acted on. All other records are skipped. When you use the for keyword with scan, it must be followed by a colon to differentiate it from a for loop.

If you use ObjectVision, you're familiar with the @PROPER command, which takes a text field and converts the first letter of every word to a capital letter. Although ObjectPAL doesn't have a proper command, you can use the format() command to achieve the same result, as the next tutorial demonstrates.

Using a *scan* Loop to Make a Field Proper

Suppose that you want to use a scan loop to change a field to a proper format. This example uses a scan loop and the format() command to change a field named Name in the CUSTOMER.DB table to a proper format. Before you make drastic changes to a table, you should always make a backup copy. This section acquaints you with the script, the scan loop, and format().

You can find the PROPER.SSL form on the disc in the \ANSWERS directory.

Step By Step

1. Make TUTORIAL your working directory. Open the CUSTOMER.DB file. Change some of the last names to all uppercase or all lowercase.

2. Choose File | New | Script and type in lines 3–16.

```
1:    ;Script :: Run
2:    method run(var eventInfo Event)
3:       Var
4:          tc      TCursor
```

```
 5:        endVar
 6:
 7:        if msgQuestion("Question?",
            "Make Name field proper?") = "Yes" then
 8:           tc.open("CUSTOMER.DB")
 9:           tc.edit()
10:           scan tc:
11:              tc."Name" = format("cl,cc", tc."Name")
12:           endScan
13:           tc.endedit()
14:           tc.close()
15:           msgInfo("","All done converting Name field")
16:        endIf
17:     endmethod
```

3. Check the syntax, save the form as PROPER.SSL, and run the script. After the script has finished executing, reopen CUSTOMER.DB. Now the Name field is in a proper format.

Analysis

In step 2, line 4 declares tc as a TCursor variable. Line 7 asks for permission to continue using a message question box. If the answer is yes, then line 8 opens the TCursor and puts it in Edit mode in line 9. In this code, the scan loop uses only three lines: lines 10–12. Line 13 ends the Edit session, and line 14 closes the TCursor. Line 15 tells the user that the program is done.

WARNING

Don't use a scan loop whenever the record number for a record might change. As mentioned earlier, it's possible for records to be encountered more than once or to be missed entirely if the record number for any record is changed. Therefore, you should never use a scan loop when you delete records or when you change the value of the primary key. Instead, use a for loop with nRecords(). An example of this technique is presented in Chapter 16.

Summary

This chapter introduced you to control structures. Control structures are broken down into two categories: branching and looping in ObjectPAL. ObjectPAL offers the immediate if (iif), the if statement, the switch block, and the try block for branching. For looping, ObjectPAL offers the while, for, forEach, and scan loops.

The main reason you purchased Paradox was to manipulate data. Manipulating data depends on data types. Chapter 11 discusses the ObjectPAL data types.

Data Types

11

What are data types? Data typing is the classifying of data into categories such as string, number, and date. This classification is necessary so that the compiler knows how to treat and store the data. For example, a number takes up more room in memory than a small integer. Chapter 5 discussed the various types or classes of methods and procedures and they have been mentioned sporadically since then. In ObjectPAL, you can declare a variable to be any of the many variable types.

How do you know the available types? You already know the answer to that question. Remember near the end of Chapter 5 when you browsed through all the variable types and their methods by selecting View | ObjectPAL Quick Lookup? Those are the variable types you can declare a variable as (see Table 11.1). The methods and procedures that correspond to them are the methods and procedures you use to manipulate them.

Table 11.1. The 50-plus variable types available in ObjectPAL.

```
ActionEvent
AnyType
Application
Array
Binary
CDOUBLE
CHANDLE
CLONG
CLONGDOUBLE
CPTR
CWORD
Currency
DDE
DataTransfer
Database
Date
DateTime
DynArray
ErrorEvent
Event
FileSystem
Form
Graphic
```

KeyEvent

Library

Logical

LongInt

Mail

Memo

Menu

MenuEvent

MouseEvent

MoveEvent

Number

Ole

OleAuto

Point

PopUpMenu

Query

Record

Report

SQL

Script

Session

SmallInt

StatusEvent

String

System

TCursor

Table

TableView

TextStream

Time

TimerEvent

Toolbar

UIObject

ValueEvent

TIP

To create an up-to-date table of class names, create and run the following one-line script (see Table 11.1):

```
enumRTLClassNames("RTLCLASS.DB")
```

This one line of code creates a table with all the current class names. Why should you do this if the preceding table has all the classes? When Borland releases a new version of Paradox, you can run this same script and check to see whether Borland added any new classes of objects.

As soon as you find a variable type with which you want to work, you declare a variable as that type in a var block. As soon as the variable is declared, you can use any of the methods in its class to manipulate it. For example, as soon as a TCursor is defined, you then can use any of the TCursor type or class of methods to manipulate it:

```
1:    var                      ;This is the start of a var structure.
2:        tc    TCursor        ;Set variable types in between.
3:    endVar                   ;This marks the end of a var structure.
4:    tc.open("ZIPCODES.DB")
```

The tc variable is a handle to a TCursor object. A TCursor is a type of object. How do data types relate to object types? Data types are simply a very important subset of all the variable types. Remember that in ObjectPAL there are more than 50 object types. All these object types are variables that you can manipulate with the appropriate method or procedure. For example, you use the data types to store data in memory. As soon as data is stored in a particular type of variable in memory, you can use the methods associated with the type or class of variable to manipulate it. Table 11.2 describes the data types and the type of data each stores.

Table 11.2. The 18 data types.

Type	Description
AnyType	Can store any basic data type (for example, string, time, date, binary, and so on)
Array	An indexed collection of data
Binary	A handle to a binary object (machine-readable data)
Currency	Money (for example, $1.00, $.05, $12.50)
Date	Calendar data (for example, 12/25/93)
DateTime	Calendar and clock data combined (for example, 10:00:00 a.m. 12/25/65)
DynArray	A dynamic array
Graphic	A bitmap image

Type	Description
Logical	True or False
LongInt	Represents relatively large integer values
Memo	Holds lots of text
Number	Floating-point values
OLE	A link to another application
Point	Information about a location onscreen
Record	A user-defined structure
SmallInt	Used to represent integer values from –32,768 to 32,767
String	Letters (for example, A–Z, 0–9, %, and $)
Time	Clock data (for example, 11:04:00 PM)

Just as you define fields in tables to store various types of data, you declare variables in ObjectPAL to store data in memory. As you can see from Table 11.3, field types in a table are related to data types in memory.

Table 11.3. ObjectPAL data types, Paradox field types, and dBASE field types.

Data Type	Paradox Field Type	dBASE Field Type
AnyType		
Array		
Binary	Binary (B)	Binary (B)
Currency	Money ($)	
Date	Date (D)	Date (D)
DateTime	TimeStamp (@)	
DynArray		
Graphic	Graphic (G)	
Logical	Logical (L)	Logical (L)
LongInt	Long Integer (I)	Float Number (F)
Memo	Memo (M)	Memo (M)
Number	Numeric-N	Number (N)
OLE	OLE (O)	OLE (O)
Point		

continues

Table 11.3. continued

Data Type	Paradox Field Type	dBASE Field Type
Record		
SmallInt	Short (S)	Number (N)
String	Alpha (A)	Character (C)
Time	Time (T)	

NEW Term

Although Paradox 5 table structures support many more data types than previous versions of Paradox, as you can see, ObjectPAL picks up where Paradox and dBASE tables leave off. There are more ObjectPAL data types than either Paradox or dBASE field types. If you wanted to store time in a dBASE table, what field type would you choose? dBASE, unlike the Paradox table structure, does not offer a time format. One technique is to use a character field size of 12 to store the characters and then use ObjectPAL to manipulate them. The important thing to note at this point is that the data types in ObjectPAL enable you to deal with more types of data than the set Paradox and dBASE field types allow. You declare or cast a variable as a particular type of variable. This is known as *type casting*.

Using *AnyType*

AnyType is the catch-all variable type for the times when you can't predict what type of variable you'll need. Table 11.4 lists all the data types AnyType accepts.

Table 11.4. AnyType **variable types.**

Array	Graphic	Point
Binary	Logical	Record
Currency	LongInt	SmallInt
Date	Memo	String
DateTime	Number	Time
DynArray	OLE	

After you declare a variable as an AnyType variable, you can use the seven AnyType methods and procedures to manipulate it. These methods are very important because most of them are the core methods for the rest of the datatypes. Following is a description of each:

blank()	Returns a blank value
dataType()	Returns a string representing the data type of a variable
isAssigned()	Reports whether a variable has been assigned a value

isBlank()	Reports whether an expression has a blank value
isFixedType()	Reports whether a variable's data type has been explicitly declared
unAssign()	Sets a variable's state to unAssigned
view()	Displays in a dialog box the value of a variable

Implicit Casting with *AnyType*

Whenever the compiler comes across a variable or value in your code, it stores it in memory. If the value was not type cast, then the compiler casts it at that time. This can create problems. For example, if you type and run the following code, you'll get an error.

```
1:    ;Button :: pushButton
2:    method pushButton(var eventInfo Event)
3:       var
4:          n       Number       ;Declare n as a number.
5:       endVar
6:
7:          ;Set n to 40000.
8:          n = 2 * 20000      ;This gives an error.
9:          n.view()
10:   endmethod
```

Why? Isn't 40,000 within the range of a Number? Yes, but when ObjectPAL came across the equation `2 * 20000`, it had to store the numbers in memory and, because the first number is an integer, the numbers were stored in temporary small integer variables. Small integers cannot store the value 40,000. To fix this, change the preceding line 8 to the following:

```
8:          n = 2.0 * 20000.0
```

More on implicit casting of numbers later when SmallInt, LongInt, and Number are discussed. For now, following are some examples of implicit casting that you can type into a button if you want:

```
1:    x = 1                    ;x is cast as a SmallInt.
2:    view(Datatype(x))        ;Displays SmallInt.
3:
4:    x = 1.1                  ;x is cast as a Number.
5:    view(Datatype(x))        ;Displays Number.
6:
7:    x = 40000                ;x is cast as a LongInt.
8:    view(Datatype(x))        ;Displays LongInt.
9:
10:   x = "Clark Lupton"       ;x is cast as a String.
11:   view(Datatype(x))        ;Displays String.
```

In the next tutorial, you use the same variable as a number and then as a string without declaring it again. It demonstrates using an AnyType variable. Several of the tutorials in this chapter are demonstrated in the form \ANSWERS\DATATYPE.FSL (see Figure 11.1).

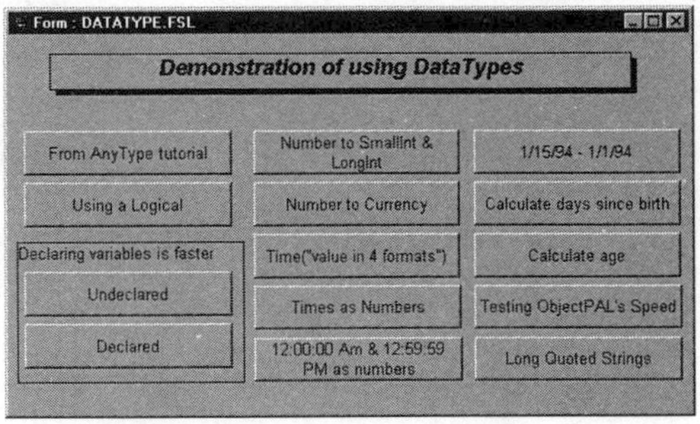

FIGURE 11.1.

The \ANSWERS\DATATYPE.FSL form demonstrates using datatypes.

Using AnyType

Suppose that you need to use *x* as both a number and a string. In this example, *x* is used first as a number, then as a string.

You can find the DATATYPE.FSL form on the disc in the \ANSWERS directory.

Step By Step

1. Change your working directory to the TUTORIAL directory, create a new form, and place a button on it.

2. Open the pushButton method of the button and add lines 3 through 13 to it.

```
1:    ;DATATYPE :: Button :: pushButton
2:    method pushButton(var eventInfo Event)
3:       var
4:          x     AnyType      ;Declare x as AnyType.
5:       endVar
6:
7:       x = 12.3          ;First use x as a Number.
8:       x.view()          ;View x.
9:       msgInfo("DataType", dataType(x))
10:
11:      x = "12.3"        ;Then use x as a String.
12:      x.view()          ;View x.
13:      msgInfo("DataType", dataType(x))
14:   endmethod
```

3. Check your syntax, save the form as DATATYPE.FSL, and run it. Click the button. First, you see the number 12.3 in a number-style viewer. After you click OK, you see a message box confirming that the current data type for x is indeed Number. After you click OK to the message box, you see the characters 12.3, but this time they are in a string box. After you click OK to the viewer, a message box confirms that x indeed is now a string.

Analysis

Line 4 declares *x* as an AnyType variable, which means that you can store many types of data in it without declaring it again. Line 7 sets *x* to the number 12.3. It is viewed with the number class viewer in line 8. In line 9, msgInfo() uses dataType() to confirm that the type of *x* has been declared by ObjectPAL as type Number.

Lines 11–13 are just like lines 7–9, except that in line 11, *x* is set to the string 12.3. In line 12, the string viewer is used when the user is shown the value. In line 13, msgInfo() confirms that, internally, ObjectPAL has changed the data type to a string type.

You Don't Have to Declare Variables, But You Should

Although *x* was specifically declared as an AnyType variable in the preceding tutorial, declaring an AnyType variable isn't required. Whenever the ObjectPAL compiler comes across a variable that hasn't been declared, it declares it as AnyType. In general, it's good programming practice to always declare variables. Get in the habit of declaring variables so that the compiler can catch typing mistakes. If you declare a siCounter variable at the form and accidentally type liCounter, the compiler will catch it when Properties | Compiler Warnings is turned on. Declaring variables also makes your code easier to read.

> **TIP**
>
> Is it a good idea to declare all variables as AnyType so that you don't have to worry about variable types? No. Avoid using AnyType variables because they slow down your code. Declaring a variable as an AnyType variable is the same as not declaring the variable at all. If you explicitly declare all your variables, your code will run faster. AnyType variables are useful when you don't know what the datatype will be.

Declared Variables Run Faster

This example demonstrates that declaring variables makes your code faster. In this example, you will create two buttons. Both buttons will beep, count to 2000, and beep again. You will notice that the button with the declared counter variable will have a shorter duration between beeps.

> You can find the DATATYPE.FSL form on the disc in the \ANSWERS directory.

Step By Step

1. Change your working directory to the TUTORIAL directory and create a new form with two buttons on it. Label them Undeclared and Declared.

2. Add lines 3–5 to the pushButton method of the Undeclared button.

```
1:    ;DATATYPE :: btnUndeclared :: pushButton
2:    method pushButton(var eventInfo Event)
3:        beep()
4:        for Counter from 1 to 2000 endFor
5:        beep()
6:    endmethod
```

3. Add lines 3–9 to the pushButton method of the Declared button.

```
 1:    ;DATATYPE :: btnDeclared :: pushButton
 2:    method pushButton(var eventInfo Event)
 3:        var
 4:            Counter SmallInt
 5:        endVar
 6:
 7:        beep()
 8:        for Counter from 1 to 2000 endFor
 9:        beep()
10:    endmethod
```

4. Check the syntax, save the form as DATATYPE.FSL, and run the form. Click both buttons. Notice how much closer together the beeps are for the button labeled Declared.

Analysis

Take a closer look at the preceding tutorial, for two reasons: to explain compile time binding and to review scope.

When the compiler compiles your source code, it casts all the variable types of the variables you have used. This process is called *binding*. When the compiler comes across a variable, it needs to find out whether the variable is declared. It first searches the method...endMethod structure in which the variable is used. Then, the compiler searches for a var...endVar structure above the current method...endMethod structure. After this, it searches the Var window of the object to which the code is attached, and then the Var window of the Object's container, and so on, until it reaches the form. When the compiler comes across the first occurrence of the variable declaration, it stops searching. If the compiler goes all the way up to the Var window of the form and the variable is not declared anywhere, then the variable is declared as AnyType.

The Logical Data Type

A variable declared as Logical can contain only two values: True or False. It can, however, be at any one of four states/values: unassigned, blank, True, or False. For example, type the following code on the pushButton method of a button:

```
 1:    ;Button :: pushButton
 2:    method pushButton(var eventInfo Event)
 3:       var
 4:          l       Logical            ;Declare l as a logical variable.
 5:       endVar
 6:
 7:          l.view("Unassigned")    ;View l.
 8:
 9:          l = blank()             ;Set l to blank.
10:          l.view("Blank")         ;View l.
11:
12:          l = True                ;Set l to True.
13:          l.view("True")          ;View l.
14:
15:          l = False               ;Set l to False.
16:          l.view("False")         ;View l.
17:    endmethod
```

A field that is either blank or zero is considered null. Whenever you store an empty field, Paradox and dBASE actually store a null. This condition for a field is called *blank* in Paradox. The ObjectPAL Logical data type is equivalent to the dBASE and Paradox Logical field types.

NEW
Term

In your ObjectPAL code, you can use Yes/No or On/Off in place of True/False, but the value that is displayed to the user is still dependent on the display format, usually True or False. If you type the following code on the pushButton method of a button, you'll notice that, although l is specifically set to Yes in line 7, True is displayed when line 8 displays a Logical view box.

```
 1:    ;Button :: pushButton
 2:    method pushButton(var eventInfo Event)
 3:       var
 4:          l       Logical
 5:       endVar
 6:
 7:          l = Yes
 8:          l.view()
 9:    endmethod
```

> **NOTE**
>
> Why use a Logical data type when you could just as easily use a String? One reason is that a Logical variable occupies only 1 byte of storage, and in computer languages, smaller is faster.

Many Methods Return a Logical

Nearly all methods and procedures return something. In many cases, they return a simple Logical True or False. You can use this return value to determine whether a method or procedure succeeded. For example, the following line of code displays True in the status bar if it can take the form out of Edit mode, and False if it can't:

```
1:    message(endEdit())
```

This simple example shows you that almost every method and procedure returns something. In most cases, you can use this fact to add error checking to your routines. For example, the following line of code displays the error box, complete with an error message when the locate() method returns False:

```
1:    if not Last_Name.locate("Last Name", "Unsicker") then
2:        errorShow()
3:    endIf
```

This and other error-checking techniques are addressed further in Chapter 29. The following tutorial shows that most methods and procedures return a value. You can return a value to a Logical variable and then display the value of the variable.

Showing a Returned *Logical* with *isFile*

Suppose that you want to find out whether a file exists. In this example, you use the fact that isFile() returns a Logical to determine whether a file exists.

> You can find the DATATYPE.FSL form on the disc in the \ANSWERS directory.

Step By Step

1. Change your working directory to the TUTORIAL directory, create a form, and add a button to it. Label the button Using a logical.

2. Add lines 3–8 to the pushButton method of the Using a Logical button.

```
1:    ;DATATYPE :: btnLogical :: pushButton
2:    method pushButton(var eventInfo Event)
3:        var
4:            lFileExist    Logical
5:        endVar
6:
7:        lFileExist = isFile("C:\\AUTOEXEC.BAT")
8:        lFileExist.view("Does file exist?")
9:    endmethod
```

3. Check the syntax, save the form as ISFILE.FSL, and run it. Click the button. The logical viewer will display True or False, depending on whether the file exists.

Analysis

In step 2, line 4 declares l as a Logical variable. isFile() returns True if the file exists and False if it doesn't. In line 7, l is given this return value from isFile(). Line 8 displays the result. Note that you passed view() a title to display.

Dealing with Numbers

Often, you need to calculate and convert numbers, such as time, date, currency, and so on. You either manipulate them or convert them so that you can manipulate them. For example, a Number is different from a String. When you have number characters stored in a String variable or Alpha field, you need to convert the string to a Number before you can use it in a calculation. ObjectPAL offers many methods and procedures for accomplishing this task. When declaring a variable as a number, you actually have three choices: Number, LongInt, and SmallInt.

Using *Number*

A Number variable is the most flexible of the three number data types and takes up the most room in memory. A Number variable can contain up to 18 significant digits, and the power of 10 can range from $\pm 3.4 * 10^{-4930}$ to $\pm 1.1 * 10^{4930}$.

Using *LongInt*

A LongInt (long integer) variable can range from $-2,147,483,648$ to $+2,147,483,647$. Why use a data type that is limited by design when you have more powerful data types? Very simply, LongInt variables occupy only four bytes of storage, and in computer terms, smaller means faster.

Using *SmallInt*

A SmallInt (small integer) variable can range from $-32,768$ to $+32,767$. Again, the reason you may want to use a data type that is limited by design when you have more powerful LongInt and Number data types is because a SmallInt variable occupies only two bytes of storage, which is half of what LongInt variables take up. A SmallInt uses up the least amount of bytes to store small numbers. In computer terms, smallest is best.

As introduced earlier, whenever ObjectPAL comes across a number, it casts the number internally as the most appropriate type of number. If the number is an integer, ObjectPAL casts the number as either a small integer, a large integer, or a number, depending on its size, as the following code indicates. If the number contains a decimal point, it is cast as a Number. If you want, type the following in the pushButton method of a button:

```
1:    msgStop("Datatype of 320", dataType(320))
```

242

This first example returns SmallInt, which takes up the smallest possible room in memory—only two bytes.

```
1:    msgStop("Datatype of 33000", dataType(33000))
```

This second example returns LongInt because the data is too large to be a SmallInt.

```
1:    msgStop("Datatype of 2200000000", dataType(2200000000))
```

This third example returns Number because the data is too large to be a LongInt.

```
1:    msgStop("Datatype of 320.0", dataType(320.0))
```

This final example is rather interesting. Although the value clearly can fit into a SmallInt, the compiler puts it into a Number because of the decimal point.

Why is this so important? Doesn't ObjectPAL take care of this for you? Well, yes and no. In most cases, you don't have to worry about it. The following code passes a syntax check but fails during runtime, however. You could pull your hair out for hours trying to figure out why. Type lines 3–8 into the pushButton method of a button and see whether you can figure out how to solve the problem. Following is the answer:

```
1:    ;Button :: pushButton
2:    method pushButton(var eventInfo Event)
3:       var
4:          si    SmallInt
5:       endVar
6:
7:       si = 60 * 24 * 24
8:       si.view()
9:    endmethod
```

When ObjectPAL comes to line 7, it casts all the numbers in the expression as small integers. When the code is executed and the three numbers are multiplied, they result in a number larger than a small integer can handle, and a runtime overflow error occurs (see Figure 11.2). This problem has many solutions, all of which rely on the fact that ObjectPAL looks at an expression as a whole and sets the data types to the lowest common data type. You simply have to make any one of the elements involved with the calculation a larger number type (for example, LongInt or Number). Line 7 can be replaced with any of the following:

Solution 1

```
7:    si = Number(60) * 24 * 24
```

The first solution casts the first number in the calculation as a Number. ObjectPAL internally casts the other two numbers, and the result is the same type.

Solution 2

```
7:    si = 60.0 * 24 * 24
```

The second solution simply uses a floating-point number (indicated by .0).

Solution 3

```
7:    si = 60. * 24 * 24
```

The third solution is a variation of the second solution. ObjectPAL checks only for the exist-ence of a decimal point in a number. It doesn't check whether the number is a floating-point number. The third solution uses this fact and simply adds a decimal point to the first of the three values.

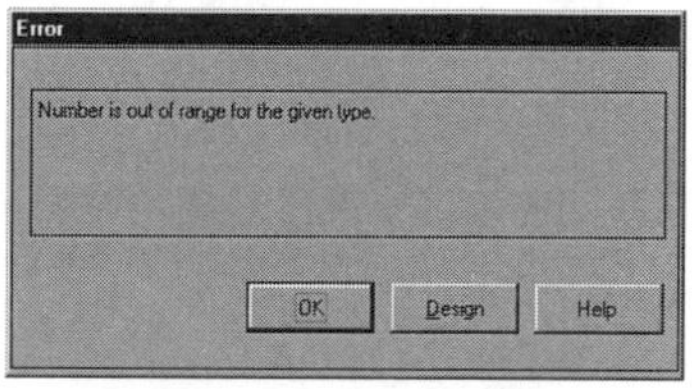

FIGURE 11.2.

If you multiply two numbers that result in a number out of a small integer's range, you get this error.

Converting *Number* to *SmallInt* and *LongInt*

Suppose that you want to convert a Number variable first to a SmallInt, and then to a LongInt. This example demonstrates how to do that. Often when you are assigning one variable to an-other, you will have to cast one variable as the other variable's type.

You can find the DATATYPE.FSL form on the disc in the \ANSWERS directory.

Step By Step

1. Change your working directory to the TUTORIAL directory. Open the DATATYPE.FSL form and put a button on it. Label the button Number to SmallInt and LongInt.

2. Add lines 3–18 to the pushButton method of the Number to SmallInt and LongInt button.

```
1:    ;DATATYPE :: btnNumber :: pushButton
2:    method pushButton(var eventInfo Event)
3:        var
4:            n       Number      ;Declare n as a number.
5:            si      SmallInt    ;Declare si as a SmallInt.
6:            li      LongInt     ;Declare li as a LongInt.
7:        endVar
8:
9:        n = 3.8             ;Set number to 3.8.
10:       n.view()            ;Displays 3.80.
11:
12:       si = SmallInt(n)    ;Set si to SmallInt of n.
13:       si.view()           ;Displays 3.
14:
15:       li = LongInt(n)     ;Set li to LongInt of n.
16:       li.view()           ;Displays 3.
```

```
17:
18:          n.view()           ;Displays 3.80.
19:      endmethod
```

3. Check the syntax, run the form, and click the button.

Analysis

The first viewer displays 3.80 in the number viewer. Note that the number is formatted according to the Windows number format (the Windows default is two decimal points). When you click OK, the number is converted internally to a SmallInt variable and is displayed in a SmallInt viewer. Note that the number was chopped down to just 3 and not rounded up to 4. Click OK again. The number is again converted, this time to a LongInt. It's displayed one last time to show you that the original *n* Number variable is unchanged.

Whenever you need a number of a different type than is declared, cast it. In this tutorial, you cast a number as both a long integer and a small integer, but you can go either way. Note, however, that converting a non-integer causes the decimal points to be stripped. For example, values of 1.1, 12.85, and .001 would be converted to 1, 12, and 0.

The Currency Data Type

A Currency variable can range from $3.4 * \pm 10^{-4930}$ to $1.1 * \pm 10^{4930}$, precise to six decimal places. The number of decimal places displayed depends on the user's Control Panel settings. The value stored in a table does not, however. A table stores the full six decimal places.

Currency variables are rounded, not truncated. Although internally, ObjectPAL keeps track of Currency variables to six decimal places, the values are rounded when they're displayed to the user. The number of decimal places depends on the user's Control Panel settings. Most users use the default of two decimal points.

If you type in the following code, ObjectPAL shows you a dialog box with the correctly rounded figure of 19.96 in a currency view box.

```
1:    ;DATATYPE :: btnPrice :: pushButton
2:    method pushButton(var eventInfo Event)
3:      var
4:        nPrice     Number        ;Declare nPrice as a number.
5:      endVar
6:
7:      nPrice = 19.9599           ;Set nPrice to a number.
8:      view(Currency(nPrice))     ;Displays 19.96.
9:    endmethod
```

The preceding code can be found on the disc under \ANSWERS\DATATYPE.FSL on the button labeled Number to Currency.

Although the number of decimal places depends on your Control Panel settings, the number will be rounded correctly. Also, note the alternative syntax used for view().

The *Date, Time,* and *DateTime* Data Types

Although Time and Date data types aren't related, each shares data and methods with the DateTime data type. When deciding between these three data types, ask yourself whether you need time in the same field as the date information. Whenever possible, separate date and time.

Using *Date*

There are differences between dates stored in a table and Date variables. The Date data type can be any valid date, whereas a Paradox table can store only dates from 01/01/100 to 12/31/9999. Use the methods and procedures to bridge the gap and manipulate date data.

You can store any valid date with the ObjectPAL Date data type. For example, type the following code into the pushButton method of a button.

```
1:    ;Button :: pushButton
2:    method pushButton(var eventInfo Event)
3:        msgInfo("Beginning Date", Date(0))
4:    endMethod
```

This displays the string 00/00/0000 in a dialog box. You can type in negative numbers that represent B.C. dates, too.

Subtracting Two Dates

If you subtract two dates, you get another date. For example, type the following code into the pushButton method of a button.

```
1:    ;Button :: pushButton
2:    method pushButton(var eventInfo Event)
3:        message(date("01/15/94") - date("01/01/94"))
4:    endMethod
```

This displays 01/14/0001 in the status bar. This information isn't very useful. Usually you want the number of days or years between the two dates. The trick to getting the number of days between two dates is to cast the result as a number. For example, type the following code into the pushButton method of a button:

```
1:    ;Button :: pushButton
2:    method pushButton(var eventInfo Event)
3:        var
4:           dBorn    Date
5:        endVar
6:
7:        dBorn = Date("01/20/1967")
8:        dBorn.view("Enter your birthdate")
9:        msgInfo("Days since your birthdate", Number(Today() - dBorn))
10:   endmethod
```

Calculating Years

To calculate years, simply cast the value as a year. For example, type the following code into the pushButton method of a button.

```
 1:    ;DATATYPE :: btnBirth :: pushButton
 2:    method pushButton(var eventInfo Event)
 3:       var
 4:          dBorn    Date
 5:       endVar
 6:
 7:          dBorn = Date("01/20/1967")
 8:          dBorn.view("Enter your birthdate")
 9:          msgInfo("Your age", Year(Today() - dBorn))
10:    endmethod
```

ANSWERS\AGE.FSL uses a similar technique to the one just demonstrated to display the number of seconds, hours, days, and years since your birth.

The *Time* Variable Type

A Time variable is stored in the format HH:MM:SS AM/PM. You could use any of the following as separators: blank, tab, space, comma, hyphen, slash, period, colon, or semicolon. If you want, type the following code into the pushButton method of a button. (All the following strings are legal time strings in ObjectPAL.)

```
 1:    ;DATATYPE :: btnTimeFormats :: pushButton
 2:    method pushButton(var eventInfo Event)
 3:       var t Time endVar
 4:          t = time("10:05:32 AM")
 5:          t.view()
 6:
 7:          t = time("10;05;32 AM")
 8:          t.view()
 9:
10:          t = time("10 05 32 AM")
11:          t.view()
12:
13:          t = time("10,05,32 AM")
14:          t.view()
15:
16:          t = time("10/05/32 AM")
17:          t.view()
18:    endMethod
```

Note that although you can type time value strings in any of the legal formats of ObjectPAL, the time in the displayed view box is the same because it is guided by the operating system. It's displayed to the user in the format specified in Control Panel. The values the user inputs must be in accordance with his or her Control Panel settings. Internally, ObjectPAL stores the time all the way down to the millisecond.

Using Time

Call `Time()` with no parameters to return the current time. For example, type the following code into the `pushButton` method of a button:

```
1:    ;Button :: pushButton
2:    method pushButton(var eventInfo Event)
3:       msgInfo("Current time", time())
4:    endMethod
```

Converting Regular Time to Military Time

The user's Control Panel settings determine whether the 12-hour time format (HH:MM:SS AM/PM) or the 24-hour (military) time format is used. Sometimes you want to convert 12-hour time to 24-hour time, however. The following routine casts a string as `Time` and then displays it in 24-hour format. You can type the code into the `pushButton` method of a button:

```
1:    ;Button :: pushButton
2:    method pushButton(var eventInfo Event)
3:       var
4:          s     String
5:          t     Time
6:       endVar
7:
8:       formatSetTimeDefault("hh:mm:ss am")
9:       s = "2:20:00 PM"
10:      t = time(s)
11:      formatAdd("24", "to(%h:%m:%s)na()np()")
12:      formatSetTimeDefault("24")
13:      t.view()
14:   endmethod
```

ANSWERS\WORLD-T.FSL demonstrates the preceding technique.

Subtracting Time

Suppose that you need to get the number of seconds between two times. Type the following into the `pushButton` method of a button:

```
1:    ;Button :: pushButton
2:    method pushButton(var eventInfo Event)
3:       var
4:          t1, t2 Time
5:       endVar
6:
7:       t1 = time("1:35:30 PM")
8:       t2 = time("2:10:15 PM")
9:       view(Number(t2 - t1) / 1000)            ;For seconds.
10:      view(Number(t2 - t1) / 1000 / 60)       ;For minutes.
11:      view(Number(t2 - t1) / 1000 / 60 / 60)  ;For hours.
12:   endmethod
```

Testing the Speed of ObjectPAL

Because there are many ways in ObjectPAL to accomplish a given task, you often need to test the speed of two routines. ObjectPAL offers, in the form of the time() method, an easy way to do this. To calculate the amount of time a scan loop takes on the Customer table, type in lines 3–19 into the pushButton method of a button.

```
1:    ;DATATYPE :: btnSpeed :: pushButton
2:    method pushButton(var eventInfo Event)
3:       var
4:          tcCustomer   TCursor
5:          tBeg, tEnd   Time
6:          nDifftime    Number
7:       endVar
8:
9:       tcCustomer.open("CUSTOMER.DB")    ;Open CUSTOMER.DB table.
10:
11:      tBeg = time()                     ;Grab current time.
12:      scan tcCustomer:
13:         ;Nothing here. Just testing scan time.
14:      endScan
15:      tEnd = time()                     ;Grab current time.
16:
17:      ;The following calculates the number of milliseconds that past.
18:      nDiffTime = number(tEnd) - number(tBeg)
19:      nDiffTime.view("Milliseconds to scan Customer table")
20:   endmethod
```

The preceding routine opens the Customer table, gets the current time, scans the customer table, and then gets the current time again. Finally, it calculates the duration of the scan loop and displays it in milliseconds. Use the preceding technique whenever you need to know how fast a set of commands takes in ObjectPAL; for example, when you discover two ways to accomplish the same task.

Using *DateTime*

DateTime is a special data type that stores both date and time values in the same variable. DateTime stores data in the form of hour-minute-second-millisecond year-month-day. The DateTime() method returns the current date and time. For example, to return the current date and time in a message information box, type line 3 into the pushButton method of a button.

```
1:    ;Button :: pushButton
2:    method pushButton(var eventInfo Event)
3:       msgInfo("Current Date & time", DateTime())
4:    endMethod
```

As an interesting experiment, you can cast values with the procedure DateTime() and display the results. This experimentation helps you to understand the numbers behind the DateTime datatype. For example, type line 3 into the pushButton method of a button.

```
1:    ;Button :: pushButton
2:    method pushButton(var eventInfo Event)
```

```
3:        msgInfo("Beginning Date/Time", DateTime(0))
4:     endmethod
```

Line 3 displays 12:00:00 AM, 00/00/0000 in a dialog box. This shows you that going back all the way to year 0 is legal in ObjectPAL. In fact, you can even use BC dates and times (negative numbers).

If you store data in an alphanumeric field type and later need to do a calculation on the value, you must cast the string in the field as a number. To cast a string as a number, use Number and DateTime() together. For example, type lines 3–8 into the pushButton method of a button.

```
1:     ;Button :: pushButton
2:     method pushButton(var eventInfo Event)
3:        var
4:           nBirth    Number
5:        endVar
6:
7:        nBirth = Number(DateTime("07:30:00 PM, January 20, 1967"))
8:        msgInfo("Lisa's Birthday", nBirth)
9:     endMethod
```

The preceding line 8 displays the number 62042700600000 in a dialog box. This isn't very useful, but you can use this code in a calculation with values (including another DateTime converted to a Number).

Dealing with Characters

When you're dealing with characters, your first choice should be the String data type. The String data type allows strings as long as 32,767 characters.

Using Quoted Strings

A quoted string typed into a method can't be more than 255 characters long. You can, however, concatenate many strings together and display the result. For example, the following assigns values to a string variable that together add up to more than 255 characters and then displays it. If you want to participate in a typing exercise, type in lines 3–11 to the pushButton method of a button.

```
1:     ;DATATYPE :: btnQuote :: pushButton
2:     method pushButton(var eventInfo Event)
3:        var
4:           sNote    String
5:        endVar
6:
7:        sNote = "The final stage in the evolution of a star,"
8:           + " whose original mass was from 1.4 to 2.5 times greater then our Sun."
9:           + " Gravitational collapse caused the star to contract to a sphere with"
10:          + " a small radius of 10 to 20 kilometers, consisting mainly of free
             neutrons."
11:          + " The density of a neutron star is a hundred million million times "
12:          + "(10 to the 14) greater than the density of water."
```

```
13:             + " Some rotating neutron stars evolve into pulsars."
14:         msgInfo("Neutron Star", sNote)
15:     endmethod
```

Using Null Characters

Use " " to represent an empty string. This is equivalent to the null character. Alternatively, you can use the blank() method to empty a string. For example, type lines 3–10 into the pushButton method of a button.

```
1:     ;Button :: pushButton
2:     method pushButton(var eventInfo Event)
3:         var
4:             s       String
5:         endVar
6:
7:         s = "Bradley Scott Unsicker"
8:         s.view()                  ;Displays Bradley Scott Unsicker.
9:         s.blank()                 ;Set s to null.
10:        s.view()                  ;Displays null.
11:    endMethod
```

Line 9 empties, or blanks out, the string. This is only one technique to empty a string. You also could replace line 6 with either of the following:

```
1:     s = ""
2:     s = blank()
```

Embedding Codes in Strings

Sometimes you might want to code some special characters or backslash codes to add to a string when it's displayed to the user. Special characters are ANSI characters not found on the keyboard. Backslash codes are the way to include some special characters in ObjectPAL. For example, \t represents a tab.

You use the string procedure chr() to display an ANSI code. Suppose that you're going to display a message to the user and you want to embed a few returns (ANSI character 13) into the text. You could use the following code (see Figure 11.3):

```
1:     ;Button :: pushButton
2:     method pushButton(var eventInfo Event)
3:         var
4:             sThreat    String
5:         endVar
6:
7:         sThreat = "You have violated the license agreement. Send me money."
8:         msgInfo("Message from programmer", "Warning!" + chr(13) + chr(13) +
            sThreat)
9:     endMethod
```

CHR.FSL demonstrates the technique of using chr(13).

This technique can add a little extra flair to your applications that other programmers might not think to include.

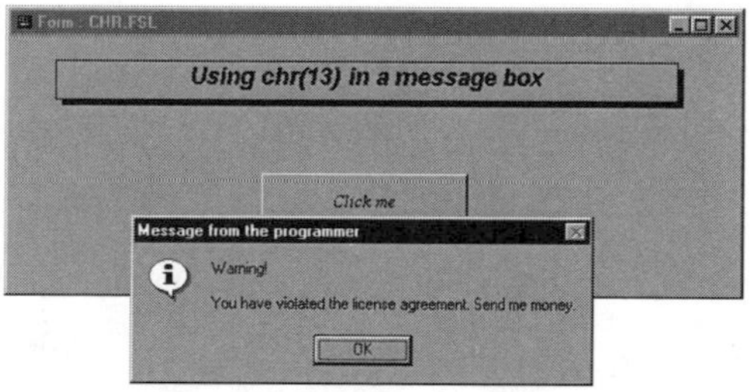

FIGURE 11.3.

An example of using the chr() *procedure to format text within a message information dialog box.*

A *keycode* is a code that represents a keyboard character in ObjectPAL scripts. A keycode can be an ASCII number, an IBM extended keycode number, or a string that represents a keyname known to Paradox. **NEW Term**

TIP

It would be easier to use the Windows and C++ standard escapes:

```
chr(13)  = \r = \n = <enter>
\t = <tab>
\b = <backspace>
```

The *Memo* Data Type

When you need to work with a string longer then 32,767 characters, use a Memo variable. As soon as you set up a Memo variable, you can use writeToFile() and readFromFile() to set and retrieve data from a Memo file. Memo fields can be as large as 512MB!

Three of the Memo type methods are of particular interest for manipulating a Memo variable: memo(), readFromFile(), and writeFromFile(). Following are descriptions of the three:

```
memo()           ;Casts a value as a Memo
readFromFile()   ;Reads a memo from a file
writeToFile()    ;Writes a memo to a file
```

The Array Data Type

An *array* is a group or series of related items identified by a single name and referenced by an index. An array is a special type of variable. It enables you to store a group of elements identified by a single name. Arrays are stored in consecutive locations in memory. Think of each one of these locations as being a cell reserved for your data; very similar to a single column Paradox table. If, for example, you declare an array with five elements, you can put a value directly in **NEW Term** cell three and later pull it out. Following this analogy, an array is very similar to a one-field table. Arrays are limited to 65,535 elements.

Using a Static Array

There are two types of arrays: *static* and *resizeable*. A static array has a fixed number of elements and uses slightly less memory than a resizeable array. A resizeable array, however, can be resized. The size of a static array is set when you declare the array, and a resizeable array is set in code after you declare it. The following is the syntax model to declare a static array:

arrayName **Array**[*size*] **dataType**

For example, the following declares a three-element array ready to store three small integers:

```
1:    var
2:        arNumbers    Array[3] SmallInt
3:    endVar
```

As soon as the array is declared, you can reference any of the elements of the array directly:

arrayName[*element*] = value

For example, the following sets the second and third elements in arNumbers to 10 and 20:

```
1:    arNumbers[2] = 10
2:    arNumbers[3] = 20
```

As soon as the elements of the array have values, you can retrieve the values much like you retrieve values from regular variables and fields. For example, the following displays the second element in the array in the status bar:

```
1:    message(arNumbers[2])
```

If you think that using an array is just like using multiple variables, you're right. One benefit of using arrays is that they group multiple variables into a single group of variables called an array. This gives you a way to address a set of values. For example, type the following piece of code into the pushButton method of a button. It uses a three-element array to store a user's first, middle, and last name. Then it displays all three variables with a single line of code.

```
1:    ;Button :: pushButton
2:    method pushButton(var eventInfo Event)
3:        var
4:            arName Array[3] String    ;Declare a 3 element fixed array.
5:        endVar
6:
7:        arName[1] = "Lester"          ;Set first element of array.
8:        arName[2] = "Earl"            ;Set second element of array.
9:        arName[3] = "Prestwood"       ;Set third element of array.
10:
11:       arName.view()                 ;View array.
12:   endmethod
```

Using a Resizeable Array

If you don't know the size of the array needed at declaration, use a resizeable array. The following is the syntax model to declare an array variable:

```
arrayName Array[] DataType
```

After you declare a resizeable array, use the setSize() method to set its size. As soon as the array is declared and its size is set, you can reference any of the elements of the array the same way you reference the elements of a static array. For example, type the following code into the pushButton method of a button. It declares a resizeable array, sets its size to 10, and fills it with numbers:

```
1:      ;Button :: pushButton
2:      method pushButton(var eventInfo Event)
3:          var
4:              myArray     Array[] SmallInt
5:              Counter     SmallInt
6:          endVar
7:
8:          myArray.setSize(10)
9:
10:         for Counter from 1 to 10
11:             myArray[Counter] = Counter
12:         endFor
13:
14:         myArray.addLast(100)
15:
16:         myArray.view()
17:     endmethod
```

Note that line 14 uses the addLast() method to add one additional element to the array before displaying it.

The following tutorial shows you how to loop through an array using a for loop with the size() method. This technique is important because an array can't use a forEach loop. (A forEach loop applies only to dynamic arrays.) Both forms ARRAY.FSL and ARRAYS.FSL in the ANSWERS directory demonstrate using arrays, dynamic arrays, and records (see Figures 11.5).

FIGURE 11.4.

\ANSWERS\ARRAY.FSL demonstrates using sets of information.

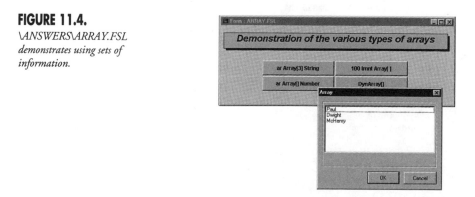

FIGURE 11.5.
ANSWERS\ARRAYS.FSL.
Use the array, DynArray,
and record data types to
store sets of information.

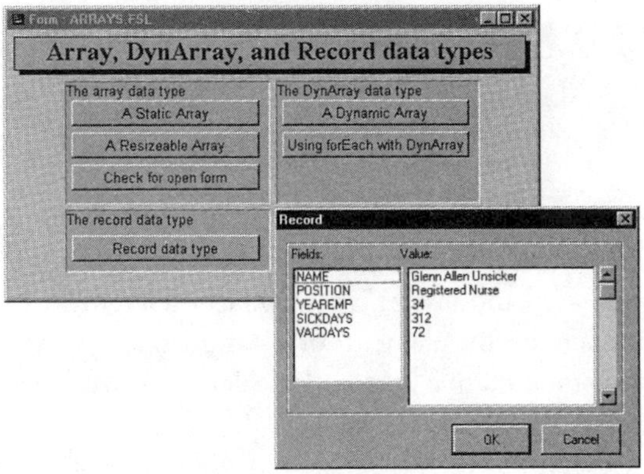

Using an Array and *enumFormNames* to Find an Open Form

Suppose that you want to use an array with the enumFormNames() procedure to check for an open form. If the form is not open, display all the open forms in an array view box.

You can find the ARRAYS.FSL form on the disc in the \ANSWERS directory.

Step By Step

1. Change your working directory to the TUTORIAL directory and create a new form. Place a button labeled Check for open form on it.

2. In the pushButton method of the button, type lines 3–18:

```
1:    ;Button :: pushButton
2:    method pushButton(var eventInfo Event)
3:       var
4:          arForms        Array[] String
5:          siCounter      SmallInt
6:       endVar
7:
8:       enumFormNames(arForms)
9:
10:      for siCounter from 1 to arForms.size()
11:         if arForms[siCounter] = "Arrays" then
12:            msgInfo("Found", "Form 'Arrays' is open")
13:            return
14:         endIf
15:      endFor
16:
17:      msgInfo("Not Found", "Form 'Arrays' is not open")
18:      arForms.view("Current forms open")
19:   endmethod
```

3. Check the syntax, save the form as ARRAY.FSL, and run it. Click the button. A dialog box indicates whether the form is open. After you click OK, the routine either stops or displays all the open forms. If a form with the name `Arrays` is open, the routine stops. Otherwise, an array view box displays all the open forms.

Analysis

In step 2, line 4 declares a resizeable array, `arForms`, that is populated in line 8 with `enumFormNames()`. Note that you don't have to set the size of the resizeable array ahead of time. Line 5 declares a `SmallInt` variable named `siCounter`. Line 10 uses `siCounter` to scan through the array from the first element to however many elements are in the array. This is determined by `arForms.size()`. Line 11 checks to see whether the current array element is `Arrays`. If it is, a message information box is displayed in line 12, and execution stops in line 13 with the keyword `return`. If the element is not `Arrays`, the loop continues. This cycle continues until either `Arrays` is found or the end of the array is reached. If the routine is never exited, line 17 tells the user that the form isn't open. Line 18 shows the user all the currently open forms.

The Details of the DynArray Data Type

A *DynArray* (dynamic array) is very similar to a regular array, except that it uses address names rather than index numbers. Just as static and resizeable arrays are for using sets of data, so is the DynArray. If you can imagine an array is similar to a single column Paradox table, then a DynArray is similar to a two-column Paradox table with the first column being the primary key. The number of elements (indexes) you can have in a DynArray is limited only by memory. An index can be up to 255 characters and is sorted in alphabetical order.

Of the many DynArray methods, the following are some of the most useful:

`contains()`	Searches a DynArray for a pattern of characters.
`empty()`	Removes all items from a DynArray.
`getKeys()`	Loads a resizeable array with the indexes of an existing DynArray.
`removeItem()`	Deletes a specified item from a DynArray.
`size()`	Returns the number of elements in a DynArray.

The following is the syntax model to declare a DynArray:

```
DynArrayName    DynArray[] dataType
```

The following declares dyn1 as a DynArray:

```
1:    var
2:        dyn1    DynArray[] SmallInt
3:    endVar
```

As soon as the array is declared, you can reference any of the elements of the DynArray directly:

```
DynArrayName[ElementName] = value
```

The following creates two elements in dyn1 and sets their values:

```
1:    myDynArray["Last_Name"] = "Megan"
2:    myDynArray["First_Name"] = "Miles"
```

As soon as the elements of a DynArray have values, you can retrieve the values much like you retrieve values from a regular array. Rather than using a numbered index, however, you use named indexes. For example, the following displays the First_Name element in the array in the status bar:

```
1:    message(myDynArray["First_Name"])
```

Now look at a completed example. Type lines 3–10 in the pushButton method of button.

```
1:    ;Button :: pushButton
2:    method pushButton(var eventInfo Event)
3:       var
4:           myDynArray    DynArray[] String
5:       endVar
6:
7:       myDynArray["Last_Name"] = "Megan"
8:       myDynArray["First_Name"] = "Miles"
9:
10:       myDynArray.view()
11:    endmethod
```

When you run the preceding code, note that the indexes are in alphabetical order.

Using *forEach*

The forEach structure enables you to loop through a DynArray, much like scan enables you to loop through a table. The syntax for forEach is as follows:

```
forEach VarName in DynArrayName
     Statements
endForEach
```

For example:

```
1:    forEach sElement in Dyn1              ;Scan through DynArray for sElement.
2:        message(DynArrayVar[sElement])    ;Display element on status bar.
3:        sleep(500)                        ;Wait for .5 seconds.
4:    endForEach                            ;End for loop.
```

The next section shows you how to move through a DynArray using a forEach loop.

Using *forEach* with *sysInfo()*

Suppose that you want to use a forEach loop to move through a DynArray of your system information, showing the user each element until you get to the IconHeight element. In addition to the forEach loop, this example acquaints you with sysInfo().

You can find the ARRAYS.FSL form on the disc in the \ANSWERS directory.

Step By Step

1. Create a new form and add a button to it. Label the button Using forEach with DynArray.

2. Add lines 3–15 to the pushButton method of the Using forEach with a DynArray button.

```
1:    ;Button :: pushButton
2:    method pushButton(var eventInfo Event)
3:        var
4:            dynSys    DynArray[] Anytype
5:            sElement String
6:        endVar
7:
8:        sysInfo(dynSys)
9:
10:       forEach sElement in dynSys
11:           if sElement = "IconHeight" then quitLoop endIf
12:           msgInfo(sElement, dynSys[sElement])
13:       endForEach
14:
15:       dynSys.view()
16:    endmethod
```

3. Check the syntax, run the form, and click the button. A message information dialog box appears for each element of the DynArray. Rather then cycle through all 30 bits of information, the program stops after the most important information is displayed. At the end of this parade of system information, a DynArray view box shows you all the elements at once.

Analysis

In step 2, line 4 declares the DynArray dynSys. Note that no size is indicated in line 3 or in the body of the code. Line 5 declares sElement as a string variable. In line 8, the sysInfo() procedure is used to put information about your system into the DynArray. s is used in line 10 to store the index name, which is used in lines 11 and 12. Lines 10–13 comprise the forEach block, which moves through each element in the DynArray, checking to see whether the element name is equal to IconHeight. If it is equal, the loop is exited with the keyword quitLoop. If the loop hasn't reached IconHeight yet, the element name and value are displayed. Finally, line 15 shows the complete DynArray all at once. In this case, a view is a better way to see all the elements of the array than looping through and showing one element at a time.

This simple example merely shows you how to loop through a DynArray and acquaints you with sysInfo(). Normally, you will do much more than this example does, using or manipulating each element as you go.

Using Custom Data Types

A custom data type is a way for you to create your own data type. You do this in a Type structure in either the Type window or in the event, much like you declare variables and constants. That is, the scope and instance of a custom type follows the same rules as a var block. The following is the syntax model:

```
type
   UserType = ExistingType
endType
```

Borland renamed the old Currency type of Paradox tables to Money, but left ObjectPAL to the same old Currency data type. If you don't like this inconsistency, then you could declare a new variable type called Money and use it in place of Currency.

```
1:    Type                        ;Begin type block.
2:         Money = Currency       ;Set custom types.
3:    endType                     ;End type block.
```

After you do this, you could use either Currency or Money whenever you deal with money. You could use either line 2 or line 6 in the following code (lines 1–3 and 5–7 declare total as a Currency data type).

```
1:    var
2:       Total       Currency
3:    endVar

1:    var
2:       Total       Money
3:    endVar
```

You will put custom types to use when you pass an Array or DynArray variable to a custom method or procedure later in Chapter 23. For now, take a closer look at the type block. Another use of the type block is to define a data type as a set or record of existing types. For example, enter lines 3–23 into the pushButton method of a button.

```
1:    ;Button :: pushButton
2:    method pushButton(var eventInfo Event)
3:       type                          ;Start type block.
4:          ctEmployee = Record        ;Start record block.
5:             Name       String       ;Set elements of record.
6:             Position   String       ;type employee.
7:             YearEmp    SmallInt
8:             SickDays   SmallInt
9:             VacDays    SmallInt
10:            endRecord                ;End record block.
11:      endType                       ;End type block.
12:
13:      var                           ;Begin var block.
14:         emp ctEmployee             ;Set emp to employee.
15:      endVar                        ;End var block.
16:
17:      emp.Name = "Glenn Allen Unsicker"
18:      emp.Position = "Registered Nurse"
19:      emp.YearEmp = 34
20:      emp.SickDays = 312
```

```
21:        emp.VacDays = 72
22:
23:        emp.view()                        ;View emp record.
24:    endmethod
```

As soon as a custom type is defined as a record, you can deal with a set of variables all at once.

Summary

The capability to manipulate data types is the core of every programming language. You now should understand that ObjectPAL is a very strong and complete programming language with powerful data types. With SmallInt, LongInt, and Number data types, you can deal with almost any number to a precision of 16 decimal points. Date, Time, and DateTime data types give you the capability to deal with the passage of time. String and Memo types enable you to manipulate characters. With Array, DynArray, and Record data types, you can manipulate sets of data. The study of data types in ObjectPAL concludes this book's discussion of the individual elements of ObjectPAL. Now that you know about all the elements of ObjectPAL, Chapter 12 brings the methods, procedures, properties, and constants of ObjectPAL into focus.

Categories of
Commands in
ObjectPAL

12

You've learned about many elements of ObjectPAL and used many of the commands. The goal of this chapter is to bring together the knowledge you have gained so far by giving you a formal review of the types of commands available in ObjectPAL: methods, procedures, constants, and properties. You can type most of the examples in this chapter (the ones you can type are indicated in the text).

Using Methods and Procedures

NEW
Term

The most often used types of commands are methods and procedures in the runtime library. The *runtime library* (RTL) is the predefined set of methods and procedures used for operating on objects (see Figure 12.1). The Types and Methods tab from the ObjectPAL Quick Lookup dialog box is the runtime library. (To display the ObjectPAL Quick Lookup dialog box, select View | ObjectPAL Quick Lookup.) Methods and procedures differ from events in that they actually do something tangible that you specify. The primary use of an event is to trigger a built-in method (an event), such as `open`, `newValue`, `mouseDown`, and `action`. An event triggers a series of code that you put between `method` and `endMethod`.

FIGURE 12.1.

The Types and Methods tab from the ObjectPAL Quick Lookup dialog box.

NEW
Term

Here are two quick definitions to remind you about the difference between a method and a procedure.

`method`—A function or command in ObjectPAL that acts on an object. A method uses dot notation to work on an object, as in `object.method()`.

`procedure`—A function or command in ObjectPAL that has no object to work on. The programmer doesn't specify an object.

The following is an example of using the `open()` method. You can type lines 3–7 into the `pushButton` of a button (make sure that your working directory is set to `TUTORIAL`).

```
1:    ;Commands :: btnMethod :: pushButton
2:    method pushButton(var eventInfo Event)
3:       var
4:          f       Form
```

```
5:        endVar
6:
7:        f.open("OV-LIKE.FSL")
8:    endMethod
```

open() is the method and the f form variable is the object. A procedure, on the other hand, has no object to work on.

> ANSWERS\COMMANDS.FSL contains all the code from this chapter. For practice, you should type in all the code from this chapter yourself. If you run into trouble, then open this form to see what went wrong.

The following is an example of using the isDir() procedure. Type line 3 into the pushButton method of a button.

```
1:    ;Commands :: btnProcedure :: pushButton
2:    method pushButton(var eventInfo Event)
3:        view(isDir("C:\\WINDOWS"))
4:    endMethod
```

isDir() is the procedure. It checks whether a directory exists.

It's not always necessary to keep in mind the difference between a method and a procedure. This book takes a formal look at the ObjectPAL language. It's enough to know that methods and procedures are two types of commands.

Using the *action()* Method

One method in the runtime library opens up a whole world of commands—the action method. As an ObjectPAL programmer, you're interested in five action constant classes: ActionDataCommands, ActionEditCommands, ActionFieldCommands, ActionMoveCommands, and ActionSelectCommands. Use these commands with the action() method. The syntax for action constants is as follows:

ObjectName.action(ActionConstant)

ObjectName is the name of the object on which you want the action to occur, such as theBox or Last_Name. The actionConstant can be any constant category whose name starts with action. If you want, you can precede this expression with an object path, as in the following:

```
1:    f.pge3.tf.action(DataNextRecord)
```

f is a handle to another form (see Chapter 13). pge3 and tf are the names of two objects contained in the form (the third page and its table frame). The constant DataNextRecord moves the cursor forward one record (if possible).

Using *Action* Constants

The constants in the `ActionDataCommands` category deal with data in a table as a whole (see Figure 12.2). They are used for navigating the pointer in a table, locking a record, posting a record, toggling Edit mode, and positioning the record pointer. Following are three examples:

```
1:      action(DataPrint)              ;Prints a form or table view.
2:      action(DataTableView)          ;Open the master table in a window.
3:      action(DataSaveCrosstab)       ;Writes the crosstab data
4:                                     ;to :PRIV:CROSSTAB.DB.
```

FIGURE 12.2.

*ActionDataCommands
deal with data as a whole.*

ActionEditCommands

In general, the constants in the `ActionEditCommands` category are used for altering data within a field (see Figure 12.3). With these constants, you can copy text to the Clipboard, enter persistent field view, access the help system, and search your text. Following are three examples:

```
1:      action(EditDropDownList)     ;Drops down pick list.
2:      action(EditEnterMemoView)    ;Enters memo view.
3:      action(EditPasteFromFile)    ;Pastes from file into current field.
```

FIGURE 12.3.

*ActionEditCommands
alter data within a field.*

ActionFieldCommands

The constants in the `ActionFieldCommands` category are used for moving between field objects (see Figure 12.4). With these constants, you can invoke and control tab order. You can move the focus forward or backward in the tab order. You can ignore the tab order and move up, down, left, or right. You can even move from one table frame to another. Following are three examples:

```
1:    action(FieldRotate)      ;Rotates columns in a table frame
2:    action(FieldNextPage)    ;Moves to the next page in a form
3:    action(FieldForward)     ;Moves one field forward
```

FIGURE 12.4.

*ActionFieldCommands
are used for moving from
field to field.*

ActionMoveCommands

The constants in the `ActionMoveCommands` category are used for positioning within a field object (see Figure 12.5). With these constants, you can move to the beginning or end of a field, move left one word, or scroll a field up or down. In general, these commands behave differently in a memo field than they do in a set of fields. Following are three examples:

```
1:    action(MoveEnd)              ;Moves to the end of the document or
2:                                 ;to last field.
3:    action(MoveLeftWord)         ;Moves cursor to word on the left.
4:    action(MoveScrollPageDown)   ;Scrolls the page image down.
```

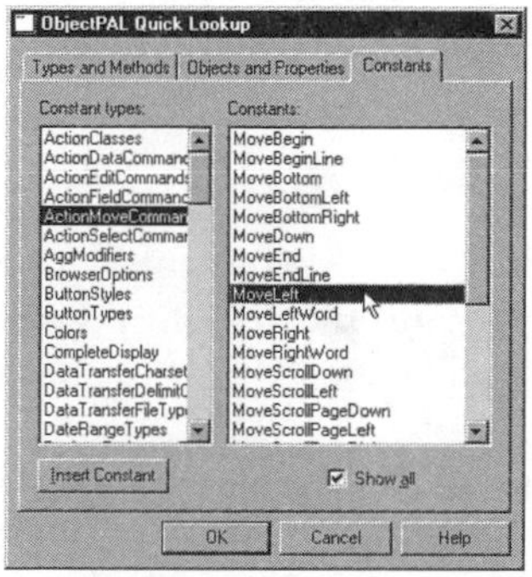

FIGURE 12.5.

*ActionMoveCommands
are used for positioning
within a field.*

ActionSelectCommands

The `ActionSelectCommands` constants are similar to the `ActionMoveCommands` constants, but you use them to select data within a field object (see Figure 12.6). With these constants, you can select from the current position to the beginning of the document. Following are three examples:

```
1:    action(SelectEnd)          ;Select to the end.
2:    action(SelectLeft)         ;Selects one character to the left.
3:    action(SelectSelectAll)    ;Selects the entire document.
```

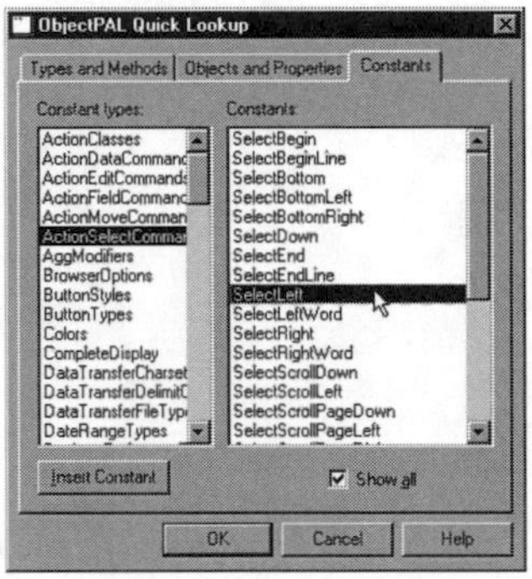

FIGURE 12.6.

ActionSelectCommands
are used for selecting data
within a field.

ANSWERS\CONSTANT.FSL demonstrates how to use move and select constants.

Browse through the online constants section by selecting View | ObjectPAL Quick Lookup and selecting the Constants tab. Select the categories whose names start with `action`. These constants are your gateway to more powerful data manipulation and, therefore, to more powerful applications.

> **TIP**
>
> If you find a constant that is not self-explanatory, search in the help for Types of Constants for a complete list of the constants, along with a description for each.

Trapping *action* Constants

In addition to executing `action` constants, you can trap for them. The basic idea is to use the `action` method and inspect the `eventInfo` variable. For example, to trap for when the form enters edit mode, type lines 3–6 in the page's `action` method.

```
1:    ;Commands :: Pge1 :: action
2:    method action(var eventInfo ActionEvent)
3:        if eventInfo.id() = DataBeginEdit then
```

```
4:          DoDefault    ;Finish moving into edit mode.
5:          beep()
6:          msgInfo("Careful", "You are now in edit mode.")
7:        endIf
8:    endmethod
```

Using *menuAction* Constants

Another method in ObjectPAL that opens up a whole world of power is menuAction(). The
menuAction() method enables you to execute any of the MenuCommand constants (see Figure 12.7).
Any time you want to execute or trap a menu-equivalent task, consider using the menuAction()
method or menuAction event.

FIGURE 12.7.

*The Constants tab from the
ObjectPAL Quick Lookup
dialog box showing the*
MenuCommands.

To display the Form Open dialog box, for example, add line 3 to the pushButton method of a
button.

```
1:    ;Commands :: btnMenuAction :: pushButton
2:    method pushButton(var eventInfo Event)
3:        menuAction(MenuFormOpen)
4:    endmethod
```

Trapping *menuAction* Constants

Just as you can trap for action constants, you can trap for MenuCommand constants. For example,
to trap for the user pressing the form maximize button, add lines 3–5 to the menuAction method
of a page.

```
1:    ;Commands :: Pge1 :: menuAction
2:    method menuAction(var eventInfo MenuEvent)
3:        if eventInfo.id() = MenuControlMaximize then
4:            disableDefault
5:        endIf
6:    endmethod
```

Using Properties

Just as you can set the values of properties using interactive Paradox, you also can set them using ObjectPAL. All properties of an object are either read-only or read-write (see Figure 12.8).

FIGURE 12.8.

The Objects and Properties tab from the ObjectPAL Quick Lookup dialog box.

Read-Only Properties

Some properties are read-only. That is, you cannot set their value. You can only read it. For example, to display the record number of the active field in a message information box whenever a button is clicked, add line 3 to the pushButton method of a button.

```
1:    ;Commands :: btnReadOnly :: pushButton
2:    method pushButton(var eventInfo Event)
3:       msgInfo("Record number", active.recNo)      ;recNo is a property.
4:    endMethod
```

> **WARNING**
>
> For the preceding code to work, the TabStop property must be set to False. If the TabStop property is set to True, focus will move to the button before the pushButton event is called. Because a button does not have a recNo property, a critical error results.

Read-Write Properties

Another type of property is a read-write property. For example, to toggle the AutoAppend property of a table frame when a button is clicked, add line 3 to the pushButton method of a button.

```
1:    ;Commands :: btnReadWrite :: pushButton
2:    method pushButton(var eventInfo Event)
3:       Customer.autoAppend = not Customer.autoAppend      ;Customer is a table
         frame.
4:    endmethod
```

Using the Form's Prefilter

The final type of command used in ObjectPAL that I am going to demonstrate in this chapter is not a command, but a programming technique. It is revisited in this chapter because it is so important and is used in the COMMANDS.FSL form, which is the form that contains all the code from this chapter. If you have typed in all the code from this chapter, then continue doing so by adding lines 3–6 and 9–20 to the form's `mouseRightDown` method.

```
1:    ;Commands :: form :: mouseRightDown
2:    method mouseRightDown(var eventInfo MouseEvent)
3:       var
4:          ui        UIObject
5:          sCode     String
6:       endVar

7:       if eventInfo.isPreFilter() then
8:          ;// This code executes for each object on the form.

9:          eventInfo.getTarget(ui)
10:         if ui.class = "Button" then
11:            sCode = ui.methodGet("pushButton")
12:            sCode.view()
13:         endIf

14:         if ui.container.class = "Button" then
15:            sCode = ui.container.methodGet("pushButton")
16:            sCode.view()
17:         endIf

18:      else
19:         ;// This code executes only for the form.

20:      endif
21:   endmethod
```

After you add this code, you can right-click any button to display the code in the `pushButton` method of it.

COMMANDS.FSL in the ANSWERS directory contains all the code from this chapter (see Figure 12.9). Hopefully, you entered all the code from this chapter yourself. If you didn't, then open this form to see the various types of commands you can use in ObjectPAL.

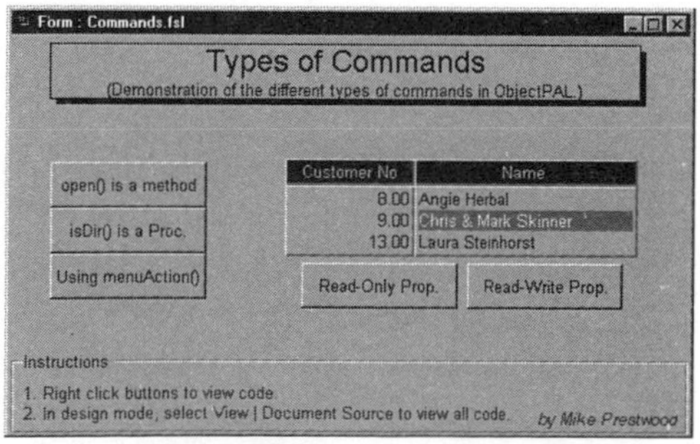

FIGURE 12.9.

COMMANDS.FSL contains all the code from this chapter.

Summary

This chapter reviewed the various types of commands available to the ObjectPAL programmer, including methods, procedures, and properties. Methods need an object to act upon while procedures know which object to work on. Properties come in two flavors: read-only and read-write. This chapter also reviewed the `action()` and `menuAction()` methods, which enable you to use constants as commands.

Finally, this chapter reviewed three important places to put code: the `action` event, the `menuAction` event, and the form's prefilter. A common use for the `action` and `menuAction` events is to trap for user actions. You also learned how to use the form's prefilter to write generic code.

You don't need to memorize all the methods, procedures, constants, keywords, control structures, and properties of ObjectPAL. What you should learn is how all the various elements of ObjectPAL are categorized and how to use them. When you need to find a command, you'll know where to check to see whether it exists and how to use it.

By now, you should feel comfortable with the categories of ObjectPAL commands. After completing the rest of this book, you will feel very comfortable with all the categories of commands in ObjectPAL and the various programming techniques used to implement them.

Part II of this book, "ObjectPAL Basics," has taught you the concepts you need in order to master ObjectPAL. Part II is the heart of this book. To get the most out of ObjectPAL, you must understand the information in Part II. Each piece of information about ObjectPAL relies on something else. If you've read other books on ObjectPAL or the ObjectPAL manuals, maybe everything in Part II made sense. If this is your first experience with ObjectPAL, however, I recommend that you review this part of the book in a few weeks.

PART

III

The Display Managers and More

Applications, Forms, and TableViews

13

A *display manager* is a group of ObjectPAL data types that includes the application, the form, the report, TableView, and the script. Except for the script, these object types are used to display data. This chapter tells you how to turn database ideas and concepts into full-featured applications, complete with buttons, that enable you to keep control of the application environment. This chapter covers handling the desktop, moving from one page in a form to another page, moving from form to form, and using a table window. You also learn about techniques that you can use to develop a complete Windows application.

Paradox uses display managers to display data. Display managers are objects that contain design objects. Following are the five types of display managers:

- Application
- Form
- TableView
- Report
- Script

This chapter deals with the Application, Form, and TableView display managers. You can read about the Report display manager in Chapter 15. Scripts are discussed in detail in Chapter 23.

The Application Display Manager

In Paradox, the application can refer to a group of files in a directory. In this chapter, application refers to the Paradox desktop. Specifically, an Application variable in ObjectPAL is an ObjectPAL data type that provides a handle to the Paradox desktop. The Application variable is one of the display manager objects.

Paradox enables you to manipulate display managers. For example, you can open, close, minimize, maximize, and move them. The first step in manipulating a display manager is to define a variable as a display manager, as in the following example:

```
1:    Var
2:        app        Application
3:        f          Form
4:        tv         TableView
5:        r          Report
6:        sc         Script
7:    endVar
```

After you define a variable, you can manipulate it with any of the object methods that belong to that object type. To set the title of the application, for example, use the following:

```
1:    var
2:        app    Application
3:    endVar
4:
5:    app.setTitle("My Custom Application")
```

After you define the application variable app, you can manipulate the app variable with any of the application methods. To browse through the various application methods, select View | ObjectPAL Quick Lookup and with the Types and Methods tab displayed, choose Application. Figure 13.1 shows the Types and Methods tab from the ObjectPAL Quick Lookup dialog box showing the application type.

FIGURE 13.1.

The Types and Methods tab from the ObjectPAL Quick Lookup dialog box.

Using *hide()*, *show()*, *minimize()*, and *maximize()*

If you want to hide the desktop and display a form, you must define the form as a dialog box. To do this, right-click on the form's title bar, select Window Style, and check the Dialog Box check box option in the Window Style panel. Figure 13.2 shows the Window Style dialog box.

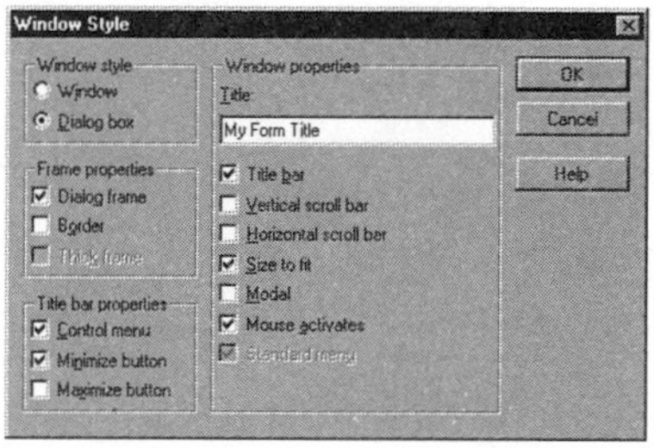

FIGURE 13.2.

The Window Style dialog box.

If the form is not a dialog box, it is a child window. As with all Windows applications, when you hide the application, all the child windows are hidden, too. Dialog boxes are not child windows and therefore, do not hide with the application. If you want show a form and hide Paradox, then define a form as a dialog box. To define a variable of type Application, for example, use the following:

```
1:    var
2:        app    Application
3:    endVar
```

Now, you can hide or show the application in View Data mode, as in the following:

```
1:    app.hide()
2:    sleep(5000)
3:    app.show(5000)
```

The form is a dialog box only when you open it in View Data mode. If you're in Design mode, running the form is not equivalent because the form is still a child window of Paradox. You must open it in View Data mode to view it as a dialog box. Table 13.1 lists the Application methods.

Table 13.1. Application methods and procedures.

```
bringToTop*

getPosition

getTitle*

hide*

isMaximized*

isMinimized*

isVisible*

maximize*

minimize*

setIcon

setPosition*

setTitle*

show*

windowClientHandle*

windowHandle*
```
*Inherited from the Form type.

The following example demonstrates how to use the hide(), show(), minimize(), and maximize() methods from the form type. These methods are important because they enable you to control your form and the Paradox desktop to achieve different looks.

Using *hide()*, *show()*, *minimize()*, and *maximize()*

Suppose that you want to create a new form with buttons that hide, show, minimize, and maximize the application and the form. After you create this form, you can use it to test different looks.

You can find the HIDE.FSL form on the disc in the \ANSWERS directory.

Step By Step

1. Change your working directory to the TUTORIAL directory and create a new form with eight buttons on it. Label the buttons Hide Application, Show Application, Maximize Application, Minimize Application, Hide Form (3 seconds), Show Form, Maximize Form, and Minimize Form. Select Properties | Form | Window Style, and choose Dialog Box from the Window Style panel (see Figure 13.3).

FIGURE 13.3.

Setup form.

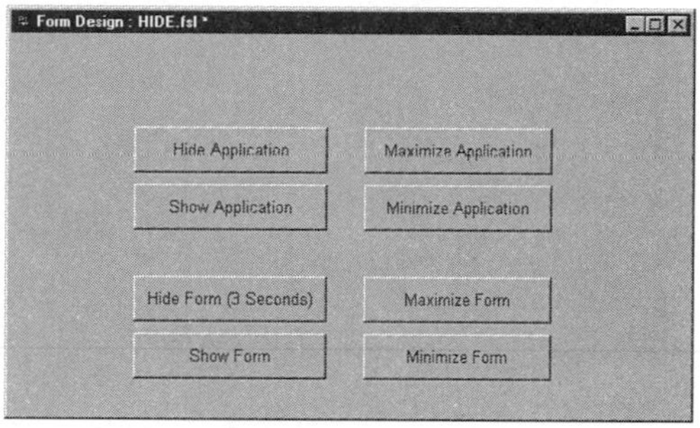

2. In the Var window of the form, add line 3.

```
1:   ;Page2 :: Var
2:   Var
3:       app    Application
4:   endVar
```

3. Add line 3 to the pushButton method of the Hide Application button.

```
1:   ;Button :: pushButton
2:   method pushButton(var eventInfo Event)
3:       app.hide()
4:   endmethod
```

4. Add line 3 to the pushButton method of the Show Application button.

```
1:   ;Button :: pushButton
2:   method pushButton(var eventInfo Event)
3:       app.show()
4:   endmethod
```

5. Add line 3 to the pushButton method of the Maximize Application button.

```
1:   ;Button :: pushButton
2:   method pushButton(var eventInfo Event)
3:       app.maximize()
4:   endmethod
```

6. Add line 3 to the pushButton method of the Minimize Application button.

```
1:    ;Button :: pushButton
2:    method pushButton(var eventInfo Event)
3:        app.minimize()
4:    endmethod
```

7. Add lines 3–5 to the pushButton method of the Hide Form (3 Seconds) button.

```
1:    ;Button :: pushButton
2:    method pushButton(var eventInfo Event)
3:        hide()
4:        sleep(3000)
5:        show()
6:    endmethod
```

8. Add line 3 to the pushButton method of the Show Form button.

```
1:    ;Button :: pushButton
2:    method pushButton(var eventInfo Event)
3:        show()
4:    endmethod
```

9. Add line 3 to the pushButton method of the Maximize Form button.

```
1:    ;Button :: pushButton
2:    method pushButton(var eventInfo Event)
3:        maximize()
4:    endmethod
```

10. Add line 3 to the pushButton method of the Minimize Form button.

```
1:    ;Button :: pushButton
2:    method pushButton(var eventInfo Event)
3:        minimize()
4:    endmethod
```

11. Check the syntax and save the form as HIDE.FSL. Close the form and then open it. Click all eight buttons in any order to see how they work. Then, select buttons in various combinations. Different combinations produce different effects (see Figure 13.4).

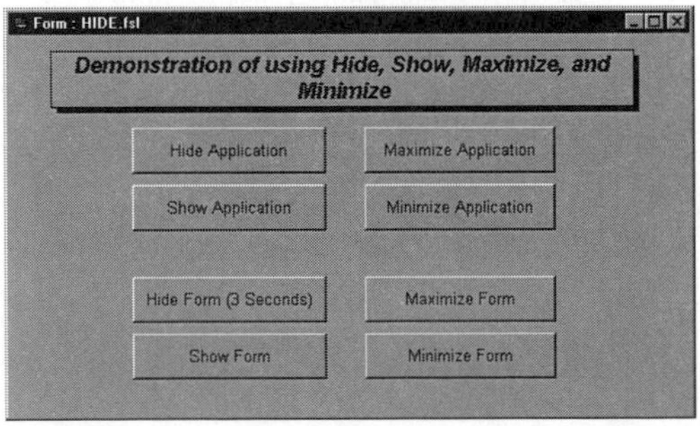

FIGURE 13.4.

HIDE.FSL demonstrates hiding an application and a form.

Analysis

In step 2, line 3 declares the application variable app. Because there is only one application—namely, the current application—you don't need to attach or open the application variable;

simply use it. This app variable is used in steps 3 through 6 to hide, show, maximize, and minimize the application; in other words, the Paradox desktop.

Steps 7 through 10 call these same procedures for the form. The only difference in syntax is that the form versions don't use the optional variable in the preceding example. You could use the name of the form or the built-in object variable `self` to refer to the form, but a variable is not needed with these methods. In addition, you could use `attach()` to attach a `Form` variable to the current form. To demonstrate this important technique, type the following into the `pushButton` method of a button.

```
1:    ;Button :: pushButton
2:    method pushButton(var eventInfo Event)
3:       var
4:          f        Form          ;Declare f as a Form variable.
5:       endVar
6:
7:       f.attach()              ;Attach f to the current form.
8:       view(f.getTitle())      ;Show title in a view box.
9:    endmethod
```

The capability of controlling the application and the form during runtime is an important part of Paradox. Use this form whenever you want to experiment with various combinations, such as minimizing and maximizing the form and the application. For example, you can hide the application and minimize the form.

The Form Display Manager

Chapter 3 discussed interactive and design issues about forms. This section discusses how to manipulate forms and pages in ObjectPAL.

Maximizing with *sysInfo()*

When designing a form, you need to consider screen size. You must decide whether your application is going to be full screen or smaller. If you choose full screen, you must decide for which resolution you're going to develop, such as 640 by 480, 800 by 600, 1024 by 768, and so on. One solution is to check the user's screen size and to make a decision based on the answer. Use the `sysInfo()` procedure to get the current user's system information. The `sysInfo()` procedure supplies much information about your system. For example, type the following into the `pushButton` method of a button.

```
1:    ;Form :: Var
2:    Var
3:       dynSys    DynArray[] AnyType  ;Variable for sysInfo()
4:    endVar
5:
6:    sysInfo(dynSys)
7:    dynSys.view()
```

After you get this information, you can extract the width of the monitor resolution and use it to decide what to do. The `FullWidth` index contains the horizontal working area in pixels in a maximized window. You can use this information to determine whether your form will fit on the screen. For example, if you develop a form for 800 by 600, you can use the following to let the user know.

```
1:    ;Form :: open
2:    if dynSys["FullWidth"] < 800 then
3:        msgStop("Startup Error!", "Form requires 800 x 600 resolution")
4:        close()
5:    endIf
```

This, unfortunately, eliminates standard VGA (640 by 480) users from using your form. A good solution to this problem is to develop all your forms with a 640 by 480 maximized resolution. In today's computer industry, most users have at least VGA. You can check whether the user is using VGA; maximize if he or she is. If the user's resolution is higher than that, the default Size to Fit setting centers the form on his or her screen (remember to check the Size to Fit property of the form). This enables users of higher-resolution monitors to get the benefit of their larger screens and still use all the screen real estate of a VGA setup.

Maximizing If the Resolution is VGA

Suppose that you want to develop a form for use on a VGA or higher-resolution monitor. If the form is open on a VGA system, then maximize the form. If the form is open on a higher-resolution system, let the default behavior take over centering the form on the desktop. This next example uses `sysInfo()` from the System class of methods and procedures and `maximize()` from the form type of methods and procedures.

You can find the VGA.FSL form on the disc in the \ANSWERS directory.

Step By Step

1. Create a form for which the size of the page is VGA, 6.67 inches by 4.11 inches. Make sure that the Size to Fit option is checked for the form.

2. In the Var window of the form, type line 3.
```
1:    ;Form :: Var
2:    Var
3:        dynSys    DynArray[] AnyType ;Variable for sysInfo()
4:    endVar
```

3. In the open method of the form, enter lines 8–11.
```
1:    ;Form :: Init
2:    method init(var eventInfo Event)
3:        sysInfo(dynSys)
4:        if dynSys["FullWidth"] = 640 then
```

```
5:          maximize()
6:        endif
7:     endmethod
```

4. Check the syntax, save the form as VGA.FSL, and run it. If you're using a VGA monitor, the form will maximize (see Figure 13.5). If you have another resolution, the form won't maximize (see Figure 13.6).

FIGURE 13.5.

VGA.FSL on a VGA system uses the full screen.

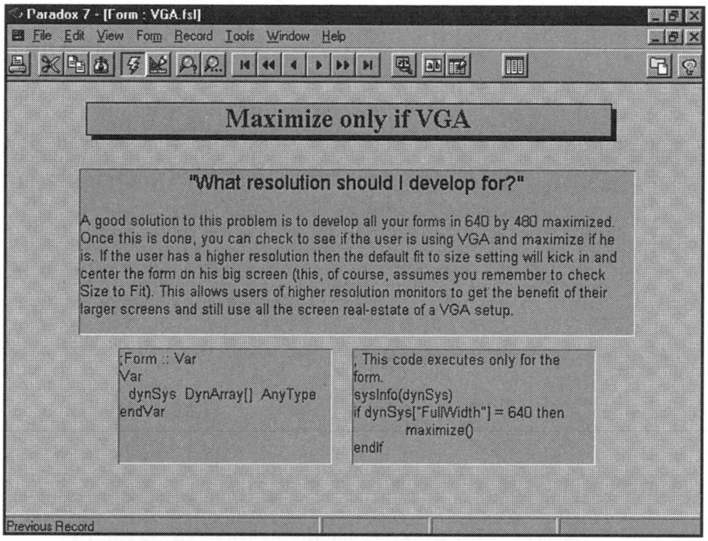

FIGURE 13.6.

VGA.FSL on a 800 by 600 SVGA system. The form is nicely fitted and centered.

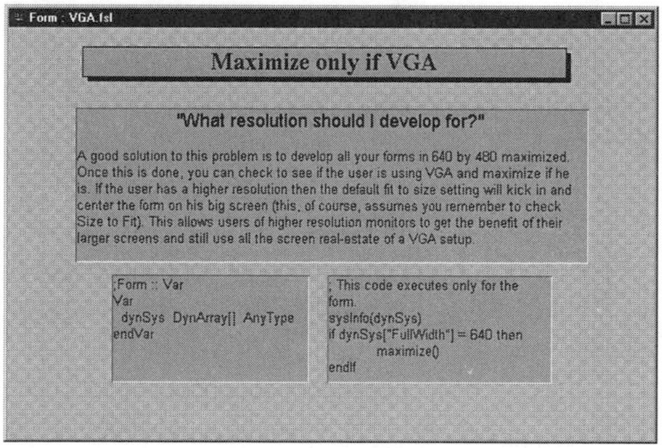

Analysis

In step 2, line 3 declares dynSys as a DynArray variable that is ready to accept any type of data. In this case, you could declare dynSys private to the open method; but the data retrieved with sysInfo() is so useful, I like to make it global to the form for use throughout the form.

In step 3, line 3 uses `sysInfo()` to grab system information and put it into the DynArray `dynSys`. Line 4 checks whether the `FullWidth` index in `dynSys` equals 640. If it does, line 5 maximizes the form.

Another technique that is not too popular is to design a form for each resolution and to use a script to decide which version to load. You also can create a dynamic form that resizes itself, depending on the resolution. This final technique is my preferred way of handling screen resolution. See the section, "Dynamic Forms," later in this chapter.

Pages and Forms

Your data model dictates whether you should use a new page or a new form. If the page that you want to add uses a table in the current data model, first consider adding a page. If a new page won't work because of size or some other reason, add a new form.

If you add another form to your application, you need to know how to move from form to form and how to pass information between forms. These two issues are discussed later in this chapter. There are two techniques to move from page to page. The first technique uses `moveTo()` and the second technique uses `moveToPage()`. To use `moveTo()`, first rename the page. Then, use `pageName.moveTo()`.

Moving from Page to Page

Suppose that you want to move back and forth from the first page in a form to the second by using buttons. This example acquaints you with `moveTo()`.

You can find the PAGES.FSL form on the disc in the \ANSWERS directory.

Step By Step

1. Create a form with two pages on it. Name the first page pge1 and the second page pge2. On pge1, create a button labeled Page Two. On pge2 create a button labeled Page One. Make sure that the pages are stacked and not tiled horizontally or vertically.

2. Add line 3 to the `pushButton` method of the Page Two button on pge1.

```
1:    ;Button :: pushButton
2:    method pushButton(var eventInfo Event)
3:        pge2.moveTo()
4:    endmethod
```

3. Add line 3 to the `pushButton` method of the Page One button on pge2.

```
1:    ;Button :: pushButton
2:    method pushButton(var eventInfo Event)
3:        pge1.moveTo()
4:    endmethod
```

4. Check the syntax, save the form as PAGES.FSL, and run it. Click the Page Two button to move to the second page. When you're on the second page, click on the Page One button to return to the first page.

Analysis

In step 2, line 3 moves to the page named pge2, and line 3 of step 3 moves to the page named pge1. An alternative technique is to use the order of the pages instead of page's UIObject name, as in the following:

```
1:      moveToPage(2)
```

Using the *positionalOrder* Property

The page has a `positionalOrder` property you can use to know which page a user is on. Use this read-write property if you need to know which page the user is currently on or to set the position of a page. The following line of code, for example, moves a page named `pgeConfig` to the top of the positional order.

```
pgeConfig.positionalOrder = 1
```

Moving from Form to Form

To open a new form, you need to do two things: define a variable as a form and use the `open()` method, as in the following:

```
1:      var
2:          f     Form
3:      endVar
4:
5:      f.open(":ALIAS:FILENAME")
```

If you specify an alias, Paradox looks in only the alias directory for the file. If you don't specify an alias, Paradox looks in the working directory. Paradox doesn't search for a form that you want to open. If you specify the following, for example,

```
1:      f.open("ORDERS.FDL")
```

Paradox looks in only the working directory for a delivered form. If you specify

```
1:      f.open("C:\DATA\ORDERS.FDL")
```

Paradox looks in only the DATA directory on drive C (it does not look in the working directory). If you specify

```
1:      f.open(":DATA:ORDERS.FDL")
```

Paradox looks in only the directory specified in the DATA alias.

Paradox looks first for the nondelivered version of a form, such as FILENAME.FSL, and then looks for its delivered version, such as FILENAME.FDL. The following searches first for ORDERS.FSL and then for ORDERS.FDL in the current working directory only.

```
1:    f.open("ORDERS")
```

If you want to search only for a specific name, use an extension, as in the following:

```
1:    f.open("ORDERS.FDL")
```

If you want to reverse the search order, use the following:

```
1:    if not f.open("ORDERS.FDL") then
2:        f.open("ORDERS.FSL")
3:    endIf
```

To move to a form that is already open, you must do three things:

1. Define a variable as a Form variable (if you haven't done so already).

2. Use the `attach()` method to attach to the form.

3. Use the `moveTo()` or `bringToTop()` method to go to the form.

Following is an example:

```
1:    var
2:        f       Form
3:    endVar
4:
5:    f.attach("Form : ORDERS.FSL")
6:    f.moveTo()
```

First, check whether the form is open. If it is, attach and move to it. If the form isn't open, you can combine the preceding methods with an `if` method, as in the following:

```
1:    var
2:        f       Form
3:    endVar
4:
5:    if f.attach("Form : ORDER.FSL") then
6:        f.moveTo()
7:    else
8:        f.open("ORDER")
9:    endIf
```

The only other problem is the title of the form. You had to specify Form : ORDER.FSL. When you're ready to deliver your forms, you must rewrite all your code to reflect the new name. In other words, you must specify Form : ORDER.FDL, which is an unsuitable situation.

You can rename the form with the `setTitle()` method and use this name with the `attach()` method. For example, on the built-in `open()` method of the form, first set the title with the following:

```
1:    ;Form2 :: open
2:    setTitle("Order Entry")
```

Then you can open either the delivered (.FDL) or nondelivered (.FSL) forms without modifying your code at delivery time if you use the following:

```
1:    ;Form1.Button :: pushButton
2:    if f.attach("Order Entry") then
3:        f.moveTo()
4:    else
5:        f.open("ORDER")
6:    endIf
```

To save yourself a line of code and some time, get into the habit of explicitly naming a form every time you create a new one. If you don't need to change the title of a form during runtime, name the form, as discussed in Chapter 3. Doing so makes it easier to attach, and the form has a more professional appearance. Rather than Form : MYFORM.FSL, you can place a more meaningful title. You might, for example, use Order Entry System. With this title, the program tries to attach to a form called Order Entry System and moves to it if attach() is successful. If attach() fails, the program attempts to open ORDER.FSL or ORDER.FDL. This is important—it's the best way to open another form. (The last example in this section adds a twist to this. It uses the if method to check whether the final open() method worked.)

Opening Another Form

Suppose that you want to open a second form or to move to that second form, depending on whether the second form is already open. The following steps demonstrate what I believe is the best way to open another form.

> You can find the FORM1.FSL form on the disc in the \ANSWERS directory.

Step By Step

1. Create two forms. In the Window Style dialog box, set the form title of one form to Form One, and save it as FORM1.FSL (see Figure 13.7). Name the other form Form Two, save it as FORM2.FSL, and close it. On Form One, put a button labeled Other form on it.

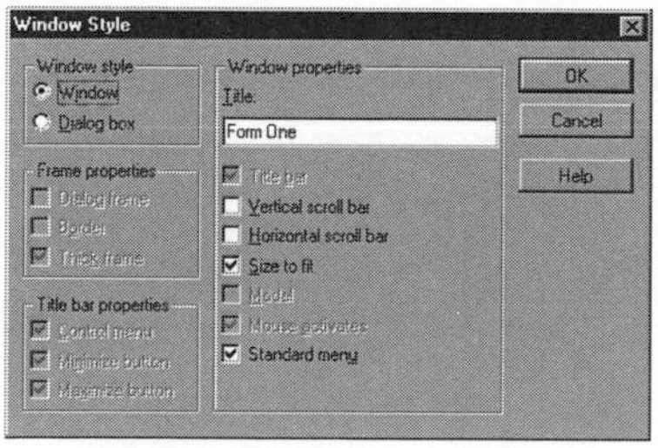

FIGURE 13.7.

The Window Style dialog box.

2. In the pushButton method of the Other Form button on Form One, add lines 3–13.

```
1:    ;Button :: pushButton
2:    method pushButton(var eventInfo Event)
3:        var
4:            f    Form
5:        endVar
6:
7:        if f.attach("Form Two") then
8:            f.moveTo()
9:        else
10:           if not f.open("FORM2") then
11:               errorShow("Form open error")
12:           endIf
13:       endIf
14:   endmethod
```

3. Check the syntax, save the form, and run it. Click the button labeled Other form. When the other form opens, leave it open and select the first form by selecting Window | 1 Form One. Click the button a second time. The second form isn't opened again. Instead, it's brought to the front very quickly (See Figure 13.8).

FIGURE 13.8.

Opening another form.

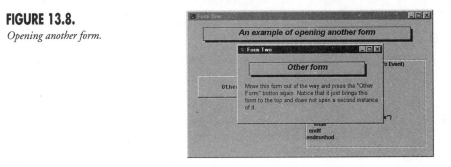

Analysis

In step 2, line 4 declares f as a Form variable. Line 7 tries to attach f to Form Two. If attach() is successful, line 8 moves control to the newly attached form. If attach() fails, the execution moves to line 10, where another if structure executes. Line 10 of the new if structure opens the FORM2 file on disk. If line 10 fails to open the form, line 11 displays the error stack with errorShow(). Line 10 uses only the name of the form; no extension is used. This enables ObjectPAL to try to open FORM2.FSL first. If FORM2.FSL doesn't exist, ObjectPAL automatically tries to open FORM2.FDL. No extra code is required.

Using an if statement is a great way to test whether a method has been successful. Use if with errorShow() whenever you can. It helps safeguard your applications, and it makes them more professional. Using if with an errorShow() is another way of developing good programming skills.

> **TIP**
>
> Whenever you open a form, report, library, or script using the open() method and do not specify a file extension, Paradox always looks first for the nondelivered .?SL file and then for the delivered .?DL file. For example, with the following line of code, Paradox first tries to open FILENAME.FSL and then FILENAME.FDL.
>
> ```
> f.open("FILENAME.")
> ```

Using *WinStyleDefault*

If you use WinStyleHidden, or any of the constants in the WindowStyles category, make sure that you also use WinStyleDefault. For example, do not do the following:

```
1:      var
2:         f        Form
3:      endVar
4:
5:      f.open("MYFORM", WinStyleHidden)        ;This is wrong.
6:      sleep(1000)
7:      f.show()
```

Instead, do the following:

```
1:      var
2:         f        Form
3:      endVar
4:
5:      f.open("MYFORM", WinStyleDefault + WinStyleHidden)        ;Correct.
6:      sleep(1000)
7:      f.show()
```

To see why, try the preceding with a dialog box style form or with a form with scroll bars. This rule also applies to reports.

Using *openAsDialog()*

Here is an example of using openAsDialog() with the WindowStyles. Create a form and in the Window Style panel, choose the Dialog Box. In the Title Bar Properties panel, turn off the Contol Menu. Open the dialog form from another form with the following:

```
1:      ;Button :: pushButton
2:      method pushButton(var eventInfo Event)
3:         var
4:            f    Form
5:         endVar
6:
7:         f.openAsDialog("MYFORM",WinStyleDefault+WinStyleModal+WinStyleControl)
8:      endMethod
```

> **NOTE**
>
> A dynamic form is a form that automatically resizes itself and all the objects it contains so that it fits when a user resizes the form. When a user changes the size of a form, the constant MenuControlSize goes through the form's menuAction method. You can trap for this constant and, after the user is finished, set the form's sizeToFit property to True.

Dynamic Forms

Suppose that you need to create a form that dynamically resizes itself when the user resizes it. The following example demonstrates how to create a form in which all the objects dynamically resize themselves when the form resizes. This example is particularly useful when developing an application for use with multiple screen resolutions.

 You can find the DYNAFORM.FSL form on the disc in the \ANSWERS directory.

Step By Step

1. Change your working directory to the TUTORIAL directory and create a new form.

2. In the setFocus method of the form, type lines 9 and 10:

```
 1:    ;Form :: setFocus
 2:    method setFocus(var eventInfo Event)
 3:
 4:        if eventInfo.isPreFilter() then
 5:        ;// This code executes for each object on the form:
 6:
 7:        else
 8:        ;// This code executes only for the form:
 9:           doDefault
10:          menuAction(MenuPropertiesZoomBestFit) ;Set zoom
                                                    ;to best
                                                    ;fit.
11:        endif
12:    endmethod
```

3. In the menuAction method of the form, type lines 7–10.

```
 1:    ;Form :: menuAction
 2:    method menuAction(var eventInfo MenuEvent)
 3:        if eventInfo.isPreFilter() then
 4:            ;// This code executes for each object on the form:
 5:        else
 6:            ;// This code executes only for the form:
 7:            if eventInfo.id() = MenuControlSize   then ;If user resizes the
            form,
```

```
 8:            doDefault                              ;make the form resize
               too.
 9:            self.sizeToFit = True
10:          endIf
11:       endif
12:    endmethod
```

4. In the `close` method of the form, type lines 8–10:

```
 1:    ;Form :: close
 2:    method close(var eventInfo Event)
 3:       if eventInfo.isPreFilter() then
 4:          ;// This code executes for each object on the form:
 5:
 6:       else
 7:          ;// This code executes only for the form:
 8:          if not isMaximized() then show() endIf ;If _maximized, show.
 9:          menuAction(MenuPropertiesZoom100)      ;Set zoom to _100%.
10:          self.sizeToFit = True                  ;Size _the form to the
               page.
11:       endif
12:    endmethod
```

5. Check the syntax, place a few objects on the form, save the form as DYNAFORM.FSL, and run it. Resize the form and notice how the page resizes itself to fit the form. The ANSWER.FSL form also uses this technique (see Figure 13.9).

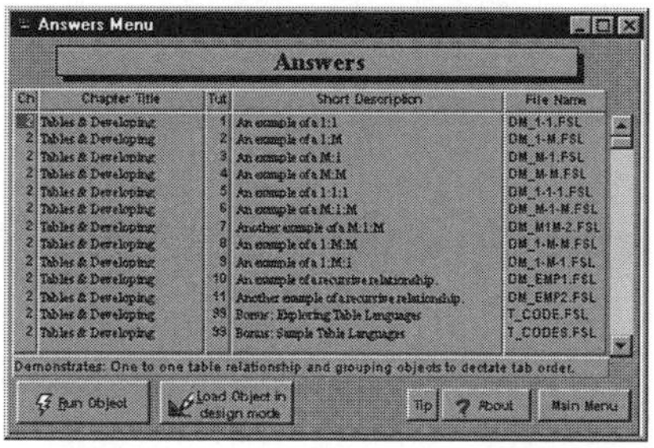

FIGURE 13.9.

ANSWER.FSL form uses this technique to dynamically resize itself.

Analysis

In step 2, line 9 executes a `doDefault`, which finishes bringing focus to the form. In line 10, the form is set to best fit. This is equivalent to the user selecting View | Zoom | Best Fit.

In step 3, the `menuAction` event of the form is used to trap for a menu event. In this case, you are trapping for `MenuControlSize` in line 7. This means that the user is resizing the form. Line 8 executes a `doDefault` so that the form will finish resizing and size the page because best fit is set. Finally, the form property `sizeToFit` is set to `True` in line 9 so that the form will match the aspect ratio of the newly resized page.

MAINMENU.FSL uses these two techniques together. All the code is located in the open method.

Using *setWorkingDir()* and *setPrivDir()*

Two important procedures are `setWorkingDir()` and `setPrivDir()`. `setPrivDir()` emulates a user selecting File | Private Directory, typing a new private directory, and clicking OK. `setWorkingDir()` does the same for your working directory. These two procedures are fairly straightforward except that the default behavior, when changing either your working or private directory, is to close all its windows. To stop this, you can trap for either `MenuChangingWork` or `MenuChangingPriv` in the `menuAction` method. The following code, for example, traps for ObjectPAL changing the working directory, and stops it from closing the form to which this code is attached.

```
1:    if eventInfo.id() = MenuChangingWork then
2:        eventInfo.setErrorCode(1)
3:    endIf
```

> **NOTE**
>
> You can disable the warning prompts that are displayed when you change working or private directories. To do this, select Edit | Preferences to display the Preferences dialog box. Then select the Advanced tab, and clear the check box for the Don't show warning prompts when changing directories option.

The next examples show you a good technique for using both `setPrivDir()` and `setWorkingDir()`.

Setting Your Private Directory

Suppose that you want to set your private directory when you open a form. Perhaps because you have a preferred private directory where you keep some favorite forms and tables. The following code will change your private directory only if needed and if the directory exists.

> You can find the PRIV1.FSL form on the disc in the \ANSWERS directory.

Step By Step

1. Change your working directory to the TUTORIAL directory and create a new form.

2. In the `init` method of the form, type lines 3–11:

```
1:    ;PRIV1 :: Form :: init
2:    method init(var eventInfo Event)
3:        var
4:            sDir    String
5:        endVar
```

```
6:          ;Set the string of your preferred private directory.
7:          sDir = "C:\\PDOXWIN\\PRIVATE"

8:          ;Change private directory if appropriate.
9:          if privDir() <> sDir and isDir(sDir) then
10:              setPrivDir(sDir)
11:          endIf
12:      endMethod
```

3. In the `menuAction` method of the form, type lines 9–11:

```
1:      ;Form :: menuAction
2:      method menuAction(var eventInfo MenuEvent)
3:
4:      if eventInfo.isPreFilter() then
5:          ;// This code executes for each object on the form:
6:
7:      else
8:          ;// This code executes only for the form:
9:          if eventInfo.id() = MenuChangingPriv then
10:             eventInfo.setErrorCode(1)   ;Prevents the form from closing.
11:          endIf
12:
13:      endif
14:
15:      endmethod
```

4. Check the syntax, save the form as PRIV1.FSL, and close it. Change your private directory to a different directory (such as C:\) and open the form. After the form opens, check the current private directory by selecting File | Private Directory.

Analysis

In step 2, line 4 declares s as a string variable. Step 14 sets sDir to a string that points to my preferred private directory. The `if` statement in lines 15–17 starts off in line 15 by checking two conditions. First, it compares the current private directory with sDir. Then, it makes sure that the directory path sDir represents exists. If both of these conditions are true, line 16 changes the private directory to sDir.

In step 3, line 9 checks for the constant MenuChangingPriv. If it is detected, line 10 sets an error code to a nonzero value.

Setting Your Working Directory

Suppose that you have code that relies on objects that are in the same directory as the form, and you want to automatically change your working directory to that directory when the form is opened. This section shows you how to accomplish this.

You can find the WORK1.FSL form on the disc in the \ANSWERS directory.

Step By Step

1. Change your working directory to the TUTORIAL directory and create a new form.

2. In the init method of the form, type lines 3–14:

```
1:    ;Form :: init
2:    method init(var eventInfo Event)
3:        var
4:            f          Form
5:            dynDir    DynArray[] String
6:        endVar

7:        ;Set working directory to this directory.
8:        f.attach()
9:        if not isFile(":WORK:ANSWERS.FSL") then
10:            splitFullFileName(f.getFileName(), dynDir)
11:            if not setWorkingDir(dynDir["Drive"] + dynDir["Path"]) then
12:                errorShow()
13:            endIf
14:        endIf
15:    endMethod
```

3. In the menuAction method of the form, type lines 8–10.

```
1:    ;Form :: menuAction
2:    method menuAction(var eventInfo MenuEvent)
3:        if eventInfo.isPreFilter() then
4:            ;// This code executes for each object on the form:
5:
6:        else
7:            ;// This code executes only for the form:
8:            if eventInfo.id() = MenuChangingWork then
9:                eventInfo.setErrorCode(1)
10:            endIf
11:        endif
12:    endmethod
```

4. Check the syntax and save the form as WORK1.FSL. Change your working directory to a different directory (such as C:\) and open the form. After the form opens, check the current working directory by selecting File | Working Directory.

Analysis

In step 2, line 4 declares f as a form variable and dyn1 as a DynArray ready to accept string values. Line 8 is rather interesting. It uses attach() to attach f to the current form. When you attach to the current form, you do not have to include its title. Line 9 checks to see whether the current working directory is the same directory the form is in. If it is not, then line 10 uses getFilename() and splitFullFileName() to extract the form's path. Line 11 sets the working directory.

Similar to the previous example, in step 3, line 9 checks for the constant MenuChangingWork. If it is detected, line 10 sets an error code to a nonzero value.

Getting User Input

With ObjectPAL you have several ways to get input from a user. You could simply place an undefined field on the form for the user to type in to. This passive way of getting user input works for many situations. Another, more decisive technique is to use a view dialog box. You already have used view() several times. Following is one more example for you to type into the pushButton method of a button:

```
1:    method pushButton(var eventInfo Event)
2:       var
3:          sName       String
4:       endVar
5:
6:       sName = "Enter your name"
7:       sName.view("Full name")
8:       if sName = "Enter your name" then
9:          ;Either user did not change text or clicked Cancel.
10:         return
11:      endIf
12:      message("Your name is " + sName)
13:   endMethod
```

You also could use some of the simple built-in dialog boxes with msgQuestion(), msgYesNoCancel(), and so on, as in the following example:

```
1:    if msgQuestion("Question", "Do you want to proceed?") = "No" then
2:       return
3:    endIf
```

Using *formReturn()*

To get more complex data input from a user, you must use another form for input. After the user types a value into an undefined field on the other form, you need to return the value from the second form to the first. You can use formReturn() to return a value from one form to another.

Using formReturn() actually requires several steps. Suppose that you want to return a value from a form form2 to form1. First, you open form2 and wait for it from form1, as in the following example:

```
1:    var
2:       f      Form
3:       s      String
4:    endVar
5:
6:    f.open("FORM2")
7:    s = string(f.wait())
```

Note that the variable s is set up to wait for a value from form2. On form2, use formReturn() to return a value to s, as in the following example:

```
1:    formReturn("Hello first form")
```

After the `form2` returns a value to `form1`, close `form2` with `close()`, as in the following example:

```
1:    f.close()
```

Following is the code for both forms:

```
1:    ;btnCallForm :: pushButton
2:    method pushButton(var eventInfo Event)
3:       var
4:          f        Form
5:          s        String
6:       endVar
7:
8:       f.open("FORM2")
9:       s = f.wait()
10:      f.close()
11:      s.view()
12:    endmethod
13:
14:    ;btnCalledForm :: pushButton
15:    method pushButton(var eventInfo Event)
16:       formReturn("Hello first form")
17:    endMethod
```

Note that the form is closed immediately after using `wait()`. Following are a couple of rules to keep in mind when using `formReturn()`.

- If `formReturn()` has a `wait()` waiting on it, `formReturn()` returns a value but does not close the current form.

- If `formReturn()` does not have a `wait()` waiting, `formReturn()` closes the form.

As long as you keep the preceding rules in mind, `formReturn()` is easy to use.

Using *formReturn()* with Dot Notation

Suppose that you need to return more than one value from a called form. This example demonstrates how to use `formReturn()` in conjunction with dot notation to return three values from the called form to the calling form. In addition, it demonstrates that text objects have a value property that you can read (and set) from another form. In this case, the calling form reads two text boxes on the called form. Finally, it demonstrates that you do not have to close the called form immediately after using `wait()`.

You can find the forms FORMRET1.FSL and FORMRET2.FSL on the disc in the \ANSWERS directory.

Step By Step

1. Change your working directory to TUTORIAL. Create two forms. On the first form, place a button labeled Call Other Form and save it as FORMRET1.FSL

(see Figure 13.10). Place two button objects on the second form, and two text objects. Label the two buttons as OK and Cancel. Name the two text boxes txt1 and txt2. Set the value of txt1 to Hello and set the value of txt2 to World (see Figure 13.11). Save this second form as FORMRET2.FSL.

Optional: Make FORMRET2.FSL a modal dialog box. This forces the user to click one of the two buttons.

FIGURE 13.10.

Setup form for FORMRET1.FSL.

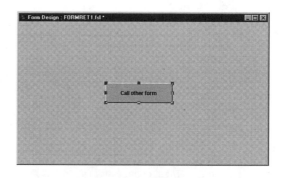

FIGURE 13.11.

Setup form for FORMRET2.FSL.

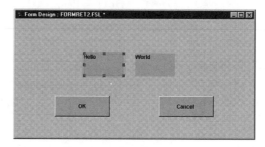

2. On the first form (FORMRET1.FSL), add lines 3–14 to the pushButton method of the button labeled Call Other Form.

```
1:   ;FORMRET1 :: btnCallForm :: pushButton
2:   method pushButton(var eventInfo Event)
3:     var
4:       fFormRet2   Form
5:       sReturnedValue, sTxt1, sTxt2   String
6:     endVar

7:     fFormRet2.open("FORMRET2")      ;Open 2nd form.
8:     sReturnedValue = string(fFormRet2.wait())   ;Wait on 2nd form.
9:     sTxt1 = fFormRet2.txt1.value    ;Grab a value from txt1 object.
10:    sTxt2 = fFormRet2.txt2.value    ;Grab a value from txt2 object.
11:    fFormRet2.close()               ;Close 2nd form.

12:    sReturnedValue.view()   ;View returned value.
13:    sTxt1.view()            ;View txt1 value.
14:    sTxt2.view()            ;View txt2 value.
15:  endmethod
```

3. On the second form (FORMRET2.FSL), add line 3 to the pushButton method of the button labeled OK.

```
1:    ;BtnOK :: pushbutton
2:    method pushButton(var eventInfo Event)
3:        formReturn("OK")
4:    endmethod
```

4. On the second form (FORMRET2.FSL), add line 3 to the pushButton method of the button labeled Cancel.

```
1:    ;BtnOK :: pushbutton
2:    method pushButton(var eventInfo Event)
3:        formReturn("Cancel")
4:    endmethod
```

5. On the second form (FORMRET2.FSL), add lines 3–11 to the form level menuAction event.

```
1:    ;Form :: menuAction
2:    method menuAction(var eventInfo MenuEvent)
3:        if eventInfo.isPreFilter() then
4:            ;// This code executes for each object on the form
5:        else
6:            ;// This code executes only for the form
7:            if eventInfo.id() = MenuControlClose then
8:                disableDefault
9:                formReturn("Cancel")
10:           endIf
11:       endIf
12:   endMethod
```

6. Check the syntax, save both forms, and close the second form (FORMRET2.FSL). Run FORMRET1.FSL and click the button. On the second form, click either the OK or Cancel button (see Figure 13.12).

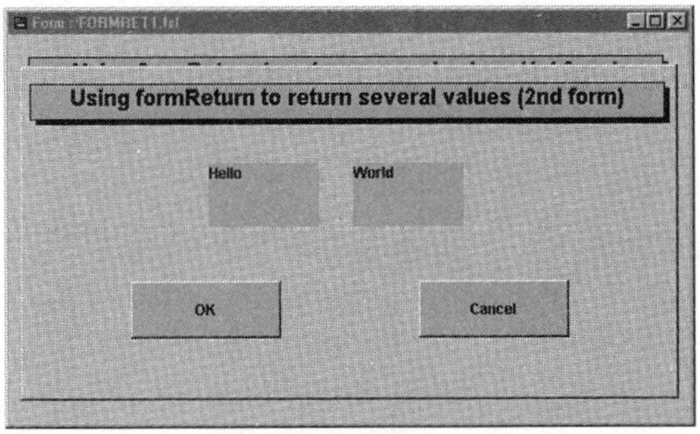

FIGURE 13.12.

FORMRET1.FSL and FORMRET2.FSL.

Analysis

In step 2, lines 4 and 5 declare fFormRet2 as a form variable and sReturnValue, sTxt1, and sTxt2 as string variables. Line 7 uses the fFormRet2 variable with open() to open the second form. Line 8 waits for the second form to return a value (pay special attention to the syntax used in this line).

Now skip over to steps 3 and 4. Line 3 in both uses `formReturn()` to return a value and control back to the calling form. It is interesting to note that, at this point, you could use `formCaller()` to find out which form is the calling form. `formCaller()` assigns the calling form to a form variable.

After `formReturn()` returns a value and control back to the calling form, the `wait()` in step 2, line 8 returns a value to the string variable `sReturnValue`. Lines 9 and 10 grab two values from two text objects on the second form. Finally, line 11 closes the second form only after you have grabbed two values from two of its text objects. Lines 12, 13, and 14 view the three values in view boxes.

Passing Values with *close()*

If you do not need to keep the second form open, then do not use `formReturn()`. Instead, just use `close()` in its place. To see this in action, follow these steps:

1. In step 2, delete lines 10, 11, 12, 14, and 15.
2. In step 3 and 4, change `formReturn()` to `close()`. For example, change `formReturn("OK")` to `close("OK")`.

If you do not need to keep the second form open, this technique of using `close()` is the preferred technique. `formReturn()` is used too much.

Passing Values Between Forms

Often, you need to pass values from one form to another. As with many things in ObjectPAL, you have several ways of approaching this task. You can't pass a variable directly from one form to another; you must use a custom method or procedure that changes or sets a variable. You can, however, change the value of a field directly.

Passing Values Directly to a UIObject

With ObjectPAL, you can pass values directly from one object to another. Because a form is an object, you also can pass values directly from one form to another. You can use statements, such as the following:

```
1:    field1Name.value = field2Name.value
```

Likewise, you can declare a `Form` variable, attach it to another form, and use dot notation to transfer values. For example, to put the value in `field1` on `form1` into `field2` on `form2`, use the following:

```
1:    var
2:       f      form
3:    endVar
4:
5:    f.attach("Form : Form2.fsl")   ;Form titles can be tricky
6:    field1.value = f.field2.value
```

This technique works well if both forms currently are open and the names of the form titles don't change. You use this technique to manipulate the `value` property of objects. After you've attached `form2` to a variable, you can expand this technique to manipulate, call, and use any of the properties of the other form's objects:

```
1:    f.box3.color = Red
2:    f.line4.visible = False
3:    f.maximize()
4:    f.hide()
5:    f.button3.pushButton()
6:    f.ID_No.locate("ID No", ID_No)
```

The following is an example of opening a form and setting a field's value:

```
1:    ;Button :: pushButton
2:    var
3:       f      Form
4:    endVar
5:
6:    f.open("MYFORM2")
7:    f.Last_Name = "Lupton"
```

This example illustrates that a form is just another object, which can be manipulated like UIObjects. As soon as you have a handle to the other form, you can manipulate it.

Passing Variables with a Table

You can write values to a table from the first form and read in the values from the other form. You use a TCursor to write to and read from a table in either the working or the private directory. You even can include a mechanism for cleaning up, or deleting, the tables when you exit the application, perhaps on the `canDepart` method of the form.

This technique works well for passing large amounts of data, nontextual data, or data you want to hang around for the next time you enter your application. To pass a sound file or a picture from one form to another, for example, use this method.

Passing Variables Through a Library

You can use a library to store and pass values. Because external objects have access only to the custom methods of a library, you must use at least two custom methods. One custom method puts the value into the library's variables; the other custom method gets the value. This technique works well if you already are using a library with your application.

This technique is valuable if you're going to open and close forms. You could write one custom method that sets a variable in the library and another that checks it. As soon as you have the two custom methods in the library, you can call them from various forms. Chapter 23 contains an example that demonstrates this technique.

Keeping Forms in Sync

With a relational database manager system such as Paradox, you often gather data into compartments. Usually, you display the data on a form in a 1:1 relationship. Occasionally, however, you need to display the data on separate forms. Having independent forms is a convenient way of displaying parts of a complete database a little at a time.

In an address book application, for example, you might separate personal information from business information. One table is connected to a form that shows personal information, such as home address, home telephone number, and so on. The other table is connected to a form that shows business information, such as title, work address, work telephone number, and so on. You might make the business form the main, or master, form and include on it a button that displays the person's home information.

When both forms are displayed, you need to keep them in sync. A form is a display manager, and display managers in Paradox are objects, just as a field is an object. Therefore, you can manipulate objects on another form. In this address book example, you can use a button to open a second form and position it on the same record or on the corresponding record. You can use two techniques to accomplish this.

You use the first technique if both forms use the same table or if they use different tables that are related. The following code represents an elegant and clean way to keep two forms in sync:

```
1:    ;button :: pushButton
2:    var
3:        f2    Form
4:    endVar
5:
6:    f2.open("homeinfo", WinStyleDefault + WinStyleHidden)
7:    f2.Last_Name.locate("Last Name", Last_Name1, "First Name", First_Name1)
8:    f2.bringToTop()
```

`Last_Name1` and `First_Name1` are two fields on the master business form.

The second technique assumes that you're using the same table in both forms. Its code is as follows:

```
1:    var
2:        tc       TCursor
3:        f        Form
4:    endVar
5:
6:    tc.attach( fldInCurrentForm )
7:    f.open("form2", WinStyleDefault + WinStyleHidden)
8:    f.fldInform2.reSync(tc)
9:    f.bringToTop()
```

Keeping Two Forms in Sync

Suppose that you have two forms that are connected to the same table or two similar tables and need to keep them in sync. This technique can be useful when displaying two forms, both of which show customer information. The following example uses dot notation and `locate()` to keep the forms in sync.

You can find the SYNC1.FSL form on the disc in the \ANSWERS directory.

Step By Step

1. Change your working directory to the TUTORIAL directory and create a new form with the Customer table in the data model. Add a button to the form and label it View Notes (see Figure 13.13). Save the form as SYNC1.FSL.

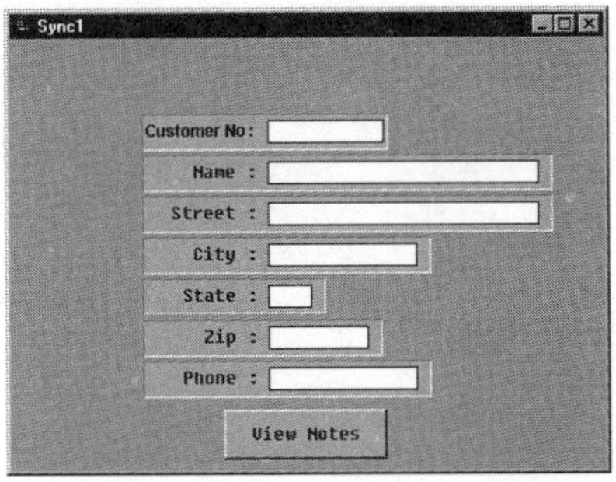

FIGURE 13.13.
SYNC1.FSL set up form.

2. Create a second form with the Custnote table in the data model. Add a button to the form and label it Close (see Figure 13.14). In the Window Style dialog box, change the title bar name to SYNC2 and save the form as SYNC2.FSL.

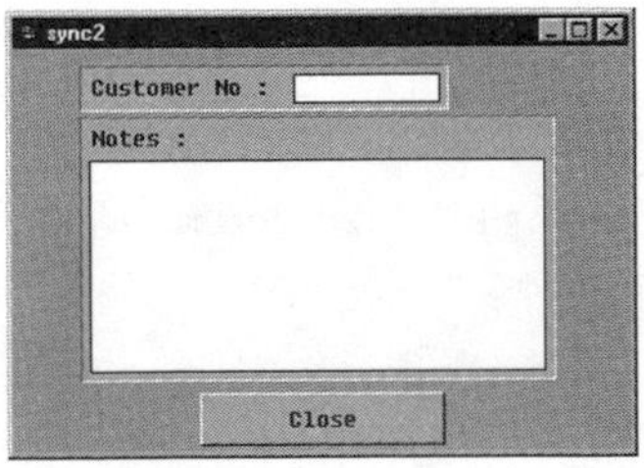

FIGURE 13.14.
SYNC2.FSL set up form.

3. In the pushButton method of the View Notes button on SYNC1.FSL, enter lines 3–17:

```
1:    ;Button :: pushButton
2:    method pushButton(var eventInfo Event)
3:        var
```

```
4:             f    Form
5:          endVar
6:
7:          if not f.attach("Sync2") then
8:              f.open("SYNC2", WinStyleDefault + WinStyleHidden)
9:          endIf
10:
11:         if not f.Customer_No.locate("Customer No", Customer_No) then
12:         f.Customer_No.edit()
13:         f.Customer_No.insertRecord()
14:         f.Customer_No = Customer_No.value
15:         endIf
16:
17:             f.bringToTop()
18:      endmethod
```

4. In the `pushButton` method of the Close button on SYNC2.FSL, type line 3:

```
1:      ;Button :: pushButton
2:      method pushButton(var eventInfo Event)
3:          close()
4:      endmethod
```

5. Check the syntax, save the forms, and run it. Move to any record and then click the View Notes button (see Figure 13.15). Enter some notes and click the Close button.

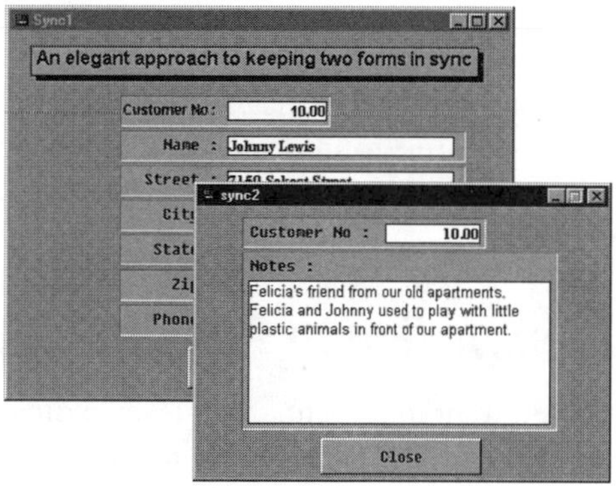

FIGURE 13.15.

SYNC1.FSL calling
SYNC2.FSL.

Analysis

In step 3, line 4 declares f as a form variable for use in lines 7 or 8 to either attach to or open SYNC2.FSL. After a handle is open, lines 11, 12, 13, and 14 use it to manipulate what record the other form is on, and then line 17 shows the form.

In step 4, line 3 closes the form and returns control back to the calling form. Also note that edit mode is automatically ended and any unposted changes to the table are posted.

The highest container level in an ObjectPAL application is the form. Often, you need to pass data from form to form. You can use any of the techniques outlined in this section to exchange data between forms or to sync forms.

Printing a Form

One of the first things you'll want to do is print a form. Unlike the report type of methods, the form type does not have a `print()` command. You can print a form from ObjectPAL, however. Just as a user can select File | Print, you can send a form to the printer with ObjectPAL. To print the current form, use either of these lines of code:

```
1:      menuAction(MenuFilePrint)    ;Emulates the menu.
2:      action(DataPrint)            ;Preferred technique.
```

You can use either of these techniques to print a form. The technique of using the `menuAction()` procedure in the preceding line 1 uses the technique to invoking a menu constant. In versions 1 and 4.5, Borland officially warns against using menu constants with this technique, for they might not work in the future. In versions since version 5, however, all the constants seem to work (at least all the constants I tested). Because menu constants are inconsistent and difficult to find, I recommend you use the action constant equivalent instead.

Preventing a User from Exiting

NEW Term

Two techniques work well for preventing the user from exiting your application. The first technique traps for the `MenuControlClose` constant with `eventInfo.id() = MenuControlClose` or `eventInfo.id() = MenuCanClose` in the `menuAction` method, and sets the `CanNotDepart` error code. The second technique uses `canDepart` of the form. Both of them use a flag. A *flag* is a variable used in a routine to indicate whether a condition has occurred. The next example demonstrates how to use `menuAction` to prevent exiting. The second technique of using `canDepart` is demonstrated next.

Using *menuAction* to Prevent Exiting

Suppose that you want to prevent a user from exiting a form unless you specify otherwise. In this example, however, the user can go into Design mode. The next example demonstrates trapping for `MenuCanClose` and `MenuControlClose` in the `menuAction` method.

You can find the NOCLOSE1.FSL form on the disc in the \ANSWERS directory.

Step By Step

1. Create a new form. On the form, place a radio button field named fldFlag. Add two choices to the radio button: Allow Close and Do Not Allow close. Figure 13.16 shows how the form should look.

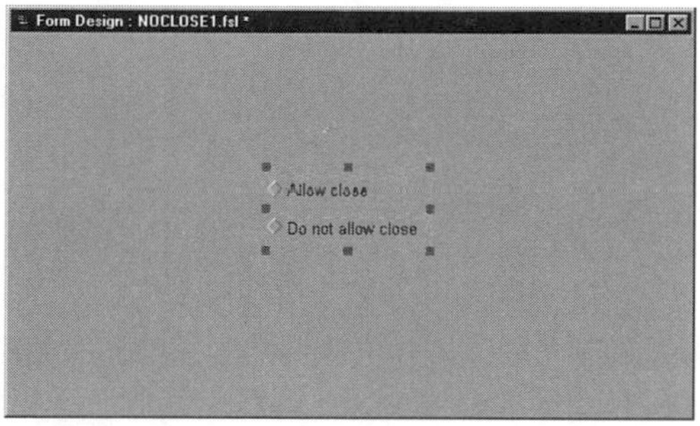

FIGURE 13.16.

NOCLOSE1.FSL. Using menuAction *to prevent the user from exiting the application.*

2. Add lines 7–12 to the menuAction method of the form.

```
1:      ;Form :: menuAction
2:      method menuAction(var eventInfo MenuEvent)
3:      if eventInfo.isPreFilter() then
4:         ;This code executes for each object on the form
5:      else
6:         ;This code executes only for the form
7:         if eventInfo.id() = MenuCanClose or
8:            eventInfo.id() = MenuControlClose then
9:            if fldFlag.value = "Do not allow close" then
10:               eventInfo.setErrorCode(CanNotDepart)
11:            endIf
12:         endIf
13:      endif
14:      endmethod
```

3. Check the syntax, save the form as NOCLOSE1.FSL, and run it. Set the field fldFlag to Do not allow close, and try all the various ways of exiting. Then, set the flag field to Allow close, and exit or move into Design mode.

Analysis

In step 2, lines 7 and 8 check for MenuCanClose and MenuControlClose. MenuControlClose is called when the user attempts to close the form, and MenuCanClose is called when the application tries to close or when the user selects Window | Close All. The menu control constants are listed online in the ObjectPAL Quick Lookup dialog box. You can use this technique to trap for any of the menu command constants. Line 9 enables you to exit. (You need a way to exit at some point in your code.) Line 10 does the real work. It sets the CanNotDepart error code.

Using *canDepart* to Prevent Exiting

Suppose that you want to prevent a user from exiting a form (including going into design mode). This next example demonstrates how to use canDepart to prevent exiting. You use the canDepart method of a form to prevent a form from closing, thereby preventing the application from closing. It also provides a way to toggle this effect on and off (perhaps with a flag field).

You can find the NOCLOSE2.FSL form on the disc in the \ANSWERS directory.

Step By Step

1. Create a new form. On the form, place a radio button field named fldFlag. The radio button field has two choices, which are Allow close and Do not allow close. The form should look like it did in the last example (refer to Figure 13.16).

2. Add lines 9–11 to the canDepart method of the form.

```
 1:    ;Form :: canDepart
 2:    method canDepart(var eventInfo MoveEvent)
 3:       if eventInfo.isPreFilter() then
 4:          ;This code executes for each object on the form
 5:
 6:       else
 7:          ;This code executes only for the form
 8:          if fldFlag.value = "Do not allow close" then
 9:             eventInfo.setErrorCode(CanNotDepart)
10:          endIf
11:       endif
12:    endmethod
```

3. Check the syntax, save the form as NOCLOSE2.FSL, and run it. Set the flag field to Do not allow close and try all the various ways of exiting. You cannot go into Design mode, as you could in the previous example. Set the flag field to Allow close, and exit.

Analysis

In step 2, line 9 checks the value of the fldFlag field. If the value is Do not allow close, line 10 sets the error code to CanNotDepart.

Both the techniques presented in this section are important. Trapping for a constant in menuAction, or action, at the form level enables you to centralize your code. Using the canDepart method and setting the error code to CanNotDepart also is useful. Both these techniques have broad uses.

The TableView Display Manager

NEW
Term

In Paradox, a *table window* is an object that displays data in its own window. A table window is what opens when you select File | Open | Table and choose a table. A TableView variable is a handle to that window. Sometimes, you want to display a table and work with it in a TableView. Although a TableView is limited in functionality, you can open and manipulate it similarly to how you open and manipulate a form. Table 13.2 lists the TableView methods and procedures.

Table 13.2. TableView methods and procedures.

```
action

bringToTop*

close

getPosition*

getTitle*

hide*

isAssigned

isMaximized*

isMinimized*

isVisible*

maximize*

minimize*

moveToRecord

open

setPosition*

setTitle*

show*

wait

windowHandle*
```

*Inherited from the Form type.

TableView Variables

Just as there are Application and Form variables, there is a variable for use with a table window. It is the TableView variable. As soon as you declare a variable as a TableView and open the TableView, you establish a handle to a table window. With that handle, you can open, wait, and close table windows, similarly to manipulating a form with a Form variable.

You also can use ObjectPAL to manipulate TableView properties. For example, you can manipulate the TableView object as a whole, such as background color, grid style, and the value of the current record. You also can manipulate the field-level data in the table (TVData), such as font characteristics and display format. Finally, you can manipulate the TableView heading (TVHeading), such as changing fonts, colors, and alignment.

The following code declares a TableView `variable` named `tv`:

```
1:    Var
2:       tv    TableView
3:    endVar
```

Because this variable now exists, you can use it to open a table window:

```
1:    tv.open("ZIPCODES.DB")
2:    tv.wait()
3:    tv.close()
```

The `TableView` `action()` method is powerful. It gives you access to many of the form methods and procedures. You can do many operations on a table, including `hide` and `show`:

```
1:    tv.hide()
2:    message("Table is hidden for 3 seconds")
3:    sleep(3000)
4:    tv.show()
```

To tell the user how to start and end Edit mode, you can use the `TableView` `setTitle()` method, as in the following:

```
1:    TableViewVar.setTitle("F9 for edit mode :: Close to return")
```

The next example demonstrates opening a table window from a button.

Displaying a *TableView* from a Button

Suppose that you want to have a button on a form display a table window. In this next example, you will declare a `TableView` variable and use the `open()` method to open up the ZIPCODES.DB table.

You can find the TVIEW1.FSL form on the disc in the \ANSWERS directory.

Step By Step

1. Set your working directory to TUTORIAL. Create a new form and put a button on it labeled ZIPCODES.DB.

2. Add lines 4–8 to the `pushButton` method, which open ZIPCODES.DB in a table window.

```
1:    ;Button :: pushButton
2:    method pushButton(var eventInfo Event)
3:       ;This routine brings up a TableView
4:       var
5:          tv    TableView
6:       endVar
7:
8:       tv.open("ZIPCODES.DB")
9:    endmethod
```

3. Check the syntax, save the form as TVIEW1.FSL, and run it. Click the button. Figure 13.17 shows how the form and table window look when you click the button.

FIGURE 13.17.

TVIEW1.FSL. How to open a table in TableView mode.

Analysis

In step 2, line 5 declares tv as a TableView variable, which line 8 uses to open the ZIPCODES.DB table.

Getting a *TableView* Ready for Input

The next step in dealing with a table window is to get it ready for data entry. You can use the action() method with constants to manipulate a table window. I like the technique presented in the next example because of its simplicity. It demonstrates how to get a table window ready for input.

Preparing *TableView* for Input

Suppose that you want to have a button on a form that opens a table window ready for input when the user clicks it. In this example, you will use the setTitle() method to set the text in the title bar of the table window, and action() to move to the end of the table, put it in Edit mode, and insert a record by moving past the last record.

You can find the TVIEW2.FSL form on the disc in the \ANSWERS directory.

Step By Step

1. Set your working directory to TUTORIAL. Create a new form and place a button on it labeled Add a Customer.

2. Add lines 4–11 to the pushButton method of the button to open Customer table window that is ready for input.

```
1:    ;Button :: pushButton
2:    method pushButton(var eventInfo Event)
3:       ;This routine brings up a table view ready for input.
4:       var
5:          tv    TableView
6:       endVar
7:
8:       tv.open("CUSTOMER.DB")
9:       tv.setTitle("Enter a record and close Table Window")
10:      tv.action(MoveEnd)
11:      tv.action(DataBeginEdit)
12:      tv.action(DataNextRecord)
13:   endmethod
```

3. Check the syntax, save the form as TVIEW2.FSL, run it, and click the button. The TableView does exactly what you told it to do, and it's ready for input. Your form should look similar to Figure 13.18. The CUSTOMER.DB table is ready for input.

FIGURE 13.18.

TVIEW2.FSL. Open for input.

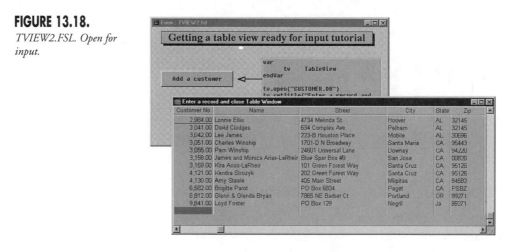

Analysis

In step 2, line 5 declares tv as a TableView variable. It's used in lines 8–11. Line 8 opens the CUSTOMER.DB table with the tv variable in a table window. Lines 9–11 use action constants to move to the end of the table, to switch into Edit mode, and to move to the next record. Now, the table window is ready for input.

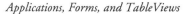

> The TVIEW3.FSL file in the \ANSWERS directory demonstrates using open(), wait(), close(), edit(), end(), and setTitle() with a TableView variable (see Figure 13.19).

FIGURE 13.19.

TVIEW3.FSL demonstrates manipulating a table window.

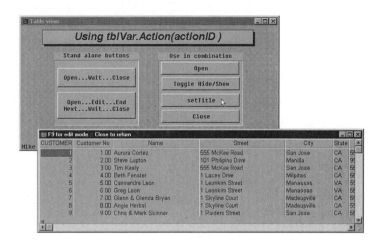

Summary

This chapter is important because it gave you control over any application you create. Now you can manipulate the application, forms, pages, and table windows. A well-designed Windows application guides a user to the correct usage of the application while giving them the freedom to explore. Later in Chapter 25, you'll learn how to add menus and toolbars to your application.

Chapter 14 discusses a topic related to display managers: queries. Chapter 15 discusses the fourth display manager—the Report display manager.

Programming with Queries

14

NEW
Term
The technique of asking questions about data by providing an example of the answer you expect is called *query by example* (QBE). You can use this tool to ask questions about your data and analyze it. A query is a means of extracting sets of information from a database or table. You can base forms and reports on a subset of your data by using a query as the first table in your data model. You can even use a live query as this first table.

You can even create queries on the fly in ObjectPAL. The Query variable is a handle to a QBE query. Table 14.1 lists the methods and procedures available in the Query type.

Table 14.1. Query methods and procedures.

```
appendRow

appendTable

checkField

checkRow

clearCheck

createAuxTables

createQBEString

enumFieldStruct

executeQBE

getAnswerFieldOrder

getAnswerName

getAnswerSortOrder

getCheck

getCriteria

getQueryRestartOptions

getRowID

getrowNo

getTableID

getTableNo

hasCriteria

insertRow

insertTable

isAssigned

isCreateAuxTables

isEmpty

isExecuteQBELocal
```

```
isQueryValid

query

readFromFile

readFromString

removeCriteria

removeRow

removeTable

setAnswerFieldOrder

setAnswerName

setAnswerSortOrder

setCriteria

setLanguageDriver

setQueryRestartOptions

setRowOp

wantInMemoryTCursor

writeQBE
```

Queries

Queries are a very important part of any database. Having a large amount of data isn't useful unless you can analyze it. Queries are what you use to analyze your data. Sometimes they are the only way to get certain information about a product. Paradox delivers a graphical QBE that makes it easier than ever to create queries and get fast answers. You can access up to 24 tables in a single query. Join, outer join, inclusion, and set operations are available for full relational queries.

QBE has two functions—namely, as an end user tool and as a way to use a subset of all the data. You can use QBE to develop specialized forms and reports.

Important Query methods and procedures are as follows:

executeQBE()	Executes a QBE query.
QUERY	Begins a QBE statement or string.
readFromFile()	Reads a QBE file into a query variable.
readFromString()	Reads a string into a query variable.
writeQBE()	Writes a Query statement to a specified file.

Displaying the Query Window

Suppose that you want to bring up the query window with a particular query. To do this, you can use sendKeys() from the system type. For example, change your working directory to the TUTORIAL directory and type line 3 into the pushButton method of a button.

```
1:   ;Button :: pushButton
2:   method pushButton(var eventInfo Event)
3:       sendKeys("%foqworld{ENTER}")   ;Emulates pressing keys.
4:   endmethod
```

sendKeys() emulates the user pressing keys. The first part of the preceding code emulates the user pressing ALT+O+Q, which is the same as selecting File | Open | Query. The second half, WORLD{ENTER}, specifies the name of the query to open and presses the Return key. Figure 14.1 shows the final result. The form ANSWERS\QUERY_O.FSL demonstrates this technique.

FIGURE 14.1.

WORLD.QBE was opened using sendKeys().

The procedure sendKeys() is addressed further in Chapter 19.

Executing a Saved Query

The term query in ObjectPAL refers to the Query variable. The Query variable is your handle to a query. Just as you can declare a Form variable and open it, you can declare a Query variable, read a file into it, and execute it. For example, change your working directory to the TUTORIAL directory and type lines 2–7 into the pushButton method of a button.

```
1:   method pushButton(var eventInfo Event)
2:       var
3:          q      Query                ;Declare a Query variable.
4:       endVar
5:
6:       q.readFromFile("WORLD.QBE")    ;Read in QBE.
7:       q.executeQBE()                 ;Execute QBE.
8:       ;Open up the ANWSER table in your private directory.
9:   endMethod
```

> **NOTE**
>
> This note is for 1.0 and 4.5 users. The procedure executeQBEFile() has been replaced with the combination of readFromFile() and executeQBE(). In versions 1.0 and 4.5, you used executeQBEFile() to execute a saved query. For backward compatibility reasons, you can still use this undocumented feature. For example:
>
> ```
> executeQBEFile("WORLD.QBE", ":PRIV:__ANS.DB")
> ```

The preceding line of code executes WORLD.QBE and generates the answer table to `:PRIV:__ANS.DB`. The new technique in version 5 is to use `readFromFile()` and `executeQBE()` from the Query type, as discussed previously.

The following example demonstrates how to run an existing query.

Running a Query from a Button

Suppose that you have an existing query, WORLD.QBE, that you want to run, show the results in a TableView, and enable Paradox to delete the answer table automatically when it exits.

You can find the form QUERY.FSL on the disc in the \ANSWERS directory.

Step By Step

1. Change your working directory to TUTORIAL. Create a new form and place a button labeled Run query file on it.

2. Add lines 3–10 to the pushButton method of the Run query file button to execute the query.

```
1:    ;Button :: pushButton
2:    method pushButton(var eventInfo Event)
3:        var
4:            q     Query            ;Declare query variable.
5:            tv    TableView
6:        endVar
7:
8:        q.readFromFile("WORLD.QBE") ;Read in QBE.
9:        q.executeQBE(":priv:__ans") ;Optional: specify answer table.
10:       tv.open(":priv:__ans")
11:   endmethod
```

3. Check the syntax, save the form as QUERY.FSL, run the form, and click the button. The query runs and creates a table named __ANS.DB in your private directory. Then the table is opened (see Figure 14.2). When you exit Paradox, the table is deleted.

Analysis

In step 2, line 4 declares a Query variable, and line 5 declares a TableView variable. Line 8 uses `readFromFile()` to read the QBE file WORLD.QBE into the q Query variable. Then `executeQBE()` is used in line 9 to run the query and create a table named __ANS.DB in your private directory.

FIGURE 14.2.

QUERY.FSL demonstrates how to run a query from ObjectPAL.

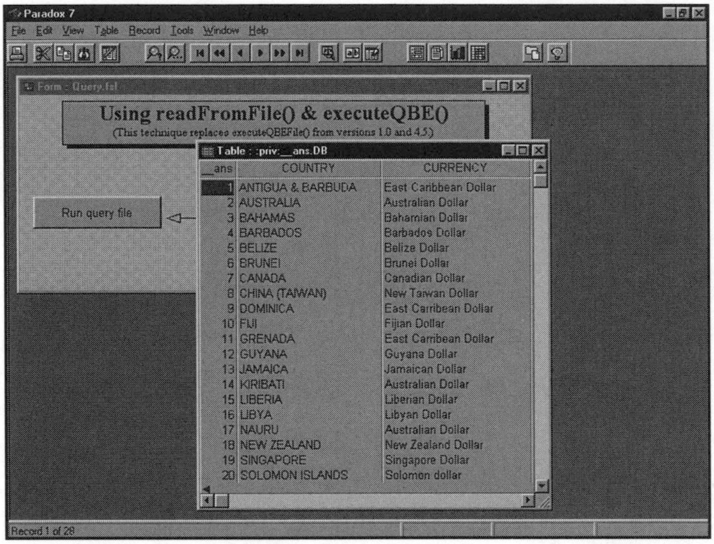

This last step of using two underscores at the beginning of a file in your private directory is important. It is also interesting because it takes advantage of an undocumented feature of Paradox. Any file in the private directory that starts with two underscores is deleted when the program is exited. This is a normal part of the clean-up process of Paradox. In addition, the files are not listed in the browser or Project Viewer.

Using a Query Statement with *executeQBE()*

In addition to executing a query file—for example, WORLD.QBE—you can code a query inside your code with ObjectPAL. First, you declare a Query variable.

```
1:   var
2:       q      Query
3:   endVar
```

Next, you use the defined Query variable to start the query section in your code. Then comes the actual Query string. For example:

```
1:   q = Query
2:          WORLD.DB | COUNTRY | CURRENCY          |
3:                   | Check   | Check ..Dollar..  |
4:   EndQuery
```

Typing all these field names, checks, and values would be a hassle, to say the least. In essence, you have to learn a whole new programming language, the QBE language. Luckily, ObjectPAL provides an easier way. A saved QBE file is simply a text file. Therefore, you can use the

Edit | Paste From option to paste the text file and alter it as needed. Then, use executeQBE() the way you did in the previous example. For example:

```
1:   q.executeQBE(":PRIV:ANSWER.DB")
```

The next example demonstrates how to use executeQBE().

Using *executeQBE*

Suppose that you want to execute a query by using the ObjectPAL Query variable.

You can find the form QUERY1.FSL on the disc in the \ANSWERS directory.

Step By Step

1. Create a new query based on WORLD.DB that queries all the records with Dollar in the CURRENCY field, as in Figure 14.3. Save the query as WORLD.QBE (this file already exists in the ANSWERS directory).

FIGURE 14.3.
WORLD.QBE query needed for example.

2. Create a new form and add a button labeled Query WORLD.DB to it.
3. The easiest way to a build a query in ObjectPAL is to build it interactively and paste it into the Editor. A QBE file is simply a text file (see Figure 14.4). It can be pasted directly into the Editor. The easiest way to do this is to use the Edit | Paste From option of the Editor. Figure 14.5 shows how the code looks after you insert the QBE file.

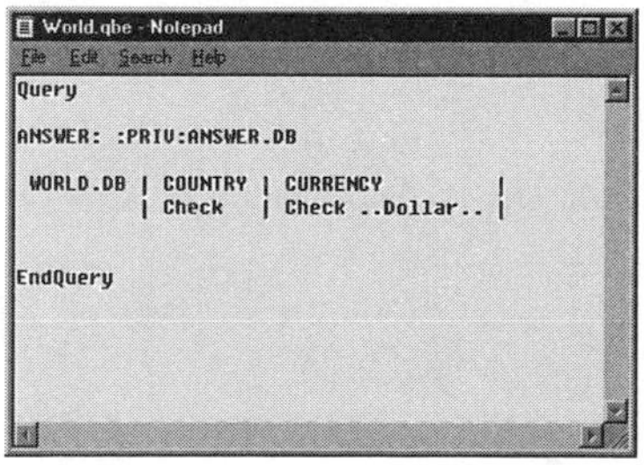

FIGURE 14.4.
The text file WORLD.QBE in Notepad.

FIGURE 14.5.

After inserting the QBE file.

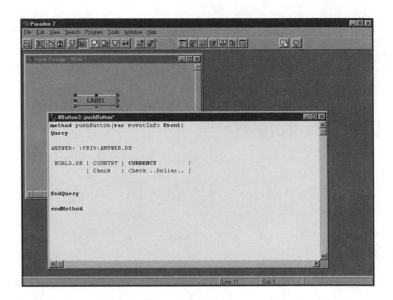

4. Alter the pushButton method of the Query WORLD.DB button as follows:

```
1:    ;Button :: pushButton
2:    method pushButton(var eventInfo Event)
3:       var
4:         q  Query
5:         tv TableView
6:       endVar
7:
8:       q = Query
9:       ANSWER: :PRIV:ANSWER.DB
10:
11:      WORLD.DB | COUNTRY | CURRENCY            |
12:               | Check   | Check ..Dollar.. |
13:
14:      EndQuery
15:
16:      executeQBE(q)
17:      tv.open(":PRIV:ANSWER.DB")
18:    endmethod
```

5. Check the syntax, save the form as QUERY1.FSL, and run it. Click the button. The query is run, and the table is shown in a table window (see Figure 14.6).

Analysis

In step 4, lines 4 and 5 declare the Query and TableView variables. Lines 8–14 contain the query that is pasted in. Only line 8 has been altered. Line 9 specifies where the answer table should be created. If you leave out line 9, the default is :PRIV:ANSWER.DB. In this case, if you delete line 9, you will get the same result. Line 16 uses executeQBE() to execute the Query variable, and line 17 displays the table that results.

FIGURE 14.6.

The QUERY1.FSL form demonstrates using executeQBE.

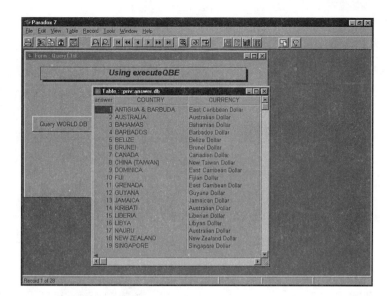

Passing a Value to a Query

You know how to execute a QBE file on disk and how to execute values stored in your code. The next step is to learn how to pass a value to a query. Often, you'll want to enable the user to enter values and to query the table for the values entered. In effect, you simulate the query editor. Use a tilde (~) variable whenever you want to pass a value to a query.

Using a Tilde (~) Variable

Suppose that you want to pass a value to a query and have the query search for that value. The next example demonstrates how to use a tilde variable to set values for a query, run the query, and display the result.

You can find the form QUERY2.FSL on the disc in the \ANSWERS directory.

Step By Step

1. Change your working directory to TUTORIAL. Create a new form. Place an unbound field named Enter_Language and labeled Enter search string. Also, place a button labeled Query World Table on the form (see Figure 14.7).

FIGURE 14.7.

Set up form for example.

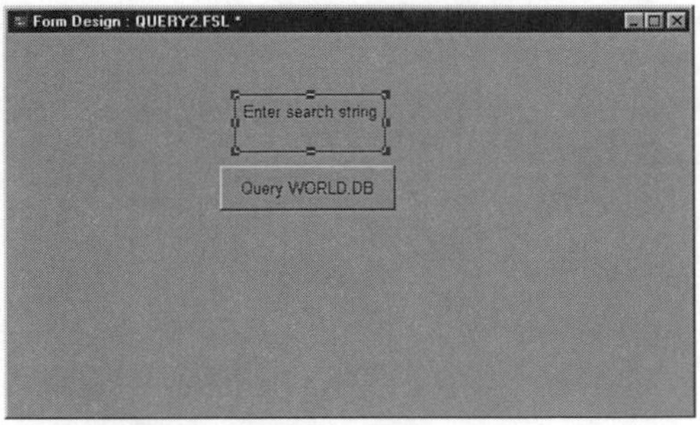

2. Before entering the code in step 3, create a query like the one shown in Figure 14.8; check the COUNTRY and LANGUAGE_1 fields and type **..English..** into the LANGUAGE_1 field. Then, paste the query directly into your code by selecting Edit | Paste From and alter it by replacing English value with the tilde and variable name (see next step).

FIGURE 14.8.

Create a query similar to QUERY2.QBE and paste it into your code.

3. Following is the altered pushButton method of the Query World Table button.

```
1:    ;Button :: pushButton
2:    method pushButton(var eventInfo Event)
3:       var
4:          q  Query
5:          tv TableView
6:          s  String
7:       endVar
8:
9:       s = Enter_Language.value
10:
11:      q = Query
12:
13:      ANSWER: :PRIV:ANSWER.DB
14:
15:      WORLD.DB | COUNTRY | LANGUAGE_1         |
16:               | Check   | Check ..~s..       |
17:
18:      EndQuery
19:
20:      executeQBE(q)
21:      tv.open(":PRIV:ANSWER.DB")
22:    endmethod
```

4. Check the syntax, save the form as QUERY2.FSL, and save it. Type a value, such as English, and click the button. The value appears. If you don't type a value into the field, all records are displayed (see Figure 14.9).

FIGURE 14.9.

QUERY2.FSL demon-strates using a tilde variable with a query.

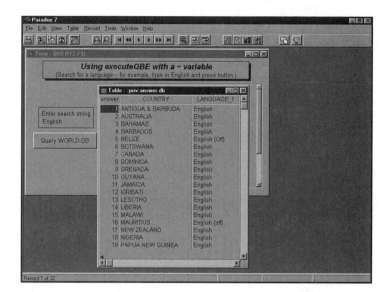

Analysis

In step 3, lines 4–6 declare the variables. Line 9 passes the value in the Enter search string field to the s variable. Lines 11–18 are the query that you pasted. Lines 11 and 16 have been altered from the value that was pasted in. Line 20 executes the Query variable, and line 21 displays the result.

Rather than bring the query editor up for the user to use (as demonstrated previously), you can simulate the query editor on a form with an interface that is more specific than File | Open | Query. Table 14.2 lists the operators you can use.

Table 14.2. Query by Example operators.

Operator	Field Types	Meaning
,	All	Specifies the AND conditions in a field
!	All except Byte & BLOB fields	Displays all the values in a field, regardless of matches
( )	N, F, D, $, S, +, I	Groups arithmetic operations
*	N, F, $, S, +, I	Multiplication
+	A, C, N, F, D, $, S, +, I	Addition or alphanumeric string concatenation
-	N, F, D, $, S, +, I	Subtraction

continues

Table 14.2. continued

Operator	Field Types	Meaning
..	A, C, N, F, D, $, S, M, FM	Any series of characters
/	N, F, $, S, +, I	Division
<	All except Byte & BLOB	Less than
<=	All except Byte & BLOB	Less than or equal to
=	All except Byte & BLOB	Equal to (optional)
>	All except Byte & BLOB	Greater than
>=	All except Byte & BLOB	Greater than or equal to
@	A, C, N, F, D, $, S, M, FM	Any single character
ALL	All except Byte & BLOB	Calculates a summary based on all the values in a group
AS	All	Specifies the name of a field in the answer table
AVERAGE	N, F, $, S, D, +, I	The average of the values in a field
BLANK	All	No value
CALC	All	Calculates a new field
CHANGETO	All except Byte and BLOB	Changes specified values in fields
Check desc	All except Byte and BLOB	Displays a field with its values sorted in descending order
Check plus	All except Byte and BLOB	Displays a field and includes duplicate values
Checkmark	All	Displays a field in the answer table
COUNT	All except Byte and BLOB	The number of values in a field
DELETE	All except Byte and BLOB	Removes records with specified values
EVERY	All except Byte and BLOB	Displays the records that match every member of the defined set
EXACTLY	All except Byte and BLOB	Displays the records that match all members of the defined set and no others
GroupBy check	All except Byte and BLOB	Specifies one group of records for a comparison that uses set comparison operators
INSERT	All except Byte and BLOB	Inserts records with specified values
LIKE	A, C	Similar to

Operator	Field Types	Meaning
MAX	All except Byte and BLOB	The highest value in a field
MIN	All except Byte and BLOB	The lowest value in a field
NO	All except Byte and BLOB	Displays the records that match no members of the defined set
NOT	All	Doesn't match
ONLY	All except Byte and BLOB	Displays the records that match only members of the defined set
OR	All	Specifies the OR conditions in a field
SET	All except Byte and BLOB	Defines specific records as a set for comparisons
SUM	N, F, $, S, +, I	The total of all the values in a field
TODAY	D	Today's date
UNIQUE	All except Byte and BLOB	Calculates a summary based on the values that appear only once in a group

NOTE

By default, SUM and AVERAGE operate on all the values in a field, whereas COUNT, MAX, and MIN operate on all values by default. You can override these default groupings by adding the word ALL or UNIQUE to a CALC statement.

Check and check descending work like check plus in BLOB fields. You can type a CALC expression in a BLOB field. You can't calculate with BLOB values, however.

Executing a Query Stored in a String

If you want, you can build a query in a string variable and then use readFromString() to read the string into a Query variable. After the query string is in a Query variable, use executeQBE() to execute it. Because you have tilde (~) variables, this technique is not really needed but can be useful. Change your working directory to the TUTORIAL directory and type lines 3–21 into the pushButton method of a button.

```
1:    ;Button :: pushButton
2:    method pushButton(var eventInfo Event)
3:        var
4:            sQuery      String       ;Declare string variable.
5:            q           Query        ;Declare query variable.
6:            tv          TableView
```

```
 7:        endVar
 8:
 9:        errorTrapOnWarnings(Yes)
10:
11:        s1 = "Query\n"
12:        s2 = "ANSWER: :PRIV:ANSWER.DB\n"
13:        s3 = "WORLD.DB ¦ COUNTRY ¦ CURRENCY            ¦\n"
14:        s4 = "         ¦ Check   ¦ Check ..Dollar.. ¦\n"
15:        s5 = "EndQuery"
16:
17:        sQuery = s1 + s2 + s3 + s4 + s5
18:
19:        q.readFromString(sQuery)
20:        q.executeQBE()
21:        if not tv.open(":PRIV:ANSWER") then errorShow() endIf
22:    endmethod
```

TIP

Here is a tip if you are having problems with a query and you are not sure whether the problem is the query string itself or something else. Use `writeQBE()` to write the Query variable out to a file, and then try to run the query interactively. In addition, you can use `isQueryValid()`, which tells you whether the query is valid. The benefit of using `writeQBE()` is that you can open the query and look at it.

Another debugging technique is to use the `errorShow()` procedure, as in the following example:

```
1:  if not q.executeQBE() then errorShow() endIf
```

Points to remember about using `readFromString()` are as follows:

- End each line of the query with \n, which represents a line feed.
- A quoted string is limited to 255 characters.
- Use multiple quoted strings for quoted strings longer than 255.
- Use the `errorShow()` procedure to check whether the query executes.

NOTE

This note is for 1.0 and 4.5 users. Those who used `executeQBEString()` should now use a combination of `readFromString()` and `executeQBE()`. In versions 1.0 and 4.5, you used `executeQBEString()` to execute a string as if it were a query block. Just as `executeQBEFile()` changed, so did `executeQBEString()`. For backward compatibility reasons, you can still use this undocumented feature. The new technique, however, is to use `readFromString()` and `executeQBE()` from the Query type, as discussed previously.

Working with Live Queries

A query is a means of extracting sets of information from a database or table. You can base forms and reports on a subset of your data by using a query as the first table in your data model. This technique is great for limiting the view of data. You can even use a live query so that you are working with the original data. The form ANSWERS\DYNASET1.FSL demonstrates this technique. It is always preferred to use a live query, but sometimes you can't. Use a nonlive query when setGenFilter() or a live query in the data model does not filter out enough records—for example, when you need unique values.

Using an In-Memory TCursor

In-memory TCursors are interesting because they are fast and they are not connected to the live data. You can ask "what if" questions of the data before writing the data to the live database. The command wantInMemoryTCursor() is used when you want to specify how a TCursor is created resulting from a query. Following is the syntax:

wantInMemoryTCursor(const **yesNo** Logical)

> **NOTE**
>
> The procedure wantInMemoryTCursor(Yes) is only necessary for queries that would normally produce live query views. If the query doesn't meet the conditions for a live query, and the answer is a TCursor, the TCursor will be in memory, nonetheless.

Specify Yes (or null) to build the TCursor in-memory; the TCursor is not connected to a table. Specify No to attach the TCursor to the live data. If you do not call wantInMemoryTCursor() before you execute a query to a TCursor, the default is the same as if you called it and passed it No; the resulting TCursor is live to the data. The exception is with multi-table queries that specify an Answer TCursor will always produce an in-memory TCursor. Here is how you use wantInMemoryTCursor() with a query to gain access to an in-memory Tcursor:

```
1:   ;Button :: pushButton
2:   method pushButton(var eventInfo Event)
3:      var
4:         qWorld           Query
5:         tcWorldQBE       TCursor
6:      endVar
7:
8:      qWorld.wantInMemoryTCursor(Yes)
9:      qWorld.readFromFile("WORLD.QBE")
10:     qWorld.executeQBE(tcWorldQBE)
11:
12:     ;Utilize in-memoy TCursor here.
13:  endMethod
```

This command also works with SQL variables. In fact, SQL variables are very similar in nature to Query variables. You manipulate them with ObjectPAL using the same techniques. You'll learn more about SQL and SQL variables later in Chapter 35. Other methods that are useful with in-memory TCursors include isInMemoryTCursor(), isView(), and instantiateView(). isInMemoryTCursor() returns True when the TCursor is an in-memory TCursor. isView() returns True if the TCursor is connected to live data. Finally, instantiateView() copies an in-memory TCursor to a physical table.

New Paradox 7 Query Methods

There are new query methods introduced with Paradox 7 to generate and modify queries using ObjectPAL. These new methods include appendTable(), setCriteria(), setQuerySortOrder(), setCheck(), and setRowOp(). These new methods are not as easy as they may seem. The following list provides a few pointers:

- You can set a row operator to check all the fields, but if you want to check all fields but one, you cannot use checkRow(), and you need to setCheck each field.

- To set the Answer table sort order, you must fill an array with every checked field. If you remove or add a field to the answer table of the query, you must fix the array and reuse setAnswerSortOrder().

- setAnswerFieldOrder() interferes with Delete, Insert, and Changeto queries. It also will inhibit removeTable().

The next example uses appendTable() to add a table to a query image, checkRow() to check all the rows of the query image, executeQBE() to run the query, and finally open() to open the answer table. Change your working directory to the TUTORIAL directory and type lines 3–14 into the pushButton event of a button.

```
 1:   ;Button :: pushButton
 2:   method pushButton(var eventInfo Event)
 3:      const
 4:         sAns = ":priv:__ans.db"  ;Path to answer table.
 5:      endConst
 6:      var
 7:         qChapters    Query
 8:         tvChapters   TableView
 9:      endVar
10:
11:      qChapters.appendTable("CHAPTERS.DB") ;Add table to query.
12:      qChapters.checkRow("CHAPTERS.DB", CheckCheck) ;Check all fields.
13:      qChapters.executeQBE(sAns) ;Execute query.
14:      tvChapters.open(sAns) ;Display table.
15:   endMethod
```

Summary

In this chapter, you learned to use a query to ask a table a question. You learned how to use sendKeys() to open up a query image for your users. You learned how to generate and use queries in ObjectPAL, how to execute a saved query, and how to execute a query string with executeQBE(). You also learned how to pass a value to a query using a tilde variable. Finally, you learned how to work with live queries, in-memory TCursors, and some of the new Paradox 7 query methods.

The questions you ask tables enable you to analyze your data. After you analyze your data, you might want to print all or part of it. You use reports, discussed in the next chapter, to print data in Paradox. Later, in Chapter 35, you learn about the SQL query language, which is yet another way to ask questions of data.

Handling Reports

A report is a tool for printing data. Reports are a way to get an organized, formatted hard copy of your data. You can communicate data with presentation-quality reports. Use this high-quality tool for the majority of your printouts. With the combination of reports and queries—and the ObjectPAL commands that enable you to use them—you can add printing capabilities to your applications.

Using Reports in ObjectPAL

The report variable is a handle to a report window. With a report variable, you can attach to an already opened report, or you can open a report. After the handle is established, you can manipulate the report. If you browse the online help and explore the Form type, Report type, and TableView type, you will see that many more Form type methods are inherited by the Report type then by the TableView type.

Opening a Report

The next bit of code demonstrates opening a report and setting the title of the report. To achieve a smooth opening of the report, note that WinStyleDefault + WinStyleHidden is used along with the show() method. Change working directories to the TUTORIAL directory and type lines 3–9 into the pushButton method of a button.

```
 1:   ;Button :: pushButton
 2:   method pushButton(var eventInfo Event)
 3:      var
 4:         r Report
 5:      endVar
 6:
 7:      r.open("REPORT", WinStyleDefault + WinStyleHidden)
 8:      r.setTitle("New report title")
 9:      r.show()  ;You can also use bringToTop().
10:   endMethod
```

Printing Reports

The first step in learning how to handle reports with ObjectPAL is learning how to print an existing report. The next two examples demonstrate how to use the print() and open() report methods.

Printing a Report from a Button

Suppose that you want to create two buttons on a form. The first button directly prints an existing report with no interaction from the user. The second button previews the report and prompts the user with the Print File dialog box.

You can find the form REPORT1.FSL on the disc in the \ANSWERS directory.

Step By Step

1. Change your working directory to TUTORIAL. Create a new form and place two buttons on it. Label the first button Print Report and the second Open then Print Report (see Figure 15.1).

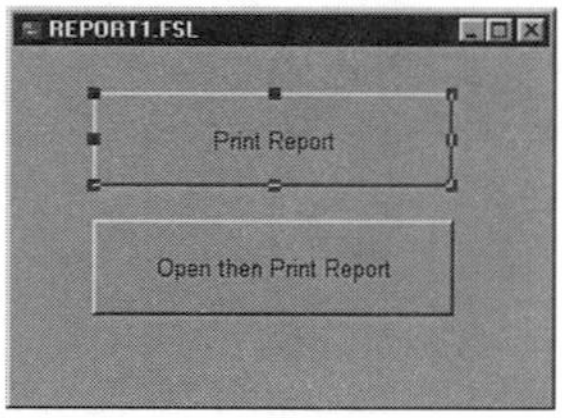

FIGURE 15.1.

*Set up form for printing
a Report tutorial.*

2. Add lines 3–7 to the pushButton method of the Print Report button.

```
1:    ;Button :: pushButton
2:    method pushButton(var eventInfo Event)
3:       var
4:         r      Report
5:       endVar
6:
7:         r.print("REPORT")
8:    endmethod
```

3. Add lines 3–8 to the pushButton method of the Open then Print Report button.

```
1:    ;Button :: pushButton
2:    method pushButton(var eventInfo Event)
3:       var
4:         r    Report
5:       endVar
6:
7:         r.open("REPORT")
8:         r.print()
9:    endmethod
```

4. Check your syntax, save the form as REPORT1.FSL, run the form, and press the Open then Print Report button.

Analysis

In steps 2 and 3, line 4 in both declares r to be a Report variable. In this case, r is a temporary variable, alive only for the duration of the method. This is important to note because, with display managers, the existence of the object (the report, in this case) does not close when the variable is destroyed. This is not true with all objects. For example, OLE and TCursor objects automatically close when the variable is destroyed. To optimize this form, you can combine these two declarations into a single declaration higher up in the containership path.

In step 2, line 7, print() is used to print the report without first previewing it. You do not need to open the report first.

In step 3, lines 7 and 8 on the second button, use open() to open the report to preview it, and use print() to display the Print File dialog box (see Figure 15.2).

FIGURE 15.2.

The Open then Print Report button previews a report and displays the Print File dialog box.

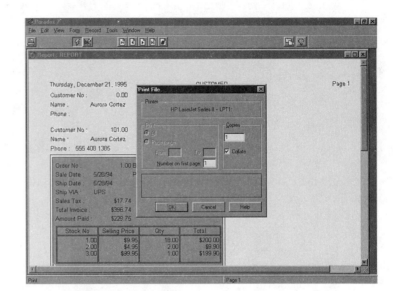

Printing a Report Based on the Current Record

In general, reports deal only with a set of data. They step through the master table one record at a time and print the report information once for every record. Often, you need to print a report based on a subset of the table or even just a single record. There are several techniques for doing this in Paradox, including using a query and using ObjectPAL. Both are demonstrated in this section. The query technique takes two steps. First, execute a query. Then, print a report that is based on the answer table for the query. In the following example, you print a report based on only the current record.

Using a Query to Print a Report Based on the Current Record

Suppose that you want to print a report based on the current record. This example uses an embedded query to generate a table with a single record in it. It also demonstrates using a temporary table to control the report.

You can find the form REPORT2.FSL on the disc in the \ANSWERS directory.

Step By Step

1. Create a query with all the fields checked based on ORDERS.DB and run it. This generates an ANSWER.DB table in your private directory, which is used in step 2.

2. Change your working directory to TUTORIAL and create a new form with the :PRIV:ANSWERS.DB, ORDERS.DB, and LINEITEM.DB tables in the data model.

3. Link the :PRIV:ANSWERS.DB table to the Orders table in a 1:1 relationship.

4. Link the Orders table to the Lineitem table in a 1:M relationship. Place a button on the form and label it Print Current Invoice. Note that you must initially create the :PRIV:ANSWER.DB table in order to link it.

5. Add lines 3–19 to the pushButton method of the Print Current Invoice button. If you would rather view the report on screen and then print it, substitute r.open("ORDER") for line 19.

```
 1:    ;Button :: pushButton
 2:    method pushButton(var eventInfo Event)
 3:       var
 4:          r    Report
 5:          q    Query
 6:          s    String
 7:       endVar
 8:
 9:       s = Order_No.value
10:       q = Query
11:       ANSWER:  :PRIV:ANSWER.DB
12:
13:       ORDERS.DB | Order No  |
14:                 | Check  ~s |
15:
16:       EndQuery
17:
18:       executeQBE(q)
19:       r.print("ORDER") ;To see report, use r.open("ORDER") instead.
20:    endmethod
```

6. Check your syntax, save the form as REPORT2.FSL, and run it. Move to the record that you want to print, and click the button.

Analysis

In step 5, line 9 takes the value from the Order_No field and puts it in the s variable. Lines 10–16 make up the query; line 14 uses the s variable. Line 18 executes the query, and line 19 prints the report. Because the report is based on the table created by the query executed in line 19, it consists of only one record.

Fully Controlling a Report

The Invoicing System, which is included on the disc that accompanies this book, demonstrates an alternate and perhaps easier technique to print the current record and maintain full control of a report. It uses setGenFilter(), setMenu(), and wait(). setGenFilter() is used to filter the data down to the current invoice. setMenu() is used to keep the user from using other menu options. Finally, wait() is used so that the user doesn't stray from the report. Following is the code in full for you to study:

```
 1:   ;btn :: pushButton
 2:   method pushButton(var eventInfo Event)
 3:      var
 4:         r              Report
 5:         m              Menu
 6:         pop            PopUpMenu
 7:         dynFilter      DynArray[] String
 8:      endVar
 9:
10:      ;Load the report hidden.
11:      if not r.load(":INVOICE:INVOICE", WinStyleDefault + WinStyleHidden) then
12:         errorShow()
13:         return
14:      endIf
15:
16:      ;Apply filter.
17:      dynFilter["Order No"] = string(Order_No.value)
18:      r.Order_No.setGenFilter(dynFilter)
19:      r.run()
20:
21:      ;Give the user only a simple menu.
22:      pop.addText("&Print...", MenuEnabled, MenuFilePrint)
23:      pop.addText("&Printer Setup...", MenuEnabled, MenuFilePrinterSetup)
24:      pop.addText("&Close", MenuEnabled, MenuControlClose)
25:      m.addPopUp("&File", pop)
26:      r.setMenu(m)
27:
28:      ;Show report and wait.
29:      r.maximize()
30:      r.wait()
31:   endMethod
```

> **WARNING**
>
> Line 17 in the preceding code works well in The Invoicing System because the field's display attributes do not display the thousands separator. If you are having trouble adopting the preceding code to your application and cannot adjust the display attributes for the field, then strip out the thousands separator using ObjectPAL's format method. For example, replace line 17 with the following line:
>
> ```
> dynFilter["Order No"] = format("EI",Order_No.Value).
> ```

Printing to a File

Sometimes, printing a report to a file is useful. For example, you can upload the file to a mainframe or take it to a service for printing. Use the generic text printer driver that comes with Windows to generate an all-text version of your report, or use a graphic printer driver for printer language files and redirect the output to a file. Either way, you can print a report to a file by setting PORT=FILE in the Windows Control Panel.

Follow these steps to print a report to a file:

Step By Step

1. If you want the file that you print to be a text-only file (no lines, frames, graphs, and so on), choose the Generic/Text Only printer driver. If it's not on the list of installed printers, install it.

> **NOTE**
>
> Viewing a report onscreen with the Generic/Text Only printer driver loaded might make your screen look irregular. The document, however, prints to a file correctly. To get rid of the irregular appearance, make sure that you design your report for the screen rather than the printer.
>
> The reason for this actually goes back to the Windows operating system itself. When Windows applications display fonts and graphics, they pull a lot of information from the printer driver. Because the Generic/Text Only printer driver has no font information, the report writer built in to Paradox does not know what to display.

If you want to keep the formatting for your report, however, choose a graphics printer driver, such as the Hewlett-Packard Series II or PostScript printer drivers. These printer drivers send printer language code to a file. This is useful for taking a printer file to an image setter.

2. From Control Panel, set up the driver to print to a file. Select the Connect button and choose File from the ports list.

3. From Paradox, choose File | Printer Setup and select the printer driver that is set up to print to a file. When you print the report, Paradox prompts you for a filename.

Manipulating the Printer Before You Print

ObjectPAL offers the capability to manipulate the printer before you print: the System Type procedures `printerGetInfo()`, `printerGetOptions()`, `printerSetCurrent()`, `printerSetOptions()`, and `enumPrinters()`. For example, to get a listing of all the available printer setups, type lines 3–8 into the `pushButton` method of a button.

```
1:   ;btn :: pushButton
2:   method pushButton(var eventInfo Event)
3:      var
4:         arPrinters        Array[] String
5:      endVar
6:
7:      enumPrinters(arPrinters)
8:      arPrinters.view("Available Printer Setups")
9:   endmethod
```

In addition to these System Type procedures, the Report Type `print()` method can control the printer.

Properties of Reports

In versions of Paradox before version 5, you had Records | Band | Sort property, RunTime | ShowAllRecords, and RunTime | ShowAllColumns. You've always had access to these properties from ObjectPAL—they were just poorly documented. FitWidth and FitHeight for table frames and MROs turned these properties on and off. In other words, selecting FitWidth and FitHeight enabled you to select these other options.

In version 7, Borland eliminated the properties `FitWidth` and `FitHeight` (only for tableframes and MROs) and added `IncludeAllData`, `ShowAllRecords`, and `ShowAllColumns`.

Using the *reportPrintInfo* Variable

Another option for changing printer orientation is to set `reportPrintInfo.orient = PrintLandscape`. The following code fragment prints a report called CUST94.RSL in landscape orientation.

```
1:   var
2:      r      Report
3:      rpi    ReportPrintInfo
4:   endVar
```

```
 5:
 6:    rpi.orient = PrintLandscape
 7:
 8:    ;Note — the file extension is optional
 9:    rpi.name = "CUST94.RSL"
10:    r.print( rpi )
```

Paper size cannot be set this way, but the number of copies, page incrementing, and starting and ending pages can be set, *if the printer driver supports these features.* To find out whether your printer driver supports these features, select File | Printer Setup: <Modify Printer Setup> <Setup>. If the Printer Setup dialog box provides fields for you to specify the number of copies, starting and ending pages, or page incrementing, then your printer driver does handle these features; otherwise, it does not.

You also can use this technique to change the master table of a report. The following code demonstrates this:

```
1:    var
2:        r        Report
3:        rpi      ReportPrintInfo
4:    endVar
5:
6:    rpi.name = "MYREPORT"
7:
8:    rpi.masterTable = "OTHER.DB"
9:    r.print(rpi)
```

Using a Custom Toolbar with a Report

Other than menus that use the standard menu constants, you can't use user-defined pull-down menus with a report because reports don't have ObjectPAL. Specifically, reports don't have a menuAction event to which you can add code. There is, however, an alternative solution. Create a small toolbar-style dialog box, then open the dialog box over the report. That is, after you preview the report, open the dialog box. Because dialog boxes are always on top, the options that you put on the dialog box are always seen; therefore, they are always active. In the following example, you launch a report and a dialog box from a button.

Adding a Toolbar to a Report

Suppose that you want to launch a report and a dialog box from a button and have the dialog box control the report. Because the second form is a dialog box, it always stays on top of the report and gives the user easy control over the report.

You can find the REPORT3.FSL form on the disc in the \ANSWERS directory.

Step By Step

1. Change your working directory to TUTORIAL. Create a new form or open an existing one, and place a button on it. Label the button Go, set the title of the form to Report Form, and save the form as REPORT3.FSL (see Figure 15.3).

FIGURE 15.3.

The Go button launches the report.

2. Now, create a small form with four buttons on it, set the form title to Options, make it a dialog box, and save it as REP—MENU.FSL. Label the four buttons Design, Maximize, Go to page 5, and Close (see Figure 15.4).

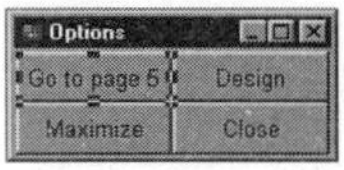

FIGURE 15.4.

REP—MENU.FSL with its title changed to Options.

3. Add lines 3–19 to the pushButton method of the Go button on the main form and save it as REPORT3.FSL.

```
 1:    ;Button :: pushButton
 2:    method pushButton(var eventInfo Event)
 3:       var
 4:          f    Form
 5:          r    Report
 6:       endVar
 7:
 8:       if r.attach("Report 1") then
 9:          r.bringToTop()
10:       else
11:          r.open("REPORT")
12:          r.setTitle("Report 1")
13:       endIf
14:
15:       if f.attach("Options") then
16:          f.moveTo()
17:       else
18:          f.open("REP-MENU")
19:       endIf
20:    endmethod
```

4. Open the REP-MENU.FSL form that you created in step 2 and add line 3 to its Var window of the page object.

```
 1:    ;Page :: Var
 2:    Var
 3:       r    Report
 4:    endVar
```

5. Add lines 3–8 to the open event method of the page object of the REP-MENU.FSL form.

```
1:    ;Page :: open
2:    method open(var eventInfo Event)
3:        if r.attach("Report 1") then
4:            r.bringToTop()
5:        else
6:            msgStop("Startup Error!",
                  "This form is only for use with Report3.fsl")
7:            close()
8:        endIf
9:    endmethod
```

6. Add line 3 to the pushButton method of the Design button on the REP-MENU.FSL form.

```
1:    ;Button :: pushButton
2:    method pushButton(var eventInfo Event)
3:        r.design()
4:    endmethod
```

7. Add line 3 to the pushButton method of the Maximize button on the REP-MENU.FSL form.

```
1:    ;Button :: pushButton
2:    method pushButton(var eventInfo Event)
3:        r.maximize()
4:    endmethod
```

8. Add line 3 to the pushButton method of the Move to Page 5 button on the REP-MENU.FSL form.

```
1:    ;Button :: pushButton
2:    method pushButton(var eventInfo Event)
3:        r.moveToPage(5)
4:    endmethod
```

9. Add lines 3 and 4 to the Close button on the REP-MENU.FSL form.

```
1:    ;Button :: pushButton
2:    method pushButton(var eventInfo Event)
3:        r.close()
4:        close()
5:    endmethod
```

10. Add lines 3–5 and 12–16 to the depart method of the REP-MENU.FSL form.

```
1:    ;Form :: depart
2:    method depart(var eventInfo MoveEvent)
3:        var
4:          f   Form
5:        endVar
6:
7:        if eventInfo.isPreFilter() then
8:            ;This code executes for each object on the form
9:        else
10:           ;This code executes only for the form
11:           if f.attach("Report Form") then
12:             f.moveTo()
13:           else
14:             f.open("REPORT3")
```

```
15:            endIf
16:         endif
17:      endmethod
```

11. Check your syntax and save both forms. Close the REP—MENU form and run the first REPORT3.FSL form. Click the Go button. The report opens first, and the dialog box opens on top of it. You can select either the pull-down menus or the buttons from the dialog box form that you created. It doesn't matter whether the report or the dialog box is active (see Figure 15.5).

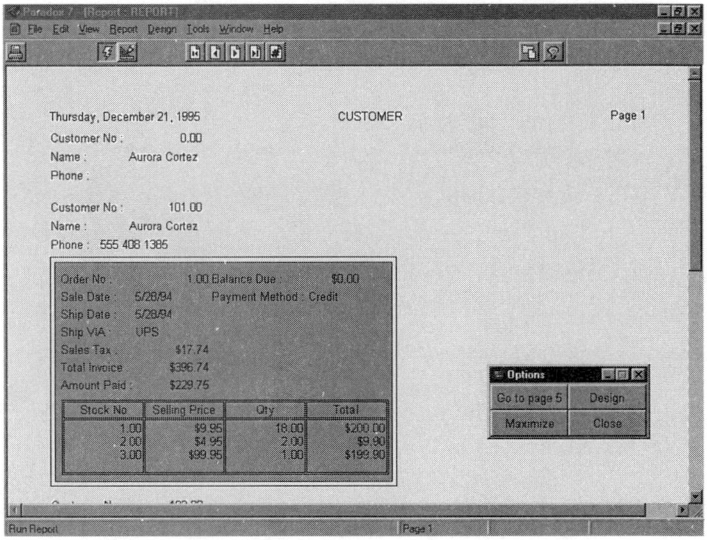

FIGURE 15.5.

REP-MENU.FSL and a report. The form always stays above the report because it's a dialog box.

Analysis

In step 3, lines 4 and 5 on the Go button of the first form declare f as a Form variable and r as a Report variable. Lines 8–13 use a Report variable to either open the report or attach to it and bring it to the top if it's open. Line 12 specifically sets a title when the report is opened. This is done so that later you can attach a Report variable to the open report. Lines 15–19 either open the small dialog box form or attach a Form variable to it and move to the small dialog box.

In step 4, Line 3 on the dialog box form declares r as a Report variable. The r Report variable is used throughout the dialog box to deal with the open report.

For example, in step 5, lines 3–8 in the open method of the dialog box establish a handle to the open report. If the report isn't open, it's assumed that the user opened the form directly. A start-up error is displayed in line 6, and the form is closed in line 7. After this form is delivered, the only way to use it is when a report named Report 1 is open.

Steps 6, 7, 8, and 9 manipulate the report on their respective buttons.

In step 10 in the var block, line 4 declares f as a Form variable. That variable is used in the depart method of the form to attach and move to the calling form. If you closed the calling form, it's reopened in line 15.

Hiding Objects in a Report

If you have a form with some hidden objects on it and want to open this form as a report, you can keep these objects hidden in the report even though there's no visible property for objects in a report. Try making the field, text, and frame of the objects white. An alternative is to open the form as a report in design mode, delete the hidden objects, and save the new report.

> **TIP**
>
> Many of the open() and load() commands can use the following:
>
> ```
> WinStyleConstants
> ```
>
> Many of the methods that open a window are overloaded with the WinStyleConstants. Therefore, the ReportVar.load() method accepts the following syntax:
>
> ```
> load("ReportName", WinStyleDefault + WinStyleHidden)
> ```
>
> This capability enables you to open a form or a report in Design mode with no impact on the screen.

Using Menus with Reports

You also can add a menu to a report using the setMenu() method. Although it was briefly introduced in this chapter, Chapter 25 discusses this technique further.

Building a Report from Scratch

Although not covered in this chapter, ObjectPAL has methods that allow you to create a report: create(), deliver(), design(), dmAddTable(), dmBuildQueryString(), dmLinkFields(), and dmLinkToIndex(). These methods enable you to create a report or form complete with a linked data model defined to UIObjects.

Summary

In this chapter, you learned about using reports and integrating them into your application. You learned how to run a report using the open() method, how to print a report with the print() method, and how to control a report with a query and with setGenFilter() and setMenu(). You also learned how to manipulate the printer before you print.

In the previous two chapters, you learned how to use and manipulate large objects in ObjectPAL. In Chapter 21, you learn how to manipulate UIObjects on a form; these chapters give you control over objects.

IV

PART

Exploring ObjectPAL

Using Table and TCursor Variables

16

A *table* is an object that consists of rows of records and columns of fields. In ObjectPAL, a Table variable is a handle to a table on disk. It's different from a TCursor variable. A TCursor variable looks at the data in a table, whereas a Table variable looks at the whole table. Table variables enable you to manipulate tables as a whole. For example, you can add records from one table to another, copy a table, and get the average value for a field. Table type methods and procedures deal with the table as a whole.

A *TCursor* (table cursor) is a pointer to a record in a table. A TCursor is a tool used to manipulate a table behind the scenes. A Table variable deals with the whole table. A TCursor variable deals with the data in a table. Specifically, a TCursor variable is a pointer to a record in a table. After you declare a TCursor variable, you can open it to a table. Once open, you then have a handle to the data in the table. When you open a TCursor, it's already pointing at the first record in the table.

Opening a Table Variable

An `open()` method is conspicuously absent from the table methods. The `attach()` method associates a Table variable with a table's filename. The extensions .DB and .DBF specify the type of table. To use a Table variable, you need to declare it, as in the following:

```
1:  var
2:     tbl  Table
3:  endVar
```

After you have a Table variable with which to work, you open it by attaching directly to a table on disk, as in the following:

```
1:  tbl.attach("CUSTOMER.DB")
```

Using Table Methods and Procedures

Many of the table methods deal with data in the table and are duplicated in the TCursor class. After you declare a Table variable and open it with `attach()`, you can use the table methods on it. The following statements, for example, are valid:

```
1:  tbl.attach("DEST.DB")
2:  tbl.cMax("Total")
3:  tbl.delete()
```

The next example puts the `cAverage()` method to work with a Table variable.

Using *cAverage()* with a Table Variable

Suppose that you want to find the average population for all the countries of the world. You can do this by using `cAverage()` and a Table variable.

You can find the TABLE1.FSL form on the disc in the \ANSWERS directory.

Step By Step

1. Change your working directory to TUTORIAL. Open a form or create a new one. Place a button labeled Average population of all the countries of the world on it.

2. Add lines 3–8 to the pushButton method of the Average population of all the countries of the world button.

```
1:   ;Button :: pushButton
2:   method pushButton(var eventInfo Event)
3:       var
4:           tbl    Table
5:       endVar
6:
7:       tbl.attach("WORLD.DB")
8:       msgInfo("Average population (millions)",
             tbl.cAverage("POPULATION_(MIL)"))
9:   endmethod
```

3. Check the syntax, save the form as TABLE1.FSL, and run it. Click the button. After a short time, the answer appears onscreen (see Figure 16.1).

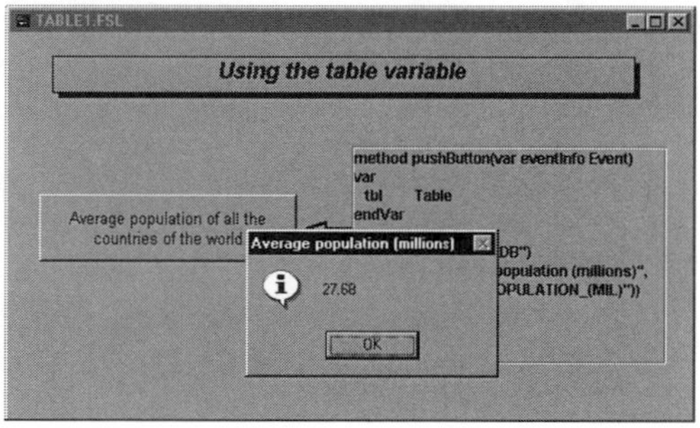

FIGURE 16.1.

*TABLE1.FSL. Using a
Table variable with
cAverage().*

Analysis

Line 4 declares the Table variable. Line 7 attaches the Table variable to the WORLD.DB table. Line 8 displays the result of cAverage().

TCursors and Invisible Access to a Table

When you use a TCursor, you can't see the changes made to a table. You can manipulate a TCursor variable just like a Table variable, however. In fact, a TCursor has many of the same methods as a UIObject. The Table type doesn't have nearly as many methods as a TCursor does. Its functionality is more limited because it operates only for the table as a whole, whereas a TCursor works directly on the data.

Think of a TCursor as a channel you open to a table. Typically, you open a TCursor with the following:

```
1:   tc.open("TABLE.DB")
```

tc is a TCursor class variable. All further references to the table can be represented by the TCursor, as in the following:

```
1:   tc.FieldName = Today()
```

In this example, quotation marks aren't used around the field name in the table. Quotation marks aren't needed for field names that have no special characters. If a field name, however, contains a special character, such as a space or a hyphen, quotation marks are required. For the sake of consistency, you might put quotation marks around all field names when you use a TCursor, as in the following example:

```
1:   tc."FieldName" = Today()
```

A TCursor works in the background. Therefore, when you manipulate a database, movement through the table doesn't appear onscreen. Because the screen isn't refreshed, changes are made quickly.

> **NOTE**
>
> In many ways, using a TCursor in ObjectPAL is like using a table on the workspace with ECHO OFF in PAL (the programming language used in Paradox for DOS).

Using a TCursor

Treat a TCursor variable like other variables. Declare it in the Var window of the object. If the method executes only once (like pushButton) or if you need a private version of the variable, declare it within the method.

In general, opening and closing a TCursor can be time consuming because opening and closing a file on a disk is slower than leaving it open. Therefore, it's best to minimize the number of times you open and close these objects. If the method you use occurs once, such as pushButton, it's okay to declare it inside the method:

```
1:   ;Button :: pushButton
2:   method pushButton(var eventInfo Event)
3:      var
4:         tc    TCursor
5:      endVar
6:
7:      tc.open("WORLD.DB")
8:      msgInfo("Current country", tc.COUNTRY)
9:   endMethod
```

Referring to Fields in a Table with a TCursor

ObjectPAL offers three ways to use a TCursor to refer to fields in a table: without quotes, with quotes, and dereferencing. For example:

```
1:  tc.Last_Name      ;Without quotes.
2:  tc."Last_Name"    ;With quotes (allows special characters).
3:  tc.(2)            ;Dereferencing with parenthesis.
```

Line 1 refers to the field with just the field name of the field as it appears in the table. If you have a field with spaces in it, such as Last Name, then you cannot use this first technique. Line 2 surrounds the field name with quotes and works with all field names. The preferred usage is to always use quotation marks. Line 3 shows how to dereference a field by surrounding it with parentheses. Line 3 is referring to the second field in the table. You also could dereference a field by using a variable, as in the following:

```
1:  var
2:     sField       String    ;Declare a variable.
3:     tcCustomer   TCursor
4:  endVar
5:  tcCustomer.open("Customer.db")
6:  sField = "Last_Name"   ;Assign a field name to the variable.
7:  view(tc.(sField))      ;Dereference the variable using parentheses.
```

Dereferencing with parentheses is a general ObjectPAL concept and is used in other places in ObjectPAL. Dereferencing is used with UIObjects, for example. You can store the name of a UIObject in a variable and use it as part of your dot notation listing the object path, as in the following example:

```
1:  var
2:     sObject      String          ;Declare a variable.
3:  endVar
4:
5:  sObject = "box1"                ;Assign an object name to the variable.
6:  pge1.(sObject).color = Red      ;Dereference the variable using parentheses.
```

For more information on dereferencing a UIObject, refer to Chapter 21.

Example of Using a TCursor to Refer to a Field

Suppose that you want to grab the name of a country and its capital from record 5. Then, position on the United States record and grab its capital. To do this, you can open a TCursor to the WORLD.DB table, grab some information, and display it to the user. The next example gets data from the WORLD.DB table using the preferred way to refer to fields referenced in a TCursor (using quotes).

You can find the TC1.FSL form on the disc in the \ANSWERS directory.

Step By Step

1. Set your working directory to TUTORIAL. Create a new form and place a button labeled Display Capitals on it.

2. Enter lines 3–12 on the pushButton method of the Display Capitals button.

```
1:  ;Button :: pushButton
2:  method pushButton(var eventInfo Event)
3:      var
4:          tc    TCursor
5:      endVar
6:
7:      tc.open("WORLD.DB")
8:      tc.moveToRecord(5)
9:      msgInfo("Capital of " + tc."COUNTRY", tc."CAPITAL")
10:     tc.locate("Country", "UNITED STATES")
11:     msgInfo("Capital of " + tc."COUNTRY", tc."CAPITAL")
12:     tc.close()
13: endmethod
```

3. Check the syntax, save the form as TC1.FSL, and run it. Click the button. The country and capital from record 5 are displayed first (see Figure 16.2). Click OK. The United States and its capital are displayed. Click OK again.

FIGURE 16.2.

TC1.FSL. Opening, displaying information from, and inserting a new record with a TCursor.

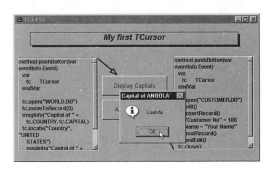

Analysis

In step 2, line 4 declares tc as a TCursor variable. Because the pushButton method occurs only when the button is clicked, you can declare the TCursor variable inside the pushButton method. The variable is redeclared every time the button is clicked, however. Therefore, a better place to declare the variable is in the button's Var window.

Line 7 opens the TCursor. Just as you can use a UIObject to move to a record, you can use a TCursor, too, as line 8 shows. Line 9 displays two values from record 5. Line 10 uses locate() to position on the record for the United States, and line 11 displays information from it. Because the data is stored in all capital letters, you must put UNITED STATES in all capitals for the `locate()` to succeed. As an alternative, you could use `ignoreCaseInLocate()` to tell Paradox to ignore the case of the letters. Line 12 closes the TCursor. This final step isn't necessary, as the TCursor will close automatically when the variable goes out of scope as the method ends. However, it's good programming to close any open TCursors when you're done with them.

Editing Data with a TCursor

With a TCursor, you can manipulate and add data directly to a table with no interaction on the form, just as you can use a UIObject to put the table connected to it into Edit mode, insert a record, and post a value. Suppose that you want to insert a new record into the CUSTOMER.DB table. To do this, open a TCursor to the CUSTOMER.DB table and insert a new record. You can perform the same tasks with a TCursor, as the following example demonstrates.

You can find the TC1.FSL form on the disc in the \ANSWERS directory.

Step By Step

1. Set your working directory to TUTORIAL. Open the TC1.FSL form you created in the last example and add a button labeled Add your Name.

2. Add lines 3–14 to the pushButton method of the Add your Name button.

```
 1: ;Button :: pushButton
 2: method pushButton(var eventInfo Event)
 3:    var
 4:         tc    TCursor
 5:    endVar
 6:
 7:    tc.open("CUSTOMER.DB")
 8:    tc.edit()
 9:    tc.insertRecord()
10:    tc."Customer No" = 100
11:    tc.Name = "Your Name"
12:    tc.postRecord() ;Post changes to table.
13:    tc.endEdit()    ;End edit mode.
14:    tc.close()      ;Close TCursor.
15: endmethod
```

3. Check the syntax, save the form, run the form, and click the button. Nothing seems to happen. Open the CUSTOMER.DB table. Now the first record is 100, and it displays your name.

Analysis

In step 2, line 4 declares `tc` as a TCursor variable. Line 7 opens the CUSTOMER.DB table. Line 7 uses the `open()` method to open the TCursor. Line 8 puts the TCursor into Edit mode.

Line 9 inserts a new record. Lines 10 and 11 set two values in the new record. Although line 12 is not really needed because ending Edit mode in line 13 posts the data, it is used here to demonstrate the postRecord() method. The postRecord() method can be useful to test whether the data you want to post to the table can be posted. Line 14 closes the TCursor and also is not needed; however, it is considered good programming practice to close any open TCursors as soon as you can.

Using *switchIndex()* with a TCursor

When you want to change the active index on a TCursor, use the switchIndex() method. The switchIndex() is in both the UIObject and TCursor types. The syntax for switchIndex() is the same, as in the following:

switchIndex([const IndexName_String][, const_stayOnRecord Logical]) Logical

To switch a table frame to a secondary index named secCity, for example, use the following:

```
1:   CUSTOMERS.switchIndex("secCity")
```

To switch back to the primary key, leave out the secondary index, as in the following example:

```
1:   CUSTOMERS.switchIndex()
```

You can use switchIndex() on a TCursor just like on a UIObject. You can even synchronize a UIObject connected to the same table with resync(). The next example demonstrates the technique of switching an index on a TCursor using ObjectPAL, and then resyncing it to the UIObject.

Example of using *switchIndex()*

Suppose that you want to sort the records in a table frame by using the primary key and the secondary index. The twist in this case is that you want to do this using a TCursor, and then synchronize it to the UIObject.

You can find the SEC-IND.FSL form on the disc in the \ANSWERS directory.

Step By Step

1. Change your working directory to the TUTORIAL directory. Create a new form with the WORLD.DB table in the data model. Choose Tabular in the Style panel in the Design Layout dialog box. Place two buttons on the form, and label them Sort by Country and Sort by Currency (see Figure 16.3).

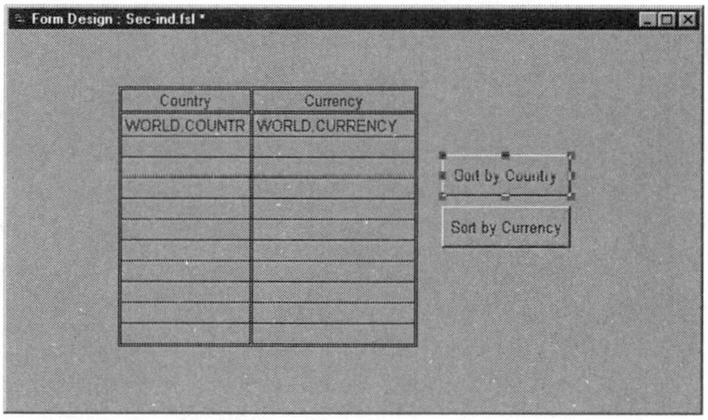

FIGURE 16.3.

Setup form.

2. Add lines 3–8 to the pushButton method of the Sort by Currency button.

```
1:  ;Button :: pushButton
2:  method pushButton(var eventInfo Event)
3:     var
4:         tc    TCursor
5:     endVar
6:
7:     tc.open("WORLD", "secCurrency")
8:     WORLD.resync(tc)
9:  endmethod
```

3. Add lines 3–9 to the pushButton method of the Sort by Country button.

```
1:  ;Button :: pushButton
2:  method pushButton(var eventInfo Event)
3:     var
4:         tc    TCursor
5:     endVar
6:
7:     tc.attach(Sec_Ind)
8:     tc.switchIndex()
9:     WORLD.resync(tc)
10: endmethod
```

4. Check your syntax, save the form as SEC-IND.FSL, and run the form. Click the Sort by Currency button; the table is now sorted by Currency, as shown in Figure 16.4. (This figure is a dressed-up version of the form you create in the "Using switchIndex with a TCursor" example.) Click the Sort by Country button to return the sort order to the primary key.

FIGURE 16.4.

The table sorted by Currency.

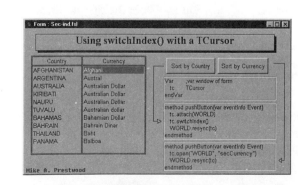

Analysis

In step 2, line 4 declares tc as a TCursor. Line 7 opens and switches the index in one step by using the alternative syntax for the TCursor open() method. Line 8 updates the screen with resync().

In step 3, line 4 declares tc as a TCursor. Lines 7–9 switch the index to the primary key. Line 8 uses switchIndex() without any parameters to switch to the primary key. These two routines can be optimized. Declaring and opening the TCursor in a higher container, for example, is more elegant.

TCursors Can Get in the Way

Sometimes you need to be wary of your own programming. An open TCursor acts like another user or session. Therefore, if an open TCursor points to or edits the same record that you are trying to edit, the error message Record already locked by this session will appear. To resolve this situation, you must move or post the TCursor. If the data you want to reach is part of the current record on the current form, always use dmget() to receive the values and dmput() to write the values. Use a TCursor only for noncurrent records.

Redeclaring TCursors

The TCursor class has both an open() and a close() method. It generally is considered good programming practice to close any TCursor you open. Any TCursor you leave open will use up resources. If you open a TCursor, should you close() it before reusing it? Although it is generally a good habit to get into, it is not necessary. Look at the following code:

```
1:  var
2:       tc TCursor
3:  endVar
4:
5:  tc.open(t1)
6:  tc.open(t2)
```

In this simple example, a TCursor is declared and used twice in a row, without ever closing the first TCursor. The question is, "Does the first instance of the tc variable close when you reopen it?" Yes.

attach() Versus open()

Many people confuse attaching and opening. You can attach a TCursor to a table window, to a UIObject, or to a TCursor variable that is already attached. This establishes an association between a new TCursor variable and an already open channel. This new TCursor variable inherits all the characteristics that apply from the attached variable. This includes edit mode, record number, and range.

When you open a TCursor, its view is the entire table. When you attach a TCursor, its view is restricted. In a multitable form, the first table in the data model is the master and controlling table. All other linked tables are detail tables. The second table shows only those records that match the current master record and are said to have a *restricted view*. When you attach a TCursor to a detail table, the TCursor inherits the restricted view of the detail table.

NEW
Term

A TCursor Can Respect a Restricted View

A table is in restricted view when it is filtered down to a subset of records. When you establish a 1:M relationship between the order numbers in the ORDERS.DB table and the records in the LINEITEM.DB table, the subset of records in the LINEITEM.DB table is restricted or filtered.

In addition to opening a TCursor in the background, you can attach a TCursor to a UIObject, which forces the TCursor to respect the restricted view of the object. For example, in a 1:M relationship, or in an active setRange(), you can attach a TCursor variable to any UIObject, and the TCursor will be restricted, just as the original UIObject is, on the same record that the UIObject is and the same edit mode.

The next example shows you how to open a TCursor by attaching it to an object already connected to the table.

Using *attach()* to Open a TCursor

Suppose that you want to display the corresponding capital of the current country. One technique for doing this is to open a TCursor to the WORLD.DB table by attaching it to a UIObject on the form and using it to grab the value. You also can use dmGet() to do this type of operation.

You can find the TC2.FSL form on the disc in the \ANSWERS directory.

Step By Step

1. Set your working directory to TUTORIAL. Create a new form that has WORLD.DB in the data model. Display only the country field. Place a button labeled Display Capital on the form (see Figure 16.5).

2. Add lines 3–9 to the pushButton method of the Display Capital button.

```
 1: ;Button :: pushButton
 2: method pushButton(var eventInfo Event)
 3:     var
 4:        tc    TCursor
 5:     endVar
 6:
 7:     tc.attach(COUNTRY)
 8:     msgInfo("Capital of " + tc.COUNTRY, tc.CAPITAL)
 9:     tc.close()
10: endmethod
```

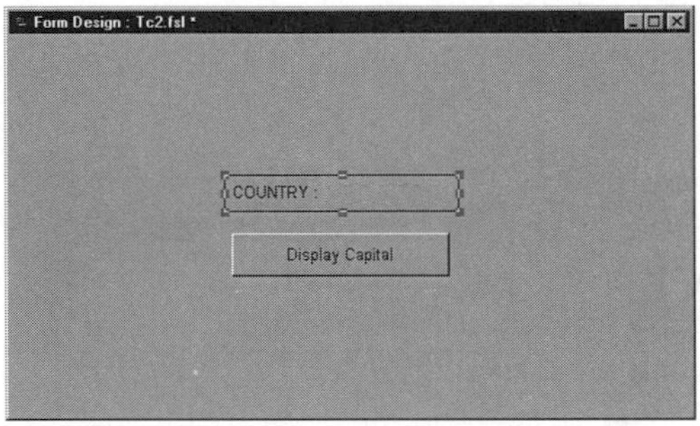

FIGURE 16.5.

Setup form.

3. Check the syntax, save the form as TC2.FSL, and run it. Position on any country you want and click the button. The capital of the country you chose is displayed (see Figure 16.6). Click OK and choose another country.

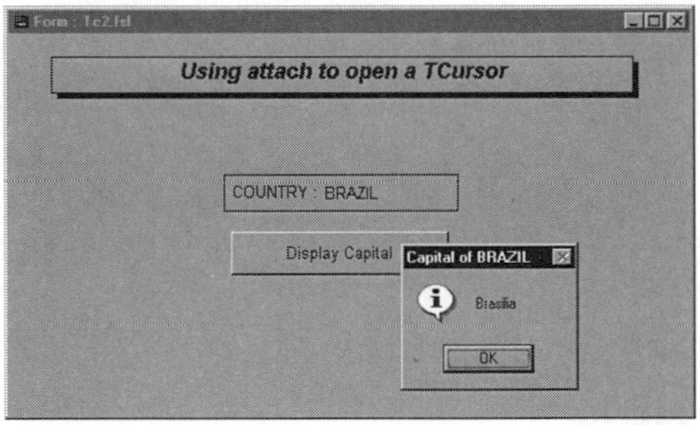

FIGURE 16.6.

TC2.FSL. Opening, displaying information from, and inserting a new record with a TCursor.

Analysis

In step 2, line 4 declares tc as a TCursor variable. Line 7 opens the TCursor by attaching it to the COUNTRY field. This technique associates the TCursor variable with the table that is bound to the field. The record number of the UIObject is inherited. Therefore, it's not necessary to use locate() to position the TCursor on the same record. Line 8 displays the capital of the current record. Line 9 closes the TCursor.

Implementing Cascade Delete Using ObjectPAL

A *cascade delete* is a setting you can set with many database products, including Borland's simpler database product, ObjectVision. Cascade delete deletes all the child records of a parent record. Because Paradox doesn't support cascade deletes, you must delete the child records. In a 1:1 relationship, this isn't a big deal. Simply delete both records in each table, as in the following:

NEW
Term

```
1:  ObjectConnectedToTableTwo.deleteRecord()
2:  ObjectConnectedToTableOne.deleteRecord()
```

This technique works quite well. You just have to remember to do it.

In a 1:M relationship, deleting child records is trickier. You have to loop through the children and delete them one at a time. As mentioned in Chapter 10, you shouldn't use a scan loop to delete records from a table. Instead, use a for loop with nRecords(), as in the following:

```
 1:  var
 2:      Counter     Number
 3:      tc          TCursor
 4:  endVar
 5:
 6:  tc.attach(ChildUIObjectName)
 7:  tc.edit()
 8:
 9:  for Counter from 1 to tc.nRecords()
10:      tc.deleteRecord()
11:  endFor
```

In this code, you attach the TCursor to the UIObject, which ensures that the TCursor will have the same restricted view that the object has. Therefore, tc.nRecords() returns the number of records in the restricted view—not the whole table.

Another technique is to use a while loop with eot(). The following code, for example, worked great in versions 1.0 and 4.5:

```
 1:  method pushButton(var eventInfo Event)
 2:      var
 3:          tc          TCursor
 4:          siCounter   SmallInt
 5:      endVar
 6:
 7:      errorTrapOnWarnings(Yes)
 8:
 9:      tc.attach(LINEITEM)        ;Attach to detail table.
10:      tc.edit()
11:
12:      ;Delete all children records.
13:      while not tc.eot()
```

```
14:        tc.deleteRecord()
15:    endWhile
16:
17:    edit()                      ;Make sure form is in edit mode.
18:    Order_No.deleteRecord()   ;Then delete the parent record.
19: endmethod
```

The preceding technique is no longer logically correct with version 5.0 because of the new interactive filter settings. The following represents the correct way to implement cascade delete in version 5:

```
1:  ;btnCascadeDelete :: pushButton
2:  method pushButton(var eventInfo Event)
3:      var
4:          tc          TCursor
5:          siCounter   SmallInt
6:      endVar
7:
8:      tc.attach(LINEITEM)       ;Attach to detail table.
9:      tc.dropGenFilter()        ;Drop any user set filters.
10:     tc.home()                 ;Put TCursor on first record.
11:     tc.edit()
12:
13:     while not tc.eot()        ;If there are any child
14:         tc.deleteRecord()     ;records, delete all of them.
15:     endWhile
16:
17:     edit()                    ;Make sure form is in edit mode.
18:     Order_No.deleteRecord()   ;Delete the parent record.
19: endmethod
```

The next example shows you how to implement cascade deletes using ObjectPAL.

Cascade Delete

Suppose that you want to delete all the children records when a user deletes their parent record. This technique is particularly important when you have implemented Prohibit referential integrity.

You can find the D-CHILD.FSL form on the disc in the \ANSWERS directory.

Step By Step

1. Set your working directory to TUTORIAL. Create a new form with ORDERS.DB and LINEITEM.DB in the data model. Link them in a 1:M relationship from ORDERS.DB to LINEITEM.DB. Group all the fields connected to the Orders table (see Figure 16.7).

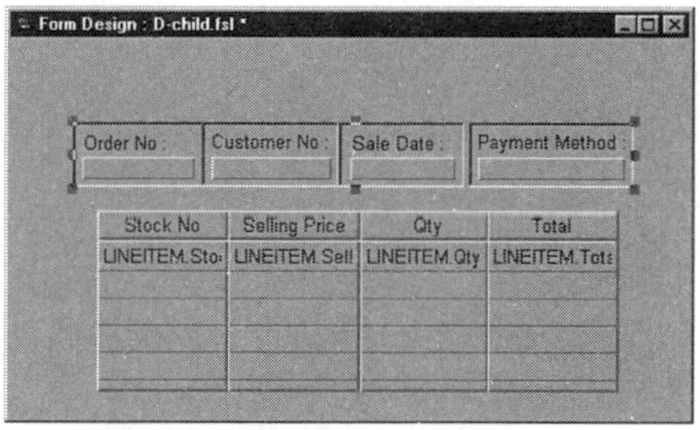

FIGURE 16.7.

Setup form.

2. Add lines 3–18 to the `action` method of the group object that is made up of all the fields from the parent table. This code deletes all the children records.

```
 1:    ;Group :: action
 2:    method action(var eventInfo ActionEvent)
 3:       var
 4:          liCounter     LongInt
 5:          tcLineItem    TCursor
 6:       endVar
 7:       if eventInfo.id() = DataDeleteRecord and isEdit() then
 8:          ;Open TCursor with UIObject restricted view.
 9:          tcLineItem.attach(LINEITEM)
10:          ;Loop through child table until all records are gone.
11:          for liCounter from 1 to tcLineItem.nRecords()
12:             tcLineItem.deleteRecord()
13:          endFor
14:          tcLineItem.close()
15:       endIf
16:       ;The default behavior occurs here and
17:       ;deletes the parent record.
18:    endmethod
```

3. Check the syntax, save the form as D-CHILD.FSL, and run it. Move to a record that has several child records and delete the parent record (see Figure 16.8).

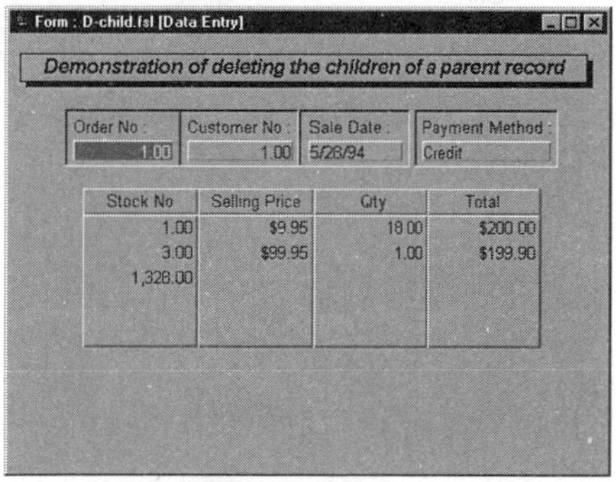

FIGURE 16.8.

D-CHILD.FSL shows an elegant technique for deleting all the children records of a parent record.

Analysis

In step 2, the var block in lines 4 and 5 declares liCounter and tc as LongInt and TCursor variables, respectively. Line 7 watches for the constant DataDeleteRecord to bubble up through the action method of the group object.

Line 9 opens the TCursor with a restricted view by attaching to the LINEITEM table frame. Note that the tc TCursor variable inherits many characteristics of the LINEITEM table frame, including its restricted view of the table and its edit mode. The for structure in lines 11–13 deletes every record in the restricted view. The for loop knows how many records are in the restricted view because of tc.nRecords() in line 11 (nRecords() returns the number of records in the table).

Line 14 closes the TCursor. In this case, you don't have to close the TCursor because the TCursor variable is declared inside the method block. This means that the TCursor's instance exists only for the duration of the action method. It's a good programming practice, however, to get in the habit of closing any TCursor that you open.

In place of the for loop in lines 11–13, you could have used a while loop, as in the following example:

```
1:   while tc.nRecords() > 0
2:       tc.deleteRecords()
3:   endWhile
```

Yet another variation on this exercise is to use the TCursor eot() method, as in the following example:

```
1:   while not tc.eot()
2:       tc.deleteRecords()
3:   endWhile
```

Why show you three different ways to accomplish the same task? For several reasons. First, to get you acquainted with the various ObjectPAL commands; and second, to show you that in ObjectPAL, there often are many ways to accomplish a single task. Which one is best? The best technique usually is the fastest or the one that uses the smallest amount of code. In this case, I believe all three are about equal.

Using *setRange()*

In versions 1 and 4.5, Borland provided the programmer with a handy but confusing method called setFilter(). setFilter() did not set a filter; it specified a range of values. This unfortunate name confused many programmers. Borland provides true filters with the setGenFilter() (discussed next) and renamed setFilter() to setRange(). All your old code that uses setFilter() still works; you just will not see setFilter() documented in the manuals, in the online help, or even when you use enumRTLMethods(). In other words, although you can use either setFilter() or setRange(), for the sake of clarity, only setRange() is documented.

setRange() is always preferred over setGenFilter() because setRange() uses the active index (either primary or secondary). This makes setRange() faster than setGenFilter().

Using *setRange()* with a TCursor

Suppose that you want to allow the user to specify a range of records they want to see—similar to live query. The technique presented in this example uses setRange() on a TCursor with the resync() method.

> You can find the SETRANGE.FSL form on the disc in the \ANSWERS directory.

Step By Step

1. Change your working directory to the TUTORIAL directory and create a new form with the Customer table in the data model and displayed in a table frame. Add two buttons labeled All Cities and Set Range of Cities. Finally, add two fields named fldStart and fldEnd (see Figure 16.9).

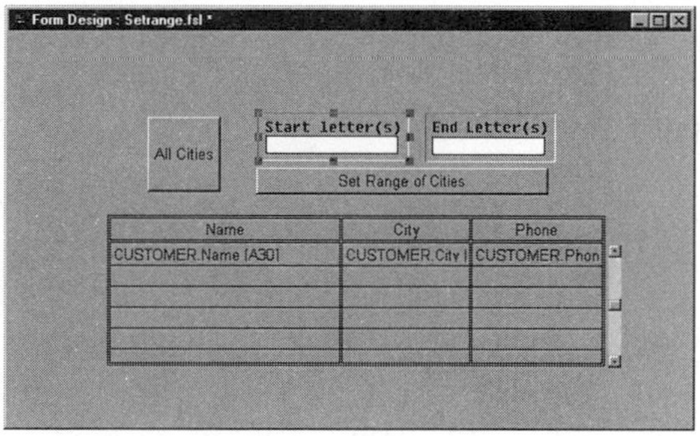

FIGURE 16.9.

Setup form for the example.

2. In the pushButton method of the Set Range of Cities, enter lines 3–11.

```
 1:    ;btnRange :: pushButton
 2:    method pushButton(var eventInfo Event)
 3:       var
 4:          tcCustomer TCursor
 5:       endVar

 6:       if not tcCustomer.open("CUSTOMER") then      ;Open TCursor.
 7:          errorShow()
 8:       endIf

 9:       tcCustomer.switchIndex("City")              ;Switch index on
                                                       TCursor.
10:       tcCustomer.setRange(fldStart.value, fldEnd.value) ;Set range of
                                                            records.
```

```
11:      CUSTOMER.resync(tcCustomer)                    ;Update the table
             frame.
12:   endmethod
```

3. In the pushButton method of the All Cities button, enter line 3.

```
1:  ;btnAll :: pushButton
2:  method pushButton(var eventInfo Event)
3:     CUSTOMER.switchIndex()
4:  endmethod
```

4. Check the syntax, save the form as SETRANGE.FSL, and run it (see Figure 16.10).

FIGURE 16.10.

SETRANGE.FSL.

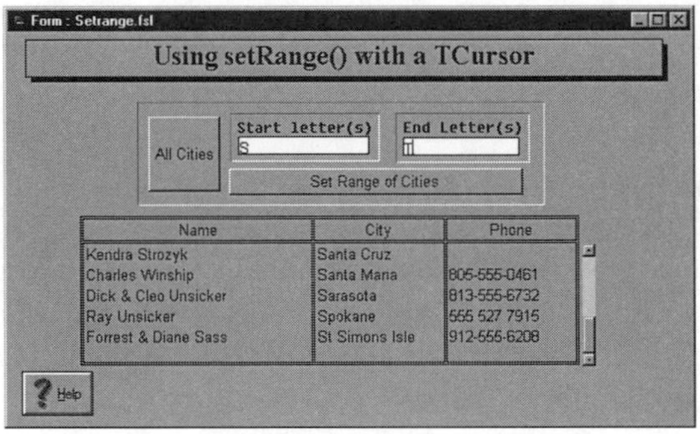

Analysis

In step 2, line 4 declares a TCursor variable for use in line 6 to open a second channel to the Customer table. This tcCustomer TCursor is used to switch the index in line 9 and set the range of records in line 10. Finally, after the TCursor has set the correct range behind the scenes, the CUSTOMER table frame is synchronized with the TCursor.

Using *setGenFilter()*

Using setGenFilter() requires two steps. First you declare a DynArray variable and populate it with the filtering data, and then you pass the DynArray to setGenFilter(). After you declare a DynArray, you assign values to it specifying the field and the values. Following are some examples of the types of formulas you can use with setGenFilter():

```
1:  var
2:     dyn  DynArray[] String
3:  endVar
4:
5:  dyn["State"] = "CA"              ;State field equals 'CA'.
6:  dyn["Total"] = "< 0"            ;Negative numbers in Total field.
7:  dyn["Total"] = "> 100, < 1000" ;Greater then 100 & less then 1000.
8:  dyn["Total"] = ">= 4, <= 8"
```

For example, to view all Orders with a Balance Due over $100.00 and less than $1,000.00, enter the following on the pushButton method of a button on a form bound to the Orders table.

Figure 16.11 shows what your form will look like.

```
1:   ;btnShowMiddle :: pushButton
2:   pushButton (var eventInfo Event)
3:   var
4:       dyn  DynArray[] String            ;Declare DynArray.
5:   endVar
6:
7:   dyn["Balance Due"] = "> 100, <1000" ;Assign filter to it.
8:   ORDERS.setGenFilter(dyn)              ;Use it with setGenFilter().
```

FIGURE 16.11.

*\ANSWERS\SETGEN1.FSL
demonstrates using
setGenFilter().*

Form : Setgen1.fsl [Data Entry]					
Demonstration of using setGenFilter()					

Customer No : Name :
1 Aurora Cortez

Order No	Sale Date	Ship Date	Total Invoice	Balance Due
101.00	7/25/94	7/25/94	$1,001.00	$1,001.00

All Orders	Positive	> 100	> 1000

Grabbing the *n* Largest Values

How do you grab the three largest values in a field? This problem often stumps database programmers. With ObjectPAL, this problem can be solved easily with a TCursor and a secondary index. You can create a secondary index based on the field you want to grab the largest three values from, activate the index, go to the end of the table, put the value in a variable, do a priorRecord(), and store the value in a variable. You also can use this technique to grab the *n* smallest values in a table.

Displaying the 10 Largest Countries

Suppose that you want to display the records for the 10 largest or smallest values in a field. In this example you use a TCursor and a secondary index to display the 10 largest countries in the world—actually, what were the 10 largest countries when WORLD.DB table was created.

You can find the TC3.FSL form on the disc in the \ANSWERS directory.

Step By Step

1. Set your working directory to TUTORIAL. Create a new form and place a button labeled 10 Largest Countries on it.
2. Add lines 4–19 to the pushButton method of the button.

```
1: ;Button :: pushButton
2: method pushButton(var eventInfo Event)
3:    var
4:       tc           TCursor
5:       ar           Array[10] String
6:       siCounter    SmallInt
7:    endVar
8:
9:    tc.open("WORLD.DB", "secArea")
10:    tc.end()
11:
12:    for siCounter from 1 to 10
13:       ar[siCounter] = tc.COUNTRY + " (" + tc."Area_(KMSQ)" + ")"
14:       tc.priorRecord()
15:    endFor
16:
17:    tc.close()
18:    ar.view("10 Largest Countries (Square Kilometers)")
19: endmethod
```

3. Check the syntax, save the form as TC3.FSL, run the form, and click the button. After a moment, the results are displayed in an array viewer (see Figure 16.12).

FIGURE 16.12.

TC3.FSL. Getting the largest values from a nonkey field using a secondary index.

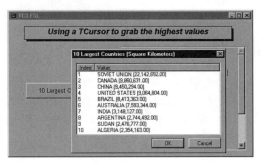

Analysis

Lines 4–6 declare the variables used for this routine. Line 5 declares a static array. Line 6 declares the siCounter variable. Line 5 declares a static array that is ready to receive 10 elements. Line 6 declares the Counter variable, which is used with the for loop later in line 12.

Line 9 opens the TCursor variable and passes it the name of the optional secondary index. Line 10 gets ready to store the values by moving to the end of the table. Because the Area secondary index is active, the end of the table is the record that has the largest number in its Area_(KMSQ) field.

Line 12 sets up the for loop to loop 10 times. Line 13 puts the first value in the first element of the array. Line 10 sets the correct record. Line 14 moves the record pointer backward one record. The loop continues for a total of 10 occurrences. Line 17 closes the TCursor (always a good idea) and line 18 displays the results.

Using Temporary Files

Sometimes, you need to create temporary tables to store information. Temporary tables are temporary because the data is needed only while the program is running. When you're done, you can delete them. One technique for deleting the tables is to use the canDepart of the form.

A better technique is to use a little-known feature built into Paradox. Whenever you quit Paradox, it deletes all the tables in the private directory whose names start with two underscores and stores them in your private directory. You can use this feature to your advantage. Whenever you create tables for temporary use in ObjectPAL, give them names that start with two underscores. Paradox takes care of deleting them for you. As a further benefit, the tables are hidden from the file browser.

This technique isn't limited to tables. In fact, it isn't limited to Paradox files. Whenever it exits, Paradox deletes all files in the private directory whose names start with two underscores. Use this feature to your advantage. Put all scratch files into your private directory, and give them filenames that start with two underscores.

Manipulating Data in a Table

There are four basic approaches to manipulating tables and records with ObjectPAL:

- Attach a Table variable to a table on disk. Then use the Table type methods to manipulate the table. (The table methods deal with the table as a whole.)
- Open a TCursor or attach it to a UIObject. Then use the TCursor class methods to manipulate the table. No manipulations are updated to the screen. If you want to update the screen, use resync().
- Use the UIObject methods to manipulate the data. Each manipulation updates the screen as it occurs.
- Send action commands to the UIObjects, such as active.action(DataNextRecord). The action commands simulate what a user does.

TIP

You can speed up a TCursor by using update(), setBatchOn(), or copyToArray(). If you use setBatchOn(), make sure to follow it with setBatchOff() every time you use it.

Copying an Entire Record with a TCursor

You can copy an entire record in a `tableFrame` by using the ObjectPal method `copyToArray()`. For the sake of simplicity, create a button on the form. In the `pushButton` method, use the following code:

```
 1:  method pushButton(var eventInfo Event)
 2:     var
 3:        recArr    Array[]    AnyType
 4:     endVar
 5:
 6:     tFrameObject.edit()
 7:     tFrameObject.copyToArray(recArr)
 8:     tFrameObject.insertAfterRecord()
 9:     tFrameObject.copyFromArray(recArr)
10:  endMethod
```

In doing this, a complete duplicate of the record will be entered after the current record. Another approach would be to attach the preceding code to the `tableframe` object using the `keyPhysical` method to monitor which key was pressed.

Autoincrementing

So far, this chapter has only touched on the power and capabilities of Table and TCursor variables. A whole book could be devoted to just these two variable types. This final section of this chapter addresses autoincrementing with the TCursor.

Paradox does have a field type to easily create an autoincrementing field. This feature was introduced with version 5. You may have reasons to use ObjectPAL to create autoincrementing fields, however.

In this section, you learn how to autoincrement using ObjectPAL. First, you autoincrement a simple field. Second, you autoincrement a nonkey field. Third, for the most elegant solution, you add locking to the routine. By studying simple and elegant methods, you learn how to implement different routines under different situations and functional programming.

Autoincrementing a field involves inserting a new record, finding the highest value, adding 1 to it, and storing the new value. You already know how to insert a new record, as in the following:

```
1:  active.insertRecord()
2:  Line_Item.insertRecord()
3:  self.action(DataInsertRecord)
4:  tc.insertRecord()
```

To get the current highest value, either move to the end of the table and put the value in a variable, or use the `cMax()` method. Either way, after you get the highest value, you need to put it into a variable.

Autoincrementing a Key Field

Suppose that you want to get the current highest value by moving to the end of the table and putting the value in a variable. First, declare a long integer variable that will hold the new number:

```
1:   var
2:        li      LongInt
3:   endVar
```

Next, move to the end of the table. Grab the current highest value and place it in the waiting variable:

```
1:   Customer_No.end()
2:   li = Customer_No
```

Now that you have the current highest value, you need to insert a new record, add 1 to the number, put the value into the field, and post the record:

```
1:   Customer_No.edit()
2:   Customer_No.insertRecord()
3:   Customer_No = li + 1
4:   Customer_No.postRecord()
```

The last line posts the record. It is important. If you don't include this line of code, the next person who tries to get the highest value won't get an accurate value.

ANSWERS\AUTO1.FSL demonstrates a simple way to autoincrement by using UIObject methods and procedures (see Figure 16.13).

FIGURE 16.13.

AUTO1.FSL.

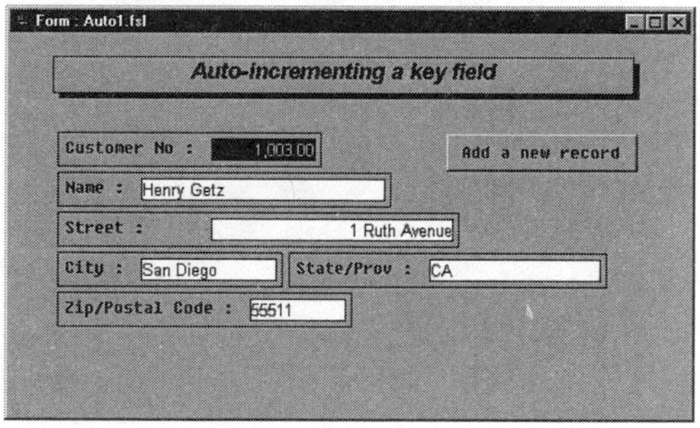

Following is the complete code:

```
1:   ;Button :: pushButton
2:   method pushButton(var eventInfo Event)
3:        var
4:             li      LongInt
5:        endVar
6:
7:        Customer_No.end()
8:        li = Customer_No
9:        Customer_No.edit()
```

```
10:        Customer_No.insertRecord()
11:        Customer_No = li + 1
12:        Customer_No.postRecord()
13:        Name.moveTo()
14:  endmethod
```

This simple example illustrates the basic steps of autoincrementing. It has many holes, how-ever. For example, the code doesn't allow for users who press the Insert key (an often-used way of inserting a record). It also is possible for two users to end up with the same number, and one user will end up with a key violation.

The next example on autoincrementing shows you how to tackle the problem of not being able to use the Insert key. It's intended only for a single-user application.

Autoincrementing for a Single User

Suppose that you want to automatically autoincrement the Customer_No field. One technique to do this is to use the action method to trap for when a user inserts a record, and increment the value at that time.

You can find the AUTO2.FSL form on the disc in the \ANSWERS directory.

Step By Step

1. Set your working directory to TUTORIAL. Create a new form with the CUSTOMER.DB table in the data model (see Figure 16.14).

FIGURE 16.14.

Setup form for example.

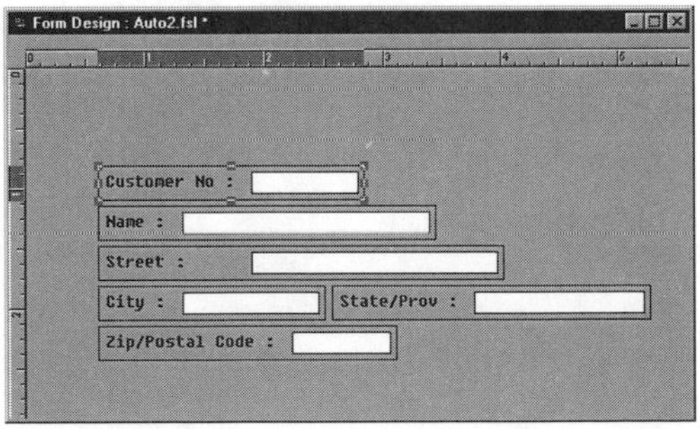

Form Design : Auto2.fsl *

```
Customer No :
Name :
Street :
City :            State/Prov :
Zip/Postal Code :
```

2. In the Var window of the page, add line 3.

```
1:  ;Page :: Var
2:  Var
3:     tc TCursor
4:  endVar
```

3. In the action method of the page, add lines 3–10.

```
1:  ;Page :: action
2:  method action(var eventInfo ActionEvent)
```

```
 3:      if eventInfo.id() = DataInsertRecord then
 4:          Customer_No.edit()
 5:          DoDefault
 6:          tc.open("CUSTOMER.DB")
 7:          Customer_No = tc.cMax("Customer No") + 1
 8:          Customer_No.postRecord()
 9:          Name.moveTo()
10:      endIf
11:  endmethod
```

4. Check the syntax, save the form as AUTO2.FSL, and run the form. Insert a record any way you want.

Analysis

In step 2, line 3 declares a TCursor in the Var window of the page. This is important. If the TCursor was declared in the `action` method, it might be redeclared thousands of times in a session—a potential problem.

In step 3, line 3 checks the event packet for `DataInsertRecord` every time an action goes to the page. After `DataInsertRecord` is detected, line 4 puts the whole form into Edit mode if it isn't in Edit mode already. Line 5 executes the default behavior. Line 6 opens a TCursor—another gateway—to the same table. Line 7 uses the TCursor with the `cMax()` method to get the highest value plus 1, and it places the new value into the Customer_No field. Line 8 posts the record. Line 9 moves the focus to the Name field as a convenience to the user.

Autoincrementing and Locking

Now you have just one more loophole to close. Theoretically, it's still possible for two users to end up with the same number. You can use autoincrementing with locks to make sure that this doesn't happen. A *lock* is a feature of the IDAPI database engine that prevents other users from viewing, changing, or locking a table or a record while one user has a lock on it. The next example uses autoincrementing with locks.

NEW
Term

Example of Autoincrementing with Locks

Suppose that you want to autoincrement a field in a multiuser environment. To do this, you need to work with locks.

You can find the AUTO3.FSL form on the disc in the \ANSWERS directory.

Step By Step

1. Set your working directory to TUTORIAL. Create a new form with the CUSTOMER.DB table in the data model (see Figure 16.15).

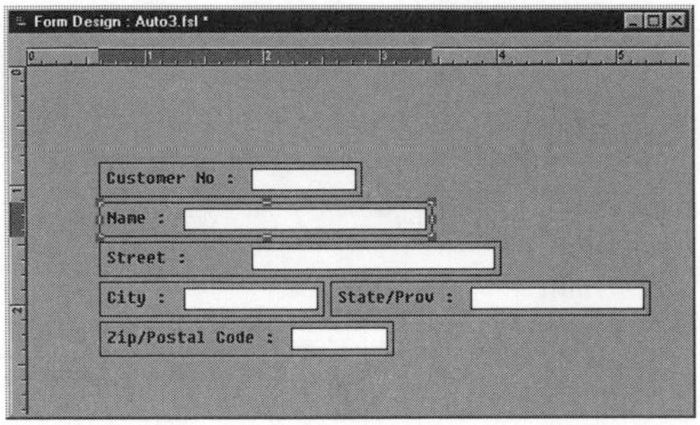

FIGURE 16.15.

Setup form for example.

2. Add lines 3 and 4 to the Var window of the page.

```
1:  ;Page :: Var
2:  Var
3:      tc              TCursor
4:      siCounter       SmallInt
5:  endVar
```

3. In the action method of the page, type lines 3–25.

```
 1:  ;Page :: action
 2:  method action(var eventInfo ActionEvent)
 3:      if eventInfo.id() = DataInsertRecord then
 4:          tc.open("INCREMNT.DB")
 5:          siCounter = 0
 6:          while not tc.lock("Full")
 7:             siCounter = siCounter + 1
 8:             message("Attempting to establish lock: " + string(siCounter))
 9:             sleep(100)
10:             if siCounter = 100 then
11:                 DisableDefault
12:                 msgStop("Warning", "Could not establish lock.")
13:                 return
14:             endIf
15:          endWhile
16:          edit()
17:          DoDefault
18:          tc.edit()
19:          tc."Customer No" = tc."Customer No" + 1
20:          tc.postRecord()
21:          Customer_No = tc."Customer No"
22:          tc.unLock("Full")
23:          Name.moveTo()
24:          tc.close()
25:      endIf
26:  endmethod
```

4. Check the syntax, save the form as AUTO3.FSL, and run the form. Insert a record.

Analysis

In step 2, lines 3 and 4 declare a TCursor and SmallInt variables for use in the action method.

In step 3, line 3 checks the event packet for `DataInsertRecord` every time an action goes to the page. When `DataInsertRecord` is detected, the elaborate autoincrementing routine begins. Line 4 opens a TCursor. Lines 6–15 attempt to put a lock on the increment table 100 times. If the program is successful, the execution skips to line 16. Otherwise, line 7 increments the counter, line 8 displays a message, and line 9 causes the program to sleep for one-tenth of a second.

Lines 10–14 check whether it is the hundredth attempt. Line 16 puts the form into Edit mode. Line 17 executes the default behavior. Lines 18–20 generate a new number. Line 21 uses the new number. Line 22 releases the incrementing table. It is important to note that this routine has two exit points. Control will leave this routine either in line 13 with the `return` keyword or at `endMethod` in line 26.

The technique you use to autoincrement your applications depends on the application and the amount of time you have.

Summary

In this chapter, you learned that Table and TCursor variables differ in fundamental ways. In general, Table variables deal with the table as a whole and TCursor variables deal with the data inside the table. When utilizing TCursor and Table variables, remember that you are utilizing another channel to the database. Table variables can lock out regular users by putting write and exclusive locks on the table. When programming a TCursor, think of the open TCursor as another user and code accordingly.

Using dm and enum Methods

17

Although manipulating the data model and setting the values of fields and table frames is discussed in other chapters, this chapter discusses manipulating the data model in general and gives specific examples. In addition, it discusses using unlinked tables in the data model and intruduces the enum category of methods.

Using the dm Methods and Procedures

The dm in dm methods stands for *data model*. With the dm methods and procedures, you can deal directly with the data model. Table 17.1 lists the dm methods and procedures.

Table 17.1. dm methods and procedures.

```
dmAddTable

dmAttach

dmBuildQueryString

dmEnumLinkFields

dmGet

dmGetProperty

dmHasTable

dmLinkToFields

dmLinkToIndex

dmPut

dmRemoveTable

dmResync

dmSetProperty

dmUnlink
```

Using *dmGet()* and *dmPut()*

Sometimes, you need values from a table in the data model for a field for which you didn't have room on your form. In those cases, dmGet() and dmPut() come in handy.

Suppose that you want to grab some values from fields in a table from the current record for which you did not have room on a form. To do this, use dwGet() and dmPut().

You can find the DMGETPUT.FSL form on the disc in the \ANSWERS directory.

Step By Step

1. Change your working directory to TUTORIAL. Create a new form with the WORLD.DB in its data model, but define only the COUNTRY field.

2. Add a button and two undefined fields to the form.

3. Label the button Change Value.

4. Change the label of the first undefined field to Value, and change its name to VField.

5. Change the display type of the second undefined field to the Radio Buttons field type, and add the following four values to its item list:

PRESIDENT

POPULATION_(MIL)

CURRENCY

LANGUAGE_1

Figure 17.1 shows how your form should look. Change the name of the form to Table_Field.

FIGURE 17.1.

Setup form for the example.

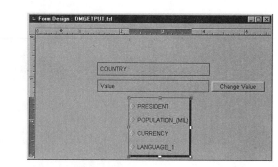

6. In the Var window of the page, add line 3.

```
1:      ;Page :: Var
2:      Var
3:         data    AnyType
4:      endVar
```

7. In the newValue method of the Table_Field field, add lines 3–6.

```
1:      ;Table_Field :: newValue
2:      method newValue(var eventInfo Event)
3:         if not self.isBlank() then
4:            dmGet("WORLD.DB", Table_Field, data)
5:            VField.value = data
6:         endIf
7:      endmethod
```

8. Add line 3 to the `newValue` method of the COUNTRY field.

```
1:    ;COUNTRY :: newValue
2:    method newValue(var eventInfo Event)
3:        if not Table_Field.isBlank() then
4:            dmGet("WORLD.DB", Table_Field, data)
5:            VField.value = data
6:        endIf
7:    endmethod
```

9. Add lines 3–7 to the `pushButton` method of the Change Value button.

```
1:    ;Button :: pushButton
2:    method pushButton(var eventInfo Event)
3:        if not Table_Field.isBlank() then
4:            edit()
5:            dmPut("WORLD.DB", Table_Field, Vfield)
6:            endEdit()
7:        endIf
8:    endmethod
```

10. Check the syntax, save the form as DMGETPUT.FSL, and run the form. Try out the various features of this form. For example, search for `United States`. You might change the name of the president from `Ronald Reagan` to `Bill Clinton`. (This shows how out-of-date the United States record is.) Figure 17.2 shows how the form looks when you use it.

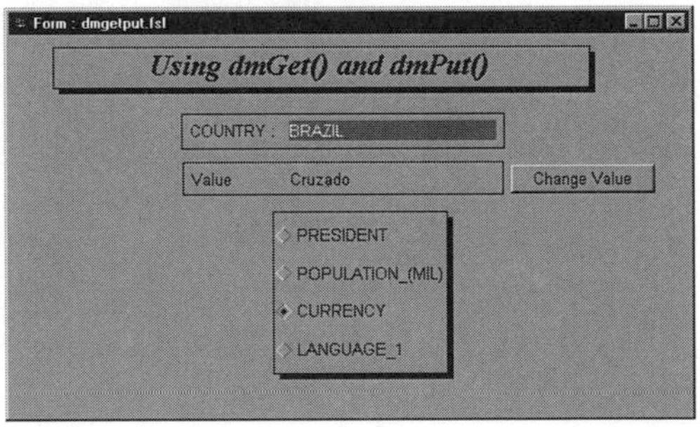

FIGURE 17.2.

DMGETPUT.FSL demonstrates using `dmGet()` *and* `dmPut()`.

Analysis

In step 6, line 3 declares `data` as an AnyType variable at the page level. This is important because `data` is used in both the Table_Field and COUNTRY fields. The page is the lowest container above both of these fields.

In step 7, lines 3–6 check whether the Table_Field field is blank. If it isn't, line 4 gets the appropriate value directly from the table and puts it first into the `data` variable and then into the VField field.

In step 8, lines 3–6 duplicate this routine for the COUNTRY field.

In step 9, lines 3–5 change the value. Line 3 makes sure that a field has been selected. Line 4 puts the form into Edit mode. Line 5 puts the changed value into the field in the table.

DM.FSL in the \ANSWERS directory demonstrates using dmBuildQueryString() and enumDataModel().

Using Unlinked Tables in the Data Model

Almost all the time, you are going to want to use the luxury of the data model. Sometimes, however, you may not need to link the tables in it. Why? One reason is that in a multiuser situation, such as Customer to Orders to Lineitem, you may have a need to have multiple data entry on customer. The problem is that the data model will lock the Customer table when you enter an order into the Order table, effectively forcing your application to be a single customer application. The trick is to emulate the data model's restricting of records without duplicating its locking scheme.

Emulate the data model by using the record object. If you have fields on the form, then surround it with a 1-by-1 MRO. After you do this, use the arrive method of the record object and use doDefault and and setFilter() on the child table or tables. Study the form NO_LINK.FSL to see this technique in detail (see Figure 17.3).

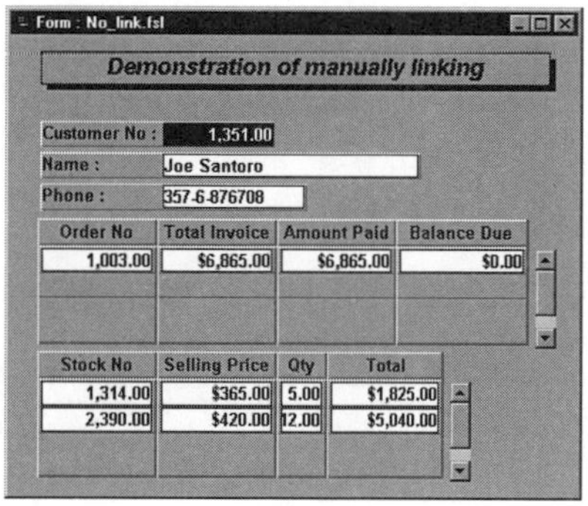

FIGURE 17.3.

NO_LINK.FSL demonstrates using unlinked tables in the data model.

The enum Category

This small chapter finishes with an interesting way to study a subject—putting it in a category. If you were studying procedures, all the procedures that give or enumerate information could be grouped in a category. This section takes a brief look at the enum methods and procedures. An *enum procedure* is a procedure that enumerates information and puts it in a table.

Using an enum Method

You use enum methods and procedures the same way you use other methods and procedures. If the enum command you want to use is a procedure, simply call it with little or no setup. To create a table on disk of all the files in a folder, for example, use the following:

```
1:   enumFolder("FILES.DB")
```

Many enum methods enable you to fill an array rather than a table on disk. To fill an array with all the files in a folder, for example, use the following:

```
1:   var
2:      ar    Array[] Anytype
3:   endVar
4:   enumFolder(ar)
5:   ar.view()
```

Finally, if the enum command is a method, you have to set up the appropriate variable first.

The following code defines tv as a TableView variable, creates a table of the current sessions in your private directory, and shows that table.

```
1:   var
2:      tv    TableView
3:   endVar
4:   enumDesktopWindowNames(":priv:sessions.db")
5:   tv.open(":priv:sessions.db")
```

The next example demonstrates using one of the enum procedures—enumFonts().

Enumerating Fonts

Suppose that you want to enumerate all your fonts and display the resulting table in a TableView. This example also acquaints you with setMouseShape().

You can find the FONTS.FSL form on the disc in the \ANSWERS directory.

Step By Step

1. Create a new form or open an existing one. Place a button labeled List Fonts on it (see Figure 17.4).

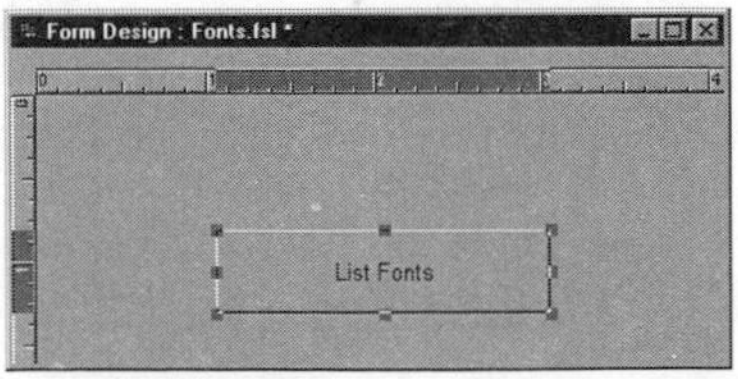

FIGURE 17.4.
Setup form for the example.

2. Add lines 3–12 to the pushButton method of the List Fonts button.

```
1:    ;Button :: pushButton
2:    method pushButton(var eventInfo Event)
3:       var
4:          tv    TableView
5:       endVar
6:
7:       message("This may take a while, searching for fonts.")
8:       setMouseShape(MouseWait)
9:       enumFonts(":PRIV:__FONTS.DB")
10:      setMouseShape(MouseArrow)
11:      message("")
12:      tv.open(":PRIV:__FONTS.DB")
13:   endmethod
```

3. Check the syntax and save your work as FONTS.FSL. Run the form and click the button. While the fonts are being enumerated, the mouse pointer turns into the waiting mouse, and a message is displayed in the status bar (see Figure 17.5).

FIGURE 17.5.

FONTS.FSL. Listing and displaying all your system fonts.

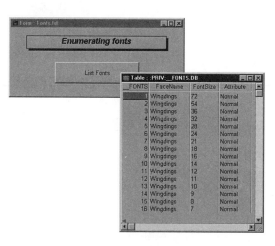

Analysis

In step 2, line 4 declares a TableView variable for use in line 12. Line 7 displays a message, letting the user know that the routine might take a long time. This message is important. The more fonts you have, the longer the routine takes, and some users have many fonts.

Line 8 reinforces the message by changing the mouse pointer to the waiting mouse. Line 9 enumerates the fonts to a table in the private directory. The two underscores preceding the name of the table are important because Paradox will automatically erase the table when it exits.

Line 10 sets the mouse pointer back to the pointer mouse, and line 11 clears the message in the status bar. Line 12 displays the TableView.

EFAMILY.FSL demonstrates using the enumFamily() method.

Summary

This chapter discussed several topics. With the dm methods and procedures, you learned you can deal directly with the data model. You learned that the trick to emulating the data model is to use the record object. If you have fields on the form, then surround it with a 1-by-1 MRO. Finally, you were introduced to the enum category of procedures.

Fields, Table Frames, and MROs

18

Fields, table frames, and multirecord objects (MRO) all display data. Table frames and MROs both have a record object; you can add a record object around a set of fields by using a 1-by-1 MRO. Fields, table frames, and MROs differ in how they display data. Although you can use many of the same techniques with all three, there are programming differences you need to keep in mind.

Handling Fields

As a developer programming a database application, you need to manipulate fields and the data in the fields. This section deals with modifying fields, setting the tab order of fields, and manipulating drop-down edit lists.

Automatically Entering Memo View

NEW Term

Memo view enables you to easily edit fields defined to a memo field. For example, the return key takes you to the next line in a memo field when in Memo view. To manually enter Memo view, press Shift+F2. To automatically enter Memo view, put the following code in the `arrive` method of a standard or formatted memo field:

```
1:    method arrive(var eventInfo MoveEvent)
2:       doDefault
3:       self.action(EditEnterMemoView)
4:    endMethod
```

The following code can be used in a `pushButton` method to move to a memo field and put the memo field into memo view:

```
1:    method pushButton(var eventInfo Event)
2:       MyMemoField.moveto()
3:       MyMemoField.action(EditEnterMemoView)
4:    endmethod
```

Setting the Tab Order of a Form

There are three commonly used techniques to set the tab stop order of a form: setting the `Next Tab Stop` property, using ObjectPAL, and using the concept of containership. The most elegant of these three solutions is the Next Tab Stop feature. The Next Tab Stop is an interactive and easy solution. For the sake of demonstrating containership and because it is very useful, however, I'll show you the third technique here: using containership.

Paradox has containership, which enables you to put a smaller object inside a larger object. You can say that the larger object contains the smaller object. You can use containership to dictate the tab order of fields by grouping them or putting them inside another object.

Suppose that you have a two-column form (a form with fields on the left and right). You put a box around the fields on the left; the box will contain those fields. Likewise, you can select all the fields and group them by selecting Design | Group. The form \ANSWERS\DM_1-1.FSL demonstrates this technique (see Figure 18.1). In this case, when you tab to the first field in the group on the left, the tab order goes through all the other fields in the group before it exits to the fields on the right.

FIGURE 18.1.

DM_1-1.FSL demonstrates grouping objects.

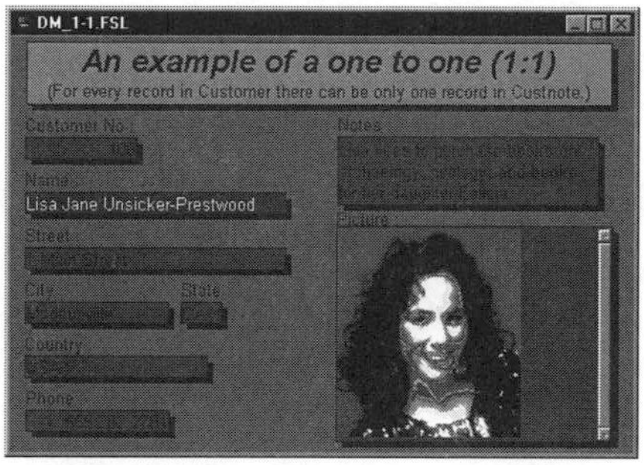

You can create a box with or without a border or group the objects. It might be a good idea to put a box around the fields on the right side of the form, too. This way, the user goes through all the fields on the right, even if some of the fields on the left are empty.

The last technique for controling tab order is to use the depart method of the object, and use objectName.moveto() to move the focus to the new object. Because version 5 introduces the new Next Tab Stop property, however, I do not recommend this technique.

On a similar note, you can set the errorCode() to CanNotDepart for the page to prevent the user from getting to the next page except through your code. To do this, you must set flags.

Drop-Down Edit Lists

Often, you want to have a pick list or a drop-down edit field available in your form when you're editing. A list field enables you to restrict the values entered into a field to those on the list. Table 18.1 lists the pertinent properties of the list object.

Table 18.1. List properties for filling a list.

Property	Description
datasource	Fills a list object with the values in a field in a table.
list.count	Specifies the number of elements in the list.
list.selection	Use to specify the currently selected item in list.
list.value	Sets the value of an item in a list.

With the properties in Table 18.1, you can control a list object. Suppose that a user needs ID numbers or items of a specific type in a list and doesn't want to have to type hundreds of ID numbers. To fill a list object, use the `dataSource` property. You can place this line of code on the list object of the drop-down edit box, as in the following example:

```
1:   self.DataSource = "[tablename.fieldname]"
```

If you use the .DB file extension when you describe your table name, you need to embed the table name in quotation marks. Because the expression is already in quotation marks, you need to use \" to represent a quotation mark. The backslash character means that the next character is taken literally, as in the following example:

```
1:   self.DataSource = "[\"tablename.db\".fieldname]"
```

To reach the list object, select the field and open the Object Tree by using the toolbar. Make sure the split pane is checked by selecting View | Both on the Object Explorer. Select the list object listed on the Object Tree, and place the code on the open method.

This technique changes the actual value of the field when you're in Edit mode. It doesn't move to the record that matches that value. The list is a list of choices that changes the value of the current field to which the drop-down edit box is attached.

Emptying a List

A list can be blanked by setting its count to 0. For example, the following code empties the list object called `lst1`:

```
1:   lst1.list.count = 0
```

Using a drop-down edit list to move to a new record, rather than change the value of the current record in that field, requires a few extra steps:

1. Make the drop-down field an undefined field. Name it DROP.

2. Add the `self.DataSource` code to the list object.

3. On the drop-down edit object (not the list object), change two methods as follows:

```
1:      ;lst1 :: open
2:      self.value = fieldname.value   ;This sets the
3:                                     ;initial value

1:      ;lst :: newValue
2:      if eventInfo.reason() = EditValue then
3:          fieldName.locate("fieldname", DROP.value)
4:      endIf
```

4. Save and execute this code. Now the drop-down edit list acts as a data navigator for your table. I don't recommend this technique for large tables because a drop-down edit list with more than a few hundred options is unmanageable. In addition, ObjectPAL limits the number of items in a list to 2,500.

The next example demonstrates how to populate a drop-down edit list.

Populating a Drop-Down Edit List

Suppose that you want to populate a drop-down edit list and to activate it whenever the user arrives on the field. This is what you learn how to do in the next example.

> You can find this form on the disc in the \ANSWERS\LIST1.FSL directory.

Step By Step

1. Set your working directory to TUTORIAL. Create a new form with three undefined fields on it. Make the middle field a drop-down edit list, and name the list object list (see Figure 18.2). This example uses only the middle undefined field. The other two fields are on the form so that you can move on and off the middle field.

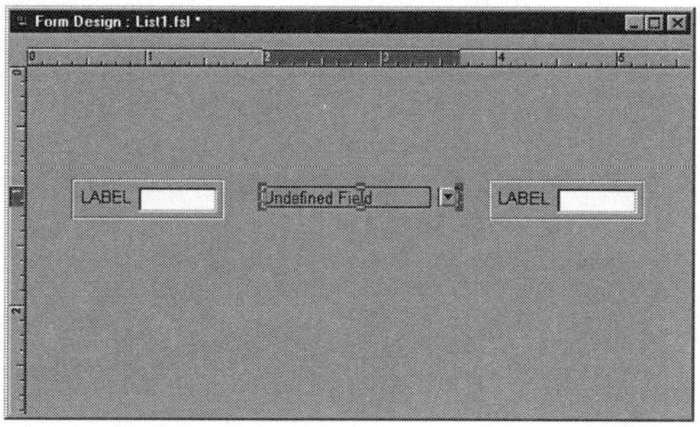

FIGURE 18.2.

Setup form for the example.

2. Add line 3 to the open method of the list object of the field.

```
1:    ;fldList :: open
2:    method open(var eventInfo Event)
3:        self.list.DataSource="[WORLD.COUNTRY]"
4:    endmethod
```

3. Add lines 3–5 to the arrive method of the field.

```
1:    ;fldList :: Arrive
2:    method arrive(var eventInfo MoveEvent)
3:        if self.isBlank() then
4:            action(EditDropDownList)
5:        endIf
6:    endmethod
```

4. Check the syntax, save the form as LIST1.FSL, and run it. Use the Tab key to move from field to field. When you arrive on the field that has the code, its drop-down edit list is displayed (see Figure 18.3). Select a value from the list, and press the Tab key. The list no longer drops down.

FIGURE 18.3.

*LIST1.FSL demonstrates
populating a list.*

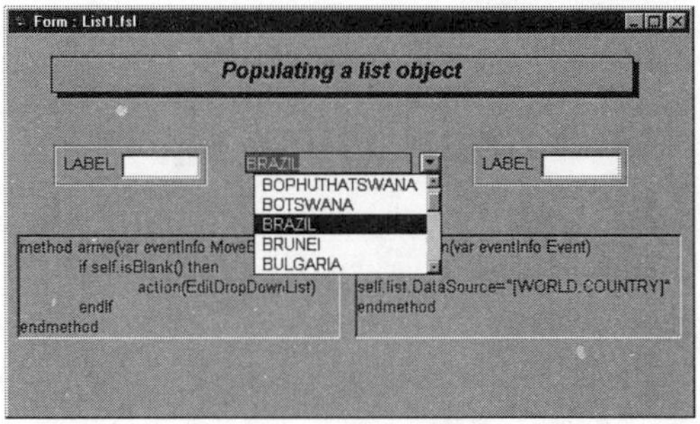

Analysis

In step 2, line 3 populates the `list` object of the field. In step 3, line 3 checks whether it has a value. If the field object is blank, line 4 drops the list for the user.

Adding Automatically to a Drop-Down List

Suppose that you want to populate a drop-down edit list and automatically add new entries to it. This next example demonstrates how to add automatically to a drop-down list.

You can find the LIST2.FSL form on the disc in the \ANSWERS directory.

Step By Step

1. Set your working directory to TUTORIAL. Create a new form with two undefined fields on it. Make the first field a drop-down edit list, and name the list object `list` (see Figure 18.4). This example uses only the first undefined field. The other field is on the form so that you can move on and off the first field.

FIGURE 18.4.

Setup form for the example.

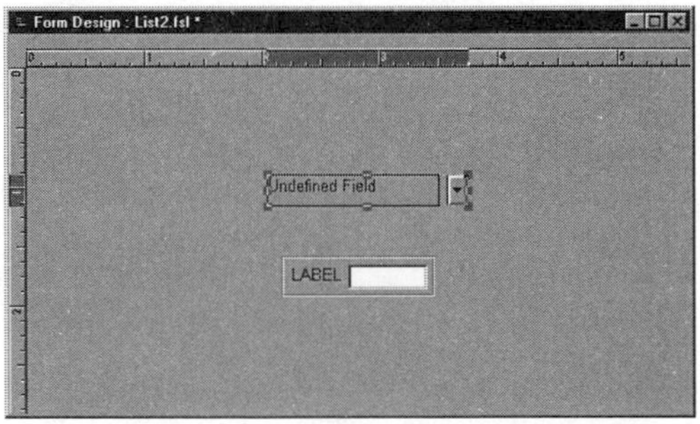

2. In the `arrive` method of the `list` object of the field, add line 3.

```
1:    ;fldList :: arrive
2:    method arrive(var eventInfo MoveEvent)
3:        self.list.DataSource="[CUSTOMER.Name]"
4:    endmethod
```

3. In the `canDepart` method of the field, add lines 3–18.

```
1:    ;fldList :: canDepart
2:    method canDepart(var eventInfo MoveEvent)
3:        var
4:            tc    TCursor
5:        endVar
6:
7:        ;Add a value if necessary.
8:        if not self.isBlank() then
9:          tc.open("CUSTOMER.DB")
10:         if not tc.locate("Name", self.value) then
11:             tc.edit()
12:             tc.insertRecord()
13:             tc."Name" = self.value
14:             tc.(1) = tc.cMax("Customer No") + 1
15:             tc.postRecord()
16:         endIf
17:         tc.close()
18:       endIf
19:   endmethod
```

4. Check the syntax, save the form as LIST2.FSL, and run it. Add a new entry to the drop-down edit list. Move off the field. Move back and drop down the edit list. Your entry has been added to the list (see figure 18.5).

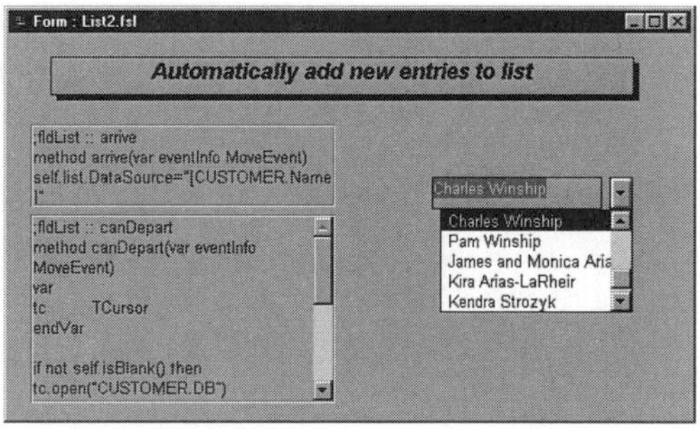

FIGURE 18.5.

LIST2.FSL demonstrates automatically adding to a list.

Analysis

In step 2, line 3 populates the `list` object of the field. The `arrive` method was selected for this task because you need the list to repopulate with the latest information every time it is selected.

In step 3, line 4 declares a TCursor variable. (A better place to declare the variable is before the method or in the Var window. To keep the code visually close together, the code in this example puts the variable inside the method.) Line 8 tests whether the field has a value in it. If it does, line 9 opens a TCursor that will be used in lines 10–15.

Line 10 tests whether the value is already in the table. If it isn't, line 11 puts the TCursor into Edit mode. Line 12 inserts a new record. Lines 13 and 14 set the values, and line 15 posts the record. Line 17 closes the TCursor.

Verifying Validity Checks

If you want to prevent the user from moving off a field when a validity check fails or when a key violation occurs within a field, use the following code:

```
1:  ;Field :: depart
2:  doDefault
3:  if self.edit() then
4:    if not self.postRecord() then
5:      errorShow()
6:      self.moveTo()
7:    endif
8:  endif
```

Table Frames

NEW
Term

A *table frame* is a design object for forms and reports that represents a table and consists of columns and rows. This section discusses how you can add sorting capibilities to table frames, highlighting records, and manipulate table frames using ObjectPAL.

Adding Column Sorting to a Table Frame

ObjectPAL is powerful and many times can complete tasks with a single line of code. To provide one-click sorting of a column of a table frame, simply add a secondary index for each column you want to sort by and add the following code to the mouseClick method of the text box in the header of the column (change the name of the secondary index to the one you created).

```
1:  ;text :: mouseClick
2:  method mouseClick(var eventInfo MouseEvent)
3:    self.switchIndex("secShortDescription")
4:  endmethod
```

Preventing the User from Going Past the End of a Table

You can use the auto-append feature of the data model to always restrict the user from going past the last record in a table frame. Suppose that you want to prevent new records from being inserted into a table that is being accessed by means of a table frame embedded in a form. You can prevent a new record from being inserted by first trapping the DataInsertRecord action constant and then disabling the code of the default event. If you just want to stop the user from inserting a new record by moving past the last record, however, then uncheck the auto-append property of the table in the data model.

PAST-END.FSL demonstrates using ObjectPAL to prevent a user from moving past the last record in a table frame.

Selecting Multiple Records from a Table Frame

Sometimes it is useful to mark a set of records permanently. dBASE does this when you delete a record. The record is marked for deletion, and it is permanently deleted when you pack the table. When you program, you often want to mark a set of records permanently. I call this mechanism a *marked list*.

To implement a marked list, include a field in the database structure called *Marked*. Make the field type A1. With code, you enable the user to select the record (such as with the spacebar or by clicking it). In turn, you place a character into the marked field of the record (such as the letter *Y* for Yes or *X* for marked).

At this point, you can do a variety of things with queries. For example, by interrogating the Marked field and looking for your character that signifies that the field is marked, you can save the answer query in another directory or do simple housekeeping chores. This is an important technique for permanently marking records. It has a broad range of uses in your applications, such as the following:

```
1:   ;Routine to mark field.
2:   ;Field :: mouseDown
3:   disableDefault
4:   if self.isBlank() then
5:      self.value = "X"
6:   else
7:      self.value = ""
8:   endIf
```

After a user marks records, you can query for the X or you can use a scan loop to loop through the table and do something with each record marked, as in the following example:

```
1:   ;Routine to handle marked field.
2:   var
3:      tc    TCursor
4:   endVar
5:
6:   tc.open("TABLE.DB")
7:   scan tc for tc."Field" = "X":
8:      ;Do something here.
9:   endScan
```

Remember that you also need to clear out the Marked field at some point, as in the following example:

```
1:   ;Routine to clear marked field.
2:   var
3:      tc    TCursor
4:   endVar
```

```
 5:
 6:  tc.open("TABLE.DB")
 7:  tc.edit()
 8:  scan tc:
 9:     tc."Marked" = ""
10: endScan
```

You can highlight an inactive table frame. In the next example, you highlight the current record of a table frame that no longer has focus.

Highlighting an Inactive Table Frame

Suppose that you want to highlight the current record of a table frame that no longer has focus. You can do this by using the color property and by knowing the event model.

 You can find the HIGHLIT1.FSL form on the disc in the \ANSWERS directory.

Step By Step

1. Change your working directory to the TUTORIAL directory. Create a new form with CUSTOMER.DB, ORDERS.DB, and LINEITEM.DB in the data model set up as a 1:M:M relationship.

2. Add a 1-by-1 MRO around the master table fields as Figure 18.6 shows.

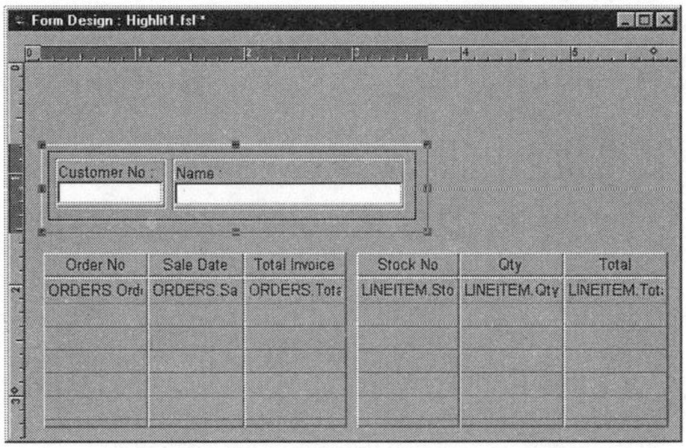

FIGURE 18.6.

Set up form for the example.

3. Name the record object of the ORDERS table frame recOrders. Without any code, you can't tell to which record records appearing in the second table frame belong.

4. In the canDepart method of the ORDERS table frame, add line 3.

```
1:   ;ORDERS :: canDepart
2:   method canDepart(var eventInfo MoveEvent)
3:      recOrders.color = Yellow
4:   endmethod
```

5. In the `canArrive` method of the ORDERS table frame, add line 3.

```
1:    ;ORDERS :: canArrive
2:    method canArrive(var eventInfo MoveEvent)
3:        recOrders.color = Transparent
4:    endmethod
```

6. Add line 3 to the `canDepart` method of the 1-by-1 MRO.

```
1:    ;mroOneByOne :: canDepart
2:    method canDepart(var eventInfo MoveEvent)
3:        recOrders.color = Transparent
4:    endmethod
```

7. Check the syntax, save the form as HIGHLIT1.FSL, and run it. Nothing seems different. Click any record in the ORDERS table frame, and then click the Name field. You still have a visual indication of which record the second table frame is on. Figure 18.7 shows that record is highlighted even when the focus is on the Name field.

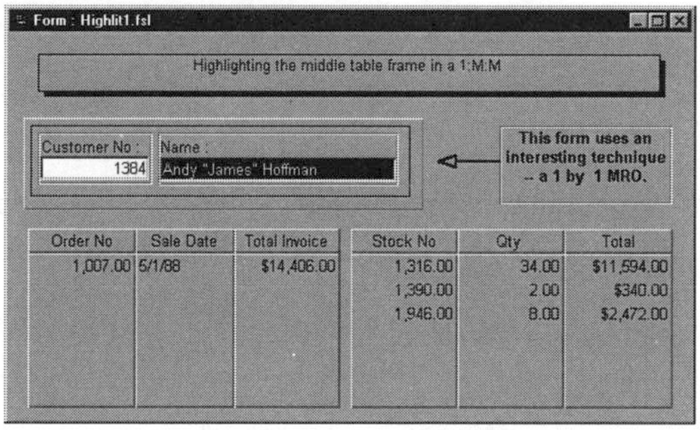

FIGURE 18.7.

HIGHLIT1.FSL demonstrates highlighting a record.

Form : Highlit1.fsl
Highlighting the middle table frame in a 1:M:M

Customer No :	Name :
1384	Andy "James" Hoffman

This form uses an interesting technique – a 1 by 1 MRO.

Order No	Sale Date	Total Invoice	Stock No	Qty	Total
1,007.00	5/1/88	$14,406.00	1,316.00	34.00	$11,594.00
			1,390.00	2.00	$340.00
			1,946.00	8.00	$2,472.00

Analysis

The technique used in this routine is interesting because of how it uses the event model. The next example shows you how to make the highlight consistent when the table frame has the focus and when it doesn't.

Highlighting a Table Frame

Suppose that you want to highlight the current record of a table frame when it has the focus and when it loses the focus. This next example builds on the concepts of the previous example.

You can find the HIGHLIT2.FSL form on the disc in the \ANSWERS directory.

Step By Step

1. Change your working directory to TUTORIAL. Create a new form with CUSTOMER.DB, ORDERS.DB, and LINEITEM.DB in the data model set up as a 1:M:M relationship (see Figure 18.8).

FIGURE 18.8.

Setup form for the example.

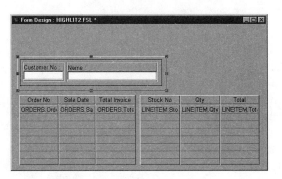

2. Add line 3 to the canArrive method of the ORDERS table frame.

```
1:      ;ORDERS :: canArrive
2:      method canArrive(var eventInfo MoveEvent)
3:          recOrders.color = Transparent
4:      endmethod
```

3. Add line 3 to the canDepart method of the ORDERS table frame.

```
1:      ;ORDERS :: canDepart
2:      method canDepart(var eventInfo MoveEvent)
3:          recOrders.color = Yellow
4:      endmethod
```

4. Add line 3 to the canDepart method of the recOrders record object.

```
1:      ;recOrders :: canDepart
2:      method canDepart(var eventInfo MoveEvent)
3:          self.color = Transparent
4:      endmethod
```

5. Add line 3 to the arrive method of the recOrders record object.

```
1:      ;recOrders :: arrive
2:      method arrive(var eventInfo MoveEvent)
3:          self.color = Yellow
4:      endmethod
```

6. Add line 3 to the canDepart method of the record object of the 1-by-1 MRO.

```
1:      ;mroOneByOne.record :: canDepart
2:      method canDepart(var eventInfo MoveEvent)
3:          recOrders.color = Transparent
4:      endmethod
```

7. Check the syntax, save the form as HIGHLIT2.FSL, and run it. Nothing seems different. Click any record in the ORDERS table frame, and then click the Name field. You still have a visual indication of which record the second table frame is on. Now, move the cursor up and down the table frame. The table frame highlight moves with the pointer (see Figure 18.9).

FIGURE 18.9.

HIGHLIT2.FSL demonstrates another technique for highlighting a table frame.

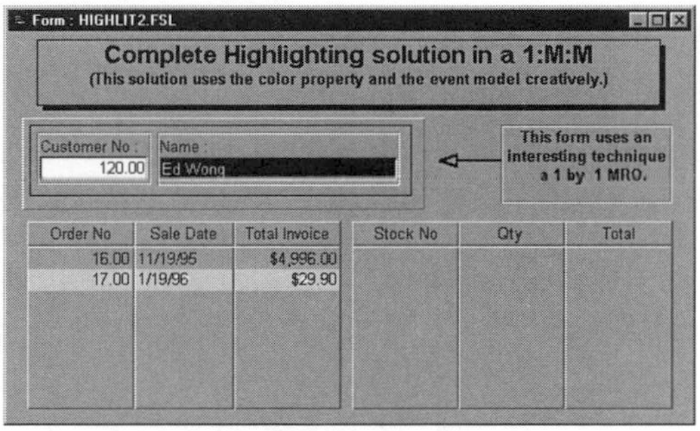

Analysis

In step 2, line 3 sets the color of the record object named `recOrders` to `Transparent`. This code occurs whenever the focus moves to the ORDERS table frame. Without this code, the highlight doesn't clear, and you end up with multiple records highlighted.

In step 3, line 3 sets the color of the current record to yellow whenever the focus leaves the table frame. In this example, nothing but the default behavior occurs when you're actually on the table frame.

In step 4, line 3 sets the record that you are leaving to `Transparent`. In step 5, line 3 sets the record on which you are arriving to `Yellow`. In step 6, line 3 changes the color of the record object to `Transparent` whenever it changes the master records.

The previous two examples compensate for the lack of a table frame marker in Paradox. Borland left out this much-needed feature. TableView objects in Paradox underline the current record. ObjectVision offers a pointer to the table object (a little arrow on the left side of an object resembling a table frame). Borland needs to add this feature in a future version of Paradox.

Selectively Highlighting Records in a Table Frame

Sometimes it is useful to highlight records of a table frame based on certain criteria. This next example demonstrates one technique for doing this.

Suppose that you want to highlight all the records in a table frame with a positive value in a certain field. This example demonstrates using the `newValue` event method with the `container` property to change the color of the record object whenever a value is updated in the field.

> You can find the HIGHLIT3.FSL form on the disc in the \ANSWERS directory.

Step By Step

1. Change your working directory to TUTORIAL. Create a new form with ORDERS.DB in the data model and displayed in a table frame (see Figure 18.10).

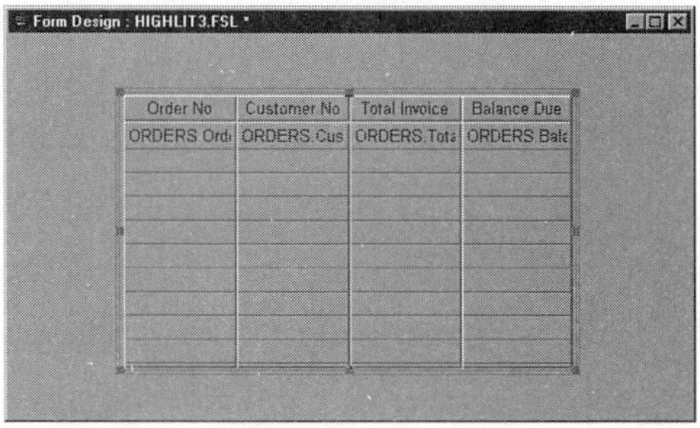

FIGURE 18.10.

Setup form for the example.

2. Add lines 3–7 to the newValue method of the Balance_Due field.

```
1:      ;Field :: newValue
2:      method newValue(var eventInfo Event)
3:          if self.value > 0 then
4:              self.container.color = Red
5:          else
6:              self.container.color = Transparent
7:          endIf
8:      endmethod
```

3. Check the syntax, save the form as HIGHLIT3.FSL, and run it. Scroll through the table frame. The records are colored red when Balance_Due is positive (see Figure 18.11).

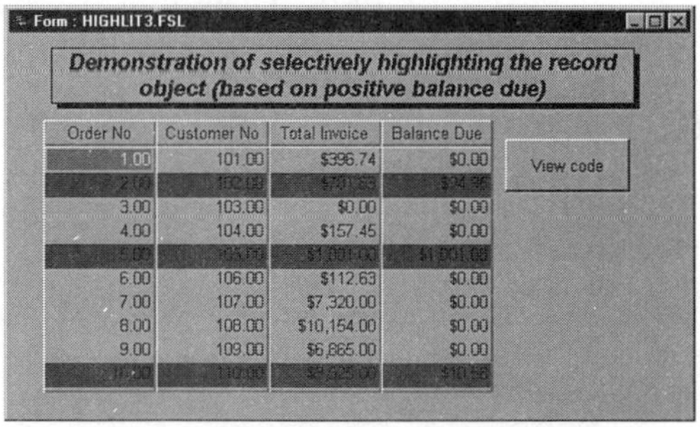

FIGURE 18.11.

HIGHLIT3.FSL demonstrates highlighting certain records based on a condition.

Analysis

In step 2, line 3 checks whether the value in the Balance_Due field is positive. If it is, line 4 sets the container's color to red. If it isn't, line 6 sets the color to Transparent.

Redefining a Table Frame with the *TableName* and *FieldName* Properties

This section discusses redefining table frames in Run mode. This next example demonstrates how to define which table is bound to a table frame.

Suppose that you want to define an undefined table frame when the user presses a button. To do this, set the `tableName` property of the table frame in the `pushButton` event method of a button.

You can find the DMADD1.FSL form on the disc in the \ANSWERS directory.

Step By Step

1. Change your working directory to TUTORIAL. Create a new form with no tables in its data model. Place a button labeled Set on the form. Add an undefined table frame to the form (see Figure 18.12).

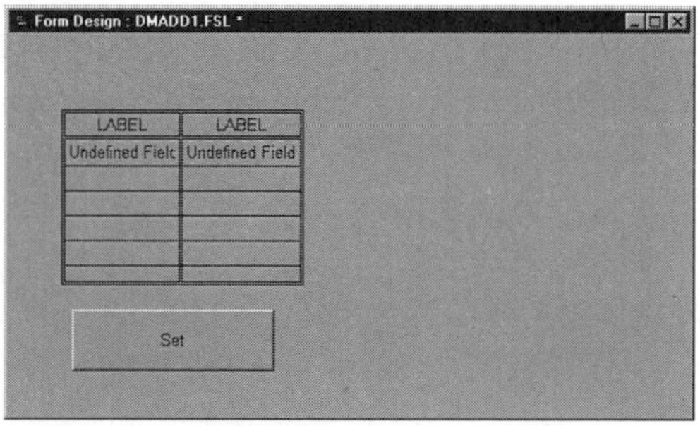

FIGURE 18.12.

Setup form for the example.

2. Add line 3 to the `pushButton` method of the Set button.

```
1:    ;Button :: pushButton
2:    method pushButton(var eventInfo Event)
3:        Table_Frame.tableName = "WORLD.DB"
4:    endmethod
```

3. Check the syntax, save the form as DMADD1.FSL, and run it. Click the Set button. The table frame has exploded from one column to all the fields in the table, as Figure 18.13 shows.

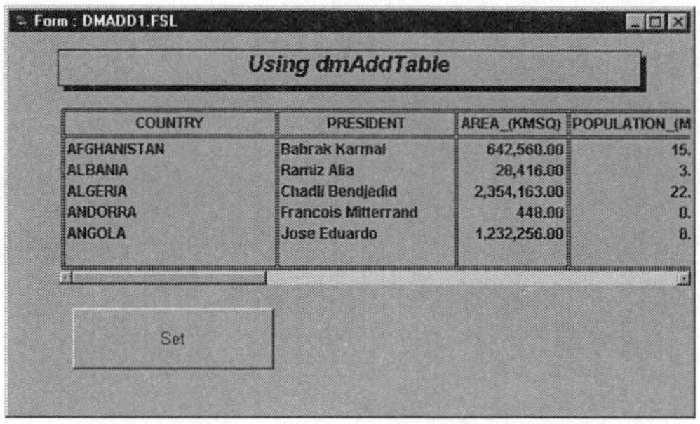

FIGURE 18.13.

DMADD1.FSL after the table frame has exploded from one column to all the fields in the table.

Analysis

Table_Frame is the name of the table frame on the form. TableName is a property of the table frame object. This code doesn't rely on dmAddTable() to add the table to the data model. Simply setting the property does that.

Defining the Columns of a Table Frame

The technique used in the preceding example is useful in some situations, such as when you want the table frame redefined. In many cases, however, you want to define just a few columns. This next example shows you a technique for doing that.

Suppose that you want to define three columns of an undefined table frame without affecting its size. To do this, do not use the tableName property; instead, use the fieldName property.

> You can find the DMADD2.FSL form on the disc in the \ANSWERS directory.

Step By Step

1. Change your working directory to TUTORIAL. Create a new form with no tables in its data model. Place a button labeled Set on the form.
2. Add an undefined table frame to the form with three columns named Col1, Col2, and Col3 (see Figure 18.14).

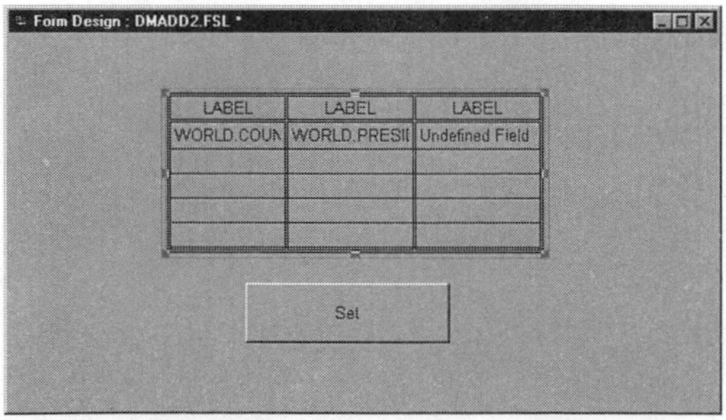

FIGURE 18.14.

Setup form for Defining the Columns of a Table Frame example.

3. Add lines 3–5 to the pushButton method of the Set button.

```
1:    ;Button :: pushButton
2:    method pushButton(var eventInfo Event)
3:        Col1.FieldName = "WORLD.COUNTRY"
4:        Col2.FieldName - "WORLD.PRESIDENT"
5:        Col3.FieldName = "WORLD.CAPITAL"
6:    endmethod
```

4. Check the syntax, save the form as DMADD2.FSL, and run it. Click the Set button. Now the columns of the table frame are defined (see Figure 18.15).

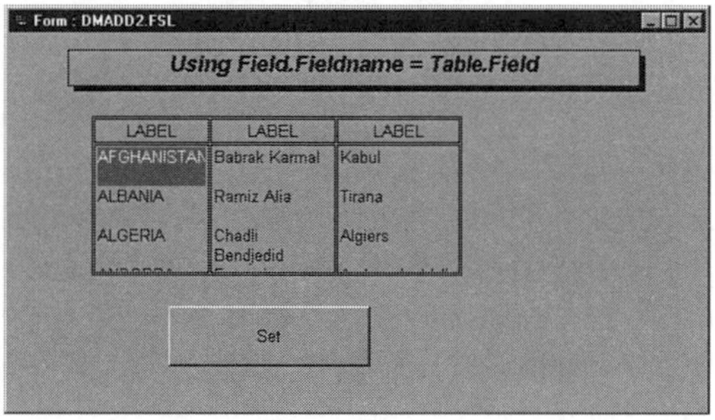

FIGURE 18.15.

DMADD2.FSL. Using the FieldName *property of a field to define the columns of a table frame.*

Analysis

In step 2, lines 3–5 set the FieldName property of all three columns. Figure 18.15 shows how the DMADD2.FSL form uses the FieldName property of a field to define the columns of a table frame. This technique doesn't alter the properties of the table. In this figure, the undefined labels and the first column are too narrow.

You can use this technique to redefine a table, too. The trick is to redefine the table frame to the null character. In the following code, WORLD is the name of the table frame.

```
1:  WORLD = ""
```

Then you can redefine the columns without a problem, as in the following example:

```
1:  Col1.FieldName = "LINEITEM.Order No"
2:  Col2.FieldName = "LINEITEM.Stock No"
3:  Col3.FieldName = "LINEITEM.Total"
```

Resizing a Table Frame

On the disc is the form ANSWERS\DMADD3.FSL, which demonstrates how to redefine and resize a table frame. Following is the pertinent code:

```
;DMADD3 :: btn :: pushButton
method pushButton(var eventInfo Event)
   delayScreenUpdates(Yes)            ;This is for a smooth look.
   tfTemp.verticalScrollBar = False   ;Turn off vertical scrollbar.
   tfTemp.TableName = "X.DB"          ;One column dummy table.
   tfTemp.design.sizeToFit = True     ;Tell the table frame to resize.
   tfTemp.TableName = "ZIPCODES.DB"   ;Bind table to table frame.
   tfTemp.verticalScrollBar = True    ;Turn on vertical scrollbar.
endmethod
```

Validating Fields at the Record Level of a Table Frame

Chapter 8 briefly discussed using the record level of a table frame to validate fields. This next example demonstrates how to use this important technique.

Suppose that you want to make sure that the user hasn't entered a date beyond today's date in the Contact Date field of the customer table. To do this, use the canDepart event method of the table frames record object. Compare the field's value with today's date using today(). If the value is greater then today's date, use setErrorcode() to prevent the user from posting the value.

You can find the RECORD1.FSL form on the disc in the \ANSWERS directory.

Step By Step

1. Set your working directory to TUTORIAL. Create a new form with the ORDERS.DB table in the data model (see Figure 18.16).

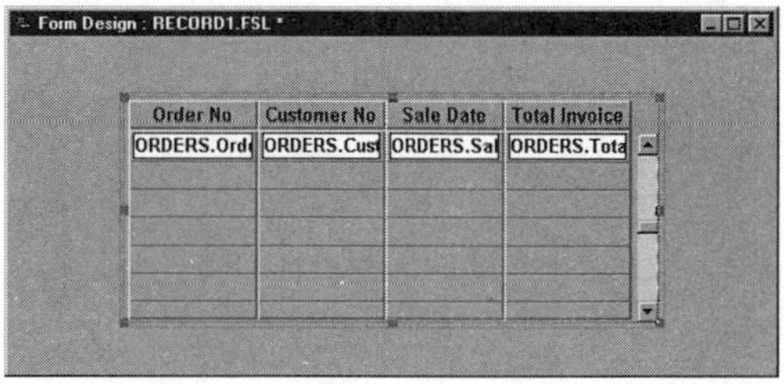

FIGURE 18.16.

Setup form for the example.

2. Add lines 3–9 to the canDepart method of the record object of the table frame bound to ORDERS.DB.

```
1:      ;TableFrame.Record :: canDepart
2:      method canDepart(var eventInfo MoveEvent)
3:         if Sale_Date.value > today() then
4:            eventInfo.setErrorCode(CanNotDepart)
5:            msgStop("Invalid Date!", "Sale date is invalid.")
6:            moveTo(Sale_Date)
7:         endIf
8:      endmethod
```

> **NOTE**
>
> You also can use a validity check at the table structure level. When you restructure a table, you can use today in the maximum validity check field. In fact, this should be your first choice for data validity.

3. Check the syntax, save your work, and run the form. Press F9 to enter Edit mode, and try to change the Sale Date field to tomorrow's date. You get a message indicating that the date is invalid, and the record turns yellow while the message is displayed (see Figure 18.17).

FIGURE 18.17.

RECORD1.FSL. Using the record object of a table name to validate values.

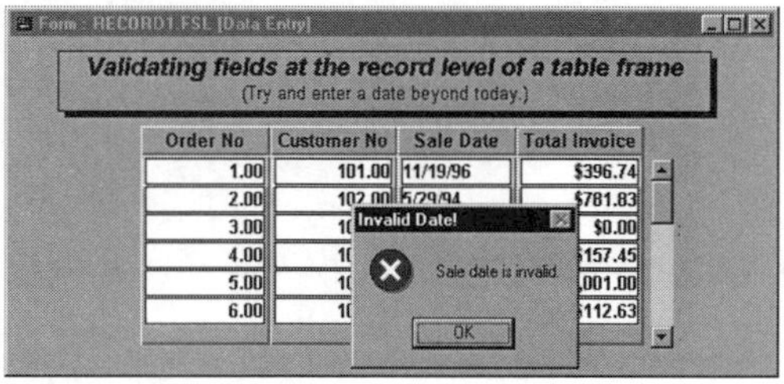

Analysis

In step 2, line 3 checks whether the date entered in the Sale_Date field is later than today's date. If it is, line 4 sets the CanNotDepart error code. Lines 5–8 notify the user of the inaccurate date by changing the color of the box to yellow, displaying a warning, and moving back to the field. You can customize your own warning system if you want.

Fly Away

Fly Away is the default behavior that occurs in a TableView and table frame when you add a new record or change the key of a record. The new or altered record moves to its ordered location in the table and appears to fly away. You can disable Fly Away with ObjectPAL. I recommend that you use the following code to disable Fly Away:

New Term

```
1:  ;Record :: action
2:  method action(var eventInfo ActionEvent)
3:  ;This code is attached to a TableFrame or MRO
4:     if eventInfo.id() = DataUnlockRecord then
5:        self.action(DataPostRecord)
6:     endIf
7:  endmethod
```

This code tells the default Paradox behavior to stay with the record as it flies away. If the record flies away as the code executes, Paradox flies with it because that's the default behavior for DataPostRecord. First, the record takes its new location. Then Paradox moves off the record. In effect, Paradox has followed the record to its new location.

Using a 1-By-1 Multirecord Object

Using the record object of a table frame to manipulate data at a record level is great, but what do you do when you have several fields? You use a 1-by-1 multirecord object (MRO) and surround the fields, which causes the MRO to bind to the underlying table.

NEW
Term
A *multirecord* object (MRO) is an object that displays several records at once in a box. It is used with forms and reports. You can use a 1-by-1 MRO to add a record object to fields on a form. This enables you to perform field validation by using the record object of the MRO in a way similar to how you use the record of a table frame. This is because the fields in the MRO are contained by a record object. Having a record object means that you can use the canDepart event to trap for record departs, among other record-oriented tasks.

The first step in using this technique is to place an MRO over the fields you want to validate (see Figure 18.18). Don't panic as your screen becomes jumbled. Next, change the MRO to a 1-by-1 MRO and resize it so that the fields fit within it. This cleans up your screen and automatically binds the record object to the underlying table (see Figure 18.19). After you set up the record object, you can use the MRO record object's methods to manipulate the data at the record level.

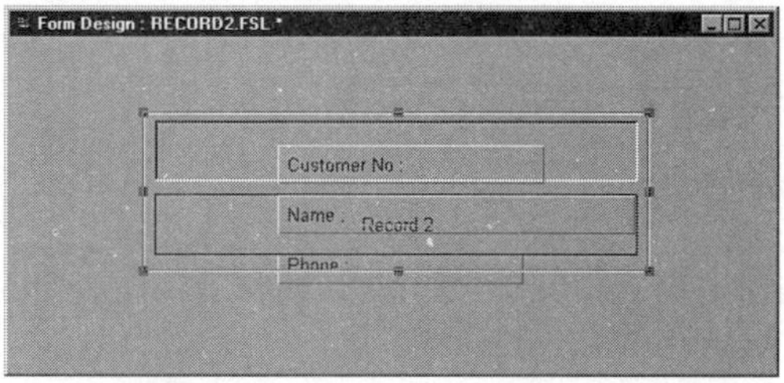

FIGURE 18.18.

The first step in using the record object of an MRO to manipulate data at the record level.

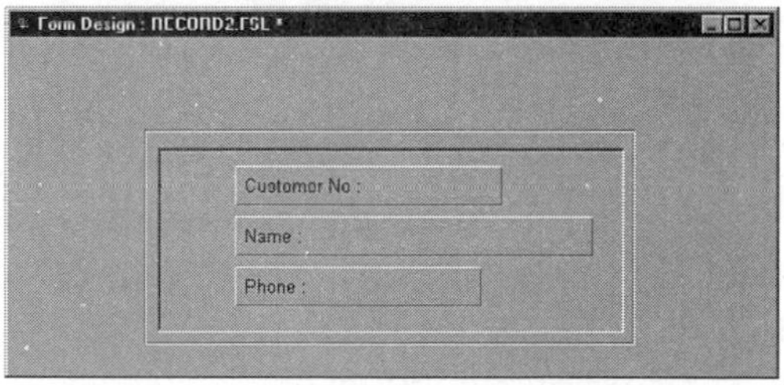

FIGURE 18.19.

The second step in using the record object of an MRO to manipulate data at the record level.

The next example demonstrates the important technique of using a 1-by-1 MRO.

Validating Fields at the Record Level by Using a Multirecord Object

Suppose that you want to make sure that the user doesn't leave the telephone number field of the customer table empty. You can do this on a group of fields by surrounding the fields with a 1-by-1 multirecord object and using the record object to trap for when the user moves from record to record.

You can find the RECORD2.FSL form on the disc in the \ANSWERS directory.

Step By Step

1. Set your working directory to TUTORIAL. Create a new form with the CUSTOMER.DB table in the data model. Create field objects and define them to Customer No, Name, and Phone, respectively (refer to Figures 18.18 and 18.19 to help set up the 1-by-1 MRO).

2. Add lines 3–9 to the canDepart method of the record object in the Multirecord object.

```
1:    ;MRO.Record :: canDepart
2:    method canDepart(var eventInfo MoveEvent)
3:       if Phone.isBlank() then
4:          eventInfo.setErrorCode(CanNotDepart)
5:          self.color = Yellow
6:          msgStop("Warning!", "Phone number required on this form.")
7:          self.color = Transparent
8:          moveTo(Phone)
9:       endIf
10:   endmethod
```

3. Check the syntax, save your work as RECORD2.FSL, and run the form. Press F9 to enter Edit mode, and try to leave the Phone field blank. You get a message indicating that the phone number is required, and the record turns yellow while the message is displayed (see Figure 18.20).

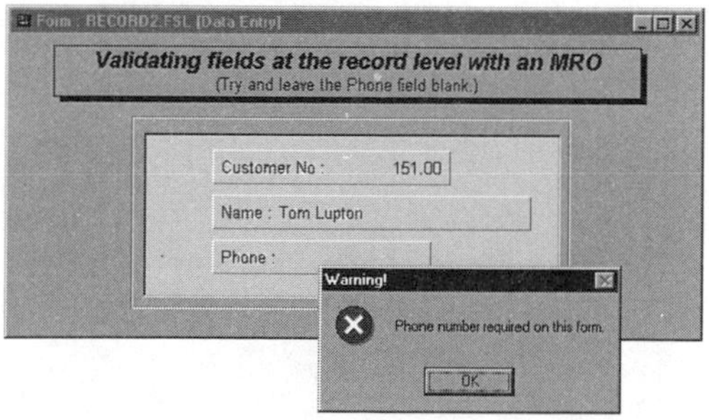

FIGURE 18.20.

RECORD2.FSL. Surrounding fields on a form with an MRO and using the record object of the MRO to validate field values.

Analysis

Line 3 checks whether the Phone field is blank. If it is, line 4 sets the `CanNotDepart` error code. Lines 5–8 notify the user by turning the box yellow, displaying a warning, and moving back to the field. You can customize these warnings to your own liking.

Summary

In this chapter, you learned how to manipulate fields, table frames, and multirecord objects. You learned about the power and ease-of-use of the multirecord's record object. You also learned that you can use the multirecord's record object with a group of fields. You also learned that you normally perform field validation at the table restructure level; you don't use ObjectPAL at all. Proper field validation must be at the table or database level. Otherwise, users could open the table directly and enter bad data. If you want to restrict input only on a particular form, however, you can use the techniques discussed in this chapter.

Manipulating Strings and Handling the Keyboard

19

IN THIS CHAPTER

It's important to be familiar with string manipulation. Most programming and macro languages, for example, have left and right string functions; that is, a single step returns the left or right *n* characters of a string. You can accomplish both these actions with the subStr() method, but the syntax is a little tricky. To assign the left three characters of a string variable s1 to the string variable s2, type the following into the pushButton method of a button:

```
 1:   ;Button :: pushButton
 2:   method pushButton(var eventInfo Event)
 3:      var
 4:         s1, s2      String
 5:      endVar
 6:
 7:      s1 = "Felicia"
 8:      s2 = s1.subStr(1, 3)
 9:      s2.view() ;Displays "Fel".
10:   endMethod
```

Doing the similar procedure with the right three characters is trickier. To assign the last three characters of s1 to s2, use the following:

```
 1:   ;Button :: pushButton
 2:   method pushButton(var eventInfo Event)
 3:      var
 4:         s1, s2      String
 5:      endVar
 6:
 7:      s1 = "Felicia"
 8:      s2 = s1.subStr(s1.size()-3, 3)
 9:      s2.view() ;Displays "cia".
10:   endMethod
```

By using the subStr() method with the size() method, you can extract from a string all the combinations of values that you need.

The Path of a Key Press

A *keycode* is a code that represents a keyboard character in ObjectPAL. A keycode can be an ASCII number, an IBM extended keycode number, or a string that represents a keyname known to Paradox. When a user presses a key on the keyboard, one of two things occurs. Either Windows processes it, or Paradox processes it. Windows processes it, for example, when the sequence Ctrl+Esc is used. When Paradox processes it, keyPhysical always sees it, and in the case of a character, keyPhysical passes the event to keyChar (see Figure 19.1).

The steps to trapping a keypress are as follows:

1. Decide whether you need to trap for a character or virtual key. If you want to trap for a character such as a, A, b, B, 1, !, or @, then use either keyPhysical or keyChar. If you want to trap for virtual keys such as F1 or Esc, then you must use keyPhysical.

FIGURE 19.1.

The path of a key event.

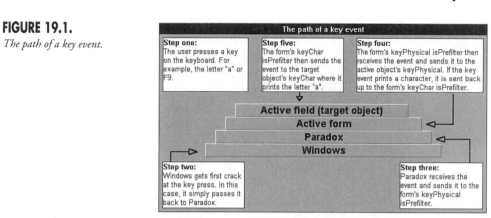

2. Decide at which level you need to trap for the key press. The two usual places are the form's prefilter or directly on the field.

3. Inspect the eventInfo packet with either char() or vChar() to trap for the key press. If case does not matter, then use vChar(). If case does matter, then use char().

NOTE

As long as a field has focus, key presses do not bubble because the key press is used up by the field. Therefore, the two best choices to trap for key presses are the form's prefilter or on the field itself.

Using *KeyEvent* Methods and Procedures

You can use the KeyEvent methods and procedures to enable you to get and set information about keystroke events. Both keyChar and keyPhysical methods are triggered by KeyEvents.

Interrupting a Loop

You can use form's prefilter with vChar() to trap a key press. For example, sometimes you may want to give the user the option of interrupting a loop. This type of control adds a touch of professionalism to your application. The following example demonstrates how you can enable the user to interrupt a loop by pressing the Esc key.

Example of Interrupting a Loop

Suppose that you want to loop to 1000 and display the counter in the status bar as the loop increments. The twist on this example is that you need to enable the user to press Esc to interrupt the loop.

> You can find the QUITLOOP.FSL form on the disc in the \ANSWERS directory.

Step By Step

1. Create a new form and place a button labeled Count to 1000 on it (see Figure 19.2).

FIGURE 19.2.

Setup form for quit loop example.

2. Add line 3 to the Var window of the form.

```
1:    ;Form :: Var
2:    Var
3:       lFlag Logical
4:    endVar
```

3. Add lines 5–7 to the keyPhysical method of the form.

```
1:    ;Form :: keyPhysical
2:    method keyPhysical(var eventInfo KeyEvent)
3:    if eventInfo.isPreFilter() then
4:       ;This code executes for each object on the form
5:       if eventInfo.vchar() = "VK_ESCAPE" then
6:         lFlag = True
7:       endIf
8:    else
9:       ;This code executes only for the form
10:   endif
11:   endmethod
```

4. Add lines 3–16 to the pushButton method of the Count to 1000 button.

```
1:    ;Button :: pushButton
2:    method pushButton(var eventInfo Event)
3:       var
4:         siCounter SmallInt
5:       endvar
6:
7:       lFlag = False
8:
```

```
 9:      for siCounter from 1 to 1000
10:        message(siCounter)
11:        sleep()
12:        if lFlag = True then
13:           message("Counting interrupted")
14:           quitloop
15:        endIf
16:      endFor
17:   endmethod
```

5. Check the syntax, run the form, and click the button. As the computer counts to 1,000, the counter is shown in the status bar. Press Esc to interrupt the loop (see Figure 19.3).

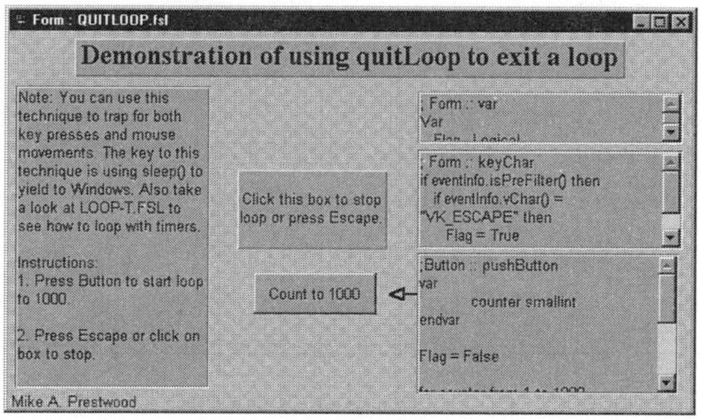

FIGURE 19.3.

QUITLOOP.FSL demonstrates the preceding technique and an additional technique using the mouse.

Analysis

In step 2, line 3 declares a variable global to the form.

In step 3, line 5 checks whether the user presses the Esc key. If the user does, line 6 sets the logical lFlag to True.

In step 4, line 4 declares a variable private to a method for use in the for loop (lines 9–16). Line 7 sets the flag to False in case the user presses Esc, setting the flag to true. Line 10 displays the value of counter in the status bar. Line 11 sleeps for the minimum amount of cycles (about 52 milliseconds), which is plenty of time to yield to Windows. This enables the Esc key to sneak in. Line 12 checks whether the flag has changed to True. If the flag is True, line 13 displays a message, and line 14 quits the loop.

> **NOTE**
>
> In place of sleep(1), you can use sleep() without a parameter—sleep(). In that case, Windows automatically permits about two events to occur.

Using *keyPhysical*

As already discussed, use keyPhysical when you want to trap for all keyboard keys. Use keyChar when you want to trap for only characters that are printable to the screen.

Echoing Keyboard Input from One Field to Another

Suppose that you created two field objects: field1 and field2. You want field2 to echo whatever you type into field1—including Backspace, Delete, and Enter—as though you were typing directly into field2. How do you do this?

A problem that often confronts users is that values aren't committed to the field until endMethod. Remember that the default behavior occurs last in a method. Therefore, when you use keyPhysical and keyChar, invoke the default behavior to commit the last keystroke, as in the following example:

```
1:   ;Field1 :: keyPhysical
2:   doDefault
3:   field2.value = self.value
```

Hiding User Input

Sometimes you need to hide user input, such as passwords or sensitive data. One technique is to make the background color the same as the text color. Showing an asterisk for each character as the user enters it, however, requires ObjectPAL. The following example shows you how to hide user input.

Example of Hiding User Input

Suppose that you want to hide user input by displaying an asterisk for each character the user types.

You can find the PASSWORD.FSL form on the disc in the \ANSWERS directory.

Step By Step

1. Create a new form with two fields a button on it (see Figure 19.4). Name the first field fldInput and label it Input. Name the second field fldPassword and label it Password.

FIGURE 19.4.

Setup form for the hiding user input example.

2. Add lines 3–18 to the keyPhysical method of the fldInput field.

```
 1:    ;fldInput :: keyPhysical
 2:    method keyPhysical(var eventInfo KeyEvent)
 3:       switch
 4:          case eventInfo.vCharCode() = VK_F8
 5:             : DoDefault
 6:          case eventInfo.vCharCode() = VK_BACK
 7:             : fldPassword.value = ""
 8:               fldInput.value = ""
 9:               DisableDefault
10:          case eventInfo.vCharCode() = VK_DELETE
11:             : fldPassword.value = ""
12:               fldInput.value = ""
13:               DisableDefault
14:          otherwise
15:             : fldPassword.value = fldPassword.value + eventInfo.char()
16:               fldInput.value = fill("*", size(fldPassword.value))
17:               DisableDefault
18:       endSwitch
19:    endMethod
```

3. Add line 3 to the mouseDown method of the fldInput field to disable moving into field view with the mouse.

```
1:    ;fldInput :: mouseDown
2:    method mouseDown(var eventInfo MouseEvent)
3:       DisableDefault
4:    endMethod
```

4. Add line 3 to the mouseDouble method of the fldInput field to disable moving into field view with the mouse.

```
1:    ;fldInput :: mouseDouble
2:    method mouseDouble(var eventInfo MouseEvent)
3:       DisableDefault
4:    endMethod
```

5. Check the syntax, save the form as PASSWORD.FSL, and run the form. Type some values into the field. Press Backspace or Delete to reset the field (see Figure 19.5).

FIGURE 19.5.

PASSWORD.FSL. One technique for hiding user input.

Analysis

In step 2, a switch statement is used to process the user's input. Note that lines 4 and 5 enable the user to move into Design mode. Lines 6–9 and lines 10–13 clear the password field. Lines 14–17 process the user's valid input.

Steps 3 and 4 disable the mouse from entering fieldview by either clicking or double-clicking the field.

This example is a beginning technique for hiding user input. For example, the user's input is echoed to a field called Password rather than directly to a variable. To make this routine work without the field, delete the field and declare a Password String variable. Remember to initiate the variable, such as when you open the form.

Another technique is to use the noEcho property on the password field and to send each keystroke there by using the UIObject keyPhysical() method on the input field's built-in keyPhysical method.

> **TIP**
>
> You can use the keyPhysical method of any object to echo keyboard input to the status bar. Put the following two lines of code into the keyPhysical method of an active object:
>
> ```
> message(eventInfo.vChar())
> sleep(250)
> ```
>
> When you run the form and press the keys on your keyboard, the vChar() name of each key is echoed to the status bar.

Limiting Keyboard Input

If you want to limit the user's input, use either the keyChar or keyPhysical methods of the input object. If you want to limit the user's input to characters, use keyChar. If you want to control all keystrokes, use keyPhysical. The next example shows you how to limit the user's input.

Limiting a User's Input

Suppose that you want to limit the user's input to uppercase, lowercase, and numbers. In addition, you want to allow a few editing keys. The technique presented here can be used to control any keys.

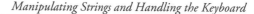 You can find the ONLYKEYS.FSL form on the disc in the \ANSWERS directory.

Step By Step

1. Create a form with a single undefined field (see Figure 19.6).

FIGURE 19.6.

Setup form for limiting a user's input example.

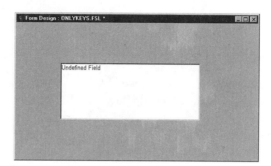

2. Add line 3 to the Var window of the form.

```
1:    ;Form :: Var
2:    Var
3:        ans  String
4:    endVar
```

3. Add lines 7–18 to the keyPhysical of the form.

```
1:    ;Form :: keyPhysical
2:    method keyPhysical(var eventInfo KeyEvent)
3:        if eventInfo.isPreFilter() then
4:            ; This code executes for each object on the form.
5:            ans = eventInfo.char()
6:            switch
7:                case eventInfo.vCharCode() = VK_DELETE  : doDefault return
8:                case eventInfo.vCharCode() = VK_BACK    : doDefault return
9:                case eventInfo.vCharCode() = VK_LEFT     : doDefault return
10:               case eventInfo.vCharCode() = VK_RIGHT    : doDefault return
11:               case ans >= "A" and ans <="z"  : doDefault return
12:               case ans >= "0" and ans <="9"  : doDefault return
13:               case ans = " "                 : doDefault return
14:               otherwise                      : disableDefault
15:            endSwitch
16:        else
17:            ; This code executes only for the form.
18:        endif
19:    endmethod
```

4. Check the syntax, save the form as ONLYKEYS.FSL, and run it. Type some characters. Be sure to try numbers, letters, and special characters (see Figure 19.7).

FIGURE 19.7.

ONLYKEYS.FSL. Limit the user's input to numbers, letters, and spaces.

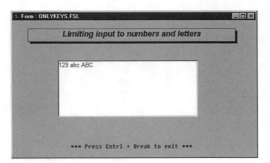

Analysis

In step 2, line 3 declares a `String` variable that is used in step 3, line 7 to capture the Windows virtual character. Because `char()` returns a null character if a nonprintable character is detected, line 17 disables the default behavior and returns control. (In this case, returning control is a way of exiting the method.) If the character is a printable character, line 7 puts its virtual character into the `String` variable. It will be used in lines 9–18. Line 14 checks for letters. Line 15 checks for numbers. Line 16 checks for the space character. Line 17 disables all other characters.

This a good routine to turn into a custom method that you can call whenever you need to limit user input. If you don't want to enable the user to enter a space, for example, delete line 16. This technique is useful when you want input for a filename. Alter this routine in other ways to suit your needs. You can't trap for everything, however. Some keys and key combinations are reserved by Windows, such as Ctrl+F4.

The FELICIA.FSL form in Figure 19.8 uses a technique similar to the one in this example. It adds pictures and sound routines to create a game that introduces an infant to the keyboard.

FIGURE 19.8.

FELICIA.FSL demonstrates trapping for keystrokes.

Character Sets

You can't store all characters in a Paradox table. This is a limitation of current computer technology. The issue is what Paradox should store to a table. For example, should it store Windows ANSI characters or OEM DOS characters? *ANSI* is an acronym for American National Standards Institute. The ANSI set consists of eight-bit codes that represent 256 standard characters, such as letters, numbers, and symbols. The ANSI set is used by Windows applications. *Extended ASCII* is a character set designed by IBM. IBM extended the standard ASCII set from seven-bit codes to eight-bit codes and added more characters. The extended ASCII set contains 256 characters.

NEW
Term

As a Windows product, the Paradox table structure has to be able to store Windows ANSI characters. Paradox supports dBASE and Paradox tables, however, and traditionally these table structures store OEM DOS characters. Therefore, Paradox must be able to deal with both character sets: the character set traditionally used by other products that used the table structures before Paradox for Windows and the character set used by Windows. In Paradox for Windows, the character set is determined by the table language driver. The problem is that although Microsoft controls both DOS and Windows, the two character sets, OEM and ANSI, are incompatible. You must decide between the two when you create your table.

One solution is to use the strict translation option of the Link tool. When strict translation is checked (the default), only the first 128 characters are stored. If you uncheck it, you enable your users to add characters that may not be supported by a different table language. There are disadvantages, however. For more information, refer to the online help on strict translation.

Using *sendKeys()*

The sendKeys() procedure sends keystrokes to the Windows message queue. The syntax for sendKeys() is as follows:

```
sendKeys(const keyText String [, const wait Logical] ) Logical
```

The *wait* argument indicates whether to send the keys immediately (True), or to wait until the current method has finished (False). In most cases, False is the preferred setting. Table 19.2 lists the keys used with sendKeys().

Table 19.2. Using sendKeys().

Key	Code
Shift	+
Control	^
Alt	%

continues

Table 19.2. continued

Key	Code
Backspace	{BACKSPACE}, {BS}, {BKSP}, {VK_BACK}
Break	{BREAK}, {VK_BREAK}
Caps Lock	{CAPSLOCK}, {VK_CAPTIAL}
Clear	{CLEAR}, {VK_CLEAR}
Del	{DELETE}, {DEL}, {VK_DELETE}
Down Arrow	{DOWN}, {VK_DOWN}
End	{END}, {VK_END}
Enter	{ENTER}, {RETURN}, {VK_RETURN} (the character ~)
Esc	{ESCAPE}, {ESC}, {VK_ESCAPE}
Help	{HELP}, {VK_HELP}
Home	{HOME}, {VK_HOME}
Ins	{INSERT}, {VK_INSERT}
Left Arrow	{LEFT}, {VK_LEFT}
Num Lock	{NUMLOCK}, {VK_NUMLOCK}
Page Down	{PGDN}, {VK_NEXT}
Page Up	{PGUP}, {VK_PRIOR}
Print Screen	{PRTSC}, {VK_SNAPSHOT}
Right Arrow	{RIGHT}, {VK_RIGHT}
Scroll Lock	{SCROLLLOCK}, {VK_SCROLL}
Tab	{TAB}, {VK_TAB}
Up Arrow	{UP}, {VK_UP}
F1	{F1}, {VK_F1}
F2	{F2}, {VK_F2}
F3	{F3}, {VK_F3}
F4	{F4}, {VK_F4}
F5	{F5}, {VK_F5}
F6	{F6}, {VK_F6}
F7	{F7}, {VK_F7}
F8	{F8}, {VK_F8}
F9	{F9}, {VK_F9}
F10	{F10}, {VK_F10}

Now type in an example to make sure you fully understand the principles of using sendKeys(). For example, the following simulates a user selecting File | Open | Form, typing ANSWERS, and pressing Enter. Type line 4 into the pushButton method of a button.

```
1:    ;Button :: pushButton
2:    method pushButton(var eventInfo Event)
3:       ;% = ALT key.
4:       sendKeys("%FOFANSWERS{ENTER}")
5:    endMethod
```

Summary

In this chapter, you learned that it is important to be familiar with string manipulation and that you can extract any combination of characters from a string with the subStr() method. In addition, you learned that when a user presses a key on the keyboard, either Windows processes it, or Paradox processes it. When Paradox processes it, keyPhysical always sees it, and in the case of a character, keyPhysical passes the event to keyChar. You learned you can use the KeyEvent methods and procedures to enable you to get and set information about keystroke events. Finally, you learned about sendKeys(), which enables you to emulate a series of key presses.

Understanding Properties

20

Paradox offers two sets of property names: end-user properties and ObjectPAL properties. The distinction is that the properties listed in the Explorer are the ObjectPAL Names for the properties you set interactively. In addition, there are many properties you can only set using ObjectPAL. If you see a property name listed in the Explorer and then look in the ObjectPAL Browser, you can paste the correct name into your code. For example, you can paste `Design.SizeToFit` as opposed to Size To Fit (from the Properties sheet). The properties displayed in the Properties sheets are end-user properties; the properties displayed in the Object Explorer are the ObjectPAL equivalents. This helps get you acquainted with the differences between the two sets of property names.

Read-Only Properties

There are two categories of properties: read/write and read-only. Figure 20.1 shows the Display Objects and Properties dialog box. You're familiar with the read/write properties. The read-only properties include `Arrived`, `BlankRecord`, `Class`, `ContainerName`, `FieldNo`, `FieldSize`, `FieldType`, `Focus`, `FullName`, `FullSize`, `IndexField`, `Locked`, and `Required`. The following statement assumes that an object named `theBox` is on a form:

```
1:  ;Button :: pushButton
2:  message("Full containership path is " + theBox.fullName)
```

FIGURE 20.1.

The Display Objects and Properties dialog box.

If you're having trouble with scope or the containership hierarchy and you need to know the full containership path of an object, use the preceding statement.

> **NOTE**
>
> Only UIObjects have properties; objects such as TCursors and strings do not.

You read and set properties in ObjectPAL by means of dot notation, just as you do with the other aspects of ObjectPAL syntax. You are familiar with the basic syntax for properties. The following two examples should look familiar:

```
1:   Last_Name.value = "Homann"
2:   theBox.color = Red
```

Following are examples of setting the value for a read/write property. If you have a box named Box1 on a form, you could put the following code on a button:

```
1:   ;Button :: pushButton
2:   method pushButton(var eventInfo Event)
3:      Box1.color = Red
4:      Box1.Frame.Color = Blue
5:      Box1.Frame.Style = DashDotFrame
6:      Box1.Frame.Thickness = LWidth3Points
7:      Box1.Pattern.Color = Yellow
8:      Box1.Pattern.Style = LatticePattern
9:   endmethod
```

No matter which property is set, the syntax is the same: *objectName.property* = constant. Use this syntax whenever you set the value of a read/write property. The previous examples set the values of properties. The syntax for reading an object's property value is similar. When you get the current value of a read/write or read-only property, you use the syntax objectName.property, which returns the current value of the object's specified property. The following code displays the current color of the object named theBox in the status bar. Usually, you use this technique to add logic to your application:

```
1:   ;Button :: pushButton
2:   method pushButton(var eventInfo Event)
3:      message(theBox.color)
4:   endmethod
```

In the following code, the value property of the field named GotoPage is used to determine whether it should display a message and move to Page2:

```
1:   ;Button :: pushButton
2:   method pushButton(var eventInfo Event)
3:      if GotoPage.value = "Page2" then
4:         message("Moving to page two")
5:         Page2.moveTo()
6:      endIf
7:   endmethod
```

Using the *first* Property of an Object

The first property returns the full containership path of the first contained object. You can display the string it returns in a message information dialog box. For example, type the following code in the pushButton method of a button. It displays the full path of the label the button contains.

```
1:   ;Button :: pushButton
2:   method pushButton(var eventInfo Event)
3:      msgInfo("Button label", self.first)
4:   endMethod
```

A more practical use of `first` is to write generic routines. Suppose that you want to change the font color of the label of a button. You could rename the button's label and use the `font.color` property of the object. This technique, however, uses up more of the symbol table, which is limited to 64K. If you change the name of an object, the name and its 4-byte address is stored in the symbol table. Therefore, use the following code instead.

```
1:   ;Button :: pushButton
2:   method pushButton(var eventInfo Event)
3:      var
4:          f      Form
5:      endVar
6:
7:      f.attach()
8:      f.(self.first).font.color = Red
9:   endMethod
```

NEW Term

Note in the preceding code two things: the use of `attach()` and parentheses. `first` returns a string, not an object. In order to use the string in ObjectPAL, you need to dereference it. *Dereferencing* is when you put the name of something in a variable and then use the variable as if you were using the name. Dereferencing an object using dot notation in ObjectPAL requires two rules: an object preceding the dereference and the use of parentheses around the dereferenced value. You need to start back in the containership path one object and then put the string in parentheses (see the preceding line 7). The following section puts this technique to work.

Toggling the Font Color of the Label of a Button

Now you'll see a full example of using the first color in context. Suppose that you want to toggle the font color of the label of a button between red and black. In this example, you make use of the first property to write a generic routine that will work with any button.

You can find the TOGGLE3.FSL form on the disc in the \ANSWERS directory.

Step By Step

1. Change your working directory to TUTORIAL and create a new form. Place a button on it.

2. Add lines 2–15 to the pushButton method. (As always, typing the comments is optional.)

```
1:   ;Button :: pushButton
2:   method pushButton(var eventInfo Event)
3:      var
4:          f      Form    ;Declare a Form variable.
5:      endVar
6:
7:      f.attach()       ;Attach to current form.
8:
9:      ;Notice the use of the Form variable and
```

```
10:        ;the use of parentheses to dereference
11:        ;the string.
12:        if f.(self.first).font.color = Red then
13:            f.(self.first).font.color = Black
14:        else
15:            f.(self.first).font.color – Red
16:        endIf
17:    endmethod
```

3. Check the syntax, save the new form as TOGGLE3.FSL, and run it (see Figure 20.2).

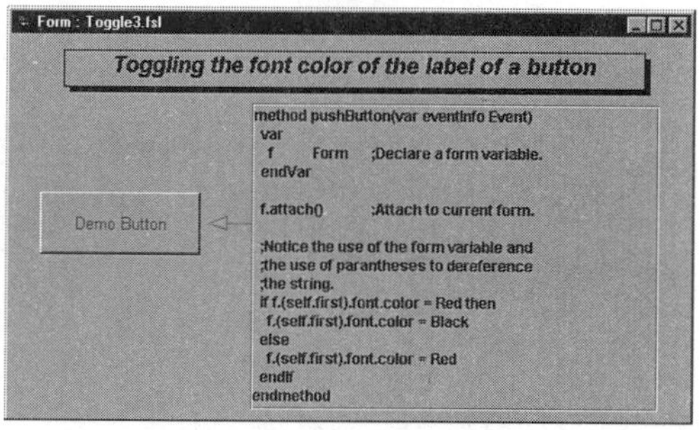

FIGURE 20.2.

TOGGLE3.FSL demonstrates using the first property.

Analysis

In step 2, line 4 declares f as a Form variable, which line 7 uses to attach to the current form. Lines 12–16 use the form variable with the object variable self and the first property to inspect and alter the color property of the button label's text.

Using the *first* and *next* Properties Together

Sometimes while creating an application, you need to manipulate a series of objects. Often times, you can create generic routines to handle a group of objects. One such technique for handling a group of objects is to use the first and next properties. The following code, for example, displays an array of all the objects inside an object named Outside. It is important to note that this code does not list the objects inside of each object.

```
1:    ;First&Next :: btnTraverse :: pushButton
2:    method pushButton(var eventInfo Event)
3:        var
4:            ui          UIObject
5:            arLayer1    Array[] String
6:            siCounter   SmallInt
7:        endVar

8:        ;Attach to the object.
9:        ui.attach(Outer)
```

```
10:        ;You must call first first.
11:        ui.attach(ui.first)
12:        arLayer1.addLast(ui.fullname)

13:        ;Now call next until next = next.
14:        siCounter = 1
15:        ui.attach(ui.next)
16:        while arLayer1[siCounter] <> ui.fullName
17:            arLayer1.addLast(ui.fullName)
18:            ui.attach(ui.next)
19:            siCounter = siCounter + 1
20:        endWhile

21:        arLayer1.view()
22:    endMethod
```

ANSWERS\FIRST&NEXT.FSL demonstrates both the first/next and
enumObjectNames() techniques for dealing with a set of objects.

Using *enumObjectNames()*

Often times, it is much easier and quicker to use enumObjectNames() and work through the
array using a for loop. The following code, for example, enumerates all the objects in the object named Outer, first displays the objects in a view box, and then displays each object one at
a time.

```
1:    ;First&Next :: btnEnum :: pushButton
2:    method pushButton(var eventInfo Event)
3:        var
4:            arObjects    Array[] String
5:            siCounter    SmallInt
6:        endVar
7:
8:        outer.enumObjectNames(arObjects)
9:        arObjects.view()
10:
11:        for siCounter from 1 to arObjects.size()
12:            ;Manipulate arObjects[siCounter] here.
13:            view(arObjects[siCounter])
14:        endFor
15:    endMethod
```

It is important to note that the preceding routine displays all the objects within an object (including the objects within the objects).

> **NOTE**
>
> When possible, use enumObjectNames() rather than enumUIObjects(). enumUIObjects()
> enumerates object information to a table and, therefore, is much slower than
> enumObjectNames().

Adding Scroll Bars to a Graphic Field

A fun exercise is to use a property that you normally set interactively in your code. This next example toggles the horizontal and vertical scroll bars on a field. If you display large amounts of data or a bitmap, you may want to add this routine to your application.

Suppose that you want to add scroll bars to a Graphic field when the user double-clicks it. To do this, you need to check whether the bitmap object currently has scroll bars. If it does, then remove them. If it doesn't, then add them.

You can find the SCROLL.FSL form on the disc in the \ANSWERS directory.

Step By Step

1. Create a new form. Place a field on the form and define the field to the Graphic field of the GRAPHICS.DB table (see Figure 20.3).

FIGURE 20.3.

Setup form for adding scroll bars example.

2. Add lines 3–15 to the mouseDouble method of the Graphic field.

```
1:    ;Field :: doubleClick
2:    method mouseDouble(var eventInfo MouseEvent)
3:       delayScreenUpdates(Yes)
4:       if self.HorizontalScrollBar = On then
5:         message("Removing scroll bars...")
6:         self.HorizontalScrollBar = Off
7:         self.VerticalScrollBar = Off
8:         message("")
9:       else
10:        message("Adding scroll bars...")
11:        self.HorizontalScrollBar = On
12:        self.VerticalScrollBar = On
13:        message("")
14:      endIf
15:      delayScreenUpdates(No)
16:    endmethod
```

3. Check your syntax and run the form. Click the graphic several times and watch the scroll bars come and go (see Figure 20.4).

FIGURE 20.4.

SCROLL.FSL demonstrates toggling scroll bars on a graphic.

Analysis

In step 2, line 3 turns on a feature that delays the drawing of the screen until the operation is complete. Without this line of code, the graphic would refresh twice, once for each scroll bar added. To see this for yourself, put a semicolon in front of line 3. This disables the line of code. Run the form. Line 4 determines whether you need to add or remove both scroll bars by checking whether the horizontal scroll bar is on.

> GRAPHIC2.FSL demonstrates toggling scroll bars by using a custom method called `toggleScrollBars()` on the form.

If the horizontal scroll bar is on in line 5, lines 5–8 remove both scroll bars. Line 5 tells the user that the scroll bars are being removed. Lines 6 and 7 turn off the horizontal and vertical scroll bars. Line 8 clears the status bar.

If the horizontal scroll bar isn't on in line 4, lines 10–13 add both scroll bars. Line 10 tells the user that the scroll bars are being added. Lines 11 and 12 turn on the horizontal and vertical scroll bars. GRAPHIC2.FSL on disk uses this routine in a custom method on the form (see Figure 20.5).

FIGURE 20.5.

GRAPHIC2.FSL. This form uses the toggle scroll bars routine in a custom method on the form.

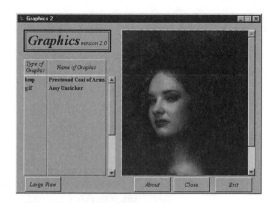

Playing Tricks with Properties

With all the various properties of objects in ObjectPAL, it is easy to do tricks and add interesting effects to your applications. You can place a box on a form, add a little code to the mouseEnter and mouseExit of the box, and watch the box fade in and out when you move over it, as in the following example:

```
1:  ;Box :: mouseEnter
2:  method mouseEnter(var eventInfo MouseEvent)
3:     box.visible = False
4:  endmethod

1:  ;Box :: mouseExit
2:  method mouseExit(var eventInfo MouseEvent)
3:     box.visible = True
4:  endmethod
```

You can find the form BOX.FSL on the disc, which demonstrates the preceding technique (see Figure 20.6).

FIGURE 20.6.

BOX.FSL demonstrates using the visible property.

Demonstration of User-Selectable Colors

Some Windows applications enable the user to adjust the colors of objects to the user's own liking. For an extra bit of professionalism, you can add this feature to your own applications.

> You can find on the disc the form SETTINGS.FSL, which demonstrates a technique that enables users to select their own colors for the form (see Figure 20.7).

The interesting bit of code in this form is in the form's Var window and open method. This code first opens a TCursor in the then portion of the open method, and then uses the TCursor to locate color values in the SETTINGS.DB table. You can edit the SETTINGS.DB table to change colors or add objects whose color is to be changed. Following is the code for both the Var window and the open event method.

FIGURE 20.7.

SETTINGS.FSL
demonstrates setting colors
based on a table.

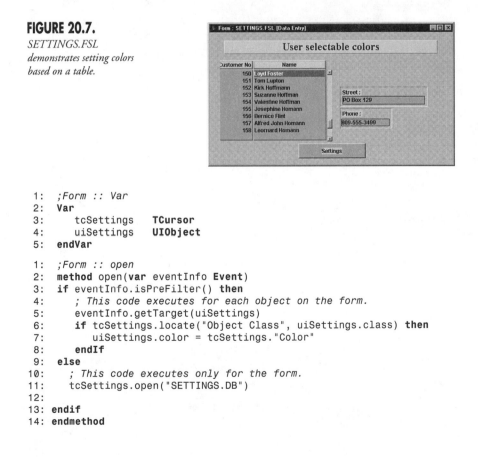

```
1:  ;Form :: Var
2:  Var
3:     tcSettings    TCursor
4:     uiSettings    UIObject
5:  endVar

1:  ;Form :: open
2:  method open(var eventInfo Event)
3:  if eventInfo.isPreFilter() then
4:     ; This code executes for each object on the form.
5:     eventInfo.getTarget(uiSettings)
6:     if tcSettings.locate("Object Class", uiSettings.class) then
7:        uiSettings.color = tcSettings."Color"
8:     endIf
9:  else
10:    ; This code executes only for the form.
11:    tcSettings.open("SETTINGS.DB")
12:
13: endif
14: endmethod
```

The other interesting bit of code is in the changeValue method of the Property_Value field on the second page. It checks to make sure that the user enters a valid color by trying to set the color property of the boxSample box (see Figure 20.8). The following is the code from the changeValue method of the Property_Value field on the second page.

```
1:   ;fld :: changeValue
2:   method changeValue(var eventInfo ValueEvent)
3:      try
4:         boxSample.color = eventInfo.newValue()
5:      onFail
6:         DisableDefault
7:         msgStop("Warning", "Invalid color")
8:      endTry
9:   endmethod
```

FIGURE 20.8.

The second page of SETTINGS.FSL.

Although the preceding technique works well for database applications, a better technique is to use an .INI file as did many Windows 3.*x* applications or use the database registration as Windows 95/NT applications use.

Using the *Enabled* Property

Enabled is a new read/write property for all UIObjects. Enabled is an interesting and powerful property that ObjectPAL programmers can use. When the Enabled property is set to False, the object and the objects that are contained in the object appear to be disabled. Specifically, the following things happen:

NEW
Term

- The object no longer responds to mouse clicks.
- You cannot move to the object.
- All text in the object becomes grayed.
- The Enabled property cascades to all the objects inside the given object.

Note the importance of this last item. For example, setting a Notebook object's Enabled property to False causes the Enabled property of every field, label, and record object inside that Notebook object also to be set to False. This makes it very easy to "disable" an entire collection of objects with one property set. Setting the Enabled property to True also cascades to all the child objects. The syntax for it is simple.

```
active.enabled = False
active.enabled = not active.enabled
```

 ANSWERS\ENABLED.FSL demonstrates the new Enabled property on text, field, and button objects, as well as a box with all three contained within it.

Summary

In this chapter, you learned about read-only and read-write properties. You also learned that using properties in ObjectPAL can be confusing because property names are inconsistent with the names you use interactively. The ObjectPAL equivalent names are different than the end-user property names. Even within Paradox, names of properties may change from one location to another. Knowing and understanding these subtle differences in properties will help make you an expert ObjectPAL programmer.

Manipulating Design
Objects

21

IN THIS CHAPTER

Objects that you place on forms and reports are UIObjects (User Interface Objects). Only UIObjects that you place on forms contain events. The form itself is also a UIObject—it has events and responds to events. Paradox takes care of painting the objects on the screen.

A *pixel* is an abbreviation for picture element. Pixels vary in size depending on your monitor. One physical pixel is one dot on your screen, regardless of resolution. Contrast this with a *twip*, which is a physical unit where 1,440 twips are equal to one inch, regardless of resolution. Most ObjectPAL properties that manipulate size are in twips, not pixels.

Using the UIObject Variable

ObjectPAL offers tremendous flexibility in manipulating UIObjects during runtime. You can either directly refer to a UIObject or attach to it and refer to it with the UIObject variable. For example, assuming a box named box1 is on a form, you can change its color with the following:

```
method pushButton(var eventInfo Event)
   box1.color = Red
endMethod
```

or with

```
method pushButton(var eventInfo Event)
   var
      ui UIObject
   endVar

   ui.attach(box1)
   ui.color = Red
endMethod
```

Obviously, in most situations the first single line of code is simpler, but the second technique is a particularly useful technique that you will often use when you do not know the name of the object a routine will be working with.

Creating UIObjects

ObjectPAL enables you to create objects in runtime. To create objects on the fly, you need to use the create() method, and you need to know about things such as points and twips. As stated earlier, a twip is what you use to measure points on the screen. A point has an x value and a y value, both of which are measured in twips. A twip is 1/1440 of an inch, or 1/20 of a printer's point. The following two examples use the create() command and a point variable to create and delete a line. create() does just what its name implies—creates objects. The type of object, where the object is created, and the dimensions of the object are all specified as part of the parameters for create().

The properties (frame, color, font, and so on) of the object produced by `create()` default to whatever the object defaults happen to be at the time the object is created. To modify the properties, you must change each individually, after the object has been created. The notation and properties specific to graphs are discussed later in this chapter.

Following, called UIObjectTypes, are the constants that correspond to the types of objects that one can create with UIObject `Create()`:

```
BandTool
BoxTool
ButtonTool
ChartTool
EllipseTool
FieldTool
GraphicTool
LineTool
NotebookTool
OleTool
PageBrkTool
PageTool
RecordTool
SelectionTool
TableFrameTool
TextTool
XtabTool
```

The parameters for `Create()` are as follows:

objectType	Corresponds to the type of object being created. For graphs, this will be `ChartTool`.
x	The x coordinate (in twips) of the upper-left corner of the object.
y	The y coordinate (in twips) of the upper-left corner of the object.
w	The width (in twips) of the object to be created.
h	The height (in twips) of the object to be created.
container	This is an optional parameter. If present, `container` must be a UIObject capable of containing the created object. In other words, you cannot place a 1000 by 1000 object within a 500 by 500 container.

A Note on Working with Groups

Normal object creation goes from the outside to inside. For example, first the page is created and then you place a box on the page. Within the box, you place a table frame. Obviously, you cannot create the box without first creating the page. Likewise, you cannot create the frame

432

without first creating the box. Unfortunately, groups work the opposite way. You cannot place a group on the page and then place objects within the group. You must first place the two objects and then place a group around these two objects.

Working with Frames

Because frames can vary in thickness, you need to allow for a border on the containing object. As a general rule of thumb, it is a good idea to give 15 twips distance between the inner object and its containing object.

Creating a Line the Same Size as the Page

Suppose that you want to allow the user to create and delete a line. To do this, you use two buttons on a form. One button creates a line, and the other deletes it.

> You can find the CREATE2.FSL form on the disc in the \ANSWERS directory.

Step By Step

1. Create a new form and place two buttons on it. Label the buttons Create Line and Delete Line (see Figure 21.1).

FIGURE 21.1.

Setup form for the example.

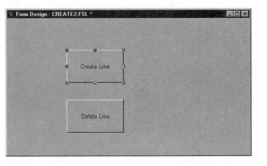

2. Add line 3 to the Var window of the page.

```
1:    ;Page :: Var
2:    Var
3:        ui UIObject
4:    endVar
```

3. Add lines 3–12 to the pushButton method of the Create Line button.

```
1:    ;Button :: pushButton
2:    method pushButton(var eventInfo Event)
3:        var
```

```
 4:          p Point
 5:        endVar
 6:        p = container.size        ;Size of page.
 7:
 8:        ui.create(LineTool, 15, p.y()-15, 0, -1000, self.container)
 9:        ui.end = point(p.x(), 0)
10:        ui.visible = True
11:      endmethod
```

4. Add line 3 to the pushButton method of the Delete Line button.

```
 1:      ;Button :: pushButton
 2:      method pushButton(var eventInfo Event)
 3:        ui.delete()
 4:      endmethod
```

5. Check your syntax, save the form as CREATE2.FSL, run the form, and click the Create Line button. After the line is created, click the Delete Line button to remove it (see Figure 21.2).

FIGURE 21.2.

CREATE2.FSL demonstrates creating and deleting a line.

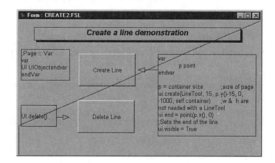

Analysis

In step 2, line 3 declares a UIObject variable named ui. After you declare a UIObject variable, you can use it to create new objects and to manipulate existing objects. In this case, the UIObject variable is created at the page level. Therefore, both buttons have access to it.

In step 3, line 4 declares p as a point variable for use in line 9. Lines 8–10 create the line, set its end point, and make it visible.

In step 4, line 3 on the second button uses the delete() method to delete the UIObject. The delete() method isn't new to you, but the UIObject version is. Earlier, you learned why many of ObjectPAL's commands are polymorphic; that is, why they behave in context. This is a good example of polymorphism. The delete() method in line 3 knows that it's working on a UIObject and handles it accordingly.

Creating a Graph from Scratch

Now that you've seen how easy the `create()` method is, type the following code into the `pushButton` method of a button:

```
 1:  ;Button :: pushButton
 2:  method pushButton(var eventInfo Event)
 3:     var
 4:        ui     UIObject        ;Declare a UIObject variable.
 5:     endVar
 6:
 7:     ui.create( ChartTool, 100, 100, 3000, 3000 ) ;Create the graph.
 8:     ui.tableName = "ORDERS.DB" ;Set graph properties.
 9:     ui.visible = True          ;Display graph.
10:  endMethod
```

The preceding code creates a graph from scratch on a form. ObjectPAL is powerful; it enables you to create all types of objects while the object to which the code is attached is running. You also can alter the properties of graphs already created.

A Simple Example of Manipulating a Graph Property

This next example is similar to the preceding example, but adds the manipulation of the `bindType` and `graphType` properties to set the graph type. Following is another example you can type into the `pushButton` method of a button:

```
 1:  ;Button :: pushButton
 2:  method pushButton(var eventInfo Event)
 3:     var
 4:        ui     UIObject
 5:     endVar
 6:
 7:     ui.create( ChartTool, 20, 20, 3000, 3000 )
 8:     ui.bindType = GraphTabular
 9:     ui.graphType = Graph2DPie
10:     ui.tableName = "ORDERS.DB"
11:     ui.visible = True
12:  endMethod
```

Using *designModified*

Sometimes you need to open another form, alter it, and close it from ObjectPAL. When you do, you are prompted to save the changes to the form; this is a very undesirable feature for a finished application. You could deliver the form and the problem would go away, or you could use the `designModified` property of the form, as in the following example:

```
 1:  f.designModified = False
```

In essence, you are telling the form that nothing was changed, when in fact it was.

This technique also works with reports. For example, the following code snippet from the Paradox Desktop opens a report and alters it:

```
 1:    var
 2:       r    Report                ;Declare r as a report variable.
 3:       ri   ReportOpenInfo        ;Declare ri as a ReportOpenInfo variable.
 4:    endVar
 5:
 6:    ri.name = "SOURCE"            ;Specify report name.
 7:    ri.masterTable = "SOURCE.DB"  ;Set master table for report.
 8:    r.open(ri)                    ;Open report.
 9:
10:    ;Set the value property of a text object.
11:    r.txtTitle.value = "Source Code for " + fldFileName.value
12:    r.show()
13:    r.designModified = False      ;Tell report it has not changed.
14:    r.wait()
```

Dereferencing a UIObject

You can create, move, size, and generally change any property of a UIObject. But how do you reference a UIObject with a variable? As discussed previously, you do so through dot notation and the use of parentheses. Referencing objects without hard-coding their names in the application adds flexibility to your routines.

When you work with several objects on a form, you might want to perform the same actions on each of the objects at different points in the code. One technique that saves many lines of code is to use a variable to reference an object. Remember the following three rules when you use a variable to reference an object:

- The statement that references an object must include a containership path. In the example that follows, Page refers to the name of the actual page in which the (Y) object resides.
- The first object in the path must not be a variable.
- Parentheses should surround the name of the variable.

Following is an example of how these rules are applied:

```
 1:    for X from 1 to 10
 2:       Y = "Box" + strVal(X) ;This evaluates Y = "Box1" for
 3:       Page.(Y).color = Blue ;the first iteration of the
 4:                             ;for loop
 5:    endFor
```

This code changes the color of the objects named Box1 through Box10 to the color blue. Remember that it's easier to access the objects if you rename them yourself. If the name of the object is the previous name suffixed by a number, such as Box1, you can use code. The sample form UIOBJECT.FSL demonstrates this technique (see Figure 21.3).

FIGURE 21.3.

*UIOBJECT.FSL. This
form uses variables for the
names of UIObjects.*

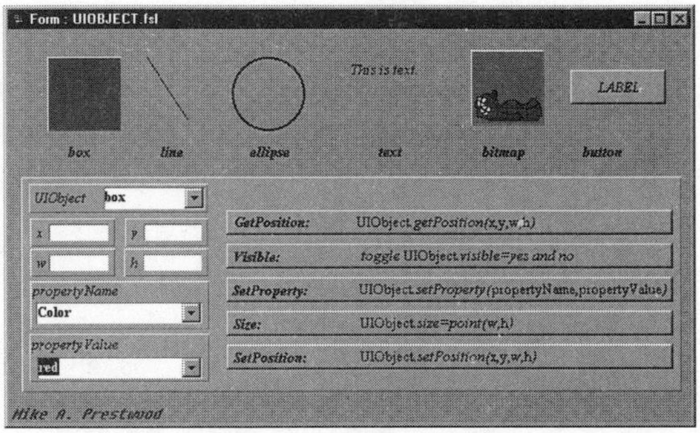

TIP

If you need to rename many objects, one right after the other, use the Object Tree. By
selecting and inspecting each object on the Object Tree, you can quickly rename many
objects.

Read-Only Properties and Dereferencing

On disc is the form READONLY.FSL, which demonstrates two important features: read-only
properties and dereferencing a UIObject. This form uses dereferencing to enable you to browse
the various read-only properties of a field.

The interesting bit of code in this form is on the pushButton method of the Display property
result button (see line 3 that follows).

```
1:  ;Button :: pushButton
2:  method pushButton(var eventInfo Event)
3:      message(pge1.(fldName.value).getProperty(fldProperty.value))
4:  endmethod
```

Line 3 uses dereferencing to use the value in the fldName field as an object. When the SS# is
selected, the line evaluates to the following:

```
1:  message(pge1.SS#.getProperty(fldProperty.value))
```

Once again, to dereference a UIObject in ObjectPAL requires two steps:

1. Start back in the containership path at least one object. In this case, pge1 contains the
   fldName field.

2. Surround the field with parentheses. This tells the compiler to evaluate what is in the
   parentheses first.

Using Timers

Timers in ObjectPAL offer a powerful way to manipulate your environment. A timer enables you to execute an event every so many milliseconds. To set a timer, use `setTimer()`, as in the following:

```
1:   setTimer(milliSeconds [,repeat])
```

For example, on the open method of any object, you can set a timer to trigger every ten seconds:

```
1:   self.setTimer(10000)
```

ANSWERS\TIMER1.FSL demonstrates the preceding line of code.

After you set the timer, add the code that you want to execute on the `timer` method of the object, as in the following example:

```
1:   method timer(var eventInfo TimerEvent)
2:     msgInfo("10 second timer", "Press OK")
3:   endmethod
```

> **NOTE**
>
> Windows timers operate at a minimum of 55 milliseconds, even if you specify less than 55 in `sleep()` or with `Timer`. Therefore, the fastest timer that you can have is every 55 milliseconds.

You can use timers for a multitude of tasks, such as the following:

- Executing a set of commands every *n* milliseconds
- Checking the system time or date to set scheduled events
- Looping every *n* milliseconds for a multitasking looping technique
- Animating objects by moving and resizing them

Animating a Box Across the Screen

This next example demonstrates how to move an object across the screen. It uses the `timer` event method and the `position` property to move a box across the screen. When the box object has reached the other side, it starts over.

You can find the TIMER2.FSL form on the disc in the \ANSWERS directory.

Step By Step

1. Create a new form with a box measuring approximately one inch by one inch (see Figure 21.4).

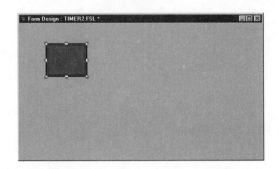

2. Add lines 3 and 4 to the Var window of the box.

```
1:    ;Box :: Var
2:    Var
3:       posPt   Point
4:       x,y     LongInt
5:    endVar
```

3. Add lines 3–6 to the open method of the box.

```
1:    ;Box :: open
2:    method open(var eventInfo Event)
3:       self.setTimer(100)
4:       posPt = self.position
5:       x = posPt.x()
6:       y = posPt.y()
7:    endmethod
```

4. Add lines 3–7 to the timer method of the box.

```
1:    ;Box :: timer
2:    method timer(var eventInfo TimerEvent)
3:       x = x + 50
4:       self.position = Point(x, y)
5:       if x > 5800 then
6:          x = 200
7:       endIf
8:    endmethod
```

5. Check your syntax and run the form. The pull-down menus still work even though the code is executing (see Figure 21.5).

FIGURE 21.5.

TIMER2.FSL demonstrates animating a UIObject.

Analysis

In step 3, line 3 starts the timer so that the code will execute 10 times a second (100/1000 = 10). Line 4 from step 2 declares posPt as a point variable so that you can get the position of the box in line 3. Line 4 in step 2 declares x and y long integers to store the values in lines 5 and 6.

Line 3 in step 4 increments *x* by 50 for use in line 4 to move the box horizontally to the right by 50 twips. Lines 5 and 6 check whether the box has traveled as far to the right as you want. If it has, line 6 repositions it to the left.

You can have a lot of fun animating your forms with timers. As an exercise, add objects to this form. You could even introduce a random moving of objects. Timers have two basic uses: for timed events and for multitasking. Use timers when you need to execute a set of commands repeatedly, or when you need to multitask one task with another.

APPS\FELICIA\FELICIA.FSL uses a similar technique to the one just demonstrated to animate a bitmap picture moving across the screen.

Looping with a Timer

Suppose that you want to enable a user to continue using his computer during a while loop that will take a long time to complete. To do this, you need to return control to Windows 95 or Windows NT. You won't see function calls in ObjectPAL that are equivalent to WaitMessage in the Windows SDK. How do you handle this situation? Because it's part of the Windows API, you can call WaitMessage directly. To do this, declare it in a Uses statement, and call it. There are, however, two better and easier techniques.

You can use two techniques, depending on how much control you want to give back to Windows. You can insert a sleep() statement in your while loop, which yields to Windows events. Depending on how complicated the while loop is, this might give you enough of a yield. You can add more sleep() statements to your code, or you can recode it to use the built-in timer method.

Set a `timer` event on a UIObject to fire every *x* milliseconds. You set *x*. Then, place one iteration of the `while` loop on the `timer` event. The iteration of the loop will process. You can vary how much you do on each `timer` event; a single iteration is the simplest example. Of course, you'll remove the `while` statement because the `timer` event controls the repetitive processing.

Table 21.1 lists the `TimerEvent` methods and procedures. Notice that `TimerEvent` has no unique methods or procedures; all of them are inherited from the base Event type.

Table 21.1. `TimerEvent` **methods and procedures.**

errorCode*
getTarget*
isFirstTime*
isPreFilter*
isTargetSelf*
reason*
setErrorCode*
setReason*
*Inherited from the Event type

Example of Looping with Timers

Suppose that you want to add three fields to a form that count up while still enabling users to use the form and Windows. You can use this technique to create loops that enable users to continue their work. In this example, you set up three independent loops that use timers and three buttons that control the three loops as a set. The first button starts the looping process. The second button causes the three loops to pause. The third button kills all three loops. To show that these three loops are multitasking, you add a table frame connected to a table. That way, you can add records while the three loops count.

You can find the LOOP-T.FSL form on the disc in the \ANSWERS directory.

Step By Step

1. Set your working directory to TUTORIAL. Create a new form, based on the WORLD.DB table, with three buttons on it. Label the buttons Start Timers, Pause Timers, and Kill Timers. Add three unlabeled, undefined fields. Name them Field1,

Field2, and Field3. Figure 21.6 shows how the form should look. In this figure, the three undefined fields and font sizes have been enlarged, and most of the columns have been deleted.

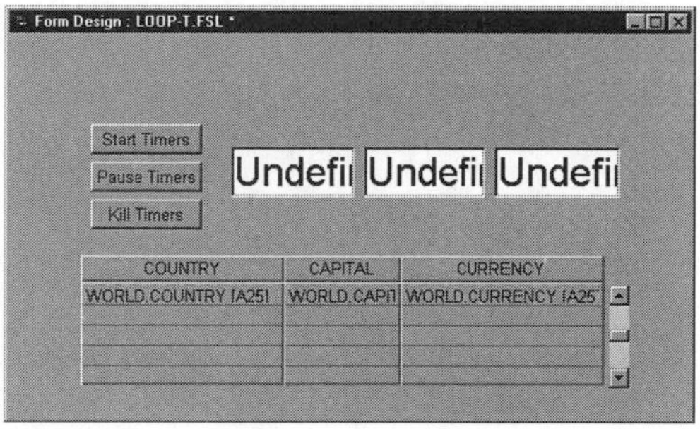

FIGURE 21.6.

Setup form for the looping with timers example.

2. Type line 3 in the Var window of the form.

```
1:   ;Form :: Var
2:   Var
3:       Counter1, Counter2, Counter3 SmallInt
4:   endVar
```

3. Type lines 3–5 in the open method of the form.

```
1:   ;Page :: open
2:   method open(var eventInfo Event)
3:       Counter1 = 0
4:       Counter2 = 0
5:       Counter3 = 0
6:   endmethod
```

4. Add lines 3–10 to the `timer` method of the Field1 field.

```
1:   ;Field :: timer
2:   method timer(var eventInfo TimerEvent)
3:       if Counter1 < 100 then
4:         Counter1 = Counter1 + 1
5:         self = Counter1
6:       else
7:         Counter1 = 0
8:         self = 0
9:         self.killTimer()
10:      endIf
11:  endmethod
```

5. Add lines 3–10 to the `timer` method of the Field2 field.

```
1:   ;Field :: timer
2:   method timer(var eventInfo TimerEvent)
3:       if Counter2 < 200 then
4:         Counter2 = Counter2 + 1
5:         self = Counter2
6:       else
7:         Counter2 = 0
8:         self = 0
9:         self.killTimer()
10:      endIf
11:  endmethod
```

6. Add lines 3–10 to the timer method of the Field3 field.

```
 1:    ;Field :: timer
 2:    method timer(var eventInfo TimerEvent)
 3:       if Counter3 < 1000 then
 4:          Counter3 = Counter3 + 1
 5:          self = Counter3
 6:       else
 7:          Counter3 = 0
 8:          self = 0
 9:          self.killTimer()
10:       endIf
11:    endmethod
```

7. Add lines 3–5 to the pushButton method of the Start Timers button.

```
 1:    ;Button :: pushButton
 2:    method pushButton(var eventInfo Event)
 3:       field1.setTimer(1000)
 4:       field2.setTimer(250)
 5:       field3.setTimer(50)
 6:    endmethod
```

8. Add lines 3–5 to the pushButton method of the Pause Timers button.

```
 1:    ;Button :: pushButton
 2:    method pushButton(var eventInfo Event)
 3:       field1.killTimer()
 4:       field2.killTimer()
 5:       field3.killTimer()
 6:    endmethod
```

9. Add lines 3–13 to the pushButton method of the Kill Timers button.

```
 1:    ;Button :: pushButton
 2:    method pushButton(var eventInfo Event)
 3:       field1.killTimer()
 4:       Counter1 = 0
 5:       Field1 = 0
 6:
 7:       field2.killTimer()
 8:       Counter2 = 0
 9:       Field2 = 0
10:
11:       field3.killTimer()
12:       Counter3 = 0
13:       Field3 = 0
14:    endmethod
```

10. Check the syntax, save the form as LOOP-T.FSL, and run the form. Click the Start Timers button and let it run a while. All three loops run at different speeds. You can use this effect to prioritize tasks. Click on the Pause Timers button; all three loops pause. When you click the Start Timers button a second time, the loops continue from where they paused. Now, use the table frame. For example, scroll up and down a few records, insert a record, and so on. Click the Kill Timers button to stop and reset all three loops. Figure 21.7 shows how the form should look after you finish this example.

FIGURE 21.7.

LOOP-T.FSL. Using timers to create multitasking.

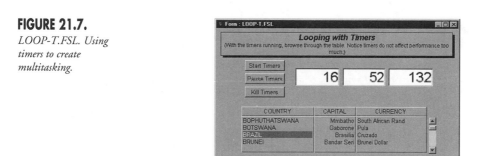

Analysis

In step 2, line 3 declares the three variables used in the three timers.

In step 3, lines 3–5 initialize the variables declared in step 2, line 3 when the form is opened.

Except for the number of times that the timers loop, the three timers are the same. In step 4, line 3, the first loop checks whether the counter variable is less than 100. If it is, line 4 increments it by 1. Line 5 sets the value of self to the value of the counter variable. This shows progress through the loop; normally, you would do something more productive. If the counter variable in line 3 isn't less than 100, line 7 sets it to 0. Line 8 sets the value of the field to 0 to indicate visually that the loop is over. Line 9 destroys the timer.

In step 7, lines 3–5 on the Start Timer button start the looping process. They dictate which loop has priority—that is, the loop speed. Line 3 sets the first timer to fire once every second, and starts it. Line 4 sets the second timer to fire once every quarter-second, and starts it. Line 5 sets the third timer to fire once every one-twentieth of a second, and starts it.

In step 8, lines 3–5 on the Pause Timer button kill the timers but don't reset the counter variables. This enables the three loops to pause and restart.

In step 9, lines 3–13 kill and reset the timers, counter variables, and field values. Using timers to multitask and pause loops is an important technique. It often will come in handy.

Toggle Buttons

How do you keep a button down? Simply disable the event prior to the pushButton method with disableDefault. For example, use the following code on the button's mouseUp method:

```
1:  disableDefault
2:  buttonName.value = True
```

Because value is assumed, you can shorten the second line of code to the following:

```
1:  buttonName = True
```

Keeping a Button Pressed

doDefault doesn't cause a button to pop up. It simply causes Paradox to immediately execute the internal code associated with a pushButton event. The button's popping up isn't part of this. The button's popping up signals the change of the button's value from True to False. If you want a button to pop up immediately, set its value to False. Having the button remain pressed, however, is a good way to signal to users that an operation stemming from the button is proceeding. The next example demonstrates how to keep a button pressed.

Toggling a Button Down and Up

Suppose that you want to toggle a button between down and up, and to set its label's text color to dark gray when the button is down. To the user, this has the effect of the button being off when it is up, and on when it is down.

You can find the TOGGLE.FSL form on the disc in the \ANSWERS directory.

Step By Step

1. Create a new form and place a button on the form, name the label on the button textObject, and change the value of the label to Toggle me (see Figure 21.8).

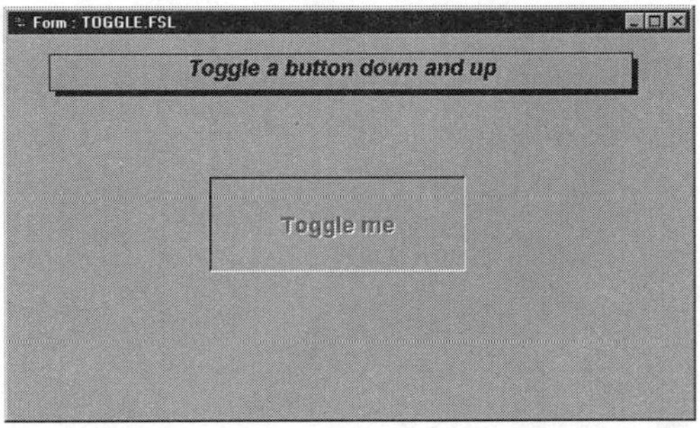

FIGURE 21.8.

TOGGLE.FSL demon-strates toggling a button up and down.

2. Add lines 3–11 to the mouseUp method of the Toggle me button.

```
1:  ;Button :: mouseUp
2:  method mouseDown(var eventInfo MouseEvent)
3:      DisableDefault
4:      if self = False then
5:          self = True
6:          self.enabled = False
7:          ;put down code here
8:      else self = False
9:          self.enabled = True
```

```
10:          ;put up code here
11:       endIf
12:    endmethod
```

3. Check your syntax, save the form as TOGGLE.FSL, run the form, and click the button. Notice that the button goes down and its label turns gray. Click it again. The button comes up and its label turns black (refer to Figure 21.8).

Analysis

In step 2, line 3 disables the default behavior. In this case, the call to pushButton is prevented. Line 4 checks whether the button is up. If the button is up, line 5 puts it down, and line 6 changes its label to dark gray. If the button is down, line 9 puts it up, and line 10 changes its label to black.

The next example shows you how to toggle among a number of buttons. While one button is down, all the other buttons are up.

Toggling Between Two Buttons

Suppose that you want to put two buttons on a form and toggle between them. If the user clicks button 1, and button 2 is down, button 1 will come up, and vice versa. In addition, you want to change a value in a field, depending on which button is down.

You can find the TOGGLE2.FSL form on the disc in the \ANSWERS directory.

Step By Step

1. Open an existing form or create a new one. Place two buttons and a field on the form. Label the two buttons Option1 and Option2, name the buttons btnOption1 and btnOption2, and name the field fldSelected (see Figure 21.9).

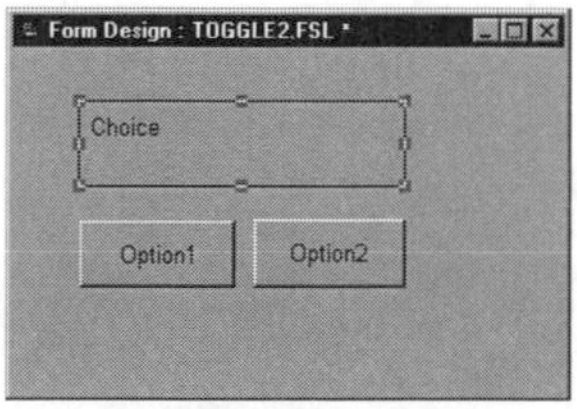

FIGURE 21.9.

Setup form for toggling a button example.

2. Add lines 3–6 to the mouseUp method of the Option1 button.

```
1:    ;btnOption1 :: mouseUp
2:    method mouseUp(var eventInfo MouseEvent)
3:       DisableDefault
4:       btnOption1 = True
5:       btnOption2 = False
6:       fldSelected.value = "Option one is down"
7:    endmethod
```

3. Add lines 3–6 to the mouseUp method of the Option2 button.

```
1:    ;btnOption2 :: mouseUp
2:    method mouseUp(var eventInfo MouseEvent)
3:       DisableDefault
4:       btnOption1.value = False
5:       btnOption2.value = True
6:       fldSelected.value = "Option two is down"
7:    endmethod
```

4. Check your syntax, save the form as TOGGLE2.FSL, run the form, and click the Option1 button. The button goes down. Now click the Option2 button. Option1 pops up, and Option2 stays down (see Figure 21.10).

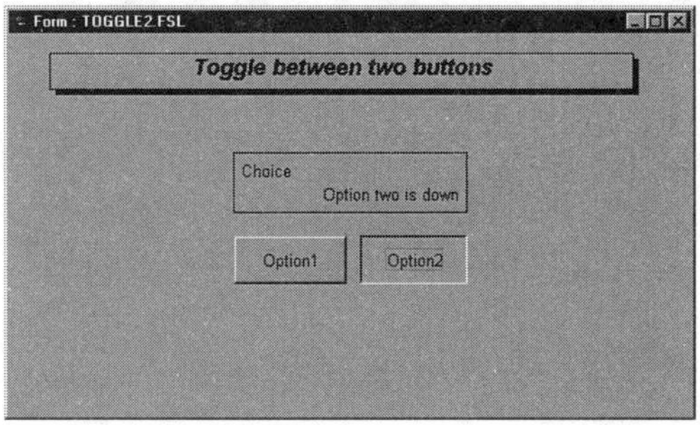

FIGURE 21.10.

TOGGLE2.FSL. This form toggles between the two buttons.

Analysis

The code for both buttons is similar. The key to holding the button down is to disable the default behavior on the mouseUp method of the button (step 2, line 3 and step 3, line 3) and to explicitly set it up or down by making its value True or False (step 2, lines 4–5 and step 3, lines 4–5). In this simple example, the only code executed controls the buttons and sets the value of the Choice_Selected field. No code is put on the pushButton method.

NOTE

Another technique for toggling between two buttons that does not require code is to use a radio button. To use this technique, place a field on a form or report, define its DisplayType as radio buttons, and then change the ButtonStyle of the button objects to pushButton.

The Form Style Creator Utility

This chapter ends by introducing a utility on the CD that creates Form style sheets from existing forms (see Figure 21.11). It uses many of the techniques outlined in this chapter, including the designModified property. Type the following code into a script or the pushButton method of a button. It automatically creates style sheets from your favorite forms. Follow the comments to see how it works.

FIGURE 21.11.

S-SHEET1.SSL startup screen.

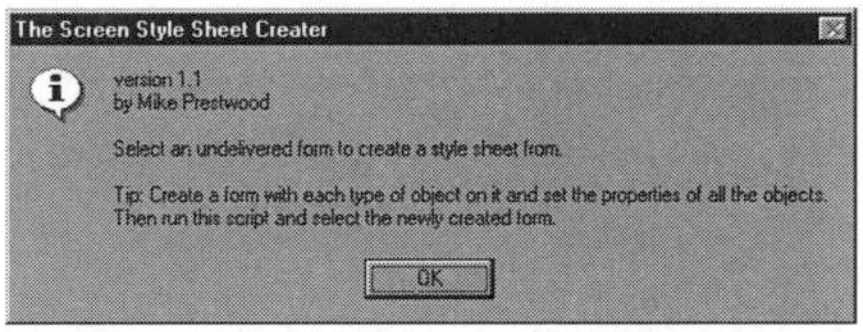

```
 1: ;S-SHEET1.SSL :: run
 2: method run(var eventInfo Event)
 3:    var
 4:       sTitle, sMessage  String
 5:       f                 Form
 6:       fbi               FileBrowserInfo
 7:       sFilename         String
 8:       sSheet            String
 9:       arObjects         Array[] Anytype
10:       arForm            Array[] Anytype
11:       siCounter         SmallInt
12:    endVar
13:
14:    errorTrapOnWarnings(Yes)
15:
16:    ;Display startup screen.
17:    sTitle = "The Screen Style Sheet Creator"
18:    sMessage = "version 1.1\nby Mike Prestwood\n\nSelect an undelivered form."
19:    msgInfo(sTitle, sMessage)
20:
21:    ;Prompt for form.
22:    fbi.allowableTypes = fbForm
23:    if fileBrowser(sFileName, fbi) then
24:    else                               ;If no file is selected,
25:       return                          ;then abort.
26:    endIf
27:
28:    setMouseShape(MouseArrow)
29:    message("Creating style sheet: extracting path")
30:
31:    ;Find path of file.
32:    errorTrapOnWarnings(No)
33:    switch
34:       case isDir(fbi.alias)
35:          : sFilename = fbi.alias + fbi.path + sFilename
36:       case sFilename.subStr(1,6) = ":PRIV:"
37:          : sFilename = sFilename.subStr(7, sFilename.size() - 6)
38:             sFilename = getAliasPath(":PRIV:") + "\\" + sFilename
```

```
39:     otherwise
40:       : sFilename = getAliasPath(fbi.alias) + "\\" + fbi.path + sFilename
41:   endSwitch
42:   errorTrapOnWarnings(Yes)
43:
44:   ;Generate style sheet name.
45:   breakApart(sFilename, arForm, ".")
46:   sSheet = arForm[1] + ".FT"
47:
48:   ;Prompt user for final time to abort.
49:   if msgQuestion("Proceed?", "Create style sheet...\n" + sSheet + "\n\nFrom
      form...\n" + sFilename + "") <> "Yes" then
50:     beep()
51:     message("Aborting...")
52:     return
53:   endIf
54:
55:   ;Create style sheet.
56:   message("Creating style sheet: loading object")
57:   f.load(sFilename, WinStyleHidden)    ;Attach to form.
58:   f.enumObjectNames(arObjects)         ;Populate array with object names.
59:
60:   message("Creating style sheet: copying styles to toolbar")
61:   setMouseShape(MouseWait)
62:   for siCounter from 1 to arObjects.size()    ;Cycle through ar and
63:     copyToToolBar(f.(arObjects[siCounter])) ;copy the object properties to
64:   endFor                                   ;the toolbar.
65:   message("Creating style sheet: saving style sheet")
66:   try
67:     f.saveStyleSheet(sSheet, True)
68:   onFail
69:     errorShow("Error saving style sheet")
70:   endTry
71:
72:   ;Finish.
73:   message("Creating style sheet: closing object")
74:   f.designModified = False            ;Tell loaded form it didn't change.
75:   f.close()                           ;Close form.
76:   setMouseShape(MouseArrow)
77:   message("Done.")
78:   sTitle = "Style Sheet Created"
79:   sMessage = sSheet + "\n\nThe above style sheet was created and is ready for
      you to use."
80:   msgInfo(sTitle, sMessage)
81:   message("")
82:endmethod
```

You can use the two style sheets, S-SHEET1.SSL and S-SHEET2.SSL, to automatically create form and report style sheets. Simply run the S-SHEET1.SSL or S-SHEET2.SSL script included on the disc in the \ANSWERS directory. When you run the script, the Open Form or Report dialog box displays, select a form or report and the style sheet is created.

Summary

In this chapter, you learned that ObjectPAL offers tremendous flexibility in manipulating and creating UIObjects during runtime. You learned that the form itself is both a display manager and a UIObject—it has events and responds to events. You can create, move, size, and generally change any property of a UIObject. You need to know about things such as points and twips. A point has an x value and a y value, both of which are measured in twips. Most ObjectPAL properties that manipulate size are in twips, not pixels. A twip is what you use to measure points on the screen.

The ObjectPAL language gives you the capability to dereference objects and use timers. You can either directly refer to a UIObject or attach to it and refer to it with the UIObject variable. Referencing objects without hard-coding their names in the application adds flexibility to your routines. Timers in ObjectPAL offer a powerful way to manipulate your environment. Timers have two basic uses: for timed events and for multitasking. Use timers when you need to execute a set of commands repeatedly, or when you need to multitask one task with another.

Importing and Exporting Data with *DataTransfer*

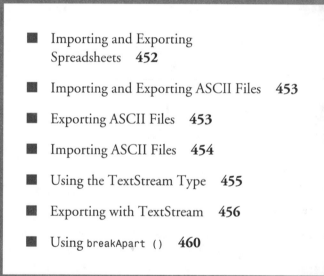

22

7 NEW Feature

With the new `DataTransfer` type, you can create, delete, import, and export data. With Paradox, you can import and export data interactively with File | Import and File | Export options. These options are very thorough and powerful.

> **NOTE**
>
> The entire `DataTransfer` type is new for version 7, but many of the methods are not. All the methods for moving data that were in the `System` type were moved to the `DataTransfer` type. Some methods are entirely new. For a complete list of all the methods that were moved from the `System` type to the `DataTransfer` type, refer to the DataType index entry in the ObjectPAL online help.

Importing and Exporting Spreadsheets

You can import or export Quattro, Excel, or Lotus spreadsheets with ObjectPAL. You pass these procedures a few parameters, and it takes over. You can use `importSpreadSheet()` to import and `exportSpreadSheet()` to export.

Using *exportSpreadSheet()*

Use `exportSpreadSheet()` when you want to export any of the following spreadsheets to a table: Quattro Pro for Windows, Quattro Pro DOS, Quattro, Lotus 2.*x*, Lotus 1.A, and Excel 3.0/4.0/5.0. Following is the syntax:

`exportSpreadSheet(const `**`fileName`**` String, const `**`tableName`**` String, [, const `
`makeRowHeaders`` Logical]) Logical`

The parameters are fairly straightforward. Specify the input spreadsheet filename with the `fileName` parameter. Specify the output table name with `tableName`. Finally, specify whether you want the spreadsheet's column labels to determine the field names of the table with `makeRowHeaders`. If successful, `exportSpreadSheet()` returns `True`; otherwise, it returns `False`. For example, the following code exports an Excel spreadsheet named SALES.XLS to a Paradox table named SALES.DB:

```
1. method pushButton(var eventInfo Event)
2.    if exportSpreadsheet("SALES.XLS", "SALES.DB", True) then
3.       message("Export successful")
4.    else
5.       message("Export not successful")
6.    endIf
7. endMethod
```

> **NOTE**
>
> You are specifying the spreadsheet format (type) with the extension on the `fileName` parameter. Valid extensions are .WB1, .WB2, and .WB3 for Quattro Pro for Windows; .WQ1 for Quattro Pro for DOS; .WKQ for Quattro; .WK1 for Lotus 2.*x*; .WKS for Lotus 1.A; and .XLS for Excel.

Importing and Exporting ASCII Files

ASCII is an acronym for American Standard Code for Information Interchange. The ASCII set consists of 7-bit codes that represent 128 standard characters—letters, numbers, and symbols. The characters in the ASCII set are the same as the first 128 characters in the extended ASCII and ANSI sets.

The meaning of the term ASCII file has expanded from its strict technical definition to something more generic. Today, ASCII can refer to any file that is composed of readable characters, even if it contains characters other than the 128 of the original set. Most programmers still restrict the definition of ASCII, however. They use the term text file when they need a more generic term.

ASCII files are important because they are the means by which file incompatible programs (especially from different computer platforms) can exchange data. More and more programs can import and export dBASE tables. More and more applications are adding Paradox to their list of import and export routines. If the program you want to bring data from or port data to supports either Paradox or dBASE, use either of those formats. You might have to work with programs that can't import or export Paradox or dBASE tables, however. In those cases, you can fall back on ASCII text files. ASCII text files are the one format that nearly all applications on all platforms can use. Text files are the common thread that enables applications and platforms to share data.

Exporting ASCII Files

To *export* a file is to convert it from a native format—either Paradox or dBASE—to a foreign format, such as ASCII. When you need data stored in either a Paradox or dBASE table in a text file, you export it. In the next two examples, you will build two of the routines used in EXPORT.FSL, which is on the disc that comes with this book (see Figure 22.1 later in this chapter). The form demonstrates how to export standard and nonstandard ASCII files.

You can use the following procedures to export data:

```
exportASCIIFix()
exportASCIIVar()
exportParadoxDOS()
exportSpreadSheet()
```

Using *exportASCIIFix()*

You use the command `exportASCIIFix()` when you want to export a table to a delimited text file. The syntax for it follows:

```
exportASCIIVar ( const tableName String, const fileName String
[ , const separator String, const delimiter String, const allFieldsDelimited
Logical,
const ansi Logical]) Logical
```

Specify `tablename` with the `tableName` parameter and specify the destination file with the `fileName` parameter. The separator and delimiter are optional parameters. Specify `True` with the `allFieldsDelimited` parameter to specify whether all fields including number and date fields should be delimited. Specify whether to use the ANSI or OEM character set with the `ansi` parameter.

The following example exports the data from the Customer table to the text file CUSTOMER.TXT. This example uses tabs to delimit field values, double quotes to enclose each value, delimits only character fields, and uses the ANSI character set.

```
1. ;Button :: pushButton
2. method pushButton(var eventInfo Event)
3.    exportASCIIVar("customer.db", "customer.txt", "\t", "\"", False, True )
4. endMethod
```

This command is similar to `exportASCIIFix()`, which exports tables to a fixed length field. `exportASCIIFix()` uses a specification file that specifies the exported field's name, type, start position, and length.

> **NOTE**
>
> `exportASCIIVar()` does not export the following field types to delimited text: memo (Paradox or dBASE), formatted memo, graphic, OLE, Byte, or binary.

Importing ASCII Files

NEW Term

When you *import* a file, you convert the data from a foreign format, such as ASCII, to a native format: either Paradox or dBASE. Importing data is the process of bringing data into dBASE, Paradox, or a variable. Normally, you can import just about anything into ObjectPAL. At the least, you can read in a file and dump it into a memo field.

You can use any of the following easy-to-use procedures to import files:

```
dlgImportAsciiFix()    ;Displays the Import Fix Data dialog box.
dlgImportAsciiVar()    ;Displays the Import Variable Data dialog box.
importASCIIFix()       ;Import data from a fix length ASCII file.
importASCIIVar()       ;Import data from a variable length ASCII file.
appendASCIIFix()       ;Append fix length ASCII data to a table.
appendASCIIVar()       ;Append variable length ASCII data to a table.
```

> **NOTE**
>
> Both appendASCIIFix() and appendASCIIVar() dramatically increase the speed of importing of text files by importing them directly to existing tables.

Using the TextStream Type

Sometimes, a client or another user will give you a table whose format isn't consistent and expect you to translate it to Paradox or dBASE. Usually, you can use a while loop to loop through the text file and convert the text. Occasionally, however, the data won't permit this. When you run into this type of data, don't waste your time. Return the table and tell the person to give you consistent data. If the user pushes, explain the specifics of why the data cannot be imported.

Suppose that you have a text field with a date field and dates such as 1193, 121293, 42593, and 12193. If the text has four or six characters, you can easily break it into 1/1/93 and 12/12/93. If the text file has five characters, you might not be able to tell what the date is supposed to be. Clearly, 42593 is 4/25/93, but 12193 could be 1/21/93 or 12/1/93. There's no way to know. The moral of the story is to make sure that the original program exports data properly.

To import data, follow these steps:

1. Open a TextStream to the text file. It can be read-only.
2. Use a while loop to loop through the text file. You can use eof to check for the end of the file.
3. Use readLine() to read one line at a time to a String variable.
4. Use the match() method to look for the names of fields, or use the breakApart() method to break each line into logical components.
5. Close the TCursor and TextStream variables.

The next two examples demonstrate routines from the IMPORT.FSL program, which is on the disc that comes with this book. The form demonstrates how to import text files into ObjectPAL, manipulate them, and store them in a Paradox table.

> **NOTE**
>
> Rather than use eof() to check for the end of the file, you can check whether readLine() was successful. If readLine() returns False, you're at the end of the file.

Exporting with TextStream

With the TextStream methods, you can export and import ASCII files in any format you want. Often, your code contains fewer than 15 lines, which is not a big deal. Table 22.1 lists the TextStream methods and procedures.

Table 22.1. TextStream methods and procedures.

```
advMatch
close
commit
create
end
eof
home
isAssigned
open
position
readChars
readLine
setPosition
size
writeLine
writeString
```

Example of Exporting Fields to an ASCII File with TextStream

Suppose that you want to export two fields of a table to an ASCII file with the fields separated by a comma. This is a common task often performed in order to transfer data to another software package.

This next example demonstrates exporting a table to an ASCII file using the TextStream type of methods. In this exercise, you will open a table with a TCursor variable and a text file with a TextStream variable. After both are open, you will scan through the table and use the writeLine() method to write the data to the text file.

You can find the EXPORT.FSL form on the disc in the \ANSWERS directory.

Step By Step

1. Change your working directory to the TUTORIAL and create a new form. Place a button labeled Export routine 1 on it.

2. Add lines 3–15 to the pushButton method of the Export routine 1 button.

```
1:    ;Button :: pushButton
2:    method pushButton(var eventInfo Event)
3:      var
4:        tc    TCursor
5:        ts    TextStream
6:      endVar
7:
8:      tc.open("EXPORT.DB")
9:      ts.open("EXPORT1.TXT", "NW")   ;N = new, W = write
10:
11:     scan tc:
12:       ts.writeLine(tc."First Name", ", ", tc."Last Name")
13:     endScan
14:     tc.close()
15:     ts.close()
16:   endmethod
```

3. Check the syntax and save the form as EXPORT.FSL. Run it and click the button. The button stays down momentarily while the table is exported (see Figure 22.1). You can use any Editor (Notepad, for example) to view the EXPORT1.TXT text file.

FIGURE 22.1.

EXPORT.FSL demonstrates exporting data.

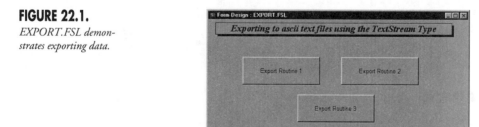

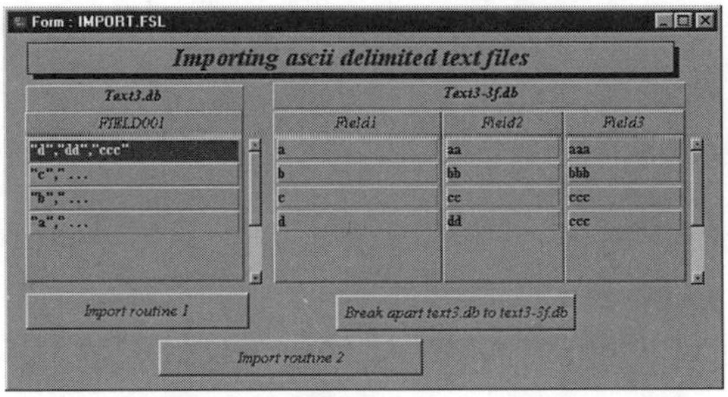

FIGURE 22.2.

The IMPORT.FSL form.

Analysis

In step 2, lines 4 and 5 declare the TCursor and TextStream variables tc and ts. Line 8 opens the TCursor, and line 9 opens the TextStream. Lines 11–13 scan through the table. Line 12 writes each record to the text file. Line 12 adds a comma and a space between the two fields. You could use a tab—chr(9)—instead. Lines 14 and 15 close both variables.

Exporting a Table to ASCII SDF Format with TextStream

NEW
Term

SDF is an acronym for standard delimited format. An SDF is a text file formatted in a particular style. Each field is enclosed in quotation marks and separated by a comma. Each line ends with a carriage return and a linefeed. This next example shows you how to export a table in SDF format.

Suppose that you want to export a Paradox table to an ASCII file in SDF format. In this next example, you export a Paradox table into a text file in standard delimited format.

You can find the EXPORT.FSL form on the disc in the \ANSWERS directory.

Step By Step

1. Change your working directory to the TUTORIAL directory and create a new form. Place a button labeled Export routine 2 on it. This label is different from the label in EXPORT.FSL (refer to Figure 22.1).

2. Add lines 3–20 to the pushButton method of the Export routine 2 button.

```
1:    ;Button :: pushButton
2:    method pushButton(var eventInfo Event)
3:       var
4:          tc        TCursor
5:          ts        TextStream
6:          s1,s2     String
7:       endVar
8:
```

```
 9:        setMouseShape(MouseWait)
10:        tc.open("EXPORT.DB")
11:        ts.open("EXPORT3.TXT", "NW")   ;N = new, W = write
12:        s1 = "\""
13:        s2 = "\","
14:
15:        scan tc:
16:          ts.writeLine(s1+tc."First Name"+s2, s1+tc."Last
                 Name"+s2,s1+tc."City"+s2, s1+tc."Hobby"+s1)
17:        endScan
18:        tc.close()
19:        ts.close()
20:        setMouseShape(MouseArrow)
21:      endMethod
```

3. Check the syntax and save the form. Run it and click the button. The button stays down momentarily while the table is exported. You can use any Editor (Notepad, for example) to view the EXPORT1.TXT text file.

Analysis

In step 2, lines 4–6 declare the TCursor, TextStream, and String variables tc, ts, s1, and s2. Line 9 sets the mouse pointer to a waiting mouse icon so that the user clearly understands to wait. Line 10 opens the TCursor, and line 11 opens the TextStream. Lines 12 and 13 define the two String variables declared in line 6. Lines 15–17 scan through the table. Line 16 writes each record to the text file.

Line 16 uses the two String variables rather than the separators. This technique has two benefits. You save effort by not having to type all the extra commas, slashes, and quotation marks. You also can easily change the separator later if you want.

Lines 18 and 19 tidy up and close both variables. Line 20 notifies the user that the routine is done by switching back to the arrow mouse icon.

Importing a Text File to a Memo Field

Suppose that you want to import a text file to a Paradox memo field—one record for each line of text—and to update the screen.

You can find the IMPORT.FSL form on the disc in the \ANSWERS directory.

Step By Step

1. Change your working directory to the TUTORIAL directory and create a new form. Place a table frame named Text3 and a button labeled Import routine 1 on it.

2. Add lines 3–20 to the pushButton method of the Import routine 1 button.

```
1:     ;Button :: pushButton
2:     method pushButton(var eventInfo Event)
3:        var
4:           tc   TCursor
5:           ts   TextStream
6:        endVar
7:
8:        tc.open("text3.db")
9:        ts.open("text3.txt","R")
10:       tc.edit()
11:
12:       while not ts.eof()
13:          tc.insertRecord()
14:          ts.readline(tc.field1)
15:          tc.postrecord()
16:       endWhile
17:
18:       Text3.resync(tc)
19:       tc.close()
20:       ts.close()
21:    endmethod
```

3. Check the syntax and save the form as IMPORT.FSL. Run it and click the button. The button stays down momentarily while the table is imported. Because TEXT3.TXT is such a small ASCII file, the table frame populates almost immediately.

Analysis

In step 2, lines 4 and 5 declare the TCursor and TextStream variables tc and ts. Line 8 opens the TCursor, and line 9 opens the TextStream. Line 10 puts the TCursor into Edit mode so that it can be used in the loop in lines 12–16. Line 12 sets up the loop and in effect says, "While not at the end of the file connected to the TextStream variable, do the following." Line 13 inserts a new blank record into the TCursor, and line 14 reads from the TextStream directly into the TCursor. Line 15 posts the new record. Line 18 updates the screen. Lines 19 and 20 tidy up and close both variables.

Using *breakApart()*

The breakApart() method from the String type is useful for both importing and exporting because it enables you to split a string into an array of substrings based on one or more separators. Following is the syntax:

breakApart (var *tokenArray* Array[ ] String [, const *separators* String])

Notice the separators parameter is optional. If you do not specify a separator, then the string is split based on spaces. The tokenArray is an Array variable you provide. Type lines 3–10 into the pushButton method of a button. This short program uses breakApart() to split a string based on spaces and periods.

```
 1:    ;Button :: pushButton
 2:    method pushButton(var eventInfo Event)
 3:       var
 4:          s        String
 5:          ar       Array[] String
 6:       endVar
 7:
 8:       s = "Mr. Daniel Raymond Unsicker"
 9:       s.breakApart(ar, ". ")
10:       ar.view("Token Strings")
11:    endMethod
```

By combining `breakApart()` with `subStr()`, you can extract any form of data you want from strings. The next example adds the `breakApart()` method to the routine. `breakApart()` is a powerful method. It can split a string into substrings based on a separator. This example also sets the mouse pointer to the waiting mouse while the import takes place.

A More Sophisticated Import Routine

This chapter ends with a slightly more sophisticated import routine. Suppose that you want to import a text file, break it apart, put the parts into the appropriate Paradox fields, and update the screen. This next example demonstrates one way to do this.

You can find the file IMPORT.FSL on the disc in the \ANSWERS directory.

Step By Step

1. Change your working directory to the TUTORIAL directory. Open the IMPORT.FSL form you created in the previous example and a button to it labeled Import Routine 2.

NOTE

If you didn't create the IMPORT.FSL form in the previous example, then create a new form with the table TEXT3-3F.DB in the data model. Place a table frame on the form and bind the table frame to the TEXT3-3F.DB table. Also place a button labeled Import Routine 2 on the form.

2. Add lines 3–29 to the `pushButton` method of the Import Routine 2 button.

```
 1:    ;Button :: pushButton
 2:    method pushButton(var eventInfo Event)
 3:       var
 4:          tc     TCursor
 5:          ts     TextStream
 6:          s      String
 7:          ar     Array[]    String
 8:       endVar
```

```
 9:
10:        setMouseShape(MouseWait)
11:        ts.open("text3.txt","R")
12:        tc.open("text3-3f.db")
13:        tc.edit()
14:
15:        while not ts.eof()
16:          ts.readline(s)
17:          s.breakApart(ar,",")
18:          tc.insertRecord()
19:          tc."Field1"=ar[1].subStr(2,size(ar[1])-2)
20:          tc."Field2"=ar[2].subStr(2,size(ar[2])-2)
21:          tc."Field3"=ar[3].subStr(2,size(ar[3])-2)
22:          tc.postRecord()
23:        endWhile
24:
25:        tc.endEdit()
26:        Table_Frame.resync(tc)
27:        tc.close()
28:        ts.close()
29:        setMouseShape(MouseArrow)
30:    endmethod
```

3. Check the syntax and save the form. Run it and click the button. The button stays down momentarily while the table is imported. Because TEXT3.TXT is such a small ASCII file, the table frame populates almost immediately.

Analysis

Lines 4–7 declare the variables needed to import and break apart an ASCII file: a TCursor, a TextStream, a String, and a resizeable Array. Line 8 sets the mouse pointer to the waiting mouse icon. Line 11 and 12 open the TCursor and the TextStream. Line 13 puts the TCursor into Edit mode so that it can be used in the loop in lines 15–23. Line 15 sets up the loop and in effect says, "While not at the end of the file connected to the TextStream variable, do the following."

Lines 16 and 17 read in a line of text and separate it into a resizeable array. Line 17 indicates that the separation uses single commas. Line 18 inserts a new blank record. Lines 19–21 strip away excess characters and use the powerful breakApart() method to put the values into this blank record. Line 22 posts the new record. Line 25 ends Edit mode, and line 26 updates the screen. Lines 27 and 28 tidy up and close both variables. Line 29 sets the mouse pointer back to an arrow.

Summary

In this chapter, you learned that importing and exporting of data with ObjectPAL can be a single line of code or, if needed, can be a complex routine. Now that you've practiced importing and exporting ASCII files, you can import or export almost any ASCII file that has consistent data. Chapter 23 discusses how you can reuse and compartmentalize your code.

Storing and Centralizing Code

IN THIS CHAPTER

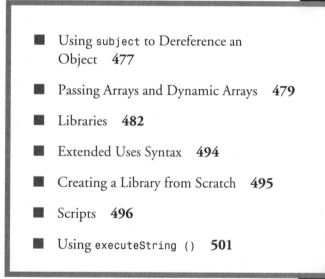

In ObjectPAL, custom methods and procedures are equivalent to subroutines. A *subroutine* is a sequence of instructions that performs a specific task, usually more than once in a program. The sequence may be invoked many times by the current program or by multiple applications. Although ObjectPAL doesn't have actual subroutines, you can think of custom methods and custom procedures as subroutines.

ObjectPAL comes with a set of methods and procedures called the runtime library. A custom method consists of methods and procedures from the runtime library, as well as registered functions from dynamic link libraries (DLLs). Think of the set of custom methods and custom procedures that you develop as your own private runtime library.

A *custom method* is a method that you create. It consists of methods and procedures from the runtime library and from other custom methods and procedures. Custom methods are subroutines that objects can access. A *custom procedure* is similar to a custom method, except that the scope for a custom procedure is much more limited. Scope determines the availability of a custom procedure to other objects.

Global Versus Private

A custom method is always global to the object. The object to which the custom method is attached and all the objects contained by it can call the custom method directly. With dot notation, objects can use the custom methods of other objects. For example, if a button has a custom method called cmMsg() on it, it can be called from another button. To experiment with this important concept, create two buttons named Button1 and Button2 and add the following code to them:

```
1:   ;Button1 :: cmMsg
2:   method cmMsg()
3:      message("Paradox tables can have up to 255 secondary indexes.")
4:   endMethod
```

```
1:   ;Button2 :: pushButton
2:   method pushButton(var eventInfo Event)
3:      Button1.cmMsg()
4:   endmethod
```

Custom procedures, on the other hand, are more limited in scope. Custom procedures have the same scope as variables. Only the object and objects contained by that object can call the custom procedure directly. In addition, dot notation doesn't work with custom procedures. A custom procedure in the Proc window of an object is global to the object. That is, an object can access its own procedure and the procedures defined in the objects that contain it. Remember, the scope of a variable depends on where it is declared; the same applies to custom methods and custom procedures. To experiment with your first custom procedure, create a button named Button3 and add the following code to its Proc method and pushButton event method:

```
1:   ;Button3 :: proc
2:   proc cpMsg()
3:      message("A BLOB field type is limited to 256 MB")
```

```
4:   endProc
5:
6:   ;Button3 :: pushButton
7:   method pushButton(var eventInfo Event)
8:      cpMsg()
9:   endmethod
```

A custom procedure can be private to a method by adding your own proc...endProc statement above or below the method line. When a custom procedure is private to a method, no other objects can call it. Likewise, no other events within the object can call it. The following is an example of a private custom procedure. The proc structure goes either above or just below the built-in method line. For example, create a button named Button4 and add lines 2–4 and line 6 to the pushButton event method:

```
1:   ;Button4 :: pushButton
2:   proc cpMsg()
3:      message("A primary index can consist of up to 255 fields")
4:   endProc
5:   method pushButton(var eventInfo Event)
6:      cpMsg()
7:   endmethod
```

Passing by Value Versus Passing by Reference

Custom methods can receive and return values. You can pass a value by value or by reference. When you pass a value to a custom method by value, you pass a copy of the value. If the custom method alters the copy, nothing happens to the original. When you pass a value to a custom method by reference, you pass a reference to the location where the value is currently stored. In other words, you are actually referring to the original value. If the custom method alters it, it is altering the original value.

Passing by value and passing by reference are common to custom methods and procedures. Take a look at the following custom method prototypes.

```
1:   method cmCode(var s String)     ;Pass by reference.
2:   method cmCode(s String)         ;Pass by value.
3:   method cmCode(Const s String)   ;Pass by reference,
4:                                   ;but not changeable.
```

If you're familiar with Pascal programming, you can see that lines 1 and 2 correspond to how you pass values to subroutines in Pascal. Line 1 has s as a var parameter that can be altered by the cmCode() method. In line 2, s is a value parameter.

In line 1, the value of s is changed. When you leave the cpCode() custom method, the value to which you changed s stays. In example 2, s is passed by value: A copy of s is given to cpCode(), and any change doesn't affect the original value. In example 3, the value is passed by reference. Because the value is a constant, the custom method can't change it. The following examples demonstrate these concepts. The form shown in Figure 23.1 demonstrates the six categories of custom procedures created in this chapter's first six examples.

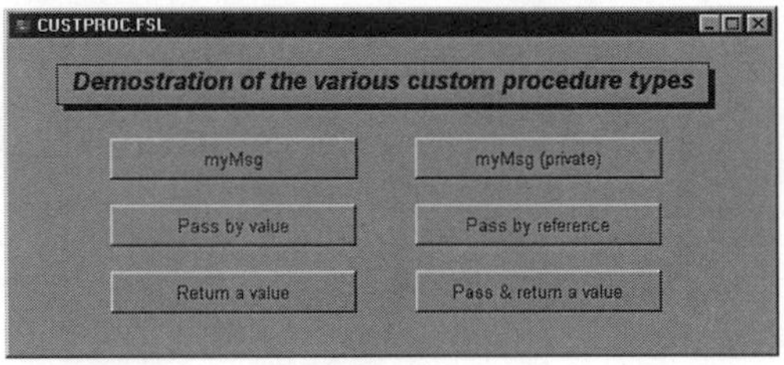

FIGURE 23.1.

CUSTPROC.FSL demonstrates the six categories of custom procedures.

My First Custom Procedure

In this next step by step example, you create and use a simple custom procedure. It demonstrates creating and using a simple custom procedure that doesn't receive or return a value. Use this type of custom procedure to compartmentalize your code into easy to understand junks of code in custom procedures.

You can find the CUSTPROC.FSL form on the disc in the \ANSWERS directory.

Step By Step

1. Change your working directory to the TUTORIAL directory, create a new form, and place a button labeled myMsg on it.

2. Alter the proc window of the myMsg button to look like the following:

```
1:   ;Button :: Proc
2:   proc cpMsg()
3:      msgInfo("PDoxWin Trivia",
                "You can use up to 24 tables in a query.")
4:   endProc
```

3. Add line 3 to the pushButton method of the myMsg button.

```
1:   ;Button :: pushButton
2:   method pushButton(var eventInfo Event)
3:      cpMsg()
4:   endmethod
```

4. Check the syntax and save the form as CUSTPROC.FSL (you are going to use this form for the next several step by step examples). Run the form and click the myMsg button. When the message appears, click OK (see Figure 23.2).

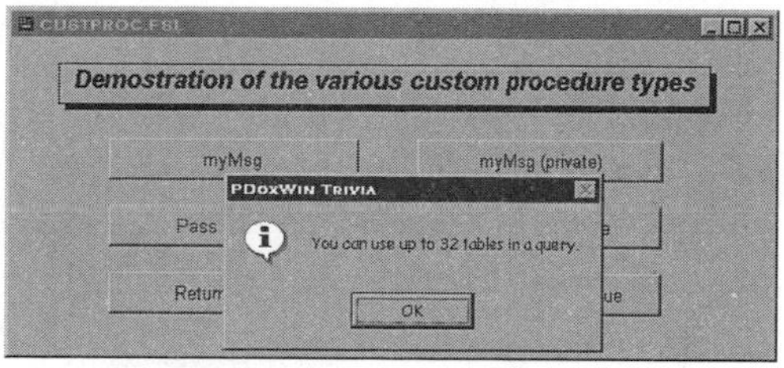

FIGURE 23.2.

CUSTPROC.FSL shows the myMsg button.

Analysis

Step 2, line 2 prototypes (sets up) the custom procedure. Nothing is in the parentheses, which indicates that the custom procedure expects to be passed nothing. The lack of code after the closing parenthesis indicates that the custom procedure returns nothing. Line 3 does the actual work.

In step 3, line 3 calls the custom method. The call passes the custom method nothing, as the lack of code in parentheses indicates.

In the next example, you create and use a private custom procedure.

My First Private Custom Procedure

This example demonstrates creating and using a simple custom procedure that doesn't receive or return a value and is private to the event.

You can find the CUSTPROC.FSL form on the disc in the \ANSWERS directory.

Step By Step

1. Open the CUSTPROC.FSL form (or create a new one). Place a button labeled myMsg (Private) on it. In this code example, the proc structure comes before the method block.

2. In the pushButton method of the button labeled myMsg (Private), add lines 2–4 above the method and line 6 below.

```
1:    ;Button :: pushButton
2:    proc cpMsg()
3:       msgStop("PDoxWin Trivia",
      "Paradox 7 tables now have descending secondary indexes ")
4:    endProc
5:    method pushButton(var eventInfo Event)
6:       cpMsg()
7:    endmethod
```

3. Check the syntax and save your work. Run the form and click the myMsg (private) button. When the message appears, click OK (see Figure 23.3).

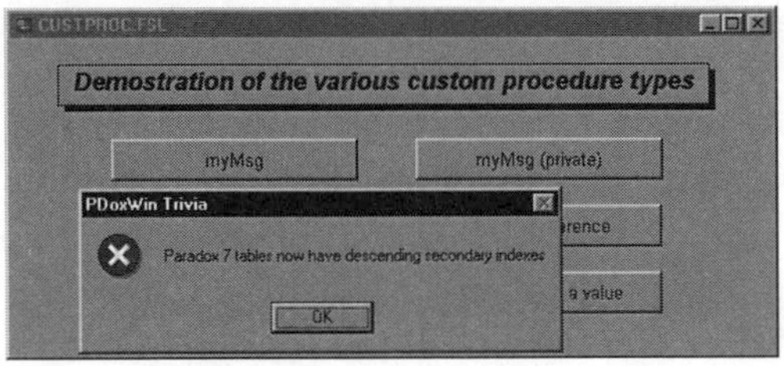

FIGURE 23.3.

*CUSTPROC.FSL shows
the myMsg button.*

Analysis

In step 2, line 2 prototypes the custom procedure exactly as it does in the previous example. Nothing is in the parentheses, which indicates that the custom procedure expects to be passed nothing. The lack of code after the closing parenthesis indicates that the custom procedure returns nothing. Line 3 does the actual work of the custom procedure. Line 6 calls the custom method. Line 6 passes the custom method nothing, again as the lack of code in the parentheses indicates.

Passing By Value to a Custom Procedure

This next step by step example demonstrates creating and using a custom procedure that receives, but doesn't return, a value. This category of custom procedure is important when writing generic custom procedures. For example, rather than referring directly to objects on forms, you can pass a UIObject variable to a custom procedure. Doing this makes the custom procedure work in more situations.

You can find the CUSTPROC.FSL form on the disc in the \ANSWERS directory.

Step By Step

1. Open the CUSTPROC.FSL form (or create a new one). Place a button labeled Pass by value on it.

2. Add line 3 to the Proc window of the Pass by value button.

```
1:    ;Button :: Proc
2:    proc cpMsg(s String)
3:        msgInfo("PDoxWin Trivia", s)
4:    endProc
```

3. Add lines 3–7 to the pushButton method of the Pass by value button.

```
1:    ;Button :: pushButton
2:    method pushButton(var eventInfo Event)
3:       var
4:          s       String
5:       endVar
6:
7:       cpMsg("Numeric fields are accurate to 15 significant digits")
8:    endmethod
```

4. Check the syntax and save your work. Run the form and click the Pass by value button. When the message appears, click OK (see Figure 23.4).

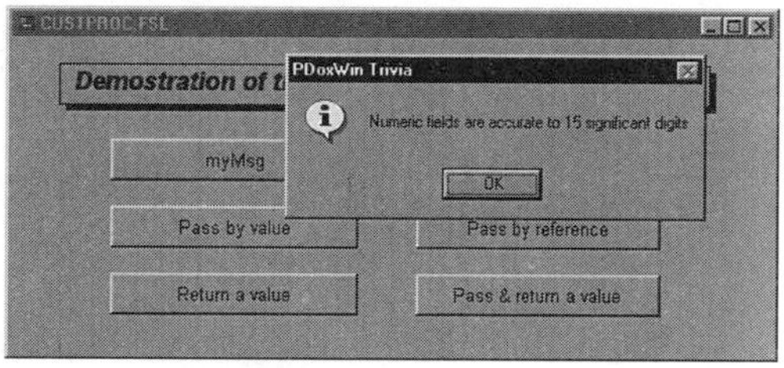

FIGURE 23.4.

CUSTPROC.FSL shows the Pass by value button.

Analysis

The custom procedures are starting to get interesting. This discussion begins with the pushButton method in step 3. Line 4 declares s as a String variable, and line 7 calls the custom method. This time, a string is passed to it.

In step 2, line 2 prototypes the custom procedure. s String, which is between the parentheses, indicates that the custom procedure expects to be passed a string. The lack of code after the closing parenthesis indicates that the custom procedure returns nothing. Line 3 does the actual work of the custom procedure. It uses the variable s.

In this example, both the calling code and the custom procedure use a String variable called s. This shows the connection between the two. In reality, both variables need only to be of the same type; they don't need to have the same name.

Passing By Reference to a Custom Procedure

This example demonstrates creating and using a custom procedure that receives a reference to a variable but doesn't return a value.

You can find the CUSTPROC.FSL form on the disc in the \ANSWERS directory.

Step By Step

1. Open the CUSTPROC.FSL form (or create a new one). Place a button labeled Pass by reference on it.

2. Add line 3 to the Proc window of the Pass by reference button.

```
1:    ;Button :: Proc
2:    proc cpMsg(var s String)
3:        msgInfo("Windows limit", s)
4:    endProc
```

3. Add lines 3–8 to the pushButton method of the Pass by reference button.

```
1:    ;Button :: pushButton
2:    method pushButton(var eventInfo Event)
3:        var
4:          sMsg       String
5:        endVar
6:
7:        sMsg = "The Registration Database replaced INI files."
8:        cpMsg(sMsg)
9:    endmethod
```

4. Check the syntax and save your work. Run the form and click the Pass by reference button. When the message appears, click OK (see Figure 23.5).

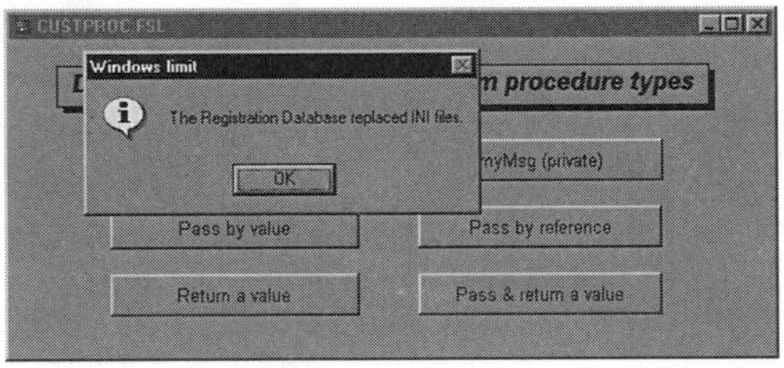

FIGURE 23.5.

CUSTPROC.FSL shows the Pass by reference button.

Analysis

This discussion begins with the pushButton method in step 3. Line 4 declares sMsg as a String variable. Line 8 calls the custom method that uses the variable sMsg. This time, a variable is passed to the custom procedure.

In step 2, line 2 prototypes the custom procedure. In this case, var sMsg String in parentheses indicates that the custom procedure expects to be passed a variable. The lack of code after the closing parenthesis indicates that the custom procedure returns nothing. Line 2 does the actual work of the custom procedure. It uses the variable sMsg.

In this example, the calling code and the custom procedure use different variable names: sMsg and s. This shows that, although the two variables have a direct connection, the connection is by reference to the same value. You could have used the same variable name.

Returning a Value from a Custom Procedure

This next step by step example demonstrates how to create and use a custom procedure that doesn't receive a value by reference but does return a value. After the procedure is created, the return value is used in a message information dialog box.

You can find the CUSTPROC.FSL form on the disc in the \ANSWERS directory.

Step By Step

1. Open the CUSTPROC.FSL form (or create a new one). Place a button labeled Return a Value on it.

2. In the Proc window of the Return a value button, add line 3.

```
1:    ;Button :: Proc
2:    proc cpNever() String
3:        return "Never duplicate a line of code!"
4:    endProc
```

3. In the pushButton method of the Return a value button, add line 3.

```
1:    ;Button :: pushButton
2:    method pushButton(var eventInfo Event)
3:        msgInfo("Message from guru", cpNever())
4:    endmethod
```

4. Check the syntax and save your work. Run the form and click the Return a value button. When the message appears, click OK (see Figure 23.6).

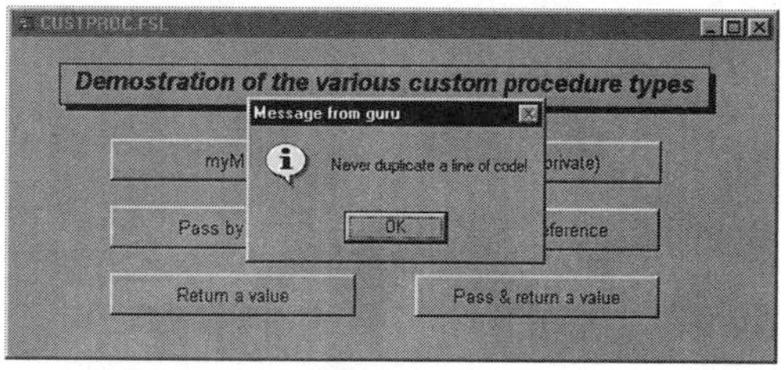

FIGURE 23.6.

CUSTPROC.FSL shows the Return a value button.

Analysis

Line 2 of step 2 prototypes the custom procedure. The lack of code in the parentheses indicates that the custom procedure expects to be passed nothing. The data declaration after the closing parenthesis indicates that the custom procedure returns a string. Line 3 does the actual work of the custom procedure. It uses the return keyword and passes back a string.

In step 3, line 3 calls the custom procedure and passes it nothing. Because the runtime library procedure msgInfo() expects a string, the custom procedure must return a value.

Sending and Returning a Value from a Custom Procedure

This example demonstrates how to create and use a custom procedure that receives a value by a reference and returns a value. After the procedure is created, the return value is used in a message information dialog box.

 You can find the CUSTPROC.FSL form on the disc in the \ANSWERS directory.

Step By Step

1. Open the CUSTPROC.FSL form (or create a new one). Place a button labeled Pass & return a value on the form.

2. Add lines 3–8 to the Proc window of the Pass & return a value button.

```
1:    ;Button :: Proc
2:    proc cpAge(var d Date) Number
3:       var
4:          n    Number
5:       endVar
6:
7:       n = year(today() - d) - 1
8:       return n
9:    endProc
```

3. Add lines 3–9 to the pushButton method of the Pass & return a value button.

```
 1:    ;Button :: pushButton
 2:    method pushButton(var eventInfo Event)
 3:       var
 4:         dBorn    Date
 5:       endVar
 6:
 7:       dBorn = date("01/08/65")
 8:       dBorn.view("Enter your birthdate")
 9:       msgInfo("Your age", cpAge(dBorn))
10:    endmethod
```

4. Check the syntax and save the form as CUSTPROC.FSL. Run the form and click the Pass & return a value button. When the first dialog box appears, type your birthdate and click OK. When the message displays your age, click OK (see Figure 23.7).

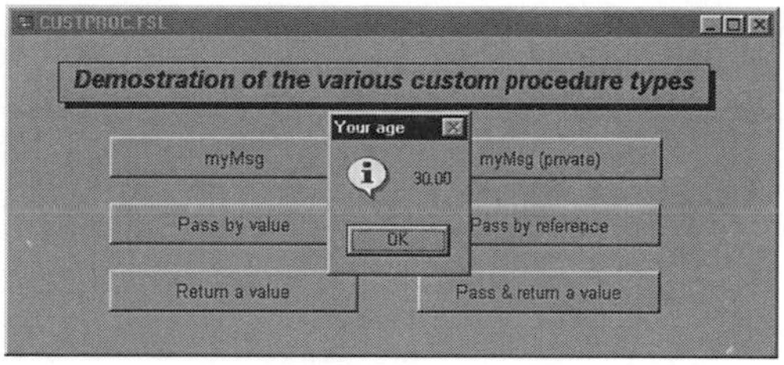

FIGURE 23.7.
*CUSTPROC.FSL shows
the Pass & return a value
button.*

Analysis

In step 2, line 2 prototypes the custom procedure. var d Date in parentheses indicates that the custom procedure expects to be passed a reference to a Date variable. The data declaration after the closing parenthesis indicates that the custom procedure returns a number. Line 4 declares n as a Number variable. It is used in line 7 to accept the result of the calculation of the number of years between today and the date passed to the custom procedure. Line 8 returns n.

In step 3, line 4 declares dBorn as a Date variable. dBorn is given a value in line 7. Line 8 enables the user to change the value with a Date View dialog box. Line 9 calls the custom procedure inside a msgInfo() procedure.

The previous six examples represent the various types of custom procedures. In a nutshell, a custom procedure can be private to the method or global to the object. Values can be passed to the custom procedure by value or by reference. Custom procedures can return a value, or not. After you master these elements, you can begin optimizing your code. Try never to duplicate a line of code. If you need to duplicate code on two objects, then consider putting the common code in a custom method or procedure and call it from both objects.

Custom Methods

Custom methods don't differ from custom procedures in any way except for scope. Whereas custom procedures can be private to a method or global to an object, custom methods are always global to an object. A custom method on an object can be called directly from any event on the object or from any event lower in the containership hierarchy. With dot notation, any object can call another object's custom method. The form shown in Figure 23.8 demonstrates custom methods. The three buttons on it are the buttons you create in the next three examples.

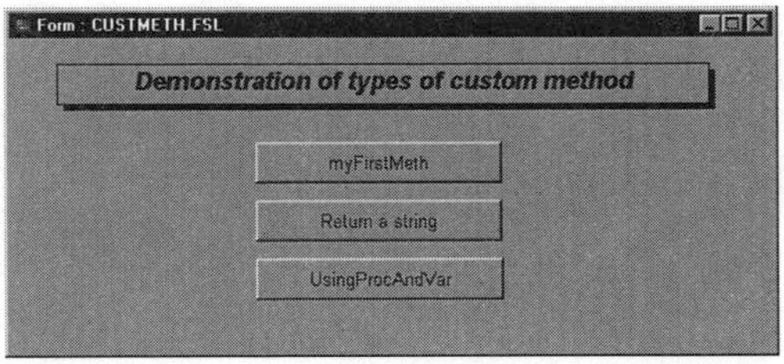

FIGURE 23.8.
CUSTMETH.FSL demonstrates three categories of custom methods.

My First Custom Method

This next step-by-step example demonstrates how to create and use a custom method that simply executes a block of code; the custom method does not accept nor return a value. In this case, the custom method asks a question.

You can find the CUSTMETH.FSL form on the disc in the \ANSWERS directory.

Step By Step

1. Change your working directory to the TUTORIAL directory, create a new form and place a button labeled myFirstMeth on it.

2. Create a new custom method called cmQuestion at the form level and add lines 3–7 to it.

```
1:    ;Form :: cmQuestion
2:    method cmQuestion()
3:       if msgQuestion("Question?",
                "Is ObjectPAL full of features?")= "Yes" then
4:          message("When you're right, you're right!")
5:       else
6:          message("How much more do you want?")
7:       endIf
8:    endmethod
```

3. Add line 3 to the pushButton method of the MyFirstMeth button.

```
1:    ;Button :: pushButton
2:    method pushButton(var eventInfo Event)
3:       cmQuestion()
4:    endmethod
```

4. Check the syntax and save the form as CUSTMETH.FSL (you will use this form for the next several step by step examples). Run the form and click the myFirstMeth button. When the first dialog box appears, answer the question. When the message appears in the status bar, you're done (see Figure 23.9).

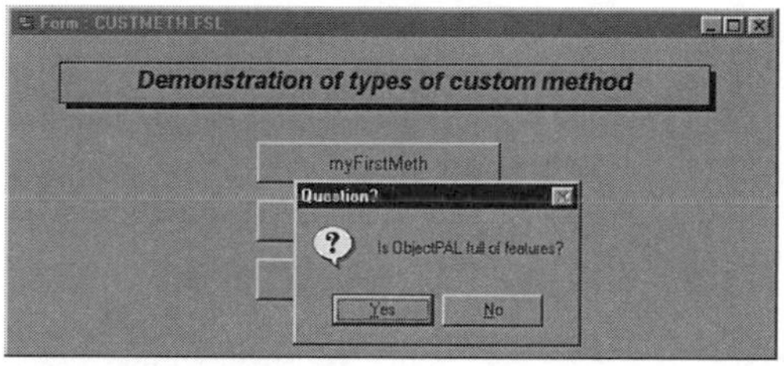

FIGURE 23.9.

CUSTMETH.FSL shows the MyFirstMeth button.

Analysis

In step 2, line 3 uses the message question dialog box to ask a question. If the user clicks Yes, the condition of the `if` structure is satisfied, and the message in line 4 appears in the status bar. If the user clicks No, the message in line 6 appears.

In step 3, line 3 starts the whole process. The syntax for calling a custom method is the same as the syntax for calling a custom procedure. Therefore, you can't use the same name for a custom procedure and for a custom method in the same object. You can, however, use the same name for both as long as they are in different objects; the scope determines whether the procedure or method is called.

For example, if you put a custom procedure named `cmQuestion` on the page level of the form created in this example, it's called from the button rather than the `cmQuestion` form-level custom method. If you look at the Object Tree by selecting Tools | Object Tree, you'll notice that the page is closer to the button than the form is.

Returning a String from a Custom Method

This next step by step example demonstrates that returning a value from a custom method is the same as returning a value from a custom procedure. Specifically, it demonstrates how to return a string from a custom method.

You can find the CUSTMETH.FSL form on the disc in the \ANSWERS directory.

Step By Step

1. Open the CUSTMETH.FSL form (or create a new one). Place a button labeled Return a string on it.

2. Create a custom method on the form level called `cmHelloWorld` and add line 3 to it.

```
1:    ;Form :: cmHelloWorld
2:    method cmHelloWorld() String
3:       return "Hello world!"
4:    endmethod
```

3. Add line 3 to the `pushButton` method of the Return a string button.

```
1:    ;Button :: pushButton
2:    method pushButton(var eventInfo Event)
3:       message(cmHelloWorld())
4:    endmethod
```

4. Check the syntax and save your work. Run the form (see Figure 23.10).

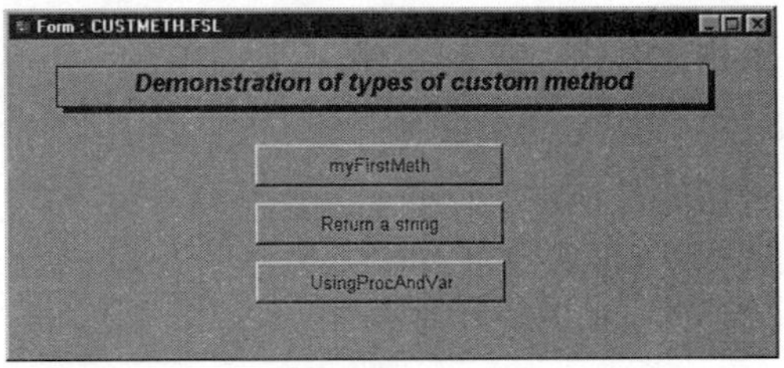

FIGURE 23.10.

CUSTPROC.FSL shows the Return a string button.

Analysis

In step 2, line 2 prototypes the custom method. As with a custom procedure, if you're going to receive or return a value, you prototype it in the first line. When you create a custom method, you prototype it as you would a custom procedure. The only difference is that a custom procedure resides in a `proc` block, whereas a custom method resides in a `method` block. Line 3 returns the string, and line 3 in step 3 calls the custom method.

Adding *proc* and *var* Structures to Custom Methods

Suppose that you need to add `proc` and `var` structures to a custom method. This example demonstrates how to add `proc` and `var` structures to a custom method.

You can find the CUSTMETH.FSL form on the disc in the \ANSWERS directory.

Step By Step

1. Open the CUSTMETH.FSL form (or create a new one). Place a button labeled UsingProcAndVar on it.

2. Create a custom method at the form level named `cmUsingProc` and add lines 2–13 to it.

```
1:    ;Form :: cmUsingProc
2:    var
3:       siCounter    SmallInt
4:    endVar
5:
6:    Proc cpCounter()
```

```
 7:          siCounter = siCounter + 1
 8:       endProc
 9:
10:    method cmUsingProc()
11:       siCounter = 9
12:       cpCounter()
13:       siCounter.view()
14:    endmethod
```

3. Add line 3 to the pushButton method of the UsingProcAndVar button.

```
1:    ;Button :: pushButton
2:    method pushButton(var eventInfo Event)
3:       cmUsingProc()
4:    endmethod
```

4. Check the syntax and save your work. Run the form and click the button. Only the number 10 appears (see Figure 23.11).

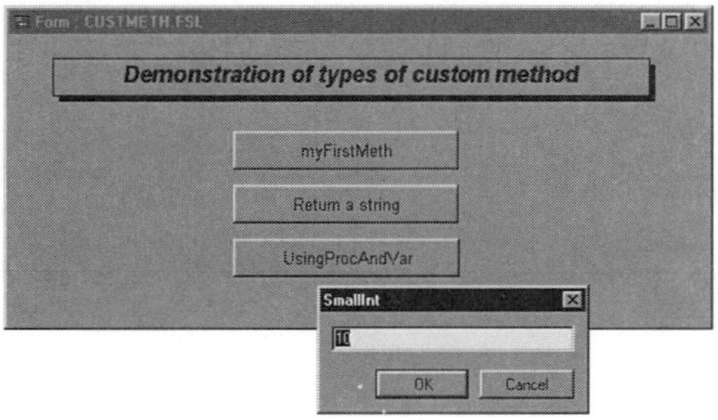

FIGURE 23.11.

CUSTPROC.FSL shows the UsingProcAndVar button.

Analysis

Step 2, lines 2–4 add a var structure to the custom method, which creates a variable private to the method. Line 3 in the var structure declares siCounter as a small integer. Lines 6–8 add a proc structure to the custom method. Line 6 prototypes the new custom procedure. Note the use of the siCounter variable. Lines 10–14 make up the actual custom method. Line 10 prototypes it. Line 11 sets the initial value for siCounter. Line 12 calls the custom procedure that increments the value. Line 13 views the variable.

In step 3, line 3 in the pushButton method of the button starts the custom method.

Using *subject* to Dereference an Object

You can pass a subject to a custom method. With dot notation, you can tell a custom method to act on another object. To do this, you use the keyword subject. The code inside the custom method can use subject to refer to the object that preceded the calling of the custom method using dot notation. This next step by step example demonstrates how to use subject and dereference an object.

Exploring ObjectPAL

Part IV

Suppose that you want to toggle the pattern of one of two ellipses, depending on the value in a field. This next step by step example dereferences a field and uses subject in a custom method to refer to the dereferenced value.

You can find the SUBJECT.FSL form on the disc in the \ANSWERS directory.

Step By Step

1. Create a new form with two ellipses on it named Ellipse1 and Ellipse2 and name the page Pge1.
2. Add a radio button field named choice with the two values Ellipse1 and Ellipse2.
3. Add a button labeled Toggle pattern. The form in Figure 23.12 uses subject with a custom method and dereferences an object.

FIGURE 23.12.

Setup form for the example.

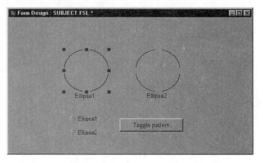

4. Create a custom method at the form level called cmToggleBackground() and add lines 3–7 to it.

```
1:    ;Form :: cmToggleBackground
2:    method cmToggleBackground()
3:       if subject.Pattern.Style = BricksPattern then
4:          subject.Pattern.Style = WeavePattern
5:       else
6:          subject.Pattern.Style = BricksPattern
7:       endIf
8:    endmethod
```

5. Add lines 3–7 to the pushButton method of the button.

```
1:    ;Button :: pushButton
2:    method pushButton(var eventInfo Event)
3:       if choice.isBlank() then
4:          return
5:       else
6:          pge1.(choice).cmToggleBackground()
7:       endIf
8:    endMethod
```

6. Check the syntax and save your work. Run the form. Select an ellipse from the choice field and click the button. Experiment with this form (see Figure 23.13).

FIGURE 23.13.

SUBJECT.FSL demonstrates using subject.

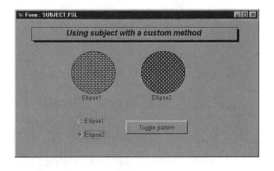

Analysis

In step 2, line 2 prototypes the custom method. Line 3 checks whether the pattern of subject is a bricks pattern. If it is, line 4 changes it to a weave pattern. If it isn't, line 6 sets it to a bricks pattern. Note the use of subject. By not hard-coding the name of the object, you can make your routines more generic and flexible.

In step 3, line 3 ensures that the choice field has a value. Otherwise, an error would occur whenever the field is left blank. If the choice field is blank, the method returns control. If a choice was made, line 6 calls the custom method. Parentheses are used around the field name, and an object is specified before the first parenthesis.

Passing Arrays and Dynamic Arrays

To pass an array or a dynamic array to a custom method or procedure, you need to set up a Type statement. The syntax checker doesn't enable you to declare an array directly, so you have to create a custom type of the array or dynamic array, as in the following example:

```
1. Type
2.    ctPassDyn = DynArray[] String
3. endType
```

After you create the custom type, you can use the custom type when you prototype your custom method (usually the first line of your custom method). For example:

```
1. method (dynSystem ctPassDyn)
2.    ;Use dynSystem here.
3. endMethod
```

This next step by step example demonstrates how to pass an array to a custom method.

Passing an Array to a Custom Method

Suppose that you need to pass an array with two elements in it to a custom method for display. To do this, you have to create a custom type of an array. Then use the custom type in the prototype line (usually the first line) of the custom method.

You can find the PASS-AR.FSL form on the disc in the \ANSWERS directory.

Step By Step

1. Create a new form and put a button labeled Pass Array on it.

2. Add line 3 to the Type window of the Pass Array button.

```
1:    ;Button :: Type
2:    Type
3:        ctPassAr = Array[2] String
4:    endType
```

3. Create a custom method called cmDisplayArray() on the Pass Array button and add line 3 to it.

```
1:    ;Button :: cmDisplayArray
2:    method cmDisplayArray(var ar ctPassAr)
3:        ar.view("Childhood friend")
4:    endMethod
```

4. Add lines 3–9 to the pushButton method of the Pass Array button.

```
1:    ;Button :: pushButton
2:    method pushButton(var eventInfo Event)
3:        var
4:          arName Array[2] String
5:        endVar
6:
7:        arName[1] = "Grant"
8:        arName[2] = "Winship"
9:        cmDisplayArray(arName)
10:   endmethod
```

5. Check the syntax and save your work. Run the form and click the button. The name Grant Winship appears in an array view dialog box, as Figure 23.14 shows.

FIGURE 23.14.

*PASS-AR.FSL demon-
strates passing an array
to a custom method.*

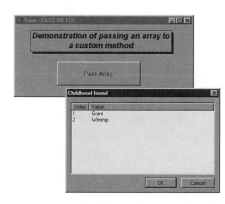

Analysis

In step 2, line 3 declares a new data type: a two-element array that is ready to receive string elements.

In step 3, line 2 uses the new data type in the custom method's prototype. The var keyword indicates that the array is passed by reference. If you leave out the var keyword, the array is passed by value. Line 3 displays the array.

In step 4, line 4 declares arName as a two-element private array that is ready to receive string values. Lines 7 and 8 populate the array. Line 9 passes the array to the custom method.

With the knowledge you gain in this chapter, you can start to reuse and compartmentalize your code. Remember to try never to duplicate a line of code and to put often-used code into custom procedures. These techniques work well for reusing code in a form. For reusing code across forms, ObjectPAL provides an object that is used only for storing code—the library.

Custom Methods Versus Custom Procedures

Is there a good rule of thumb to when to use a custom procedure? Functionally, the rule of thumb should be to always use custom procedures unless the code is called from outside of the containership hierarchy. Unfortunately, however, the reality is that it's too much of a pain for most people to do this because of Paradox's incapability to present a list of custom procedures and jump directly to a specific one. Any Proc or Method window is limited to 32K, which is dedicated to one method as opposed to shared among many procs. This limits the wide use of custom procedures to just 32K per Proc window. The following is a list of differences between custom methods and custom procedures:

- Custom procedures are accessed slightly faster than custom methods.
- Custom procedures are protected from usage outside its immediate containership path and custom methods are not. Any object can call a custom method with dot notation including forms someone else creates.
- Custom procedures are limited by scope.
- Custom procedures use the caller's built-in UIObject values (such as `self`).

The extra speed of procedures is not execution speed, but access speed. This implies that the advantage of procedures decreases as the size of the procedure increases. The biggest advantage of custom procedures, and the only real motivation for their use is their faster access speed. However, speed is not that much of an issue in the decision because the difference in access time between custom methods and custom procedures is negligible. In addition, the scope is easily controlled by containership. If anything, use a custom procedure for `Action` method calls to keep code out of `Action`, and because it is called so often, the performance may show.

Libraries

NEW Term

A *library* is a Paradox object that stores custom ObjectPAL code. A library is useful for storing and maintaining frequently used routines and for sharing custom methods and variables among forms, scripts, and other libraries.

In a library, you can store custom methods, custom procedures, variables, constants, and user-defined types. Think of a library as a place to store often-used routines. It's the key to reusing your code and therefore, is a time-saver. The more you use libraries, the more time and energy you will save. You code a library similar to the way in which you code a form. Select File | New | Library and add custom methods. You don't run a library. Instead, from your forms, you access the custom methods that you create in a library.

Characteristics of a Library

You never run a library. With ObjectPAL, you open and use the custom methods in a library, but you never run a library. A library doesn't contain objects. It can contain up to 64K of compiled code stored in custom methods and custom procedures.

NEW Term

The object variable *self* has different meanings, depending on when it's used. When it's used in a library, `self` refers to the calling object. When it's used in a form, `self` refers to the object to which the code is attached.

`self` refers to the calling object, not the library. This makes sense, although it's different than when another object's custom methods use `self`.

The scope of a library is determined by where you declare its variable and by how you open it (with or without the constant `PrivateToForm`). Although you can open a library from any point in the containership path, the placement of the Library variable determines which objects can see it. The form's Var window is a good place to declare a library's variable.

Every library has a built-in open, `close`, and `error` method. The open and `close` methods work just like a form's open and `close` methods. open is a good place to initialize variables. `error` is called when code in the library generates an error. The `error` method is a good place to trap for errors that the library itself might generate. By default, the `error` method calls the built-in `error` method of the form that called that particular custom method.

A library is a complete unit, just like a form. With a library, however, external objects have access only to the library's custom methods. Although a library can't contain objects, it has Var, Const, and Type windows for declaring, setting, and defining variables. A library also has Procs and Uses windows for writing procedures and accessing other libraries and DLLs. You access all these items by writing custom methods that utilize them.

The custom methods you write in a library can be self-contained—that is, each method contains all the commands within its own code. By using custom methods, you can access variables, constants, types, and procedures inside a library. You can even get to a library's Uses window to call functions from other libraries or DLLs. Table 23.1 lists the Library methods and procedures.

Table 23.1. Library methods and procedures.

```
close

create

deliver*

enumSource

enumSourceToFile

execmethod

isCompileWithDebug*

load*

methodDelete*

methodGet*

methodSet*

open

save*

setCompileWithDebug*
```

*Inherited from the `Form` type.

Libraries enable you to do the following:

- Reuse your code
- Centralize your code
- Set and retrieve variables in the Var window
- Call custom procedures in the Procs window

When should you use a library? Whenever you repeat code, create a custom method. Whenever you want to use a custom method on more than one form, put it in a library.

Opening a Library with *open()*

Use open() to give access to a library. You must declare a library first. As soon as you declare a variable, you use the open() command to open it. The syntax is as follows:

```
libvar.open( libName String [ GlobalToDesktop ¦ PrivateToForm] ) Logical
```

Following are two examples:

```
1:   lib.open("LIBRARY")
2:   lib.open("LIBRARY", PrivateToForm)
```

Closing a Library with *close()*

Closing a library frees up memory. Although it's not always necessary, you can close a library with the close() method. For example, the following closes the lib library variable:

```
1:   lib.close()
```

Steps in Using a Library

This next section takes you on a short, guided tour of creating and using a library. The following section presents a step by step example of using a library.

1. Create a custom method in a library. By means of custom methods, you can access all the various components of a library.

2. Declare the Library variable. You need to declare a Library variable on every form with which you want to use a particular library. A good place to declare a Library variable is on the Var method of the form, as in the following:

    ```
    1:   ;Form :: Var
    2:   var
    3:      lib Library
    4:   endVar
    ```

3. Open the library. After you declare the Library variable, you can use it to open the library. The syntax for opening a library is as follows:

    ```
    library.open(Filename)
    ```

> **NOTE**
>
> Note that if you leave the second parameter blank, Paradox assumes that it is
> `GlobalToDesktop`.

A good place to open a form's library is in the form's `init` method, as in the following:

```
1:    ;Form :: init
2:    method init(var eventInfo Event)
3:        lib.open("LIBRARY")
4:    endMethod
```

Note that this statement doesn't specify an extension. Paradox automatically looks for LIBRARY.LSL first and then for LIBRARY.LDL.

> **NOTE**
>
> Use the `open()` command on all the forms in an application. Libraries don't have an
> `attach()` command. It is implied by `open()`.

4a. Declare the custom method or methods in the Uses window or use the extended Uses syntax discussed later in this chapter. If you don't use the extended Uses syntax, then every method you want to use from a library must be declared in the Uses window of the object you want to use it in. The syntax to prototype each custom method follows:

```
1. Uses ObjectPAL
2.    methodName( [[var ¦ const] argList]) [returnType]
3. endUses
```

A good place for this is in the form's Uses window:

```
1: Uses ObjectPAL
2:    cmMsg()
3: endUses
```

4b. To use Paradox 7's new extended Uses, all you need to do is the following:

```
1. Uses ObjectPAL
2.    "LIBRARY1.LSL" "LIBRARY2.LSL"
3. endUses
```

All the custom method prototypes, types, and constants from both LIBRARY1 and LIBRARY2 are bound at compile time. You can find more information on extended Uses later in this chapter.

5. Use the `custom` method. After the `custom` method is set up for use, you must use proper dot notation to call it. The syntax for using a custom method from a library is as follows:

libraryVariable.**customMethod**([*argList*]) [**ReturnValue**]

For example:

```
1:  lib.cmMsg()
```

The syntax of `object.method()` is consistent throughout ObjectPAL. If an object with the name `box` has code on its built-in `mouseClick` method, you can access that code with `box.mouseClick()` from any other object. When this code executes, the UIObject method `mouseClick()` calls the built-in `mouseClick` method for a UIObject.

How do you know when you can call the code in a built-in method of an object? Easy, if the runtime library has a method equivalent, then you can use it, for example, `mouseClick()` and `pushButton()`.

The form LIBRARY.FSL demonstrates how to open and use a library with dot notation. It uses two libraries—LIBRARY.FSL and LIBRARY2.FSL.

Use enum procedures to document your code. You can use `enumSource()` and `enumSourceToFile()` to send all the code from a library to a table or a text file. The syntax for these two procedures is as follows:

```
LibVar.enumSource("TABLE.DB")
```

and

```
LibVar.enumSourceToFile("FILE.TXT")
```

After you use an enum procedure, it's easy to create a form or a text file that documents your library. This technique works with forms, libraries, and scripts.

Example of Using a Library

This next step by step example demonstrates how to create a new library, put a simple custom method in it that displays a message, and then use it.

You can find the LIB-TUT1.FSL form on the disc in the \ANSWERS directory.

Step By Step

1. Create a new library by selecting File | New | Library. A new Library object appears. Figure 23.15 shows this form in development.

FIGURE 23.15.

LIB-TUT1.LSL in development. Note that a library has only three built-in methods.

2. Display the Methods tab of the Object Explorer (select Tools | Object Explorer and select the Methods tab) Double click the <New Method> option. Type **errorMsg** in the New Method dialog box and select OK (see Figure 23.15).

3. Edit the newly created errorMsg() custom method to look like the following:

```
1:     ;LIB-TUT :: errorMsg
2:     method errorMsg()
3:        msgStop("Warning",
                    "Execution stopped, press OK to continue")
4:     endmethod
```

4. Check the syntax, exit the edit window, and save the library as LIB-TUT.LSL. You can close the library if you want, but you don't have to.

5. Create a new form. Edit the form's Var window to look like the following:

```
1:     ;Form :: Var
2:     var
3:        lib  Library
4:     endVar
```

6. Open the library in the init method of the form with the following:

```
1:     ;Form :: ini
2:     method init(var eventInfo Event)
3:        lib.open("LIB-TUT")
4:     endMethod
```

7. Prototype the custom method in the Uses window of the form as follows:

```
1:     ;Form :: Uses
2:     Uses ObjectPAL
3:        errorMsg()
4:     endUses
```

> **NOTE**
>
> Line 7 of this step by step example is a good place to briefly show you extended Uses syntax. Instead of placing the prototype of the custom method in line 3, you could simply put the library name, as in the following example:
>
> ```
> LIB-TUT.LSL
> ```
>
> You can read more on extended uses later in this chapter.

8. Place a button on the form, and alter its pushButton method as follows:

```
1:    ;Button :: pushButton
2:    method pushButton(var eventInfo Event)
3:        lib.errorMsg()
4:    endMethod
```

9. Save your work and run the form (see Figure 23.16).

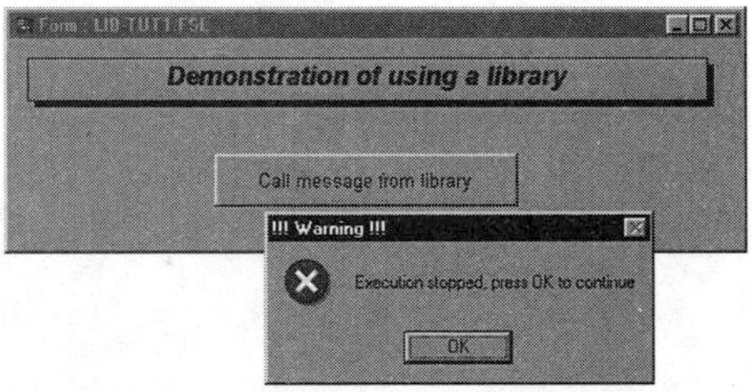

FIGURE 23.16.

*LIB-TUT1.FSL. This form
demonstrates how to use a
library—namely,
LIB-TUT.LSL.*

Analysis

In step 3, lines 2–4 make up the actual custom method. In step 5, line 3 declares the lib variable. The lib variable is used in step 6, line 2 to open the library. In step 7, lines 2 and 3 prototype the custom method. In step 8, line 2 calls the custom method.

Passing Variables Through a Library

Passing variables from form to form and from form to library comes close to making up for the lack of a true global variable in ObjectPAL. Occasionally, you need a system-wide control mechanism, or you need to store a piece of data from a form in a library for later use. A variable in a library enables you to emulate a true global variable. The next example shows you how to put variables into and get variables from a library.

Passing a Variable Between Forms

Suppose that you want to pass a value from one form to another through a library. Because you are using a library, both forms don't have to be open at the same time.

You can find the LIB1.FSL and the LIB2.FSL forms on the disc in the \ANSWERS directory.

Step By Step

1. Change the working directory to a directory other than TUTORIAL. Create two forms and save the forms as LIB1.FSL and LIB2.FSL, respectively. Put a button labeled Put

on the LIB1.FSL and a button labeled Get on the LIB2.FSL. Create a library and save it as LIB.LSL (see Figure 23.17).

FIGURE 23.17.

Passing a variable from one form to another form by means of a library.

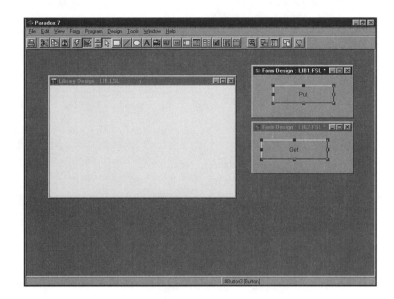

2. Create a new library and line 3 to the Var window of the library.

```
1:    ;Library :: Var
2:    Var
3:        s1,s2 String
4:    endVar
```

3. Create a new custom method in the library called cmPutString1() and add line 3 to it.

```
1:    ;Library :: cmPutString1
2:    method cmPutString1(s String)
3:        s1 = s
4:    endmethod
```

4. Create a new custom method in the library called cmPutString2() and add line 3 to it.

```
1:    ;Library :: cmPutString2
2:    method cmPutString2(s String)
3:        s2 = s
4:    endmethod
```

5. Create a new custom method in the library called cmGetString1() and add line 3 to it.

```
1:    ;Library :: cmGetString1
2:    method cmGetString1() String
3:        return s1
4:    endmethod
```

6. Create a new custom method in the library called cmGetString2() and add line 3 to it. Save the library as LIB.LSL.

```
1:    ;Library :: cmGetString2
2:    method cmGetString2() String
3:        return s2
4:    endmethod
```

7. Create a new form and add lines 3 and 4 to the Uses window of the first form.

```
1:    ;Form :: Uses
2:    Uses ObjectPal
3:        cmPutString1(s String)
4:        cmPutString2(s String)
5:    endUses
```

8. Add line 3 to the Var window of the first form.

```
1:    ;Form :: Var
2:    Var
3:        lib Library
4:    endVar
```

9. Add lines 3–5 to the pushButton method of the Put button on the first form. Save the form as LIB1.FSL.

```
1:    ;Button :: pushButton
2:    method pushButton(var eventInfo Event)
3:        lib.open("LIB")
4:        lib.cmPutString1("Keith")
5:        lib.cmPutString2("Kinnamont")
6:    endmethod
```

10. Add lines 3 and 4 to the Uses window of the second form.

```
1:    ;Form :: Uses
2:    Uses ObjectPAL
3:        cmGetString1() String
4:        cmGetString2() String
5:    endUses
```

11. Add line 3 to the Var window of the second form.

```
1:    ;Form :: Var
2:    Var
3:        lib Library
4:    endVar
```

12. Add lines 3 and 4 to the pushButton method of the Get button on the second form. Save the form as LIB2.FSL.

```
1:    ;Button :: pushButton
2:    method pushButton(var eventInfo Event)
3:        lib.open("lib.lsl")
4:        msgInfo("Childhood friend", lib.cmGetString1() + " " +
            lib.cmGetString2())
5:    endmethod
```

13. Check the syntax and save all the various elements (the forms and the library). Close the library and run both forms. Click the Put button on the first form, and then click the Get button on the second form (see Figure 23.18).

WARNING

If you close LIB1.FSL before you open LIB2.FSL, the library is closed and reopened, losing any variables you had set.

Analysis

In step 2, line 3 declares two `String` variables in the library Var window. The variables are global to the library.

Line 2 in steps 3, 4, 5, and 6 prototypes the four custom methods. Line 3 in steps 3, 4, 5, and 6 either sets or returns a variable.

In step 7, lines 3 and 4 prototype the library's custom methods in the Uses window of the first form.

In step 8, line 3 declares `lib` as a Library variable that is used to open the library in step 9, line 3.

In step 9, lines 4 and 5 call two of the four custom methods in the library.

In step 10, lines 3 and 4 prototype the other two custom methods in the library.

In step 11, line 3 declares `lib` as a `Library` variable that is used in step 12.

FIGURE 23.18.

LIB.1.FSL and LIB.2.FSL demonstrate passing a value through a library.

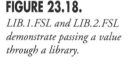

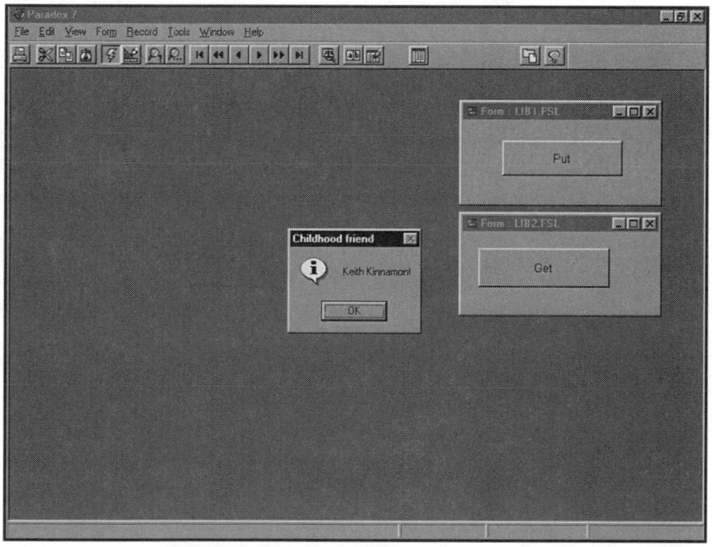

In step 12, line 3 opens the library for the second form. Line 4 uses the two `cmGetString1()` and `cmGetString2()` custom methods in a message information dialog box.

Calling a Library Custom Method from Another Library

A library can access the custom methods in other libraries, as the next example demonstrates. This example is a good example of reusing code. Although it often takes more time to reuse code than to copy and paste, the benefits are significant. By reusing as much code as possible, you will make your applications more powerful. They will contain fewer bugs and should be smaller, too.

Suppose that you need to call a custom method in a library that calls another custom method in another library. You can do this with dot notation. In fact, you can use the technique you learn in this step by step example in either forms or libraries to call custom methods from either forms or libraries.

You can find the LIB-TUT2.FSL, LIB-TUT2.LSL, and LIB-TUT3.LSL forms in the \ANSWERS directory.

Step By Step

1. Create a new form and place on it a button labeled as follows: Call Lib-Tut2, which calls Lib-Tut3.

2. After you complete steps 1 through 5, create a new library for steps 6 through 9; save it as LIB-TUT2.LSL.

3. Create another library for step 10; save it as LIB-TUT3.LSL.

4. Add line 3 to the Var window of the Call Lib-Tut2 button.

```
1:    ;Button :: Var
2:    Var
3:        lib  Library
4:    endVar
```

5. Add line 3 to the open method of the Call Lib-Tut2 button.

```
1:    ;Button :: open
2:    method open(var eventInfo Event)
3:        lib.open("LIB-TUT2.LSL")
4:    endMethod
```

6. Add line 3 to the Uses window of the Call Lib-Tut2 button.

```
1:    ;Button :: Uses
2:    Uses ObjectPAL
3:        cmFromLib2()
4:    endUses
```

7. Add line 3 to the pushButton method of the Call Lib-Tut2 button.

```
1:    ;Button :: pushButton
2:    method pushButton(var eventInfo Event)
```

```
3:          lib.cmFromLib2()
4:      endmethod
```

8. Add line 3 to the Var window of the LIB-TUT2 library.

```
1:      ;Library :: Var
2:      Var
3:          libLIBTUT3  Library
4:      endVar
```

9. Add line 3 to the open method of the LIB-TUT2 library.

```
1:      ;Library :: open
2:      method open(var eventInfo Event)
3:          libLIBTUT3.open("LIB-TUT3")
4:      endMethod
```

10. Add line 3 to the Uses window of the LIB-TUT2 library.

```
1:      ;Library :: Uses
2:      Uses ObjectPAL
3:          cmMsg()
4:      endUses
```

11. Create a custom method called cmFromLib2() in the LIB-TUT2 library.

```
1:      ;Library :: cmFromLib2
2:      method cmFromLib2()
3:          LibLIBTUT3.msg()
4:      endmethod
```

12. Create a custom method called cmMsg() in the LIB-TUT3 library and add line 3 to it.

```
1:      ;Library :: cmMsg
2:      method cmMsg()
3:          msgInfo("From LIB-TUT3", "Reuse as much code as possible")
4:      endMethod
```

13. Check the syntax and save your work. Run the form and click the Call Lib-Tut2, which calls Lib-Tut3 button. When the message appears, click OK (see Figure 23.19).

FIGURE 23.19.

LIB-TUT2.FSL demonstrates calling a custom method from another library.

Analysis

All the code that opens the first library is on the same object—the button. Because the Library variable is declared on the button in step 2, line 3, no other objects on the form can use the library. This keeps all the code for this example together. In actual practice, however, you will want to move the Library variable up the containership path to a more accessible location.

In step 3, line 3 indicates that the form is to use methods found in the LIB-TUT2.LSL library. The library is opened in the open method of the button. It doesn't matter where the library is opened. The only thing that matters is that the library is opened.

In step 4, line 3 prototypes the custom method cmFromLib2 called in the pushButton method in step 5, line 3.

Steps 6, 7, and 8 from the first library are similar to the code from the button. I purposefully have kept this example simple. The first library, however, usually does much more than what it does here. Take the message in step 10, line 3 to heart. It's the reason for this example.

Extended Uses Syntax

New to version 7 is a feature called *extended uses* that enables ObjectPAL to use compile time binding for the first time. Compile time binding enables the compiler to resolve code at the time the code is compiled. Extended uses enables you to utilize libraries easier as well as do some things you couldn't do before. Following are the three things that it enables you to do:

- You can utilize the custom types you have defined in a library or form in another library or form without having to write the code again.
- You can utilize the constants you have defined in a library or form in another library or form without having to write the code again.
- You can utilize the custom methods from a library or form from another library or form without having to prototype the custom methods.

In C, compile time binding is accomplished with the #include command. In Pascal, it is accomplished with the Uses statement (similar in nature to ObjectPAL's uses statement). Following is the syntax for doing compile time binding in ObjectPAL:

```
Uses ObjectPAL
    ["fileName"]*
endUses
```

For example, assume that you have a library you use just for constants, a library just for custom types, and a library for custom methods. Following is the code you need in the Uses window of the form to give your code the capability to utilize all the constants, types, and custom methods from the libraries:

```
1:    ;Form :: Uses
2:    Uses ObjectPAL
3:        "constants.lsl"
4:        "types.lsl"
5:        "methods.lsl"
6:    endUses
```

Now in your code, you can utilize the constants from the CONSTANTS.LSL library, and the types from the TYPES.LSL LIBRARY. In addition, although the two files, CONSTANTS.LSL and TYPES.LSL, need to be around while you deliver the form that utilizes them, the libraries do not need to be around after you deliver the form. The types and constants have been bound at delivery time.

The custom methods from the METHODS.LSL library are not quite that easy to use, but they almost are. You still have to open the library just as you learned earlier in this chapter; however, you do not have to prototype each method—the compiler does that for you at compile time. Following is an example of using an imaginary `cmMyMethod()` custom method in METHODS.LSL.

```
 1. Uses ObjectPAL
 2.    ;Step 1 - specify library.
 3.    "methods.lsl"
 4. endUses
 5. method pushButton(var eventInfo Event)
 6.    var
 7.       libMethods Library
 8.    endVar
 9.
10.    ;Step 2 - Open library.
11.    libMethods.open("methods")   ;Can be methods.lsl or methods.ldl.
12.    ;Step 3 - Call method using dot notation.
13.    libMethods.cmMyMethod()
14. endMethod
```

When you deliver your application, you still need to distribute a copy of the library (either .LSL or .FDL).

Creating a Library from Scratch

The form LIB-CR.FSL demonstrates creating a library from scratch and then using it (see Figure 23.20). Following is the pertinent code from the `pushButton` method:

```
 1:  ;Button :: pushButton
 2:  method pushButton(var eventInfo Event)
 3:     var
 4:        lib  Library
 5:     endVar
 6:
 7:     ;Create library.
 8:     lib.create()
 9:     lib.methodSet("cmMessage", "method cmMessage() msgInfo(\"From new
        library\", \"Hello World!\") endMethod")
10:     lib.save("test")
11:     lib.close()
12:
13:     ;Use library.
14:     lib.open("test")
15:     lib.cmMessage()
16:  endmethod
```

Following is the pertinent code from the button's Uses method:

```
1:   ;Button :: Uses
2:   Uses ObjectPAL
3:      cmMessage()
4:   endUses
```

FIGURE 23.20.

LIB-CR.FSL demonstrates creating and using a library.

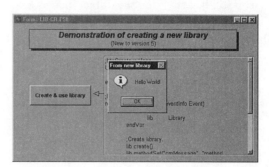

Scripts

A *script* is a Paradox object that consists of ObjectPAL code that can be run independently of a form or called from ObjectPAL. Unlike a form or a report, a script has no objects. Unlike a library, a script can be run without ObjectPAL.

The code for a script isn't attached to a form. Libraries exist. So why would you need or want scripts? Scripts are used to store code. It also is sometimes useful to give users a way to run code by selecting File | Open | Script without displaying a UIObject.

Scripts are excellent when you aren't using a UIObject, such as a form. Because libraries require a UIObject (you can't open and run a library from Interactive mode), scripts are a way to give users the capability to run code interactively. You can run a script with the ObjectPAL procedure play(). The syntax for play() is as follows:

```
play(ScriptName) AnyType
```

Use play() to play a script from ObjectPAL. In this example, play() searches first for ENUM.SSL and then for ENUM.SDL. After the correct file is found, the statements in the script are executed, as in the following example:

```
1:   Play("ENUM")
```

The next example shows you how to write and run a script. You run the script by either selecting File | Open | Script or playing it from a button.

> **NOTE**
>
> Here are some notes to keep in mind when developing a script:
>
> ■ No menus are possible with scripts.
>
> ■ Do not use the form type wait(), as in f.wait().

Writing a Script

Suppose that you want to create four tables of ObjectPAL information for use as reference material. This next step by step example demonstrates how to create and use a script by generating reference tables for your own use.

> You can find the ENUM.SSL form on the disc in the \ANSWERS directory.

Step By Step

1. Set your working directory to the TUTORIAL directory. Select File | New | Script. The Edit window for the run event method appears (see Figure 23.21).

FIGURE 23.21.

The run method of the script.

2. Add lines 3–13 to the run method of the script.

```
 1:    ;Script :: run
 2:    method run(var eventInfo Event)
 3:        message("Sending RTL constants to RTLCONST.DB ...")
 4:        enumRTLConstants("RTLCONST.DB")
 5:
 6:        message("Sending RTL class names to RTLCLASS.DB ...")
 7:        enumRTLClassNames("RTLCLASS.DB")
 8:
 9:        message("Sending RTL methods to RTLMETH.DB ...")
10:        enumRTLMethods("RTLMETH.DB")
```

```
11:
12:        message("Sending UIObject classes to CLASSES.DB ...")
13:        enumUIClasses("CLASSES.DB")
14:     endmethod
```

3. Check the syntax, save the script as ENUM.SSL, and run it. You also could run the script from a form. To do this, place a button on a form and use the play() procedure to run the script, as in the following example:

```
1:   ;Button :: pushButton
2:   method pushButton(var eventInfo Event)
3:     play("ENUM")
4:   endmethod
```

Analysis

In step 2, lines 3, 6, 9, and 12 send messages to the status line. Lines 4, 7, 10, and 13 enumerate information to their respective tables.

Sending Table Structures to Text Files

Paradox lacks an easy way to grab the structure of all the tables in a directory. A feature that does this would be very useful. After all, a directory full of tables is considered a database in Paradox. This example demonstrates how to grab the structure for all the tables in a directory. Specifically, it creates a text file of the structure with the same name as each table.

Sending Structures to Text Files

Suppose that you want to create a text file of the structure of every Paradox table in a directory. This next script uses the TextStream type along with the FileSystem, and TCursor types to write the structure of every Paradox table to a text file.

You can find the STRUCT.SSL form on the disc in the \ANSWERS directory.

Step By Step

1. Select File | New | Script and type lines 3–50 into the run method of the script.

```
1:   ;Script :: Run
2:   method run(var eventInfo Event)
3:     var
4:       sDir, s1, s2, s3, s4, S      String
5:       fs               FileSystem
6:       arTable          Array[]   String
7:       siCounter        SmallInt
8:       tc1, tc2         TCursor
9:       ts               TextStream
```

```
10:        endVar
11:
12:        ;Get path of tables
13:        sDir = getAliasPath("work")
14:        sDir.view("Enter path of tables")
15:
16:        ;Make sure "\" is at end of sDir variable (the path)
17:        if sDir.subStr(size(sDir)) <> "\\" then
18:          sDir = sDir + "\\"
19:        endIf
20:
21:        ;Get all .db tables from directory
22:        fs.enumFileList(sDir + "*.db", arTable)
23:        arTable.view("Cancel button does nothing")
24:
25:        ;Process each table
26:        setMouseShape(MouseWait)
27:        for siCounter from 1 to arTable.size()
28:         ;Display message in status bar
29:         message("Processing: " + arTable[siCounter])
30:
31:         ;Create struct.db in private directory
32:         tc1.open(sDir + arTable[siCounter])
33:         tc1.enumFieldStruct(":PRIV:STRUCT.DB")
34:
35:         ;Open text file
36:         splitFullFileName(sDir + arTable[siCounter], s1, s2, s3, s4)
37:         ts.open(s1 + s2 + s3 + ".TXT","NW")
38:
39:         ;Write table to text file")
40:         TC2.open(":PRIV:STRUCT.DB")
41:         scan tc2:
42:             ts.writeLine(TC2."Field Name", chr(9), TC2."Type", chr(9),
43:             tc2."size", chr(9), TC2."Key")
44:         endScan
45:
46:         tc1.close()
47:         tc2.close()
48:         ts.close()
49:        endFor
50:        setMouseShape(MouseArrow)
51:        message("All done.")
52:    endMethod
```

2. Check the syntax and save your work. Run the script. As each structure is written, a message appears in the status bar.

Analysis

In step 1, lines 3–10 make up the var block, which declares all the variables used in the script. Lines 13 and 14 set the directory. Line 13 uses getAliasPath() to get the path of the current working directory and assigns it to the sDir variable.

The user sees the initial path in line 14, where he or she can change it. Lines 17–19 make sure that \ appears at the end of the path. In line 22, enumFileList() uses the path to put all the

Paradox tables into the resizable arTable array. Line 23, which isn't required for this routine, displays the list of tables.

Lines 25–48 loop through the list of tables stored in arTable and write out the ASCII files. Lines 25 and 49 set the mouse pointer to the waiting mouse and back.

This routine is great, but it can be improved. For example, you could add a print option to each table. Also, view() is not the best option to use because it might mislead the user into thinking that he or she can cancel the process. To make the code more interesting, add a feature that creates tables with the same name as the table in a subdirectory of the destination directory.

Although a script has limited use, it enables a user to select File | Open | Script to perform a set of chores. Likewise, a script is a good place to store code. Occasionally, it is useful to start off an application with a script.

ObjectPAL offers many ways to reuse and compartmentalize your code by means of custom methods in forms, custom methods in libraries, and scripts. It might not always seem that you have time to use these code-saving features. A few extra minutes now, however, will save you hours later.

Returning a Value from a Script to a Form

How do you have a script return a value back to a form? One way to return a value from a script back to a form is to use formReturn(), as in the following:

```
1:   method run(var eventInfo Event)
2:     var
3:        n Number
4:     endVar
5:
6:     n = 5
7:     formReturn(n)
8:   endMethod
```

Following is an example in the pushButton method of a button playing a script:

```
1:   method pushbutton(var eventInfo Event)
2:     var
3:        any   AnyType
4:     endvar
5:
6:     any = play("scriptname")
7:   endmethod
```

Running a Script from a Form

When I run a script from within a form, the form won't close until the script is done running. Why? The script uses a method called run to handle execution of ObjectPAL code when it opens. The script is considered by the form to be one of its own methods running. Because no form can close while a method is being executed, it will remain open until the script finishes execution.

Using *executeString()*

The `executeString()` procedure is similar to a script in that it enables you to execute a bit of code. The syntax is as follows:

executeString(const *scriptText* String) AnyType

This procedure provides a way to build and execute dynamic methods. There are a few quirks to be aware of concerning `executeString()`. These quirks are related to the fact that `executeString()` generates and executes a temporary script at runtime. Here are some notes on using `executeString()`.

- You can declare types, constants, and variables within the string, but you cannot use the `Uses` clause.
- To return a value from `executeString`, you must use `formReturn()`.
- If the string contains syntax errors, the Script window is left on the desktop.

The following is a simple example of using `executeString()` that you can type into the `pushButton` method of a button.

```
1. ;Button :: pushButton
2. method pushButton(var eventInfo Event)
3.    var
4.       sCode        String
5.    endVar
6.
7.    sCode = "message(\"This is a test.\")"
8.    executeString(sCode)
9. endMethod
```

Summary

In this chapter, you learned that custom procedures, custom methods, libraries, and scripts are devices you can use to compartmentalize and organize your code. When your code is well organized, you can reuse more of it.

In ObjectPAL, custom methods and procedures are equivalent to subroutines. ObjectPAL comes with a set of methods and procedures called the runtime library. A custom method consists of methods and procedures from the runtime library, as well as registered functions from dynamic link libraries (DLLs). Think of the set of custom methods and custom procedures that you develop as your own private runtime library.

A custom procedure is similar to a custom method, except that the scope for a custom procedure is much more limited. Scope determines the availability of a custom procedure to other objects. A custom method is always global to the object.

A library is a Paradox object that stores custom ObjectPAL code. A library is useful for storing and maintaining frequently used routines and for sharing custom methods and variables among forms, scripts, and other libraries. Although you learned how to prototype custom methods by specifying each custom method, you also learned about the easier extended uses syntax.

A script is a Paradox object that consists of ObjectPAL code that can be run independently of a form or called from ObjectPAL. Unlike a form or a report, a script doesn't have any objects. Unlike a library, a script can be run without ObjectPAL.

Exploring *action* and *menuAction* Methods

24

IN THIS CHAPTER

Whenever you interact with Paradox, you generate either an Action or MenuAction constant. For example, when you select a menu item, a constant is sent to the built-in menuAction method. If the constant maps to an Action constant, an equivalent Action constant then is sent to the built-in action method. For example, when you select File | Print, the constant MenuFilePrint is sent to the form's menuAction method. Since MenuFilePrint maps to the action constant DataPrint, DataPrint is sent to action. In the events action and menuAction, you can trap for nearly every user interaction. In addition, using the action() and menuAction() methods you can invoke or imitate nearly any user interaction by sending Action and MenuAction constants to the built-in action and menuAction methods.

Identifying Action and Error Constants

Sometimes it is necessary to identify a constant. Either you need to trap for it or you want to execute it. Either way, finding the action constant that maps to a specific task can be daunting. This section helps you understand action constants better by breaking them up into the action classes.

Table 24.1 lists the action classes. As you can see by Table 24.1, most action events do not bubble. In fact, only ActionDataCommands bubble. You can use eventInfo.actionClass() to return the class of an action event.

Table 24.1. Categories of ActionEvents.

ActionEvent	*Bubble?*	*Description of Action*
ActionDataCommands	Yes	Deal with the whole form
ActionEditCommands	No	Deal with editing data
ActionFieldCommands	No	Move from field to field
ActionMoveCommands	No	Move the cursor within a field
ActionSelectCommands	No	Select data within a field

Using constantValueToName() enables you to extract the name of a constant from a number. The syntax for constantValueToName() is as follows:

```
constantValueToName ( const groupName String, const value AnyType, var constName
String ) Logical
```

This method is very helpful in developing an application when you want to know which actions are being triggered. The one weakness of this method is that you have to specify the group type. For example, you have to specify ActionDataCommand, ActionMoveCommand, Error, and so on.

The following code snippet from ANSWERS\ID_ACTIONS.FSL demonstrates how to extract the name of an action or error constant from eventInfo (see Figure 24.1). For demonstration purposes, this code is called from the action method of the form; this code displays every action generated and every error generated. It uses actionClass() to extract the class of action constant. It also demonstrates using a list object to scroll values. It uses a private custom procedure which helps make it structured.

FIGURE 24.1.

ID_ACTIONS.FSL demonstrates identifying action and error constants.

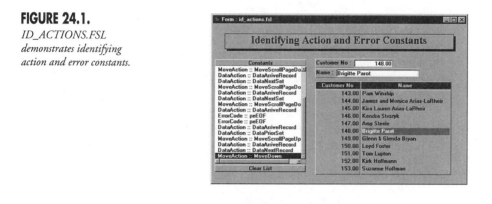

Read through the code and see whether you can follow the logic; start from the method prototype line. After you read through this code, then run the ID_ACIONS.FSL form in the Answers directory to see it running and to experiment with various interactive tasks that cause actions and errors.

```
1:    ;ID_Actions :: Form :: cmIdentifyConstant
2:    proc cpDisplayConstant(sConstantType String, sConstant String)
3:        ;Display constant class & constant in list field.
4:        ;This procedure is used by cmIdentifyConstant.
5:        beep()
6:        lstConstant'list.selection = lstConstant'list.count + 1
7:        lstConstant'list.value = sConstantType + " :: " + sConstant
8:    endProc
9:
10:   method cmIdentifyConstant(var eventInfo ActionEvent)
11:       ;Identify constant.
12:       var
13:           sConstant       String
14:           siConstantType  SmallInt
15:           sConstantType   String
16:           siID            SmallInt
17:       endVar
18:
19:       ;Check for an error.
20:       if eventInfo.errorCode() <> peOk then
21:           constantValueToName("Errors", eventInfo.errorCode(), sConstant)
22:           cpDisplayConstant("ErrorCode", sConstant)
23:           return
24:       endif
```

```
25:
26:          ;Identify action constant.
27:          siConstantType = eventInfo.actionClass()
28:          siID = eventInfo.id()
29:          switch
30:             case siConstantType = DataAction
31:                :  sConstantType = "DataAction"
32:                   constantValueToName("ActionDataCommands", siID, sConstant)
33:             case siConstantType = EditAction
34:                :  sConstantType = "EditAction"
35:                   constantValueToName("ActionEditCommands", siID, sConstant)
36:             case siConstantType = FieldAction
37:                :  sConstantType = "FieldAction"
38:                   constantValueToName("ActionFieldCommands", siID, sConstant)
39:             case siConstantType = MoveAction
40:                :  sConstantType = "MoveAction"
41:                   constantValueToName("ActionMoveCommands", siID, sConstant)
42:             case siConstantType = SelectAction
43:                :  sConstantType = "SelectAction"
44:                   constantValueToName("ActionSelectCommands", siID, sConstant)
45:             otherwise
46:                :  ;This should never get called.
47:                   sConstantType = "unknown"
48:                   sConstant = "unknown"
49:          endSwitch
50:
51:          cpDisplayConstant(sConstantType, sConstant)
52:       endMethod
```

The following code calls the custom method. Notice that `doDefault` is called before `eventInfo` is passed to the custom method.

```
1:     ;ID_actions.fsl :: Form :: action
2:     method action(var eventInfo ActionEvent)
3:
4:        if eventInfo.isPreFilter() then
5:           ;// This code executes for each object on the form
6:           ;//
7:           DoDefault
8:           cmIdentifyConstant(eventInfo)
9:        else
10:           ;// This code executes only for the form
11:           ;//
12:
13:        endIf
14:
15:     endMethod
```

You might want to put a variation of the preceding custom method into your standard library—perhaps alter it to return the action constant. After you do this, you can use it from time to time when you code to determine an action constant name that is giving you problems.

On the disc is the DEV-SRC\LIBRARIES\SECRETS.LSL library with a custom method that contains a modified version of the preceding custom method.

> **TIP**
>
> To send a list of all the constants to a table, create and run the following one-line script:
>
> ```
> enumRTLConstants("CONST.DB")
> ```
>
> This script creates a table that has all constants, including all the error constants. Use this table to create reports in any order you like.

Manipulating a Memo Field

To manipulate the font attributes and text of a memo field use the action() method. The basic technique is to pass the action() method an action constant:

object.action(**ActionConstant**)

For example, the following is from the SelectSelectAll button from the CONSTANT.FSL form included on the disc:

```
1:  ;Form :: Var
2:  method pushButton(var eventInfo Event)
3:     fldMemo.action(SelectSelectAll)
4:  endMethod
```

On the disc is the form CONSTANT.FSL, which demonstrates using the ActionSelectCommands and ActionMoveCommands constants (see Figure 24.2).

FIGURE 24.2.

CONSTANT.FSL demonstrates manipulating a memo field.

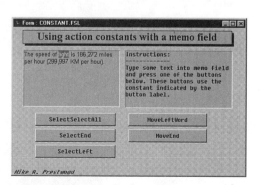

Time and Date Stamping a Memo Field

On the disc is the form ANSWERS\STAMP-IT.FSL, which demonstrates using the ActionEditCommands and ActionMoveCommands constants (see Figure 24.3).

FIGURE 24.3.

STAMP-IT.FSL demonstrates time and date stamping a memo field.

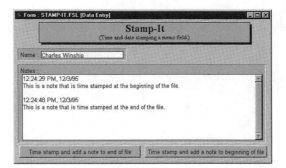

To time stamp and add a note to the end of a memo field, use lines 3–7.

```
1:   ;Button :: pushButton
2:   method pushButton(var eventInfo Event)
3:     edit()
4:     Notes.moveTo()
5:     Notes.value = Notes.value + chr(13) + String(DateTime()) + chr(13)
6:     Notes.action(EditEnterMemoView)
7:     Notes.action(MoveEnd)
8:   endmethod
```

To time stamp and add a note to the beginning of the memo field, use lines 3–8.

```
1:   ;Button :: pushButton
2:   method pushButton(var eventInfo Event)
3:     edit()
4:     Notes.moveTo()
5:     Notes.value = String(DateTime()) + chr(13) + chr(13) + Notes.value
6:     Notes.action(EditEnterMemoView)
7:     Notes.action(MoveBegin)
8:     Notes.action(MoveDown)
9:   endmethod
```

Identifying *menuAction* Constants

You can use the form \ANSWERS\MENUID.FSL to browse and test menu constants (see Figure 24.4).

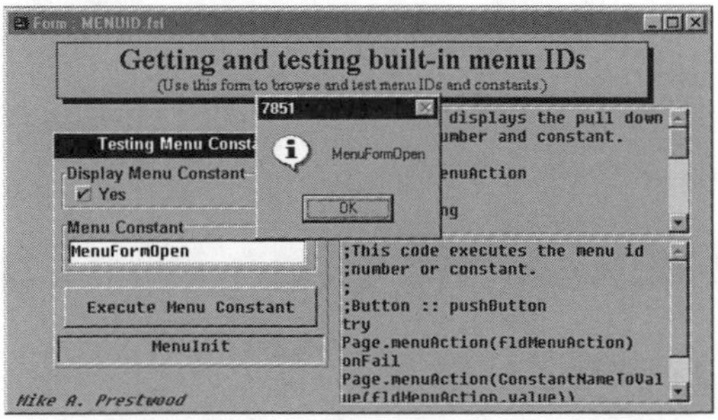

FIGURE 24.4.

MENUID.FSL.

Following are the steps to using the MENUID form:

1. Select a menu option to generate a menu constant.

2. Put the constant or number in the MenuAction field (the constant is always pre-ferred). You can just click on the constant displayed below the Execute Menu Con-stant button.

3. Press the button to make sure it works.

The interesting bit of code is in the page's menuAction method and in the pushButton method of the button. The following is the code in menuAction which traps the menu constants.

```
1:    ;MENUID :: page :: menuAction
2:    method menuAction(var eventInfo MenuEvent)
3:    var
4:        s    String
5:    endVar
6:
7:    if eventInfo.isPreFilter() then
8:        ;// This code executes for each object on the form:
9:
10:   else
11:       ;// This code executes only for the form:
12:       switch
13:          case eventInfo.id() = MenuInit
14:              :    ;Occurs when the menu option is selected.
15:                   ;Do nothing.
16:          case eventInfo.id() = MenuBuild
17:              :    ;Occurs when the menu is first built.
18:                   ;Do nothing.
19:          case eventInfo.id() = MenuControlKeyMenu
20:              :    ;Menu selected via a key press.
21:                   ;Do nothing.
22:          otherwise
23:              :    if fldDisplay.value = "Yes" then
24:                       constantValueToName("MenuCommands", eventInfo.id(), s)
25:                       msgInfo(eventInfo.id(), s)
26:                   endIf
27:       endSwitch
28:       constantValueToName("MenuCommands", eventInfo.id(), s)
29:       fldStatus.value = s
30:   endmethod
```

The following is the code in the pushButton method of the button which uses a try block to first try to execute a MenuCommand number, and then uses a constant.

```
1:    ;MENUID :: btnExecute :: pushButton
2:    method pushButton(var eventInfo Event)
3:        ;Try to execute number.
4:        try
5:            menuAction(fldMenuAction)
6:        onFail
7:            ;Convert string to number.
8:            try
9:                menuAction(ConstantNameToValue(fldMenuAction.value))
10:           onFail
```

```
11:            msgStop("Warning", "Invalid menu constant.")
12:         endTry
13:      endTry
14:   endmethod
```

Summary

In this chapter, you learned you can imitate nearly any user interaction by sending action and menuAction constants to the action and menuAction event methods using the action() and menuAction() methods. In addition, you learned how to trap for most user interactions in the action and menuAction event methods.

Using Menus, Toolbars, and the File System

25

A *pop-up menu* is the vertical list of options that usually becomes attached to a menu; however, it does not have to be attached. In other words, you can use pop-up menus without a menu. Most Borland applications use pop-up menus heavily. When you right-click an object in Paradox, the Property Inspector that appears is a pop-up menu. This section explores how to use pop-up menus with a menu variable.

You can use some of the methods and procedures from the Menu type in addition to the `PopUpMenu` methods and procedures. Table 25.1 lists the `PopUpMenu` class methods and procedures.

Table 25.1. `PopUpMenu` **class methods and procedures.**

addArray	contains*
addBar	count*
addBreak	empty*
addPopUp	isAssigned**
addSeparator	remove*
addStaticText	show
addText	switchMenu

*Inherited from the Menu type.

**Inherited from the `AnyType` type.

Using a Pop-Up Menu

Stand-alone pop-up menus do not trigger `menuAction`. That is, when a user selects an option from a stand-alone pop-up menu, no event is sent to `menuAction`. Therefore, you cannot trap for stand-alone pop-up menus with `menuAction`. How, then, do you trap for the user's selection? You use `show()` to display the pop-up menu. Fortunately, `show()` returns the user's selection in a string. Therefore, use the following syntax:

```
1:  s = pop1.show()
2:  if s = "Option1" then
3:    ;Execute option1 code here.
4:  endIf
```

Pull-Down Menus

A *menu* is a set of options. Typically, a menu is a list that appears horizontally across the menu bar of an application. Menus in ObjectPAL also can take the form of buttons on a form, pull-down menus, or pop-up menus. A *pull-down menu* is a list of items that appears when you choose a menu item from the horizontal menu list. A pull-down menu displays further options for you to choose.

Maneuvering within Windows applications has become quite elaborate. With Paradox, the user can use the built-in pull-down menus, the Toolbar, and the Property Inspector. As a programmer, you can leave the Paradox default menu in place, trap for the menu constants in the menuAction method, and execute your own code in place of the default behavior. You also can remove the Toolbar with hideToolbar(). You even can get rid of the built-in menus and use your own menus instead.

You can add pop-up menus that are similar to the Property Inspector, and the menus can pop up anywhere onscreen. Although Paradox doesn't support a custom Toolbar or balloon help—which is becoming popular—it does offer the programmer much control. Table 25.2 lists the Menu methods and procedures.

Table 25.2. Menu class methods and procedures.

addArray	getMenuChoiceAttributeById
addBreak	hasMenuChoiceAttribute
addPopUp	isAssigned*
addStaticText	remove
addText	removeMenu
contains	setMenuChoiceAttribute
count	setMenuChoiceAttributeById
empty	show
getMenuChoiceAttribute	

*Inherited from the AnyType type

Where to Put Code

When you use custom menus in ObjectPAL, you must do two things: build the menu and process the user's input. The usual place to define a menu is in the arrive method of the form or page.

If you plan to change the menus in a particular form when you move from one page to another, however, create your menus on the arrive method of each page. In fact, a good rule of thumb is always to build and show menus on the arrive method of the page. That way, if you ever need to add a menu to the form, you can add it to another page, which is the most logical breaking point.

To process user input, use the menuAction method of the page. The following steps outline a good technique for capturing and processing user input:

1. Declare a String variable that catches menuAction constants in step 2.

2. Use sAns = eventInfo.menuChoice().

3. Use a switch structure to process the user's choice.

Unique Entry Menus

It's simple to set up a menu that always has a unique entry. For example, File | Save and Record | Save selections wouldn't work together because Save is duplicated in two pull-down menus. If you need duplicate menu options, use a menu ID number.

The following steps outline how to set up a unique entry menu:

1. Define your variables. You need to define a Menu variable for the menu itself and a PopUpMenu variable for each pull-down menu you want. For example, you might use the following code on the Var window of the page:

```
1:  var
2:    m      Menu
3:    pop    PopUpMenu
4:  endVar
```

2. Build the menu. Construct the pull-down menus, attach them to entries in the menu, and show the menu. Use the addText() method to add entries to the PopUpMenu variable. For example, you might use the following code on the arrive method of the page:

```
1:  pop.addText("Cut")
2:  pop.addText("Copy")
3:  pop.addText("Paste")
```

3. Add PopUpMenu to a menu bar item. Attach the constructed PopUpMenu variable to an entry on the Menu variable. For example, you might use the following code immediately after the code shown in step 2:

```
1:  m.addPopUp("Edit", pop)
```

4. Display the menu. You display the Menu variable with the show() method:

```
1:  m.show()
```

5. Trap for user responses. After you construct the menu, you must decide what each menu option does. In the menuAction method—usually the menuAction method of the page—you trap for the selection and act on that selection. For example, you can declare a String variable, trap for menuChoice() with eventInfo.menuChoice(), and use the switch statement to act on that selection.

```
1:    var
2:       sAns String       ;Declare sAns as a String variable.
3:    endVar
4:
5:    sAns = eventInfo.menuChoice() ;Capture user selection.
6:
7:    ;Process user selection.
8:    Switch
9:       case sAns = "Cut"   : active.action(EditCutSelection)
10:       case sAns = "Copy"  : active.action(EditCopySelection)
11:       case sAns = "Paste" : active.action(EditPaste)
12:    endSwitch
```

The next example uses the CUSTOMER.DB table from the files that come with Paradox.

Duplicating the Paradox Menu

There are times you need to create your own menu system, yet retain a few of the Paradox menu options. You can duplicate the Paradox menu and send the correct constant to the built-in `menuAction` method in one step, as in the following:

```
1:    pop.addText("&Tile", MenuEnabled, MenuWindowTile)
```

This technique is particularly important now that you can add a menu to a report because menus can respond only to menu constants. You can read more about this technique, later in this chapter.

Building a Unique Entry Menu

Suppose that you want to build a functional, two-entry, pull-down menu. File | Exit closes the form, and Edit | Cut, Edit | Copy, and Edit | Paste cuts, copies, and pastes text. This next step by step example uses Menu and PopUpMenu method types to build and use a pull-down menu.

You can find the MENU-1.FSL form on the disc in the \ANSWERS directory.

Step By Step

1. Create a form based on the CUSTOMER.DB table located in the \TUTORIAL directory. You can make it as fancy as you want, but a simple form is all that you need (see Figure 25.1).

FIGURE 25.1.

Setup form for the example.

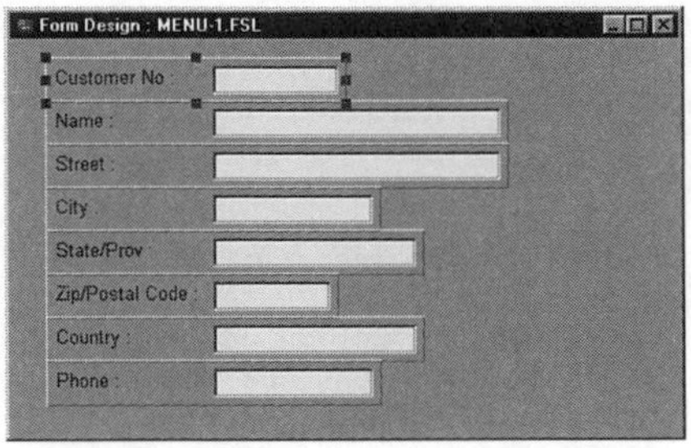

2. Define the variables in the Var window of the page.

```
1:    ;Page :: Var
2:    Var
3:        m                  Menu
4:        sAns               String
5:        popFile, popEdit   PopUpMenu
6:    endVar
```

3. Build and show the menu in the arrive method of the page.

```
1:    ;Page :: arrive
2:    method arrive(var eventInfo MoveEvent)
3:        ;Build File menu.
4:        popFile.addText("Exit")
5:        m.addPopUp("File", popFile)
6:
7:        ;Build Edit menu.
8:        popEdit.addText("Cut")
9:        popEdit.addText("Copy")
10:       popEdit.addSeparator()
11:       popEdit.addText("Paste")
12:       m.addPopUp("Edit", popEdit)
13:
14:       ;Display menu.
15:       m.show()
16:   endMethod
```

4. Trap for user selections in the menuAction of the page.

```
1:    ;Page :: menuAction
2:    method menuAction(var eventInfo MenuEvent)
3:        sAns = eventInfo.menuChoice()
4:
5:        switch
6:           case sAns = "Exit"  : close()
7:           case sAns = "Cut"   : active.action(EditCutSelection)
8:           case sAns = "Copy"  : active.action(EditCopySelection)
9:           case sAns = "Paste" : active.action(EditPaste)
10:       endSwitch
11:   endmethod
```

5. Check the syntax, save the form as MENU-1.FSL, and run it (see Figure 25.2).

FIGURE 25.2.

*MENU-1.FSL demon-
strates building and using a
menu.*

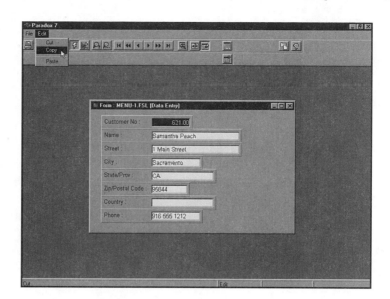

Analysis

In step 2, lines 3–5 declare the variables. A good place in which to declare the menu variables is in the Var window of the page. If you declare the String variable sAns in the menuAction method, it is redeclared every time a user chooses a menu option. It makes only a minor difference here, but it can make a significant difference in a large application. It is slightly more elegant to declare the variable static, as in the Var window of the page.

Step 3 builds and shows the menu. Line 4 adds text to the popFile variable, and line 5 attaches popFile to the menu variable. Lines 8–11 add text to the popEdit variable. Line 10 adds a line to the menu between Copy and Paste with the addSeparator() method. Line 12 attaches the popEdit variable to the m menu variable. Now, two pop-up menus are attached to m. Line 15 uses the show method.

Step 4 processes the user's selection. Line 3 grabs the user's selection and puts it into the sAns String variable. Lines 5–10 check which selection the user has selected and respond accordingly.

Dressing Up a Menu

Most programs use hot keys, bars, and other features to enhance the look of their menus. To dress up a menu in Paradox with ObjectPAL, you use a combination of ObjectPAL methods and embedded ASCII codes.

518

For example, you can use the following to dress up a menu:

```
& = accelerator (underlines character)
\008 = all the way to the right like Help
\009 = tab use only on a sub menu
addSeparator()
addBreak()
addBar()
```

Using Menu ID Numbers

Menu IDs enable you to have identical menu options. This next step by step example shows you how to build a menu by using menu IDs. In it, you build a menu that is identical to the one in the previous example, but this time the menu uses menu IDs.

You can find the MENU-2.FSL form on the disc in the \ANSWERS directory.

Step By Step

1. Change your working directory to the TUTORIAL directory and create a new form.

2. Define the variables in the Var window of the form.

```
1:    ;Page :: Var
2:    Var
3:        m                  Menu
4:        popFile, popEdit   PopUpMenu
5:        siAns              SmallInt
6:    endVar
```

3. Build and show the menu in the page's arrive method.

```
 1:    ;Page :: arrive
 2:    method arrive(var eventInfo MoveEvent)
 3:        ;Build File menu
 4:        popFile.addText("Exit", MenuEnabled, UserMenu + 101)
 5:        m.addPopUp("File", popFile)
 6:
 7:        ;Build Edit menu
 8:        popEdit.addText("Cut", MenuEnabled, UserMenu + 201)
 9:        popEdit.addText("Copy", MenuEnabled, UserMenu + 202)
10:    popEdit.addSeparator()
11:        popEdit.addText("Paste", MenuEnabled, UserMenu + 203)
12:        m.addPopUp("Edit", popEdit)
13:
14:        ;Display menu
15:        m.show()
16:    endMethod
```

4. Trap for the menu selection in the page's menuAction method.

```
1:    ;Page :: menuAction
2:    method menuAction(var eventInfo MenuEvent)
3:        siAns = eventInfo.id()
4:
```

```
 5:         Switch
 6:           case siAns = UserMenu + 101
 7:              :  close()
 8:           case siAns = UserMenu + 201
 9:               : active.action(EditCutSelection)
10:          case siAns = UserMenu + 202
11:              : active.action(EditCopySelection)
12:          case siAns = UserMenu + 203
13:              : active.action(EditPaste)
14:        endSwitch
15:      endmethod
```

5. Check the syntax, save the form as MENU-2.FSL, and run it (see Figure 25.3).

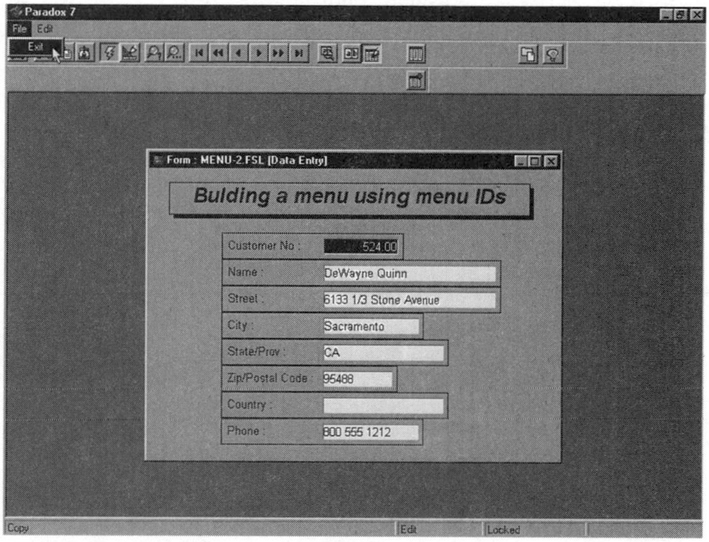

FIGURE 25.3.

MENU-2.FSL demonstrates using Menu IDs.

Analysis

The only lines analyzed here are those that deal with using menu IDs. For analysis of the other lines, refer to the Analysis section in the preceding example.

In step 2, line 5 declares a SmallInt variable for use in step 4.

In step 3, line 4 and lines 8–11 use the third syntax variation to assign return values to the menu options. They use the UserMenu built-in constant, which gives you the base value allowed in this version of Paradox. The numbering system used here and in the manuals is only by convention; with this version, you can use any numbers up to 2000 that you want . To verify the maximum number you can use with the constant UserMenu, type line 3 into the pushButton method of a button.

```
1:    ;Button :: pushButton
2:    method pushButton(var eventInfo Event)
3:       view(UserMenuMax - UserMenu)     ;Displays 2000.
4:    endmethod
```

It's a good idea to use the first digit of the menu ID for its left-to-right position and the next two digits for its top-to-bottom position. MenuEnabled is used because syntax 3 of addText() requires a MenuChoiceAttributes constant.

In step 4, lines 5–14 process the user's selection in the menuAction method. Lines 6–12 must use UserMenu because UserMenu was used earlier.

Using the *MenuInit* Constant

When you activate a menu, the first event isn't MenuChoice(); it's MenuInit. This occurs just before the item or pull-down menu is displayed. It's your last-minute chance to change the status of the menu items. You might want to add the following code:

```
1:  if eventinfo.id() <> MenuInit then
2:      sChoice = eventInfo.menuChoice()
3:      view(sChoice)
4:  endif
```

> **NOTE**
>
> Use MenuEnabled only when you're creating menus. Use setMenuChoiceAttributes() later to modify them.

Table 25.3 lists the menu choice attributes.

Table 25.3. Menu choice attributes.

Attribute	Description
MenuChecked	Displays a checkmark before the menu option.
MenuDisabled	Disables the menu option.
MenuEnabled	Activates the menu option.
MenuGrayed	Grays a menu option and deactivates it.
MenuHilited	Highlights the menu option.
MenuNotChecked	Removes a checkmark.
MenuNotGrayed	Displays the item normally.
MenuNotHilited	Turns off an option's highlight.

Cascading Pull-Down Menus

A *cascading menu* is the object that pops up when a pull-down menu or a pop-up menu displays another pop-up menu. This next step by step example shows you how to build a cascading menu.

NEW
Term

You can find the MENU-3.FSL form on the disc in the \ANSWERS directory.

Step By Step

1. Change your working directory to the TUTORIAL directory and create a new form.

2. Define the variables in the page's Var window.

```
1:    ;Page :: Var
2:    Var
3:       m                         Menu
4:       popFile, popEdit, popCut  PopUpMenu
5:       sAns                      String
6:    endVar
```

3. Build the menus in the page's arrive method.

```
1:    ;Page :: arrive
2:    method arrive(var eventInfo MoveEvent)
3:       ;Build File menu
4:       popFile.addText("Exit")
5:       m.addPopUp("File", popFile)
6:
7:       ;Build Cut sub menu
8:       popCut.addText("Text")
9:       popCut.addText("Record")
10:      popEdit.addPopUp("Cut", popCut)
11:
12:      ;Build Edit menu
13:      popEdit.addText("Copy")
14:      popEdit.addSeparator()
15:      popEdit.addText("Paste")
16:      m.addPopUp("Edit", popEdit)
17:
18:      ;Display menu
19:      m.show()
20:   endMethod
```

4. Trap for user input in the page's menuAction method.

```
1:    ;Page :: menuAction
2:    method menuAction(var eventInfo MenuEvent)
3:       sAns = eventInfo.menuChoice()
4:
5:       Switch
6:         case sAns = "Exit"
7:             : close()
```

```
 8:            case sAns = "Text"
 9:                 : active.action(EditCutSelection)
10:            case sAns = "Record"
11:                 : active.action(DataDeleteRecord)
12:            case sAns = "Copy"
13:                 : active.action(EditCopySelection)
14:            case sAns = "Paste"   : active.action(EditPaste)
15:         endSwitch
16:      endmethod
```

5. Check the syntax, save the form as MENU-3.FSL, and run it. Figure 25.4 shows how the MENU-3.FSL form looks.

FIGURE 25.4.

MENU-3.FSL demonstrates cascading menus.

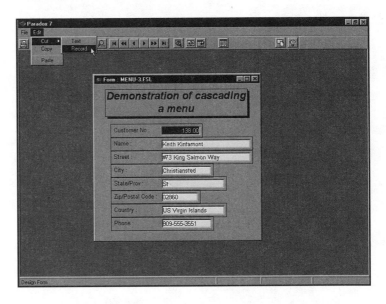

Analysis

The only lines analyzed here are those that deal with using cascading menus. For analysis of the other lines, refer to the Analysis sections in the previous two examples.

In step 2, line 4 uses an extra pop-up menu variable, popCut.

In step 3, lines 8 and 9 add two entries to the pop-up menu variable popCut. Line 10 adds popCut to popEdit. Lines 13–15 construct the rest of the popEdit pop-up menu. Line 16 adds this cascaded menu to the m menu variable. Line 19 displays the results.

Step 4 processes the user's menu choice.

You can use this technique to cascade as many times as you need. Don't overuse cascading menus. You can use one or two cascades, but anything more becomes cumbersome for the user and takes up memory.

Menu Constants Have Duplicates

ObjectPAL is a very rich language. In fact, you often can accomplish a single task in two or three different ways. Many menu constants have duplicate constants in other classes. The menu constant `MenuFilePrint`, for example, has a `DataAction` constant `DataPrint`. Because Borland might change the menu constant in the future, use the other class constants whenever possible. Rather than print your form with `menuAction(MenuFilePrint)`, for example, use `action(DataPrint)`.

> **NOTE**
>
> Don't confuse the `menuAction()` procedure with the `menuAction` built-in event method. The `menuAction()` procedure is used to execute a MenuAction constant while the `menuAction` event method is used to trap for MenuAction constants.

Overcoming the Pop-Up Menu Limit

When you display more items than will fit onscreen, the pop-up menu keeps going, preventing you from being able to see the options offscreen. You can use the `mod()` method to determine how many columns you need to display, and build the pop-up menu accordingly.

You can use Paradox as a model. Paradox displays many fonts by using a two-step approach. When there are too many fonts to display on a pop-up, Paradox displays *n* items with the string `More` as the last option. When the user selects that item, a dialog box that displays all the fonts in a table frame object appears. This solution is easy for the user to use, and it's straightforward to implement. An alternative is to write code that wraps the menu items to multiple columns.

The number of items is limited to 35. You can change this limit, however. Although Borland imposed this limit, it actually comes from Windows. Windows creates menus in the USER segment, which is limited to 64K. Many other objects must share this same segment of memory. If the USER segment is nearly full, don't create a new ObjectPAL menu. If the USER segment becomes too full, Windows will crash in ways and places over which Paradox has no control.

> **TIP**
>
> Borland set a limit of 35 options for each pop-up menu that you build. If you want to create a single pop-up with more than 35 options, use the undocumented `menuSetLimit()` procedure, as in the following example:
>
> `menuSetLimit(NumberOfItems)`

During the testing of the product, when ObjectPAL programmers tried to create menus with hundreds of items, they got General Protection Faults from Windows. As a rule of thumb for user interfaces, don't create menus or pop-up menus with a large number of items. It's too difficult to select one from the list. For this reason, Borland put an artificial limit of 35 items for each top-level menu, pop-up menu, and submenu. If you need to increase this limit, use menuSetLimit (*NumberOfItems*).

Doing this overrides the artificial limit, but it opens up the possibility of Windows crashing if you include too many options. How many is too many? That depends on your system and the applications that are currently running. Use menuSetLimit() at your own risk for two reasons: first, you could end up with an unstable application, and second, Borland may take out any undocumented software in the future. The form ANSWERS\POPUP100.FSL demonstrates using menuSetLimit() (see Figure 25.5).

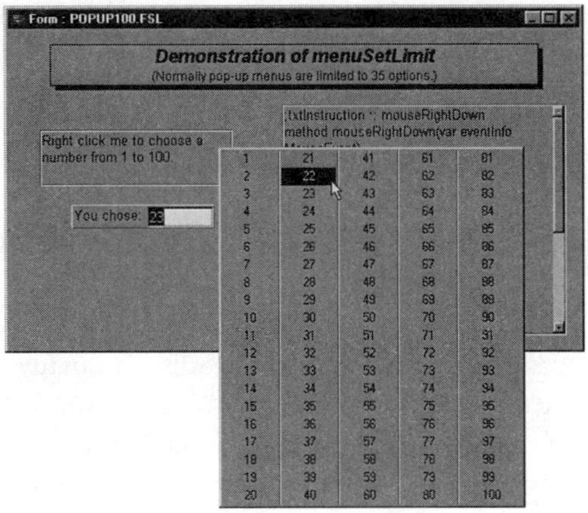

FIGURE 25.5.

POPUP100.FSL demonstrates building pop-up menus with more than 35 options.

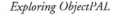

Following is the pertinent code from POPUP100.FSL from the mouseRightDown method of the txtInstruction text object.

```
 1:   ;txtInstruction :: mouseRightDown
 2:   method mouseRightDown(var eventInfo MouseEvent)
 3:     var
 4:        si1Counter   SmallInt
 5:        si2Counter   SmallInt
 6:        popChose     PopUpMenu
 7:     endVar
 8:
 9:     si2Counter = 0
10:
11:     menuSetLimit(200)
12:
13:     for si1Counter from 1 to 100
14:         popChose.addText(si1Counter)
15:
```

```
16:        si2Counter = si2Counter + 1
17:        if si2Counter = 20 then
18:          popChose.addBar()
19:          si2Counter = 0
20:        endIf
21:    endFor
22:
23:    fldChose = popChose.show()
24: endmethod
```

Creating a Pull-Down Menu on a Form

Although ObjectPAL doesn't have an explicit command for putting pull-down menus on a form, you can simulate one by using `PopUpMenu`, a box, and a text object. This next step by step example shows you how to create a pull-down menu on a form.

You can find the MENU-4.FSL form on the disc in the \ANSWERS directory.

Step By Step

1. Create a form with a long white box at the top that resembles a menu bar. Add two text objects labeled File and Quit (see Figure 25.6).

FIGURE 25.6.

Setup form for MENU-4.FSL example.

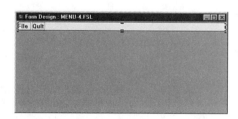

2. Create a custom method called `cmFileMenu()` at the form level and add lines 3–23 to it.

```
1:    ;FileText :: cmFileMenu
2:    method cmFileMenu()
3:       var
4:          p              PopUpMenu
5:          sChoice        String
6:       endVar
7:
8:       oldforgroundcolor = subject.font.color
9:       oldbackgroundcolor = subject.color
10:      subject.color = DarkBlue
11:      subject.font.color = White
12:
13:      p.addtext("Option1")
14:      p.addtext("Option2")
```

```
15:
16:        sChoice = p.show(20,300)
17:        subject.color = oldbackgroundcolor
18:        subject.font.color = oldforgroundcolor
19:
20:        switch
21:           case sChoice = "Option1" : msgInfo("", "Option 1")
22:           case sChoice = "Option2" : msgInfo("", "Option 2")
23:        endSwitch
24:     endmethod
```

3. Call the custom method for the first time by adding line 3 to the mouseDown method of the FileText object.

```
1:     ;FileText :: mouseDown
2:     method mouseDown(var eventInfo MouseEvent)
3:        cmFileMenu()
4:     endmethod
```

4. Call the custom method for the second time by adding line 3 to the mouseClick method of the FileText object.

```
1:     ;FileText :: mouseClick
2:     method mouseClick(var eventInfo MouseEvent)
3:        cmFileMenu()
4:     endmethod
```

5. Add lines 3–13 to the mouseClick method QuitText box.

```
1:     ;QuitText :: mouseClick
2:     method mouseClick(var eventInfo MouseEvent)
3:        oldforgroundcolor = self.font.color   ;Original colors.
4:        oldbackgroundcolor = self.color
5:        self.color = DarkBlue   ;Sets new colors
6:        self.font.color = White
7:
8:        if msgQuestion("Quit?", "Are you sure?") = "Yes" then
9:           close()
10:       endIf
11:
12:       self.color=oldbackgroundcolor   ;Back to original.
13:       self.font.color=oldforgroundcolor
14:    endmethod
```

6. Save the form as MENU-4.FSL and run it. Select the three options set up in this example. Figure 25.7 shows two sets of pull-down menus.

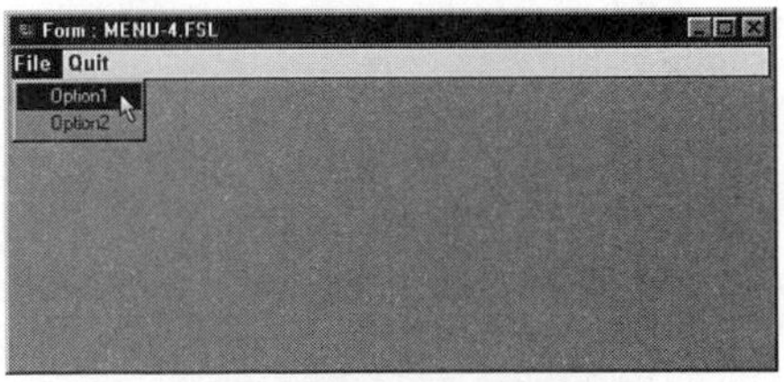

FIGURE 25.7.

MENU-4.FSL. There are two sets of pull-down menus.

In the preceding example, notice that the custom method is at the form level. It was placed at the form level only for convenience of this example. An even better technique would be to move the custom method to the box that contains the text boxes rather than all the way up at the form level. This would make the menu box object a self-contained object that can you can paste from form to form.

The form shown in Figure 25.8, PULLDOWN.FSL, demonstrates a technique for simulating pull-down menus on a form. It was developed for this book by Dave Orriss, Jr. when Dave worked at Borland.

FIGURE 25.8.

PULLDOWN.FSL.
Simulating pull-down
menus on a form.

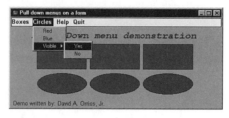

The *BuildMenu* and *MenuInit* Constants

You can trap for all MenuCommand constants in the menuAction method, including MenuBuild and MenuInit. The MenuBuild constant reports when the desktop is building a menu. The MenuInit constant reports when the user selects a menu option from a pull-down menu. With these two constants, you can trap for when a menu is built or when a user selects a menu option.

Using *setMenu( )* with a Report

The default menus that display with a report enable the user to do many tasks you may not want, such as opening a table. Suppose that you want to use just a limited set of menu options with a report. This next example uses setMenu() to add menus to a report.

You can find the SETMENU.FSL form on the disc in the \ANSWERS directory.

Step By Step

1. Change your working directory to the TUTORIAL directory, create a new form, and place a button on it.

2. In the pushButton method, type lines 3–17:

```
1:   ;Button :: mouseClick
2:   method pushButton(var eventInfo Event)
3:     var
4:       r     Report
5:       m     Menu
6:       pop   PopUpMenu
7:     endVar
8:
9:     r.open("REPORT", WinStyleDefault + WinStyleMaximize)
10:
11:    pop.addText("&Print...", MenuEnabled, MenuFilePrint)
12:    pop.addText("&Printer Setup...", MenuEnabled, MenuFilePrinterSetup)
13:    pop.addText("&Close", MenuEnabled, MenuControlClose)
14:    m.addPopUp("&File", pop)
15:
16:    r.setMenu(m)
17:  endmethod
```

3. Check the syntax, save the form as SETMENU.FSL, and run it (see Figure 25.9).

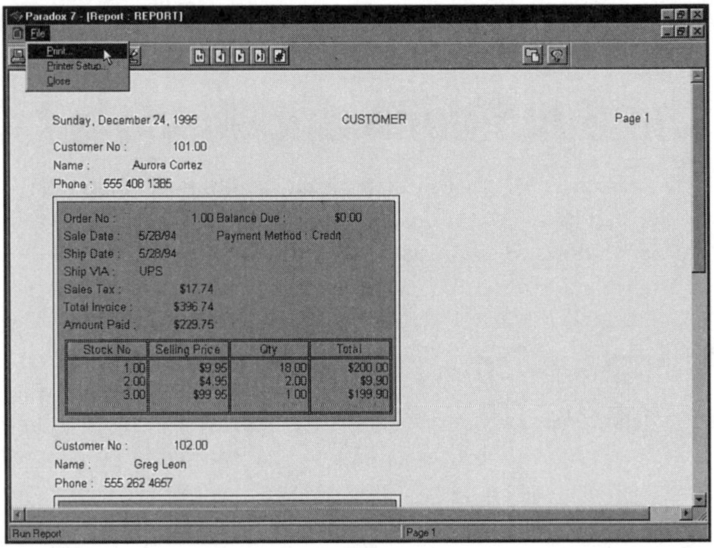

FIGURE 25.9.

SETMENU.FSL adding a menu to a report.

Analysis

In step 2, line 9 opens the REPORT.RSL with the r Report variable declared in line 4. Lines 11–14 build the menu and line 16 attaches it to the report using the r Report variable. It is important to note the use of menu constants in lines 11–13. You can add menu options only to reports that call existing menu constants. Therefore, using menus on reports is somewhat limited.

Modifying Existing Toolbars

You can use the new Toolbar type to alter existing toolbars or create your own. You can use the Toolbar class attach() to bind a variable to an existing toolbar. After you have a handle to a toolbar, you can remove buttons with removeButton() and add them with addButton(). The following is the syntax for attach():

attach (const *toolbarName* String) Logical

The attach() method binds the toolbar variable toolbarName to a variable. You can attach to any toolbars you create or to the standard toolbar. To attach to the standard toolbar, specify Standard for toolbarName. The following example demonstrates using attach() to bind a Toolbar variable to the standard toolbar:

```
var
    tbStandard    Toolbar
endVar
tbStandard.attach("Standard")
```

After you attach to a toolbar, you can remove buttons with removeButton(). The following is the syntax for removeButton():

removeButton (const *idCluster* SmallInt, const *idNum* SmallInt) Logical

You specify which cluster of toolbar buttons with idCluster. The cluster is specified left to right, starting from 0. The position of the button within a cluster also is specified left to right, starting with 0. For example, the Run button which is five buttons over is in cluster 2, and button 0. Type the following code snippet into the pushButton method of a button:

```
 1:    ;Button :: pushButton
 2:    method pushButton(var eventInfo Event)
 3:        var
 4:            tbStandard   ToolBar
 5:        endVar
 6:
 7:        tbStandard.attach("Standard")
 8:        tbStandard.removeButton(0, 0) ;Print.
 9:        tbStandard.removeButton(2, 1) ;Run.
10:        tbStandard.removeButton(2, 0) ;Design.
11:        tbStandard.removeButton(8, 0) ;TableView.
12:    endMethod
```

The preceding short program attached to the standard toolbar with line 7, and removed several buttons with lines 8–11. The buttons it removed you probably don't want because they give the user too much control in a data access form.

Just as you can remove buttons, you also can add your own using addButton():

```
1.    addButton ( const idCluster SmallInt, const buttonType SmallInt, const
      idCommand SmallInt, const grBmp Graphic, const buttonHelp String ) Logical
2.    addButton ( const idCluster SmallInt, const buttonType SmallInt, const
      idCommand SmallInt, const idBmp SmallInt, const buttonHelp String ) Logical
```

The `idCluster` parameter is the same as for `removeButton()`. The `buttonType` parameter enables you to specify the type of button to add to the toolbar, such as the following:

- `ToolbarButtonPush`
- `ToolbarButtonRadio`
- `ToolbarButtonRepeat`
- `ToolbarButtonToggle`

The `idCommand` parameter specifies which menu constant to send to the active form's `menuAction` method. The only difference between the two versions of syntax is the fourth parameter, which enables you to specify either a bitmap or a constant that maps to an existing bitmap (see Table 25.4). The final parameter is a string for the pop-up hint that appears when the mouse moves over the button. The following adds a button to the standard toolbar in the eighth cluster that displays the Add Table dialog box.

```
1: ;Button :: pushButton
2: method pushButton(var eventInfo Event)
3:   var
4:       tbStandard  ToolBar
5:   endVar
6:
7:   tbStandard.attach("Standard")
8:   tbStandard.addButton(8, ToolbarButtonPush, MenuFileTableAdd, BitmapAddTable,
      "Add Table")
9: endMethod
```

Table 25.4. The `Bitmap` constants.

BitmapAddBand
BitmapAddTable
BitmapAddToCat
BitmapAlignBottom
BitmapAlignCenter
BitmapAlignLeft
BitmapAlignMiddle
BitmapAlignRight
BitmapAlignTop
BitmapBookTool
BitmapBoxTool
BitmapBringToFront
BitmapButtonTool
BitmapCancel
BitmapChartTool

```
BitmapChkSyntax

BitmapCoEdit

BitmapCompile

BitmapDataBegin

BitmapDataEnd

BitmapDataModel

BitmapDataNextRecord

BitmapDataNextSet

BitmapDataPriorRecord

BitmapDataPriorSet

BitmapDelTable

BitmapDesignMode

BitmapDoJoin

BitmapDuplicate

BitmapEditAnswer

BitmapEditCopy

BitmapEditCut

BitmapEditPaste

BitmapEllipseTool

BitmapFieldTool

BitmapFilter

BitmapFirstPage

BitmapFldView

BitmapFontAttribBold

BitmapFontAttribItalic

BitmapFontAttribStrikeout

BitmapFontAttribUnderline

BitmapGotoPage

BitmapGraphicTool

BitmapGroup

BitmapHelp

BitmapHSpacing

BitmapLastPage

BitmapLineSpace1
```

continues

Table 25.4. continued

BitmapLineSpace15

BitmapLineSpace2

BitmapLineSpace25

BitmapLineSpace3

BitmapLineSpace35

BitmapLineTool

BitmapLinkDm

BitmapLoadDm

BitmapMaxHeight

BitmapMaxWidth

BitmapMinHeight

BitmapMinWidth

BitmapNextPage

BitmapNextWarn

BitmapObjectTree

BitmapOk

BitmapOleTool

BitmapOpenExpert

BitmapOpenForm

BitmapOpenLibrary

BitmapOpenProject

BitmapOpenQbe

BitmapOpenReport

BitmapOpenScript

BitmapOpenSql

BitmapOpenTable

BitmapOpenTutor

BitmapPageBreak

BitmapPickTool

BitmapPrevPage

BitmapPrint

BitmapQuickForm

BitmapQuickGraph

```
BitmapQuickReport
BitmapQuickXTab
BitmapRecordTool
BitmapRemoveFromCat
BitmapRestructure
BitmapRun
BitmapSave
BitmapSaveDm
BitmapSendToBack
BitmapSetBreak
BitmapSetOrgin
BitmapSetWatch
BitmapShowSQL
BitmapSortAnswer
BitmapSpeedExit
BitmapSrchNext
BitmapSrchValue
BitmapStepInto
BitmapStepOver
BitmapStop
BitmapTableFrameTool
BitmapTButton
BitmapTComboBox
BitmapTextCenter
BitmapTextJustify
BitmapTextLeft
BitmapTextRight
BitmapTextTool
BitmapTGuage
BitmapTHeader
BitmapTListBox
BitmapTSpinEdit
BitmapViewBreak
BitmapViewCallStack
```

continues

Table 25.4. continued

```
BitmapViewDebugger

BitmapViewMethods

BitmapViewSource

BitmapViewTracer

BitmapViewTypes

BitmapViewWatch

BitmapVSpacing

BitmapXtabTool
```

Creating New Toolbars

You also can create your own toolbars with create(), using the following syntax:

create (const ***toolbarName*** String [, const ***parentToolbarName*** String]) Logical

The toolbarName parameter can be any string you want except for Standard. The toolbarName identifies the toolbar and appears in the title bar when the toolbar is not docked. The following example creates a toolbar that includes one button:

```
 1: ;Button :: pushButton
 2: method pushButton(var eventInfo Event)
 3:     var
 4:         tbMyToolbar   ToolBar
 5:     endVar
 6:
 7:     tbMyToolbar.create("MyToolbar")
 8:     tbMyToolbar.addButton(0, ToolbarButtonPush, MenuFileTableAdd,
        BitmapAddTable, "Add Table")
 9:     ;Add more buttons here.
10: EndMethod
```

> **NOTE**
>
> Paradox 7 standard bitmap size is 22 pixels wide and 21 pixels high. Winword 7 is 22 pixels wide and 20 high. It doesn't really matter which you use—it is up to you. However, when adding icons to the Standard toolbar, use bitmaps that are 22 by 21 pixels.

Simulating a Toolbar on a Form

Toolbars don't exist at the form level, but you can simulate one. One technique is to create a screen shot of the Paradox desktop (with the toolbar). Open Paintbrush and cut out Paradox's toolbar. Add it to your form, and add methods to each button.

The following steps give you an overview of how to create a form-level toolbar:

1. Click the Print Screen button on your keyboard while Paradox is showing. This sends a bitmap to the Clipboard.
2. Launch Paintbrush and paste the image into it.
3. Cut out only the toolbar (or only the parts that you want).
4. Paste the image into your form.
5. Add a transparent box over every Toolbar option.
6. Add code to the mouseClick method of each transparent box.

This technique works, but no option on the toolbar has the appearance of pressing in as with normal toolbar buttons. If you want to go through the trouble, you can use two bitmaps and toggle their visible properties or place a bitmap inside a real button.

One final technique is to use a graphic as a button by toggling its frame between Inside3DFrame and Outside3DFrame. This technique is demonstrated in the Paradox desktop and because the form is a delivered form, the following code is pertinent. Add a bitmap to a form and add the following code:

```
1: ;Bitmap :: mouseDown
2: method mouseDown(var eventInfo MouseEvent)
3:    self.Frame.Style = Inside3DFrame    ;Make frame pop in.
4: endmethod
1: ;Bitmap :: mouseUp
2: method mouseUp(var eventInfo MouseEvent)
3:    self.Frame.Style = Outside3DFrame   ;Make frame pop out.
4: endmethod
```

The interesting thing about using mouseDown, mouseUp, and mouseClick is that mouseClick is called only when the pointer is inside the boundary of the object for both the mouseDown and mouseUp methods. Using all three methods makes your custom-created button behave just like a real button. You can execute any code you want in the mouseClick, but following is the code that is executed in the mouseClick method of the light bulb bitmap on the Paradox desktop:

```
 1:;Bitmap :: mouseClick
 2: var
 3:    siQuestion     SmallInt
 4: endVar
 5: method mouseClick(var eventInfo MouseEvent)
 6:    if not siQuestion.isAssigned() then
 7:       siQuestion = 1
 8:    endIf
 9:
10:    switch
11:       case siQuestion = 1
12:          :  msgInfo("About this screen", "This screen is the main screen.")
13:             siQuestion = 2
14:       case siQuestion = 2
15:          :  msgInfo("Keyboard Short Cuts", "Ctrl+M = Paradox Desktop Menu")
16:             siQuestion = 3
17:       case siQuestion = 3
18:          :  msgInfo("Tip / Hint", "Run multiple instances to increase your
              productivity.")
19:             siQuestion = 1
20: endSwitch
21: endmethod
```

Simulating a Floating Toolbar

You also can use a separate form to simulate a floating toolbar. Create a form that is long and thin like the Paradox floating toolbar. Put buttons or pictures on it. Then, make the form a dialog box. If the form isn't a dialog box, it's hidden every time the user selects the main form. Chapter 15 contains an example of this technique.

FileSystem Methods and Procedures

With the FileSystem commands, you can change your working directory, manipulate files on a disk, get the time and date from a file, and so on. Table 25.5 lists the FileSystem methods and procedures.

Table 25.5. FileSystem **methods and procedures.**

accessRights
clearDirLock
copy
delete
deleteDir
drives
enumFileList
existDrive
findFirst

findNext

freeDiskSpace

fullName

getDir

getDrive

getFileAccessRights

getValidFileExtensions

isAssigned

isDir

isFile

isFixed

isRemote

isRemovable

isValidFile

makeDir

name

privDir

rename

setDir

setDirLock

setDrive

setFileAccessRights

setPrivDir

setWorkingDir

shortName

size

splitFullFileName

startUpDir

time

totalDiskSpace

windowsDir

windowsSystemDir

workingDir

Changing Your Working Directory

To change working directories, use the setWorkingDir() method. This is particularly useful when you open a form. On the open of the form, type the following:

```
1:    var
2:       f        Form
3:       dynPath  DynArray[] String
4:    endVar
5:
6:    f.attach()
7:    splitFullFileName(f.getFileName(), dynPath)
8:    setWorkingDir(dynPath["Drive"] + dynPath["Path"])
```

The default behavior when you change working directories is to close all the objects that are open on the Paradox desktop. To prevent the currently opened objects from closing, use the following in the form's menuAction:

```
1:    if eventInfo.id() = MenuChangingWork then
2:       eventInfo.setErrorCode(1)
3:    endIf
```

It is important to note that you cannot execute any code after calling setWorkingDir() in the open method. If you want to execute code after changing working directories, then trap for the MenuChangedWork constant in menuAction, as in the following:

```
1:    if eventInfo.id() = MenuChangedWork then
2:       ;Execute more code here.
3:    endIf
```

Both setWorkingDir() and setPrivDir() are posted actions. Therefore, the logical value returned by them reports whether the action was posted (placed in the event queue)—not whether the directory was changed. Instead, use a try block to see whether the directory changed. Do not depend on the return value.

Changing the Working Directory of a Form

Suppose that you want to automatically change working directories when a form opens. In this case, you want to change the working directory to the same directory the form is in.

You can find the WORK1.FSL form on the disc in the \ANSWERS directory.

Step By Step

1. Change your working directory to TUTORIAL and create a new form.
2. Add lines 3–13 to the init method of the form.

```
1:    ;Form :: init
2:    method init(var eventInfo Event)
3:        var
4:           f    Form
5:           dyn1 DynArray[] String
6:        endVar
7:        f.attach()
8:        if not isFile(":WORK:WORK1.FSL") then
9:            splitFullFileName(f.getFileName(), dyn1)
10:           if not setWorkingDir(dyn1["Drive"] + dyn1["Path"]) then
11:               errorShow()
12:           endIf
13:        endIf
14:    endmethod
```

3. Add lines 9–11 to the menuAction method of the form.

```
1:    ;Form :: menuAction
2:    method menuAction(var eventInfo MenuEvent)
3:
4:        if eventInfo.isPreFilter() then
5:           ;This code executes for each object on the form:
6:
7:        else
8:           ;This code executes only for the form:
9:           if eventInfo.id() = MenuChangingWork then
10:               eventInfo.setErrorCode(1)
11:           endIf
12:        endif
13:    endmethod
```

4. Check the syntax, save the new form as WORK1.FSL, and close it. Change your
working directory to another directory and open up the form by browsing for it.
When it opens, notice what your working directory is set to (see Figure 25.10).

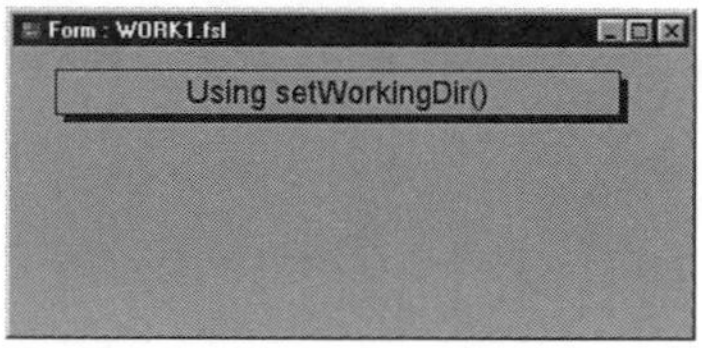

FIGURE 25.10.

*WORK1.FSL demonstrates
changing your working
directory.*

Analysis

In step 2, line 15 attaches to the current form with the Form variable declared in line 4. Line 16
checks to see whether the current file is in the working directory, and if it is not, proceeds with
lines 17–20. Line 17 grabs the current path and puts it into the dyn1 DynArray that was declared in line 5. Line 18 uses the DynArray to set the working directory and displays an error
in line 19 if it fails.

In step 3, line 9 checks the eventInfo ID for the constant MenuChangingWork. If the current ID
is MenuChangingWork, then a nonzero error code is set in line 10.

One other constant of interest when you're changing working directories is `MenuChangedWork`. This constant flows through `menuAction` after the working directory has successfully changed. You can use this, for example, to let the user know what the new working directory is whenever the working directory has changed. For example:

```
1: ;Form :: menuAction
2: if eventInfo.id() = MenuChangedWork then
3:    message("New working directory: " + workingDir())
4: endIf
```

Finding the Path of a File

Suppose that you want to add a routine to a button that opens up the Paradox browser, browse for a file, select a file, and place its full path in a field. (This task is harder than it should be.)

You can find the FINDPATH.FSL form on the disc in the \ANSWERS directory.

Step By Step

1. Change your working directory to the TUTORIAL directory and create a new form with a field and a button on it. Name the field fldFile and label the button Browse (see Figure 25.11).

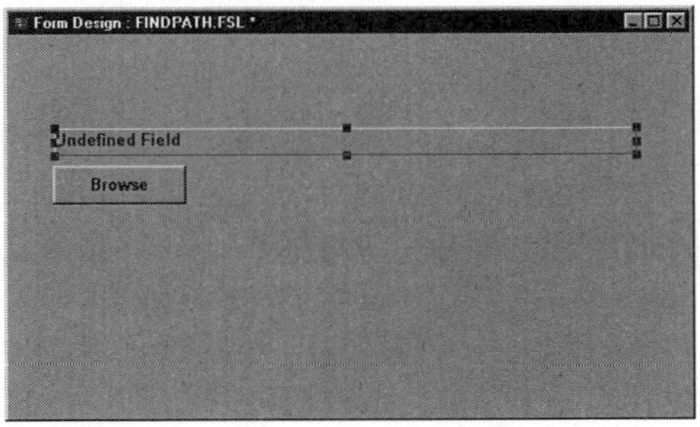

FIGURE 25.11.

Setup form for the example.

2. In the pushButton method, type lines 3–23.

```
1:    ;Button :: pushButton
2:    method pushButton(var eventInfo Event)
3:       var
4:         sFilename   String
5:         fbi         FileBrowserInfo
6:       endVar
7:
8:       if fileBrowser(sFileName, fbi) then
9:             ;A File was selected.
10:      else       ;If no file is selected,
```

```
11:          return   ;then return.
12:        endIf
13:
14:        ;Find path of file.
15:        switch
16:          case isDir(fbi.alias)
17:             : fldFile.value = fbi.alias + fbi.path + sFilename
18:          case sFilename.subStr(1,6) = ":PRIV:"
19:             : sFilename = sFilename.subStr(7, sFilename.size() - 6)
20:                fldFile.value = getAliasPath(":PRIV:") + "\\" + sFilename
21:          otherwise
22:             : fldFile.value = getAliasPath(fbi.alias) + "\\" + fbi.path
                 _+ sFilename
23:        endSwitch
24:      endmethod
```

3. Check the syntax, save the form as FINDPATH.FSL, and run it (see Figure 25.12). Click the Browse button and choose a file. Try choosing files from the current working directory and from another directory using an alias.

FIGURE 25.12.

FINDPATH.FSL demonstrates finding the path of a file.

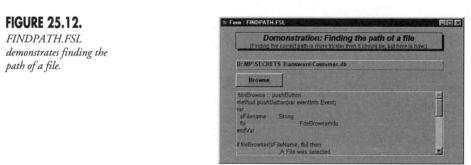

Analysis

In step 2, lines 3–6 declare an `sFilename` string variable to receive the name of the file in line 8 and an `fbi` FileBrowserInfo variable for use with `fileBrowser()`, also in line 8. Lines 15–23 determine the path of the file.

In the next example, you set up a way to launch a file by double-clicking on its filename.

Finding a Set of Files

Suppose that you want to create a form that lists all the files in a directory and enables the user to launch a file by double-clicking its filename. This next step by step example uses the FileSystem methods to search your Windows directory for .EXE files and puts them in a list field. When the user double-clicks on a filename, the .EXE file is launched.

You can find the FINDFILE.FSL form on the disc in the \ANSWERS directory.

Step By Step

1. Create a new form with two undefined fields. Label the first undefined field Search For, and change its name to SearchForField (see Figure 25.13).

FIGURE 25.13.

Setup form for the example.

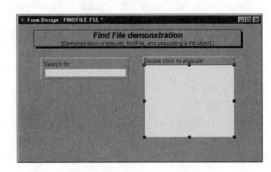

2. Make the second undefined field a list field; change its name to fldResult and its list to FileList. Figure 25.14 shows the Object Tree of the list field. The list object is inside the field object.

FIGURE 25.14.

The Object Tree of the list field.

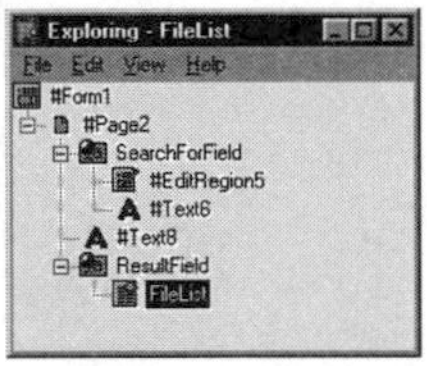

3. Place a text object above the fldResult field with the text Double click to execute. Figure 25.15 shows how your form should now look.

FIGURE 25.15.

Add instructions via a text object.

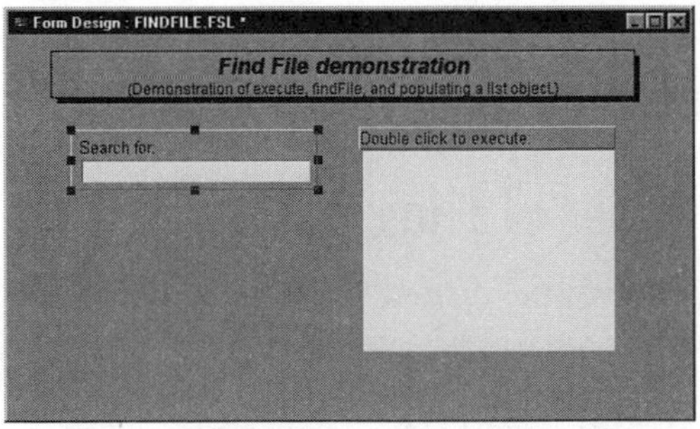

4. Add line 3 to the Var window of the Search for field.

```
1:    ;SearchForField :: Var
2:    Var
3:        fs FileSystem
4:    endVar
```

5. Add lines 3 and 4 to the open method of the Search for field.

```
1:    ;SearchForField :: open
2:    method open(var eventInfo Event)
3:       doDefault
4:       self.value = windowsDir() + "\\*.EXE"
5:    endmethod
```

6. Add lines 3–17 to the newValue method of the Search for field.

```
1:    ;SearchForField :: newValue
2:    method newValue(var eventInfo Event)
3:       if not SearchForField.isBlank() then
4:         if fs.findFirst(SearchForField) then
5:            fldResult.FileList.list.count = 0
6:            fldResult.FileList.list.selection = 1
7:            fldResult.FileList.list.value = FS.name()
8:            while FS.findNext()
9:                fldResult.FileList.list.selection =
                      fldResult.FileList.list.selection +1
10:               fldResult.FileList.list.value = FS.name()
11:           endWhile
12:         else
13:            fldResult.FileList.list.count = 0
14:            fldResult.FileList.list.selection = 1
15:            fldResult.FileList.list.value = "File not found"
16:         endIf
17:       endIf
18:    endmethod
```

7. Add lines 3–7 to the mouseDouble method of the fldResult field.

```
1:    ;fldResult :: mouseDouble
2:    method mouseDouble(var eventInfo MouseEvent)
3:       try
4:          execute(fldResult.value)
5:       onFail
6:          msgStop("Warning", "Could not launch file")
7:       endTry
8:    endMethod
```

8. Check the syntax and save the form. Run the form. All the .EXE files from your Windows directory are listed. If you double-click a file, it will execute (see Figure 25.16). Change the extension to .HLP. If .HLP is associated with WINHELP.EXE like the Windows default, you can double-click any Help file to launch it. Now, type in an invalid extension, such as .XYZ. The words File not found appear.

FIGURE 25.16.

*FINDFILE.FSL
demonstrates finding a
group of files.*

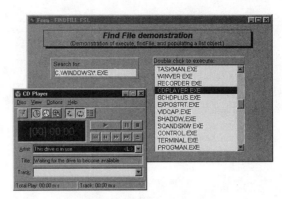

Analysis

In step 4, line 3 sets up fs as a FileSystem variable. It's used later in step 6.

In step 5, line 4 populates the Search for field after invoking the default behavior.

In step 6, line 3 checks the value, and line 9 uses it and the fs System variable to find the first occurrence of the search criteria. If nothing is found, the execution skips to line 14. Lines 14–16 clear the list and set the first value to File not found. If line 3 finds a file, lines 5–7 clear the list and set the initial value, and lines 8–12 loop through and populate the rest of the list.

In step 7, lines 3–7 attempt to launch the value that you double-click. These lines use a try block. If you don't use a try block, ObjectPAL will display abstract errors when the file isn't found. In other words, many ObjectPAL errors are meant for the programmer. You might want to use a try structure to test your code. If it fails, display a more meaningful message to the end user.

Summary

In this chapter, you learned about pull-down menus, toolbars, and how the FileSystem gives the user a sense of control. With the techniques you learned in this chapter, you can give your users control over your applications. Remember to be consistent within an application. If you develop a particularly attractive look and feel for one application, you might want to use it with all your applications.

Launching Applications

26

IN THIS CHAPTER

This chapter shows you how to add more power to Paradox through the use of, and communication with, other applications. You'll learn how to quickly and easily add other applications to your application—true object-oriented programming (plug and go).

The open architecture of Paradox means that there are few limits to the types of applications you can create. Through DLLs, Paradox supports direct access to functions written in traditional programming languages. Paradox also offers full support for DDE and OLE. In addition, you can execute commands to launch anything Windows can launch (discussed in this chapter). This includes Windows and DOS applications and batch files. You can use the `execute()` procedure to easily include other applications in the applications you develop (see Table 26.1 for the commands). Doing so gives the user easy access to those applications and increases the functionality of your applications.

Table 26.1. The two `execute()` commands.

Command	Class	Description
execute	DDE	Sends a command via a DDE link
execute	System	Executes an application

Executing Windows Applications

Sometimes it's useful to start another application from within a form, such as the Windows Notepad or Calculator. Many applications, such as Quicken for Windows, provide the user such access to other programs through icons or pushbuttons. Paradox makes it easy to implement this type of feature; it takes just one line of code that uses the `execute()` procedure. The following example starts the Calculator program from the `pushButton` method of a button object:

```
1:  ;Button :: push Button
2:  method pushButton(var eventInfo Event)
3:    if not execute("CALC.EXE") then
4:       msgStop("Error", "Unable to start application.")
5:    endif
6:  endmethod
```

NOTE

Remember that two backslashes (\\) take the place of a single backslash (\) whenever you need to include a single backslash in a string. When you use the `execute()` command, you pass it a string to execute—for example, C:\\IDAPI\\IDAPICFG.EXE.

Executing DOS Applications

In addition to executing Windows applications, you can execute anything Windows can execute, including DOS applications. For example, to start a DOS session, you could execute a batch .BAT file or the COMMAND.COM directly, as in the following:

```
1:   ;Button :: pushButton
2:   method pushButton(var eventInfo Event)
3:     execute("COMMAND.COM")
4:   endmethod
```

Using execute( ) with *switchMenu*

The following example adds the most useful Windows and DOS applications to a button. After you create these four buttons, you can simply copy and paste from them into any application you develop.

A *desk accessory* is a term usually used in the Macintosh world to refer to a small application that adds functionality to an application. You can create or use small Windows or Paradox applications with your application.

New
Term

Example of Using *execute( )* with *switchMenu*

Suppose that you want to set up four buttons. The first button will launch several common Windows applications. The second will launch the Paradox accessory applications. The third will launch the Paradox help files, and the fourth will launch several common DOS applications. This next step by step example accomplishes this by using switchMenu and execute().

You can find the DA.FSL form on the disc in the \ANSWERS directory.

Step By Step

1. Create a form with four buttons on it. Label them WinApp Desk Accessories, DOS Desk Accessories, PDoxWin Desk Accessories, and PDoxWin Info.

2. Add lines 3–6 to the `pushButton` method of the DOS Desk Accessories button.

```
1:    ;Button :: pushButton
2:    method pushButton(var eventInfo Event)
3:       switchMenu
4:         case "DOS" : execute("COMMAND.COM")
5:         case "Edit" : execute("EDIT.COM")
6:       endSwitchMenu
7:    endmethod
```

3. Add lines 3–8 to the `pushButton` method of the PDoxWin Info button.

```
1: ;Button :: pushButton
2: method pushButton(var eventInfo Event)
3:    switchMenu
4:       case "PDoxWin Help"    : execute("winhelp.exe pdox.hlp")
5:       case "OPal Help"       : execute("winhelp.exe opal.hlp")
6:       case "TUtility Help"   : execute("winhelp.exe tutility.hlp")
7:       case "BDE Help"        : execute("winhelp.exe bdecfg32.hlp")
8:    endSwitchMenu
9: endmethod
```

4. Add lines 3–10 to the `pushButton` method of the WinApps Desk Accessories button.

```
1: ;Button :: pushButton
2:  method pushButton(var eventInfo Event)
3:    switchMenu
4:       case "Calculator"    : execute("calc.exe")
5:       case "Control Panel" : execute("control.exe")
6:       case "Explorer"      : execute("EXPLORER.EXE /n,/e,C:\\")
7:       case "File Manager"  : execute("winfile.exe")
8:       case "Notepad"       : execute("notepad.exe")
9:       case "Sysedit"       : execute("Sysedit.exe")
10:    endSwitchMenu
11: endmethod
```

5. Check the syntax, save your work, and run the form. Click any of the buttons to display its pop-up menu and make a selection (see Figure 26.1). If the selection you choose doesn't execute, make sure that it is in your DOS path.

FIGURE 26.1.

Using `execute()` *and* `switchMenu` *to simulate four desk accessory-style buttons.*

Analysis

This example demonstrated an easy way to build pop-up menus and process the user's choice. All four `switchMenu` statements are basically the same, so just the first statement in step 2 is analyzed. Line 3 uses the keyword `switchMenu` to start the `switch` menu block. This is similar to the way in which you start a `switch` block. Lines 4–6 build and display the menu options and launch the appropriate application.

> **NOTE**
>
> When using `execute()`, the path that is searched is Paradox's startup directory, the Window's directory, the Window's system directory, and then the DOS path.

Executing DOS Batch Files

A *batch file* is a text file that contains one or more DOS commands. A batch file always has an extension of .BAT. The commands in a batch file are executed sequentially. In Chapter 4, you learned that you can use all you know about computers with Paradox. For example, maybe you're familiar with batch files and feel comfortable writing them. If you have the following batch file saved as BATCH.BAT, NEW *Term*

```
1:   echo.
2:   CLS
3:   echo *** Listing of files ***
4:   echo.
5:   dir  C:\ ¦more
6:   echo.
7:   pause
```

you could execute the batch file with the following:

```
1:   execute("BATCH.BAT")
```

Most of the time, you won't find batch files too useful, mainly because of the many and broad features of ObjectPAL. Occasionally, however, you'll find that batch files are a convenient, easy, and fast way to accomplish a set of tasks. For example, you could use a batch file to run a set of DOS back-up programs and use a timer in ObjectPAL to start the whole process.

Using DOS Batch Files in ObjectPAL

You also can use batch files to redirect the output of a DOS application to a text file on a disk, and then use Notepad to view it. The next example demonstrates the technique of integrating a batch file into ObjectPAL. Use a batch file to redirect the output of the DOS DIR command to a text file, and then view the text file in an Editor.

> You can find the BATCH.FSL form on the disc in the \ANSWERS directory.

Step By Step

1. Change your working directory to TUTORIAL and create a new form with two buttons on it. Label them Create Directory Tree and View Directory Tree (see Figure 26.2). In this example, the batch file, ANSWERS\TREE.BAT, is already created and on the disc.

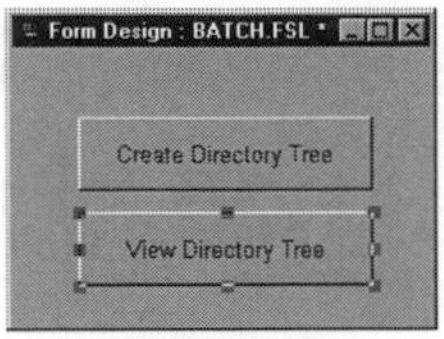

FIGURE 26.2.

*Setup form for executing
a batch file example.*

2. Add lines 3–10 to the pushButton method of the Create Directory Tree button.

```
1:    ;Button :: pushButton
2:    method pushButton(var eventInfo Event)
3:      var
4:        s1,s2      String
5:      endVar
6:
7:      s2 = "C:\\"
8:      s2.view("Enter a path to view")
9:      s1 = getAliasPath("work")
10:     execute(s1 + "\\TREE.BAT " + s2 + " " + s1 + "\\TREE.TXT")
11:   endmethod
```

3. Add line 3 to the pushButton method of the View Directory Tree button.

```
1:    ;Button :: pushButton
2:    method pushButton(var eventInfo Event)
3:        execute("WORDPAD.EXE " + getAliasPath("work") +"\\TREE.TXT")
4:    endmethod
```

4. Check the syntax, save your work, and run the form. Click the Create Directory Tree button, and then either click OK or change the path and click OK. Press any key to continue the batch file. When your disk light goes out, click the View Directory Tree button (see Figure 26.3).

FIGURE 26.3.

*Using execute() to
integrate DOS batch files
into your application.*

Analysis

In step 2, line 4 declares two `String` variables for use in lines 7–10. Line 7 sets the initial directory path that will be passed to the batch file in line 10. Line 8 offers the user a chance to change the default path. Line 9 sets the path for the location of the batch file and the destination of the resulting text file. Line 10 executes the batch file and passes it the parameters you built.

In step 3, line 3 on the `pushButton` method of the other button enables the user to view the resulting text file using Microsoft Write (refer to Figure 26.3).

NOTE

The preceding example called WORDPAD.EXE and not WRITE.EXE or NOTEPAD.EXE. Both Microsoft Write and Notepad came with Windows 3.*x.* In Windows 95, WordPad replaces both. An interesting feature of Windows 95 is that if you call Microsoft Write or Notepad, WordPad is automatically called instead. To test this, replace WORDPAD.EXE in step 3, code line 3 with either NOTEPAD.EXE or WRITE.EXE.

Summary

This chapter showed you how to add more power to Paradox through the use of and communication with other applications. You learned you can execute commands to launch anything Windows can launch. This includes Windows and DOS applications and batch files. Doing so gives the user easy access to those applications and increases the functionality of your applications. You learned how to quickly and easily add other applications to your application.

The open architecture of Paradox means that there are very few limits to the kinds of applications you can create. Through DLLs, Paradox supports direct access to functions written in traditional programming languages (DLLs are discussed more in Chapter 31). Paradox also offers full support for DDE and OLE (discussed in Chapter 27).

Using DDE, OLE, and OLEAuto

27

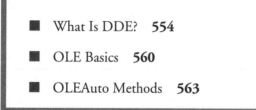

Dynamic data exchange (DDE) and *object linking and embedding* (OLE) are two protocols, or standards, that Microsoft asks makers of Windows applications to support. Both provide easy ways to exchange data with another Windows application. Although DDE and OLE are primarily interactive user features, you can carry out some interesting tasks with them in ObjectPAL.

The primary difference between DDE and OLE has to do with what each one sends. DDE sends data and commands between two applications. OLE either embeds data directly into another application, or stores information about a link to a specific piece of data. You can store OLE data in an OLE field type of a table. You cannot store DDE links in a table.

What Is DDE?

DDE is a powerful tool for Windows programmers. DDE in ObjectPAL enables you to do three things: send values to another application, get values from another application, and send commands to another application.

NEW Term

Just as you have a client and a server in a network environment, you have a DDE client and a DDE server when you establish a DDE link between two applications. The application that is the source—that is, the provider—of the data is the *server*. The application that receives the data is the *client*. Paradox is only a DDE client with ObjectPAL. Therefore, you can send and receive values, but Paradox must be the application that does the sending and receiving. In other words, another application can't tell Paradox to send or receive data.

DDE Basics

NEW Term

The term *DDE* stands for *Dynamic Data Exchange*, which is a way for two or more applications to share data. A DDE link is distinctly different from an OLE link. Use DDE to exchange bits of data and execute DDE commands. Use OLE to embed objects from one application into another. The application that receives data from the server application is the *DDE client*. The *DDE server* is the application that responds to the calling application (that is, the client) in a DDE or OLE conversation, usually by sending data. The client application is responsible for starting the DDE or OLE conversation. A *DDE topic* is the subject of a DDE conversation. Usually, it is the name of a data file of the application. A *DDE item* is the piece of data sent between applications.

What DDE Can Do for You

DDE sends and receives one piece of data or a command at a time. This means that you can use DDE to send the value of a single field or a complete table. You can send several single values one after another. With DDE, you can send text, field information, or even a bitmap. For example, you can put a button on a form that tells your word processor to open a document. Then you can send it values and tell it to print.

Not every application can exchange data with Paradox. For example, DOS applications don't support DDE. Most—but not all—Windows applications support DDE. Applications that support DDE include Quattro Pro for Windows, Excel, Word for Windows, WordPerfect for Windows, ObjectVision, and Quicken for Windows. Small utilities often don't support DDE.

Most programmers stay away from DDE because they think that it's difficult. The funny thing, however, is that DDE isn't difficult. In fact, only four commands in ObjectPAL deal with DDE. Table 27.1 lists the DDE methods and procedures.

Table 27.1. DDE methods and procedures.

Method	*Description*
close	Closes a DDE link.
execute	Sends a command by means of a DDE link.
open	Opens a DDE link to another application.
setItem	Specifies an item in a DDE conversation.

The Windows Registration Database

The Windows *registration database* is a system-wide source of information, listing the server applications that support the DDE/OLE protocol, the names of the executable files for these applications, the verbs for classes of objects, and whether an object-handler library exists for a given class of object (see Figure 27.1).

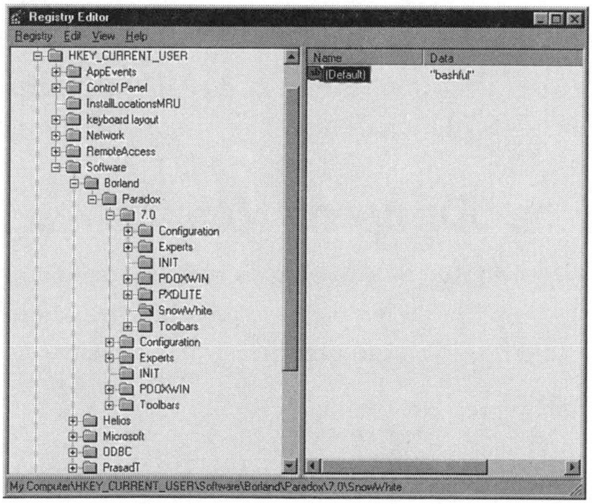

NEW
Term

FIGURE 27.1.

The registration database.

When a DDE or an OLE server is installed, the correct information about the server is stored in the registration database. The registration database is a big part of Windows 95 and Windows NT and stores information about your software and hardware. You can access the registration database by running the REGEDIT.EXE application. If a program that supports DDE or OLE is merely copied to a workstation, problems with DDE and OLE can occur. For example, a DDE server must be in the DOS PATH.

How to Use DDE from ObjectPAL

You must establish all DDE and OLE links for a form from Paradox. You can do this interactively or through ObjectPAL. You can't use another application's macro or a programming language to establish a link with a form.

To establish a DDE link with another application through ObjectPAL, you need to know the following three things:

- The name of the other application
- What the other application uses as a DDE topic
- What the other application uses as a DDE item

The name of the application almost always is the name of the executable. For example, Word for Windows uses WINWORD, and ObjectVision uses VISION.

The DDE topic almost always is the name of the document with which you want to establish the link. For example, Word for Windows uses the document name, such as README.DOC, and ObjectVision uses the application name, such as ORDER.OVD. When using the document name, remember to include the path to the document.

The DDE item is trickier. In most cases, you must consult the manual of the other application to find out what it uses for the DDE item. Usually, the DDE item is an element of the document—in other words, an element of the DDE topic. For example, Word for Windows uses the document's bookmarks, and ObjectVision uses the application's field names.

Using the DDE *open()* Method

You can think of DDE links as conversations between two applications. One application must ask the other application if it wants to talk about a particular subject or topic. You do this with the open() method. You can use three syntax models:

```
open (const server String)

open (const server String, const topic String)

open (const server String, const topic String, const item String)
```

As always, first you must declare a variable, as in the following example:

```
1:   var
2:       ddeWinWord    DDE
3:   endVar
```

As soon as you have a variable to work with, you can use one of the three syntax models to establish a link. With syntax 1, you ask the other application whether it wants to talk. You can use the following techniques to establish links with most DDE-compatible applications.

The following line of code asks Word for Windows whether it can talk:

```
1:   ddeWinWord.open("WINWORD")
```

If Word for Windows isn't open already but it's in your DOS path, this command launches it. After a conversation, or link, is established, you can use the `execute()` method to execute a command in the other application.

In most cases, however, you won't use syntax 1 because it doesn't establish a topic. The following command uses syntax 2. It opens a link and establishes a topic with Word for Windows.

```
1:   ddeVar.open("WINWORD", "C:\\WINWORD\\DATA\\README.DOC")
```

Syntax 3 of the DDE :: Open method enables you to specify the application, topic, and item, as in the following:

```
1:   ddeVar.open("WINWORD", "C:\\WINWORD\\DATA\\README.DOC", "MyBookMark")
```

Executing DDE Commands

To enable you to control other applications with DDE, ObjectPAL offers the `execute()` command. You can use ObjectPAL to send commands to other applications. You use the same macro command structure that the controlled application understands. For Word for Windows, this is WordBasic. You can search the Word for Windows help screen to find the WordBasic commands.

If you only want to print the document, you don't need to establish an item. The following line of code uses the `execute()` command to tell Word for Windows to print the document:

```
1:   ddeVar.execute("[FilePrintDefault]")
```

NOTE

Do not confuse the DDE type `execute()` with the system type `execute()`. The DDE `execute()` sends the `string` command to an application via a DDE link. The system `execute()` executes or runs a Windows or DOS application. The nature of the DDE `execute()` command varies from one application to another. Commands sent to Excel probably won't work in Quattro Pro or in a word processor.

Using *setItem()*

If you want to exchange data, you must send (or in DDE terminology, *poke*) the data into another application or get information from it. To do this, open a DDE channel, use the `setItem()` method, and assign the data as a value to the DDE variable. If the README.DOC document has a `LastName` bookmark, you can set the item of conversation to it with the following statement:

```
1:   ddeVar.setItem("LastName")
```

Otherwise, you can use syntax 3. For example, the following opens a conversation and sets both the topic and the item in one line of code:

```
1:   ddeVar.open("WINWORD", "C:\\WINWORD\\DATA\\README.DOC", "LastName")
```

After you establish the link, or gateway, you can use regular dot notation to manipulate the data in the open document. For example, to get a value from the established DDE item and to put it in a variable, you can use the following code:

```
1:   var
2:      Last_Name String
3:   endVar
4:
5:   Last_Name = ddeVar
```

Setting the value in the other application is just as easy. For example, the following statement sets the item in the other application to the value in the variable named `Last_Name`:

```
1:   ddeVar = Last_Name
```

Now, put all these statements together. The code looks like the following:

```
1:    ;button :: pushButton
2:    method pushButton(var eventInfo Event)
3:       var
4:          ddeVar       DDE
5:          Last_Name    String
6:       endVar
7:
8:       ddeVar.open("WINWORD", "C:\\WINWORD\\DATA\\README.DOC", "LastName")
9:       Last_Name = ddeVar
10:      Last_Name.view("Value in Word")
11:      ddeVar = "Ault"
12:      Last_Name = ddeVar
13:      Last_Name.view("New value in Word")
14:   endMethod
```

Exchanging Multiple Values

So far, this chapter has discussed sending and receiving only single values. You might be wondering how you send multiple values. To do so, first use the `setItem()` method to set the item. Next, send or receive the value. Then, use `setItem()` again to establish a new item of discussion. In DDE terminology, that is a new item within the current topic.

The following code builds on the README.DOC example. It sends three different values to three different bookmarks. It assumes that you already have established the three bookmarks in Word for Windows:

```
1:  ddeVar.setItem("LastName")
2:  ddeVar = Last_Name
3:
4:  ddeVar.setItem("FirstName")
5:  ddeVar = First_Name
6:
7:  ddeVar.setItem("PhoneNumber")
8:  ddeVar = Phone_Number
```

Paradox makes asynchronous transmissions. This means that Paradox waits for the other program to respond. This waiting doesn't always occur correctly. This means you might need to put a `sleep()` command in your code to wait for the server to respond to certain requests. As a rule of thumb, if a DDE command fails when it sends or gets values or when it sends commands, put a `sleep(100)` command between the two lines of code. This tells Paradox to sleep for one-tenth of a second. In computer time, this is usually plenty of time for the other application to return a message.

Starting the Other Application Ahead of Time

If you want, you can launch an application before you establish the DDE link. For example, you can launch Word for Windows ahead of time with code such as the following:

```
1:  ;Button :: pushButton
2:  method pushButton(var eventInfo Event)
3:     execute("WINWORD.EXE C:\\WINWORD\\README.DOC")
4:  endmethod
```

This approach offers no real advantage. Sometimes, however, you want to enable the user to open the application ahead of time without doing any DDE exchanges.

The form in Figure 27.2 demonstrates how to link to Word for Windows, send and get values, and print. You must have Word for Windows in your path for this form to work. When you tell Word for Windows to print, the system doesn't switch to Word for Windows. Instead, the Printing dialog box from Word for Windows appears over Paradox.

> You can use DDE to spell check a field with Word for Windows. Take a look at the information database (\APPS\INFO\INFO.FSL) for an example of this technique. Also note that you can use this technique to check grammar.

Sometimes, you might want to send a large text field to Word for Windows for spell checking. When the spell checking is done, you retrieve the text file. The form in Figure 27.2 demonstrates how you can do this. Table 27.2 lists sample DDE applications, names, topics, and items. For the applications, case doesn't matter.

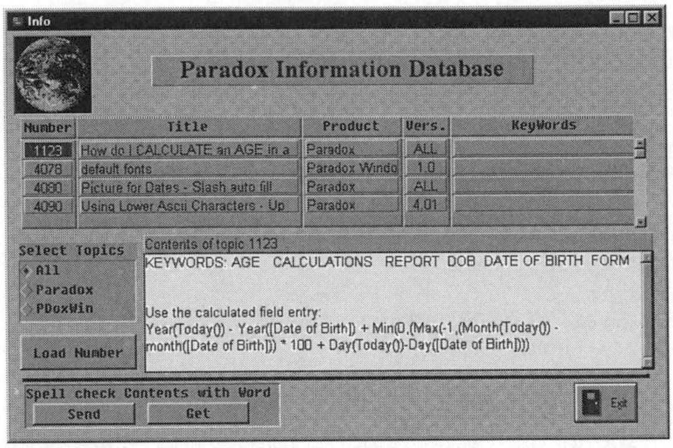

FIGURE 27.2.
APPS\INFO\INFO.FSL uses Word for Windows to spell check text.

Table 27.2. Sample DDE applications, names, topics, and items.

Program	Application	DDE Topic	DDE Item
ObjectVision	Vision	OVD filename	Field name
Paradox	PDoxWin	Table filename	Field name
Word for Windows	WinWord	Document	Bookmark
WordPerfect for	WPWin	Document	not supported Win. v5
WordPerfect for	WPWin60_Macros	Document	not supported Win. v6
Quicken for	Quicken	System	SysItems, Windows ReturnMessage, Key

Limitations of DDE

DDE in Paradox is limited. You can't send values from another application to a Paradox form. You must use ObjectPAL to get the values from the other application. This is simply a matter of what has control. Paradox must have control, except when you use a TableView object. Another limitation is that Paradox doesn't support the system topic, which is a general-purpose topic that some applications support. Paradox can't exchange data through the system topic.

OLE Basics

NEW
Term

The term *OLE* stands for *object linking and embedding*. You use OLE to insert files from OLE servers into a Paradox table using the OLE field type or to an OLE object on a form or report. An *OLE client* is an application that uses the documents provided by an OLE server. Paradox is both an OLE server and client. An *OLE server* is an application that can provide access to its documents by means of OLE. An *OLE object* is the object the server shares. This object is similar to the document that an OLE server can save. An OLE object is stored in the OLE client much as a document is stored on a disk. An *OLE variable* is a handle to an OLE object. You use an OLE variable in ObjectPAL to manipulate an OLE object.

Using OLE

OLE is another tool that enables you to take advantage of another application. OLE enables you to insert objects created by OLE servers into forms and reports, or you can use them in fields of a table. You can use OLE to manage large numbers of files on disk. For example, you might browse through a database of AutoCAD drawings, which is actually a Windows metafile snapshot of a data file. Then, double-click on the drawing you want. The OLE link automatically brings up AutoCAD and feeds it the correct file. OLE fields enable you to store objects from other Windows applications in your database. You can create a database of your word processing documents or spreadsheets and manage them with Paradox.

OLE Version 1

Currently, two types of OLE are on the market: object linking and object embedding. Can Paradox OLE embed, link, or both? You can link to files using the command-line option in Windows Object Packager or through DDE Paste Link into a table's alphanumeric field.

OLE Version 2

Paradox now supports version two of OLE. With OLE 2, you can use the other application right in your database application; including its menus.

OLE Controls

OLE Controls (or OCX controls) are new to Windows 95/NT. The OLE control is a 32-bit version of the old 16-bit VBX controls. OLE controls are portable to DEC Alpha, MIPS, Apple Macintosh, and PowerPC environments.

Paradox 7.0 enables you to embed 32-bit OLE Custom Controls (OCXs) into Paradox forms. OCXs can be a complex miniature application such as an editor, spreadsheet, or even a graph engine. Each OCX surfaces methods, properties, and/or events, which the user can set and call during runtime or design-time.

Because OLE controls are a separate application running as a subprocess of Paradox, you will find the behavior is different from normal Paradox objects. Each OCX has its own child window on the form and its own message queue. This gives the OCX its own event model.

ObjectPAL and OLE

Through ObjectPAL, you can use Paradox as a client or server. You can use ObjectPAL to send data from Paradox to another application or to get values from another application. In ObjectPAL, you can retrieve data in two ways: from a table or from the Clipboard.

OLE Methods and Procedures

You can use the OLE methods and procedures and most of the methods and procedures from the AnyType type. Table 27.3 lists the OLE class of procedures and methods.

Table 27.3. OLE methods and procedures.

```
blank*

canLinkFromClipboard

canReadFromClipboard

dataType*

edit

enumServerClassNames

enumVerbs

getServerName

insertObject

isAssigned*

isBlank*

isFixedType*

isLinked

linkFromClipboard

readFromClipboard

writeToClipboard

unAssign*

updateLinkNow
```
*Inherited by the Anytype type

Table 27.4 describes some of the more important OLE methods.

Table 27.4. OLE methods and procedures descriptions.

Method	Description
canReadFromClipboard	Reports whether an OLE object can be pasted from the Clipboard into an OLE variable.
edit	Launches the OLE server and enables the user to edit the object or take another action.
enumVerbs	Creates a DynArray that lists the actions supported by the OLE server.
getServerName	Returns the name of the OLE server for an OLE object.
readFromClipboard	Pastes an OLE object from the Clipboard into an OLE variable.
writeToClipboard	Copies an OLE variable to the Clipboard.

OLEAuto Methods

OLE Automation is a way to manipulate an application's objects from outside that application. OLE Automation uses OLE's component object model, but can be implemented independently from the rest of OLE. With OLE Automation, you can do the following:

- Create objects for programming tools and macro languages.
- Create and manipulate objects from one application exposed in another.
- Create tools that access and manipulate objects.

Using *enumAutomationServers* ()

The procedure enumAutomationServers() reads the registry on the current machine and gathers all the available OLE servers, with a programmable interface. Following is the syntax:

enumAutomationServers (var *servers* Array[ ] String) Logical :

You can type in the following code into the pushButton method of button to list all the available OLE servers on your machine:

```
1: ;Button :: pushButton
2: method pushButton(var eventInfo Event)
3:    var
4:        dynServers    DynArray[] String
5:    endVar
6:
7:    enumautomationservers(dynServers)
8:    dynServers.view("Available OLE Automation Servers")
9: endMethod
```

Using *open*, *enumMethods*, and *version*

The open, enumMethods, and version methods enable you to open an OLE server and extract information. Following is the syntax for each:

open (const *serverName* String) Logical

enumMethods (var **methods** DynArray[ ] String) Logical

version ( ) String

The following example opens the Paradox OLE server and enumerates its methods to a dynamic array. Finally, it displays the version number.

```
 1: ;Button :: pushButton
 2: method pushButton(var eventInfo Event)
 3:    var
 4:       oa            OLEAuto
 5:       dynMethods    DynArray[] String
 6:    endVar
 7:
 8:    ;Open server.
 9:    oa.open("Paradox.Application")
10:
11:    ;Display methods
12:    oa.enumMethods(dynMethods)
13:    dynMethods.view("Paradox Methods")
14:
15:    ;Display version.
16:    view(oa.version())
17: endMethod
```

The OLEAuto methods enumObjects() and enumProperties() enable you to extract other types of information from OLE servers.

NOTE

Some of these methods of an OLE control might not be accessible by ObjectPAL because their types are not supported, in which case the prototype will show an asterisk (*).

Native Windows Controls

Paradox provides support for *native window controls* (NWC) to be used in forms. To ObjectPAL, native windows controls and OLE controls are virtually identical. Paradox has an OCX type wrapper inside of the Paradox form system so that native controls behave like OLE controls. All the OLEAuto programming concepts are applicable to native windows controls. The only difference (and benefit) is that there is no .OCX file (the code is stored in the Paradox DLLs). Table 27.5 lists all the OLEAuto methods and procedures.

Table 27.5. OLEAuto methods and procedures.

```
attach

close

enumAutomationServers

enumConstants

enumConstantValues

enumControls

enumEvents

enumMethods

enumObjects

enumProperties

enumServerInfo

first

invoke

next

open

openObjectTypeInfo

openTypeInfo

registerControl

unregisterControl

version
```

The New ^ Operator

Among the OLE Automation methods included with Paradox 7 (such as `FormOpen()`, `ScriptOpen()`, and so on), is `delete()`, which deletes a named file. The following is an example of using `delete()` with an OLEAuto variable.

NEW Feature

```
1: var
2:    oa OLEAuto
3: endvar
4: oa.open("Paradox.application")
5: oa.delete("customer.db")
```

In the preceding code, there is a conflict with the existing `delete()` method. You must use the new ^ operator (as in `oa^delete()`) which unambiguously identifies the method as an OLE method. An ObjectPAL method always overrides an automation method when using dot notation. Use the ^ to refer to automation methods in which there may be a conflict with an existing ObjectPAL method.

Using *enumServerClassNames()*

Use enumServerClassNames() to find the OLE servers on your system—specifically, the OLE verbs. For example, a Microsoft Word for Windows server name is either Microsoft Word 6.0 Document or Microsoft Word 6.0 Picture. The corresponding OLE verb you use in ObjectPAL to refer to the OLE server is either Word.Document.6 or Word.Picture.6. You find this information with the following code:

```
 1:  ;btnServers :: pushButton
 2:  method pushButton(var eventInfo Event)
 3:    var
 4:       dyn   DynArray[] AnyType
 5:       o     OLE
 6:    endVar
 7:
 8:    o.enumServerClassNames(dyn)
 9:    dyn.view("OLE Servers on system")
10: endmethod
```

Type the preceding code into the pushButton method of a button on a form. Run the form and click the button.

Using *insertObject()*

You can use insertObject() to insert a linked or embedded OLE object into an OLE variable. Following is the syntax for insertObject().

insertObject ( ) Logical

insertObject (const *fileName* String , const *link* Logical) Logical

insertObject (const *className* String) Logical

The first syntax is just like choosing Edit | Insert Object. In the second syntax, you insert the name of a file. Finally, in the third syntax, you specify the class of the object to insert. For example, place a button and an OLE object on a form and type the following into the pushButton method of a button:

```
 1:  ;btnInsertOLE :: pushButton
 2:  var
 3:    o  OLE
 4:  endVar
 5:  method pushButton(var eventInfo Event)
 6:    if not o.insertObject() then
 7:        errorShow()
 8:        fldOLE.value = o
 9:    endIf
10: endMethod
```

Using OLE Type *edit()*

The `edit()` method launches the OLE server application and gives control to the user when used with an OLE object. The argument `oleText` is a string that Paradox passes to the server application. Many server applications can display `oleText` in the title bar. For example, the following is the syntax template for `OLE :: edit`.

edit (const ***oleText*** String, const ***verb*** SmallInt) Logical

`edit` passes `verb` to the application server to specify an action to take. `verb` is an integer that corresponds to one of the OLE server's action constants. The meaning of `verb` varies from application to application, so a `verb` that is appropriate for one application may not be for another. Usually, you can pass an OLE server the number 1 to play or display the OLE object.

Using *CanReadFromClipboard()*

With ObjectPAL, you can read OLE data directly from the Windows Clipboard. You can use `canReadFromClipboard()` to test whether anything is on the Clipboard. The syntax is as follows:

canReadFromClipboard ( ) Logical

This method is useful in a routine that informs the user whether an operation is possible. `canReadFromClipboard()` returns `True` if an OLE object can be read from the Clipboard into an OLE variable; otherwise, it returns `False`. For example, type the following into the `pushButton` method of a button:

```
1:   ;Button :: pushButton
2:   method pushButton(var eventInfo Event)
3:      var
4:         o OLE
5:      endVar
6:
7:      view(o.canReadFromClipboard)
8:   endMethod
```

> **NOTE**
>
> Another technique you can use is to use the `timer` event method and check the result of `enumWindowNames()`. As an alternative to `enumWindowNames()`, you could use the Windows API `FindWindow` function for the OLE server's window title. When it is gone, kill the timer and assign the OLE variable.

Summary

In this chapter, you learned about DDE, OLE, OCX and the new OLEAuto type. All provide easy ways to exchange data with another Windows application. Although DDE and OLE are primarily interactive user features, you can carry out some interesting tasks with them in ObjectPAL. The primary difference between DDE and OLE has to do with what each one sends. DDE sends data and commands between two applications. OLE either embeds data directly into another application, or stores information about a link to a specific piece of data. OCX is an extension of OLE you can use to extend the objects in Paradox.

In Chapter 28, you'll learn more about how Paradox interacts with other applications.

Multimedia and ObjectPAL

28

IN THIS CHAPTER

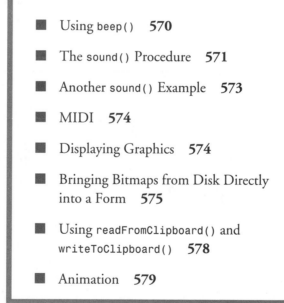

This chapter discusses two ways in which you can add sound to your Paradox applications—with built-in ObjectPAL methods and procedures, and with the Windows multimedia DLL. The beep() command in ObjectPAL enables you to beep your PC's speaker; it sounds the Windows default beep. The sound() command enables you to play sounds by using a sound card. It creates a sound of a specified frequency and duration. You use the Windows multimedia DLL to play .WAV files and other MCI files.

Using *beep()*

NEW
Term

A *beep* in computer programming terms is an audible sound produced by a computer speaker. beep() is a command in some computer languages, including ObjectPAL. You can use the beep() command to beep almost any computer (except for one that doesn't have even a small speaker). One way in which you can add sound to your applications is with the simple beep() procedure. beep() belongs to the System class of procedures. For example, to make every button in your application beep, use the beep() procedure in the isPreFilter of the form as in the following:

```
1:      ;Form :: pushButton
2:      method pushButton(var eventInfo Event)
3:          if eventInfo.isPreFilter() then
4:              ;This code executes for each object on the form
5:              beep()
6:          else
7:              ;This code executes only for the form
8:          endif
9:      endmethod
```

You can expand this technique and set it up as a configuration option.

Using *beep()* in *isPreFilter*

Suppose that you want to use the beep() procedure globally so that every button beeps when a setup field has the value Yes in it. This step by step example uses the prefilter section of the pushButton event of the form to trap for the pushButton event. Whenever a user presses a button, the pushButton event is sent first to the form's pushButton event where the code here causes the computer to beep.

You can find the BEEP.FSL form on the disc in the \ANSWERS directory.

Step By Step

1. Create a new form with a check box field named Beep that has the values Yes and No. Add two buttons to the form. You don't need to label them; they are used only for demonstration (see Figure 28.1).

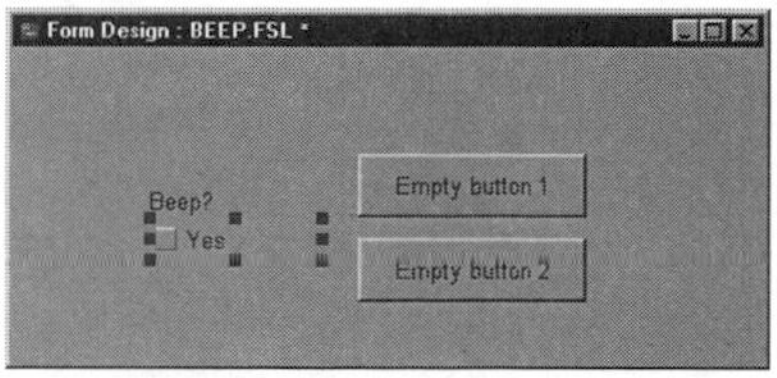

FIGURE 28.1.

Setup form for example.

2. Add line 5 to the form's pushButton method.

```
1:    ;Form :: pushButton
2:    method pushButton(var eventInfo Event)
3:    if eventInfo.isPreFilter() then
4:       ;This code executes for each object on the form
5:       if Beep = "Yes" then beep() endIf
6:    else
7:       ;This code executes only for the form
8:
9:    endIf
10:   endMethod
```

3. Check the syntax, run the form, and click the buttons. In this case, the dummy buttons do nothing but beep (see Figure 28.2).

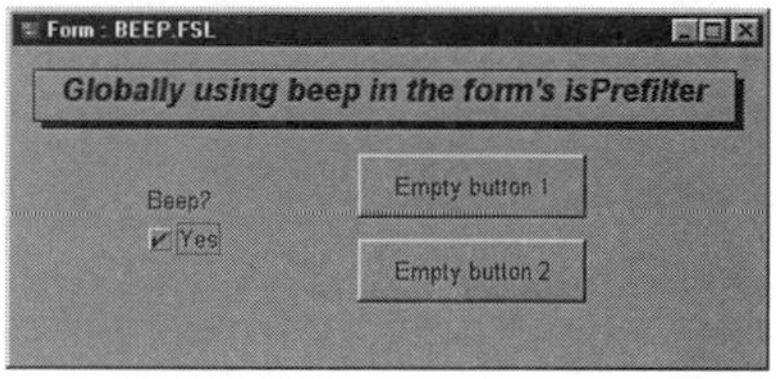

FIGURE 28.2.

BEEP.FSL. Using beep in the isPreFilter section of the pushButton method of the form to globally make every button beep.

Analysis

In step 2, line 5 checks whether the field named Beep is set to Yes. If it is, line 5 causes the computer to beep. What is powerful about this example is not this one line of code but rather the placement of this one line of code. Whenever a button is clicked, the method is sent first to the form's prefilter and then to the target object.

The *sound()* Procedure

sound() belongs to the System class of procedures. It creates a sound of a specified frequency and duration. The syntax for the sound procedure is as follows:

```
sound (const freqHertz, const durationMilliSecs LongInt)
```

sound() creates a sound of a specified frequency in Hertz (freqHertz) for a specified length of time in milliseconds (durationMilliSecs). The frequency values can range from 1 to 50,000 Hz. The audible limit for the human ear is approximately 16 Hz to 20,000 Hz.

Table 28.1 lists eight tones that you can use to construct your own melodies.

Table 28.1. Common tones.

Tone	Description
sound(130,240)	130 is C1
sound(146,240)	146 is D1
sound(164,240)	164 is E1
sound(174,240)	174 is F1
sound(195,240)	195 is G1
sound(220,240)	220 is A2
sound(249,240)	249 is B2
sound(265,240)	265 is C2

NOTE

In MIDI terminology, each note is given a number. For example, C2 is the same note as C1, but an octave higher.

Table 28.2 lists a duration for each type of note. Use the values when you create melodies.

Table 28.2. Common durations.

Note	Duration in Milliseconds
Whole note	960
Half note	480
Quarter note	240
Eighth note	120
Sixteenth note	60

The following code plays a C major scale in eighth notes except for the final C, which is a half note. Type lines 3–10 in the pushButton method of a button.

```
1:  ;Button :: pushButton
2:  method pushButton(var eventInfo Event)
3:      sound(130,120)
4:      sound(146,120)
5:      sound(164,120)
```

```
 6:        sound(174,120)
 7:        sound(195,120)
 8:        sound(220,120)
 9:        sound(249,120)
10:        sound(265,480)
11.  endmethod
```

You can use other elements of ObjectPAL to create interesting effects. See the following section for an example.

Another *sound()* Example

The following step by step example uses the ObjectPAL method rand() with the sound() procedure to play a random melody whenever the user clicks a button.

Creating Sounds of Random Duration

Suppose that you want to create a random note played for a random duration. To do this, use the rand() method to play a random note for a random duration. You should make sure that the note is within hearing range and has at least a certain minimum duration.

> You can find the SOUNDS.FSL form on the disc in the \ANSWERS directory.

Step By Step

1. Create a new form and place a button on it. Label it Using sound() with rand().

2. Add lines 3–20 to the pushButton method of the Using sound() with rand() button.

```
 1:    ;Button :: pushButton
 2:    method pushButton(var eventInfo Event)
 3:       var
 4:          freq, dur Number
 5:       endVar
 6:
 7:       freq = 0
 8:       dur = 0
 9:
10:       while freq < 110
11:          freq = rand()*1000
12:       endWhile
13:
14:       while dur < 60
15:          dur = rand() * 300
16:       endWhile
17:
18:       sound(freq, dur)
19:       sound(freq + 65, dur)
20:       sound(freq + 70, dur * 2)
21:    endmethod
```

3. Check the syntax, save the form as SOUNDS.FSL, run the form, and click the button. Figure 28.3 shows the SOUNDS.FSL form with three ways to add sound to your applications using beep(), sound(), and .WAV files.

FIGURE 28.3.

SOUNDS.FSL. Using beep(), sound(), *and* .WAV *files.*

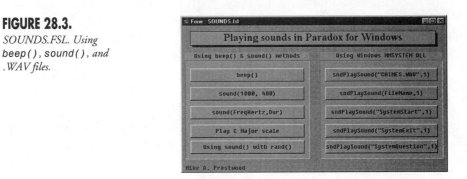

Analysis

In step 2, line 4 declares Number variables that will be used with rand() and sound(). Lines 7–8 set the variables you need. All variables must be set to a value before you can use them. Lines 10–12 generate a number that produces an audible tone. Lines 14–16 generate a reasonable duration. Anything shorter than 60 milliseconds is too short to be used in the routine in lines 18–20. Lines 18–20 play the first, third, and fifth notes of a major scale. These are the same notes in a major chord.

MIDI

NEW
Term

The term *MIDI* is an acronym for *musical instrument digital interface.* MIDI is a standard protocol that computers and musical instruments use to communicate with and control one another. Currently, Paradox doesn't support MIDI. If you need MIDI support, you have to call a DLL. Another, less elegant solution is to use an OLE field with a media player to play MIDI files.

Displaying Graphics

Graphics add flair and visual excitement to your forms. Pasting static graphics is fairly straightforward. In fact, Chapter 3 encouraged you to use graphics this way. Switching graphics while a form is running adds even more visual excitement to your applications and makes them more fun to use.

Graphics Methods and Procedures

ObjectPAL offers several methods you can use to read and write graphics from the Clipboard or directly from a file. Table 28.3 lists the Graphic class methods and procedures.

Table 28.3. The Graphic methods and procedures.

```
blank*

dataType*

isAssigned*

isBlank*

isFixedType*

readFromClipboard

readFromFile

writeToClipboard

writeToFile
```
*Inherited from `AnyType`

Bringing Bitmaps from Disk Directly into a Form

If a table is too large because too many graphics have been pasted into it, you can use the graphic `readFromFile()` method in a form to read the files in directly from disk. This has the benefit of storing the images outside of a table.

Displaying Bitmaps

This example demonstrates listing files on a disk and selectively reading them in with `readFromFile()`, and then displaying them on a form.

You can find the BMP.FSL form on the disc in the \ANSWERS directory.

Step By Step

1. Create a new form with a list field, a labeled field, and a button.
2. Label the button Display bitmap. Name the list field BMPField and its list object FileList. Name the labeled field SearchForField and change its label to Search For (see Figure 28.4).

FIGURE 28.4.

Setup form for displaying bitmaps example.

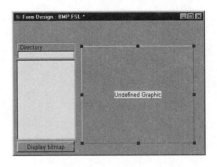

3. Add line 3 to the Var window of the form.

```
1:    ;Form :: Var
2:    Var
3:        fs    FileSystem
4:    endVar
```

4. Add line 3 to the open method of the SearchForField field.

```
1:    ;Field :: open
2:    method open(var eventInfo Event)
3:        self = windowsDir() + "\\*.BMP"
4:    endmethod
```

5. Add lines 3–18 to the newValue method of the SearchForField field.

```
1:    ;Field :: newValue
2:    method newValue(var eventInfo Event)
3:        if not SearchForField.isBlank() then
4:          if fs.findFirst(SearchForField) then
5:             BMPField.FileList.list.count = 0
6:             BMPField.FileList.list.selection = 1
7:             BMPField.FileList.list.value = fs.name()
8:             while fs.findNext()
9:               BMPField.FileList.list.selection =
10:              BMPField.FileList.list.selection +1
11:              BMPField.FileList.list.value = FS.name()
12:            endWhile
13:          else
14:             BMPField.FileList.list.count = 0
15:             BMPField.FileList.list.selection = 1
16:             BMPField.FileList.list.value = "File not found"
17:          endIf
18:        endIf
19:    endmethod
```

6. Add lines 3–10 to the `pushButton` method of the Display bitmap button.

```
1:    ;Button :: pushButton
2:    method pushButton(var eventInfo Event)
3:       var
4:          g Graphic
5:          s1, s2, s3, s4 String
6:       endVar
7:
8:       splitFullFileName(fs.fullName(),s1, s2, s3, s4)
9:       g.readFromFile(s1 + s2 + BMPField)
10:      GraphicField = g
11:   endmethod
```

7. Check the syntax, save your work, and run the form. Select a bitmap and click the button to display it. Your form should look similar to Figure 28.5 when you're done with this example.

FIGURE 28.5.

BMP.FSL. Listing and displaying bitmaps.

Analysis

You're already familiar with steps 2 through 5. They were used in the example called "Finding a File," in Chapter 25.

In step 6, line 4 declares a graphics variable for use in lines 9 and 10. Line 5 declares four `String` variables for use with `splitFullFileName()` in line 8. Line 8 splits the current file system variable into its four components: drive letter, path, filename, and file extension.

Line 9 uses the drive letter (stored in `s1`), the path (stored in `s2`), and the user's selection to read in a bitmap from a disk. Line 10 sets the value for the `GraphicField` object to the bitmap brought into `g`.

You can use the technique you learned in this example to load files from a disk. You even can apply this technique to a table frame by following these steps:

1. Create a table with an alphanumeric field.
2. In each record, place the name of the graphics file with the full path.
3. Create a tabular form that is bound to the table that you created.
4. Place a graphics object.

5. In the `arrive` method of the tableFrame field object, place the following code:

```
 1:   ;TableFrame.Field :: arrive
 2:   method arrive(var eventInfo MoveEvent)
 3:      var
 4:         g Graphic
 5:         s String
 6:      endVar
 7:
 8:      s = tableframeFieldObjectName
 9:      g.readFromFile(s)
10:      graphicObjectName = g
11:   endMethod
```

As you scroll through the records, the graphics file is read into the graphics object. You don't need to be in Edit mode. You also might check the read-only property of the `tableFrame` field object.

Sound and graphics add flair to your applications and make them fun to use. You might not always have the time to add these extra features to your applications, but your users will appreciate it when you do.

Another technique to read a file in from diskette is to use the `value` property of a graphic field. The form \APPS\FELICIA\FELICIA.FSL uses this technique. The interesting piece of code is a procedure that is part of the timer method of the bitmap. Note that line 6 below uses the `value` property of the graphic object.

```
1:   Proc cpFindBitmap()
2:      if not fs.findNext() then
3:         fs.findFirst(windowsDir() + "\\*.BMP")
4:      endIf
5:
6:      self.value = windowsDir() + "\\" + fs.name()
7:   endProc
```

Using *readFromClipboard()* and *writeToClipboard()*

On the disc included with this book is the form GRAPHICS.FSL, which is a simple demonstration of using `readFromClipboard()` and `writeToClipboard()` (see Figure 28.6). This form writes to the Clipboard the graphics on the left and then reads that graphics from the Clipboard into the object on the right.

```
1:   ;Button :: pushButton
2:   method pushButton(var eventInfo Event)
3:      var
4:         bmpOriginal Graphic
5:         bmpTemp     Graphic
6:      endVar
7:
8:      bmpOriginal = bmp1.value
```

```
 9:     bmpOriginal.writeToClipBoard()
10:
11:     bmpTemp.readFromClipboard()
12:
13:     bmp2.value = bmpTemp
14:  endmethod
```

FIGURE 28.6.

GRAPHICS.FSL demonstrates reading bitmaps from disk.

Animation

There are many ways to create and play animation in ObjectPAL. You can animate with a TCursor and a Graphic field by cycling through the table. You can animate using the `visible` property, making one picture or element visible at a time. A similar technique is to use `bringToFront()`. Finally, you can use OLE to play AVI files (short movies). See the file ANSWERS\OLE2.FSL for an example of playing an AVI file (see Figure 28.7). After you embed the OLE object, you can use the following code to play any Media Manager object. In this example, the user just clicks the object.

```
1:  ;Object :: Var
2:  Var
3:    o  OLE
4:  endVar
```

```
1:  ;Object :: mouseClick
2:  method mouseClick(var eventInfo MouseEvent)
3:    o = self.value
4:    o.edit("", 0)
5:  endmethod
```

> **TIP**
>
> My favorite way to animate in ObjectPAL is to read in all the graphics from a table into an array and then cycle through the graphics.

FIGURE 28.7.

OLE2.FSL playing an .AVI animation file with Media Player.

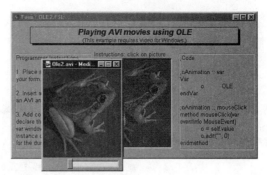

Using a Table to Animate

Suppose that you want to add a spinning animation to your application to add that extra bit of flair. This next step by step example uses a table with graphics in it to store the images. The images are then read into an array of graphics (now all the images are in memory). Once the images are in memory, a `timer` event is used to cycle through and display the images.

You can find the ANIMATE.FSL form on the disc in the \ANSWERS directory.

Step By Step

1. Change your working directory to the TUTORIAL directory and create a new form with an undefined graphic field on it (see Figure 28.8).

FIGURE 28.8.

Setup form for using table to animate example.

2. In the open method of the undefined graphic field, type lines 3–5:

```
1:    ;fldGraphic :: open
2:      Var
3:        lDirectionFlag    Logical
4:        lPosition         SmallInt
5:        arAnimation       Array[] Graphic
6:      endVar
```

Chapter 28

3. In the open method of the undefined graphic field, type lines 3–18:

```
1:    ;fldGraphic :: open
2:    method open(var eventInfo Event)
3:       var
4:          to TCursor
5:       endVar
6:
7:       DoDefault              ;Finish opening object.
8:
9:       tc.open("ANIMATE.DB")
10:
11:      scan tc:
12:         arAnimation.setSize(arAnimation.size() + 1)
13:         arAnimation[tc.recNo()] = tc.(2)
14:      endScan
15:
16:      lPosition = 1          ;Set starting position.
17:      lDirectionFlag = True ;Set start direction.
18:      self.setTimer(100)     ;Set speed of animation.
19:   endmethod
```

4. In the timer method of the undefined graphic field, type lines 3–19:

```
1:    ;fldGraphic :: timer
2:    method timer(var eventInfo TimerEvent)
3:       switch
4:        case lDirectionFlag = True :              ;Forward direction.
5:         if lPosition = arAnimation.size() then;If at end,
6:            lDirectionFlag = False               ;move backward.
7:         else
8:            self = arAnimation[lPosition]
9:            lPosition = lPosition + 1
10:        endIf
11:
12:        case lDirectionFlag = False :  ;Backward direction.
13:         if lPosition = 1 then
14:            lDirectionFlag = True       ;Next time move forward.
15:         else
16:            self = arAnimation[lPosition]
17:            lPosition = lPosition - 1
18:        endIf
19:      endSwitch
20:   endmethod
```

5. Check the syntax, save the form as ANIMATE.FSL, and run it (see Figure 28.9).

FIGURE 28.9.

The ANIMATE.FSL form demonstrates animating spinning objects.

Analysis

Step 3 uses a TCursor and a scan loop to read in all the graphic images into an array of graphic variables.

Step 4 cycles through the Array forward and then backward. This gives the images a sense of animation.

Summary

In this chapter, you learned two ways in which to add sound to your Paradox applications with beep() and sound(). The beep() command in ObjectPAL enables you to beep your PC's speaker. The sound() command enables you to play sounds by using a sound card. You also learned about how to add animation to your applications using a TCursor and a Graphic field by cycling through graphics. Finally, you learned how to use OLE to play AVI files (short movies).

Special Topics

V

PART

Debugging and Dealing with Runtime Errors

29

Until now, it's been assumed that you are an excellent typist. Occasionally, you might have typed a routine incorrectly. In those cases, you either spotted the typo and debugged the routine or ran the program from the ANSWERS directory. This next section formally introduces the Debugger. It gives you the tools you need to debug your code with confidence.

ObjectPAL offers an advanced debugging tool called the ObjectPAL Debugger. The Debugger is a set of features built into the ObjectPAL Editor that helps you debug your application. With the debugger, you can inspect variables, list the events called, step through code, and monitor various elements of your application.

Using the Debugger

The debugger included in Paradox is very powerful. You can view your running application using the following debugger windows: Breakpoints, Call Stack, Watches, Tracer, and Debugger (see Figure 29.1).

FIGURE 29.1.

The new enhanced debugger.

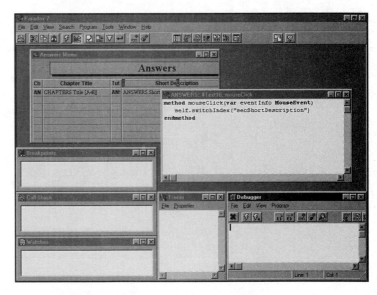

Entering and Exiting the Debugger

Any time that you are in the ObjectPAL Editor, you can open any of the five ObjectPAL Debugger windows from the View menu or with the appropriate Toolbar icons. If your form or script is running, you can enter the Debugger in three ways:

■ If Compile with Debug is checked, add a debug() procedure to your code and run the form.

- If Enable Ctrl+Break is checked, use Ctrl+Break when the form is running.
- Set a breakpoint and run the form.

Placing a debug() statement in a method has the same effect as setting a breakpoint at a line. The advantage of debug() is that it is saved with the source code, so you don't have to keep resetting it as you would with a breakpoint. The setting for Compile with Debug is saved with the form and determines whether debug() statements are ignored. When this option isn't checked, debug() statements are ignored. There is no need to uncheck this option before you deliver a form because the compiler strips out all debug() statements before it compiles. Using the debug() statement will not interrupt execution when the user runs the form.

To use the debug() procedure, follow these steps:

1. Place debug() in your code.
2. Make sure that Compile with Debug is checked.
3. Run the form.

One advantage of using the debug() procedure instead of setting a breakpoint is the capability to use it conditionally. For example:

```
1:    if siCounter > 100 then
2:        ;Execute code.
3:    else
4:        debug()
5:    endIf
```

> **NOTE**
>
> When using a debug() statement in a library, the Compile with Debug option must be selected from within the library for it to take effect.

The Breakpoints Window

A *breakpoint* is a flag that you can set in your code that stops a form during runtime and enters the Debugger. The Debugger enables you to inspect variables, step through your code, and much more. The most common way of entering the Debugger is by setting a breakpoint. When you choose Program | Toggle Breakpoint, the visual minus sign appears next to the active line (see Figure 29.2). Go ahead and type the code that you see in Figure 29.2, put the cursor on the second msgStop(), and select Program | Toggle Breakpoint. In addition to selecting Toggle Breakpoint, you can double-click to the left of the line of code where you want to place a breakpoint.

NEW
Term

FIGURE 29.2.

Setting a breakpoint.

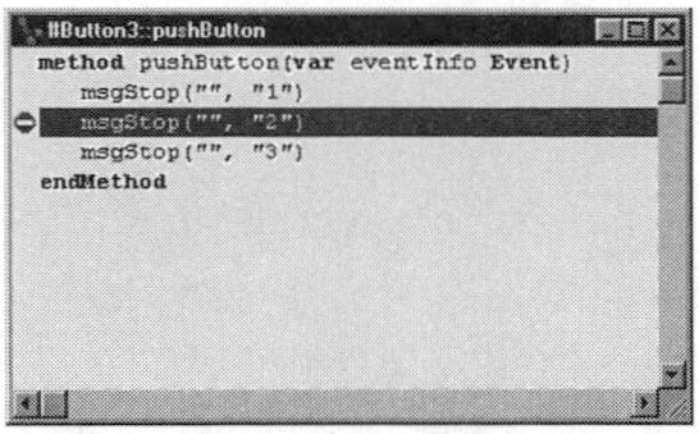

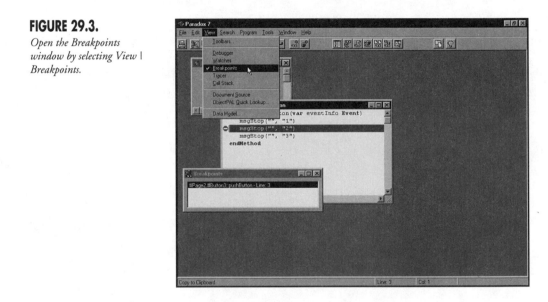

To see the currently set breakpoints, toggle the Breakpoints window open by selecting View | Breakpoints (see Figure 29.3). Right-click the Breakpoints window to gain access to its menu.

FIGURE 29.3.

Open the Breakpoints window by selecting View | Breakpoints.

When you run the form, execution stops at the second `msgInfo()`—right where you placed the breakpoint (see Figure 29.4). Note that the pointer turns into a stop sign while you are in debug mode.

When you are in debug mode, you have many options. For now, just select Program | Run or press F8 to continue execution. To use breakpoints, follow these steps:

1. Select the method in which you want to put a breakpoint—for example, `pushButton`, `newValue`, and so on.

2. Place the cursor on the line on which you want the breakpoint to occur.

3. Select Program | Toggle Breakpoint.

4. Run the form.

5. To view the current breakpoints, select View | Breakpoints to display the Breakpoints windows.

FIGURE 29.4.

Stopping at a breakpoint opens the Debugger window.

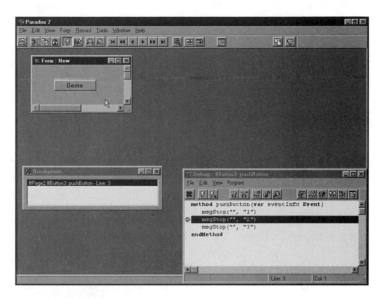

The Call Stack Window

The Call Stack window is used after execution stops at a breakpoint. Select View | Call Stack to toggle the Call Stack window open. The Call Stack window lists all the events, custom methods, and custom procedures called since the form started running. The most recently called routine and its caller are listed first. This process continues all the way back to the first method or procedure.

The Call Stack window is most useful when you want to know where you are. For example, if you've called several custom methods in your code and you want to verify that a certain custom method was called, use View | Call Stack. To use the Call Stack window, follow these steps:

1. Set a breakpoint at the place in your code from which you want to start viewing the stack.
2. Run the form.
3. When the breakpoint occurs, select View | Call Stack. A list of all the called methods appears. Right-click the Call Stack window to view its menu.

The Watch Window

The Watch window enables you to watch variables as your form executes. To toggle the Watches window open, select View | Watches. To add a watch, select Program | Add Watch, or right-click on the Watch window (see Figure 29.5).

FIGURE 29.5.
*The Watch window allows
you to watch variables.*

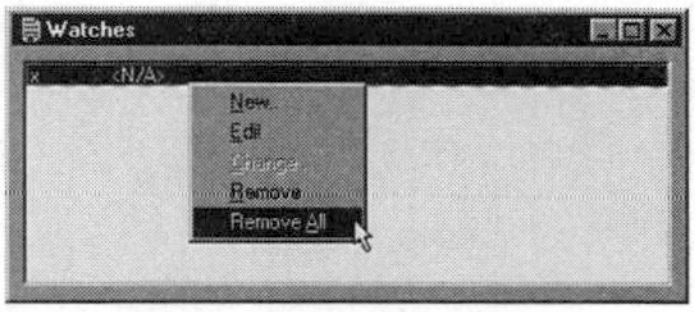

The Tracer Window

ObjectPAL offers a powerful tracing utility that enables you to view the behind-the-scenes activity of your application. You can start the tracer before you run your form while in the Editor. A window that logs all the activity of your code and the events pops up.

The Properties | Tracer On option in the Tracer window toggles the tracer on. When the form is open, a window opens that traces the form, script, or report.

The Properties | Show Code option in the Tracer window toggles on and off whether the Tracer lists each line of code as it executes.

The Properties | Built-Ins option in the Tracer window allows you to select any events that you wish to trace. If you check the Properties | Tracer On option and you haven't selected any events to trace, the ObjectPAL tracer opens a window and lists each line of code as it executes. Use this method to trace only the code that you write. This is a wonderful way to find the location of a problem. To trace your code, follow these steps:

1. Make sure that Program | Compile with Debug is checked in the main Paradox menu.
2. Select Properties | Tracer On from the Tracer menu. Make sure that no built-in methods are checked.
3. Make sure that Properties | Show Code is checked from the Tracer menu.
4. Run the form.

> **NOTE**
>
> The tracer requires that you have Program | Compile with Debug checked in order to trace your code. Compile with Debug has no effect on tracing built-in event methods.

Tracing Built-In Methods

In addition to tracing only your code, you can trace your code and the events. If you check the View | Tracer option and select some events to trace, the ObjectPAL tracer opens a window and lists each line of code and each event as it executes.

Checking an event indicates that you want that method traced; unchecked methods are not traced. It doesn't matter whether the method has code attached to it. If you check the method, it will be traced. Figure 29.6 shows the Select Built-In Methods for Tracing dialog box with the action method select. The action method is perhaps the most important event to trace.

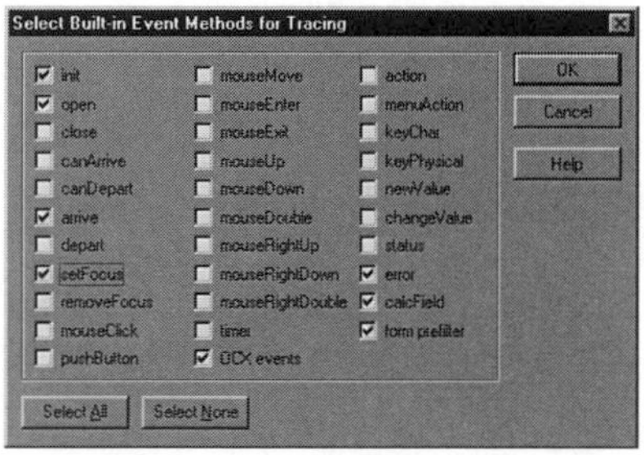

FIGURE 29.6.

The Select Built-In Event Methods for Tracing dialog box.

When the box labeled Form Prefilter is checked, methods are traced as they execute for the form and for the intended target object. Otherwise, methods are traced only for the target object. Your settings for these options are saved with the form, so you don't have to check them every time you want to trace execution. When the Tracer is open, execution proceeds normally. ObjectPAL provides procedures for controlling the tracer. To trace your code and the events, follow these steps:

1. Select Properties | Built-In Events. Choose the built-in event methods that you want to trace (see Figure 29.6 shown previously). You can check any combination of methods, but the fewer you check, the better. It will be easier to follow.

2. Make sure that Properties | Trace On is checked.

3. Run the form.

You also can use the tracerOn() procedure in your ObjectPAL code, but you still have to manually select the combination of methods that you want to trace.

The Debugger Window

You can get into and out of the Debugger, but what can you do with it? When execution stops at a breakpoint, you can inspect variables. Paradox has a built-in way to check a variable's value at a certain point in your code. To check a value, set a break at the point in your code at which you want to check a variable, and run the form. When your program breaks, select Program | Inspect to inspect as many different variables as you want.

There are three steps in inspecting a variable:

1. Set a breakpoint at the place in your code where you want to view a variable.
2. Run the form.
3. When the breakpoint occurs, select Program | Inspect from the Debug window and type the name of the variable that you want to see.

The options in the Debugger window fall into these four categories:

- Entering and exiting the Debugger
- Inspecting variables
- Stepping through the application
- Monitoring the application

The following paragraphs describe the more important options in the Debugger.

Program | Run: You can select this option before or after you set breakpoints or while you're in the Debugger. Using this option is equivalent to selecting Form | View Data. If you haven't set any breakpoints, Run does nothing extra. After you set breakpoints, select Program | Run to run the form. Paradox saves all attached methods, compiles the code, and runs the form. When Paradox encounters a breakpoint, execution halts and a Debugger window opens. In effect, this is how you enter the Debugger. When you're in a Debugger window, this option enables you to continue execution from the breakpoint.

Program | Step Over: Select Program | Step Over to step through your code line by line. You can use this option after execution stops at a breakpoint.

Program | Step Into: Select Program | Step Into to step through every line in a custom procedure. You can use this option after execution stops at a breakpoint.

Program | Stop Execution: Select Program | Stop Execution to exit the Debugger. This option halts execution and closes any Debugger windows. You can use this option after execution stops at a breakpoint.

Program | Inspect: Select Program | Inspect to display and change the value of a variable. You can use this option when execution stops at a breakpoint.

Program | Origin: Select Program | Origin to return to the method that contains the current breakpoint. The cursor will appear on the line that contains the breakpoint. You can use this convenient feature when execution suspends at a breakpoint and your screen becomes cluttered.

Program | Compile with Debug: Check Program | Compile with Debug to stop execution when the debug() statement is encountered. Placing a debug() statement in a method has the same effect as setting a breakpoint at that line. Unlike a breakpoint, the debug() procedure can be saved as part of your code. This option tells Paradox to provide more detailed error information. In most situations, I recommend that you leave Compile with Debug checked, even if you never use the debug() statement.

WARNING

When do you want to uncheck Compile with Debug? Breakpoints can be saved in code. Leaving on Compile with Debug during development is okay, but it is recommended that you turn it off if you plan to distribute non-delivered forms, libraries, or scripts. With Compile with Debug checked, your form, library, or script is about one-third larger and runs slower. For best performance, turn off Compile with Debug if you distribute undelivered forms, libraries, or scripts.

Enable Ctrl+Break: If you check Enable Ctrl+Break, pressing Ctrl+Break in the ObjectPAL Preferences dialog box, execution suspends and opens a Debugger window that contains the active method or procedure. This operation is similar to setting a breakpoint. If Enable Ctrl+Break to Debugger isn't checked, pressing Ctrl+Break still works, but it only halts execution. Although Ctrl+Break halts the execution of ObjectPAL methods and procedures, other operations, such as queries, are not affected.

It is also important to note that Enable Ctrl+Break will stop execution when Ctrl+Break is pressed, but you must also check Compile with Debug in order for Ctrl+Break to enter the Debugger.

TIP

Here is an undocumented tip. If you're like most programmers, the default error messages make sense most of the time, but not always. Select Program | Compile with Debug to get better error messages from the compiler. This applies even if you don't use the debug() procedure.

The Enable Ctrl+Break Option

To get into the Debugger easily, use the Enable Ctrl+Break option and press Ctrl+Break. This technique suspends execution when your form is running. It enables you to decide on the fly whether—and where—you want to interrupt execution. Although this technique is less precise than setting a specific breakpoint or using the debug() procedure, you'll like its flexibility. To use Ctrl+Break, follow these steps:

1. Select the Edit | Developer Preferences and check the Enable Ctrl+Break option on the General tab.

2. Run the form.

3. Press Ctrl+Break when you want to move into the Debugger.

Stepping Through Your Application

Selecting Program | Step Over enables you to step through your code line by line. Selecting Program | Step Into enables you to step through every line in a method and through every line in a custom procedure that it calls.

To step through your code, follow these steps:

1. Set a breakpoint at the place in your code that you want to start stepping through.
2. Run the form.
3. When the breakpoint occurs, select Program | Step Into or Program | Step Over to execute the next piece of code.

If you want to try this, make sure that Compile with Debug is checked. Place the following code on a button and run the form:

```
1:     ;Button :: pushButton
2:     method pushButton(var eventInfo Event)
3:        debug()
4:
5:        message("1")
6:        message("2")
7:        message("3")
8:        message("4")
9:     endmethod
```

After you run the form, click the button. The Debugger window opens. Select Program | Step Into repeatedly to step through the messages.

Debugging Without the Debugger

The Debugger is wonderful. Often, however, it's just as easy to debug code without the Debugger as it is to set a breakpoint and go into the Debugger. This section discusses general debugging techniques.

Debugging means locating the places where your application or routine doesn't work—but also the places where it does. If you're debugging, you're at a place where your application doesn't work, and you need to get to a place where it does work. One popular technique is to strip code and objects until something works, and then rebuild. ObjectPAL offers several ways to debug without the Debugger.

Types of Errors

A *logic error* is an error in thinking. Often, you try to code something that doesn't make sense because it's a logic error. Logic errors are among the most difficult types of errors to diagnose. If you knew that your thinking was wrong, you wouldn't try to implement the code in the first place! A *runtime error* is an error that occurs while a form is being run, even though the routine has passed a syntax check. A *syntax error* is an error that occurs because of an incorrectly expressed statement. Syntax errors usually occur when you mistype a command or when you attempt to use a command that doesn't exist.

> **TIP**
>
> If you want tighter, cleaner code, turn on the Compiler Warnings option. It gives you better control over your code. For example, not declaring variables slows down your code. The Compiler Warnings option catches undeclared variables and warns you. To turn on this option, go into the ObjectPAL Editor and select Properties | Compiler Warnings.

Use an *if* Statement to See Whether a Routine Is Successful

A technique commonly used for error checking is to use an `if` statement. Many methods and procedures return a Logical, and display or do one thing when a routine succeeds and another when it fails. For example, type the following into the `pushButton` method of a button.

```
1:  ;Button :: pushButton
2:  method pushButton(var eventInfo Event)
3:    if isFile("AUTOEXEC.BAT") then   ;If exists, then
4:      message("File exists")         ;display "File exists".
5:    else                             ;If not,
6:      message("File does not exist") ;dislplay "File does not".
7:    endIf
8:  endMethod
```

I used a variation of the preceding error-checking routine in the form `open` routines in an earlier chapter:

```
1:  if f.attach("My Form") then   ;MY FORM is a title.
2:    f.moveTo()
3:  else
4:    f.open("MYFORM")            ;MYFORM is a filename.
5:  endIf
```

You can use an `if` structure for many methods and procedures to give the user a better user-oriented message than the programmer-oriented, built-in error messages. For example, type the following code into the `pushButton` method of a button:

```
1:    ;Button :: pushButton
2:    method pushButton(var eventInfo Event)
3:      var
4:        tbl  Table
5:      endVar
```

```
 6:
 7:        if isTable("WORLD.DB") then
 8:            tbl.attach("WORLD.DB")
 9:        else
10:            msgStop("Oops!", "Could not find WORLD.DB. Check your working
               directory")
11:        endIf
12:    endMethod
```

`Table.attach()` returns `True` if the Table variable is associated with the table name. It doesn't report whether it is a valid table, or even that the file exists!

Use *errorShow()* in an *if* Statement

With Paradox, you can utilize the built-in error stack. To do this, you use the `errorShow()` procedure. The `errorShow()` procedure displays the error dialog box with the current error information from the error stack. For example, type the following code into the `pushButton` method of a button:

```
 1: ;Button :: pushButton
 2: method pushButton(var eventInfo Event)
 3:   var
 4:       tc TCursor
 5:   endVar
 6:
 7:   if not tc.open("xyz") then
 8:       errorShow("Table xyz is missing or corrupt", "Try rebuilding or
            reinstalling")
 9:   endIf
10: endMethod
```

If the open method fails for any reason, an error message is displayed. You won't see benefits of this type of error checking while you develop. Instead, the benefits come when users use your program. Without this extra code, you might get a telephone call from a user who says, "The program doesn't work. When I click this button, nothing happens." With the extra code, the user would get a specific message—for example, an error saying that a table doesn't exist (see Figure 29.7). The user could check whether the table exists on the disk, and you would be spared the telephone call.

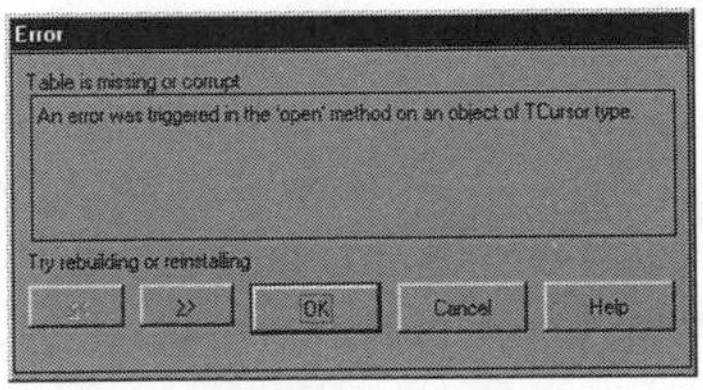

FIGURE 29.7.

Using the `errorShow()`
procedure.

The `errorShow()` procedure also can accept two optional string parameters that you can use to add text to the error box. When you use hundreds of `errorShow()` procedures in a large project, adding text to the error box can really help. The following is the complete syntax for `errorShow()`:

```
errorShow( [const topHelp String, [const bottomHelp String]] )
```

You can use topHelp and bottomHelp for anything you wish, but here is a suggestion. Use the topHelp for the name of the object followed by the path to the code, and bottomHelp for extra information. For example:

```
1:  if not tc.open("LINEITEM") then
2:     errorShow("Secrets.fsl :: button1 :: pushButton", "Open routine failed")
3:  endIf
```

Use *view()* to View a Variable

Sometimes, it's convenient to use view() to view a variable in your code. view() also provides a stopping point that can help you narrow down a problem. For example, type the following into the pushButton method of a button.

```
 1:    ;Button :: pushButton
 2:    method pushButton(var eventInfo Event)
 3:       var
 4:          s1, s2, s3 String
 5:       endVar
 6:
 7:       s1 = "Tim"
 8:       s1.view()
 9:       s2 = "Keely"
10:       s2.view()
11:       s3 = s1 + " " + s2
12:       s3.view()
13:    endMethod
```

This code doesn't shed light on any problems because it has no bugs. The code demonstrates, however, how view(), heavily used, breaks a large piece of code into smaller parts. If a problem existed, you might get a view box before the problem appeared. That would enable you to get closer to the problem. The closer you are to a problem, the easier it is to fix. You also can turn on the Compile with Debug option to receive better error messages.

Table 29.1 describes many methods and procedures that you can use to deal with errors.

Table 29.1. Methods and procedures used for dealing with errors.

Method or Procedure	Description
errorCode	Reports the status of the error flag
getTarget	Returns the name of the target of an event
isFirstTime	Reports whether the form is handling an event for the first time before it dispatches it
isPreFilter	Reports whether the form is handling a form event

continues

Table 29.1. continued

Method or Procedure	Description
isTargetSelf	Reports whether an object is the target of an event
reason	Reports why an event occurred
setErrorCode	Sets the error code for an event
setReason	Specifies a reason for generating an event
constantNameToValue	Returns the numeric value of a constant
constantValueToName	Returns the name of a constant
debug	Halts execution of a method and invokes the Debugger id Compile with Debug is checked
errorClear	Clears the error stack
errorCode	Returns a number that lists the most recent runtime error or error condition
errorLog	Adds information to the error stack
errorHasErrorCode	Check the error stack for a specific error
errorHasNativeErrorCode	Checks the error stack for a specific SQL error
errorMessage	Returns the text of the most recent error message
errorNativeCode	Returns the error code from an SQL server
errorPop	Removes the top layer of information from the error stack
errorShow	Displays an error dialog box
errorTrapOnWarnings	Specifies whether ObjectPAL handles warning errors as critical errors
isErrorTrapOnWarnings	Specifies whether errorTrapOnWarnings is toggled on
fail	Causes a method to fail
tracerClear	Clears the Tracer window
tracerHide	Hides the Tracer window
tracerOff	Closes the Tracer window
tracerOn	Activates code tracing
tracerSave	Saves the contents of the Tracer window to a file
tracerShow	Makes the Tracer window visible
tracerToTop	Makes the Tracer window the top window
tracerWrite	Writes a message to the Tracer window

Use *msgInfo()* and *sleep()* to Overcome Timing Problems

You can use msgInfo(), msgStop(), or any procedure that stops execution to fix or at least test for timing problems. Occasionally, timing problems interfere with your code. For example, you might open a TCursor too close to a running query. Or, you might have too many forms closing too quickly for Windows to handle, and a GPF (general protection fault) results. Whenever you suspect that timing might be causing a problem, use msgInfo() to stop execution as a test. If using msgInfo() solves the problem, use sleep(100) to put the code to sleep for one-tenth of a second between the tasks.

Use the *fullName* Property

If you're having trouble with scope or the containership hierarchy and you need to know the full containership path of an object, use the following example. It assumes that an object named theBox is on a form:

```
1:    ;Button :: pushButton
2:    method pushButton(var eventInfo Event)
3:        message("Full containership path is " + theBox.fullName)
4:    endMethod
```

Sometimes you'll be surprised about the full path of an object. Using the fullName property involves checking yourself. Some people call this type of debugging a reality check because you test your own perception of what's going on. If you're absolutely positive that an object has a certain path, do a reality check with fullName.

Using the Object Tree

Another way to check an object's path is to use the Object Tree inspector. The Object Tree is part of the Object Explorer and is a visual hierarchical display of a form and its containers. The Object Tree is most valuable when you come back to your own old code or analyze someone else's application. It's also a valuable everyday tool for opening many methods and for accessing stacked objects more easily. You can even print the Object Tree for a permanent printed record (see Figure 29.8).

FIGURE 29.8.

The Object Tree enables you to see all the objects.

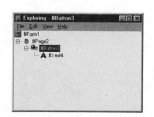

Warning and Critical Errors

In ObjectPAL, two levels of errors occur: warning errors and critical errors. Because warning errors aren't critical errors, they display nothing during runtime, or, at most, a message in the status bar. A key violation error is an example of this type of error. If you want to include a higher level of error trapping in your applications, use one of the following techniques:

■ If the method or procedure returns a Logical, use it in an if statement.

■ Use errorShow() to display the built-in error messages.

■ Use a try structure to trap for errors.

Warning errors do not stop execution, whereas critical errors do. To illustrate, type the following code into the pushButton method of a button.

```
 1:   ;btn1 :: pushButton
 2:   method pushButton(var eventInfo Event)
 3:     var
 4:        tc   TCursor
 5:     endVar
 6:
 7:     errorTrapOnWarnings(No)        ;Make sure warning errors
 8:                                    ;stay warning errors.
 9:
10:   msgInfo("", "Before error")
11:   tc.open("123xyz")               ;123xyz does not exist.
12:   msgInfo("", "After error")      ;This message does appear.
13: endmethod
```

Now, raise the warning error to a critical error. Type the following:

```
 1:   method pushButton(var eventInfo Event)
 2:     var
 3:        tc   TCursor
 4:     endVar
 5:
 6:     errorTrapOnWarnings(Yes)       ;Raise warning errors to
 7:                                    ;critical errors.
 8:
 9:     msgInfo("", "Before error")
10:   tc.open("123xyz")               ;123xyz does not exist.
11:   msgInfo("", "After error")      ;Note that this message never appears.
12: endmethod
```

This is an important part of dealing with errors. Note that warning errors do not stop execution of code, whereas critical errors do (see Figure 29.9).

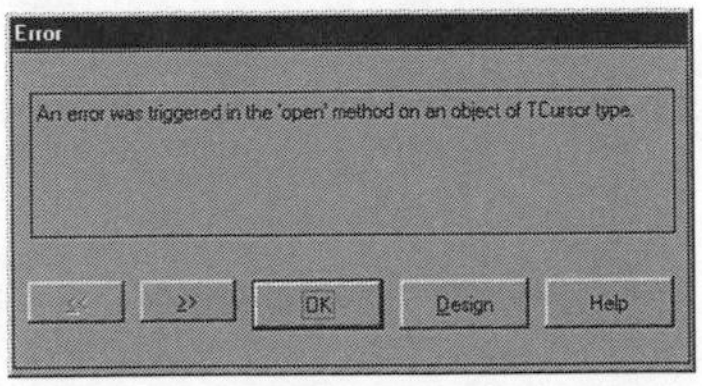

FIGURE 29.9.

Critical errors stop execution.

Using the *try* Structure

To deal with errors yourself, you can place a `try` structure around your code. If an error is detected, you can use `reTry`, execute optional code, or display an error message that's better or more complete than the built-in error message. The following code uses a variation of this technique. It displays the built-in error messages, which normally wouldn't be triggered:

```
1:   errorTrapOnWarnings(yes)
2:   try
3:      ;Your code here
4:   onFail
5:      msgStop( errorCode(), errorMessage() )
6:      ;You could also use errorShow()
7:   endTry
```

Use `errorTrapOnWarnings(Yes)` to raise warning errors to critical. If you wish to write really tight ObjectPAL code, do the following three things:

- Use `errorTrapOnWarnings(Yes)` in the open method of every form.
- Make sure that Properties | Show Compiler Warnings is checked for every form.
- Make sure that Properties | Compile with Debug is checked for every form.

Sometimes, however, you will want to turn off `errorTrapOnWarnings()`. The most common time is when you are using the warning error in an `if` statement.

Another technique to raise warning errors to critical is with `setReason()`. Suppose that you wish to use `setReason()` to raise warning errors to critical. You might wish to use this technique when filtering out reasons. Add lines 2–4 to the error method of the form.

```
1:   ;Form :: Error Prefilter
2:   method pushButton(var eventInfo Event)
3:      if eventInfo.reason() = ErrorWarning then
4:          eventInfo.setReason(ErrorCritical)
5:      endIf
6:   endMethod
```

The `errorTrapOnWarnings(Yes)` makes warning errors critical errors. Specifically, it has the effect of the following:

- The built-in `error` method will be called.
- The standard error dialog box will be shown.
- `onFail` will be called in a try structure.
- The next line of code will not execute.

Using the Built-In *error* Event Method

So far, I haven't discussed the built-in `error` method. Despite what you might think, the built-in `error` method is not the preferred place to put code. The reason is that the built-in error method is always called after the error occurs. Most of the time, you are going to want to know before the error occurs so that you can take appropriate steps. Sometimes, however, you will want to simply add to or alter an error message.

Table 29.2 lists the ErrorEvent methods and procedures.

Table 29.2. ErrorEvent methods and procedures.

```
errorCode*

getTarget*

isFirstTime*

isPreFilter*

isTargetSelf*

reason

setErrorCode*

setReason
```
*Inherited from the Event type.

Using *errorHasErrorCode()*

In addition to the ErrorEvent methods and procedures, there are several System type methods and procedures you can use for handling errors. For example, you can use `errorHasErrorCode()` to check whether a specific error code is in the error stack. The syntax is as follows:

errorHasErrorCode(const *errorCode* SmallInt) Logical

This procedure was introduced in version 4.5 and is very useful, because a test like this:

```
1:  if errorCode() = peKeyViol then
2:    ;Your code here.
3:  endIf
```

would fail if another error occurred after the key violation because the key violation error would not be on top of the error stack; it would be second or third. The following code would detect the key violation, no matter where the error code is in the error stack:

```
1:  if errorHasErrorCode(peKeyViol) then
2:    ;Your code here.
3:  endIf
```

Overcoming a *Cannot Modify Data During Refresh* Error

If you attempt to put a value into a field while the field is updating, you get a runtime error. The following code is supposed to enable the user to type into either column, and the other column should calculate automatically. This sounds easy, but the code generates an error.

```
1:    ;Total_Column :: newValue
2:    method newValue(var eventInfo Event)
3:       x2 = self * 2
4:    endmethod
5:
6:    ;Calculated_Column :: changeValue
7:    method changeValue(var eventInfo ValueEvent)
8:       Total = self * .5
9:    endmethod
```

Like many obstacles in ObjectPAL, a Cannot modify data during refresh error seems insurmountable, but it isn't. The following example shows a way to overcome this error. Although a more elegant solution to this problem might exist, the technique illustrated in this example works well. It's a good example of working with the event model instead of against it. This technique uses flags to overcome conditional problems. It also demonstrates that nearly any problem in ObjectPAL can be overcome.

Overcoming a *Cannot Modify Data During Refresh* Error

Suppose that you want to work around the Cannot modify data during refresh error. In this case, the specific goal is to enable the user to type into either the Total or the x2 columns. The x2 column is a calculation based on data in the Total column.

You can find the ERROR2.FSL form on the disc in the \ANSWERS directory.

Step By Step

1. Set the working directory to TUTORIAL. Create a new form that has LINEITEM.DB in the data model. Add a column labeled x2 (see Figure 29.10).

2. Add line 3 to the Var window of the page.

```
1:    ;Page :: Var
2:    Var
3:       Flag Logical
4:    endVar
```

3. Add lines 3–5 to the newValue method of the x2 field in the column.

```
1:    ;Field :: newValue
2:    method newValue(var eventInfo Event)
3:       Flag = False
4:       x2 = self * 2
5:       Flag = True
6:    endmethod
```

4. Add lines 3–6 to the changeValue method of the Total field in the column.

```
1:    ;UndefinedField :: changeValue
2:    method changeValue(var eventInfo ValueEvent)
3:       if Flag = True then
4:          DoDefault
5:          Total = self * .5
6:       endIf
7:    endmethod
```

5. Check the syntax, save the form as ERROR2.FSL, and run the form. Scroll the table frame up and down. Then, change the values in both the Total and x2 columns. Figure 29.11 shows that the cursor is in the last column. Using a calculated field wouldn't have worked because the user couldn't have edited the value.

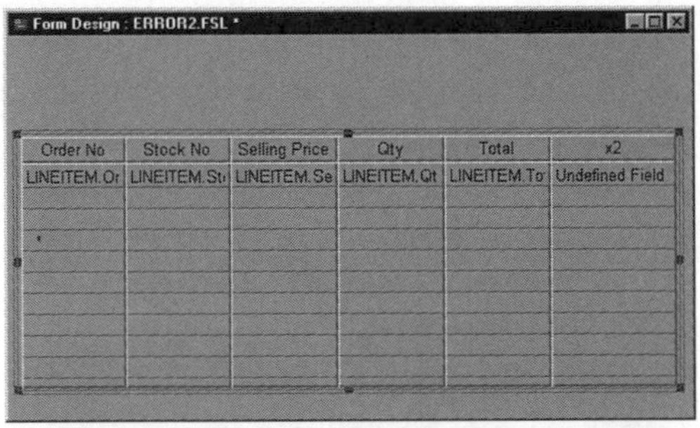

FIGURE 29.10.

Setup form for example.

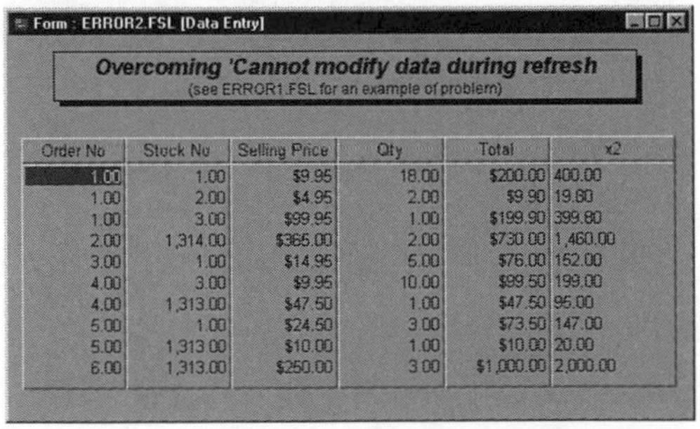

FIGURE 29.11.

Overcoming the Cannot modify data during refresh *error.*

Analysis

Step 2, line 3 declares a logical flag variable for use with both methods. This flag enables the methods to communicate with each other. In effect, the Total field tells the x2 field not to execute its code at key moments.

Steps 3 and 4 are intertwined. Look at them twice. The first time, assume that the user changes the value in the x2 field. In step 3, line 3 sets the flag to False. Line 4 changes the value in x2. Because line 3 in step 4 checks the flag and sets it to False, the newValue code is skipped. Line 5 sets the flag back to True in case the user wants to change the value in x2.

Now assume that the user changes the value in the Total field. Line 3 in step 4 checks whether the flag is set to True; at this point, it is. Line 4 implements the default behavior (commits the displayed value). Line 5 changes the Total field to the new value by implementing the same code just discussed.

This example is a good example of how to use the tools that are available to overcome an obstacle. This process is often difficult to carry out, and it sometimes requires creative thinking. If you are racking your brain trying to figure out how to do something, take a break. Go fishing, play table tennis, or do something. When you come back to the problem later, your mind will be fresh.

The built-in newValue method has three reasons to execute, refreshing the displayed value in the object:

- **FieldValue:** The newValue method executes when the user types in a new value. Note that there's no way with this event to tell the difference between a refresh across the network or a refresh in which the user changed the value of a field.

- **EditValue:** The newValue method executes when the user selects a value from a drop-down list.

- **StartupValue:** If a value was specified when the form was opened, newValue will execute.

Basically, data should never be changed in a newValue. You can almost always use changeValue to get the desired effect after a doDefault. If you must use newValue, use the following technique to deal with the error message:

```
1:    ;fld :: newValue
2:    if eventInfo.reason() = FieldValue then
3:        postAction(UserAction + 1)
4:    endIf
```

```
1:    ;fld :: action
2:    if eventInfo.id() = UserAction + 1 then
3:        x2 = self * 2
4:    endIf
```

This posts a custom action using Paradox's internal "flags" (actions), thus dealing with the problem more elegantly. Now that you understand using flags to overcome an error, you'll learn about using ObjectPAL's built-in flags to accomplish the same thing more elegantly.

Rounding Errors

The blame for another type of runtime error, rounding errors, can definitely be assigned to the computer. Take, for example, the following three rounding errors.

■ Compare .35 entered in a numeric field to see whether it is less than .35. You'll find out that Paradox thinks it is.

■ message(.1+.1+.1+.1+.1+.1+.1+.1+.1+.1=1) returns False.

■ Add .7 in one numeric field to .3 in another number field. Then, compare them to 1. You'll find that Paradox believes they are not equal. For example, view((a.value + b.value) = 1) returns False.

These examples are typical of floating-point number handling in C, C++, and other low-level programming languages. Paradox for DOS, however, handles it correctly. Also, Paradox for DOS provides a consistent, predictable value when the round() function is used; that is, banker's rounding (rounding to two significant digits).

Using *compileInformation()*

To find out detailed information about your form and the code within it, use compileInformation(). For example, type the following code on the pushButton method of a button.

```
1:    ;Button :: pushButton
2:    method pushButton(var eventInfo Event)
3:        var
4:            dyn   DynArray[] Anytype
5:        endVar
6:
7:        CompileInformation(dyn)
8:        dyn.view()
9:    endmethod
```

Note that compileInformation() reports on the last form to compile. Therefore, either put a button on the form in question or open and use the form with the compile information button on it after you open the form you want to inspect.

Summary

In this chapter, you learned that all programmers have their own ways of debugging. Now that you have the basics down, you can develop a style of your own. When problems arise, you'll be able to isolate them quickly. You'll be able to correct your mistakes, straighten out your logic, or find a solution that works around the problem.

The Event Model Revisited

30

Now that you have explored ObjectPAL in depth, you're ready to revisit the event model. As discussed previously, events are triggered by internal, external, and special events. In this chapter, you review the three categories of events and the paths they follow.

Internal Events

NEW
Term

Internal events are events generated by Paradox. A good case study example of an internal event is open. The open event occurs from outer container inward. The form is opened, then the page, and then the objects in the page. The `canArrive`, `arrive`, and `setFocus` methods also trigger from outer container inward.

Internal events are generated by Paradox. Like external events, internal events go first to the form and then to the target object. Unlike external and special events, internal events do not bubble. In simple terms, the event dies at the target. In other words, the complete path for an internal event is sent to the form and back to the object.

Take a closer look at the default behavior of each internal event. Internal methods are always called either from other internal methods or from an external built-in event. Paradox has many built-in default behaviors. The following sections describe the internal events and their default behaviors.

The *init* Event

7
NEW
Feature

New to version 7 is the built-in event method called `init`. The `init` method is called once when a form is opened. The primary use for the `init` method is for initialization code. The only object that supports this method is the form object itself; all other UIObjects within the form do not have this method. The chief benefit of this method, unlike all other form level methods, is that it does not have a `prefilter` clause. Now, you have control over what happens before the open method. In previous versions of ObjectPAL, the open method was called from a pre-wired C routine that the developers of Paradox wrote.

> **Default behavior:** The default behavior of `init` is to call open. You should note that when you use `disableDefault` in `init` the form and all the objects within the form are still opened. However, any code in the open methods of all objects does not execute. You have, in fact, disabled the code in the object's open methods. To stop a form from opening, set an error code in the `init` method using `eventInfo.setErrorCode(CanNotArrive)` as shown in Chapter 7.

The *open* and *close* Events

Every object has to be opened and is eventually closed. The open event is called only once for every object, starting with the form, then the page, then the objects contained by the page, and finally the objects contained within that container. After the first page is completely open, the process starts over with the next page in the form. Remember that the prefilter of the form sees the open event before the target object sees it.

Default behavior: The default code for open calls the open method for each of the objects it contains. Then the open method for each one of these objects calls the open method for the objects it contains, and so on. If you use DisableDefault in the open of an object, the object and the objects it contains are still opened. The appearance is that DisableDefault has no effect; however, it does. DisableDefault in the open method prevents the code in the open method of the objects it contains from executing. If a table is bound to the object, the object also opens the table. The default behavior for the close method acts in the same way.

Effect of errors: Any errors abort the open process and put the object in Design mode. For example, eventInfo.setErrorCode(1) prevents an object from opening and puts the object in Design mode.

The *canArrive* Event

The canArrive method occurs before movement to an object is permitted. Think of canArrive as asking permission to move to the object. Contrary to what is implied in the manuals, canArrive is not used just for restricting entrance to a field. You can use this method to execute almost any kind of code just before arriving on an object.

Default behavior: The canArrive method blocks arrival for records beyond the end of a table—except, of course, when you are in Edit mode and the Auto-Append data model property is checked. Any object whose tab stop property is unchecked also is blocked. You can't disable the default behavior using DisableDefault. Instead use

eventInfo.setErrorCode(CanNotArrive).

EventInfo: The eventInfo packet for the canArrive method is type MoveEvent. The reasons for a MoveEvent are PalMove, RefreshMove, ShutDownMove, StartupMove, and UserMove. Suppose that you want to know whether a move was made by ObjectPAL or by a user. You could use the following in canArrive:

```
1:   Switch
2:     case eventInfo.reason() = PalMove
3:        : message("ObjectPAL move")
4:     case eventInfo.reason() = UserMove
5:        : message("move by user")
6:   endSwitch
```

The MoveEvent eventInfo packet has a unique method called getDestination(), which enables you to know which object the user is trying to move to. Suppose that you want to know whether a user is going to move to either of two fields, such as Last_Name or First_Name, and you want to do this at the form level. You can use the following:

```
1:   ;Form :: canArrive prefilter
2:   method canArrive(var eventInfo MoveEvent)
```

```
 3:    var
 4:       ui UIObject
 5:    endVar
 6:    if eventInfo.isPreFilter() then
 7:       ;// This code executes for each object on the form
 8:    else
 9:       ;// This code executes only for the form
10:    eventInfo.getDestination(ui)
11:    if ui.name = "Last_Name" or  ui.name = "First_Name" then
12:       ;Execute code here.
13:    endIf
14:    endMethod
```

Effect of errors: Any error denies permission to arrive on the object. Suppose that you want to stop movement to a field. You could use the following code in the `canArrive` built-in event method:

```
eventInfo.setErrorCode(1)
```

ObjectPAL does provide the constant `CanNotArrive` to humanize the language a bit. As an alternative to using any nonzero value, you could use the following:

```
eventInfo.setErrorCode(CanNotArrive)
```

The *arrive* Event

The `arrive` method is executed after movement has arrived on an object. An `arrive` method can be called only after a `canArrive` method. You can use the `inserting` and `blankRecord` properties to tell when a record is being inserted and when a record is blank.

> **Default behavior**: `arrive` calls the `arrive` method of the objects it contains. This process occurs inward, that is, from the outer container in—the form, the page, the objects in the page, and so on. Pages, table frames, and multirecord objects move to the first tab stop object they contain. When you arrive on a field or a record, the object is made current. If you're in Edit mode, an editing window appears when the field is touched, in FieldView or MemoView. If the object is a drop-down edit list, the focus moves to the list. If the object is a radio button, the focus moves to the first button.
>
> **EventInfo**: The `eventInfo` packet for `arrive` is type `MoveEvent`. See "EventInfo" in the section "The *canArrive* Event."
>
> **Effect of error**: Any error prevents arriving on the object. Visually, an error means that no object becomes focus. `DisableDefault` seems to have the same effect as setting an error. As usual, the preferred way to stop the behavior is to set an error.

The *setFocus* Event

The `setFocus` method occurs every time an object gets the focus.

Default behavior: If the object getting the focus is contained in another object, setFocus is called for each container—from the outermost container inward. For example, if a page contains a box, which contains a field, setFocus is triggered first for the page, next for the box, and then for the field. In an edit field, the default code highlights the currently selected edit region and causes the insertion point to blink. The focus property is set to True, and the status message reports the number of the current record and the total number of records. For buttons, if the tab stop property is set, a dotted rectangle appears around the label.

The *canDepart* Event

The canDepart method is triggered before a move off an object.

Default behavior: Field objects try to post their contents and trip changeValue. If the record is a changed record, the object tries to commit the current record. If the record is locked, the form tries to unlock it.

EventInfo: The eventInfo packet for canDepart is type MoveEvent. See "EventInfo" in the section "The *canArrive* Event."

The *removeFocus* Event

The removeFocus method occurs when an object loses the focus.

Default behavior: On field objects, the flashing insertion point and highlight are removed. On a button, the dotted rectangle is removed. The object's focus property is set to False. This is called for the active object and its containers.

EventInfo: The eventInfo packet for removeFocus is type Event.

The *depart* Event

After canDepart and removeFocus have executed successfully, the depart method is called.

Default behavior: Field objects close their edit windows and then Paradox repaints and cleans up the screen.

EventInfo: The eventInfo packet for depart is type MoveEvent. The reasons for a MoveEvent are PalMove, RefreshMove, ShutDownMove, StartupMove, and UserMove. All these event reasons are self-explanatory except perhaps for RefreshMove. An example of when RefreshMove is generated is when data is updated by scrolling through a table.

Effect of error: Any nonzero value stops the departure from a field or a page. For example, eventInfo.setErrorCode(CanNotDepart) in the depart method of a field or page keeps focus on the current field or page. In the case of a page, however, focus is lost. Therefore, a better location to execute this code for all objects is in canDepart. Setting the error code in the depart method of the form does not stop the form from closing.

The *mouseEnter* Event

The mouseEnter method is generated whenever the mouse pointer enters an object.

> **Default behavior**: Form, page, and button objects set the pointer to an arrow. Field objects set the pointer to an I-beam. If a button has received a mouseDown but not a mouseUp, and is still down, its value toggles from False to True. You can disable this default behavior by using DisableDefault in mouseEnter.

The *mouseExit* Event

The mouseExit method is generated whenever the mouse pointer exits an object.

> **Default behavior**: Field objects set the pointer back to the arrow. If a button has received a mouseDown but not a mouseUp, and is still down, its value toggles from True to False. You can disable this default behavior by using DisableDefault in mouseEnter.

External Events

NEW
Term

External events are generated by the user interacting with a form. Keep in mind, however, that ObjectPAL can trigger some external events.

Now take a closer look at the default behavior of each external event. Both internal and external events go first to the form and then to the target object. External events, however, unlike internal events, bubble back up to the form. Paradox has many built-in default behaviors. The default behavior for an external method is to pass the event to its container, which is how it bubbles up to the form. The following sections explain the default behavior of the external events that do something in addition to bubbling their events.

The *mouseDown* Event

The mouseDown method occurs when the left mouse button is pressed.

> **Default behavior**: If the object is a field that is active, the field is put into field view. If the object is a button with its tab stop property set to True, the button becomes active. A button's value is toggled from False to True. You can verify this value by typing the following code into the pushButton method of a button:

```
1:  ;Button :: pushButton
2:  method mouseDown(var eventInfo MouseEvent)
3:     message(self.value)
4:     sleep(500)
5:     DoDefault
6:     message(self.value)
7   endmethod
```

EventInfo: The eventInfo packet for mouseDown contains the mouse coordinates in twips relative to the last object that executed a mouseEnter method.

The *mouseRightDown* Event

The mouseRightDown method occurs when the right mouse button is pressed. It is the same as the mouseDown method, except that it uses the right mouse button instead.

Default behavior: If the object is a formatted memo, a graphic, OLE, or an undefined field, a pop-up menu appears.

The *mouseUp* Event

The mouseUp method occurs when the left mouse button is released. mouseUp is called for the last object that received a mouseDown method. Therefore, an object always sees the mouseDown and mouseUp methods in a pair.

Default behavior: If you select text, mouseUp ends the selection. If the object is a button and the pointer is still inside the button, mouseUp calls the pushButton method.

The mouseRightUp method is the same as the mouseUp method, except that it uses the right mouse button instead.

The *mouseDouble* Event

The mouseDouble method occurs when the left mouse button is double-clicked.

Default behavior: A field object enters field view.

The mouseRightDouble method is the same as the mouseDouble method, except that it uses the right mouse button.

The *mouseMove* Event

The movement of the mouse is tracked with the mouseMove method. Whenever the pointer is moved within an object, the mouseMove method is triggered.

Default behavior: An active edit field checks the state of the Shift key. If the Shift key is down (or pressed), the selection is extended. If necessary, an active graphic field scrolls the graphic. When you press and hold the mouse button inside an object, the mouseMove method of the object is called until you release the button (even when the pointer moves outside the object).

The *keyPhysical* Event

The keyPhysical method occurs whenever any key is pressed and each time a key is autorepeated. keyPhysical includes all the physical keys on the keyboard, including the character keys, the function keys, and the Alt, Ctrl, and Esc keys.

> **Default behavior**: A keystroke goes first to Windows and then to Paradox, which gives it to the form's prefilter. The form sends it to the active object for processing. The object determines whether the keystroke represents an action or a display character. Actions are passed to the action method, and display characters are passed to keyChar.

The *keyChar* Event

The keyChar method occurs whenever a character key is pressed. Actually, the keyPhysical method for the active object sends action events such as nextRecord() to the action method, and it sends characters such as *a* to keyChar; if a keyPhysical does not map to an action, then it calls keyChar.

> **Default behavior**: If the active object is a field in Edit mode, a lock is put on the record before the first character is inserted.
>
> If the active object is a button and the character is a spacebar, the button's pushButton method is called without calling mouseDown or mouseUp. In other words, your code in mouseDown and mouseUp does not execute. (Remember, a button can be active only if its tab stop is set to True.)

The *action* Event

The action method is called frequently. It executes when it is sent an action keystroke KeyEvent from keyPhysical, when a MenuEvent from menuAction maps to a menu option, or when a method calls for an action. An example of a method calling for an action is UIObject.postRecord(). In this case, the postRecord() calls for a DataPostRecord. The constant DataPostRecord is sent to the event action. You can send Action commands to action using the action() method.

> **Default behavior**: The default behavior for action is to perform the pending action. You can think of the default behavior for action as DO_IT! It's default behavior is extensive because all actions go through it. For example, Page Down moves to the next record, F9 toggles Edit mode, and Alt+Tab task-switches to another application.

The *menuAction* Event

The menuAction method occurs when a menu option or Toolbar icon is selected. You can send MenuCommands to menuAction using the menuAction() method.

Default behavior: The option is sent first to the form's menuAction method for processing and then to the active object.

The *error* Event

The error method occurs after an error is encountered. Because error is always triggered after an error, trap for errors in the action method.

Default behavior: An error is passed to its container until it gets to the form. The form might or might not display a message, depending on the severity of the error; that is, depending on whether the error is a Warning or Critical level. All critical errors produce the error dialog box. Warning errors, on the other hand, may or may not display a message in the status bar. You can trap for errors and alter this default behavior in the form's action method.

The *status* Event

The status method occurs whenever a message is displayed in the status bar.

Default behavior: The default behavior of status is too extensive to be described here. In short, any time you see a message in one of the four status areas, it has gone through the built-in status method. For example, whenever a key violation occurs, a message is sent to the status window.

Special Events

Special events are specific to a few objects, such as a field's newValue method. The following sections explain the default behavior of the special events.

The *pushButton* Event

Only button objects and the form have a pushButton method. Some field display types are actually composite objects that include buttons; fields themselves never have a pushButton. For example, a field displayed as a check box is composed of a field, a button, and a text object.

The form, which has all the events, acts like a dispatcher. The pushButton method occurs when the pointer is inside an object for both the mouseDown and mouseUp methods. In fact, mouseUp calls mouseClick, which then calls pushButton.

Default behavior: Button objects visually depress and pop out. Check boxes check or uncheck. Radio buttons push in or pop out. If the tab stop property is set to True, the focus moves to it.

The *newValue* Event

Only fields and the form have a newValue method. The newValue method is triggered after the value in a field changes. newValue is triggered even if the value is changed only onscreen. The form's open method also triggers newValue for each field object in the form. The changeValue method, on the other hand, is triggered by a change in a table.

The *changeValue* Event

The changeValue method is triggered before a value in a table is changed. If you have code on both changeValue and newValue, the code on changeValue occurs first, before the value changes. newValue is triggered after the value changes. Therefore, if you want to do validity checks on a field, do them in changeValue. To fully understand the relationship between DoDefault, self.value, and eventInfo.newValue(), enter the following code into the changeValue method of a field bound to a table and then change the value:

```
 1:  ;Field :: changeValue
 2:  method changeValue(var eventInfo ValueEvent)
 3:     ;Before default behavior.
 4:     view(self.value, "self before DoDefault")
 5:     view(string(eventInfo.newValue()), "newValue before DoDefault")
 6:
 7:     DoDefault
 8:
 9:     ;After default behavior.
10:     view(self.value, "self after DoDefault")
11:     view(string(eventInfo.newValue()), "newValue after DoDefault")
12:  endmethod
```

Moving a Text Box During Run Mode

Enabling the user to move objects around during Run mode is very useful. In ObjectPAL, you can enable the user to move an object around to reveal something behind it, or you can enable the user to move an object to a new location. The following example shows you how to move an object around. When you let go (mouseUp), the object snaps back to its original position. You could use this technique for many tasks. For example, you could use this technique in a game to reveal answers or offer clues.

Example of Moving a Text Box

Suppose that you want to enable the user to move text fields around but not place them while the form is in View Data mode.

You can find the MOVER.FSL form on the disc in the \ANSWERS directory.

Step By Step

1. Create a form with several text boxes on it. Give them various frames and colors (see Figure 30.1).

FIGURE 30.1.

Setting up a form for the example.

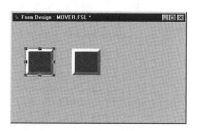

2. Add lines 3–5 to the Var window of the form:

```
1:      ;Form :: Var
2:      Var
3:          x,y,x1,y1,w,h  SmallInt
4:          ui             UIObject
5:          sTargetClass   String
6:      endVar
```

3. Add line 3 to the init method of the form:

```
1:      ;Form :: init
2:      method init(var eventInfo Event)
3:          sTargetClass = ""
4:      endmethod
```

4. Add lines 8–10 to the mouseDown of the form:

```
1:      ;Form :: mouseDown
2:      method mouseDown(var eventInfo MouseEvent)
3:          if eventInfo.isprefilter() then
4:              ;This code executes for each object on the form
5:
6:          else
7:              ;This code executes only for the form
8:              eventinfo.getTarget(ui)
9:              ui.getPosition(x1, y1, w, h)
10:             sTargetClass = ui.class
11:         endif
12:     endmethod
```

5. Add lines 3–5 and 11–17 to the mouseMove of the form:

```
1:      ;Form :: mouseMove
2:      method mouseMove(var eventInfo MouseEvent)
3:          var
4:              liX, liY   LongInt
5:          endVar
6:          if eventInfo.isprefilter() then
7:              ;This code executes for each object on the form
8:
9:          else
```

```
10:            ;This code executes only for the form
11:            if eventinfo.isLeftDown() and
12:               sTargetClass = "Text" then
13:               liX = eventinfo.x()
14:               liY = eventinfo.y()
15:               ui.getPosition(x, y, w, h)
16:               ui.setPosition(x + liX - 400, y + liY - 400, w, h)
17:            endif
18:         endif
19:      endmethod
```

6. Add line 8 to the mouseUp of the form:

```
1:      ;Form :: mouseUp
2:      method mouseUp(var eventInfo MouseEvent)
3:         if eventInfo.isprefilter() then
4:            ;This code executes for each object on the form
5:
6:         else
7:            ;This code executes only for the form
8:            ui.setPosition(x1,y1,w,h)
9:         endif
10:      endmethod
```

7. Check the syntax, save the form as MOVER.FSL, and run the form. Click and drag any text box you placed on the form to move it. When you let go (mouseUp), the object snaps back to its original location (see Figure 30.2).

FIGURE 30.2.

MOVER.FSL. Moving objects during runtime.

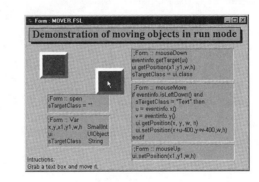

Analysis

In step 2, lines 3–5 declare all the variables needed in the Var window of the form.

When the form is opened, line 3 in step 3 initializes the targetclass variable for use later.

In step 4, lines 8–10 get the original size and location of the object that the user clicks. This information is used later to set the object back to its original position in mouseUp (the snapping-back effect).

Step 5 executes the fun code. Lines 8–14 move the object with the pointer. Lines 8 and 9 check to see whether the left mouse button is down and whether the target is the object you want (in this case, a text object). If both conditions are satisfied, lines 10 and 11 get the current position of the pointer. Line 12 gets the current position of the object. Line 13 uses the two values to set the new position of the object. Lines 8–14 are what create the "glued to the pointer" effect.

In step 6, line 8 activates when the mouse button is released and sets the object back to its old position. An interesting effect is to remark out line 8 and run the form. Notice that when you move all the objects around, they stay in the new location! You aren't prompted to save your changes when you exit the form, however. This means that you can't design a form while it's running. This limitation is logical because forms are compiled.

Redirecting Status Messages

You can use `reason()` in the status event to trap for a particular category of messages and redirect either with `setReason()` or `statusValue()` (see Table 30.1).

Table 30.1. Sections of the status bar.

Constant	Description
StatusWindow	The left largest area on the status bar
ModeWindow1	First small window right of the status area
ModeWindow2	Second small window right of the status area
ModeWindow3	Third small window right of the status area (rightmost window)

To redirect status messages to a field, use the following code in the prefilter of the status method:

```
1:  if eventInfo.reason() = StatusWindow then
2:     fldStatus.value = eventInfo.statusValue()
3:  endIf
```

Case Study Trapping for the Down Arrow in *keyPhysical*

Trapping for the down arrow in `keyPhysical` presents some interesting problems when combined with `doDefault` and `disableDefault`. For example, suppose that you put the following code on the `keyPhysical` method of a field named Name. Figure 30.3 shows what happens when the code is executed.

```
1:  ;fldName :: keyPhysical
2:  method keyPhysical(var eventInfo KeyEvent)
3:     if eventInfo.vCharCode() = VK_DOWN then
4:        Total_Invoice.moveTo()
5:     endIf
6:  endmethod
```

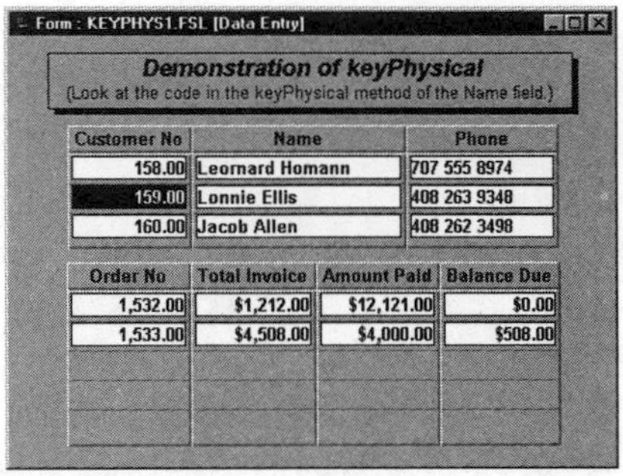

FIGURE 30.3.

KEYPHYS1.FSL demonstrates trapping for keyPhysical.

What do you think will happen when the user presses the down arrow while on the Name field? The goal is to jump from the Name field to the Total_Invoice field when the user presses the down-arrow key. The code, however, appears to have no effect. What actually happens is the focus does move to the Total_Invoice field, but immediately moves back to the Name field (this time on the next record down). This movement occurs because the default behavior executes after the move.

Now consider the following code:

```
1:  ;fldName :: keyPhysical
2:  method keyPhysical(var eventInfo KeyEvent)
3:    if eventInfo.vCharCode() = VK_DOWN then
4:      doDefault
5:      Total_Invoice.moveTo()
6:    endIf
7:  endmethod
```

Now, what do you think will happen when the user presses the down arrow while on the Name field? In this case, the code appears to do the job. The focus is indeed on Total_Invoice. What actually occurs, however, is that the focus moves first to the Name field of the next record and then to the destination; this move is invoked by the doDefault.

What if you have code on the arrive of Name? It, of course, would execute.

Finally, consider the following code:

```
1:  ;fldName :: keyPhysical
2:  method keyPhysical(var eventInfo KeyEvent)
3:    if eventInfo.vCharCode() = VK_DOWN then
4:      disableDefault
5:      Total_Invoice.moveTo()
6:    endIf
7:  endmethod
```

Now the code works just the way you want. In this case, you disable the default behavior and in essence pretend that the keystroke never occurred.

Chapter 30

Passing *eventInfo*

Just like you can pass variables to a custom method, you can pass the eventInfo variable to a custom method. You can use this technique to centralize your code further. For example, you can pass the eventInfo up to a library routine to handle all errors.

Inspecting *eventInfo*

You can use the technique of passing eventInfo to inspect the eventInfo by creating your own custom method. For example, the following custom method displays information about an ActionEvent when passed eventInfo. Create a form based on the customer table (see Figure 30.4). Type it into a custom method named cmActionEvent() at the form level, as follows:

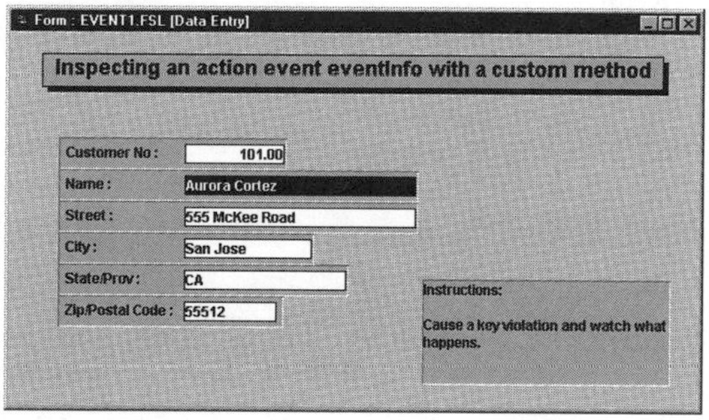

FIGURE 30.4.

EVENT1.FSL demonstrates inspecting eventInfo.

```
1:   ;Form :: cmActionEvent
2:   method cmActionEvent(var eventInfo ActionEvent)
3:     var
4:        ui  UIObject
5:     endVar
6:
7:     eventInfo.getTarget(ui)
8:
9:     dynEventInfo["actionClass"] = eventInfo.actionClass()
10:    dynEventInfo["errorCode"] = eventInfo.errorCode()
11:    nEventInfo["getTarget Name"] = ui.name
12:    dynEventInfo["getTarget Value"] = ui.value
13:    dynEventInfo["getTarget Container Name"] = ui.container.name
14:    dynEventInfo["id"] = eventInfo.id()
15:    dynEventInfo["isFirstTime"] = eventInfo.isFirstTime()
16:    dynEventInfo["isprefilter"] = eventInfo.isprefilter()
17:    dynEventInfo["isTargetSelf"] = eventInfo.isTargetSelf()
18:    dynEventInfo["Reason"] = eventInfo.reason()
19:
20:    dynEventInfo.view("View Eventinfo")
21:  endmethod
```

Next, pass it an `ActionEvent` `eventInfo` variable. For example, type the following code into the action method of the form:

```
1:    ;EVENT1 :: Form :: action
2:    method action(var eventInfo ActionEvent)
3:      if eventInfo.isprefilter() then
4:        ;// This code executes for each object on the form
5:        ;//
6:        if eventInfo.id() = DataUnlockRecord or
7:            eventInfo.id() = DataPostRecord then
8:          DoDefault
9:          if eventInfo.errorCode() = peKeyViol then
10:            msgStop("Warning",
                      "Key violation\n\nLet's inspect the action event
                      eventInfo.")
11:            cmActionEvent(eventInfo)
12:          endIf
13:        endIf
14:      else
15:        ;// This code executes only for the form
16:        ;//
17:      endIf
18:    endMethod
```

Next, run the form and cause a key violation (see Figure 30.5).

FIGURE 30.5.

EVENT1.FSL showing the contents of `eventInfo`.

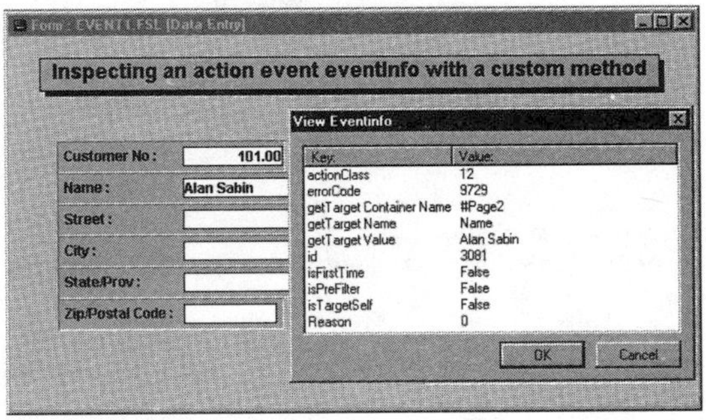

Creating and Sending Your Own Events

You have already learned about `action()` and `menuAction()` to generate built-in `Action` and `MenuAction` constants. Now, you're ready to learn about `broadcastAction()` and `postAction()`, which work similar to `action()`. They send `Action` constants to the `action` method. `broadcastAction()` sends an `Action` constant to the action method of an object and all the objects it contains. `postAction()` sends the `Action` constant to a queue for delayed execution. `postAction()` is most useful when working with `newValue`.

In general, avoid placing code in `newValue` except when you're using `postAction()`. The `newValue` event is called when the data underneath a field changes, or when you click a list member (such as a radio button or list box). While you are in a `newValue` method, you are coming out of the heart of a recalc/repaint loop inside the newValue method. Therefore, you cannot modify the value of a bound field. The solution is to use newValue sparingly, and when you do use it, use postAction(). For example,

```
self.postAction(UserAction + 1)
```

Using postAction() has the effect of queuing up a user-defined action call to the object receiving the newValue. As soon as the newValue is done executing and the system has completed the refresh loop, the built-in action() fires, and you can trap for this action with the following:

```
1:  If eventInfo.id() = UserAction + 1 then
2:     ;Do here what you would have done in newValue.
3:  endif
```

The end effect is the same, but the code is much safer and easier to debug.

If you have a common set of code (such as a calculation), which you were putting in newValue, then you can trigger this calculation from anywhere in your application simply by calling the action() or postAction() method for this object, thus making your code more reusable.

In a newValue, you can write many things that are harmless, such as writing to unbound fields or changing display properties. Many programmers try to do "database stuff" inside a newValue, and this kind of programming isn't good. When in doubt, use postAction() to send a custom action ID to self and trap for the custom action ID in the action method. Your safety will be guaranteed because the action code cannot execute until the recalc/repaint cycle is complete.

Events Can Cause Events

In an event-driven environment such as Paradox for Windows, an event often creates another event before the first event finishes. In effect, you can have several events occurring at the same time. (Some developers have mistakenly called this a *secondary event stream*. Furthermore, they have mistakenly referred to the first event as the *primary event stream*. I do not use that terminology here because it just confuses the issue.) Suffice it to say, just as Windows sends messages from application to application, Paradox sends messages from object to object.

Using the Built-In Error Codes

Rather than always just setting the error code to a nonzero value, try using built-in error constants whenever possible. The following example enforces uniqueness in a table and checks whether the field is required. This example is interesting because it uses the peReqdErr and peKeyViol constants instead of just a nonzero value.

```
1:  ;Record :: action
2:  var
3:     tc TCursor
4:  endvar
5:
```

```
 6:  ;check for required field
 7:  if isBlank(Ship_Via) and self.locked then
 8:     eventinfo.setErrorCode(peReqdErr)
 9:     return
10: endif
11:
12: ;Key violation check
13: tc.attach(ORDERS)
14: if tc.locate("Order_No", Order_No.value) then
15:    if tc.recNo()<> self.recNo then
16:       eventinfo.setErrorCode(peKeyViol)
17:    endif
18: endIf
```

Note that the preceding code works for both Paradox and dBASE tables; it works even though dBASE tables do not use the concept of keys and therefore cannot have a key violation.

Moving Focus to a Box

Although only fields and buttons have tab stop properties, you can still move focus to an object other than a field or a button—for example, a box. ObjectPAL offers the flexibility for you to move focus to any object. Suppose that you have a box named *box1* on your form. You can move focus to it by using box1.moveTo(). To the user, the only visual difference is that no object onscreen appears to have focus.

Summary

In this chapter, you learned that events are triggered by internal, external, and special events. You learned that internal events are events generated by Paradox. Like external events, internal events go first to the form and then to the target object. Unlike external and special events, internal events do not bubble. In general, external events are events generated by the user interacting with a form.

In this chapter, you completed your knowledge of generating your own events by learning about postAction() and broadcastAction() (you previously learned about action() and menuAction()).

Using and
Writing DLLs

31

New
Term

The term *DLL* is an acronym for dynamic link library. A DLL is a type of application used by other applications. It usually contains a library of functions. A DLL is a module of executable Windows code that other applications can use. Typically, a DLL has several functions or modules that can be called. Just as you can run Windows .EXE applications within Windows, a Windows application can run or use a function in a DLL. The function is loaded on demand and linked at runtime. If the DLL is a good Windows DLL, the function is unloaded when you no longer need the code. This chapter provides a general overview of how to register and use a DLL in Paradox for Windows.

What's in a DLL?

Your hard drive has many DLLs with thousands of functions in them—all the files with a .DLL extension. The problem with using DLLs on your hard drive is that they were never designed for any other program except the original to call. So how do you find out what commands or functions are in them? Some utilities dump the header of a DLL into a file, but they usually aren't worth the time that it takes to reverse-engineer a DLL. If you're writing a DLL, you know what the calls are. If you purchase a DLL, its documentation tells you.

In general, the DLL interface is intended for people who already know how to write DLLs or who are willing to invest the time and effort to learn. The DLL interface also is intended for people who know how to hook into third-party DLLs written explicitly for this purpose. Using a DLL that has no documentation or that is written for a particular application is difficult—and in many cases, impossible. For example, many DLLs on the Borland BBS and CompuServe were written specifically and only for ObjectVision. Some of these DLLs do things that simply don't apply to any other application. That doesn't mean that none of the ObjectVision DLLs work with Paradox—some do. It does mean, however, that two categories of DLLs are in use—specific and general. With proper documentation, most of the general DLLs will work within ObjectPAL. All the Paradox-specific DLLs will work. As for the rest, you have to try them on a case-by-case basis.

Most DLLs designed to be called from another product come with documentation that lists the available functions, parameter data types, and return values. After you have this information, you can link and call the DLLs from Paradox. Without this information, you might have a hard time figuring out how to call those DLLs.

Where Do You Get DLLs?

You can write your own DLLs, download them for free from BBSs, or buy them. You also can ask the producers of the products on your hard disk to let you use the DLLs and provide you with documentation. This method of getting access to the DLLs in which you're interested is reliable and reasonable. If you want to write your own DLL, you will find the template later in this chapter to be helpful.

Using a DLL

To use a function in a DLL, you first must register it. In ObjectPAL, you register DLLs in the Uses window of an object. You call the code in the Uses window from the object or the object's containership path. Use the following template:

```
uses libraryName
[function([paramList])[retType][[callConv ["linkName"]]]]*
endUses
```

For example, suppose that you have a DLL with the filename STRINGS.DLL. It contains a function called scramble. You register it with code like this:

```
1:  Uses Strings
2:    scramble(text cptr) cptr
3:  endUses
```

After you register a DLL function, you can call it just like any runtime library method or procedure. In the next example, you pass a number to a DLL. The DLL returns the number and some characters. In other words, you send a value to a DLL and receive an altered value. The goal is to use ObjectPAL to pass a number to a DLL that will pass back a string and the same number. Make sure that you use the correct parameters.

Example of Using a DLL

This example demonstrates how to use a DLL. Specifically, you learn how to pass a number to a DLL that will pass back a string and the same number.

> You can find the HELLO.FSL form on the disc in the \ANSWERS directory.

Step By Step

1. Change your working directory to TUTORIAL\DLL. Create a new form and place a button labeled Use DLL on it.

2. Alter the Uses window of the form to look like lines 2–4.
    ```
    1:   ;Form :: Uses
    2:   Uses Hello
    3:      getHelloString(text cWord) cptr
    4:   endUses
    ```

3. Add lines 3–8 to the pushButton method of the Use DLL button.
    ```
    1:   ;Button :: pushButton
    2:   method pushButton(var eventInfo Event)
    3:      var
    4:        s   String
    5:      endVar
    6:
    ```

```
7:        s = getHelloString(3)
8:        s.view()
9:     endmethod
```

4. Check the syntax, save the form as HELLO.FSL, run it, and click the Use DLL button. Almost immediately, a string dialog box appears. Click OK. Figure 31.1 shows how the HELLO.FSL form should look when you're done.

FIGURE 31.1.

HELLO.FSL demonstrates using a DLL.

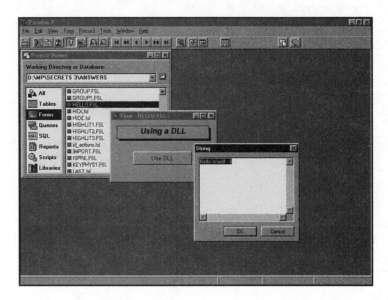

Analysis

In step 2, line 2 tells ObjectPAL which function is in HELLO.DLL. No path or extension is used. ObjectPAL automatically searches the current directory, the Windows directory, and all the directories on the path for the DLL. Line 3 prototypes the function in the DLL. You prototype DLLs similarly to custom methods. In this case, the DLL function is called getHelloString. It takes a single parameter and returns a string.

In step 3, line 4 declares a String variable so that there is a place in which to store the string returned by the DLL in line 7. Line 8 shows you the result in a String View dialog box.

DLLs and Data Types

When you use or register DLLs with another application, you need to know how the other application deals with data types. Table 31.1 lists the names of the different data types that ObjectPAL, C/C++, and Pascal use.

Note that not all the data types a DLL may use are listed in Table 31.1. If the DLL (or Windows API call) you want to use needs to receive or pass back a variable other than the data types listed in Table 32.1, you need to use a wrapper DLL. A *wrapper DLL* is an intermediate DLL that can communicate on behalf of Paradox for Windows with the DLL. For example, if you need to pass an array to a DLL, you could use a wrapper DLL. The wrapper DLL can take several strings from ObjectPAL, convert them to an array, and pass the array to the DLL. This process also holds true for a C structure.

Table 31.1. The DLL data types.

Data Type	Uses Keyword	ObjectPAL Type	C/C++ Type	Pascal Type
16-bit integer	CWORD	SmallInt	short (short int)	Integer
32-bit integer	CLONG	LongInt	long (long int)	Longint
Natural integer (*)	CLONG (*)	LongInt (*)	int	Integer
64-bit floating-point number	CDOUBLE	Number	double	Double
80-bit floating-point number	CLONGDOUBLE	Number	long double	Extended
String pointer	CPTR	String	char *	Pchar
Binary or graphic data	CHANDLE	Binary, Graphic	HANDLE (Windows)	THandle

---

NOTE

The only place these special ObjectPAL data types are valid is in the uses Window. Use CWORD, CLONG, CDOUBLE, DLONGDOUBLE, CPTR, and CHANDLE in the Uses window to prototype functions in DLLs.

- CWORD corresponds to SmallInt.
- CLONG corresponds to LongInt.
- CDOUBLE and CLONGDOUBLE correspond to Number.
- CPTR corresponds to String.
- CHANDLE corresponds to Binary or Graphic.

Passing By Value

Just as custom methods utilize the concept of passing by value versus passing by reference, so do DLLs. Here is an example of passing by value:

C data type:	`Long Int`
C syntax:	`void pascal far _loadds cproc(long int value)`
In Uses block:	`cproc(value CLONG)`
ObjectPAL call:	`cproc(si) or cproc(li)`

Passing By Reference

The following is an example of passing by reference. Note that the DLL data type used in the Uses windows is `CPTR`, which is a C pointer. A C pointer points to a memory location.

C data type:	`Long Int *`
C syntax:	`void pascal far _loadds`
	`cproc(long int * value)`
In Uses block:	`cproc(value CPTR)`
ObjectPAL call:	`cproc(li)`

Common Error Messages

When you misspell a DLL or function (remember, functions are case-sensitive), or if the DLL is not found, you get the error message displayed in Figure 31.2 when you try to run the form.

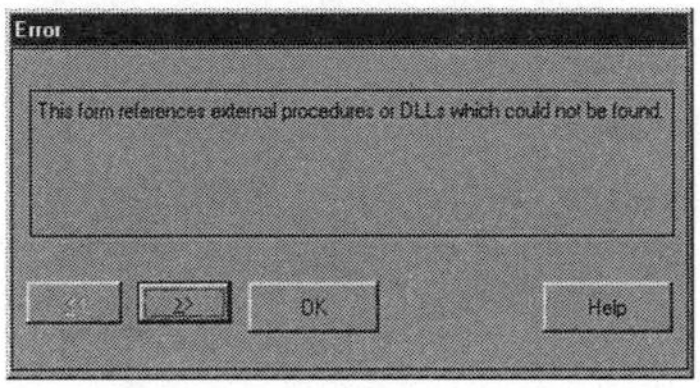

FIGURE 31.2.

The error message displayed when the DLL or DLL function cannot be found.

This form references external procedures or DLLs which could not be found.

NEW Term

When you try to pass a DLL the wrong data type, you get the syntax error message illustrated in Figure 31.3. This error message also occurs if you try to pass by value and you mean to pass by reference (or vice versa). This error is known as a *reference mismatch*. In particular, this error message occurs when you try to pass a constant and you prototype to pass by reference. The status bar in Figure 31.3 shows the error you get.

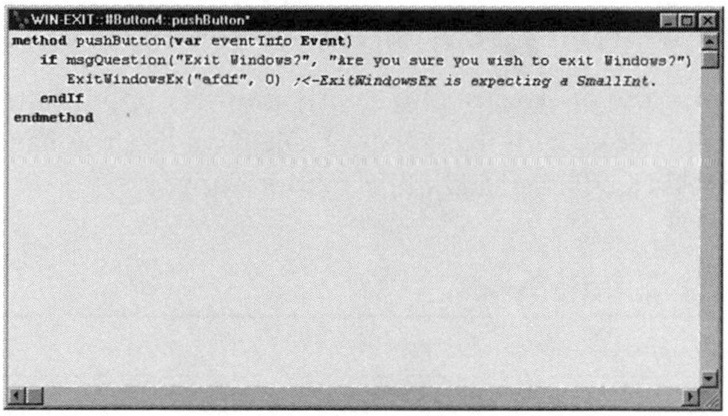

FIGURE 31.3.

The error message displayed when you try to pass a function something other than what it is proto-typed for.

Passing an Array to a DLL

The DLL you want to use, for example, needs to pass an array back to Paradox. How do you accomplish this task? Because you cannot pass an array to a DLL or back to Paradox, you need to write an intermediate DLL that can then pass the data one element at a time to the DLL and back to Paradox. This type of intermediate DLL is known as a *wrapper* because, in a sense, it wraps itself around the DLL.

NEW Term

Passing a String to a DLL

Why does Paradox cause a GPF when you pass a string of one size to a DLL, make it larger in the DLL, and return the larger string? You need to set the maximum size of the string ahead of time. Be careful to set the maximum length of the variable in your ObjectPAL code. For example:

```
1:    var
2:        x    String
3:    endVar
4:
5:    x = "12345678901234567890"
```

Passing a Null to a DLL

To pass a null to a DLL, you use the CWORD data type and pass a 0 (zero).

Passing a Logical

To pass a logical to a DLL, you use a CWORD and pass a 0 for False and a 1 for True (any nonzero value represents a True).

DLLs, Data Types, and ObjectVision Parameters

When you use or register DLLs with another application, you need to know how the other application deals with data types. Table 31.2 lists the names of the different data types that ObjectPAL, C, Pascal, and ObjectVision support.

Table 31.2. Data types.

Date Type	ObjectPAL	C	Pascal	ObjectVision
16-bit integer	CWORD	int	Integer	I, H, or A
32-bit integer	CLONG	long	Longint	J
64-bit floating-point number	CDOUBLE	double	Double	B point number
80-bit floating-point number	DLONGDOUBLE	long double	Extended	
Pointer	CPTR	char far	String	C
Binary	CWORD	handle	THandle	y graphic data

> **NOTE**
>
> Page 160 of the ObjectVision reference guide lists all 19 data types that ObjectVision supports when it deals with DLLs. You can't use an ObjectVision DLL with Paradox if it uses a data type other than the seven data types listed for ObjectVision in Table 31.2.

CPTR Is a Pointer

A string null pointer in ObjectPAL is not the same as a null pointer in C. If you need to pass a null string to a DLL, use CWORD set as 0. If you pass a string by reference—that is, by CPTR—don't modify the length of the string with the DLL.

A DLL with a return value of a string actually is a pointer to a memory address that defines the beginning of the string that is returned. You might have to define the maximize size of the string in ObjectPAL before you call this DLL. Here's an example. Suppose that the DLL function takes an Integer as an argument and returns a string no longer than 30 characters.

```
1:    ;Button :: Uses statement
2:    Uses MYDLL
3:        MyFunction(const MyNum CWORD) CPTR
4:    endUses

1:    ;ObjectPAL Method
2:    Method pushButton(var eventInfo MouseEvent)
3:        var
4:           sMyString String
5:           siMyInteger SmallInt
6:        endVar
7:
8:        ;Initialize variables
9:        siMyInteger = 10
10:       sMyString = "123456789012345678901234567890"
11:
12:       ;Call DLL function
13:       sMyString=MyFunction(iMyInteger)
14:
15:       ;Examine results
16:       sMyString.view("Result")
17:   endMethod
```

Summary

In this chapter, you learned that a DLL is a type of application used by other applications. You also learned that a DLL is a module of executable Windows code. This chapter provided a general overview of how to register and use a DLL in Paradox for Windows. In Chapter 32, you build on your knowledge of DLLs with a study of the Windows 95 API.

Using the Windows API

NEW
Term
The term *API* is an acronym for application programming interface. The Windows API is the set of DLLs that makes up Windows 95 and NT. It comprises all the functions, messages, data structures, data types, statements, and files that a programmer needs for developing Windows 95/NT applications.

Windows 95/NT itself is just several big DLLs, including the very useful User32.exe. Many of the DLLs that Windows 95/NT uses don't end with the customary .DLL extension. The API is full of functions of which you can take advantage. How do you know what functions are in there, and how do you figure out how to use them?

Using the Windows 95 and NT API

Many companies, including Borland, offer a set of API reference guides. These guides describe the Microsoft Windows 95/NT API and list all the functions, messages, data structures, data types, statements, and files that a programmer needs for developing Windows 95/NT applications. You can buy an API reference guide for about $35.

Changes from Windows 3.x

In Windows 3.1, you could do the following:

```
Uses USER
   MessageBox(hWnd CWORD, msgTxt CPTR, msgCaption CPTR, boxStyle CWORD) CWORD
endUses
```

This structure is incorrect for Windows 95/NT. You should refer to a Win32 API reference to check on any other changes that may have happened to the Windows API.

The following section talks about the API in general and gives specific useful examples that extend Paradox.

The Five Steps to Using a Windows 95 and NT API Function

When you're dealing with a large subject, such as using API functions, having clear-cut goals is nice. The following is an overview of the five steps you need to follow when you want to use an API function:

1. Set a goal.
2. Check ObjectPAL. Make sure that the function is not already duplicated in ObjectPAL.

3. Find the API function. You can use any source you want; the online help for BCW 4.5, Delphi 2.0, and Microsoft Visual C++ are perhaps the best.

4. Find the name of the DLL from which the function comes. Finding the DLL is a little more difficult because most other compilers automatically use the correct DLL when calling an API function. A handy source for this information is the Delphi 2.0 Windows API help file.

5. Prototype the function. Use a Uses window in ObjectPAL to prototype a function in a DLL. Use the special ObjectPAL data types to choose an appropriate data type to which you can map. Refer to the online help or the header file for the appropriate `typedef` definition to find valid data.

Following these five steps makes tackling the Windows 95 and Windows NT API manageable.

Hungarian Notation

The API consists of Hungarian notation for variable names. Table 32.1 lists variable prefixes with corresponding variable types.

Table 32.1. Hungarian notation.

Prefix	Variable Type
b	BOOL (int)
by	BYTE (unsigned char)
c	char
cx, cy	short (used as x or y length, c stands for count)
dw	DWORD (unsigned long)
h	Handle
i	int
l	LONG (long)
n	short or int
p	point
s	string
sz	string terminated by a zero
u	unsigned
w	WORD (unsigned int)
x, y	short (used as x or y coordinate)

Reading Documentation on API Calls

To call an API function that shuts down Windows, you call a Windows function called
`exitWindows` from User32.exe.

API Syntax:

```
BOOL ExitWindows(dwReturnCode, reserved)
```

Parameters:

```
DWORD dwReturnCode; /* return or restart code    */
UINT  reserved    ; /* reserved; must be zero    */
```

Description:

The `ExitWindows` function can restart Windows, terminate Windows and return control to
MS-DOS, or terminate Windows and restart the system. Windows sends the `WM_QUERYENDSESSION`
message to notify all applications that a request has been made to restart or terminate Windows. If all applications "agree" to terminate, Windows sends the `WM_ENDSESSION` message to all
applications before terminating.

> **NOTE**
>
> In C, a `/*    */` combination remarks out the characters between the asterisks.

The following is a translated `Uses` statement:

```
1:  Uses User32
2:     ExitWindows(reserved CDOUBLE, returncode CLONG)
3:  endUses
```

The following is the ObjectPAL call to API:

```
1:  method pushButton(var eventInfo Event)
2:     if msgQuestion("Exit Windows?", " ") = "Yes" then
3:        ExitWindows(0, 0)
4:     endIf
5:  endmethod
```

Translating from Hex to Decimal

ObjectPAL has two procedures for translating to and from hexadecimal: `toHex()` and `fromHex()`.
Of these two, `fromHex()` is of particular interest in this discussion of the Windows 95 and NT
API because API functions are most often documented using hexadecimal numbers. To convert a hexadecimal number to a decimal number, type the following code into the `pushButton`
method of a button:

```
1:  ;Button :: pushButton
2:  method pushButton(var eventInfo Event)
```

```
3:      var
4:         s    String
5:         li   LongInt
6:      endVar
7:
8:      ;Hexadecimal value to convert (for example "0x00010")
9:      s = "Enter Hex number"
10:     s.view("Hex value to convert")
11:     li = fromHex(s)
12:     li.view(s)
13:   endMethod
```

Examples of Making Windows 95 and NT API Calls

This next section continues your quest into the Windows 95 and NT API by showing several common API calls.

Exiting Windows with the Windows 95 and NT API

To call an API function that shuts down Windows, you call a Windows function from USER32.EXE:

```
1:  Uses User32
2:     ExitWindows(reserved CDOUBLE, returncode CWORD) CWORD
3:  endUses
```

The following example shows you step-by-step that once you register a function from the Windows 95 and NT API, you can use it just like any ObjectPAL procedure. For this example, suppose that you want to exit Windows when a user presses a button on a form. This example uses the exitWindows function. (For more options on using this function, refer to the Windows SDK or API reference guides.)

You can find the WIN-EXIT.FSL form on the disc in the \ANSWERS directory.

Step By Step

1. Set your working directory to the TUTORIAL directory, create a new form, and place a button on it. Label it Exit Windows.

2. Add line 5 to the Uses window of the Exit Windows button.

```
1:      ;Button :: Uses
2:      Uses User32
3:         ;The return value is zero if one or more applications
4:         ;refuse to terminate.
5:         ExitWindows(reserved cdouble, returncode cword) Number
6:      endUses
```

3. Add lines 3–5 to the pushButton method of the Exit Windows button.

```
1:    ;Button :: pushButton
2:    method pushButton(var eventInfo Event)
3:        if msgQuestion("Exit Windows?",
      "Are you sure you wish to exit Windows?") = "Yes" then
4:            ExitWindows(0, 0)
5:        endIf
6:    endmethod
```

4. Check the syntax and save the form as WIN-EXIT.FSL. Run the form and click the Exit Windows button. You exit not only Paradox but also Windows itself (see Figure 32.1).

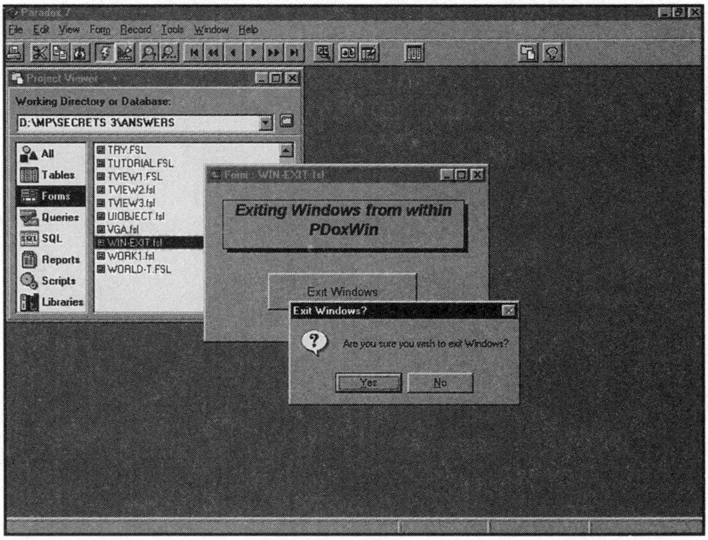

FIGURE 32.1.

WIN-EXIT.FSL demonstrates using the Windows API.

Analysis

In step 2, line 2 tells ObjectPAL which function is in the User32.exe DLL. No path or extension is used. ObjectPAL automatically searches the current directory, the Windows directory, and all the directories on the path. Line 5 prototypes the function in the DLL. You prototype DLLs similarly to custom methods. In this case, the DLL function is called exitWindows. It takes two parameters and returns a number.

In step 3, line 3 prompts the user with a message question dialog box. If the answer to the question is yes, line 4 calls the function, which exits Windows. This button is completely self-contained; all the code is in it. Now that you have created it, you can copy and paste the button into any application that you want.

Using *IsWindow*

You use the API function IsWindow from User32 when you want to determine whether a window handle is valid. Following is the correct Uses prototype:

```
Uses User32
    IsWindow(WinHandle CLONG) CLONG
endUses
```

The WinHandle parameter is a long integer representing the window handle. You can retrieve all the window handles to a dynamic array by using enumWindowHandles() or to a table by using enumDesktopWindowNames(). The second example gives you much more information. The return value from IsWindow is either 0 or a nonzero value. Valid window handles return 0, and invalid window handles return a nonzero value.

Here is how you use IsWindow to find the first valid window handle available on your system:

```
 1:   ;Button :: pushButton
 2:   Uses User32
 3:       IsWindow(WinHandle CLONG) CLONG
 4:   endUses
 5:   method pushButton(var eventInfo Event)
 6:       var
 7:           liWindow        LongInt
 8:           liCounter       LongInt
 9:       endVar
10:
11:       liCounter = 1
12:       for liCounter from 1 to 100000
13:           if IsWindow(liCounter) <> 0 then
14:               ;Valid Window handle.
15:               msgInfo("Valid Window Handle", String(liCounter) + " is a valid
                   window handle")
16:               quitloop
17:           else
18:               ;Invalid Window handle.
19:               message(String(liCounter) + " is not a valid window handle")
20:           endIf
21:       endFor
22:   endMethod
```

The Windows 95/NT API includes many functions you can use to manipulate Windows. Examples are AnyPopUp, ArrangeIconicWindows, BringWindowToTop, GetTopWindow, IsChild, and SetParent.

Checking the State of the Numlock Key

This next example enables you to check the state of the Numlock key using the User32 module of the Windows 95 and Windows NT API. Alter the pushButton method of a button as follows:

```
1:   ;Button :: pushButton
2:   Uses User32
3:     GetKeyState(vkey CWORD) CWORD
4:   endUses
5:
6:   method pushButton(var eventInfo Event)
7:       if getkeystate(VK_NUMLOCK) = 1 then
8:           msgInfo("Numkey is...", "locked")
9:       else
10:          msgInfo("Numkey is...", "unlocked")
12:      endIf
12:  endmethod
```

Switching to Another Application

This next example demonstrates how to switch to another Windows 95 or Windows NT application using the Windows 95 and NT API. Alter the pushButton method of a button as follows:

```
1:   ;Button :: pushButton
2:   Uses User32
3:     BringWindowToTop(WinHandle CWORD)
4:   endUses
5:
6:   method pushButton(var eventInfo Event)
7:       var
8:          tc   TCursor
9:          s    SmallInt
10:      endVar
11:
12:      enumWindowNames("WinNames.db")
13:
14:      tc.open("WinNames.db")
15:
16:      if tc.locate("WindowName", "Untitled - Notepad") then
17:          s = tc.handle
18:          bringWindowToTop(s)
19:      else
20:          execute("notepad.exe")
21:      endIf
22:  endmethod
```

Using TAPI to Dial the Phone

The final example in this chapter demonstrates how to dial the phone using the Windows 95 and NT TAPI interface. Alter the pushButton method of a button as follows:

```
1:   ;Button :: pushButton
2:   method pushButton(var eventInfo Event)
3:       var
4:          sPhoneNumber   String
5:          sName          String
6:       endVar
7:
8:       ;Prompt for number to dial.
9:       sPhoneNumber = "1234567"
```

```
10:        sPhoneNumber.view("Enter phone number to dial")
11:        if sPhoneNumber = "1234567" then return endIf
12:
13:        ;Who are you calling?
14:        sName = ""
15:        sName.view("Who are you calling? [optional]")
16:
17:        ;Dial number.
18:        cmDialPhone(sPhoneNumber, sName)
19:    endmethod
```

Next, add the following custom method to the form.

```
1:    ;Form :: cmDialPhone
2:    Uses Tapi32
3:        ;Dial the phone.
4:        tapiRequestMakeCall(sNumber CPTR, sAppName CPTR, sLogName CPTR, sComment
           CPTR) CLONG
5:    endUses
6:    method cmDialPhone(sNumber String, sLogName String)
7:        var
8:            arNumber      Array[] String
9:            siCounter     SmallInt
10:        endVar
11:
12:        ;Take out non-number characters commonly used in phone numbers.
13:        breakapart(sNumber, arNumber, "()-/ ")
14:        sNumber = "" ;Reset number.
15:        for siCounter from 1 to arNumber.size()
16:            sNumber = sNumber + arNumber[siCounter]
17:        endFor
18:
19:        tapiRequestMakeCall(sNumber, "Paradox 7", sLogName, "")
20:    endMethod
```

Run the form, click the button, and type in a phone number you want to call.

Summary

In this chapter, you learned that the API is the set of DLLs that makes up Windows 95 and NT. It comprises all the functions, messages, data structures, data types, statements, and files that a programmer needs for developing Windows 95/NT applications. You learned a technique for finding and using the functions in the Windows 95/NT API.

The System, Session, and Binary Types

33

This chapter introduces you to the system, session, and binary type. The System commands add functional programming power to ObjectPAL. For example, you can use them to beep the system speaker or read from and write to .INI files or the registry. The Session type gives you a channel to the database engine. For example, with the Session type you can add an alias. The Binary type enables you to deal with binary data. For example, you can use the Binary type to store zip files in a Paradox table. Finally, this chapter concludes with an introduction to the concept of a data dictionary by introducing you to a Paradox data dictionary.

The Registry and .INI Files

In versions of Windows prior to Windows 95, configuration information was stored in initialization (.INI) files. For example, if you used Windows 3.1, you probably are familiar with WIN.INI and SYSTEM.INI. In Windows 95, the registry stores such information and more. The registry holds information about the computer hardware configuration, installed software, settings, preferences, and file associations. Should you still use .INI files in Windows 95? You bet. However, use them sparingly. Your first choice for information about your software should be the registry, and only when you run into a reason not to use the registry should you use initialization files. For example, the *Programmer's Guide to Microsoft Windows 95* (Microsoft Press, 1995) recommends creating an initialization file if the information exceeds a few thousand bytes.

Using .INI Files

ObjectPAL offers a convenient way to read and write .INI files. You can, for example, write to your own custom .INI file using writeProfileString(). After you create a file, you can read it using readProfileString(). Here is the syntax for both functions:

writeProfileString(const *FileName* String, const *Section* String, const *Key* String, const *Value* String) Logical
readProfileString(const *FileName* String, const *Section* String, const *Key* String) String

The *FileName* is the .INI file you want to create or edit. The *Section* is the word bound with square brackets (do not include the square brackets with these procedures). Each section contains one or more *Keys*. Each *Key* has an associated *Value*. For example, to set a value called MYAPP.INI in an .INI file, type lines 3 and 4 of the following into the pushButton method of a button:

```
1:   ;btnWriteProfile :: pushButton
2:   method pushButton(var eventInfo Event)
3:      writeProfileString("MYAPP.INI", "Colors", "Background",  "White")
4:      writeProfileString("MYAPP.INI", "Colors", "Foreground",  "Black")
5:   endMethod
```

The preceding code creates the file MYAPP.INI in your Windows directory with the following text:

```
[Colors]
Background=White
Foreground=Black
```

You could then use this information to customize your application. When you open the application, read in the following values and set the foreground and background colors. For example, type the following code into the pushButton method of a button:

```
 1:    ;btnReadProfile :: pushButton
 2:    method pushButton(var eventInfo Event)
 3:       var
 4:          sBG, sFG String
 5:       endVar
 6:
 7:       sBG = readProfileString("MYAPP.INI", "Colors", "Background")
 8:       sFG = readProfileString("MYAPP.INI", "Colors", "Foreground")
 9:
10:       sBG.view("Background Color")
11:       sFG.view("Forground Color")
12:    endMethod
```

Then you can use these two variables to set colors in your application. For example, the following code uses the two variables defined in the preceding code to set the colors of a box. (Do not type this example; the preceding variable is declared private to the pushButton method and is out of scope from the box.)

```
 1:    box1 :: open
 2:    doDefault
 3:    self.color = sBG
 4:    self.frame.color = sFG
```

I have always found it annoying that programs put unnecessary files in my Windows directory. If you share my opinion, another good location for .INI files is the same directory as the files that use it. For example, the following uses getAliasPath() to write the .INI file to the current working directory.

```
writeProfileString(getAliasPath("WORK") + "\\MYAPP.INI",
"Colors", "Background", "White")
```

Because the new standard for Windows 95 is to use the registry for most of your setting information, I suggest to you that if you choose to use a .INI file, then you should create it in the same directory as the object using it. Otherwise, use the registry. INI files are convenient because they don't rely on another form, library, or table to store information. In addition, they store information from one session to another.

Registry Methods

The preferred method of storing software information is to use the registry. ObjectPAL offers several methods for manipulating the registry; they include `setRegistryValue()`, `getRegistryValue()`, `deleteRegistryValue()`, `searchRegistry()`, `enumRegistryKeys()`, and `enumRegistryValueNames()`.

Using *setRegistryValue()* and *getRegistryValue()*

The `setRegistryValue()` method sets a value in the registry. Here is the syntax:

```
setRegistryValue ( const key String, const value String,
const data AnyType, const rootKey LongInt) Logical
```

If either the *key* or *value* does not exist, it will be created.

The `rootKey` is analogous to a directory drive. The `rootkey` should be set with the predefined constants: `regKeyCurrentUser`, `regKeyClassesRoot`, `regKeyLocalMachine`, or `regKeyUser`.

The following example sets the current ObjectPAL level in the registry:

```
 1: ;Button :: pushButton
 2: method pushButton(var eventInfo Event)
 3:    var
 4:       sKey, sValue, sData, sLevel    String
 5:    endVar
 6:
 7:    sKey = "Software\\Borland\\Paradox\\7.0\\PDOXWIN\\Properties"
 8:    sValue = "Level"
 9:    sData = "Advanced"
10:    setRegistryValue( sKey, sValue, sData, regKeyCurrentUser )
11: endMethod
```

> **NOTE**
>
> The preceding usage of `setRegistry()` value is only an example of how to use the procedure. In actual practice, you should use the new `setUserLevel()` and `getUserLevel()`.

`getRegistryValue()` is the counterpart to `setRegistryValue()`. It retrieves a value from the registry. Here is the syntax:

```
getRegistryValue ( const key String, const value String ,
const rootKey LongInt ) AnyType
```

The following example gets the current ObjectPAL level from the registry:

```
 1: ;Button :: pushButton
 2: method pushButton(var eventInfo Event)
```

```
 3:    var
 4:       sLevel, sKey, sValue    String
 5:    endVar
 6:
 7:    sKey = "Software\\Borland\\Paradox\\7.0\\PDOXWIN\\Properties"
 8.    sValue = "Level"
 9:    sLevel = getRegistryValue(sKey, sValue, regKeyCurrentUser )
10:    sLevel.view("ObjectPAL Level")
11: endMethod
```

Notice that the syntax for `getRegistryValue()` shows that it returns a value of type `AnyType`. `sLevel` is of type `string` because you knew ahead of time what the return type would be. If you don't, then return the value to a variable of type `AnyType`. Setting and retrieving values from the Windows 95 registry is easy when you're using Paradox 7.

Using Aliases

As an ObjectPAL programmer, you probably have dealt with aliases already. Programming aliases involves checking for the existence of the alias, adding it if it does not exist, and saving the BDE configuration file. With the Session methods and procedures, you can check for, list, add, and save aliases.

If you're really ambitious, you might add error-checking routines to make sure that the alias has a valid directory. For example, you can use `getAliasPath()` to check whether an alias exists. You can use `addAlias()` to create a new alias. You can use `setAliasPath()` to set the path for an existing alias; this function isn't needed if you use `addAlias()`. You also can use `saveCFG()` to save the alias permanently. The example in the next section shows you how to check for and add an alias in the current session.

> **NOTE**
>
> You can use the `saveCFG()` method without a parameter to save the configuration to the current (active) configuration file.

Using the Alias in the Current Session

Suppose that you want to create a button on a form that checks whether an alias exists and that adds the alias if it doesn't exist.

> You can find the ALIAS.FSL form on the disc in the \ANSWERS directory.

Step By Step

1. Create a new form and place a button on it. Label the button Go.

2. Add lines 3–11 to the pushButton method of the Go button:

```
 1: ;Button :: pushButton
 2: method pushButton(var eventInfo Event)
 3:    if getAliasPath("Secrets3_Answers") = blank() then
 4:       if isFile("ALIAS.FSL") then
 5:          addAlias("Secrets3_Answers", "Standard", getAliasPath(":work:"))
 7:          msgInfo("Secrets3_Answers alias added",
                getAliasPath("Secrets3_Answers"))
 8:       else
 9:          msgStop("Startup Error", "This form is not in the current
                working directory.")
10:          close()
11:       endIf
12:    endIf
13: endMethod
```

3. Check the syntax, save the form as ALIAS.FSL, run the form, and click the button. If the Secrets3_Answers alias doesn't exist, it's added and a message information box appears. If the form isn't in your working directory, a stop message box pops up, and the form closes (see Figure 33.1).

FIGURE 33.1.

ALIAS.FSL demonstrates how to add an alias.

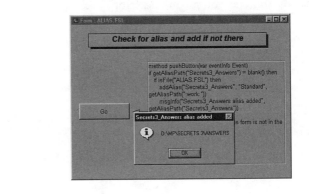

Analysis

In step 2, line 3 checks whether the Secrets3_Answers alias exists by checking whether its path is empty. For an alternative, you could use enumAliasNames() to write all the alias names to a table on a disk and scan the table for the name. That's too much work, though. (You can use or omit the colons.)

Line 4 makes sure that the form is in the current working directory. This is important because line 5 adds an alias based on the current working directory. That way, if a user attempts to open the form from a different directory, a bad alias isn't added. Instead, line 8 displays an error message, and line 9 closes the form.

Adding a Permanent Alias

In this example, you learn how to add a permanent alias automatically when the form opens. To do this, you need to check whether an alias exists and add it if it doesn't exist.

> You can find the ALIAS2.FSL form on the disc in the \ANSWERS directory.

Step By Step

1. Remove the Secrets3_Answers alias added in the preceding example and create a new blank form.

2. Alter the init method of the form to look like the following:

```
1: ;Form :: init
2: proc cpAddSecrets3_Answers()
3:;This custom procedure adds an alias.
4:     addAlias("Secrets3_Answers", "Standard",  getAliasPath(":work:"))
5:     if not saveCFG() then
6:         errorShow()
7:     endIf
8:     msgInfo("Secrets3_Answers alias added",
         getAliasPath("Secrets3_Answers"))
9: endProc
10:
11: proc cpAliasError()
12:;This custom procedure displays an error message and closes.
13:     msgStop("Startup Error", "This form is not in the current working
         directory.")
14:     close()
15: endProc
16:
17: method init(var eventInfo Event)
18:     switch
19:        case getAliasPath("Secrets3_Answers") = blank()
20:           :  if isFile("ALIAS2.FSL") then
21:                 cpAddSecrets3_Answers()
22:              else
23:                 cpAliasError()
24:              endIf
25:        otherwise
26:           :  if getAliasPath("Secret3") <> getAliasPath(":work:") then
27:                 if isFile("ALIAS2.FSL") then
28:                    cpAddSecrets3_Answers()
29:                 else
30:                    cpAliasError()
31:                 endIf
32:              endIf
33:     endSwitch
34: :: endMethod
```

3. Check the syntax and run the form. If the Secrets3_Answers alias doesn't exist, it's added and a message information box appears. If the form isn't in your working

directory, a stop message box pops up, and the form closes. If the Secrets3_Answers alias exists and its path needs to be changed to the new current working directory, the path is changed, and the configuration file is saved (see Figure 33.2).

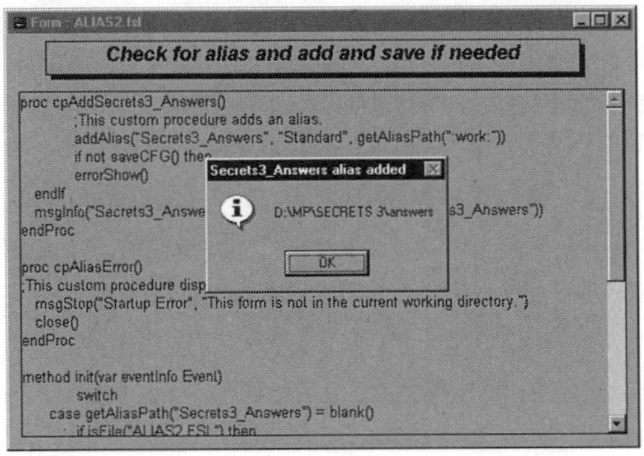

FIGURE 33.2.

ALIAS2.FSL demonstrates adding an alias permanently.

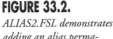

Analysis

The `init` event method uses a switch statement to check whether the alias should be added. The `cpAddSecrets3_Answers()` custom procedure adds and saves the alias. If there is an error, the `cpAliasError()` custom procedure displays an error message.

This example of checking for an alias and adding or updating it is elegant programming. It isn't elegant because of its simplicity, but rather because of its thoroughness. If the user forgets to create an alias, the alias is created for him or her. If the user moves the application directory, the alias is updated for him or her. Although you might not want to implement this routine on all your applications, you should if you're designing for sale an application that uses an alias.

The Dialog Category

All system dialog procedures start with `dlg`. These dialog procedures interactively bring up many—but not all—of the dialog boxes available. The next example in the next section looks at six of them.

Using Dialog Procedures

In this example, you learn how to use the system dialog procedures by studying six of them: `dlgDelete()`, `dlgCreate()`, `dlgCopy()`, `dlgSort()`, `dlgNetSetLocks()`, and `dlgNetWho()`.

You can find the DLG.FSL form on the disc in the \ANSWERS directory.

Step By Step

1. Change your working directory to TUTORIAL. Create a new form with six buttons. Label the buttons Create TEMP table, Delete TEMP table, Copy WORLD.DB, Sort World table, Lock/Unlock a table, and Show Current Users (see Figure 33.3).

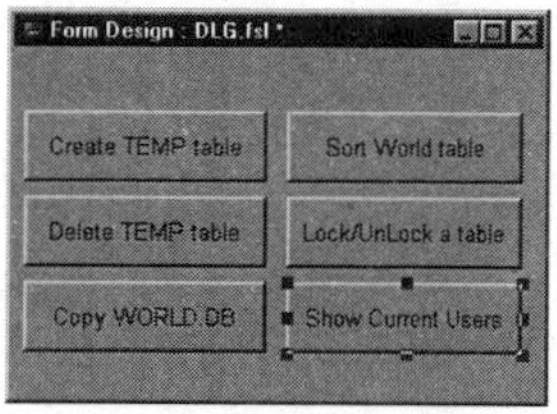

FIGURE 33.3.

Setup form for the example.

2. Add line 3 to the pushButton method of the Delete TEMP table button.

```
1:    ;Button :: pushButton
2:    method pushButton(var eventInfo Event)
3:        dlgDelete("TEMP")
4:    endMethod
```

3. Add line 3 to the pushButton method of the Create TEMP table button.

```
1:    ;Button :: pushButton
2:    method pushButton(var eventInfo Event)
3:        dlgCreate("TEMP")
4:    endMethod
```

4. Add the Copy WORLD.DB button, as follows:

```
1:    ;Button :: pushButton
2:    method pushButton(var eventInfo Event)
3:        dlgCopy("WORLD")
4:    endMethod
```

5. Add line 3 to the pushButton method of the Sort World table button.

```
1:    ;Button :: pushButton
2:    method pushButton(var eventInfo Event)
3:        dlgSort("WORLD")
4:    endMethod
```

6. Add line 3 to the pushButton method of the Lock/Unlock a table button.

```
1:    ;Button :: pushButton
2:    method pushButton(var eventInfo Event)
3:        dlgNetSetLocks()
4:    endMethod
```

7. Add line 3 to the pushButton method of the Show Current Users button.

```
1:    ;Button :: pushButton
2:    method pushButton(var eventInfo Event)
3:        dlgNetWho()
4:    endMethod
```

8. Check the syntax and save the form. Run the form. Click all six buttons in any order to see how they work. Figure 33.4 shows the Sort Table dialog box.

FIGURE 33.4.

*DLG.FSL and the Sort
Table dialog box.*

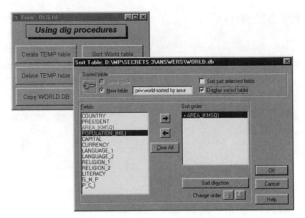

Analysis

The dialog procedures are fairly straightforward. The only interesting thing is that they have two types of syntax. One type of syntax requires a table name; the other one does not.

You should explore the other 12 system dialog procedures. Add the ones of interest to you to the form that you created in this example.

About the Binary Type

Use the Binary data type for data that only the computer understands; Paradox does not know how to interpret the data. The Binary variable is a handle you can establish to a binary object. Table 33.1 lists the Binary methods and procedures.

Table 33.1. The Binary methods and procedures.

```
blank*

clipboardErase

clipboardHasFormat

dataType*

enumClipboardFormats

isAssigned*

isBlank*

isFixedType*

readFromClipboard

readFromFile

size
```

```
writeToClipboard

writeToFile
```

*Inherited from the AnyType type

On the disc, the form BINARY.FSL in the \ANSWERS directory demonstrates many of the Binary methods and procedures (see Figure 33.5).

FIGURE 33.5.

BINARY.FSL demonstrates many of the binary methods.

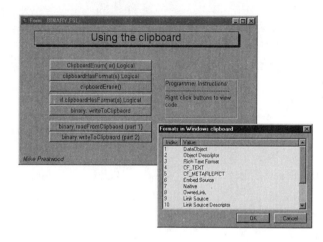

For example, type lines 3–9 into the pushButton method of a button to display the formats currently in the Windows Clipboard:

```
 1:  ;Button :: pushButton
 2:  method pushButton(var eventInfo Event)
 3:     var
 4:        b      Binary
 5:        ar     Array[] String
 6:     endVar
 7:
 8:     b.enumClipboardFormats( ar )
 9:     ar.view("Formats in Windows clipboard")
10:  endmethod
```

Storing Objects Using the Clipboard Viewer

You can use the Clipboard Viewer that comes with Windows to store code. This technique of storing code is better than saving files to a disk as individual text files. Plus, you can store objects and code listings in the same place. You can read and write to the Clipboard using writeToClipboard() and readFromClipboard().

Creating a Data Dictionary

NEW Term

A *data dictionary* is a set of tables that describes a database. A database in Paradox is roughly defined as all the files in a directory. Suppose that you want to create a data dictionary for all the files in a directory.

> On the disc is a script that builds a data dictionary of your application. The script is \ANSWERS\DD_BUILD.SSL. Especially handy is the table that stores all the source code, DD_SRC.DB (see Table 33.2). You can use this table to search globally through the source code of all the forms, scripts, and libraries of an entire directory. Run this script on the files in the ANSWERS directory; then create a quick form based on the DD_SRC.DB table, and browse all the source code.

Table 33.2. Prestwood's data dictionary.

Table	Description
DD_F.DB	Listing of forms
DD_FILES.DB	Listing of all files (including non-Paradox files)
DD_L.DB	Listing of libraries
DD_Q.DB	Listing of queries
DD_R.DB	Listing of reports
DD_S.DB	Listing of scripts
DD_SQL.DB	Listing of SQL source files
DD_SRC.DB	Listing of source code for forms, scripts, and libraries
DD_T.DB	Listing of tables

Although this data dictionary is useful, currently it does have limitations. The following are the limitations of DD_BUILD.SSL:

- Supports only Paradox tables.
- Deals with files only in the same directory (does not recurse subdirectories).
- Generates tables in the same directory as files.
- Does not scan through each table and delete the references to the data dictionary files. If you do not want to have the data dictionary files take up room in the data dictionary tables, then use a scan loop to go through each table that starts with DD_ and delete every entry that starts with DD_.

> **NOTE**
>
> I upgrade this Data Dictionary all the time. Visit the Internet site of Prestwood Enterprises for information on how to contact me for the latest version (http://www.impex.com/prestwood).

Summary

This chapter was a catchall for the System, Session, and Binary types and just touched on the power in these three types. Of particular interest are the use of aliases and the data dictionary; these two items will probably become part of your everyday use.

Networking

34

**NEW
*Term***

A network is a system of interconnected computer systems and terminals that share software and data. Communicating with other applications enables you to increase the functionality and usability of your applications. This chapter teaches you how to create multiuser applications.

Network programming features enable you to create multiuser applications easily. And Paradox offers the best data connectivity available to Paradox and dBASE tables. Each major release of Paradox since version 2.0 has improved table structures.

Converting Your Application to a Network Application

**NEW
*Term***

The central, or controlling, computer in a local area network is the *server*. Although it could be used like a regular computer, a server usually is dedicated to sending and receiving data from devices that are connected to a network. A *client* is a device that receives data from the server in a local area network.

Any application you create in Paradox is fully networkable—automatically. It doesn't matter whether you use Paradox or dBASE table structures. Paradox for Windows obeys all the rules of networking for both Paradox and dBASE.

You still need to be concerned about multiple users, but you don't have to do anything other than properly install and set up Paradox in order to network your application. Most problems that come up in a network environment deal with users who step on or run into other users. This issue is almost always about conflicting locks. Your first and main task when establishing a network application is to install it and set it up properly. Half the battle to networking successfully with Paradox is installing and setting up Paradox correctly. After you correctly install and set up all your applications, networking is transparent—and painless.

Installing Paradox on a Network

This section gives you an overview of the three possible configurations you can use to install Paradox on a network.

**NEW
*Term***

The worst and slowest configuration is to install everything on the network. With this setup, the only files you install locally are the boot files on your local hard drive—or even worse, on a single floppy disk. All other files—including utilities, Windows, Paradox, your application, net files, and data files—are on the server, susceptible to network traffic and breakdowns. This setup is called a *diskless workstation*. I don't recommend it. Given that the price for hard drives has plummeted, no company should use this setup.

The best and fastest configuration is to install everything locally, if you can. This configuration includes DOS, Windows, Paradox, and your application. The only files that go on the network are the net files and data files. This setup requires the most hard drive space, but it offers the most convenience and speed of the three setups.

A compromise solution is to install some necessary files on the network and some files locally. If you use this setup, I recommend that you keep DOS, Windows, and Paradox local and put just your application, the data files, and the net files on the network. For a further compromise, you could keep DOS, Windows, and the BDE files local and put the rest of the files—Paradox, your application, the data files, and the net files—on the network. This setup requires less hard drive space and offers moderate speed.

The best place to put files is in the place that gives you the most convenience and speed. Therefore, you should install DOS, Windows, Paradox, and your application files locally and store only the net files and data tables on the network. Paradox does run in all three configurations, however. You can install the Paradox files either locally or on a network hard drive (perhaps F:\WINAPPS\PDOXWIN). Each user must have read, open, scan, and execute rights to the directory in which you install Paradox (or its equivalent on networks that aren't Novell networks).

Where to Install BDE Files

BDE is an acronym for *Borland Database Engine*. BDE is the engine of the Windows versions of Paradox and dBASE. Without it, you can't access any database tables. Borland's decision to separate the engine from the application enables Borland to upgrade both independently and use the engine in other applications. Just as the DOS Paradox engine is available separately for C, C++, and Pascal programmers, the BDE engine is available for C, C++, and Pascal programmers and goes by the name of the Borland Database Engine.

NEW
Term

You can put the BDE files in either the default Windows system directory or in another directory (such as F:\WINAPP\BDE). If Paradox is the only application on your network that is aware of Paradox, you can install the BDE files in the Paradox directory. I advise that you don't, however. Each user should have read, open, scan, and execute rights to the directory that contains the BDE files.

Configuring the BDE Engine

After you've installed all the files in their appropriate places, you still must deal with setup and configuration.

The BDE engine configuration file holds network-specific configuration information. Its default name is IDAPI32.CFG. This file stores the location of the network control file and the list of database aliases, among other things.

To set the network control file, run the Configuration Utility program, BDECFG32.EXE, in the Paradox group (see Figure 34.1). Type the location of the Paradox network control file and click OK. As soon as you specify a network control file, Paradox is ready to access data over the network. Users who want or need their own IDAPI32.CFG files can copy it from this location.

FIGURE 34.1.

The BDE Configuration
Utility dialog box.

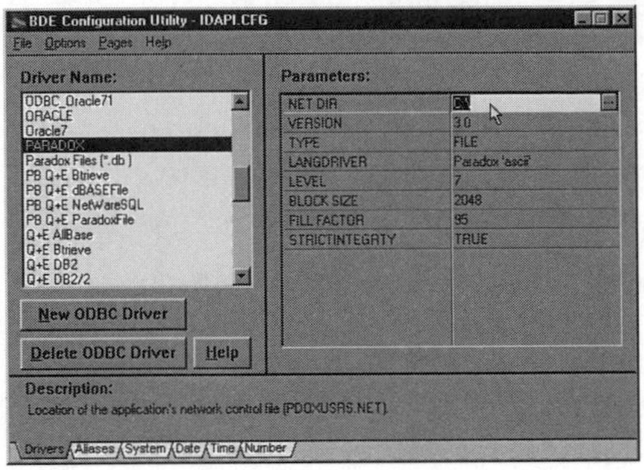

You also use the BDE Configuration Utility program to set whether BDE shares local tables with other programs that use the Paradox 4.0 locking protocol.

The Network Control File

The *network control file* is a file that controls items such as table and directory access. A network control file is often called a *net file*. The Paradox network control file, PDOXUSRS.NET, serves as the reference point for all the lock files created by Paradox. Each lock file references the network control file. Therefore, all the users must map to the same network control file using the same path but not necessarily the same drive letter. For example, one machine can use T:\NETFILES\PARADOX, and another machine can use G:\NETFILES\PARADOX. The drive letter does not matter as long as the path is the same.

The Paradox Startup Sequence

When Paradox starts, it attempts to access the network control file specified in the BDE configuration file. If a PDOXUSRS.NET file is available, Paradox opens it. If Paradox doesn't find a PDOXUSRS.NET file, it creates a new PDOXUSRS.NET file and continues with the startup process.

After Paradox successfully opens the PDOXUSRS.NET file, it places an exclusive PARADOX.LCK file in a designated directory for temporary files. If it can't place that exclusive PARADOX.LCK file, Paradox shuts itself down. After it secures a directory for temporary files, Paradox places a shareable PARADOX.LCK file in a directory with data files. The initialization is complete, and Paradox is ready to open its first table.

Concurrency

Application *concurrency* is the simultaneous use of applications. It can be confusing with all the different applications—especially when the various versions of the programs support different locking protocols and, therefore, different levels of concurrency. The following section lists the issues involved in multiuser environments. Then you'll learn how to configure applications that are aware of Paradox.

NEW
Term

Paradox Locking Protocols

A *lock* is a device that prevents other users from viewing, changing, or locking a table while one user is working with it. One networking feature of Paradox is locking. Powerful record-locking technology increases your productivity in multiuser performance and functionality. Multiuser locking is mostly automatic for both the end user and the programmer. Paradox also offers screen refresh. Changes made by other multiple users are immediately refreshed onscreen.

NEW
Term

Paradox has two locking protocols: the protocol introduced with Paradox 2.0 and the protocol introduced with Paradox 4.0. These two protocols are incompatible with each other. The locking protocol has no bearing on the type of table a program can work with. However, the locking protocol does determine which applications can network together; that is, what applications can access a table at the same time. A few programs can support both locking protocols, but even these programs can support only one protocol at a time.

Five versions of the Paradox Engine are in wide use: namely, Paradox Engine 2.0, Paradox Engine 3.0, ODAPI, IDAPI, and the new BDE engine. Paradox 1.0 and 4.5 for Windows use ODAPI, Paradox 5 for Windows uses IDAPI, and Paradox 7 for Windows 95 and Windows NT utilizes the BDE engine. In addition to the Paradox line of products, other products use versions of the Paradox Engines. When you implement a network application, understanding which products use which engine is important. Table 34.1 lists which products support each locking protocol.

Table 34.1. The Paradox locking protocols and the programs that support each one.

Paradox 2.0	*Paradox 4.0*	*Both Protocols*
Paradox 2.0–3.5	Paradox 4.0 & 4.5	Paradox Engine 3.0
Paradox Runtime 2.0–3.5	Paradox Runtime 4.0	Quattro Pro
Paradox Engine 1.0–2.0	Quick Reports 1.0	Quattro Pro 4.0
ObjectVision 1.0–2.0	ODAPI/IDAPI/BDE	ObjectVision 2.1

continues

Table 34.1. continued

Paradox 2.0	*Paradox 4.0*	*Both Protocols*
Quattro Pro 2.0–3.0 SideKick 2.0	Paradox for Windows (all versions)	Crystal Reports 1.1–2.0

The Paradox 2.0 Locking Protocol

The Paradox 2.0 locking protocol is the older protocol used in older products. As Table 34.1 indicates, many older Borland applications use this locking protocol. The designation Paradox 2.0 locking protocol represents this level of concurrency. In today's network environment, it's somewhat dated.

The Paradox 4.0 Locking Protocol

As Table 34.1 shows, not all versions of Paradox for Windows support the Paradox 2.0 locking protocol. This means that Paradox for Windows can't network with the products in the first column of that table. Usually, you simply need to upgrade. For example, users of ObjectVision 2.0 must upgrade to version 2.1 to network with both ObjectVision and Paradox. The Paradox 4.0 locking protocol is the only protocol available for the BDE engine.

Applications written with version 3.0 of the Paradox Engine library can switch the locking protocol that they use. The designation Paradox 4.0 locking protocol represents this style of locking and concurrency.

In a multiuser environment, the Paradox 4.0 locking protocol maintains concurrency through the PDOXUSRS.NET file. All users who want to share Paradox tables must point to the same PDOXUSRS.NET file by using the same path; they don't necessarily have to use the same drive letter. Paradox places a PDOXUSRS.LCK and an exclusive PARADOX.LCK file in each directory in which tables are being accessed. These locks prevent previous versions of Paradox from accessing files in the same directory. Each user who wants to share tables in that directory must map that directory in the same way by using the same path but not necessarily the same drive letter. Then Paradox places all the locking information for that table in the PDOXUSRS.LCK file. This reduces the number of files that are needed.

Table Locks Used by Engine 3.0, ODAPI, IDAPI, and BDE

Paradox 4.0 places each table lock in the directory locking file, PDOXUSRS.LCK. It no longer uses the separate table lock file of previous versions. For example, suppose that three users are viewing the CUSTOMER.DB table, and one user is restructuring the ORDERS.DB table.

The PDOXUSRS.LCK file will list a shareable lock for each of the three users who are viewing the CUSTOMER.DB table and an exclusive lock on ORDERS.DB for the user who is restructuring that table.

What Gets a Directory Lock

Because Paradox, the Paradox Engine, and ODAPI/IDAPI/BDE place a lock file in the directory that contains the tables, the first locking protocol to get to the directory owns it. If that locking protocol is the Paradox 2.0 locking protocol, any version of Paradox 2.0–3.5 or Paradox Engine 1.0–2.0 or 3.0 in compatible locking mode has concurrent access to the directory and to all files in that directory. For example, if the first locking protocol to use a directory is Paradox 7 with the BDE, only Engine 3.0 and ODAPI, IDAPI, and BDE applications have access to the tables in that directory.

Private Directory

Paradox for Windows and Paradox for DOS require a directory for storing temporary files, such as the answer tables from queries. When Paradox starts, it places exclusive PDOXUSRS.LCK and PARADOX.LCK files in the private directory and designates that directory as the location for temporary files. This designation means that other Paradox users can't access tables in that directory. This restricted access occurs only if Local Share is turned on in the BDE Configuration file.

Benefits of the Paradox 4.0 Locking Protocol

The Paradox 4.0 locking protocol replaces the form lock with a new locking protocol called a *group lock*. The Paradox 4.0 locking protocol also removes separate table lock files, thus reducing the number of files needed to maintain concurrent access. These improvements increase table concurrency, reduce network access time, and reduce downtime. Table 34.2 lists the methods and procedures that deal with locks in Paradox 7.

NEW Term

Table 34.2. Methods and procedures that deal with locks.

Method or Procedure	Class	Description
enumLocks	TCursor	Creates a Paradox table that lists the locks currently applied to a TCursor
enumLocks	UIObject	Creates a Paradox table that lists the locks currently applied to a UIObject and returns the number of locks
lock	Session	Locks one or more tables

continues

Table 34.2. continued

Method or Procedure	Class	Description
lock	Table	Locks a specified table
lock	TCursor	Places specified locks on a specified table
lockRecord	TCursor	Puts a write lock on the current record
lockRecord	UIObject	Puts a write lock on the current record
lockStatus	TCursor	Returns the number of times that a lock has been placed on a table
lockStatus	UIObject	Returns the number of locks on a table
unLock	TC/TBL	Removes a specified lock
unLockRecord	TC/UI	Removes the current lock

Table 34.3 compares the locks in Paradox for DOS to the locks in Paradox for Windows.

Table 34.3. Locks in Paradox for DOS and Paradox 7 for Windows.

Paradox 4.0	Paradox for Windows
write lock	read lock
prevent write lock	No equivalent; Paradox displays Unknown but respects prevent lock
group lock	Equivalent to a lock on the referential integrity master
Equivalent to write	write lock and prevent write lock
full lock	exclusive lock
prevent full lock	open lock

> **NOTE**
>
> A Paradox image lock is a lock placed on the TableView (.TV file) so that a second user sharing the table can't modify any properties.

Sending Messages Over a Network

You often use a network to communicate with other users connected to it. Two types of communicating systems are regularly used: messaging systems and mailing systems. In a messaging—or broadcasting—system, the other user must be logged onto the network. A mail system stores messages for later use; the other user doesn't have to be logged onto the network. If you don't already have a messaging system or if you want to include a messaging feature in your application, you can use ObjectPAL. Often, including a way to send messages from one user to another in your application is useful.

The example in the following section demonstrates a technique for sending messages across a network. It uses a common table with a timer. You use the timer to check whether the table has a message for you. If it does, you display the message and then delete it. You don't need to be connected to a network to go through this example.

Example of Sending Messages Over a Network

For this example, suppose that you want to add the capability to your application to send messages across the network to another user.

You can find the NET-MSG.FSL form on the disc in the \ANSWERS directory.

Step By Step

1. Create a new form and place a field and a button on it (see Figure 34.2). Change the field's label to FromNetUserName, and name the field FromField. Label the button Send a message.

FIGURE 34.2.

*Setting up the form
for the example.*

2. Add lines 3 and 4 to the Var window of the form:

```
1:    ;Form :: Var
2:    Var
3:       toStr, msg  String
4:       tc          TCursor
5:    endVar
```

3. Add lines 3 and 4 to the init method of the form:

```
1:    ;Form :: init
2:    method init(var eventInfo Event)
3:       self.setTimer(5000)
4:       tc.open("NET-MSG.DB")
5:    endmethod
```

4. Add line 3 to the open method of the FromField field:

```
1:      ;Field :: open
2:      method open(var eventInfo Event)
3:          self = getNetUserName()
4:      endmethod
```

5. Add line 8 to the timer method of the form:

```
1:      ;Form :: timer
2:      method timer(var eventInfo TimerEvent)
3:      if eventInfo.isPreFilter() then
4:          ;This code executes for each object on the form
5:
6:      else
7:          ;This code executes only for the form
8:          checkMsg()
9:      endif
10:     endmethod
```

6. Create a custom method called sendMsg() at the form level and add lines 3–22 to it, as follows:

```
1:      ;Form :: sendMsg
2:      method sendMsg()
3:          toStr = "All or username"
4:          toStr.view("Send message to?")
5:          if toStr = "All or username" then
6:              return
7:          endIf
8:
9:          msg = "Enter up to 30 characters"
10:         msg.view("Enter message")
11:         if msg = "Enter up to 30 characters" then
12:             return
13:         endIf
14:
15:         tc.edit()
16:         tc.insertRecord()
17:         tc."DateTime Stamp" = DateTime()
18:         tc."To" = toStr
19:         tc."From" = FromField
20:         tc.message = msg
21:         tc.postRecord()
22:         tc.endEdit()
23:     endmethod
```

7. Create another custom method at the form level, this time called checkMsg(), and add lines 3–20 to it, as follows:

```
1:      ;Form :: checkMsg
2:      method checkMsg()
3:          var
4:              s1, s2, s3 String
5:          endVar
```

```
 6:
 7:          if FromField.isBlank() then
 8:              return
 9:          endIf
10:
11:          if tc.locate("To", FromField) then
12:              s1 = tc."To"
13:              s2 = tc."From"
14:              s3 = tc."Message"
15:              tc.edit()
16:              tc.deleteRecord()
17:              msgInfo("*** Broadcast Message ***", "To: " + s1 +
          chr(13) + "From: " + s2 + chr(13) + chr(13) + s3)
18:              tc.endEdit()
19:          endIf
20:          checkAll()
21:      endmethod
```

8. Create one more custom method at the form level, this time called checkAll(), and add lines 3–11 to it, as follows:

```
 1:    ;Form :: checkAll
 2:    method checkAll()
 3:       if tc.locate("To", "All") then
 4:          if tc."DateTime Stamp" < DateTime() - (1000 * 5) then
 5:             tc.edit()
 6:             tc.deleteRecord()
 7:             tc.endEdit()
 8:          else
 9:             msgInfo("*** Broadcast Message ***", "To: " +
                  _    tc."To" + chr(13) + "From: " + tc."From" +
                  _    chr(13) + chr(13) + tc."Message")
10:          endIf
11:       endIf
12:    endmethod
```

9. Add line 3 to the pushButton method of the Send a message button:

```
 1:    ;Button :: pushButton
 2:    method pushButton(var eventInfo Event)
 3:       sendMsg()
 4:    endmethod
```

10. Check the syntax, save your work, and run the form. If the wrong name or no user name shows up in the FromField field, type a user name. The customary user name is your first initial and last name. Send yourself a message. Click the Send a message button and type your network user name—in other words, the value in the FromField field. Click OK. When the Enter Message dialog box appears, enter a message and click OK. Within five seconds, your message should appear. Figure 34.3 shows how the form looks when you are done with this example.

FIGURE 34.3.

NET-MSG.FSL. Sending a message by means of a table and a timer through the network using Paradox.

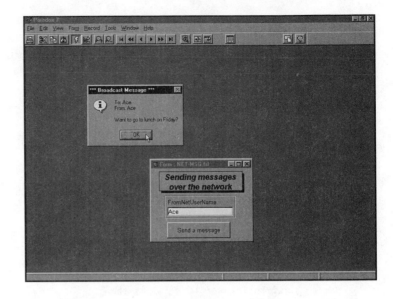

Analysis

In step 2, line 3 declares the two String variables used to store the name of the "To" user and the message. Line 4 declares a TCursor variable.

In step 3, line 3 sets the timer to trip every five seconds. Line 4 opens the TCursor. The TCursor is left open for the duration of the form to minimize how often a TCursor is opened. You might want to put error checking on line 4. That way, if the user is unable to open the table, he or she gets an error. For example, if two users pointing to different net files try to access the table at the same time, the second user gets an appropriate error message.

In step 4, line 3 attempts to get the name of the current network user and store it in FromField—that is, the field labeled FromNetUserName.

In step 5, line 8 on the `timer` method of the form calls the `checkMsg()` custom method.

In step 6, line 2 prototypes the `sendMsg()` custom method. This custom method is passed no value and returns no value. Lines 3 and 4 set the value for `toStr` and prompt the user to enter the network user name of the individual or the word `All`. Line 5 ensures that the user changed the value. If the user didn't, line 6 aborts the routine with `return`. Lines 9 and 10 set the value for `msg` and prompt the user to enter a message of up to 30 characters. Line 11 makes sure that the user changed the value. If he or she didn't, the routine is aborted in line 12. Note that there is no error checking to make sure that the user types 30 characters or fewer. Lines 15–22 place the TCursor into Edit mode, insert a record, date and timestamp the new record, set the values, post the record, and end Edit mode.

In step 7, line 2 prototypes the checkMsg() custom method. This custom method is passed no value and returns no value. Line 4 declares three String variables used to store the complete message. Line 7 makes sure that a current network user is defined. If a user isn't defined, line 8 aborts the routine. Line 11 checks whether a message for the user exists in the table. If one does, lines 12–14 grab the values and place them into String variables. Lines 15 and 16 delete the record so that the user doesn't get the same message more than once. Line 17 displays the message, and line 18 ends Edit mode.

In step 8, line 2 prototypes the checkAll() custom method. This custom method is passed no value and returns no value. Except for line 4, this routine is similar to the checkMsg() routine. Line 4 checks whether the All message is older than five seconds. If it is, line 6 deletes it without displaying it. Line 4 uses 5*1000 rather than 5000. This line illustrates a technique for using milliseconds. Thinking in terms of milliseconds is difficult. You may find it easier if you break the milliseconds into an equation. For example, how long is 3,600,000 milliseconds? (Where's Rain Man when you need him?) One thousand milliseconds—that is, one second—times 60 equals one minute. One minute times 60 equals an hour. You can see that 1000*60*60 is clearer than 3,600,000.

In step 9, line 3 calls the sendMsg() custom method, which starts the whole process.

You can simplify this routine so that it only sends a broadcast to everyone, or you can add to it to make it do more. If you want to include a way to display a message on all the terminals in your application without establishing the "To" and "From" users, you can strip down this routine. You also can add more groups than only "All." You can add a configuration that enables users to set things such as their personal user names or how often messages are checked. To take this technique to its limits, blow it up into a full-fledged mail system complete with storage—in other words, copy the message to a private table.

Summary

In this chapter, you learned that Paradox comes ready to use a network. Whether you buy a single version or a network license, you get the same functionality. This functionality extends to your applications; all your applications are ready for the network. The only real issues left are configuration, setup, and multiuser considerations.

Developing SQL Applications

35

This chapter focuses on using Paradox as a client/server development tool. It does not talk about connecting; it is assumed you have already connected. If you are having trouble connecting to a particular SQL server, then refer to the *Connection Guide* for that particular server. This chapter does review what a user can do interactively with Paradox and how to use ObjectPAL with SQL servers.

Who should read this chapter? Anyone interested in getting started with SQL and client/server applications. This chapter also covers using SQL on local tables—Paradox and dBASE tables. Do you need to be connected to a server? No, the first part of this chapter talks about SQL concepts and what you can do with SQL on local tables. Everybody can read the first half of this chapter up to the section titled "Interactive SQL."

About SQL

Structured Query Language (SQL) was developed to create a standard for accessing database information. The ANSI standard for SQL allows a user to become familiar with the commands needed to query many different types of data. After you learn ANSI SQL, you then can query many different databases.

Is SQL a solid standard? Yes and no. Yes, the core ANSI SQL commands are solid and consistent from vendor to vendor. Every vendor, however, adds capability to its version of SQL. These improvements are expected because ANSI SQL does not go far enough to cover every feature of every high-end DBMS.

The SQL standard is used by many companies for their high-end products. They include Oracle, Sybase, Microsoft SQL, Informix, and Borland's Interbase. Borland also provides the capability to use standard ANSI SQL commands on local Paradox and dBASE tables.

Using SQL on Local Tables

Although SQL by definition is a standard, various flavors are on the market. Borland, too, has its own flavor of SQL. Local SQL is built on a modified version of the InterBase SQL parser. The parser turns the SQL statements into QBE syntax, and then executes or translates it into BDE function calls.

> **NOTE**
>
> Version 7 is now SQL ANSI 92 compliant. This means that you can use any ANSI 92-compliant SQL statement. You therefore can go out and buy any SQL primer book that is compliant to ANSI 92.

Supported Syntax

Local SQL (sometimes called *client-based SQL*) is a subset of ANSI 92 SQL enhanced to support Paradox and dBASE (standard) naming conventions for tables and fields (columns in SQL terminology).

Naming Tables

ANSI SQL confines each table or column name to a single word consisting of alphanumeric characters and the underscore. Local SQL, however, is enhanced to support more comprehensive names. Local SQL supports full file and path specifications for table names (including Alias support).

Enclose table names with path or filename extensions in single or double quotation marks. For example,

```
select * from 'customer.dbf'
select * from ":work:customer.dbf"
```

> **NOTE**
>
> If you omit the file extension for a local table name, the table is assumed to be the table type specified in the Default Driver setting in the System page of the BDE Configuration Utility.

Column Names

Local SQL also supports Paradox's field names as long as these names are enclosed in single or double quotation marks and prefaced with a SQL table name or table correlation name. For example,

```
select o."Order No"
from Orders o
```

Supported SQL Statements

The SQL statements are broken into Data Manipulation Language (DML) and Data Definition Language (DDL). DML statements are used for handling data (selecting, inserting, updating, and deleting), and DDL statements handle the creating, altering, and dropping of tables, and the creating and dropping of indexes.

Table 35.1. Supported SQL keywords.

Category	Supported Keywords
DML statements	SELECT, INSERT, UPDATE, and DELETE
DML clauses	FROM, WHERE, ORDER BY, GROUP BY, HAVING, and UNION
Aggregate functions	SUM(), AVG(), MIN(), MAX(), COUNT(), and COUNT(*)
String functions	UPPER(), LOWER(), TRIM(), and SUBSTRING()
Operators	+, -, *, /, <, >, =, <>, IS NULL, IS NOTNULL, >=, =<, AND, OR, NOT, ¦¦, and LIKE
DDL statements	CREATE TABLE, ALTER TABLE, DROP TABLE, CREATE INDEX, DROP INDEX, and CREATE VIEW

SQL Query Properties

Figure 35.1 shows the Answer tab of the Query Properties dialog box for SQL queries. The following is a short description of each feature:

Live query view: This option enables you to work with the live data generated from a SQL statement (see "Constrained Updates" later in this list for related information).

Answer table: This option enables you to specify if you want a Paradox or dBASE answer table. In addition, it enables you to specify the name of the table.

Figure 35.2 shows the SQL tab of the Query Properties dialog box for SQL queries. The fol-

FIGURE 35.1.

The Answer tab of the Query Properties dialog box.

lowing is a short description of each feature:

Queries against remote tables: This panel affects only remote SQL data. It enables you to specify whether a SQL statement is run locally or on the remote server. The Run query remotely option is the fastest.

Auxiliary table options: This panel enables you to specify whether auxiliary tables are created. For faster queries, select Fast queries. To retain the ability to undo a SQL statement, select Generate auxiliary tables to create the necessary tables.

Constrained Updates: This option affects live queries only. If it is checked, you can enter values that match the select criteria only.

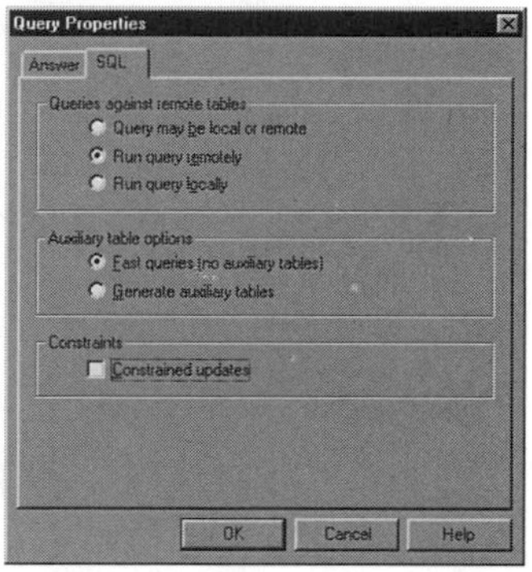

FIGURE 35.2.

The SQL tab of the Query Properties dialog box.

A SQL Primer

In this section, you learn about ANSI SQL as it applies to local Paradox and dBASE tables in a step by step tutorial format. ANSI SQL is a rich query language. Each command supports many different keywords and parameters. To really learn SQL, you need to get a good ANSI SQL book. You can get started with this section and some of the Paradox and dBASE local tables located in the TUTORIAL directory. After you learn this core syntax, you can use it with any SQL DBMS including Oracle, Sybase, MS SQL, Informix, and Gupta.

Using *select*

In this first step into SQL, you learn how to query your local Paradox tables with SQL. Here, you query the Customer and Orders tables using the SQL select command. The syntax for select is quite elaborate. For now, the basic syntax you need is as follows:

```
select criteria
from tablename
[where whereCriteria]
[order by orderBy]
```

Step By Step

1. Change your working directory to the TUTORIAL directory, and select File | New | SQL File. The SQL Editor opens, ready for you to type and execute a single SQL statement. Your screen should now look like Figure 35.3.

FIGURE 35.3.
The SQL Editor.

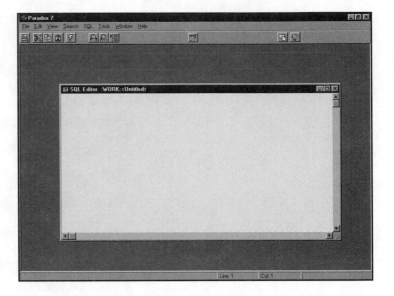

2. In place of *criteria*, you can place the names of columns or an *, which signifies all columns. Type the following SQL statement and save it as SQL-LS1.SQL:

```
1:  select *
2:  from Customer
```

NOTE

Notice that the .DB extension for the preceding Customer table is not specified. If you do not specify an extension, Paradox assumes that you are querying a Paradox table. To specify the .DB extension or a dBASE .DBF extension, add the extension and surround the name with quotes (such as "CUSTOMER.DB").

3. Run the SQL query by pressing F8. Your screen should look similar to Figure 35.4.

4. Next, specify the names of the columns you want to see separated by commas and ending with a space. Type the following, save it as SQL-LS2.SQL, and run the SQL statement. Your screen should then look similar to Figure 35.5.

```
1:  select Name, Phone
2:  from Customer
```

5. The count clause enables you to count records. For example, type the following SQL statement into the SQL Editor to find out how many records are in the Customer table:

```
1:  select count(*)
2:  from Customer
```

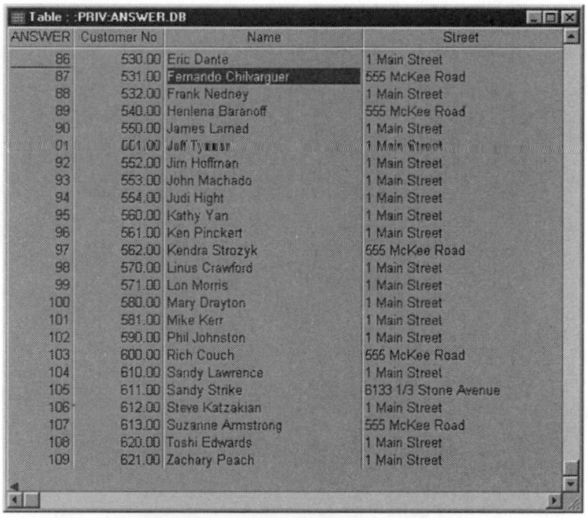

FIGURE 35.4.

Using the select *command.*

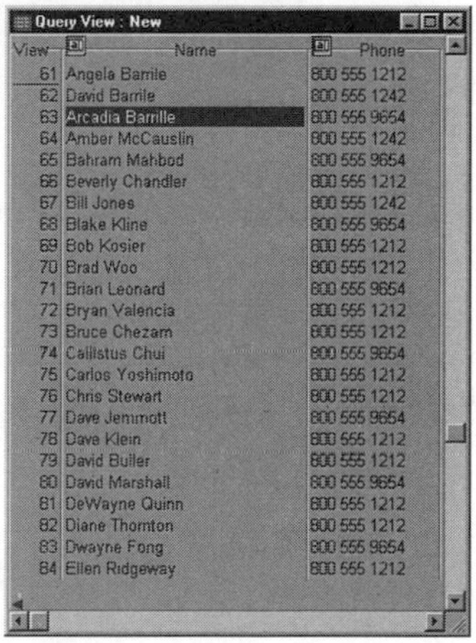

FIGURE 35.5.

Specifying columns using select.

6. The where clause enables you to narrow down your search criteria. Using this clause is similar to specifying example elements in Paradox's QBE. Refer to Table 35.1 to see which of the many aggregates and operators are supported by local SQL. Next, use the where clause to specify that you want to see only the records where *City* is equal to *Madeupville.* To do this, type the following, save it as SQL-LS3.SQL, and run it. Your screen should look similar to Figure 35.6.

```
1:  select *
2:  from Customer
3:  where City = "Madeupville"
```

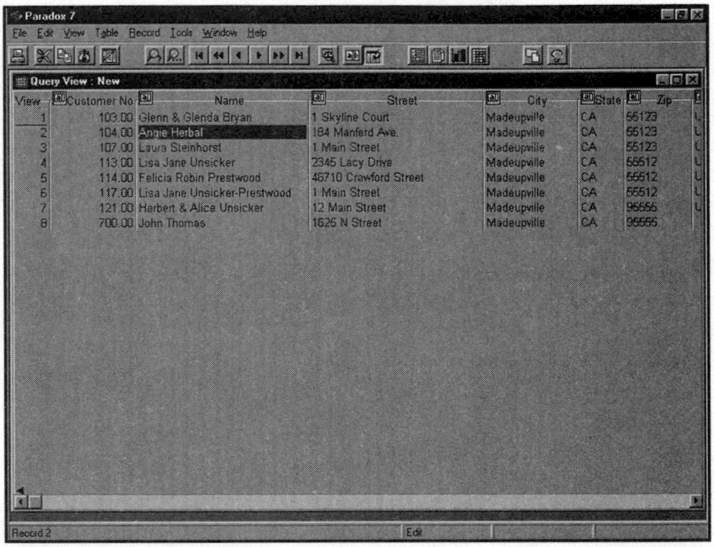

FIGURE 35.6.

Using the where *clause with* select.

7. You also can use the where clause to link tables similar to how the Data Model does. For example, the following links the Customer and Orders tables. Type, save as SQL-LS4.SQL, and run the following SQL statement. Your screen should look similar to Figure 35.7. (Note the use of the table name and quotation marks around the fields in line 1. Any field name that contains spaces requires quotation marks.)

```
1:  select Customer."Customer No", Customer."Name", Orders."Order No"
2:  from Customer, Orders
3:  where Customer."Customer No" = Orders."Customer No"
```

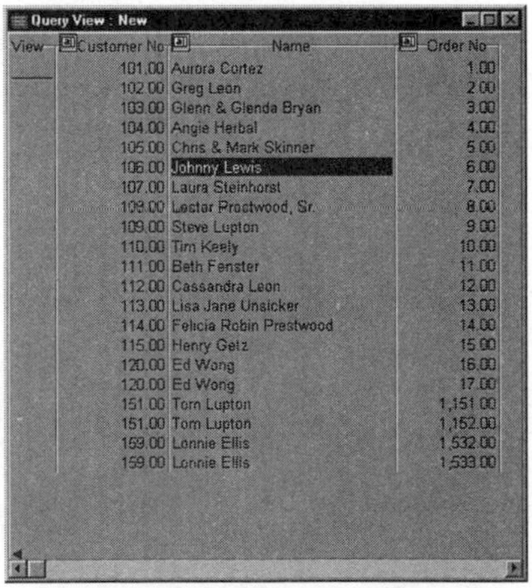

FIGURE 35.7.

Joining tables using select.

Commenting SQL Files

You can add a comment to any SQL file using the C-like comment /* and */, such as the following:

```
/* This is a comment. */
```

Using *distinct, union,* and *order by*

The distinct keyword prevents duplicate values. The union clause enables you to combine one or more select statements to produce a single result. The order by clause specifies how to order the data. Here is an example of using all three:

```
select distinct p.Name from 'Customer.db' p
union select d.Name from 'Customer.dbf' d
order by p.Name
```

Step By Step

1. This example uses a where clause and the and clause. It links the Customer and Orders table on Customer No and displays the five columns (some from each table) where the *Balance Due* is not 0. Type **save as SQL-LS5.SQL**, and run the following SQL statement:

   ```
   1:  /* SQL-LS5.SQL */
   2:  select Customer."Customer No", Customer."Name",
   3:      Customer."Phone", Orders."Order No", Orders."Balance Due"
   4:  from Customer, Orders
   5:  where Customer."Customer No" = Orders."Customer No"
   6:      and Orders."Balance Due" <> 0
   ```

2. This example introduces the order clause, which enables you to sort the answer table. Type **save as SQL-LS6.SQL**, and run the following SQL statement:

   ```
   1:  /* SQL-LS6.SQL */
   2:  select Customer."Customer No", Customer."Name",
   3:  Customer."Phone"
   4:  from Customer
   5:  order by Name
   ```

3. This example demonstrates linking two tables and ordering by one of the fields. Type **save as SQL-LS7.SQL**, and run the following SQL statement:

   ```
   1:  /* SQL-LS7.SQL */
   2:  select Orders."Order No", Orders."Balance Due",
   3:      Lineitem."Stock No"
   4:  from Orders, Lineitem
   5:  where Orders."Order No" = Lineitem."Order No"
   6:  order by Orders."Balance Due"
   ```

4. This example demonstrates sorting in a descending order. When you use descending, you must also use distinct. Type **save as SQL-LS8.SQL**, and run the following SQL statement:

```
1:  /* SQL-LS8.SQL */
2:  select distinct Orders."Order No", Orders."Balance Due",
3:      Lineitem."Stock No"
4:  from Orders, Lineitem
5:  where Orders."Order No" = Lineitem."Order No"
6:  order by Orders."Balance Due" descending
```

Heterogeneous Joins

As previously mentioned, local SQL supports aliases when referencing table names. This way, you can execute heterogeneous joins; that is, joins of more than one table type. For example, you could create a SQL statement that joins Paradox, Oracle, and Informix tables in a single SQL query.

NEW Term

Heterogeneous joins are table links between two or more different types of tables. Because Paradox uses the BDE, you can easily link various heterogeneous tables. For example, the following joins a Paradox table to a dBASE table:

```
select p.Name, p.'Customer No', d.Customer from
"Customer.db" p,
"Customer.dbf" d
where p.'Name' = d.'Name'
```

Finally, here are some more select statements you can try. Keep your working directory set to the TUTORIAL directory and type and run any or all of them.

Using *insert*

The syntax for insert is not nearly as elaborate as the syntax for select, but it is still fairly substantial. Paradox supports only a small subset, however. For now, the basic syntax you will use is as follows:

```
insert into tableName
([columnName1 [, columnName2] [, columnName3]...])
values ([value1 [, value2] [, value3]...])
```

Step By Step

1. The next SQL statement uses insert to insert a new record into the Customer table. Type the following, save it as SQL-LI2.SQL, run the SQL statement, and then open the table. Your screen should look similar to Figure 35.8.

   ```
   1:  insert into Customer
   2:  (Customer."Customer No", Customer."Name")
   3:  values (0, 'Aurora Cortez')
   ```

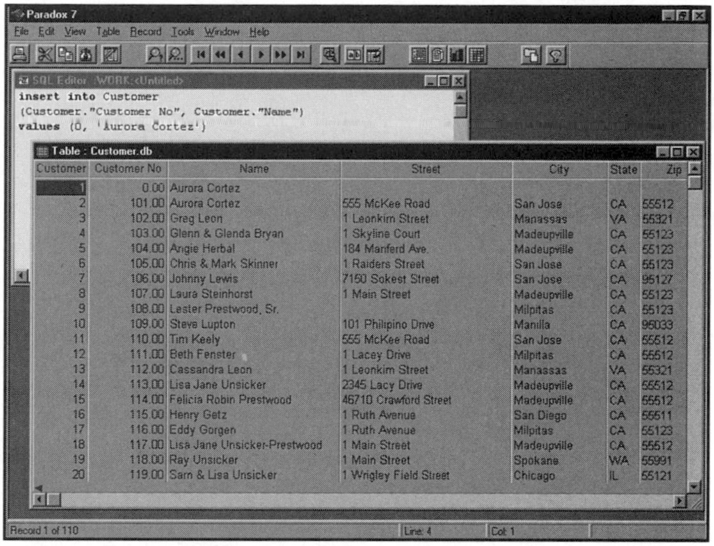

FIGURE 35.8.

Using insert *on a local table.*

2. The next SQL statement uses insert with a nested select statement to add the records from CUSTOMER.DBF into CUSTOMER.DB.

```
/* Add one table to another. */
insert into "Customer.db"
select * from "customer.dbf"
```

Using *update*

The syntax for update also is not as elaborate as the syntax for select, but it is still fairly substantial. For now, the basic syntax you will use is as follows:

```
update tableName
set setcriteria
where wherecriteria
```

The update command is very powerful, so be cautious when using it. One mistyped word can change all the data in your table.

Step By Step

1. For your first example, suppose that Sandy Jones got married and she now wants to use her married name. The update command enables you to change the Customer table. Type the following SQL statement, save it as SQL-LU1.SQL, and execute it.

```
1:  update Customer
2:  set Name = "Sandy Kowalski"
3:  where Name = "Sandy Jones"
```

2. The next `update` statement assumes the entire town of *Madeupville* was magically moved to Illinois. Type the following SQL statement, save it as SQL-LU2.SQL, and execute it.

```
1:  update Customer
2:  set State = "IL"
3:  where City = "Madeupville"
```

3. This next `update` statement accomplishes a similar task as step 2, but this SQL statement demonstrates how to specify and update multiple columns. Type the following SQL statement, save it as SQL-LU3.SQL, and execute it.

```
1:  update Customer
2:  set City = "SJ", State = "IL"
3:  where City = "San Jose" and State = "CA"
```

Using *delete*

The syntax for `delete` is fairly straightforward. The basic syntax you will use is as follows:

```
delete from tableName
where whereCriteria
```

Step By Step

1. Suppose that you want to delete a record or set of records from a database. The `delete` command enables you to do so. Type the following SQL statement, save it as SQL-LD1.SQL, and execute it.

```
1:  delete from Customer
2:  where Name = 'Aurora Cortez'
```

2. This final `delete` example adds a comment and the and clause. Suppose that you want to delete all the customers from a table where the customers are in Sacramento, CA. Type the following SQL statement, save it as SQL-LD2.SQL, and execute it.

```
1:  /* SQL-LD2.SQL */
2:  delete from Customer
3:  where City = "Sacramento" and State = "CA"
```

Using *create table* and *drop table*

The create table SQL commands enable you to create tables. The interesting thing about creating tables with create table is that the `create table` statement is often portable to other database servers. For example, all the create table SQL statements in this section work on Local Interbase and on Oracle. The syntax for `create table` is as follows:

```
create table tableName (fieldName fieldType [, fieldName fieldType...])
```

Use the following field types: SMALLINT, INT, DECIMAL(x,y), NUMERIC(x,y), FLOAT(x,y), CHAR(n), DATE, BOOLEAN, BLOB(n,s), TIME, TIMESTAMP, MONEY, AUTOINC, and BYTES(n).

Step By Step

1. Create a table, as follows:

```
1:  create table test
2:  (field1 char(20))
```

2. Delete it, as follows:

```
1:  drop table test
```

3. Create one more table for use with the following index examples:

```
1:  create table Contacts
2:  (Name char(20), Phone char(15), Age SmallInt)
```

Using *create table* with the Primary Key Constraint

You can create primary keys with the primary key constraint. The syntax for create table using the option primary key constraint is as follows:

```
create table tableName (fieldName fieldType [, fieldName fieldType...]
[, primary key (fieldName [,fieldname…]])
```

Step By Step

1. The following is a create table example using the optional primary key constraint:

```
/* Create emp table with a primary key. */
CREATE TABLE "emp"
    (
    SSN char(11),
    Last_Name char(20),
    First_Name char(15),
    Salary numeric(10,2),
    Dept_No smallint,
    PRIMARY KEY (SSN)
    )
```

2. To delete the primary key, execute the following SQL statement:

```
1:  drop index Contacts.primary
```

NOTE

You cannot create a primary key using create index; you must create the primary key at the time you use create table.

Using *create index* and *drop index*

This example shows how to use create index and drop index.

Step By Step

1. To add a secondary index, execute the following SQL statement:

```
create index secLastFirst
on emp (Last_Name, First_Name)
```

2. To delete the newly created secondary index, execute the following SQL statement:

```
1:    drop index emp.secLastFirst
```

Using Embedded SQL on Local Tables

Just as you can embed query code into your ObjectPAL code and execute it using `executeQBE()`, you can embed SQL code and execute it using `executeSQL()`. What is interesting is that embedded SQL statements work on local tables, too. For example, type the following code into the `pushButton` method of a button:

```
 1:   ;Button :: pushButton
 2:   method pushButton(var eventInfo Event)
 3:       var
 4:               q      SQL
 5:               tc     TCursor
 6:               db     Database
 7:               tv     TableView
 8:       endVar
 9:
10:       q = SQL
11:           select Customer."Customer No", Customer."Name", Customer."Phone"
12:           from Customer
13:           where not Phone is null
14:       endSQL
15:
16:       db.open("WORK")
17:       q.executeSQL(db, ":PRIV:ANSWER.DB")
18:       tv.open(":PRIV:ANSWER.DB")
19:   endMethod
```

The Client/Server Model

New Term

In a client/server model, the database processes are shared between the client and the server. This is called *distributed processing*. In the case of Paradox, Paradox is the client, and any of the SQL servers that BDE can use can be the server. Oracle, Sybase, Informix, and Borland's Interbase are examples of SQL servers. For example, when you connect Paradox to an Oracle server, the database processes are divided between the server and Paradox.

Paradox provides access to SQL servers through Borland's SQL Link for Windows. When Paradox communicates with a SQL server, queries—commands—from Paradox need to be in the dialect of the particular server. The link provides this translation and sends the appropriate commands to the server. Because the link is fairly transparent, you do not have to learn SQL.

Back End/Front End

In a client/server model, the SQL server is called the *back end*. A client application, such as Paradox, is called the *front end*. When you set up a very large database, you generally have two software-buying considerations: the back end and the front end. Typical back-end servers include Borland's Interbase, Oracle, Sybase, Microsoft SQL, and Informix. Typical front-end servers include Paradox for Windows, Paradox for DOS, Access, and dBASE for Windows.

NEW Term

Columns and Rows

Sometimes, just getting used to the terminology of a new subject helps you to understand it. In SQL server terms, a *column* is the same as a Paradox table field's name, and a *row* is the same as a record.

NEW Term

Overview of Database Application Architectures

Database application architecture has more to do with the software development life cycle than it has to do with Paradox. However, understanding database application architecture is important because it will have a major impact on any large application you develop. Deciding the basic architecture of any application you develop is one of the final steps you undertake when you do your system analysis. You need to decide between a single-user and multiuser application. If you decide that you need a multiuser application, you need to decide between a multiuser network application and a client/server application. Finally, if you decide on a client/server application, you need to decide among a two-tier, three-tier, or multi-tier application.

Single-User Applications

A single-user application contains both the data and application on the same machine. Local tables include Paradox and dBASE and Local Interbase. This type of application is also known as one-tier development because both the application and data reside on the same machine.

> **NOTE**
>
> Local Interbase is a cross between the local table and the client/server concepts.
> Although you can develop client/server applications with Local Interbase, one proces-
> sor processes both the application requests and manages and serves data. The great
> thing about Local Interbase is that it enables you to develop a client/server application
> on a single machine and move the data to another processor such as a Windows NT
> server, NLM server, or UNIX server. Personal Oracle is similar to Local Interbase.

Multiuser Applications

Multiuser one-tier applications are similar to single-user applications. The main difference is
that the data is moved to the network. This way, multiple users can access the data. However,
this setup is not client/server because the data is still processed by Paradox on a single machine—
a single tier. Refer to Chapter 34 for more information on creating multiuser applications.

Client/Server Applications (Fat Client Versus Thin Client)

Client/server applications (two-tier development) split the processing needed to set and retrieve
data between two processors, or two tiers. In general, client/server applications are either fat or
thin.

A *fat client application* contains most of the business rules and data integrity on the client (in
this case, in Paradox using ObjectPAL). Sometimes program architects like to use this model
because they have very strong clients. I have even heard of this design architecture referred to
as the muscular client model because a typical client machine today runs at over 100MHz and
has more than 16 megabytes of RAM.

A *thin client application* moves as much of the business rules and data integrity to the server as
possible—for example, calculations, required fields, and data link enforcement. This process is
accomplished by using data integrity rules such as referential integrity, stored procedures, and
triggers. In general, thin client architectures are considered better because they spread more of
the processing onto the server, and server machines are generally more powerful than client
machines. Most companies today creating client/server applications try to create thin client
applications.

Multi-Tier Development

A hot topic in database development today is multi-tiered development. You are already familiar with two-tier or client/server development. Two-tiered development separates the application and data management to two computers (a client and a server). Multi-tiered development
takes this to the next logical step by moving more of the processing to another server. It breaks
up the application into more than just two logical separations.

Paradox is good at developing the presentation layer, and servers including Interbase, Oracle, Sybase, and Informix are good for developing the database layer. Room is left for the middle layer (some refer to it as the *application server layer*). You can, for example, place business rules, replication schemes, and data translation rules on the middle layer. You can build the middle layer yourself using languages such as C and C++, or you can buy software designed to aid in the development of middle-ware. Some of the more popular middle-ware applications on the market include EZ-RPC, Entera, and RPC Painter.

Paradox 1.0 for Windows was Well-Suited for Multiuser Applications

Paradox 1.0 for Windows was geared toward single-user and multiuser applications. Because version 1.0 was not able to connect to a SQL back-end server, your only choices were to develop a front end to tables on your hard drive or on the network. Version 7.0 is great for both single-user and multiuser applications.

Paradox 4.5/5.0 for Windows was Adapted for Client/Server Applications

Paradox 4.5 and 5.0 for Windows were still geared toward one-tier and multiuser applications, but they could handle client/server development. The connections to SQL servers seemed like an add-on to the product. For example, the interface to SQL servers was different than the interface to local tables. Even though Borland had the Interbase server product for several years, client/server was still new to them, and they did not do it well. It was obvious that SQL server support was an afterthought and that a complete redesign of the interface was needed. This complete redesign came with version 7.

Paradox 7 for Windows 95 and NT is Well-Suited for Client/Server Applications

Paradox 7 for Windows 95 is geared toward single-user, multiuser, and client/server applications but not multi-tiered development. SQL support is now integrated into the Paradox menus, and Borland has matured as a client/server provider. Borland's strongest leaps are with its engine. The Borland Engine is now in its third generation; it has progressed from ODAPI, through IDAPI, and now to BDE. At Borland, more emphasis is now put on client/server. Paradox is still not geared toward multi-tiered development. Although Paradox can use a network, various protocols, many back-end servers, and so on through the BDE, the BDE still has to run on the same machine as Paradox. In a multi-tiered application, Paradox is a good tool to use to build the front end, and it can work with middle-ware packages.

Interactive SQL

Before you jump into SQL and ObjectPAL, review what Paradox for Windows can do interactively with SQL. As a front end for SQL, Paradox for Windows rivals anything on the market. Your first experience may well lead you to the same conclusion. When you access SQL tables, you'll notice a few differences from using Paradox tables. The following are some of the obvious features to note:

- You can open a SQL in a table window by choosing File | Open | Table. Note that you can directly edit the data in the table.

- In previous versions of Paradox, many tasks with SQL servers were accomplished through an add-on utility called SQL Tools. This Paradox form was full of bugs and awkward to use. Creating SQL tables, adding data to a SQL table, restructuring, and so on have now been integrated into the standard Paradox menus. In general, you simply use the option you want and select the SQL alias you want to work with.

- You can create a quick form based on a SQL table. Press F9 to go into Edit mode. The default setting for Read-only for all tables in the data is unchecked. Leave this option turned off to edit data. Also worth mentioning is that you need to execute forceRefresh() with table frames to update data altered by other users, but not with fields.

- When you query SQL tables with the QBE, note that the SQL button shows you the equivalent QBE query in SQL. If you are familiar with Borland's Query by Example (QBE), then you might want to always use it—rather than SQL—to query both local and SQL tables. If you know SQL or have an interest in learning it, however, you can use the SQL Editor built into Paradox.

- When you use the SQL File (or query SQL tables with SQL), note that you do not put a semicolon at the end of a SQL statement as you do with other SQL Editors. Also note that you can execute only a single line of SQL at a time.

- You can use SQL statements with local tables.

- You can base a report on a SQL table or SQL statement. By now, you may have noticed that the link to SQL tables is nearly transparent. Borland has provided an extremely easy-to-use SQL front end.

- The button on the vertical scroll bar in a table frame behaves differently than with Paradox tables. While you view remote tables in Paradox, the data is cached. Paradox reads only part of a remote table—unlike a local table. Performance would suffer if the SQL link had to ask the server for the table size and record position while scrolling through the table.

Answer Set

Whenever you access data on a SQL server, you create an answer set. When you open a table in a SQL database in a table window, you can call the data you are currently viewing an *answer set*. When you execute a specific SQL query—either through a QBE query or a SQL file—you refer to the data returned by the server as an answer set.

NEW
Term

Note on Cached Data

Paradox may have occasional delays when accessing data. Paradox is fairly fast at retrieving data if the data is within the set of cached data. If Paradox has to request a new set of records, however, the SQL link slows down because Paradox has to either generate a fetch or select for the new data. Using indexes—for example, a primary key on Oracle tables—greatly speeds up performance, and this issue is no longer a concern.

ObjectPAL and SQL

With ObjectPAL, you can establish a connection to a SQL server. You can use TCursors and Table variables almost exactly the same way you do with local tables. You can embed SQL code in your ObjectPAL code; this includes any server-specific extensions. For example, you can have ObjectPAL, QBE, SQL, and Oracle's PL/SQL all in one event. ObjectPAL also supports the use of transactions. You can even trap for errors.

Connecting via an Existing Alias

To connect to an existing alias, use the Database open method. The syntax for the Database open method is as follows:

open (const *aliasName* String) Logical

The following is a simple example:

```
1:   ;Button :: pushButton
2:   method pushButton(var eventInfo Event)
3:      var
4:         dbSQL    Database
5:      endVar
6:
7:      dbSQL.open(":Godzilla2:")
8:   endMethod
```

In the preceding example, the user is prompted to enter his or her password. If you know the user's password you can use it in ObjectPAL so that the user doesn't have to enter it. To enter the password for the user, use the following syntax:

open ([const *aliasName* String,] [const *ses* Session,] [const *parms* DynArray])
➥Logical

The following is another simple example of using the Database open method passing the alias a username and password:

```
 1:  ;Button :: pushButton
 2:  method pushButton(var eventInfo Event)
 3:     var
 4:        dbSQL        Database
 5:        dynAlias     DynArray[]  AnyType
 6:     endVar
 7:
 8:     dynAlias["USER NAME"]  = "guest"
 9:     dynAlias["PASSWORD"]   = "guest"
10:     dbSQL.open(":Godzilla2:", dynAlias)
11:  endMethod
```

Connecting via a New Alias

The following example demonstrates connecting to an Oracle server without a preexisting alias:

```
 1:  ;Button :: pushButton
 2:  method pushButton(var eventInfo Event)
 3:    var
 4:       tv          TableView
 5:       dbSQL       Database
 6:       dynAlias    DynArray[] String
 7:    endVar
 8:
 9:    dynAlias["SERVER NAME"]         = "Godzilla2"
10:   dynAlias["USER NAME"]          = "guest"
11:   dynAlias["OPEN MODE"]          = "READ/WRITE"
12:   dynAlias["SCHEMA CACHE SIZE"] = "8"
13:   dynAlias["NET PROTOCOL"]       = "SPX/IPX"
14:   dynAlias["LANGDRIVER"]         = ""
15:   dynAlias["SQLQRYMODE"]         = ""
16:   dynAlias["PASSWORD"]           = "guest"
17:
18:   addAlias("Godzilla2_guest", "Oracle", dynAlias)
19:   dbSQL.open("Godzilla2_guest", dynAlias)
20:   tv.open(":godzilla2_guest:ksmith.customer")
21: endmethod
```

Disconnecting is actually quite simple. As you do with so many other objects in ObjectPAL, you simply close it. Assuming that the SQL Database variable DbSQL from the preceding example is within scope, the following line of code closes the connection:

```
1:  dbSQL.close()
```

SQL and *TCursor* and *Table* Variables

New Term

In the preceding example, you used a TableView variable to open up a TableView of a SQL table. The following code shows that you can use TCursor and Table variables with the same techniques with which you are already familiar. A *cursor* is a pointer to a row in a SQL answer set. Cursors are implemented in ObjectPAL as a TCursor object. This next example shows you how to copy a table from the server to a local hard drive:

```
 1:    ;Button :: pushButton
 2:    method pushButton(var eventInfo Event)
 3:       var
 4:            tc    TCursor    ;Declare a TCursor variable.
 5:       endVar
 0.
 7:       tc.open(":Godzilla2:rspitz.customer") ;Open table on server.
 8:       tc.copy(":work:customer")             ;Copy table.
 9:       tc.close()                            ;Close table.
10:    endmethod
```

This example shows how to copy a table from your local hard drive to the server:

```
 1:    ;Button :: pushButton
 2:    method pushButton(var eventInfo Event)
 3:       var
 4:            tc    TCursor
 5:       endVar
 6:
 7     errorTrapOnWarnings(Yes)
 8:    try
 9:        tc.open(":work:customer.db")
10:        tc.copy(":godzilla2:rspitz.test")
11:        tc.close()
12:    onFail
13:        errorShow()
14:    endTry
15:    endmethod
```

NOTE

Although TCursor and Table variables work with SQL data, for the sake of speed, using a SQL query is always better. Therefore, try to do what you want with a query first and then fall back to using a TCursor only when a SQL query is not possible.

Executing a SQL Query in ObjectPAL

The executeSQL() method works just like the Query equivalent executeQBE(). After you define the SQL variable, then you execute it using executeSQL(). The following example shows how to execute an existing SQL file. In ObjectPAL, the technique is similar to executing an existing QBE file.

```
 1:    ;Button :: pushButton
 2:    method pushButton(var eventInfo Event)
 3:       var
 4:          sqlEXESQL    SQL
 5:          tvAnswer     TableView
 6:       endVar
 7:
 8:    sqlEXESQL.readFromFile(":WORK:EXECSQL.SQL")
 9:    sqlEXESQL.executeSQL(db, ":PRIV:ANSWER.DB")
10:
```

```
11:     tvAnswer.open(":PRIV:ANSWER.DB")
12: endmethod
```

You assign a SQL variable to a SQL string in any of the following three ways: embedding SQL in ObjectPAL, reading it in from a string, or reading it in from a file. You used `readFromFile()` previously to read in a SQL file and execute it. The next three examples use embedded SQL, embedded SQL with a tilde variable, and `readFromString()` to assign a SQL variable a SQL statement and then use `executeSQL()` to execute it.

Embedded SQL

The capability to place SQL commands within another programming language enables you to extend that language. This capability is called *embedding SQL*, and it means that you can actually embed SQL commands inside ObjectPAL. The following example shows how to embed SQL statements into your ObjectPAL code. Again, just as you can embed query code, you can embed ObjectPAL code.

```
 1:     ;Button :: pushButton
 2:     method pushButton(var eventInfo Event)
 3:        var
 4:           sqlVar     SQL
 5:           tvLike     TableView
 6:        endVar
 7:
 8:        ;Define SQL variable.
 9:        sqlVar = SQL
10:
11:     select * from ksmith.customer
12:
13:        endSQL
14:
15:        ;Execute SQL variable.
16:        executeSQL(db, sqlVar, ":PRIV:__LIKE")
17:
18:        ;View answer table.
19:        tvLike.open(":PRIV:__LIKE")
20:     endmethod
```

The next SQL query example demonstrates how to use a tilde variable to pass a SQL statement some data. This process is just like passing a tilde variable to an embedded query.

```
 1:     ;Button :: pushButton
 2:     method pushButton(var eventInfo Event)
 3:        var
 4:           sqlVar     SQL
 5:           tvLike     TableView
 6:           s          String
 7:        endVar
 8:
 9:        s = "ksmith.customer"
10:        s.view("Enter SQL table name")
11:
12:        sqlVar = SQL
13:
```

```
14:            select * from ~s
15:
16:        endSQL
17:
18:        executeSQL(db, sqlVar, ":PRIV:__LIKE")
19:        tvLike.open(".PRIV.__LIKE")
20:     endmethod
```

This final SQL query example demonstrates how to use a SQL string. This process is just like using a query string.

```
1:     ;Button :: pushButton
2:     method pushButton(var eventInfo Event)
3:        var
4:            s            String      ;Declare a String variable.
5:            sTilde       String
6:            sqlVar       SQL         ;Declare a SQL variable
7:            tv           TableView   ;Declare a TableView variable.
8:        endVar
9:
10:       ;Assign string values.
11:       sTilde = "Dive"
12:
13:       s = "SELECT LAST_NAME, FIRST_NAME, COMPANY, PHONE " +
14:           "FROM    CONTACTS " +
15:           "WHERE   COMPANY LIKE '%" + sTilde + "%'"
16:
17:       ;Read string values into a SQL variable.
18:       sqlVar.readFromString(s)
19:
20:       ;Execute SQL statement.
21:       sqlVar.executeSQL(db, ":PRIV:ANSWER.DB")
22:
23:       ;Open answer table.
24:       tv.open(":PRIV:ANSWER.DB")
25:    endmethod
```

Using *errorHasNativeErrorCode()*

errorHasNativeErrorCode() checks the error stack for a specific SQL error code. It is equivalent to errorHasErrorCode(), except that it checks for SQL error codes. The syntax is as follows:

errorHasNativeErrorCode(const errCode LongInt) Logical

Executing Locally or Executing on the Server

If a QBE query generates SQL code, the query executes on the server; otherwise, the query executes locally. A query that executes on the server may take a long time, so knowing beforehand where it will execute can be useful. You also should note that a local SQL query may take longer than on the server. As the programmer, you must experiment and use the best choice.

You can use the following methods to find out whether your SQL code will execute locally or on the server. The following reports whether a QBE query will be executed locally or on a server:

```
isExecuteQBELocal()
```

The complete syntax is as follows:

isExecuteQBELocal(const *qbeVar* Query) Logical

The next example displays one of two messages in a message stop dialog box, depending on whether the SQL query is to be executed locally or on the server:

```
 1:  ;Button :: pushButton
 2:  method pushButton(var eventInfo Event)
 3:     var
 4:        qAnswer    Query
 5:     endVar
 6:     qAnswer = Query
 7:
 8:            ANSWER: :PRIV:ANSWER.DB
 9:
10:            :IB_ALIAS:CONTACTS | LAST_NAME  | FIRST_NAME      | COMPANY    |
11:                               | CheckPlus  | CheckPlus Ron   | CheckPlus  |
12:                               | CheckPlus  | CheckPlus Phil  | CheckPlus  |
13:
14:     endQuery
15:     if isExecuteQBELocal(qAnswer) then
16:        beep()
17:        msgStop("WARNING", "Query Will Run Locally, This May Take Longer.")
18:     else
19:        msgInfo("Query Status", "This Query Will Run Remotely.")
20:     endIf
21: endmethod
```

Transactions: The Protocol for Communication

NEW
Term

Client applications such as Paradox communicate with SQL database servers with a unit of work called a *transaction*. Although a transaction is perceived as a single operation, a transaction may consist of a number of operations. For example, a single transaction could update multiple records. If you want to have some control over undeleting changes to your data, then use the following methods and procedures:

beginTransaction()	Starts a transaction on a server
commitTransaction()	Commits all changes within a transaction
rollbackTransaction()	Rolls back all changes within a transaction (undo feature)

Commit and Rollback Overview

The term *commit* is part of a concept for entering data. The idea is to enter data into a temporary table and commit, or copy, the data to a main table. The term *rollback* is also part of a concept for entering data. The idea is to enter data into a temporary table with the opportunity to empty the temporary table and to leave the main table untouched. The term *two-phase commits* applies this idea over a wide area network. With two-phase commits, you can have data entry from anywhere in the world.

NEW
Term

In the following example, the first record 1001 is posted to the table and then undone with the rollback:

```
 1:  ;Button :: pushButton
 2:  method pushButton(var eventInfo Event)
 3:      var
 4:          dbSQL       Database
 5:          tc          TCursor
 6:      endVar
 7:
 8:      dbSQL.open(":Server1:")
 9:      dbSQL.beginTransaction()
10:      tc.open(":Server1:guest.customer")
11:      tc.insertRecord()
12:      tc.(1) = 1001
13:      tc.(2) = "Mike Prestwood"
14:      tc.postRecord()
15:      dbSQL.rollbackTransaction()      ;Un-inserts record 1001.
16:      dbSQL.begintransaction()
17:      tc.(1) = 1002
18:      tc.(2) = "Lisa Prestwood"
19:      dbSQL.commitTransaction()        ;Commits record 1002.
20:      tc.close()
21:  endMethod
```

Statement Atomicity

In ObjectPAL, all database commands are committed immediately. For example, a single QBE query, a single ObjectPAL table append, and a single edit operation are examples of commands that are executed and committed to the database immediately.

NOTES ON TRANSACTIONS AND INFORMIX

The following are some notes on Informix and Paradox:

Implicit/Explicit Transactions: Each of the three Informix database types supports different rules for implicit and explicit transaction starting.

ANSI-Compliant Databases: Start an implicit transaction. You can start a transaction only after a COMMIT WORK, CREATE DATABASE, DATABASE, ROLLBACK WORK, or START DATABASE statement (they probably autocommit a transaction). If you attempt to close a database without ending the transaction, an error may occur.

> **AutoCommit Transactions.** The following classes of SQL statements automatically commit a transaction in Informix. You are guaranteed that there is no active transaction after one of the following statements has been executed: COMMIT WORK, ROLLBACK, CREATE DATABASE, START DATABASE, DATABASE (select a db for use).
>
> As far as Data Definition statements are concerned, if they are executed inside a transaction, they will not be committed unless you commit the transaction. If no transaction exists, they will be committed when completed. For example, no AutoCommit exists for DDL statements.
>
> For INFORMIX-SE, DDL statements are autocommitted when a transaction is started. They do not end an active transaction, however.

Views

NEW
Term

A *view* is a virtual table that represents a part of the database or the whole database. The following is a list of various types of views:

- A vertical subset of columns from a single relation. This type of view limits the columns displayed.

- A horizontal subset of records from a single relation. This type of view limits the records displayed.

- A combined vertical and horizontal subset of records from a single relation. This type of view limits the number of records displayed.

- A subset of records from many relations. This type of view usually performs a join operation.

You can use a view to ensure security and for convenience; you can allow users to see only columns or values as necessary. Views can also enable users to see the bigger picture; for example, you can simplify a complex join into a manageable package. You create a view using the SQL command create view. The syntax is as follows:

```
create view [<owner.>]<view name>
[(<column name>[, <column name>...])
as <SELECT statement>
```

Triggers and Stored Procedures

NEW
Term

Triggers are procedures stored in the database that help you enforce both business and data relationship rules. With a trigger, you can keep summary data up to date, take actions based on what data a user enters, and enforce business rules such as no out-of-state checks accepted.

A trigger can occur when you either update, insert, or delete values. A trigger is like a Paradox validity check in which you can put code. In a way, triggers are analogous to events in a form, and stored procedures are analogous to custom methods.

Creating and Using a Sybase Trigger

The following is a simple example of how you might create and use a trigger in Sybase to ensure data integrity. On the SQL side, you create an update trigger on a table's column.

```
1:  create trigger updatetrigger on sqlTableName
2:  for update as
3:  if update(columnName)
4:     begin
5:        raiserror 30000 'Cannot change values in this. Changes have been
           discarded.'
6:        rollback transaction
7:     end
```

To raise or see the error in Paradox, use the error method. For example,

```
1:  ;tableframe :: error
2:  method error(var eventInfo ErrorEvent)
3:     if eventinfo.reason() = ErrorWarning then
4:        eventinfo.setReason(ErrorCritical)
5:     endIf
6:  endmethod
```

Or you can use `errorTrapOnWarnings(Yes)`. This rudimentary example should help you get started using triggers.

Summary

This chapter introduced you to Paradox as a client/server development tool. You also reviewed what a user can do interactively with Paradox and how to use ObjectPAL with SQL servers. Then you got started using SQL. Now that you are familiar with ANSI SQL, you can begin to query many different databases.

Developing Large Applications

36

So far, this book has taught you elements of coding an application. At this point, you have all the knowledge you need to code an application. This final chapter introduces concepts needed to develop an entire application.

Gaining the ability to develop large applications as an individual or as a small or large development shop requires that you set up a process for developing software and document it. Many methodologies for developing software exist. This chapter will introduce you to what is needed to develop large applications. Its intent is to start you thinking about the big picture and to spark your interest in the software life cycle. Whether you are an individual or part of a large development shop, I hope you will go out and pick up a few books on the software life cycle.

In addition, this chapter talks about documenting and delivering your application, testing, GPFs, and some Paradox-specific issues.

Waterfall Versus RAD

With the *waterfall* approach to developing software, one phase of the development cycle follows the other and the user is involved only at the beginning during the requirements gathering phase and at the end during the acceptance phase. The requirements gathering in the waterfall approach is critical and unless it is 100 percent perfect, the project will fall short. With the rapid application development (*RAD*) approach to developing software, the user is heavily involved all throughout the development process. In true RAD development, software is often very focused on a specific task. If you need to create several applications for a single client, then true RAD can lead to several independent applications that do not communicate and sometimes overlap in functionality.

My preference is for a modified RAD approach to development. In a modified RAD approach, emphasis is placed on thoroughly gathering requirements and involving the user in both the coding and testing phase of development.

Development Charter

NEW
Term

As an independent developer, you should step back and analyze what you are trying to accomplish for your business. One technique for expressing your main goals is to write them down in a development charter. A *development charter* lists general guidelines you use while doing business with your clients. You can even include the charter along with your business proposal. The following is an example development charter:

SAMPLE DEVELOPMENT CHARTER

We are responsible for designing, developing, and delivering a software system that meets the needs of your business. This includes the following responsibilities:

1. Upon identification of work processes that can be automated using a custom-designed database software solution, work with the client to create a schedule that includes software development, deployment, and fall-back plans.

2. Along with the executive sponsor, prioritize software requirements.

3. Design the presentation layer of the software application in a joint effort with the business participants and executive sponsor.

4. Deliver applications on time and under budget.

5. Follow up with the user community after delivery of systems to identify any improvements to make or defects to correct.

6. Provide quality guidance to all to ensure that processes are designed to build quality into the software we deliver. This guidance ensures that our delivered applications are continually improving and strengthening.

The Software Development Cycle

The software development cycle, also known as *full cycle development*, is the process of developing a software application. Without a set process, the end application is likely to be buggy, not meet the users' needs, and take too long to develop.

NEW
Term

The purpose of this section is to define the software development cycle as it affects the development team and the user community. The cycle itself is composed of a series of steps punctuated with milestones. These steps lead from the analysis of a new application to its development, testing, and eventual deployment. Each step is defined in detail.

An approximate duration for each step, if applicable, is given for example only; the estimation assumes five developers, one business analyst, one quality assurance tester, and a medium-sized application. The estimates are included only for reference. The actual duration will depend on many factors including quality of business requirements analysis, complexity of the requirements, talent pool of programmers, and testing plan.

Remember that the application development cycle is a developing process that is revised on an ongoing basis. You should not consider it to be set in stone, but it should act as a guideline and you should use it in accordance to the needs of the current cycle.

Overview of the Life Cycle of a New Application

The following is a list of the steps in the application development cycle:

1. Requirements Gathering
2. Requirements Freeze

3. Requirements Sign-Off
4. Design Session
   a. Database Specification (Logical Design)
   b. Software Specification (Logical Design)
5. Database Freeze (Logical DB Specification Implementation)
6. Development
   a. Module Coding
   b. Programmer Integration Testing
   c. Resolution of Existing Bugs
   d. Code Optimization
8. Development of Help File and User Manual
9. Application Stabilization
10. Quality Assurance Building
11. Quality Assurance Iterations/Discrepancy Resolution
    a. Test Data Creation
    b. Unit Testing by Programmers and Quality Assurance
    c. Integration Testing
    d. Regression Testing
    e. Running Test Scenarios
    f. Stress Testing
12. User Acceptance
13. Application Deployment

Gathering Requirements

Requirements are collected by the business analysts, system architect, and development participants. The average duration needed to gather requirements is directly proportional to the size of the application. Five days is usually sufficient for a medium-sized application. New requirements for the application are gathered until the requirements freeze. The business analyst also needs to identify the requirements critical for the application to be accepted by the executive sponsor at an acceptance meeting.

The requirements report should be broken down into logical categories—for example, business rules, data input, data output, reports, external hardware and software requirements, user expected response times, security, and finally, open issues. The project manager should create a set of questions to weigh the quality of the business requirements. Examples include "Are all the report formats specified?" "Are all the tasks the user wants to accomplish specified?" "Is success clearly identified?" "Are any of the programmers uneasy about any of the requirements?" and so on.

Dealing with Business Rules

Creating a database isn't just about creating tables and linking them. It is also about implementing business rules on the data. For example, in an invoicing system, you need to multiply quantity times price to get each line total on an invoice. Then you sum up the line total and multiply it by the local tax rate and perhaps add shipping costs. These are all business rules. Another less obvious business rule might be to start charging interest on invoices that still have a balance due after 30 days. If you're a database consultant, remember to ask your client about all his or her business rules and incorporate as many as appropriate into your database application.

Reviewing Requirements

The requirements freeze represents the point at which new requirements are moved to the next development cycle. Any new requirement after this point must be approved by the project manager if it is to be included in the current development cycle. The project manager is responsible for keeping the scope of the project within the boundaries agreed upon between him or her and the executive sponsor.

Signing Off Requirements

After you have defined the user requirements, then you should have the executive sponsor sign off on the requirements list.

> **TIP**
>
> When you're finishing an application for a client, nothing is more frustrating than the client telling you that the application is all wrong. Do yourself a favor: During or shortly after the planning stage, be sure to echo to the client what you heard him or her say. Also consider putting your general plan in writing and have both you and your client sign it. This approach makes you a more professional consultant.

Deliverable: Functional Requirements Document

From the time your client agrees to hire you to create an application to the time you actually deliver the application can be a long time—in some cases, more than a year. Keeping your client in the loop and up to date is important. An excellent way to update your client is to have regularly scheduled status meetings. Another way is to give the client status reports as you reach each milestone.

The Functional Requirements Document is a formal gathering of statements that specifies what the software must do or how it must be structured. This document includes a list of features, business rules, and calculations.

Deliverable: User Interface Requirements Document

The User Interface Requirements Document represents how the application will look and feel. Although you have already received input from the user, a good next step is to prototype the application and demonstrate the prototype to the users with the goal of either having the users approve it or refine it.

Designing Database and Software

In a session away from the user community, the development team creates the database and software specifications. The software specification lead is the system architect, and the database specification lead is the DBA. If you have all the correct participants and the requirements analysis is good, you can usually nail down the initial database and software specifications in a day or two.

Business analysts and the development team meet to discuss viability of implementation and specific details of new requirements for clarification to development and quality assurance team. Development assigns a specific developer or developers to each new requirement based on the ownership of the module affected.

Each assigned developer estimates the time requirements for the new requirement to the project management (the estimation phase could take an additional day or two). The project manager then compiles all the information into a project plan.

Each developer is responsible for adding to the software specification and is responsible for creating a test scenario for any requirements he or she implements.

Planning from the Top Down

Any programmer with any experience will tell you that planning an application is just as important as getting started on it. In other words, the first step in designing a database application is to sit down, take some time, and think through the process.

Creating Your Tables

In a separate session with your client, sit down and gather all the data components and categorize them into tables. After you gather the business rules and data components, you need to decide on table structures. Whether you're developing a complete invoicing system or an application that just keeps track of phone numbers, planning your table structures correctly can save you hours of work later. Although Paradox makes it easy to restructure your tables later, you can never recover the time and frustration wasted because of poorly designed table structures.

As you develop your tables, think about the data model. The data model is a diagram of the table relationships for a form. Each form has only one data model. With the Data Model dialog box (select Form | Data Model), you can bind tables to documents and specify how they are linked to one another. In particular, think about all the possible relationships between tables that you need for this project. What fields will make this table unique? What fields must be in common?

Develop your tables with your primary keys in mind. (Chapter 2 discussed this point further.) Increasing or decreasing the length of your fields is easy in Paradox, so keep in mind the minimum size needed as you develop your field lengths. A little careful planning can save you hours of backtracking later. Remember to plan and create your tables with the data model in mind before you start working on your forms.

Deliverable: Software Specification

The Software Specification Document represents an interpretation of the Functional Requirements Document and the User Interface Requirements Document. This document represents how you are going to implement the software features. It is a detailed description of the required characteristics of the application.

Deliverable: Database Specification

The database design is also based on the requirements. Do not hide the database you are creating from your client. Show it to him or her. The Database Specification Document is a good place to do that.

Deliverable: Test Plan

The user should be involved with creating the test plan for the software. That way, the software will work the way the users want it to.

Freezing the Database

Freezing the database is the milestone where the DBA implements the database specification. This is an important milestone to reach on time because, in general, very little coding can occur until the database is stable.

Coding Software

You are probably most familiar with the coding phase of the software development life cycle. This book focused on this phase, which includes module coding, programmer integration testing, resolution of existing bugs, and optimization of code. This phase can take anywhere from three to eight weeks on a medium-sized application.

Programmers develop new features as described in the Development Specification into the application. The business analysts and the development participants are enlisted by the programmers to verify that the new features are developed. This step ensures correctness. This point is also a good time to involve your quality assurance department. The quality assurance team can test the software against both the user requirements and the software specification.

Freezing the User Interface

The user interface freeze (UI Freeze) is necessary so that the developer(s) developing the help file and manual can start finalizing the documentation on how to use the application. This milestone also helps keep the development process moving because it forces the developer, analysts, and the development participants to decide on the look and feel of the application and specific menu and window designs.

Developing the Help File and Manual

Once the UI Freeze occurs, you can dedicate some resources to documenting how the user is going to use the application. If you are a single developer, then this step obviously cannot start until after the development is done. In a single-user environment, this is likely to delay the deployment of the application.

Freezing Features

Development ceases to develop any new features. This Freeze date is the final deadline for functional changes to the application.

Debugging Software

In the debugging phase, the development team tests new features and fixes any anomalies. These tests include unit and integration testing. In unit testing, each developer tests his or her own work. In integration testing, each developer tests his or her work integrated with everyone else's work including the final help file.

Testing Software

The project manager moves control of the software from the programmers to the quality assurance group along with the user requirements and software manual. The quality assurance team conducts initial acceptance testing to verify that the application is stable enough to begin a formal test cycle.

This development period is dedicated to resolving existing discrepancies in the application and verifying the application against the user requirements. (You learn more about testing later in this chapter.)

User Acceptance

The business analyst and project manager present the application to the executive sponsor. Usually, the system architect demonstrates the software for the executive sponsor. Development participants usually do not need to attend the acceptance meeting because they have seen the software all throughout the development cycle. At this point, you can have the executive sponsor sign an acceptance contract that lists the critical features needed for acceptance of the software gathered in the first step.

Deliverable: User Acceptance Agreement

When you deliver the software to your client, have the executive sponsor sign an acceptance agreement after demonstrating the software. The User Acceptance Agreement should list the critical features required to accept the product.

Deploying the Application

Deploying the application is, of course, the final step in developing an application. Do yourself and your client a favor, and take some time to develop a fall-back plan in the event you deploy the software and something goes wrong. If, for example, the company for which you are developing software has an existing software application, create a backup plan to return to it in case the software you are developing fails for any reason. If your clients have a manual procedure, make sure that they are prepared to return to it if needed.

Multi-Programmer Developing

When developing a large application, you will need to program in a team environment. Programming in a team environment is dramatically different than programming by yourself.

Dividing and Conquering

The most dramatic part of getting used to programming in a multi-programming environment is getting used to the fact that you are not in charge of all the code. The best way to accomplish this it to divide up the responsibility of the program among all the programmers, with no over-lapping assignments. This way, you establish pride of ownership, and each programmer can do his or her best to make modules complete and bug-free.

Establishing Programmer Roles

Depending on the size of the team created, you can have any of the following roles: grunt pro-grammer, lead programmer, architect, project leader, QA tester, unit tester, business analyst, user interface expert, and so on. The role a particular programmer will fill depends on his or her programming skills, how well he or she gets along with others, his or her leadership capa-bilities, and finally his or her knowledge of the requirements, design specification, and data-base.

Development Roles

Whether you are an individual developer or part of a team, you need to fully understand the various roles individuals play during the software development life cycle.

Development Team

No matter how many individuals are involved with a large project, the development team usu-ally consists of a project manager, a business analyst, a system architect, and one or more lead programmers. Even in multi-programmer development teams, an individual may commonly fill more than one role. If you are an individual developer, you fill all the development team roles.

Project Manager

The project manager is the glue that keeps the project moving. He or she may be a technical or non-technical project manager. Although it is not usually recommended, the technical project manager often doubles as the system architect. In either case, the project manager is respon-sible for coordinating efforts among the user community and the development team. Usually, the programmers, analysts, and quality assurance personnel report directly to him or her. In addition, the project manager is responsible for any documentation needed to complete the project.

Business Analyst

The business analyst can work either for the user community or the development team. This person coordinates, gathers, refines, defines, and prioritizes the various user requirements.

Database Administrator

The database administrator (DBA) takes the business requirements and develops the database specification. The database specification contains all the table names, field definitions, data restrictions, trigger definitions, and stored procedure definitions. The DBA is also responsible for creating and modifying the database.

System Architect

The system architect takes the business requirements and the database specification and develops the software specification at the highest level. The system architect is also responsible for selecting the tools used for development.

Lead Programmer

The lead programmer works with the system architect to flush out the details of the software specification. The lead programmer understands the big picture; he or she understands the goals and high-level architecture of the application.

Programmer

A regular programmer works with the lead programmer to code specific tasks. This level programmer may not understand the whole picture. In fact, this position is usually told very specifically what and how to code.

User Community

As a software developer, you need to identify the key players in the user community for whom you are developing an application. Identify who will be using the software and get them involved in the design and testing of the software while it is being developed.

Executive Sponsor

The executive sponsor is responsible for final decisions. Often, conflicts may arise among the development participants, and only the executive sponsor can resolve them. Also, the executive sponsor signs off on requirements, accepts the application, and usually pays for the application.

Development Participant

A development participant is the person who at first deals with the business analyst and system architects to define and refine requirements. If you are using the Rapid Application Development (RAD) process, the development participants also participate during development with the programmers, approving the features as they are implemented. Finally, the development participants are involved at the end of the process in beta testing.

Versioning Software

Versioning software enables you to keep track of various versions of the same file. This way, you can roll back to any version of the file that you have checked into the versioning software. Versioning software tracks and organizes all revisions of all files associated with a project. It also enables developers in a multi-programmer environment to lock files being developed to safeguard against duplicate development.

One such commercial versioning software I recommend is PVCS. PVCS (Project Version Control System) is a third-party software program created to track the revisions of files associated with a project. It has become one of the standard versioning software applications in the industry.

Revision Numbers

To begin developing on a file, the developer must first create a slot in the versioning software for the file. When the file is checked back into the versioning software, it assigns a new incremental revision number to that revision of the file—for example, 1.0, 1.1, 1.2, and so on. With most versioning software, the developer may assign a higher revision number at the time the document is checked in.

New Term — Versioning the software allows for a chronological sequence of revisions of a specific file and can be the primary source for identifying which version of a file you want to retrieve when something goes wrong. These revisions are usually stored in an *archive file,* a special file created to hold all revisions of a specific file.

Promotion Groups

Many versioning software products, such as PVCS, allow a revision to belong to one of a number of user-defined promotion groups. Promotion groups are used as flags to identify which revision of a file is available to be delivered as a part of the next build of the software.

You could, for example, maintain three development groups labeled Development, Test, and Deployed. You can use Development for files that are being worked on. You can then promote files from Development to Test when the file is ready to be tested with the rest of the software.

Finally, if all the files in Test work well together, you could promote all the files to Deployed and deliver the software to your client. This system enables to keep developing while someone else tests your software.

Conventions

You should develop or adopt a coding convention. Perhaps consider developing or adopting both a general coding convention and an ObjectPAL-specific coding convention. For more information on coding conventions, refer to Appendix C.

Documenting Your Application

You can employ many methodologies for documenting a large software project. The following sections describe some of the documentation I use when creating large applications. Should you create all these documents for every project? No. The size and importance of the project determines how much documentation is called for.

Business Proposal

Sometimes known as the project charter, the business proposal contains the general information about your company, values, mission, and very high-level information about the project or projects you are going to deliver for the client.

Project Plan

The project plan contains the detail steps needed to complete the project, who is assigned to each task, how much each task costs to complete, and more. One popular tool for creating such a plan today is Microsoft Project (see Figure 36.1).

Creating a Software Developer's Guide

A Software Developer's Guide is a manual written by programmers for programmers. Its intention is to aid the coding and debugging of the application. In addition, you can use this guide to document programmer procedures such as how to use whatever versioning software you use and overall design considerations. Additionally, the Software Developer's Guide is a good place to put miscellaneous notes that do not belong in any other document.

The Software Developer's Guide often includes a section titled "Application Style Guide," which documents how the application should look and feel. As you learned in Chapter 3, you should be consistent in how you design software. In a multi-programmer environment, consistency is difficult to accomplish with a style guide. Either as part of the Software Developer's Guide or separately, you should document the user interface of your application.

FIGURE 36.1.

Microsoft Project showing a project plan in a gantt chart view.

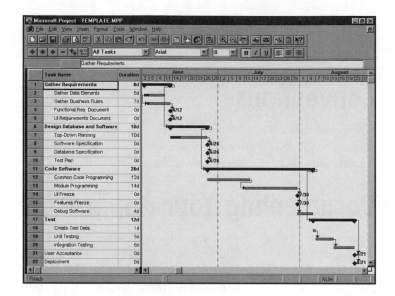

Using Paradox's Data Model Designer

Paradox comes with a very handy tool, the Data Model Designer (select Tools | Data Model Designer). With it, you can easily document local and remote databases. Figure 36.2 shows the data model of The Invoicing System. You can even print the data model and put it in a common location accessible by all programmers.

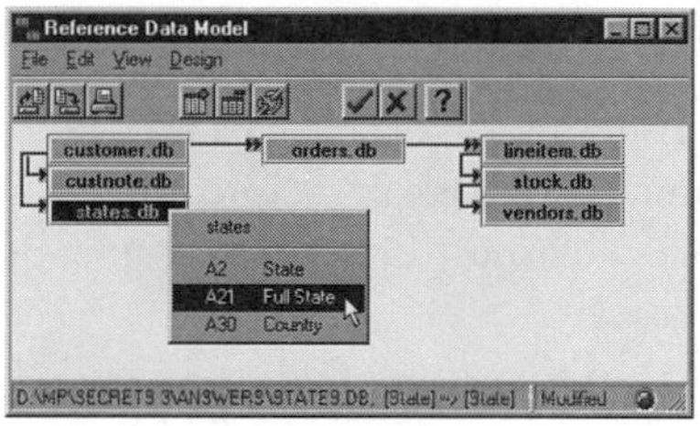

FIGURE 36.2.

The data model from The Invoicing System.

Creating a CRUD Matrix

NEW
Term

CRUD is an acronym that stands for Create, Read, Update, and Delete. A *CRUD matrix* documents what objects (forms, reports, libraries, and scripts) access what data elements in a database. It can help you test your software on large projects. The resolution can either be at the table level or the field level.

Bug-Free Software

Many programmers assume that when they reuse bug-free code in object-oriented programming, it will still work. If all the elements are bug free, the code remains bug free when it's reused. This assumption sometimes holds true, but often it does not. Because you are using the code within a new container, it might not work. You must test the code and debug it again. Therefore, although the components can work fine, the application might be buggy or poorly pasted together. Bug free doesn't necessarily mean well designed.

You can accomplish complicated and sophisticated tasks by using Paradox interactively. If Paradox is bug free, the applications that you develop also will be bug free. This doesn't mean that your applications are well designed, however. Borland's job is to make Paradox as free of bugs as possible. Your job is to make sure that the applications you develop with Paradox are well designed.

What Is an Anomaly?

An error or mistake in a program is a *bug*. An *anomaly* is a nice way to say bug. Is Paradox a bug-free program? Of course not. Paradox isn't without its problems; no software company could make that claim about any application. Paradox has so few bugs, however, that it is a testimony to the quality of its overall design and its use of object-oriented technology.

NEW
Term

The anomalies discussed in the following sections are documented in the SECRETS2.HLP help file that comes with the support files for this book.

How Do You Address Anomalies?

Anomalies are a fact of computing—and especially programming. As much as you might try, avoiding them is often difficult. By the time you read this chapter, Borland might have already released the next version, which could take care of many of its anomalies. The next version might even address anomalies that you never have—and never will—run into.

You can distinguish three kinds of anomalies: configuration anomalies, gotchas, and WADs. A *configuration anomaly* is a conflict between Paradox and another application or the hardware. A *gotcha* is an anomaly that both you and Borland think shouldn't happen. A *WAD*—short for works as designed—refers to product behavior that you dislike, even though it was designed intentionally.

NEW
Term

Anomalies That Are WADs

NEW
Term

A *WAD* is behavior that a product's designers intended. For example, some users don't like the way in which the bands within a report are adjusted. The adjustment feels awkward to them. Many of these users have called Borland to say that the report section was broken. The problem, of course, is that these users don't understand how the product works. The report doesn't have a bug; the users simply need some guidance on how to use it.

In the computer industry, you can always look at a feature in several ways. Companies put in some features and take out others for a multitude of reasons. If you disagree with Borland International on a particular feature, write a product suggestion letter to let the company know how you feel. Then forget about it. There's no possible way that a major feature in Paradox will get changed overnight. You can, however, affect how the product is changed and enhanced in the long run.

Testing

NEW
Term

The *alpha test* cycle is the preliminary testing of a new product in which research and development are still in progress. The *beta test* is a stage in product testing in which testing is done with actual users in the users' environment.

Before you deliver your forms and put your application into production, you need to test it. Borland, for example, has a large team of engineers who test Paradox. The series of tests each quality assurance engineer puts Paradox through can take up to three days to complete—and this is for just one small section of the product. You don't have to go through such extensive testing, but you owe it to your users to do at least some testing. The following sections offer some hints and tips on testing your completed application.

Creating Test Data

Test data is especially created to test the operation of a given program. Usually, one or more hand-calculated results or otherwise known results is associated with test data so that the program under test may be validated. Also data known to be invalid are used as test data.

Developing Test Scenarios

Develop test scenarios with your users so that you can standardize your tests. After you develop a set of standard tests, you can often automate the tests with automated testing software. This type of software is similar to the Windows recorder provided with Windows 3.0 and 3.1. Automated testing software can record mouse movements and keyboard presses.

Unit Testing

Unit testing is the testing of a unit. A unit is a recognized section of a program—for example, a form or group of forms. The programmer who programmed the unit usually performs the unit testing.

Integration Testing

After all programmers are done writing their modules, the modules need to be integrated and tested. This phase of testing tests how well all the units and modules fit together. On large projects, you often go through a build process during which you bring all the application objects together for testing. This can include all the Paradox objects from the various programmers and a new database. This is where versioning software such as Intersolv's PVCS come in handy because it can keep track of all the latest objects ready for the build process while the programmers continue coding.

Regression Testing

Regression tests are performed on a previously verified program whenever it is extended or corrected. In other words, you test all the bugs that were fixed. This step guarantees that previously identified bugs do not reappear in the program.

Testing the Boundaries

Testing boundaries is also known as *stress testing*. Stress testing is ensuring through trial operations that the program or system will continue to perform reliably in spite of data inaccuracies and extraordinary data volumes. Try your application with very large tables and empty tables. Run it on systems with the least amount of memory Paradox will run on—4MB. Log any errors you come across for final testing. Finally, play a game of "what if." For example,

- What if the user uses a corrupt table?
- What if the table gets moved or deleted?
- What if the user starts up using the wrong working directory?

Try to add your own questions to this list.

> **TIP**
>
> If possible, find someone else to exercise your program. As the programmer, you have certain ideas of how a user will use your application. These ideas probably apply to about half the users.

Running Every Feature Three Times

Test each feature three times. Sometimes, errors in logic don't show up until the second or even the third time through a sequence of events.

Protecting Your Application

Protecting your application means that users can't edit your application, even if they own Paradox. In addition, you want to restrict the users' movements through your application. You don't want users to exit without your permission. Also, you don't want users to be able to alter your applications. To protect your applications, you need to do only two things: password-protect your data tables and deliver your forms, reports, libraries, and scripts.

Delivering Your Application

NEW
Term

The final step in the development cycle is to *deliver* all the forms, scripts, libraries, and reports. In ObjectPAL, it's the process of compiling an object for a special Paradox-only dynamic link library. I recommend that you deliver your forms occasionally as you develop for testing. If you haven't been doing so, you should start.

The Delivery System is on disc. This script, \ANSWERS\DELIVER.SSL, delivers all the forms, scripts, libraries, and reports in a directory.

Customizing Paradox

Many programmers want to give their Paradox applications a custom look and feel. Using an icon editor—PDXWIN32.EXE—you can change the custom icon that Paradox uses. In addition, you can open many of the DLLs that Paradox uses and alter its resources. You make these changes using Borland's Windows Resource Workshop or another resource editor. You also can edit splash screens and bitmaps, menus and string tables, and dialog boxes.

NOTE

An undocumented registry setting loads a custom bitmap in place of Paradox's normal startup screen. To change the startup screen, create the following new string values:

```
MyOwnSplashScreen=BITMAP.BMP
SplashScreenTextColor = <RGB Value>
```

under

```
HKEY_CURRENT_USER\Software\Borland\Paradox\7.0\Configuration
```

The bitmap must be in the Paradox startup directory. The RGB value is in the form 0 0 0. For example, use 0 255 0 for bright green. The text color is for the Borland copyright string and the username and company name strings (the latter can be set to "" in the registry). You cannot remove the Borland copyright strings.

Summary

In this chapter, you learned that to successfully develop a large application means that you must have a defined process in place. This chapter touched on many parts of the full software development life cycle and introduced you to many of the basic concepts needed to start developing your own software development methodology. This chapter also encouraged you to plan, document, and fully test the software you develop.

That's a Wrap

Most of the examples that you went through in this book were geared toward accomplishing a specific task, learning a particular technique, or explaining a concept. Now that you have finished this book, it's up to you to put what you've learned in this book and elsewhere to work. You're ready to take on a whole project. Remember to keep this book and support software handy.

One of the reasons that I got into programming—and the reason that I wrote this book—is that I love to create. Creating things gives us all a sense of accomplishment and the feeling that we have added something to this world. Paradox is one of the best tools that you can use to create applications. Take advantage of it!

INDEX

SYMBOLS

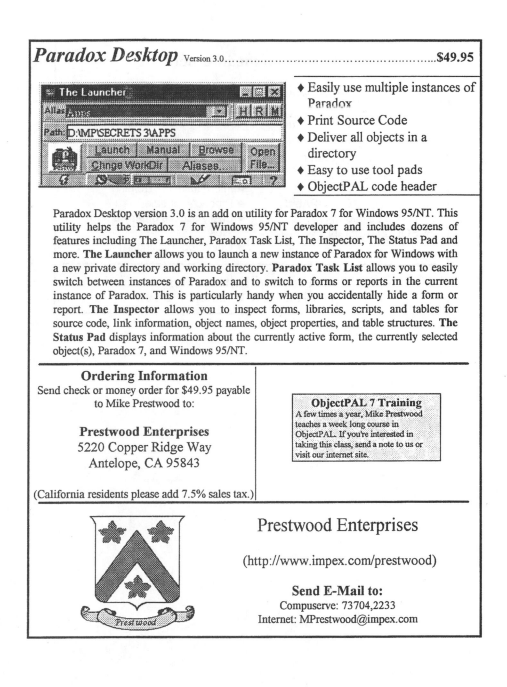

- Professional Web Services
- Free Online Estimates
- Consulting

INTERNET SERVICES

(916)564-6506
info@impex.com

For More Information:

http://www.impex.com

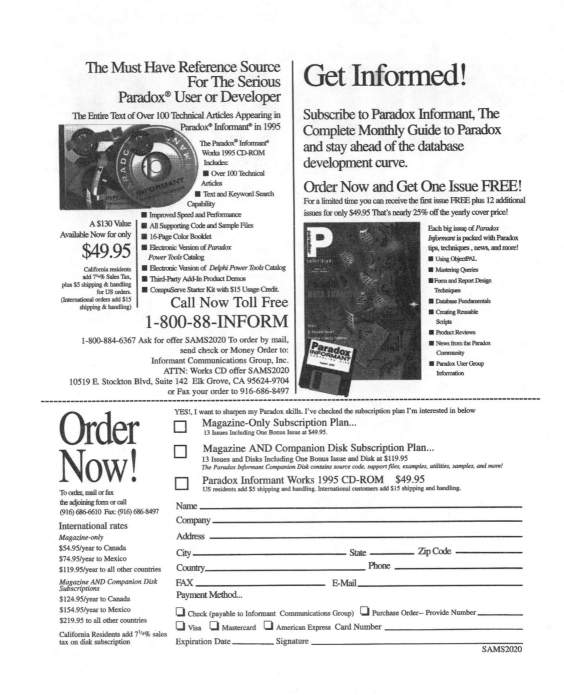

ProtoView DataTable
The Fastest Grid Component Anywhere

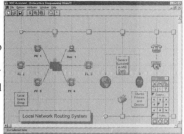

DataTable is an industrial grid control. DataTable strength lies in its ability to handle massive amounts of data in an efficient manner. With a compact size, only 90K of memory, virtual memory, and advanced data cache scheme, DataTable is clearly designed for industrial, real-world applications.
Set colors, fonts, and picture formatting for cells. Has built-in column sorting. It's visual and easy. Supports the clipboard, hidden columns, row, and column selection and resizing. Cells may have drop-down combo boxes or check boxes. Full message and property set. MFC classes and message based programming interface. 16- and 32-bit DLL version, VBX and OCX available. Source code is available.
New features include bitmaps in cells, horizontal and vertical splitter window, numeric column totaling, column searching, cell overwriting, improved keyboard handling, auto row insert, region selection, European formatting for date, time, and numbers, and 3D effects. Windows 95-compatible look.

ProtoView Interactive Diagramming Object
The Visual Way to Add Diagramming To Your Application

The Interactive Diagramming Object gives you advanced capabilities for creating easy to read diagrams. Choose from a wide assortment of shapes, pictures, lines, and arrows to design pleasing presentation visuals, outlines, process flows, hierarchy charts, floor plans, and much more.
With it you can: load and save diagrams, set colors, fonts and 3D effects, create custom design palettes, and respond to notifications and events for complete program control. It supports diagrams of any size with scrolling, zooming, printing, and the clipboard. Simply drop the IDO on a form and it's ready to go. It's easy to use and easy to program. Whether you want to explain a process or present a plan, the IDO helps you effectively communicate ideas and create applications that are more powerful, yet easier to use. Available as OCX or DLL. Source code is available.

ProtoView Interface Component Set
Polished User Interface Components

PICS offers sophisticated controls for calendar, date, time, and numeric input using your choice of odometer, LED readout, and normal display. Add to these a slick looking percent/gauge control, multi-directional spin button, a stereo volume control, and fancy icon buttons. You also get a font and point size selection control for your toolbars or dialogs. Also included are 21 PICS button controls with bitmap images.
You also get a powerful hierarchical list box that includes: setting unlimited number of bitmaps per list, lines between bitmaps and names, over 100 functions for complete control of subtrees, selection, display, search and item manipulation.
Complete on-line help, MFC classes, and message based programming interface. 16- and 32-bit DLL, VBX, and OCX available. Source code is available. Windows 95 compatible look. With PICS you can create the sharpest looking applications in no time at all.

ProtoView Visual Help Builder
The Fastest Way To Build Help Systems!

The ProtoView Visual Help Builder is the fastest way to author help systems. Developers can document an application, whether they have that application's "source" programs or not. With a few clicks of the mouse, ProtoView Visual Help Builder captures every dialog box, menu, and control field of an application and creates a full blown help system. Only ProtoView Visual Help Builder brings you these innovative features. Add multimedia support for video, sound, and high-res graphics. It provides the advanced features you need to create help systems, including macros, secondary windows, multiple hotspot graphics, help topics, hypertext links, jumps, browse sequences, and more.
Integrates into version control software. Includes help compiler. Requires Microsoft Word 2.0/6.0/7.0.

Add to Your Sams Library Today with the Best Books for Programming, Operating Systems, and New Technologies

The easiest way to order is to pick up the phone and call
1-800-428-5331
between 9:00 a.m. and 5:00 p.m. EST.
For faster service please have your credit card available.

ISBN	Quantity	Description of Item	Unit Cost	Total Cost
0-672-30858-4		Delphi 2 Unleashed (Book/CD-ROM)	$55.00	
0-672-30914-9		Delphi 2 Developer's Guide, 2E (Book/CD-ROM)	$59.99	
0-672-30863-0		Teach Yourself Delphi 2 in 21 Days	$29.99	
0-672-30851-7		Teach Yourself Database Programming with Delphi in 21 Days (Book/CD-ROM)	$39.99	
0-672-30876-2		Borland C++ 5 Unleashed (Book/CD-ROM)	$49.99	
0-672-30474-0		Windows 95 Unleashed (Book/CD-ROM)	$39.99	
0-672-30902-5		Windows NT 3.51 Unleashed, 3E (Book/CD-ROM)	$49.99	
0-57521-041-X		The Internet Unleashed 1996 (Book/CD-ROM)	$49.99	
0-57521-040-1		The World Wide Web Unleashed 1996 (Book/CD-ROM)	$49.99	
❏ 3 ½" Disk		Shipping and Handling: See information below.		
❏ 5 ¼" Disk		TOTAL		

Shipping and Handling: $4.00 for the first book, and $1.75 for each additional book. Floppy disk: add $1.75 for shipping and handling. If you need to have it NOW, we can ship product to you in 24 hours for an additional charge of approximately $18.00, and you will receive your item overnight or in two days. Overseas shipping and handling adds $2.00 per book and $8.00 for up to three disks. Prices subject to change. Call for availability and pricing information on latest editions.

201 W. 103rd Street, Indianapolis, Indiana 46290

1-800-428-5331 — Orders   1-800-835-3202 — FAX   1-800-858-7674 — Customer Service

Book ISBN 0-672-30895-9

Installing the CD-ROM

The companion CD-ROM contains sample programs developed by the author, full retail versions of EditPro 3.5 from EditPro Corporation and Protoview's DataTable Spreadsheet/Grid Control, plus an assortment of third-party tools and product demos. The disc is designed to be explored using a browser program. Using Sams' Guide to the CD-ROM browser, you can view information concerning products and companies, and install programs with a single click of the mouse. To install the browser, follow these steps:

Windows 3.1 Installation Instructions

1. Insert the CD-ROM disc into your CD-ROM drive.
2. From File Manager or Program Manager, choose Run from the File menu.
3. Type *<drive>***setup** and press Enter, where *<drive>* corresponds to the drive letter of your CD-ROM. For example, if your CD-ROM is drive D:, type D:\SETUP and press Enter.
4. The installation creates a program manager group named Paradox 7 Unleashed. To browse the CD-ROM, double-click on the Guide to the CD-ROM icon inside this Program Manager group.

Windows 95 Installation Instructions

1. Insert the CD-ROM disc into your CD-ROM drive. If the AutoPlay feature of your Windows 95 system is enabled, the setup program will start automatically.

2. If the setup program does not start automatically, double-click on the My Computer icon.

3. Double-click on the icon representing your CD-ROM drive.

4. Double-click on the icon titled SETUP.EXE to run the installation program. Follow the onscreen instructions that appear. When setup ends, the Guide to the CD-ROM program starts up, so that you can begin browsing immediately.

Following installation, you can restart the Guide to the CD-ROM program by clicking the Start button, selecting Programs, and then selecting Paradox 7 Unleashed and Guide to the CD-ROM.

NOTE

The Guide to the CD-ROM program requires at least 256 colors. For best results, set your monitor to display between 256 and 64,000 colors. A screen resolution of 640 by 480 pixels also is recommended. If necessary, adjust your monitor settings before using the CD-ROM.